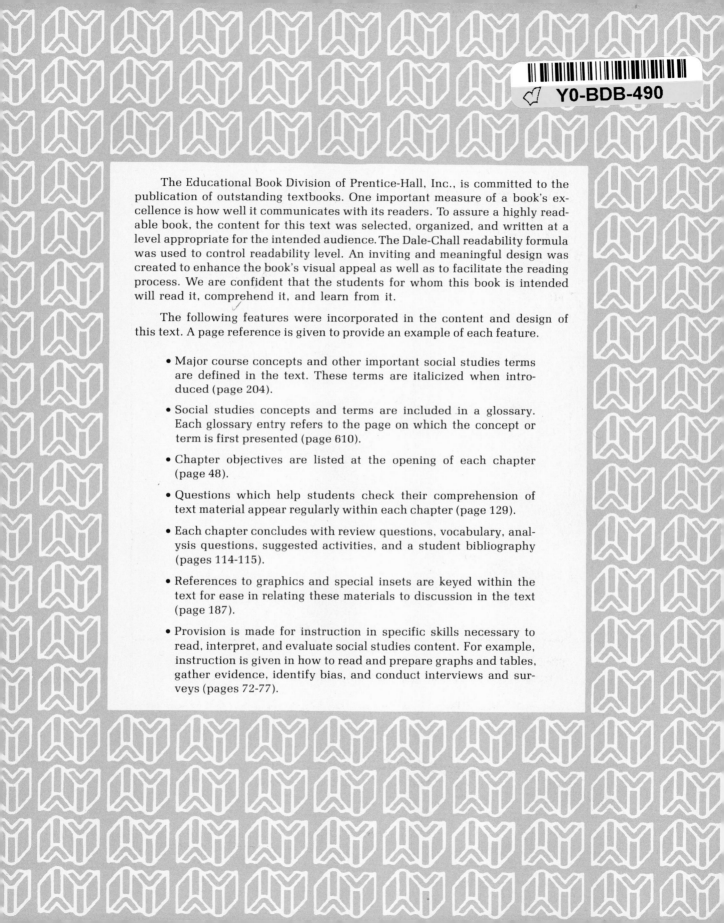

The Educational Book Division of Prentice-Hall, Inc., is committed to the publication of outstanding textbooks. One important measure of a book's excellence is how well it communicates with its readers. To assure a highly readable book, the content for this text was selected, organized, and written at a level appropriate for the intended audience. The Dale-Chall readability formula was used to control readability level. An inviting and meaningful design was created to enhance the book's visual appeal as well as to facilitate the reading process. We are confident that the students for whom this book is intended will read it, comprehend it, and learn from it.

The following features were incorporated in the content and design of this text. A page reference is given to provide an example of each feature.

- Major course concepts and other important social studies terms are defined in the text. These terms are italicized when introduced (page 204).

- Social studies concepts and terms are included in a glossary. Each glossary entry refers to the page on which the concept or term is first presented (page 610).

- Chapter objectives are listed at the opening of each chapter (page 48).

- Questions which help students check their comprehension of text material appear regularly within each chapter (page 129).

- Each chapter concludes with review questions, vocabulary, analysis questions, suggested activities, and a student bibliography (pages 114-115).

- References to graphics and special insets are keyed within the text for ease in relating these materials to discussion in the text (page 187).

- Provision is made for instruction in specific skills necessary to read, interpret, and evaluate social studies content. For example, instruction is given in how to read and prepare graphs and tables, gather evidence, identify bias, and conduct interviews and surveys (pages 72-77).

AMERICAN GOVERNMENT

Comparing
Political Experiences

This book is based on materials completed by the High School Political Science Curriculum Project, sponsored by the American Political Science Association with funds provided by the National Science Foundation. The Directors of the Project were Judith Gillespie, Howard Mehlinger, and John Patrick.

AMERICAN GOVERNMENT

Comparing Political Experiences

Judith Gillespie
Stuart Lazarus

Prentice-Hall, Inc., Englewood Cliffs, New Jersey

SUPPLEMENTARY MATERIALS

Teacher's Guide
Skills and Evaluation Package

© Copyright 1979 by American Political Science
Association

A course developed by the High School Political
Science Curriculum Project, sponsored by the
American Political Science Association with funds
provided by the National Science Foundation.

ISBN 0-13-026807-0   10 9 8 7 6 5

Maps, graphs, and charts by Lee Ames & Zak Ltd.
Cover photo: Leo DeWys, Inc.
Cover and text design by Diane Irene Kachalsky
Photo research by Libby Corlett Forsyth

PRENTICE-HALL INTERNATIONAL, INC., London
PRENTICE-HALL OF AUSTRALIA, PTY. LTD., Sydney
PRENTICE-HALL OF CANADA, LTD., Toronto
PRENTICE-HALL OF INDIA PRIVATE LTD., New Delhi
PRENTICE-HALL OF JAPAN, INC., Tokyo
PRENTICE-HALL OF SOUTHEAST ASIA PTE. LTD., Singapore
WHITEHALL BOOKS LIMITED, WELLINGTON, New Zealand

acknowledgments/sources

UNIT ONE Page 36: From Joshua Miller, "ACORN and Citizen
Education," June 7, 1977. 53: From The Nation, June 16, 1969,
pp. 749-750. With permission. The Nation copyright 1969. 53-
54: From Ebony, July 1973, pp. 133-134. Reprinted by permission of Ebony Magazine, copyright 1973 by Johnson Publishing
Company, Inc. 101t: From "McGovern: Up From the Grass
Roots," Newsweek, April 17, 1972, pp. 26, 31. Copyright 1972
by Newsweek, Inc. All rights reserved. Reprinted by permission.
101b: From Gordon Weil, The Long Shot: George McGovern
Runs for President (New York: W.W. Norton & Co.), 1973, p. 66.
108: The Gallop Poll. 109: The Gallop Poll. 111-112: With per-
mission of Catherine Norris. 112: © 1976 by The New York
Times Company. Reprinted by permission. 112-113: With per-
mission of Charlotte Zietlow. 113t: With permission of Ed and
Barb Olson. 113b: With permission of Bill Peters. 123t: Con-
gressional Quarterly, July 27, 1974. 123b: © 1977 by The New
York Times Company. Reprinted by permission. 124-125:
Adapted from "Grassroots Lobbying Blitz Overrides Ford's 59th
Veto," American Teacher, October 1976, pp. 10-11. 127: From
Caesar Chavez, "The Organizer's Tale," Ramparts, Vol. 5, No. 2,
1966, p. 46. Copyright 1966 by Ramparts Magazine, Inc. re-
printed by permission. 130-132: Adapted from "John Dewey's
Giant Killers," The Grass Roots Primer (San Francisco: Sierra
Club, 1975) pp. 54-63. 165-167: With permission of Frank
Powers.

UNIT TWO Page 209: © 1976 by The New York Times Company.
Reprinted by permission. 214: Quotation used with permission
of Action for Children's Television. 235b: Adapted from John
W. Lesow, "Litter and the Nonreturnable Beverage Container:
A Comparative Analysis," Environmental Law, Vol. 2, 1971,
p. 208. 261t: From David R. Berman, State and Local Politics,
Second Edition. Copyright © 1978 by Holbrook Press, Inc. Subsidiary of Allyn and Bacon, Inc., Boston. Adapted with permission. 261b: Adapted from Dvorin/Misner, Governments Within
the States, © 1971, Addison-Wesley, Reading, Massachusetts.
Reprinted with permission. 262: Office of Laurence R. Sprecher,
City Manager, Beaverton, Oregon. 294: With permission of
Dr. Pearl Chase. 295: With permission of James Bottoms.
296-297: With permission of Hal Conklin. 299: With permission of Leo Martinez.

Acknowledgments continue on page 627.

4

contents

unit 1
The Political Life of Citizens, 16

5

unit 2
State and Local Political Activities, 172

6

unit 3
National Political Systems, 310

7

unit 4
Global Political Systems, 492

graphic features

case studies

reference materials

THE UNITED STATES

★   *Capital City*

●   *Other City*

ADMISSION TO THE UNION

Alabama	1819	Montana	1889
Alaska	1959	Nebraska	1867
Arizona	1912	Nevada	1864
Arkansas	1836	New Hampshire	1788
California	1850	New Jersey	1787
Colorado	1876	New Mexico	1912
Connecticut	1788	New York	1788
Delaware	1787	North Carolina	1789
Florida	1845	North Dakota	1889
Georgia	1788	Ohio	1803
Hawaii	1959	Oklahoma	1907
Idaho	1890	Oregon	1859
Illinois	1818	Pennsylvania	1787
Indiana	1816	Rhode Island	1790
Iowa	1846	South Carolina	1788
Kansas	1861	South Dakota	1889
Kentucky	1792	Tennessee	1796
Louisiana	1812	Texas	1845
Maine	1820	Utah	1896
Maryland	1788	Vermont	1791
Massachusetts	1788	Virginia	1788
Michigan	1837	Washington	1889
Minnesota	1858	West Virginia	1863
Mississippi	1817	Wisconsin	1848
Missouri	1821	Wyoming	1890

0	100	200	300 Miles
0	200	400	Kilometers

13

preface

The desire to improve citizenship is not new to our day and age. Greek scholars dating back to Plato called for strengthening the mental and physical capacities of citizens in order to develop a truly participatory democracy. Thomas Jefferson saw the need for citizenship education, and he called for an emphasis on citizenship in the education of youth. The famous educator John Dewey wanted students to learn about politics and to use their knowledge as citizens in a democracy. Responsible citizenship has certainly been a major objective for social studies teachers in our country for many years.

While the concern with citizenship education has occurred throughout history, key elements toward realizing this goal have not always been fully integrated. The purpose of *American Government: Comparing Political Experiences* is to promote citizenship education through three dimensions—knowledge, basic intellectual skills, and participation skills. We believe that each of these dimensions must be explored, learned, and practiced for effective citizenship to work.

The knowledge dimension of citizenship education involves learning about the structure and function of government as well as about the operation of political groups. As revealed by the preceding table of contents, this text begins with a study of the political life of citizens. The text then delves into a study of government institutions and activities, beginning at the state level, moving through the national level, and then concluding with an analysis of political institutions at the international level. A focus throughout the book is on how political institutions relate to citizens— how citizens can become involved in and affect these institutions.

A second key element of citizenship education is teaching basic intellectual skills. These skills are presented systematically, and students are encouraged to apply these skills through suggested activities in the text. We hope that students will have ample opportunity throughout the course to learn these skills and to apply them in school and community settings.

An important dimension of citizenship which is often neglected in government courses is participation. It is important to know and to inquire. It is equally important to be able to participate effectively. This does not mean that everyone must participate in every political decision. It does mean, however, that students who wish to be active citizens should be able to participate when and if they choose and to make wise choices when they do participate. One of the central aims of this course is to give students opportunities to learn and practice key participation skills.

None of these dimensions of citizenship stands alone. It is important that they be integrated in studying the political process. It is equally important that students realize how they can apply these dimensions to political activities in their everyday lives.

We expect that you will use this course flexibly. Many teachers and students have field tested experimental versions of this course and have given us valuable feedback. We hope that we have developed a course which will be a successful experience in government and citizenship. How you use this text is up to you. Regardless of how the course is sequenced, we hope that teachers in classrooms across the United States will produce active, sensitive, and future-oriented citizens as a result.

Judith Gillespie
Stuart Lazarus

acknowledgments

Many individuals contributed to the High School Political Science Curriculum Project, which generated this book. Acknowledgments cannot be extended to each person individually here. We have received substantial help from national and state associations, political scientists, social studies educators, teachers across the country and, of course, our most persistent and important critics, high school students.

The American Political Science Association was the grantee institution for funds provided by the National Science Foundation. We thank Thomas Mann, Sheilah Koeppen Mann, and Evron Kirkpatrick at APSA headquarters for their significant efforts on behalf of the Project. We are also grateful to L.O. Binder, Jean Intermaggio, Ray Hannapel, and Alexander Barton from the Foundation who gave us their support at crucial periods in our work.

The American Political Science Association's Committee on Pre-Collegiate Education played a major role in monitoring the Project. Special thanks go to Richard Snyder, Chairperson of the Committee. Individuals on the Committee who helped in initiating the Project, in policy planning, and in reviewing the materials include Paul Abramson, Lee Anderson, Stephen Bailey, David Easton, Laurily Epstein, F. Chris Garcia, Fred Greenstein, Robert Lane, Harold Lasswell, Leslie McLemore, Howard Mehlinger, Jewel Prestage, Frank Sorauf, Judith Torney, and Harmon Ziegler. We also wish to thank two Committee staff associates, Judith Kies and Richard Remy.

The Social Studies Development Center served as the working base for the Project. Colleagues at the Center contributed ideas and advice at every stage. The Project was directed by Judith Gillespie, Howard Mehlinger and John Patrick. We owe much of our success to Howard and John. Howard provided untiring support for Project staff and activities. John's creative work in the development of experimental materials made an invaluable contribution to our efforts.

Several individuals have aided in development, evaluation, and dissemination activities. Toby Bonwit, Robert Hanvey, Joel Pett, Jean Wagner, and B'Ann Wright helped us in developing instructional activities. Sam Christie, Dave Lambert, Mike Stentz, and the staff at National Evaluation Systems worked on the evaluation of the program.

To our graduate assistants—Ron Banaszak, Lynn Fontana, Ron Pahl, Murray Print, Ellen Sampson, Martin Sampson and Bruce Smith—we owe much more than words can describe.

Seven high school teachers worked on the Project as teacher associates. Pat Basa, Regis Birckbichler, Ed Brennan, Tom Castellano, Tony Codianni, Dick Kraft, and Dave Victor contributed important feedback and teacher perspectives in the development of the materials.

Many, many thanks are extended to over one hundred pilot teachers across the nation and their students who cared enough to be critical and who made the pilot test an exciting learning experience for the authors. This book is vastly improved by their efforts. University consultants who visited schools, reviewed manuscripts, and hosted conferences also added measurably to the revisions which resulted in this volume.

Acknowledgments are also due to individuals and groups who made personal contributions to the citizen participation chapters in each of the units. We extend our appreciation to Matt Witt of the United Mine Workers of America in Washington, D.C., and to other members of the union who contributed to our study of the mine workers; to Tony Codianni for the idea of going to Santa Barbara, and to Robert Easton and Hal Conklin for their service in contacting community members there; to citizens of the city of Boston for their contribution to the idea of a civil rights unit, and to John O'Connor and Linda Scher for their help in the field work; and to J.D. McConnell, R. Gordon Redshaw and Evan Bridgewater at Cummins Engine Company for their work in the development of materials on multinational corporations.

Special thanks go to Diane Davis for her administrative work and her manuscript typing. Other typists without whom we would not have completed the manuscript include Cathi Eagan, Jane Leitzman, Mary Kay Preuss and Lynn Young.

As our acknowledgments reveal, *American Government: Comparing Political Experiences* is the result of efforts of literally hundreds of individuals across the United States. To each of you we extend our most heartfelt thanks.

Judith Gillespie
Stuart Lazarus

unit 1

The Political Life
of Citizens

Chapter Objectives

★ To learn the meaning of government and citizenship

★ To analyze what governments do

★ To compare different kinds of governments

★ To analyze the rights and duties of citizenship

★ To develop skills in participating as an observer

chapter 1

GOVERNMENT and CITIZENSHIP

If your spacecraft landed on a strange and uninhabited planet, you and your companions would find yourselves in a new world. You could create from scratch whatever ways of living you needed and wanted. You might structure society very differently from what you had known in your old world. But one thing is almost certain: sooner or later you and your companions would form some sort of government. You would choose leaders, and you would make rules to guide your life together.

Governments have existed in societies for thousands of years. In all societies governments perform certain important functions for members, such as providing order and security. However, governments take many different forms. The governments of France or England, the government of the United States, and the government in your local community may operate in very different ways. Nevertheless, all these governments serve the common needs of their members.

In this chapter you'll learn that groups such as labor unions, social clubs, and neighborhood organizations also have governments of their own. Indeed, in today's world, governments vary from the small organization that governs your student body to the giant organization that governs the United States. How these governments operate, how they affect your life, and how you can affect them will be the focus of this book.

What Is Government?

The word *government* comes from Greek and Latin words meaning "to steer or guide a boat." A *government* is an organization that makes and enforces rules to guide a group of people. In your state, for example, voters, the governor, judges, legislators, and thousands of state employees work together to make and enforce rules that guide the state.

When you think about it, rules are made and enforced in many groups—corporations, labor unions, clubs, and churches, for example. Your student council is a government. Its rules apply to all students in your school. In the same way, General Motors has a government. Corporate officers, stockholders, and managers make and enforce rules that affect all employees of the company.

KINDS of GOVERNMENT

There is an important distinction between governments like those in corporations and clubs and governments like that of the United States. Our national government can be classified as a *public government*. A public government has the right to make and enforce rules that apply to everyone living within its domain. Your state government is a public government, as are the government of the United States and the government of your city.

Public government does not allow voluntary membership. For example, if you live in Arizona, the laws of the state government apply to you. You are not free to decide whether you want to be a part of the group which must obey these laws. Of course, you may move to another state or to another country. However, once you get there, you are bound to obey the laws of the public government of your new place of residence.

A *private government,* on the other hand, does not make and enforce rules for the general public. Private governments are formed to govern social groups, work groups, political groups, and the like. A private government has the right and duty to make and enforce rules and to provide services for only those people who belong to the group. For example, the League of Women Voters is an organization with a private government. The League is involved in getting information on political issues and candidates to voters. Members of the League study issues and express their views on policies which are important to them. Rules

Since 1970, Native American tribal councils, such as this Sioux council in South Dakota, have assumed greater control over housing, hospitals, and schools on Native American reservations. Is a tribal council a public or private government?

which govern the League of Women Voters pertain only to the goals and activities of this group. The AFL-CIO, an organization of labor unions, is another example of private government. Its members elect officers to lead the organization, and these officers make and enforce rules which apply only to the members of the AFL-CIO.

Members of groups with private governments are more or less free to join or drop out of the group. If they don't approve of the rules or how they are enforced, they may quit the group. Dropping out of the group may mean forfeiting certain privileges, but nevertheless the decision to belong or not is a personal, voluntary choice.

In looking at these two types of governments, it is important to see that the public government always controls the private government. The public government makes rules which the private government must obey. The state and city regulate school attendance; the student council cannot legally ignore those regulations. The federal government taxes corporations; the private company must pay those taxes.

Both public and private governments exist at different levels. There are local, state, national, and international governments. Examples of public governments at each of these four levels are easy to name. What examples of private governments can you identify at each level?

Power and Decision-making. In public and private governments at every level there are important differences in the distribution of power. The table on page 22 describes some of the traditional categories into which governments have been classified in terms of power and decision-making.

In an autocracy or dictatorship, for example, power normally is held by one person or small group. Decisions are made by this group without the consent of citizens. A democracy, on the other hand, gives people a direct part in electing those who govern and an indirect part in influencing decision-making. An oligarchy is a mix of autocratic

and democratic forms, with wealth generally serving as the basis of power.

After you study the table carefully, read the following case about a school government. Compare the government at Aztlan High School to the kinds of government described in the table.

★ Decision-making at Aztlan High

Aztlan High is a southwestern high school with students of Mexican-Spanish-Indian origin. Both Spanish and English can be heard in its corridors. In the courtyard stands a statue of an Aztec warrior, a symbol of the culture and a gathering place for students.

For many years, the Aztlan student government was run by a small group of executive officers. As one student said: "No one was really involved in government. It wasn't talked about much." But in the 1970s, a group of students organized to improve student representation and responsibility in school government.

Joined by the activities director and the school administration, the group drew up a plan which called for an elected, representative Student Senate. The plan was approved by the entire student body, the principal, and the community. This proposal called for annual popular elections and bi-weekly open meetings with flexible, published agendas.

Today, the channels of communication work well at Aztlan. The new Student Senate puts out a weekly bulletin to communicate with students, and seeks student opinions and proposals for new activities. The Senate has been instrumental in purchasing a school van for transporting students to sports events. Senate representatives also have worked with the community to raise funds for community services and to improve town-school communication.

The Senate has been effective in making constructive changes in some school policies. For example, members worked closely

Categories of Government

FORM OF GOVERNMENT	DERIVATION OF NAME	DEFINITION	EXAMPLES WITH YEARS OF POWER OR INFLUENCE
Autocracy Dictatorship	*Autokratēs* (Greek): ruling by oneself *Dictatus* (Latin): assert, pronounce. In ancient Rome, an official given absolute power for a limited time.	A government controlled by one person or group not responsible to the people or their elected representatives. Ruler(s) hold all power.	Russia: Peter the Great 1672–1725 Portugal: Antonio Salazar 1932–68 Uganda: Idi Amin 1971–
Monarchy	*Monos* (Latin): alone *Archein* (Greek): to rule	A government headed by a king, queen, or emperor. Usually, monarch inherits power. Today most are limited by constitutions and share power with an elected parliament.	<u>Absolute</u> Saudi Arabia: King Khalid 1975– <u>Constitutional</u> Great Britain: Elizabeth II 1952–
Oligarchy	*Oligo* (Greek): small *Archein* (Greek): to rule	A government controlled by a small group. Power often based on wealth, military might, or social position.	Venice: During Renaissance, 1400s and 1500s
Fascism	*Fascis* (Latin): bundle. Bundle of rods wrapped around an ax and carried before ancient Roman magistrate to show authority.	A one-party dictatorship with absolute power for and glorification of dictator. Private ownership of economy with heavy government regulation.	Italy: Benito Mussolini 1922–43 Germany: Adolph Hitler 1933–45
Communism	*Communis* (Latin): shared by all or many	The goal is to establish collective, classless society in which the people own all land and capital, control power, and share profits equally. In practice, a government with severe restrictions on individual rights and an economy controlled by the government.	USSR: Since 1917 People's Republic of China: Since 1949
Democracy	*Demos* (Greek): the people *Kratein* (Greek): to rule	A government in which the people hold authority and rule either directly or indirectly, through elected representatives. Government protects individual liberties. An indirect democracy is known as a republic.	<u>Direct</u> Ancient Athens: 6th Century B.C. New England town meetings <u>Indirect</u> U.S.: 1783–present Canada: 1867–present
Anarchy	*Anarchos* (Greek): without a leader	A society with no government. In theory, all people enjoy complete freedom.	Never used to set up a government. Famous advocates: Jean-Pierre Proudhon 1809–65 Emma Goldman 1869–1940

with Aztlan's principal to change the passing time between classes from five to ten minutes. According to the principal, "I meet often with the students . . . At one meeting they presented some good reasons why we should extend the passing time . . . So, I tried walking from one side of the campus to the other in the time between classes. . . . You know, it took me three minutes longer than the allotted time!" The passing time was extended by a vote of teachers, administrators, and students.

Aztlan High School's Student Senate has given students an important share in responsibility for decision-making.

1. What similarities can you find between government at Aztlan High School and the kinds of government described on page 22?
2. What are some of the rules made and enforced by one government with which you are familiar?
3. Distinguish between public and private government. Give examples of each.

WHY DO WE NEED GOVERNMENTS? There are many theories about why people form governments. (Some of the most important of these theories are described on page 24.) For as long as groups of people have lived together, they have made and enforced rules to guide their relationships. In small groups, like a family, these rules are usually informal sets of understandings among group members. Parents and children, sisters and brothers follow certain agreed-upon patterns of behavior with one another.

Larger groups need formal rules to govern their relationships. In a large group of people, it is more difficult for everyone to agree informally. And there are more decisions to be made for the group. Imagine the chaos that would result if every family in the United States today provided its own police, fire, and sanitation services; its own roads; its own armed forces; and its own laws! A government, then, allows a society to accomplish what individuals cannot do alone.

Early American Governments. The earliest governments in America were formed by groups of Native Americans. Later, the first European colonists established rules to guide their lives in the New World. Here are two descriptions of situations involving these early governments. As you read each story, think about the reasons why the governments were formed.

★ **The Iroquois League**

The name Iroquois applies to a group of approximately twelve large and five or six small Native American tribes that lived in the United States before the arrival of European settlers. The Iroquois were renowned warriors. When united against a common enemy, they were virtually unbeatable. Several of these tribes invaded the Mohawk Valley area of New York State, eventually driving out the Algonquian who had been living there. However, soon after the departure of the Algonquian, the Iroquois tribes began fierce attacks against each other. Legend says that the valley was red with the blood of Iroquois warriors.

The situation became especially bad during the mid-sixteenth century. At that time, two Iroquois men began to preach the idea of a *confederation* (or union) of Iroquois tribes. They hoped to end the bloodshed among themselves and also provide a strong defense against attacks from outside. The reformers were Dekanawidah, a Huron, and his disciple and preacher, Hiawatha, a Mohawk chief.

At first, the men's idea for a confederation was rebuffed; each Iroquois tribe felt strongly about its independence. The reformers persisted in preaching for an

Theories of Government

Since the time of the Greek philosopher Aristotle (384–322 B.C.), people have discussed and written about the development of the state. The *state*, in this sense, is the power or authority represented by a group of people living in a defined geographical area and organized under one government. That government can govern without higher authority.

Many theories on the origin of the state have been proposed in the course of history. Some of them, like the views below, have had a major impact on modern-day government.

The Social Contract. Thomas Hobbes (1588–1679) believed that before the creation of the state, people lived in a "natural condition." At that time, each person enjoyed the "natural right" to act in any way. There was total freedom, but also constant warfare, as people competed fiercely for limited resources.

Thomas Hobbes

According to Hobbes, these horrible conditions eventually forced people to form a *social contract*. People gave to the state a part of their natural right to act freely. In doing so, the people also empowered the state to create and enforce laws which they promised to obey. The state, in return, protected the security of all the people within its boundaries.

Hobbes' idea that a social contract formed the basis of the state influenced the thinking of other political philosophers, particularly John Locke (1632–1704) and Jean Jacques Rousseau (1712–1778). Locke believed that the foundation of the state rested on the social contract, and that the foundation of government rested on the trust of the people. Thus, any government that failed to protect the life, liberty, and property of its citizens could be changed or replaced. Rousseau maintained that all authority ultimately rested with the "general will" of the people.

Socialism. Karl Marx (1818–1883) maintained that the state had been created to promote capitalism. (*Capitalism* is an economic system in which all or most of the means of production and distribution are privately owned and operated for profit.) To Marx, capitalism was an unfair system in which workers were exploited by a wealthy ruling class. Marx believed that capitalism would eventually destroy itself in a revolution of the workers. They would seize the means of production and make ownership of them public. (This economic system is called *socialism*.)

Friedrich Engels (1820–1895), a friend of Marx, and later Vladimir Lenin (1870–1924), leader of the Russian Revolution, explained the fate of the state after such a "socialist revolution." According to Engels, a pure classless society would not emerge immediately. Instead, the state and many of its institutions would still exist and take the form of a "dictatorship of the proletariat" (workers).

In time, the state would prove unnecessary. A *communist* society would eventually evolve. Engels believed that in this communist society each person would have complete freedom. Because of the complexities of economic life, there would be institutions and rules, but no means of enforcing them. According to Engels, enforcement would be unnecessary, since everyone would act to promote the general good.

Iroquois league. They pointed out that it was precisely this freedom that had brought intertribal warfare and death. Sometime between 1570 and 1600, the reformers succeeded in convincing five tribes—Mohawk, Seneca, Cayuga, Onondaga, and Oneida—to join what was called the League of Five Nations. About 1715, the Tuscarora joined the confederation, and it became the League of Six Nations.

The plan for the League was soundly based on Iroquoian culture, which helped to assure its success. There was an unwritten constitution that called for the creation of a common representative body. This council consisted of clan and tribal chiefs, and a group of 50 specially appointed *sachems*. These were peace chiefs who had jurisdiction over all intertribal matters.

The council was required to meet at least once every five years at the main Onondaga village. In practice, it generally met every summer. Although the number of representatives from different tribes varied, each tribe had only one vote, and unanimity was required for all decisions. Disputes among member tribes had to be arbitrated by the council. However, the council had no control over the internal affairs of each tribe. Thus, each member tribe had almost total freedom, but was also bound by the unanimous decisions of the council. Some historians believe that the organization of the League influenced the European colonists in their early efforts to unite.

The League eventually became one of the best organized and most powerful Native American confederations in North America. It was successful in ending violence among its members and in defeating its enemies, including the French during the seventeenth century. However, it did not prevent members from attacking neighboring tribes, including Iroquoian people who were not League members.

During the American Revolution, the six League members split over the issue of which side to support in the conflict. The Oneida and Tuscarora supported the Americans, and the rest threw their support to the British. The colonial victory brought a virtual end to the League in 1784.

★ The Pilgrims and the Mayflower Compact

In 1608, a group of Pilgrims, members of a religious sect, left England to seek religious freedom. They settled in Leyden, Holland. As you know, the Pilgrims had been persecuted in England for refusing to recognize the authority of the Church of England over their private religious beliefs and practices. In Holland, the Pilgrims found religious freedom, but they suffered many economic and cultural hardships. Unable to earn a living and upset that their children were becoming more Dutch than English, the Pilgrims sought a better place to live.

They approached Sir Edwin Sandys, who controlled the London Company. That organization administered all the affairs of the Virginia colony. It was there, in the wilderness of the New World, that the Pilgrims wished to settle and build their "New England."

Although he did not support the Pilgrims' religious views, Sandys granted their charter request. The Pilgrims found financial backers and formed a joint-stock company. In September 1620, they sailed from England for the New World. They numbered about 100 strong, approximately one-third from Leyden and the rest from England.

The 66-day passage across the Atlantic Ocean was difficult. When the Pilgrims finally approached the continent, fierce winds and navigational errors took them farther north than they had planned. Instead of landing in the Virginia colony, they found themselves at the inside tip of Cape Cod near Provincetown harbor. Weary of the cold, storm-tossed December seas, many aboard wished to anchor the ship anyway.

However, the Pilgrim leaders faced a serious problem. Some in the group claimed that if they landed, they would be free of all

Before landing in the New World, the Pilgrims gathered in the cabin of their ship to sign the Mayflower Compact. With this document they established a government to guide their activities as they started their new life.

government control, since they would be outside the boundaries of the Virginia colony. The Pilgrim leaders realized that once they landed, they would face many problems that would require group cooperation to solve. Without authority, there would be no way to maintain order and discipline. In time, they thought, the group would be sure to fail. Therefore the Pilgrim leaders wrote the Mayflower Compact, which was signed by all free Pilgrim men aboard ship.

The Mayflower Compact is a simple document, but its importance cannot be overlooked. It is the first example of self-government by European colonists in the New World. Part of it reads:

"We whose names are underwritten . . . having undertaken for the glory of God, and the advancement of the Christian faith, and the honour of our king and country, a voyage to plant the first colony in the Northern parts of Virginia . . . Do by these Presents, solemnly and mutually in the presence of God and one another covenant [contract] and combine ourselves into a civil Body Politick, for our better ordering and preservation and furtherance of the ends aforesaid; and by virtue hereof do enact, constitute, and frame such just and equal laws, ordinances, Acts, constitution, and officers as shall be thought most meet [suitable] and convenient for the general good of the Colony; unto which we promise all due submission and obedience. . . . "

Making a Constitution. When the American colonies declared their independence from England in 1776, it was necessary for them to establish governments for the new states. In the Declaration of Independence the colonists informed England of the reasons for the formation of a new government. The Declaration says, in part:

"We hold these truths to be self-evident, that all men are created equal, that they are endowed by their Creator with certain unalienable [not transferable] Rights, that among these are Life, Liberty and the pursuit of Happiness. That to secure these rights, Governments are instituted among Men, deriving their just powers from the consent of the governed; That whenever any Form of Government becomes destructive of these ends, it is the Right of the People to alter or to abolish it, and to institute new Government, laying its foundation on such principles and organizing its powers in such form as to them shall seem most likely to effect [cause] their Safety and Happiness."

In forming a government for the newly united states, one of the first steps was to create a constitution. A *constitution* is a set of basic rules and principles of a government; it presents a plan for governing. Most constitutions are written documents. Some are unwritten but are known and agreed upon by group members. Governments of all sizes and varieties, both public and private, have constitutions which define the structure of the government and the rights of its citizens or members.

The first constitution of the United States was called the Articles of Confederation. When this plan for government proved unsuccessful, state leaders met to create a new plan and a new constitution. Almost 200 years after it was conceived, this written document, titled the Constitution of the United States of America, is still the basis for the government of our nation.

You will be studying the Constitution in great detail in this course. As a first step, a study of the *preamble,* or introduction, to the Constitution will show you the basic reasons why the people of the United States formed the government outlined in this document. The preamble reads as follows:

"We, the People of the United States, in Order to form a more perfect Union, establish Justice, insure domestic Tranquility, provide for the common defense, promote the general Welfare, and secure the Blessings of liberty to ourselves and our Posterity, do ordain and establish this Constitution for the United States of America."

The creators of the Constitution listed six reasons why they were establishing a government. What does each of the phrases mean to you?

1. To form a more perfect union
2. To establish justice
3. To insure domestic tranquility
4. To provide for the common defense
5. To promote the general welfare
6. To secure the blessings of liberty

The Constitution of the United States gives reasons for the formation of a national government. The following example describes why a small community decided to form a government where none had existed before.

★ **Government in Kimberling City**

Kimberling City is located in the southern Missouri Ozarks. For a long time, people have been living there without the need for any form of official city government. However, by 1973, there were over 900 people

The Second Continental Congress appointed this committee to draft a Declaration of Independence. Its members included Benjamin Franklin, Thomas Jefferson, John Adams, Robert R. Livingston, and Roger Sherman. Most of the Declaration was actually written by Jefferson.

living in the area, and people began to question whether a government might bring them important services. Many said that they also needed a plan for future growth.

Out of 900 people, 517 voters went to the polls. Of these, 324 voted for a city government, which was formed under Missouri laws for local government.

A comprehensive plan was then drawn up for the city, stating the goals of the residents in regard to their city government. Some of the goals were:

1. To maintain and improve the existing character of the city.

2. To encourage a good urban design.

3. To plan for community facilities that would preserve the clean air and water.

4. To ensure a sense of privacy and healthful living environment.

5. To plan land-use allocations and public facilities and services that would meet the needs of the future.

6. To maintain a continuing program of public communication in order to keep planning goals constantly before the eyes of the citizens.

After this, a comprehensive survey was done to find out citizens' opinions on the plan for government. Citizens were asked to list what they thought the city government should do. The three most commonly listed items were (1) to repair the streets and improve drainage; (2) to install sewers and stop lake pollution; (3) to enforce city ordinances, especially zoning and building codes.

1. Why were governments formed by the Iroquois, the Pilgrims, the American colonists, and the citizens of Kimberling City?

2. In your opinion, what are the three most important reasons for forming a government?

3. What is a constitution?

4. Compare the views of Hobbes and Marx on the role of government.

WHAT DO GOVERNMENTS DO?

You have been examining reasons why people form governments, reasons that reflect people's expectations of what governments will do for them. Remember that a government is established by men and women who want the government to create certain conditions for a group. The Iroquois, the Pilgrims, the framers of the Constitution, the citizens of Kimberling City—all formed governments to do specific things for them that they could not accomplish without government.

When you begin to think about what governments do for people, many different kinds of activities may come to your mind, like collecting taxes, building schools, and passing laws. If you include private governments, you'll probably think about ways in which the officers and rules of groups such as clubs, churches, and student governments guide the activities of those groups.

All these functions of government can be grouped into several major classifications. Not all governments perform all these functions. However, these are basic areas in which many governments act.

1. Governments can provide representation.

2. Governments can provide order and security.

3. Governments can provide services.

4. Governments can manage relations with other governments.

Governments Can Provide Representation. A major function of a government like the United States government is to provide representation for its more than 200 million people. As you know, it would be impossible for every person to perform every function of government. Instead, citizens elect representatives to manage the government. This is known as an indirect democracy, or a republic. The President and members of Congress are elected representatives of the American people. These representatives make decisions for the people of this country. In the same way, student councils in schools give students representation in the school government. A union also represents its members. On a larger scale, the United Nations provides representation for large as well as small nations in an international forum.

Governments Can Provide Order and Security. A vital job of any public government is to maintain order and security in a society. Governments do this by making and enforcing laws and by providing institutions like armies, police departments, and agencies of diplomacy which work to keep order and peace for the society.

In what ways do governments make and enforce laws? First, they establish how rules will be made; in other words, they determine who will make decisions about laws and how they will decide.

In our national government, the Constitution establishes the ways that many rules are made. The decision-making process in Congress, for example, is specified in the Constitution; the Constitution says that a majority of members of Congress can make a decision to pass or reject a law. This majority rule is a crucial factor in the operation of the government. If everyone had to agree on everything, the government wouldn't be able to accomplish very much. On the other hand, if one person could make all decisions, we would not have the representative government that the framers of the Constitution wanted to establish. Rules about how to make rules determine the way that all other decisions will be made.

Governments also provide security and order by making and enforcing new rules. When automobiles became popular, cities and states had to make rules to keep order on the roads. Companies make rules about

This woman is voting for a town council member. By this action she is choosing someone to represent her in local government.

Governments provide many
services to their members.
Public governments protect
citizens from fire and
disease. They also build
roads and preserve historic
landmarks, such as
Independence Hall.

safety in working conditions. Presidents have signed arms limitation agreements to slow down the nuclear arms race.

In addition, public governments maintain institutions and personnel who work to keep order and security. Police officers seek to enforce laws for the community. The armed forces protect the nation in case of war. Diplomats and advisers work around the world to further the interests of peace.

Governments Can Provide Services. Governments are able to provide their members with important services. Public governments build roads, schools, and parks. They provide public housing for people who need it and financial assistance for people who cannot earn enough money. These services are invaluable in the operation of society. Try to imagine life in your town without government-built roads or schools, without any aid for poor people, without any fire or police departments, without any environmental protection.

Private governments provide services too. Unions, for example, organize negotiating teams that bargain to improve members' wages, safety, and health benefits. They often build hospitals and retirement homes for members.

Governments are able to provide services for several reasons, most important of which are money and centralization. Almost all governments collect money from members in the form of taxes or dues. This money is used to pay for the functions of government, including services. Figure 1-1 is a chart of government expenditures, including the cost of services.

By centralizing people and money government can efficiently accomplish much more than individuals can. One fire department can serve an entire city, but few individuals or even neighborhoods have the knowledge or money to provide full fire protection for themselves.

Governments Can Manage Relations with Other Governments. Imagine what it would be like if all the people who live in the United States had to negotiate a peace treaty with all the people in another country. It would be impossible. So, a major role of governments is to represent members of the group in relations with other governments. Local governments manage relations with state and national governments. National governments manage relations with other national governments. International organizations like the United Nations manage relations among groups of nations.

Private governments also manage relations with other governments. The government of a union negotiates with the government of a corporation. The leaders of the Pep Club represent members in dealing with the school administration.

Basically, these relationships fall into three categories. First, governments manage relations involving security and conflict. For example, the governments of two nations may decide that they will wage war against one another; the governments of those nations can also negotiate a peace. Intergovernmental relations also take place in private governments, such as when leaders of a block association negotiate with the city to improve neighborhood safety.

Second, governments manage relations which involve economics. National governments, for example, make rules about trade with other countries. They give aid to needy countries. They manage the flow of money from one nation to another.

Third, governments manage relations involving human relationships. They make rules about who can travel where, and when. They establish regulations regarding the international exchange of information in the media or the exchange of scholars and performers. They deal with human rights.

1. Describe the four major functions of government.

2. Provide a new example of each function.

3. Make a list of all the government services you can think of that affect your life directly. How would your life be different if governments did not provide public services?

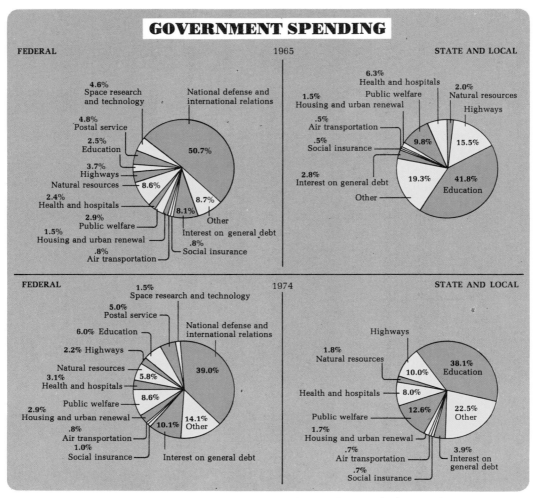

Figure 1-1

Source: Statistical Abstract of the U.S. 1966
Statistical Abstract of the U.S. 1976

What Is Citizenship?

"Today, for the first time, I shall be celebrating Thanksgiving Day as an American citizen. And, as for millions of Americans before me, this will be a day of thanks for the dreams that come true...."

These words, spoken in 1970 by a Polish immigrant, express the value of citizenship to a new citizen of this country. The word *citizenship* comes from the Latin word *civitas,* which means "citizens united in a community." Strictly speaking, citizenship means membership in a nation. It can also refer to membership in a smaller unit of government, such as a state or city. Therefore, at the same time that people are citizens of the United States, they are citizens of the states and cities in which they live.

HOW to BECOME a CITIZEN There are two ways to become a citizen of the United States—by birth and by naturalization. (Other nations also use these rules to determine citizenship.) Those born in any one of the 50 states, in the District of Columbia, or in any American territory are citizens of the United States at birth, regardless of the nationality of their parents. Thus, whether your parents are American- or foreign-born, you can be a citizen of this country as long as you were born on United States territory. A child born in a foreign country can also be an American citizen if one parent is an American citizen. If the family lives abroad for an extended time, the child born abroad must come to live in the United States for at least five years between the ages of 14 and 28 in order to retain United States citizenship.

Naturalization is the legal process by which a person changes citizenship from one country to another. Naturalized citizens of the United States have the same rights and duties as natural-born citizens, except that they cannot be elected president or vice-president of the nation.

In the United States, a foreign-born person who is living in our country but is not yet a citizen is called an *alien*. To become a naturalized citizen of this country, an alien must be at least 18 years of age and must have been legally admitted to the United States as a permanent resident. An applicant for naturalization must live in the United States for five years. This includes a six-month residence in the state where an application is filed.

The first official step toward citizenship is to file a petition for naturalization. This petition must be sent to the nearest office of the Immigration and Naturalization Service, a division of the United States Department of Justice. An alien must then appear in an interview before a naturalization examiner with two United States citizen witnesses who have known the alien for the last five years. These witnesses give testimony regarding the alien's character. An alien must be of good moral character and believe in the principles of the United States Constitution.

During this interview an alien is asked to demonstrate an ability to read, write, and speak English. The examiner also asks questions to test the alien's knowledge of United States history and government. The examiner then makes a recommendation to the naturalization court.

About 30 days after the interview, the alien appears in court before a judge for final hearings. If the court approves an alien's petition for naturalization, the alien takes an

Becoming a citizen of the United States is an important event in the lives of these new citizens. They are taking the oath of allegiance in Hackensack, New Jersey.

33

oath pledging loyalty to the United States and renouncing loyalty to any other country. The alien receives a certificate of naturalization and is then officially a citizen of the United States.

> 1. In what ways can a person become a United States citizen?
> 2. Explain the process of naturalization.

RIGHTS and DUTIES of CITIZENSHIP

In this book, when we speak of citizenship we will usually mean something broader than national identity. Citizenship in the United States involves both rights and duties. Those rights which apply to all American citizens are defined in the United States Constitution and its amendments. (An *amendment* is a change or addition. Amendments to the Constitution are official changes of the original document.) These rights include the right to freedom of assembly, freedom of religion, free speech, the right to vote, and equal protection under the law. In addition, citizens have the right to all the privileges and services offered under local, state, and national laws.

The right to freedom of assembly means that citizens have the right to gather together in groups. Citizens sometimes participate in groups for the purpose of influencing local, state, or national government in some way. Sometimes they gather together to publicly evaluate the performance of elected leaders in office. Citizens also have the right to gather together in religious groups and to worship as they choose.

Freedom of speech allows citizens to express their views on important issues. Citizens have the right to speak out against government actions they think are unwise or wrong.

At the same time that Americans have these rights, they also have the duty to support their government, obey its laws, and defend it in time of war. To be worth anything, rights must be defended and used. For example, many people believe that citizens have the duty as well as the right to vote for their leaders in government. If citizens think their leaders are inefficient, they should support an opposing candidate and vote the leaders out of office. By the same token, if citizens think their leaders are doing a good job, it is important that they vote to re-elect them. Many people also believe that if a government official is not doing an effective job, citizens have the duty to bring this out publicly.

Citizens can fulfill their civic duties in a number of other ways also. (*Civic* means "related to citizenship.") Serving on juries, serving in the armed forces, taking part in community projects, and joining groups which seek to influence government are important kinds of civic participation.

As citizens of the United States, our rights and duties of citizenship are part of our behavior in our families, schools, businesses, and social groups. Citizenship protects our rights and defines our responsibilities in all the groups we belong to. For example, the right of due process under the law protects you as a high school student just as it protects adult members of your family. It is important to realize that private governments (such as your school or social groups) often define a special set of rights and duties unique to membership in those groups. These special rules cannot, however, deny you the rights you have as a citizen of this country.

Each of us is also a citizen of the global community. As such we have the right to seek changes to help better our world. We also have the duty to respect the rights of other nations and the values of other cultures.

An important right and duty of citizens is to join others in public action to improve their lives. Read the following case on citizen action in Arkansas and decide which rights and duties of citizenship were exercised by the organization known as ACORN.

34

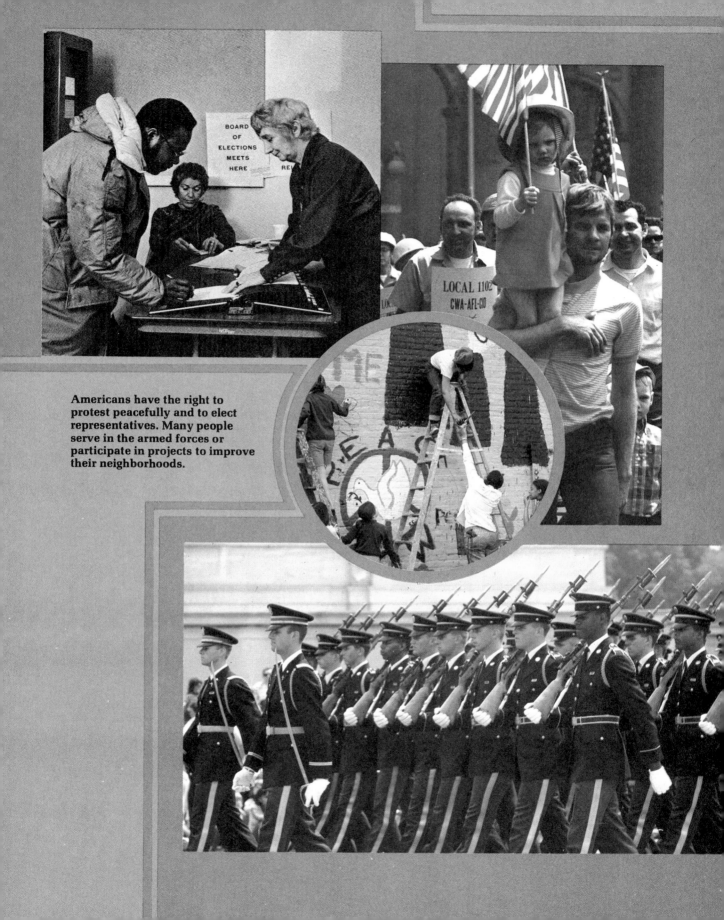

Americans have the right to protest peacefully and to elect representatives. Many people serve in the armed forces or participate in projects to improve their neighborhoods.

★ ACORN and Citizenship

The year 1970 was a memorable one in Little Rock, Arkansas. It was then that Wade Rathke, Director of the National Welfare Rights Organization, and local citizens decided to begin to act instead of to react to local concerns that were bothering them. In the hope of improving community life, they organized the Association of Community Organizations for Reform Now, popularly referred to as ACORN.

When ACORN first started, it organized various neighborhood projects in Little Rock. Generally, the members had small-scale goals, such as improving garbage collection and getting traffic lights installed. They felt that accomplishing their goals was important. They believed that people needed to feel successful in order to move on to bigger things.

Once the members learned that they could do things by organizing, they set their goals higher. They began successful campaigns for lower utility rates and for revised tax assessments. They also supported candidates for local office.

By 1977, ACORN was active in 11 states—Arkansas, Missouri, Texas, Louisiana, Tennessee, Florida, Colorado, Nevada, Iowa, Pennsylvania, and South Dakota. ACORN had become a collection of over 150 neighborhood organizations which boasted more than 10,000 member families. Its membership was approximately 60 percent white and 40 percent black.

ACORN has been successful. It has helped communities obtain better roads, stop signs at dangerous intersections, and better drainage for flooded yards. For example, W. Willard Johnson, Chairperson of the Arkansas Board of ACORN, had complained for years about poor drainage that caused flooding in his Little Rock home. In joining ACORN, he and his neighbors worked together to get a $960,000 federal grant to rework ditches and streets in their neighborhood.

The philosophy of ACORN and its relationship to citizens was reflected in a statement by Joshua Miller, an ACORN organizer. Here are parts of his statement:

"ACORN believes that a citizen education program must be founded on participation.

"Unless people have the experience of citizenship, citizen education can mean little to them. Unless people have power and are faced with the choices that come from holding power, discussions about political values ring hollow. Essential in the theory of citizenship is its practice.

"An essential aim of the ACORN organizing model is to increase citizen participation. One of the reasons ACORN organizes neighborhood groups instead of just state-wide or nation-wide structures is to allow more members to learn and to exercise leadership skills.

"An essential goal of every ACORN campaign, at both the local and state levels, is to develop skills of leadership and membership. In the course of a campaign many members learn how to write a statement, make a public speech, face the media, and develop strategy. ACORN members learn about political power by confronting it and exercising it."

1. What rights and duties of citizenship are shown in this case?
2. What examples of the functions of government can you find in this case? Is ACORN an example of public or private government?
3. Does your community have an organization similar to ACORN? If it does, briefly describe the organization and what it has accomplished. If there is no such organization in your community, think about whether one is needed and the kinds of concerns it could tackle.

Citizen Roles in Group Activities

The ACORN experience is an example of citizen participation. As in any group, members of ACORN contributed in different ways to group projects. They also gave varying amounts of their time and efforts. In other words, those people played different roles as they participated in political activities. A *role* is a way of acting in a group.

For example, in an army we expect a general and a private to act in different ways. They have different roles. The general gives orders, and the private is expected to follow orders. Different players on a basketball team also have different roles. For example, the center is expected to be a good rebounder. The guards are supposed to be playmakers. The coach has the right and duty to teach the players how to improve their game, and referees have the responsibility of enforcing the rules of the game.

FOUR PARTICIPANT ROLES In this section you will examine four different roles that people can and do play in group activity.

Understanding these roles enables you to take part in group activity more effectively. It is also important to understand the interaction that occurs between people as they participate according to these roles.

People who participate in groups usually find themselves in one or more of these roles: (1) observer, (2) supporter, (3) advocate, or (4) organizer. Each role has its own characteristics.

Some people tend to play one role more than others. However, most people perform each of the four roles at one time or another. It depends on the situation, the needs of the group, and the interests and abilities of the group members.

The Observer Role. Observers watch the action in a group. They listen carefully and notice who does what. Observers help a group reach its goals by spotting problems in group procedures and making suggestions about how to overcome them. Most citizens play the role of observer at one time or another. For example, most citizens act as observers during political campaigns. They read newspaper articles and watch television programs about the candidates. They may even attend rallies and listen to speeches given by the candidates.

Think about a person like Joseph Hartley, who belongs to the Drama Club in his school. He is most often an observer in this group. When the group is discussing different actions that might be taken, Joe usually listens and thinks carefully about what is said. He sometimes gathers information to answer questions that are raised. He makes suggestions to other club members about what they might do based on the information and observations he offers them. Other members often listen to Joe. They have learned to trust his observations. Observers tend to be less active than others. But a careful observer, such as Joe, can be a valuable group member.

The Supporter Role. Supporters are devoted to backing group projects. They are more active members of a group than observers are. After a decision is made, they do the work needed to carry it out. Without supporters, a group could not follow through on its plans. Supporters also try to help group members with clashing opinions settle their differences. Supporters do this in order to support the group effort, to help keep the group together. However, a good supporter is not a "blind" follower. The good supporter thinks carefully and critically before deciding what to do.

Many citizens act as supporters in election campaigns. People who work at the campaign headquarters of a candidate are acting as supporters. They make phone calls and they stuff envelopes with campaign

These students assume different participant roles in their school's Drama Club. Identify the observer, supporter, advocate, and organizer in the photographs.

literature. They participate in rallies and perform other tasks in behalf of their candidate.

A person like Jane Kerr, another member of the Drama Club in her school, tends to be a supporter of that group. When decisions are made, she works hard to carry them out under the direction of the club's leader. Jane is also known as a peacemaker in the club. She helps members with clashing opinions to settle their differences for the good of the group by offering compromise solutions.

More initiative is needed to play the supporter role than to act as an observer. Hard work and personal commitment are also usually involved.

The Advocate Role. Advocates take sides in a conflict. They try to influence others to agree with them. An advocate can state a position clearly and present reasons to try to convince others. Citizens who write editorials in newspapers, urging voters to back one candidate rather than another, are acting as advocates.

One of the most common acts of advocacy is standing up and speaking out on issues. United States senators advocate various positions every day. For example, when the 18-year-old vote was being debated in the Senate, Barry Goldwater played an advocate role when he testified before a Senate committee. He said:

> "I support extending the vote to young citizens because I know it is right. Young Americans can raise families, hold jobs, be taxed, be tried in adult courts and be trusted on the public highways; and yet they are not allowed to vote. Youth today is better informed than any previous generation. I hold that there is no sensible reason for denying the vote to 18-year-olds."

The amendment was approved in the Senate not long afterward. Effective advocates such as Senator Goldwater aided its success.

Once again consider a school setting. Felipe Garcia, for example, often takes the advocate role in meetings of the Drama Club. He is a good thinker and a skilled speaker. When the club is trying to decide on a course of action, Felipe usually gives his opinions and tries to persuade other members to agree with him.

Felipe is also an active supporter in the group. When decisions are made, he often helps to carry them out. However, Felipe thinks carefully before he acts. So he is not likely to follow the leadership of those he believes to be unwise or unfair.

The Organizer Role. Organizers are leaders and managers. They plan and manage group activities. They are active in setting group goals and influencing people to work together to reach those goals. They make sure that the group makes decisions and that the decisions are then carried out.

People who act as campaign managers are organizers. They manage people and events in the effort to elect their candidate to public office. Other kinds of organizers, such as civil rights leader Martin Luther King, Jr., have mobilized entire portions of the population behind important causes. Interest group leaders such as the heads of major labor unions commonly organize large groups in order to make their voices heard.

Maria Krokindes is the president of the School Drama Club. She is a leader and organizer. She is bright, outgoing, and persuasive. She can motivate group members to carry out group decisions, and she can plan activities for the group. To be an organizer requires more initiative and activity than performance of the other participant roles.

Remember that a person may assume different participant roles at various times. For example, Maria Krokindes, chief organizer of the Drama Club, sometimes takes an advocate position in that group. She may give her opinion on an issue such as whether the club should present one play instead of another. At other times, she is a careful observer of club members' discussion so that she can maintain a "sense of the meeting." And she always supports club

José

Mary

Georgina

Michael

Rita

Patrick

activities by helping in the same way any other member would. Because everyone plays all roles at some time, it is important to develop skills in each one.

Here is a fictional situation in which people play the several participant roles just discussed. Read the dialogue and decide what role or roles each person is playing.

★ How Much Help for Lisa Jimmerson?

Imagine the following situation: The Citizens for Good Government is a community group working to improve public services in the city. The group backs candidates for public office who seem likely to improve the city government. Thus, the group has decided to back Lisa Jimmerson's bid to become mayor. Group members believe that Lisa Jimmerson's leadership will bring the kinds of changes they are seeking. In the following discussion, group members are trying to decide how much money they can afford to contribute to Ms. Jimmerson's campaign.

Michael: How are we going to help Lisa Jimmerson win the mayoral election?

José: Well, for one thing, we can give $2,000 to her campaign fund.

Mary: That's too much. We haven't got that kind of money. I say we should donate only $500.

José: That's ridiculous. She needs all the money she can get to win this race. If we're really for her, we should give as much as possible.

Mary: I disagree, José! If Lisa gets $2,000 of our precious cash, then I'm walking out of this club.

Rita: Calm down, Mary. We all know you want the best for the group, and we respect you for it. We aren't going to do anything without including you in it. But you ought to give José's idea a fair hearing. He might be right. How about it, José?

José: Yes, I think it's a decent idea. I believe we should give Lisa Jimmerson some real support.

Rita: What do other people think about José's idea? Should we donate $2,000 to Lisa's campaign?

Patrick: That's a bit too much, but I think we can afford to give her $1,200.

Michael: That sounds like a good compromise. Let's take a vote on it. All in favor say "aye."

Georgina: Wait a minute! I haven't said much because I've been listening carefully and thinking. I don't think we're ready to decide yet. We need to study this situation some more.

Michael: I think you're right Georgina. Okay, before we decide what to do we need to have a committee study the situation and make a recommendation. Georgina, I want you, Mary, José, Patrick, and Rita to be on this committee. Rita, you be chairperson of the committee. Let's move ahead on this as quickly as possible.

1. What role or roles is each person playing? Explain.
2. What is the importance of each role to the success of the group?

CITIZENS as OBSERVERS

The exercise on the following three pages will help you develop skills in acting as an observer. Remember that a successful observer follows these guidelines. A good observer:

1. Listens carefully to group discussions.
2. When necessary, obtains information about the issue under discussion.
3. Makes suggestions to the group about actions that might be taken or decisions that should be made.

A parking garage controversy in the fictional town of Andersonville is presented in this exercise. Read about the controversy and the views presented in the profiles. Then be prepared to take the observer role in working out a solution to the problem.

The observer in this photograph is listening carefully to what is being said. He may be able to help these girls solve their problems.

★ The Observer Role

The Parking Garage Controversy

Andersonville is an average-sized community in the United States. The town shopping center is an active area where local community members have owned small businesses for a long time.

As the town has grown in size, the shopping area has become more and more crowded, and parking space has become hard to find. A local merchant has recently proposed tearing down one of the older stores and building a six-story parking garage in its place. This would increase the number of parking spaces available in town and relieve congestion in the streets. The idea has created vigorous debate among the people of Andersonville.

The Andersonville Town Council has met once to consider whether or not the parking garage should be permitted in the town. The council members' opinions are as varied as those of other community residents. Some council members believe that the multistory garage would help bring new revenue to the city, and this would encourage further business development. Others feel that it would be an unattractive sight and that it would contribute to rather than relieve the traffic problem.

The Town Council will meet several times to discuss the issue. Community members are prepared to voice their opinions and to support their opinions with facts.

Profile: Mr. / Mrs. Hickman

The Hickmans have lived in Andersonville all of their lives. They were born, raised, and married in Andersonville, and they are now bringing up their children there. They feel that adequate parking is necessary for the town. And they think that a parking garage can be built which will not destroy the small-town feeling of the community. In their opinion the parking lots which are presently scattered throughout the downtown area are ugly, and they would rather see stores and park areas built in their place.

They think this could be done if a new garage provides needed parking space.

The Hickmans also know that the town needs revenue. They share with others the belief that by attracting new businesses to Andersonville the community would receive additional income. For these reasons the Hickmans are planning to go to the Town Council meetings to register their support of the proposed multistory garage. They are also meeting with small groups of residents to formulate recommendations.

Profile: Mr. / Mrs. Bentley

Like the Hickmans, the Bentleys have lived in Andersonville all their lives. The Bentleys like Andersonville the way it is, and they don't want it to change.

No shop in town is over two stories high, and they think that a six-story building would destroy the attractiveness of the shopping area. They point to the possibility that additional parking facilities might encourage people from nearby towns to shop in Andersonville. The resulting traffic would clog the streets. There would be pollution and delays in getting from one place to another. The Bentleys also fear that large shopping malls might be a next step, which would change the entire atmosphere of the town.

The Bentleys have written carefully worded letters to the editor of the local newspaper, speaking out against the parking garage proposal. They are also meeting with other residents to discuss the issue.

Profile: The Observer

You have recently moved to Andersonville from a nearby city. Aware that there is a controversy over the possible building of a parking garage in Andersonville, you are anxious to learn more about the issue. As a concerned citizen, you attend the meeting of the Andersonville Town Council to discuss the proposed parking garage.

Activities

As you have learned, observers can be very important in group activities. Observers at the Andersonville Town Council meetings, for example, could offer a great deal in helping to resolve the controversial parking garage question.

Reread the characteristics of a good observer, pages 37 and 41. Then review the material you have just read about the parking garage controversy. Do one of the two following assignments. Your teacher will tell you which assignment to follow.

Assignment 1

a. Write position papers explaining the views of Mr./Mrs. Hickman and Mr./Mrs. Bentley on the parking garage issue. Both community members will present their views at town council meetings.

b. Imagine that you are an observer at the town council meeting at which Mr./Mrs. Hickman and Mr./Mrs. Bentley speak. As an observer who has listened to both people,

1. What questions do you have about the ideas presented?
2. What additional information do you need to form an opinion on the question?
3. What suggestions would you offer to resolve the situation?

Assignment 2

a. With two of your classmates, form a group of three for discussion of the Andersonville parking garage controversy. One person should play the part of Mr./Mrs. Hickman, a second person should play the part of Mr./Mrs. Bentley, and the third person should be an observer. In your group of three, Mr./Mrs. Hickman and Mr./Mrs. Bentley should present their ideas to one another on the garage question. Each should try to convince the other to agree with his or her position. The observer should follow the guidelines for playing the observer role.

b. Each person in your group should answer these questions:

1. What major topics were discussed?
2. Did the observer in your group enter the conversation in any way? If so, how?
3. What kinds of ideas did the observer suggest or do to aid in solving the controversy?
4. How might you act effectively as an observer in a school or community group to which you belong?

1. What is a government? What are its main functions for a group?
2. Make an outline of reasons for forming a government. Include these groups on your chart: the Iroquois, the Pilgrims, the Americans who wrote the Constitution, and the citizens of Kimberling City.
3. What is a constitution? Describe ways in which a constitution can reflect reasons for forming a government.
4. How do governments provide order and security for a group?
5. How do governments provide representation?
6. What services can governments provide?
7. How do governments manage relations with other governments? In what way is this a form of representation?
8. Describe the naturalization process for acquiring United States citizenship.
9. What are some of the rights and duties of citizenship in the United States?
10. Give a brief description of each of the four citizen roles described in this chapter.

Define the following terms.

government	public government	civic
constitution	private government	role
capitalism	citizenship	observer
socialism	naturalization	supporter
state	alien	advocate
confederation	amendment	organizer

1. List the different types of public and private governments that affect you. For example, you obey the rules of the federal, state, and local governments. Then, in essay form, analyze the reasons why membership in each of these governments is necessary. In other words, what functions does each perform?
2. According to Karl Marx and Friedrich Engels, the goal of communism is the establishment of a classless society in which there is no need for a government. Based on your reading of this chapter, do you think that

it is possible for a group of people to live together without a formal government? Explain why or why not.

3. List the four major areas in which most governments act. Then select what you consider to be the most important purpose of government. Explain why, using examples from the textbook, newspapers, or your community to support your answer.

4. People voluntarily join private governments. In other words, they willingly permit the government to enforce its rules. What are some of the reasons that a person might decide to become part of a private government, such as the League of Women Voters or the AFL-CIO? What rights and duties do members have in the organization?

5. Being a United States citizen means fulfilling certain civic duties. What are some of the duties that you can and do perform? What additional responsibilities do you expect to assume after you leave high school? For example, you will probably serve on a jury.

6. Reread the ACORN study. Then select a problem in your town or community. Based on your study of government thus far, write a proposal for an organization to solve the problem that you have chosen. In your proposal include the functions of the organization and the rights and the duties of the citizens who join.

Chapter Activities

1. Choose one area in which public government provides services for citizens. Write a story, play, or newspaper article describing an imaginary situation in which government suddenly stopped providing that service.

2. Obtain a copy of the constitution of any public or private government. Analyze the document in terms of what it tells you about the expectations of the people who made the constitution and what basic rules for government it establishes.

3. Act as an observer in a group to which you belong. Keep a diary in which you record your participation. At the end of your observation, evaluate your performance.

Chapter Bibliography

Backroom Politics: How Your Local Politicians Work, Why Your Government Doesn't and What You Can Do About It, Bill and Nancy Boyarsky (J. P. Tarcher: Los Angeles, CA), 1974.

A good account of what active citizen groups can do, written in a case study, journalistic style.

Citizen Action: Vital Force for Change, William M. Kitzmiller and Richard Ottinger, (Center for a Voluntary Society, Washington, DC), 1971.
> A study of the citizen action movement in America, focusing on five case studies of organizations.

The Story of the Declaration of Independence, Dumas Malone (Oxford University Press: New York, NY), 1976.
> A clearly written discussion of the Declaration of Independence, giving special attention to each of the signers.

Selected Readings in Citizen Education (National Conference on "Education and Citizenship: Responsibilities for the Common Good." Kansas City, MO), 1976.
> Contains articles on aspects of citizen education including politics, economics, the family, and ethnic groups.

A Public Citizen's Action Manual, Donald K. Ross (Grossman Publishers: New York, NY), 1973.
> Highlights how citizens can bring about changes in areas such as health, taxes, and making government responsive to their needs.

People Helping People: U. S. Volunteers in Action, (U. S. News and World Report: Washington, DC), 1977.
> A guide to volunteers and organizations active in fields like health, environment, crime, welfare, housing, and education.

Chapter Objectives

★ To learn the meaning of politics
★ To learn the meaning of political resources
★ To identify important political resources
★ To analyze variations in resources among groups in American society
★ To develop the skill of gathering evidence

chapter 2

POLITICS and POLITICAL RESOURCES

In Chapter 1 you learned about government and citizenship. With this base of understanding it is now important for you to learn how public government in the United States works. What does it do? How does it accomplish what it does? For this understanding you need to examine a basic idea for the entire course—politics. By exploring the idea of politics you will learn about political resources, a central part of political life.

Not all people have the same amount or kind of resources. In American society, for example, you can identify basic differences in resources among age groups, between men and women, and among ethnic groups. The knowledge of these variations in resources is essential to an understanding of differences in political activities among these groups.

Skills are an important resource for effective citizenship. Throughout this course you will be introduced to a variety of skills that are necessary for participation in political activity. They can be called citizenship skills. The first of them, presented in Chapter 2, is the skill of gathering evidence. Knowing how to find information can be important in many aspects of your life, particularly in forming opinions and making decisions. In political situations, the skill of gathering evidence becomes an essential part of effective citizenship.

What Is Politics?

Government operates through a process called *politics*. Politics goes on daily in city halls, county courthouses, state legislatures, and in our national Capitol. The people involved in politics include mayors, governors, judges, lawmakers, and members of various citizen's groups. Because these people take part in political events, they can be called *political actors*. The term "political actors" is useful as a general label under which to categorize all people who participate in any kind of political activity.

Politics also goes on around you every day in your home, school, and social groups after school. Who takes part? Do you? Do your parents and friends ever participate in politics? What is politics anyway?

GROUPS, ACTIVITIES, RESOURCES

One definition of politics involves three key ideas. These ideas are *groups*, *activities*, and *resources*.

First of all, politics is activity within groups. It is part of interaction among people. Action which you take alone and which affects you alone is not political action. When you decide what time to get up in the morning, you are not making a political decision! But when your class decides how to spend its class treasury, the activity is a political one.

Not all group activity is political. What makes any action political, in addition to its involvement with a group, is its involvement with resources. When you consider resources you may think about the oil that heats your home or the money you use to buy food. In other words, a resource is something you use to satisfy needs or accomplish certain goals. When resources are used in politics they can be called *political resources*.

One example of a political resource is the vote. Citizens use this resource to accomplish the goal of electing a particular person to office. The activity of voting is one way in which citizens can influence the direction and policies of government. They can vote for persons who reflect their own positions on governmental issues.

Resources are a part of politics in two ways. They are *used* in political activities, and they can be *distributed* as a result of those activities. You have already considered the use of your vote as a political resource. In the same way, for example, you can use status—your position in a group—as a political resource. Think about candidates in an election. Some may have high status based on political or social experience, personal wealth, family name, or some other characteristic. This high status can be used by candidates to persuade voters to select them in the election. On the other hand, status is also distributed as a result of the election. The winner gains higher status than the losers. The winner also may be in a position to distribute additional status by appointing others to important jobs in a new administration.

You can examine the groups, activities, and resources in any political action. Suppose you write a letter asking your representative in Congress to vote in favor of spending federal money on school lunch programs. The resources you use in this activity are your skill in communicating and your importance to the representative as a voter. The group which is affected is the American people. By communicating your stand on an issue to your representative you will have an effect on his or her decision to vote "yes" or "no" on the issue. That decision affects the federal government's distribution of money—an important resource.

In summary then, politics is activity in which resources are used and distributed in a group.

1. What examples of politics can you think of? Try to explain the relationship between resources and activities in each example.
2. What skills do you think a person needs to function well in political situations?

POLITICS in ACTION An election campaign is an excellent situation in which to examine politics in action. The following case is about Tom Bradley and his election as mayor of Los Angeles, one of the largest cities in the United States. Bradley ran for mayor in 1969 and was defeated. He ran again for mayor in 1973, and this time he won. He was reelected in 1977.

Bradley is the first black person to be elected mayor of Los Angeles. In 1973 there were 2,621 black people in the United States who held elected office. This figure included 82 black mayors. When Bradley became the nation's 83rd black mayor, he was part of a general movement for increased black participation in the political process.

A series of black mayors had been elected in major cities before 1973. Carl Stokes was elected mayor of Cleveland in 1967. He was the first black man in this country to be elected mayor of a major city. Richard Hatcher was elected mayor of Gary, Indiana, in 1968. Following him, Kenneth Gibson became mayor of Newark, New Jersey, in 1970. Thus by the time Bradley was elected, black people in several major United States cities had won mayoral elections.

Bradley's victory was not won by a black coalition against a white minority. (This had been the case in some other cities.) Blacks comprise only about 18 percent of Los Angeles' population. The population is also 14 percent Mexican-American. The majority of people living in Los Angeles are white, and almost half of this majority white population voted for Bradley in 1973.

As you read the following case, see if you can identify the resources and activities which Bradley used to achieve his goal.

★ **Making a Difference in Los Angeles**

For Tom Bradley, winning the election for mayor of Los Angeles in 1973 was a success story. What aided Bradley in his victory? Much of the answer lies in Tom Bradley himself. Bradley's story goes back to Calvert, Texas, a small town where his father

Tom Bradley shakes hands with supporters during his first campaign for mayor of Los Angeles in 1969. Bradley lost the run-off election to Mayor Sam Yorty that year.

was a farm worker. The family moved to Los Angeles in 1923. There Bradley attended an almost exclusively white high school where he was nicknamed "Long Tom," because of his 6'4" height. He became a football and track star.

Bradley then went on to U.C.L.A. for his college work. He married, and joined the Los Angeles police force. A member of the police force for 21 years, Bradley rose to the rank of police lieutenant. While on the force, he was active in community relations. He tried to better the understanding between the police force and ghetto residents. During the evenings Bradley continued his schooling and soon earned a law degree.

Bradley left the police department in 1963, after he won a seat on the Los Angeles City Council. He served on the City Council until his election in 1973 as mayor. During his years on the police force and City Council, Bradley had the opportunity to learn many skills. Most important, he learned how to deal with people, how to make necessary compromises, and how to be an efficient administrator.

Bradley's quest for the mayor's office began officially in 1969. In the spring of that year he entered the Los Angeles mayoral primary. (Los Angeles conducts a *non-partisan* mayoral primary. This means that the names of eligible candidates from all parties are put on the same ballot. The two candidates with the highest number of votes then face each other in a run-off contest.) Bradley was one of the top two candidates in the primary. He faced the mayor of eight years, Sam Yorty, in the election run-off.

A great many resources were put at Bradley's command at this time. The traditionally conservative and influential *Los Angeles Times* came out in support of Bradley. In addition, he was endorsed by well-known political figures. For example, prominent senators and representatives—Democrats as well as Republicans—came out for Tom Bradley. His bid for the mayor's office was given support in national newspapers and had wide coverage. Therefore, he had national visibility and the backing of key political figures.

Bradley ran well among blacks in Los Angeles, who hoped that through him they would receive more benefits from the city. He also ran well in some Mexican-American communities; however, most white people did not vote for Bradley. Bradley was an unknown. Many whites did not know whether they could trust him. And at the time racial prejudice and violence were high.

Mayor Tom Bradley of Los Angeles answers questions during his first term in office.

Despite the support given to him, Tom Bradley lost the 1969 election to Sam Yorty. But Bradley did not feel personally defeated. Part of his reaction to Mayor Yorty's reelection victory was as follows:

"We have worked for victory. Not for a man, but for an idea. Not for a partisan victory, but a victory for principle. We have tried to prove that the democratic process can work. Never give up that hope. I have lived by that belief all my life, and I will not give up now. This city, this nation, does not begin or end with one man. Keep faith with what we are trying to do."

As Bradley stated on the eve of his defeat, he believed in democratic principles. He vowed to go on fighting for them. Bradley wanted people to be proud of Los Angeles. He believed the city should serve its diverse citizenry. He would spend four years campaigning to become known, to become trusted, and to become a popular alternative to the incumbent mayor. (An *incumbent* is a person currently holding an office.)

Tom Bradley faced Sam Yorty once again in the 1973 mayoral election. This time Bradley hired an experienced manager to run his election campaign. In this attempt Bradley put together media advertising that was unequaled for a mayor's race. He spent more than a million dollars in the campaign. About half this money went for television commercials.

Bradley also went to the people directly. He campaigned in every section of Los Angeles, speaking at rallies, before church groups, and at events where people could get to know him.

Tom Bradley also had a program. He made many promises to the citizens of Los Angeles. He promised to reduce crime and to establish a rapid transit system. He promised to bring about government reform and new social programs for minorities and the poor. He called for a crash development of detoxification centers for drug addicts. He called for the use of volunteer community patrols to curb street crime and gang violence. In each of these cases, he demonstrated a sincere interest in the people of Los Angeles and in solving problems which plagued the city.

Bradley received help from various organizations in the 1973 campaign, including labor unions and other interest groups. One important source of support came from black church groups. In Los Angeles a group called Concerned Clergy to Elect Bradley was formed. Once organized, the Concerned Clergy met weekly to campaign and to plan a strategy for getting the vote for Bradley. Ministers from the major black and white congregations gathered together in this effort. Members of the Concerned Clergy organized telephone campaigns, set up registration centers, and became registrars of voters themselves. Prior to election day, a mass rally was held at the Second Baptist Church in Los Angeles. The pastor of this church was Thomas Kilgore, a founder of the Southern Christian Leadership Conference. For twenty years Kilgore was a personal adviser to the late Martin Luther King, Jr. This rally was attended by black people from all over the city. It gave visibility and important momentum to the Bradley campaign.

Because of a good campaign, loyal followers, and citizen dissatisfaction with Mayor Yorty, Bradley won the mayoral election in 1973. He captured 56 percent of the popular vote. The election results represented the support of voters from many ethnic groups who wanted a change in leadership. Approximately half of the white population of Los Angeles cast its vote for Bradley. The tables had been turned from 1969 to 1973 through a strong campaign and a personality who could attract the majority vote.

As Bradley himself said,

"When I ran against him [Yorty] in 1969, I was known by only 7 percent of the people in this city. The fears he stirred in people and the uncertainty came because I wasn't known. When this election started, I was known by 95 percent of the people so it was a considerably different situation.

"I have been working from the day of that defeat in 1969, not only to become better known, but to have people understand what I'm all about. I worked with them in their communities and their neighborhoods on their problems. I wasn't just a councilman from *my* district. I think that helped greatly in establishing not only identification but some clear picture of how I will work to serve all the people of this city."

In 1977, at the end of his first term as mayor, Bradley was reelected.

1. What was Tom Bradley's goal? What activities did he take part in to achieve his goal? See if you can pick out the resources he used.
2. How did citizen participation contribute to Bradley's 1973 success?
3. What advantages might an incumbent have in an election campaign?

TYPES of POLITICAL RESOURCES

Anything that can be used to accomplish goals or satisfy needs in a group can be a political resource. In general, political resources can be grouped in categories. In this section you will be examining the categories of wealth, votes, ideas, skills, status, and information.

You also will learn about the various ways in which resources function in political life. Basically, those with more political resources are in a position to have greater political influence than those with fewer resources. The more resources people have, the better they can accomplish their goals.

Wealth. As you can imagine, money is a key resource for political action. Candi-

dates for elective office depend on money to run effective campaigns. In many elections, those candidates with the most money to spend have a stronger chance of election over their opponents. Their money can buy more publicity and more exposure to the public.

The costs involved in running for office, particularly national office, can be staggering. This is especially true when the expenses involved in publicity and staffing are added up. For example, in the 1976 presidential contest, a total of $70 million was spent by the 28 people who sought the Republican and Democratic nominations. Fund raising—the attempt to increase financial resources—is thus a critical campaign activity.

Money spent to support a candidate can have a long-term effect on how resources are distributed in society. Those who win election to office are then in a position to put into practice their beliefs about which groups of people should receive what kinds of benefits.

Money also supports activities directed at informing and influencing government officials of citizens' views. Obviously, individuals with money to contribute to candidates and to the political party of their choice are in a particularly strong position to make their views known.

Money as a political resource is important to all kinds of groups, not just to those involved in election activity. Businesses, social groups, and community groups in your town, for example, all rely on money for the services and influence it brings. Money pays for the services of people with knowledge and skills needed to help a group achieve its goals.

Votes. As you learned earlier, your vote is a very important political resource. You probably think of voting as the process of choosing among several candidates. In fact, to *vote* means to make any formal choice. The choice may be among candidates, among ideas, among objects. In many

54

Many political resources are represented here. Nelson Rockefeller, in the top photograph, had great personal wealth. He also had status, because he served as governor of New York and later as vice-president of the United States. Many Americans, like the man in the center, use the newspaper as a source of important political information. The campaign workers in the bottom photograph provide their candidate with the resources of loyalty, support, time, and effort.

situations, the choice is deciding "yes" or "no" on a certain issue. School boards, town councils, state commissions, and our national law-making bodies operate on different levels. However, they all use the vote to make choices in decision-making situations.

For the individual citizen, the vote is a very precious political resource. In a representative democracy such as ours, in which leaders are elected by the people, the vote allows people to determine who runs their government. Citizens are also given the opportunity to express their opinions on public issues by voting.

Ideas. Ideas as solutions to problems, ideas as guidelines to follow, ideas as beliefs to cherish—all can be extremely important in political activity. Why? Because people often act as a result of ideas they believe in. In the United States, the important ideas of democracy, freedom, and equality form the basis of our laws and of our actions toward one another. These ideas have shaped the course of United States history since our nation's birth.

When people run for office—government office or office in a private organization—they usually present their ideas on a set of issues. These ideas often represent the candidates' positions on how certain questions or problems should be dealt with. People will vote for a candidate on the basis of the candidate's ideas. Those who can influence others by their ideas have a key resource at their disposal.

Ideas also can take the form of loyalty. For example, school spirit is an idea that creates feelings of loyalty. This idea can be a meaningful political resource. A leader who has people's loyalty has crucial support in making and enforcing rules. At the same time, loyal leaders have strong feelings of responsibility toward their followers, feelings which can be a resource for that group.

1. Which of the political resources discussed so far do you think that you have? Explain.

2. Which of these resources might you use effectively in a group to which you belong? Explain.

Skills. We often talk about people with "experience" and how important that is in political activity. People respect leaders who have been through tough situations and who have been able to resolve important issues. Experience in political situations involves the development of a number of skills. Five of these skills are discussed here.

Skill in *public speaking* is very important in trying to influence other people. Today, very few people in a representative democracy can be leaders unless they possess this skill. Good public speakers are able to persuade others to understand and agree with their point of view. They can present sound arguments in support of their ideas. They are willing to air their ideas before groups of people. Good speakers usually speak clearly, and very effective speakers can move a crowd to action.

Think of political leaders in the news. It is quite likely that many of these people have strong speaking ability. Now think of leaders in your school and in your town. Which of these people have, in your opinion, well-developed skill in public speaking?

Working in groups is another important skill which can serve as a political resource. Working effectively in groups means knowing how to get along with other people, how to set clear objectives, how to divide tasks among group members, and how to get a job done. Groups which function well are also able to follow alternative plans if their original scheme does not work. Groups which don't function well are not able to reach their goals.

Bargaining skill is also important as a political resource. A great deal of political activity involves give and take. Sometimes a person has to give in on a certain point in order to gain on another. Good bargainers know how to convince others. They know how to make necessary trades on issues.

They know when to stand firm when they think the other side is wrong. Such negotiation between people and groups with opposing views is a normal part of political life.

Skill in *decision-making* is another key resource in political activities. Knowing when and how to make wise choices is a key to effective leadership and action. So is understanding the process by which decisions are made. Decisions are made every day in all kinds of political settings. The basics of skilled decision-making, however, are the same no matter what the situation.

Differences of opinion among people and groups are common. They are to be expected in political life, especially when people are competing for limited services and other benefits. Indeed, many believe that conflict is itself the heart of politics. Ability in *settling differences* is therefore a valued skill. Conflict need not be violent. A clash of ideas on what action should be taken or on what strategy to use can produce conflict which is nonviolent but serious nonetheless. Good political leaders know how to make conflict a productive force. They can find ways of cooperation. These are fundamental skills no political leader can do without.

> 1. Which of the political skills just discussed do you think you have at the present time?
> 2. Which of these skills might be valuable to you in a group to which you belong?

Status. "Status" refers to the authority that a person has and the amount of respect that person receives from others. A high or low status indicates a person's position in a group. When people talk about status, they generally think in terms of high status.

Some people have *formal status.* Those who hold official positions in government, business, education, or other walks of life have formal status. The president of the United States has high formal status because of the authority and responsibility which

the office of president holds. The head of a corporation, the chief of police, and the superintendent of education in your town have high status also because of the authority of their offices.

Informal status is the position someone has in relationship to other people based on friendship, trust, and common experience. Informal status is created by the network of friends and relationships that a person establishes. Those who win the admiration of others find that they enjoy high status, even if they hold no formal position at all. Very often admiration is gained because of the ideas and skills that individuals possess.

How can high status work as a political resource? People often listen carefully to those in authority and those they respect. They will often follow their suggestions. Status is therefore a very important source of power.

Information. Information is a necessary resource for those who want to vote wisely, to act intelligently on issues confronting them, and to make decisions about how to use their time and energy. For instance, citizens need to know the basic facts about the world energy situation if they are to understand national energy programs.

Basically, those who are "in the know" have more political power than those who are not. Being "in the know" includes knowing how government works—who the sources of power are, how they can be reached, how to get answers to your questions.

Other Resources. Wealth, votes, ideas, skills, status, and information are very important political resources, but they are certainly not the only examples. Anything which a person uses to gain goals in political situations can be thought of as a political resource.

Public approval, for example, can also be thought of as a resource. Public officials and independent agencies often conduct polls to find out what people think about policies, issues, and leaders. Leaders like the president of the United States often quote the results of poll statistics to say that most Americans support their policies. This approval gives a leader an important base of political power. The leader is then in a position to exert influence on members of Congress to win support for programs.

Having a majority or at least a large number of people to back one's cause can be a most effective political resource. This is true in government or in everyday political situations. Being able to say "we think" instead of "I think" carries with it the approval and support of others.

Support in the form of *time and effort* devoted by volunteers is another important resource. Sharing a person's ideals is a major part of loyalty. Knowing that a person can be trusted is another major factor. Loyalty often motivates people to take action on behalf of others. For example, most local elections and, indeed, many national elections, are run by loyal volunteers. These volunteers put in personal time, effort, and energy that candidates could not afford to pay for. The hard work of loyal volunteers can provide the necessary momentum that a candidate needs to wage a successful campaign.

In yet another frame of reference, think about how important sheer *numbers* can be to the success of a national movement. For example, the number of followers who supported Martin Luther King, Jr., when he led the civil rights movement in the 1950s and 1960s was extremely important to him as he sought additional support for the civil rights cause.

1. What other examples of political resources can you think of?
2. In what ways can these resources be used? (Think of situations and experiences which are common to your own life as well as to government and public elections.)

The following case will help you identify political resources in a typical school situation. The case is a fictional one, and it takes place in a high school perhaps very similar to yours. The case shows how political resources are used by students on an everyday basis. As you read, think about the political resources of each person described.

★ **The Student Lounge**

The Student Action Club at Jefferson High School was organized three years ago. The club was founded by students who wanted to modify the dress code. They thought students should be allowed to wear casual clothes, such as jeans and sandals, to school. The students who worked with the Student Action Club were successful in their efforts, and the dress code was relaxed.

Since the dress code issue, however, the club has done very little. People have raised some other problems, but no one has wanted to become involved enough to work on them. The club has dwindled to a dozen members who meet once in a while to talk.

Recently, however, club meetings have become more exciting. Members are talking about a new issue—whether students can have their own lounge in school. Many students want a place where they can relax and spend time together (even do homework) before and after school. There are several areas in the school which could be made into a student lounge.

The club seems to have an issue, but it doesn't have a membership. Most students stopped coming to meetings long ago. Jackie, the club president, is concerned. How can the club put together a group to look into this question? They clearly need people, but not just anyone. They need to form a working group which can get things done quickly and efficiently.

Jackie raised the issue at the Tuesday meeting of the club. The five people who attended were enthusiastic. They talked about their needs, and agreed that they want people to look into the tasks involved in arranging for a student lounge. They also need people who can influence others, including teachers and administrators, to support the student lounge proposal. Well-respected people who can calmly and clearly discuss the student lounge proposal with others will be important in this task. Finally, the club decided it needs people with ideas about how possible problems can be solved. It needs students who can work up plans that people in school will rally behind.

Everyone agreed that the Student Action Club needs help in several important areas. They adjourned the meeting with the promise that they would think about these needs. Each club member agreed to prepare a list of names of people who could help them.

Following are descriptions of people who might be asked by the Student Action Club to help investigate the student lounge issue. If you could choose just two students to become members of the club, which of these two do you think would have the most to offer? Why?

with money to buy furniture or equipment for a lounge. Barbara has many ideas about various activities the class might undertake with its money. She will be important in planning and winning support for these activities. The lounge is only one idea among several which she considers to be important.

Ronald (Ron) Mackey

Ron is a good student, and he is respected by his teachers and classmates. In the past he has been able to win teacher support for activities that students wanted to undertake. Although Ron is not an official leader in any school organizations, he has been useful in convincing teachers of the soundness of student views.

Sam Turner

Sam Turner is well liked by many students. He is quarterback of the school's championship football team, knows many students, and works easily with others. However, Sam does not have much influence with teachers. And, he does not know procedures for dealing with the school administration. He is a "go-getter," though, and most students listen to him.

Barbara Banks

Barbara is treasurer of the senior class and oversees the $250 raised by the class early this year. The seniors are the only ones

Chris Chavez

Chris Chavez is editor of the student newspaper. Under his direction the editorial staff of the school newspaper frequently polls students, teachers, and administrators to find out their views on school problems. Chris has consistently run a paper which presents issues fully and clearly. The teachers and the principal sometimes disagree with his editorials, but generally they respect his point of view.

Chris is an idea man. His editorials usually reflect both careful thought about an issue and alternative plans for how a problem can be solved. He rarely has led students in "causes," but he often has valuable suggestions about effective courses of action. For

59

example, his suggestions helped bring about agreement on the new school dress code.

Marv Rosen

Marv has been pushing for a student lounge since he was a freshman. He was principal author of the revised student dress code. He knows the school rules better than any other student. Marv has done a lot of research on student lounges at other schools—how they were created, what happened when they first began, and what reasons students give for using such a room.

Marv has often tried to get students to push the lounge issue, but without success. He has fresh ideas and facts to back his case, but students have been too busy with other activities. Marv is a man with an idea, but without much of a following.

Jennie Larkin

Jennie Larkin is an excellent debater who has led the school debating team to many victories over the last two years. Jennie is respected by students, teachers, and administrators, since she has brought recognition to the school and community.

Because of her skills, Jennie has much influence with the principal. The principal is often persuaded on school issues after listening to Jennie's arguments. Jennie worked hard on the dress code issue. She developed a good argument which the principal used in support of the new code when the issue was brought before the school board.

1. What might each person be able to contribute to the success of the Student Action Club?
2. Which two of these people do you think have the most valuable resources? Why?

Variations in Political Resources

So far we have been talking about resources that people *can* have. It is also important to know what resources people actually *do* have. When you investigate the resources people really possess, you see that some people have many more resources than others. Consider the resources of someone living alone in the desert without a large community nearby. Compare that person's resources for influencing politics to those of the governor of California!

Knowing who has more resources and who has fewer is a very important part of understanding the realities of political activity. People who have more resources than others can have more influence or power in the system. They also can gain even more resources. Remember what you learned earlier: Having some resources helps you gain

more resources, just as "success breeds success."

If you want to investigate variations in resources you need to know what kinds of information provide good *indicators* of resources. For example a person's personal income indicates how much wealth he or she has as a resource. A person's job can indicate his or her status in society. The amount of formal education a person has can indicate that person's probable resources in knowledge and skills. By comparing the average personal income, jobs, and education of different groups of people you can learn significant facts about variations in resources among those groups.

As you analyze variations in income, jobs, and education, you will see significant differences among the resources of groups in

American society. However, when people with few resources work together to accomplish goals, they become much more powerful. The strength of numbers becomes a resource in itself. The civil rights movement is an outstanding example of this.

DIFFERENCES in INCOME Income tells us how much money a person earns. High income can be a valuable political resource. It gives a person money which can be used to support candidates and campaigns. People with higher incomes often have more time to devote to politics than people with lower incomes have. Those with higher incomes usually have more political influence than people with lower incomes have. Thus, information about income is one indicator of the political resources that an individual can contribute to any political situation.

Figure 2–1 shows the percentage of families in the United States at certain levels of income in 1975. (Study the material entitled *Reading a Pie Graph* on page 62.) Notice

Figure 2-1

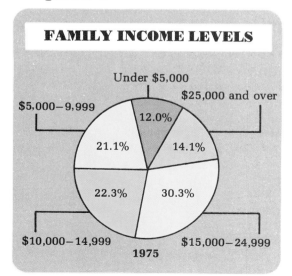

Rounding off of figures may cause figures to total slightly less than 100%.

Source: Statistical Abstract of the U.S. 1976

Figure 2-2

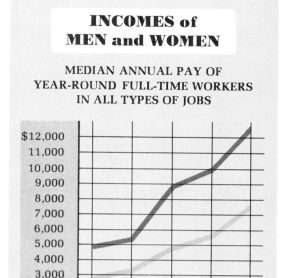

Source: Statistical Abstract of the U.S. 1976

that 14.1 percent earned more than $25,000 in 1975. In that year 12.1 percent earned less than $5,000. That portion of the American population with very low incomes had little or no money or time to use as a political resource. What money they had was used to buy food, clothing, and other necessities. On the other hand, those with high incomes had more money, time, and skills to use as a political resource.

Figure 2–2 shows the median incomes of males and females from 1955 to 1975. (Study the material entitled *Reading a Line Graph* on page 64.) For example, the graph shows that in 1955 the median income for women was about $2,700. This means that half of the women in the United States earned less than this amount and half of the women earned more. The graph shows that most women still tend to earn less money each year than men do. In 1975 the median

61

Reading a Pie Graph

Look in several textbooks or in recent copies of newspapers and you will probably find graphs and charts. Despite the fact that they contain condensed information, many people skip over graphs and charts, thinking they are difficult to read. In fact, they are easy to understand. You just need practice. Graphs and charts help to show the relationship between two or more sets of information. There are several types of graphs—*pie graphs*, *line graphs*, and *bar graphs*.

Figure 2-1 is an example of a pie graph. The pie as a whole represents the total number of American families in 1975. It is divided into several sections, each of which represents an income level. For example, one section represents those American families who earned $10,000-$14,999 in 1975. According to census figures, the incomes of 22.3% of American families in that year fell into this salary range.

The information contained in the pie graph could also be presented in this way:

INCOME LEVEL	PERCENT OF FAMILIES IN THE UNITED STATES, 1975
Under $5,000	12.0
$5,000–$9,999	21.1
$10,000–$14,999	22.3
$15,000–$24,999	30.3
$25,000 and over	14.1

Suppose you were given the information in the two columns above and were then asked to present this information in a pie graph. Your first step would be to determine what the whole pie represents. In this case it represents American families in 1975. Then you would determine how many sections you'd need to divide your pie into and how large each section would have to be. In this example the pie is divided into five sections. Let's take one section and decide how large it should be.

In 1975, 30.3%, or slightly less than one third, of American families earned $15,000-$24,999. Therefore, a section which is roughly one third of the pie should be reserved for the $15,000-$24,999 income category. Similarly, 20.1%, or roughly one fifth, of American families earned $5,000-$9,999 in 1975. Thus another section measuring roughly one fifth of the pie should be drawn to represent the $5,000-$9,999 income category. The other sections should be figured out in the same way.

Because the number of families in each income level is shown according to percent, which is based on 100, it is helpful to think of the pie as divided into 100 sections. Thirty of these sections represent the $15,000-$24,999 category, 20 of them represent the $5,000-$9,999 category, and so on.

What advantage is there to presenting information in a pie graph instead of in two columns as shown above?

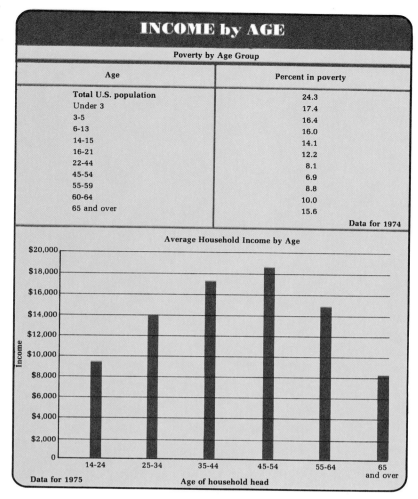

Figure 2-3

INCOME by AGE	

Poverty by Age Group

Age	Percent in poverty
Total U.S. population	24.3
Under 3	17.4
3-5	16.4
6-13	16.0
14-15	14.1
16-21	12.2
22-44	8.1
45-54	6.9
55-59	8.8
60-64	10.0
65 and over	15.6

Data for 1974

income of male workers was between $12,000 and $13,000. The median for females was about $7,500.

In general, women were likely to have less income than men to use as a political resource. However, the graph also shows that women's median income increased from 1955 to 1974. In that period, women improved their income and their ability to use political resources at a *greater* rate than men. This must be taken into consideration when you make the generalization that men usually earn more than women.

As you study these data, keep in mind that these statistics show the broad picture. There are always exceptions to every generality. For example, Figure 2-2 shows that, in general, women earn less than men. However, some women make more money per

year than many men do, and have more money to use as a political resource. These women are exceptions to the generalizations based on the graph.

The data shown in Figure 2-3 provides information about the incomes of adults in different age groups. The statistics show that younger people and older people tend to earn less than those in the middle-age category. This means that young people and older adults have less money to offer to the political process. On the other hand, they may have more time than working people in the 35 to 64 age group.

In the United States there are also wide variations in income based on racial and ethnic identity. As you can see in Figure 2-4, the income of whites and nonwhites in 1975 was very different. In general, there are both

Reading a Line Graph

Figure 2–2 is an example of a line graph. To read the graph, look first at the line that runs up and down. This vertical line is called the *vertical axis*. In Figure 2–2 the vertical axis shows income levels. Now look at the line that runs sideways. This line is called the *horizontal axis*. In Figure 2–2 the horizontal axis is a time line spanning the years 1955-1974.

The two lines drawn in color on the graph show the median annual pay of year-round, full-time workers in all types of jobs. The figures are broken down for men and women separately. *Median* refers to the midway point. In this graph, median annual pay means that for each income figure shown, half the women (or men) earned more and half earned less than this figure.

To determine the median annual pay for men in the year 1970, locate 1970 on the horizontal axis. Then, run the eraser of your pencil up to the line labelled "men." If you look over to the vertical axis, you'll see that the median annual pay of year-round full-time male workers in 1970 was about $9,300. What was the median annual pay for women in 1960? In 1970? In what year was the median income for men over $11,000?

Let's imagine that you were given the following information:

MEDIAN YEARLY INCOME of GRANDVIEW CITIZENS	
YEAR	**YEARLY INCOME**
1970	$7,000
1971	6,900
1972	7,500
1973	8,000
1974	8,400
1975	8,600
1976	9,000
1977	9,300
1978	9,700

To convert this information into a line graph, you should first create a horizontal axis and a vertical axis. The horizontal axis could represent the years, and the vertical axis could show yearly income. (Or, you could do this in reverse.) Any axis should be subdivided into even intervals. On this graph, for example, the axis showing the income should be divided into even intervals of $1,000. To plot out the median yearly income of Grandview citizens, first find 1970 on its axis. Then, run the eraser of your pencil up to a point even with $7,000. Place a round pencil mark at that point. Follow the same procedure in plotting the median income for each of the other years. Then connect the marks with one another. The result will be a line graph. The line itself will not be a straight line. But like Figure 2–2, the graph will present information in linear fashion.

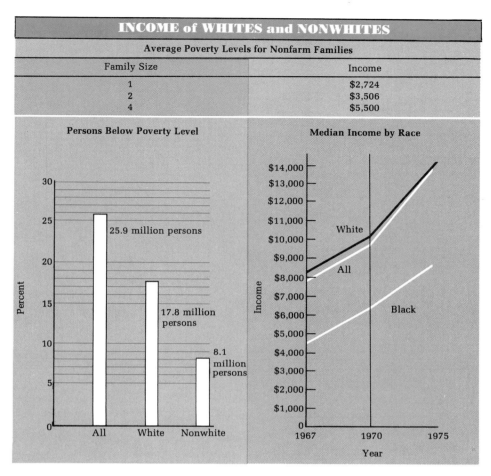

Figure 2-4

rich and poor people in every racial and ethnic group. However, the economic position of minority groups tends to be considerably less favorable than that of whites in the United States. This condition, like the condition of women, has improved and median incomes have increased slightly.

1. On the basis of income, rank the following people in terms of who is most likely to have the greatest political resources.
   a. A 17-year-old female
   b. A 45-year-old male
   c. A 68-year-old male
   d. A 38-year-old female
2. Which ones of the following general statements do you think accurately describe what you have learned from the charts, tables, and graphs on personal income?
   a. Women tend to earn more money than men in the United States.
   b. The older a person is the higher his or her income will be.
   c. In the United States the median income for whites is greater than that for blacks or Hispanic Americans.
   d. More whites than blacks live in poverty in the United States.
   e. White, middle-class, middle-aged males generally have more political resources than other groups in the United States do.
   f. Generally, the financial situation for women and minority groups has improved.

JOB STATUS of WOMEN in GOVERNMENT and BUSINESS

1. In 1975, of all elected officials in the United States, between 5% and 7% were women.

2. In 1977, about 12,000 women held elective offices, but this represented only 10% of elected officials. There were 2 female governors (Ella Grasso, D.-Conn.; Dixie Lee Ray, D.-Wash.), 18 female members of the U.S. House of Representatives, and 2 female members of the president's cabinet. There were no women in the U.S. Senate.

3. In 1967, there were 27.5 million women in the U.S. labor force.

4. In 1977, there were 37 million women in the U.S. labor force. Of these 6.16 million, or 16%, held professional jobs.

5. An April 1977 survey of influential Americans by *U.S. News and World Report* listed 2 women among the 30 people selected. The women mentioned were Katherine Graham, publisher of *The Washington Post*, and Rosalynn Carter.

Figure 2-5

DIFFERENCES in JOB STATUS

Statistics about job status can tell you what percentage of a group hold high-level positions in government, business, schools, and other important sectors of our society. People in top jobs usually have high status in their communities and are in positions to influence political activity on many levels. Thus, information about job status is another indicator of political resources.

Figures 2–5, 2–6, and 2–7 provide information about who holds top jobs in government, business, schools, and various professional fields. Use this information to answer questions that follow the data cards. Think about what these data tell you about who is likely to have more or fewer political resources.

1. Which of the following statements do you believe accurately describe variations in job status in the United States?

    a. Males tend to have more high-status jobs than females do, although the percentage of females in high-status jobs has increased over the years.

    b. Middle-aged Americans tend to have better job status than young or older Americans do.

Figure 2-6

TOP JOBS by AGE

1. In 1977 the majority of top jobs in business, industry, and government were held by people between the ages of 35 and 65. Most people past the age of 65 had retired.

2. The law in most states prevents anyone under 30 years old from becoming governor. The Constitution requires a person to be at least 30 years old to be elected Senator and 25 years old to be elected to the House.

3. In 1977 the average age of members of the House was 49. The average age of members of the Senate was 54.

4. Of the 30 people selected by a *U.S. News and World Report* survey as the most influential in the U.S., none chosen were under 35 years old. Most were between 40 and 65 years old.

WHITES and NONWHITES in HIGH STATUS JOBS

1. In 1977, of the 435 members of the House, 411 were white, 16 were black, 2 were Oriental, and 6 were Hispanic.

2. In 1977, of the 100 members of the Senate, 96 were white, 1 was black, and 3 were Oriental.

3. In 1970, there were fewer than 2,000 black elected officials in the United States. By 1975 this number had risen to slightly more than 3,500.

4. Since 1970, more Hispanic Americans have become involved in government. The first two Mexican-Americans to be elected governor took office in 1975. Jerry Apodaca became governor of New Mexico, and Raoul Castro became governor of Arizona in that year.

5. In 1965, there were about 70 black state and federal judges in the United States. By 1975 this number increased to 360, which represented three percent of state and federal judges at that time.

Figure 2-7

c. Whites tend to have more high-status jobs than nonwhites do. However, the percentage of nonwhites gaining high-status jobs, particularly in government, has increased over the years.

d. White, middle-aged males have a higher job status than most other groups in society do.

2. How would you compare these findings with those about income? Make some general statements about variations in both income and job indicators among groups in the United States.

3. How can formal education affect a person's job status?

DIFFERENCES in FORMAL EDUCATION

Formal education is education that takes place in an institution of learning like a school or university. Although you can learn many valuable skills and acquire almost unlimited amounts of knowledge outside a school or university, it is almost impossible to measure this kind of education. Statistics can tell us about formal education, however.

Information about variations in formal education is an indicator of great differences in other political resources, such as skills, information, and status. Those who have completed more years of schooling tend to have more knowledge, to acquire more skills, and to use their knowledge and skills to gain higher status jobs. These resources can be used to influence political activity.

Figures 2–8, 2–9, and 2–10 provide data about the formal education of various groups in the United States. (Study the materials entitled *Reading a Table* and *Reading a Bar Graph* on pages 70 and 71.) As you can see from the tables, a very small percentage of women are students at professional schools. However that percentage is

Figure 2-8

WOMEN in PROFESSIONAL SCHOOLS

PROFESSION	WOMEN AS PERCENT TOTAL ENROLLMENT	
	1960	1976
Architecture	5	11
Dentistry	1	11
Engineering	1[a]	9
Law	4	26
Medicine	6	22
Optometry	1[a]	13
Pharmacy	12	36
Veterinary Medicine	4	26

[a]Less than one percent

Source: John B. Parrish, University of Illinois

67

Political resources vary across different groups in American society. Women and members of minority groups have traditionally had less education and jobs with less status. How do these photographs indicate that this situation is changing?

EDUCATION of WHITES and NONWHITES

1. In 1975, 64.5% of the white population 25 years old and over had completed four years of high school or more.

2. In 1975, 51.7% of Hispanic Americans between 25 and 29 had completed four years of high school. Only 14.5% of Hispanic Americans over 65 had completed high school.

3. Between 1965 and 1975, enrollment of blacks in college increased from 274,000 to 948,000. In 1965, 4.2% of all blacks eligible for college were enrolled in colleges. By 1975 the percentage had increased to 6.5%.

4. Between 1965 and 1975, enrollment of whites in college increased from 5,317,000 to 8,516,000. In 1965, 11.3% of all whites eligible for college were enrolled in colleges. By 1975 the percentage had decreased to 8.7%.

5. In 1975, 6.3% of Hispanic Americans 25 years old and over had completed college.

Figure 2-9

increasing. You can also see that the educational attainment of minorities is not as high as that of whites. Women in minority groups tend to have more formal education than their male counterparts. However, there is an increase in the percentage of people in minorities who have completed high school and college.

1. Based on these data, what statements can you make about the educational attainment of various groups in our society?

2. Review what you have learned about income, occupation, and education as indicators of political resources. Now imagine you are a candidate for public office. You can choose people from the following two groups to work with you in a campaign. What do members from each group have to offer to your campaign?

Group A: Approximately 30 members of mixed racial and occupational backgrounds. Most members have high incomes and have completed a college education. All are young women.

Group B: Approximately 30 members. All are white middle-aged males who work at a local factory. Most have medium incomes and have completed a high school education.

3. Write a description of the political resources of two groups with which you are familiar. Compare the variations of resources of the two groups. Is each group successful politically? Why?

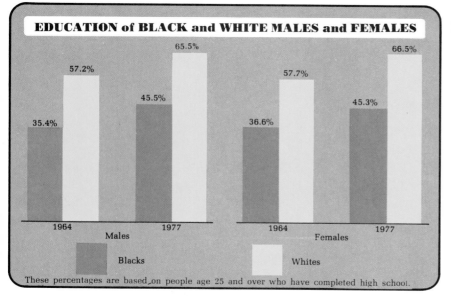

EDUCATION of BLACK and WHITE MALES and FEMALES   **Figure 2-10**

These percentages are based on people age 25 and over who have completed high school.

Reading a Table

Figure 2–8 is an example of a table. Tables are similar to graphs in that they both provide information in a simple and easy-to-read format. Tables are designed using *columns* and *rows*. Figure 2–8 has, for instance, three columns and six rows. The column on the far left presents the names of several different professions. The other two columns present the percentage of women students at professional schools in the years 1960 and 1974. Each row presents the name of a profession and the percentage of women students who studied at schools that train for this profession in the years shown.

To determine the percentage of women students who studied for a particular profession in a given year, first choose one of the professions listed. Then move horizontally across the table to the year you want. For example, to figure out the proportion of female students who studied medicine in 1974, first locate "Medicine" in the professions column. Then move across the row to the 1974 column. In 1974, 18% of all medical students were women.

Which profession shown had the highest percentage of female students in 1960? Which had the lowest? Answer these same questions for 1974.

Construct a table which presents the following information.

Population of Ringtown	1950— 15,000	Population of Oakmont	1950— 84,000
	1960— 19,000		1960— 60,000
	1970— 23,000		1970— 50,000
Population of Springfield	1950— 500	Population of Snowboro	1950— 28,000
	1960— 10,000		1960— 127,000
	1970— 25,000		1970— 500,000
Population of Bedlam	1950— 72,000	Population of Liberty Square	1950— 900
	1960— 74,000		1960— 800
	1970— 75,000		1970— 1,100

Reading a Bar Graph

Figure 2–10 contains two sets of bar graphs. Set 1 shows the percentage of males who completed four years of high school in the years 1964 and 1977. As you can see, the information is categorized by racial or ethnic background. Set 2 presents the same information for females. The legend in the lower left-hand corner of Figure 2–10 provides the key to reading the graphs. The bar graphs suggest several kinds of comparisons.
1. For each year it is possible to compare by race the percentage of men and women who completed four years of high school.

2. It is also possible to compare educational attainment across years. For example, marked gains were made between 1964 and 1977 for both black people and white people.
3. Sets 1 and 2 allow us to compare educational attainment by sex. Do there seem to be major differences in the number of males and females who completed four years of high school in the years shown?

A bar graph can also be constructed showing a horizontal and a vertical axis. Consider the following bar graph. (The bar graphs here and in Figure 2–10 are vertical, but horizontal bar graphs can be made.)

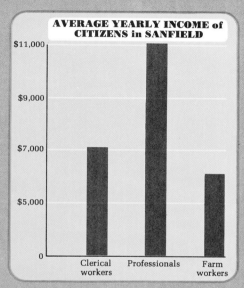

What does the vertical axis in the above example show? What does the horizontal axis show? What advantage is there to presenting information in bar graph form?

Prepare a bar graph to illustrate the following information. You will find it helpful to use a horizontal and a vertical axis in making this graph.

AGE GROUP	NUMBER OF EMPLOYED CITIZENS IN DILLEN CITY
20–40	1,000
40–60	3,000
60 and over	600

As you encounter graphs in this book as well as in other sources, study them carefully to gain as much information as possible. Remember to:
1. Determine what type of graph you are studying—pie graph, line graph, or bar graph.
2. Determine the kind of information presented on the horizontal axis and on the vertical axis (when these exist).
3. Relate the information on one axis to the information on the other axis.

The Skill of Gathering Evidence

The statistics you have just studied provide valuable information on resource variations in the United States. That information itself is a resource. It can be used to accomplish goals such as better understanding political power.

The more information you have, the more effective you can be as a citizen. You need information in order to have well-based opinions and take intelligent stands on issues. You need information in order to make rational, intelligent decisions. You need information in order to influence others.

The kind of information that is most useful to you as a citizen is information that furnishes proof, that provides an explanation. This kind of information is called *evidence*. Let's look at some information that is evidence. The statement, "The mayor of our city is Ralph Andrews," communicates information, but it probably does not prove or explain anything. On the other hand, assume you were trying to decide whom to vote for in the next mayoral election. Information like the following might be evidence on which you could make a decision to vote for Ralph Andrews:

Andrews supports the proposed new youth center, which you favor.

Andrews has been given the highest rating of all candidates by the Citizen Review Panel.

Andrews has promised to increase personnel in the police and fire departments by 25 percent.

All this information is evidence that tells you that Andrews is the best candidate for mayor. The evidence becomes the basis for your decision about whom to vote for in the election. Any wise political decision is based on evidence.

Since evidence is such a valuable commodity to you as a citizen, it is important for you to learn how to work with it. You need to know how to find evidence in sources available to you. You should also learn how to generate, or produce, evidence by compiling information from your own observation, surveys, or interviews. And you should know how to interpret and use evidence. You'll learn these skills in each unit of this course, beginning with the skill of gathering evidence.

IDENTIFYING a TOPIC To gather evidence you must begin by deciding exactly what topic you want to investigate, what question you want to answer. For example, you might want to inquire about resources of older people in your city. Formulate a clearly stated question on your topic of investigation: What resources do older people in our city have? You have decided to investigate the resources of a specific group, older people in your city. You have stated a *topic question*. Now you are ready to gather evidence to answer that question.

ASKING QUESTIONS In order to answer your topic question—What resources do older people in our city have?—you should pose another set of questions to yourself. By answering these *related questions* you will answer your topic question. For example, in thinking about resources you might come up with these questions to be answered:

1. Do the older people in our city have money?

2. What skills do they have?

3. Who supports the interests of the city's older people?

4. What is the status of older people in our city?

The answers to these questions will tell you something about the resources of older people in your city.

> Choose a topic about which you would like to gather evidence. Write a topic question and 4 or 5 related questions that will help you answer your topic question. Save the questions.

Asking the right questions is a key to gathering evidence. To find out about anything, you must ask questions that lead to the facts you need to have. You can be certain that if your questions don't make sense, your answers won't make sense.

There are certain criteria with which you can determine whether or not a question is a good one. These criteria should be used to judge both topic questions and secondary questions. Good questions are:

1. Significant.
2. Directly related to your goal.
3. Stated clearly.

Significance. First, questions should be significant. A significant question leads to useful and important answers. Before spending your time, effort, energy to answer a question, you should always ask: "What difference will it make to anybody if I answer this question? Is this worth knowing about? Or, will people say 'So what?' when I am finished with my work?"

Common sense can help you decide whether a question is significant or not. For example, it would be foolish to spend much time or effort trying to answer this question: Are citizens with big feet more likely to participate in politics than those with small feet? This question may be related to your purpose of finding out who is more or less likely to take part in election campaigns. However, it is not very significant! In con-

trast, here is a more significant question: Are female or male citizens in our town more likely to participate in election campaigns?

> Write three topic questions that you think are significant.

Relationship to Goal. A second rule, or criterion, for asking good questions is to relate them directly to your goal. Suppose you are interested in finding out how many governments exist in your school. To gather evidence about this topic, you must first form a topic question. That question should be directly connected to your purpose or goal of finding out just how many governments exist in your school. Your related questions must apply directly to your topic question. Here is a sequence of questions that is directly related to the goal of finding out about the governments in your school:

Topic Question: What governments exist in my school?

Related Questions:

1. What organized groups exist in my school?
2. In each group, are there official rules that guide members?
3. In each group, who makes rules? Who enforces rules?

Because each of these questions is directly related to your goal, the answers you get, the evidence you gather, will be directly related to your goal. On the other hand, a question like "How many schools are there in this city?" is not directly related to your goal. The answer to that question will not tell you anything about the governments in your school.

> Review the questions you wrote at the beginning of this section. Were your related questions directly tied to your topic question? Rewrite any questions that need a stronger relationship to your goal.

Clarity. A third rule says questions should be stated clearly. A clear question is easily understood and helps you focus on exactly what you need to know. This is a clear question: What special political skills would help candidates win elections? This question is likely to mean the same thing to everyone who tries to anwer it. When you research this question, your goal is obvious and understandable.

This is an unclear question: Do citizens in our school think they are slick politicos? It is not clear because it includes slang words—"slick politicos"—which are ambiguous. You can't gather evidence about "slick politicos" if you don't know what they are!

This is another example of an unclear question: Who participates more? This question is too vague and general. It does not tell what individuals or groups you are asking about. It doesn't tell what kinds of participation you want to know about. It also does not specify the place about which you will see evidence; it doesn't focus on whether you're asking about participation in a school, in a city, in a labor union, or wherever.

> Choose two topics. Write a clear and an unclear question about each topic.

You probably have heard people say, "If you ask a silly question, you'll get a silly answer." This advice is very important to you in your job as an evidence-gatherer. Answers are only as good as the questions which prompt them. You will ask questions which make sense if you follow these three rules:

1. Questions should be significant.
2. Questions should be directly related to your goal.
3. Questions should be stated clearly.

CHOOSING SOURCES of INFORMATION

Now that you understand how to ask good questions to guide your evidence gathering, you are ready to begin collecting information. Your first step in this process is to choose sources of information. Where and how are you going to look for evidence? In later units you will learn skills for generating your own evidence by means of surveys, interviews, and other techniques. First, however, you should learn how to find evidence already available. Often, there are many different sources you can use in order to gather evidence. Here are some examples:

You can locate many valuable sources of information in a public or school library.

1. You can gather books on the topic of interest to you.
2. You can look at magazine and newspaper articles.
3. You can look at surveys of voters, public opinion, needs for housing developments, or other topics.
4. You can look at census data to find out the characteristics of a population.
5. You can read records of proceedings of hearings and meetings of the city council or other organizations.
6. You can go to meetings of organizations such as the school council or a local political club.
7. You can watch television and gather information from the news or other special programs.

All these sources can provide data for the kinds of questions you might want to answer. In fact, you could probably think of some other sources that you might use.

> On a separate piece of paper list at least three additional sources you know in which you can obtain information.

Having so many sources through which you could get evidence means that you need to make a choice. You probably cannot gather information from all these sources.

The big question, then, is how you choose among alternative sources. The answer depends on a great many factors. However, there are some general rules that you can follow in evaluating and choosing sources.

Number. First, the number of sources you consult is important. Generally, the more sources of information you have, the better evidence you are likely to gather. You might, for example, get some information from a television news program. Then, you might supplement that with newspaper articles. You might then read a book or check a source of collected data, such as a survey of popular opinion. You could also talk with people directly. In general, the more sources of information you have behind any question that you ask, the better off you are in terms of presenting your case before other people and being knowledgeable about what you are doing.

Relevance. A second important criterion is relevance. What sources of information are most relevant to your topic? If you are investigating the qualifications of a city council candidate, an encyclopedia will not give you any useful information. Instead, you should read or listen to the candidate's speeches, consult newspaper articles that report the candidate's actions and statements, and find out the official positions the candidate supports.

Accessibility. A third criterion is accessibility. Choose sources which are possible for you to find and use. A newspaper from London dated 1879 may be the best source of evidence on a given subject, but you may have no access to hundred-year-old English newspapers. When you make a list of sources for any question, be sure that you consider how much time you have to answer the question and the kinds of sources which are most easily obtainable.

Up-to-Date. Fourth, the source should be as up-to-date as possible. Often materials can be revised based on new knowledge. If there is a question about the first or second edition of a book, or about new versus older information, you will want to get that information which is the most current. Unless you are answering a question about a particular historical event, you should have records which represent the most up-to-date information.

Directness. A fifth criterion is directness. Do you want to know what somebody said about what somebody said? For example, suppose you are looking for evidence to answer a question on whether the city should have built a controversial new housing project. A news editorial is not as direct a source as statistics on city housing or photographs of areas before and after the housing was constructed.

Think about the five criteria as you answer the questions below:

1. If you were trying to identify sources which would help you back your opinion of the need to have middle-income housing in your neighborhood, which would be the best source?
   a. Library books on the development of your neighborhood
   b. Yesterday's newspaper information about the socio-economic characteristics of your neighbors
   c. The mayor's opinion about what kind of housing there should be

2. If you want to identify sources to support your opinion that the city should not put up a billboard in your neighborhood, which would be the best?
   a. Information from the local corporations about the need to advertise
   b. Information from your father who is a city council member about the council members' opinions about the billboard
   c. City ordinances regarding putting up of billboards in your neighborhood

3. If the school council had just voted to suspend students who were late to class, and you wanted to rally support to override their vote, which source would be best?
   a. The proceedings of the council meeting in which the vote was taken
   b. People who had attended the high school ten years ago
   c. The history of the school council

4. Write a topic question and list as many sources as you can that would meet the standards for good sources for evidence on that topic.

EVALUATING INFORMATION Once you have formulated your questions and chosen possible sources of information, you are ready to begin the actual collecting of evidence. Not all the information you find in the sources you consult will be useful evidence. So, you need to know how to evaluate what you

Recording information accurately is an important step in gathering evidence.

read and hear. The actual interpretation of evidence—what does it mean? how accurate is it? upon what is this statement based?—is a skill you will learn in Unit 2. The serious interpretation of your information takes place after you have collected it. However, as you initially find information you should make some basic judgments about whether or not the information is worth collecting. You should evaluate the information's potential use as evidence.

Selection. First, you should evaluate the selection of the information. In a newspaper or magazine article, what was the source of information? Do you think that the author is reporting all the facts or has he or she selected only some facts to report? Is the author of the article reporting from firsthand experience or is he or she repeating what someone else said or saw?

There are different standards for judging the selection of information in a survey or poll. First of all, the portion of the population included in the survey or poll should be large. The larger the portion, the more representative it is likely to be. Also, the kinds of people studied should be representative. You do not question only white, upper-class eighteen-year-olds if you want to survey the opinions of the American people. Finally, the survey or poll should have been conducted systematically. The same question should have been asked of everyone who is counted. The same criteria should be applied to everyone.

Time. Second, you should look at the time period in which the information was collected. Is the information out of date? On the other hand, is the information so recent that it does not have the historical depth that you might need?

Relationship. Another very important standard by which you must evaluate information is its relationship to your questions. If you are trying to find information to answer a question about how a city council is run, you do not want to collect information on the local police station. A source may seem very promising but turn out to have excellent information on the wrong subject or the wrong aspect of a subject. It is important to recognize when information is relevant and when it is not.

RECORDING INFORMATION When you find information that you think will be useful in answering your questions, you should record it accurately. Accuracy is a key to gathering good evidence. You must copy a quote or a set of statistics exactly as they appear in the source. If you are listening to a speech or the proceedings of a meeting, make precise notes, particularly if you later want to quote the statements of particular people.

In addition, make careful note of the source of your information. Write down the name and date of a book, newspaper, or magazine, along with the page on which the information appeared and the name of its author. In the case of a meeting, note the time, location, and participants.

You have learned a number of steps in the valuable skill of gathering evidence. You should know how to

1. Identify a topic.

2. Ask good questions.

3. Choose sources of information.

4. Evaluate information.

5. Record information.

Following the procedures for each of these steps, you can gather evidence that will give you an important resource for citizenship. Good evidence will help you form sound opinions and make rational decisions about public issues.

Chapter Review

1. What is politics? What are resources?
2. Give examples of several political situations, identifying the resources, activities, and groups involved.
3. Make a chart of political resources. On your chart, list various categories of resources—skills, wealth, status, etc. Give examples of ways in which each resource is used in politics.
4. (a) Describe resources that would be important to a candidate for election. (b) Then, describe resources that might be redistributed in an election. (c) What resources did Tom Bradley use in his 1973 victory in Los Angeles? What resources did he have in 1973 that he had not had in 1969?
5. What significant variations in income exist in the United States? How are these variations related to politics?
6. What significant variations in job status exist in the United States? How are these variations related to politics?
7. What significant variations in amount of formal education exist in the United States? How are these variations related to politics?
8. Outline the steps in gathering evidence.
9. What are the criteria for asking good questions?
10. What are the criteria for evaluating sources of information? for evaluating information itself?

Chapter Vocabulary

Define the following terms.

politics	formal education	horizontal axis
resources	evidence	vertical axis
vote	indicator	incumbent
status	median	

Chapter Analysis

1. In your school system several groups of people have an impact on school policy—teachers, administrators, parents, and students. What political resources does each of these groups possess? How can they use these resources to affect decision-making in the school?
2. Choose a group with which you are familiar. Analyze the ways in which the group engages in politics. What resources are used and distributed by the group? What are the group's goals? What activities does the group perform to reach these goals?
3. Describe the resources that are available to you. Assume that you are a candidate for president of the student council. Which of your re-

78

sources do you think would most contribute to a successful campaign? Explain why.

4. List the activities in which you participate each week. Determine which are political and which are not. In paragraph form, explain the reasons for each of your decisions.

5. If you want to find out about a presidential candidate, what would be some possible sources of information? Of these, which do you think would be the most valuable in determining your vote? Explain.

Chapter Activities

1. Make a collection of newspaper and magazine reports that describe activities or situations that you think are political. In each article, point out the resources, activities, and groups involved.

2. Identify a political leader whom you would like to study. Read about his or her political activities. Then, analyze the resources the leader uses and distributes.

3. Investigate some issues being debated in Congress. Select one that is of importance to you, and write a letter to your senator or representative expressing your views on the subject.

4. Prepare graphs and tables to profile your community graphically. In other words, prepare different types of graphs showing such things as income levels, occupations, or types of businesses.

Chapter Bibliography

Politics, Power, Polls and School Elections, Ralph M. Kimbrough and Michael Y. Nunnery (McCutchan: Berkeley, CA), 1971.
Describes how citizens need and use resources to become active in educational issues in their community.

Statistical Abstract of the United States: annual editions (U. S. Department of Commerce, Washington, DC), 1976.
An invaluable source of statistics on many aspects of American life. Useful for analyzing variations in resources.

Justice in Everyday Life: The Way It Really Works, edited by Howard Zinn (William Morrow: New York, NY), 1974.
Composed of short, easy-to read articles which describe questions of politics and justice. Focuses on police, courts, prisons, housing, work, health, schools, and "fighting back."

Politics in Action: How to Make Change Happen, William Muehl (Association Press: New York, NY), 1972.
Outlines how citizens can become active in politics. Chapter 3, "Sources of Political Power," focuses on various political resources which enable people to participate in politics.

Chapter Objectives

★ To learn what elections are and how they are conducted

★ To apply knowledge about political resources to elections

★ To analyze how citizens use resources to participate in elections

chapter 3

CITIZENS and ELECTIONS

Elections are among the most important and exciting events in American political life. It is through elections that government leaders are selected for office. Election activity is especially significant because it is a process in which many Americans take part. In fact, more people participate in voting than in any other type of political activity.

Elections are good examples of how citizens can and do use political resources. As you learned in Chapter 2, political resources are the key to winning elections. People across the United States contribute time, money, knowledge, and skills to candidates for a wide range of offices. Volunteer as well as paid campaign workers raise money, make speeches, and arrange publicity for the candidates they want to see elected. Throughout this chapter, you will apply your knowledge about how political resources can be used in election campaigns.

As you read the chapter, think about ways in which you can participate in elections. In the next election, will you support a candidate? If so, in what ways will you lend support?

The Election Process

An *election* is a way to make a choice by voting. Elections are held in private as well as public governments. This chapter deals solely, however, with elections in the public sphere.

Public elections are the means by which American citizens choose their leaders in government. Competing candidates for office often have different beliefs about what government ought to do. Or, they may differ on how government should perform its functions. These differences encourage citizens to consider their own political preferences carefully as they decide how to vote.

In the United States, elections are held at the local, state, and national levels. At each level, elections have similar features. Perhaps the most common feature is the presence of *political parties,* organizations whose main purpose is to win elections for the candidates they sponsor.

KINDS of ELECTIONS There are several kinds of elections in the United States involving candidates for office: primary elections, general elections, special elections, and recall elections. In addition, there are two kinds of elections involving laws: the initiative and the referendum.

Generally, elections in the United States are *partisan*. This means that candidates run for office on the basis of political party identification and support. In some cases, though, local and state offices are filled by candidates who do not run on a party ticket. These are called *nonpartisan* elections.

Primary Elections. In primary elections—sometimes called "direct primaries"—the members of political parties nominate the parties' candidates for office. As you probably know, to *nominate* means to select, or put forward.

Usually, primary voters nominate one person to represent their party for each office that is to be contested in a later election. For example, when Edward Koch ran for mayor of New York City in 1977, he was one of seven candidates in the Democratic mayoral primary. These seven competed for the party's nomination in a primary election held in September. As the primary election winner, Edward Koch was the New York City Democratic party's choice to face the candidates of other political parties in a November election.

Primary elections are used in all states, though some use the primary only for certain offices. Primaries are strictly regulated by state law. States determine the date on which primaries are held (usually in the spring). In general, states control primary election conduct.

Almost all states have *closed primary elections*. This means that only voters who have identified themselves as party members can take part in their party's primary election. Usually, citizens are asked to declare political party preference when they register to vote. By indicating preference for one party, a voter is considered a member of that party. Voters are not forced to declare party preference, but unless they do they cannot vote in a closed primary.

Some states (including Alaska, Idaho, Michigan, Minnesota, Montana, North Dakota, and Wisconsin) have *open primary elections*. This means that voters do not have to declare their party preference in order to vote in a primary. Usually when voters arrive at the polling place on primary election day, they are given the ballots of all the parties who are holding primaries. (A *ballot* is a piece of paper used to record a vote.) Usually just the Democratic and Republican parties are involved. In the voting booth, voters select the ballot of the party whose candidates they want to choose among. Thus, someone can vote to nominate Democratic candidates even though he or she usually votes Republican.

The state of Washington, which also conducts open primaries, runs them differently. Under its system voters are given only one ballot. This ballot contains the names of all candidates in all parties seeking nominations for all offices. For each office, voters may nominate a candidate in only one party. Voters may, however, switch from one party to another in considering party candidates for different offices.

General Elections. Voters make their final choices in selecting government officials in general elections. In most states, general elections for state and national office are held in November in the even-numbered years.

Special Elections. Sometimes a public office is vacated before a regularly scheduled election. The officeholder may die or become too ill to work. For example, Mayor Richard J. Daley of Chicago died during the first year of his fifth four-year term. A special election was called to fill the vacancy. In the special primary election, Michael Bilandic beat three others to win the Democratic party nomination. The Republicans nominated Dennis Black. Later, in a special general election, Bilandic defeated Black.

Sometimes a vacancy is created when an officeholder takes a new job. For example, in 1976 Brock Adams, a Democrat, was reelected to Congress from the Seventh District of the state of Washington. Soon after, he left his seat in Congress to become the head of the federal Department of Transportation. A special election was held to replace Adams. This time the Republican candidate won the congressional seat.

Recall Elections. In 13 states, citizens may remove state government officials from office before their terms are finished. The procedure is called a recall election. This type of election may also be held in many communities to remove local government officials. Recall elections may be called when a certain number of citizens sign a petition asking for such an election. The public official(s) named in the petition must face the challenge of opposition candidates. The outcome determines if the official(s) stays in office to complete the term. Recall elections are usually held when the public believes that an officeholder is not properly carrying out the responsibilities of office. Recalling an official is a complex procedure, which is not frequently carried out.

Referendum. In some states, citizens also have the opportunity to decide the fate of proposed laws or laws which have already been passed. There are two kinds of procedures which permit voters to decide about laws. These are the *referendum* and the *initiative*.

In a *popular referendum* voters petition to have the right to accept or reject a law which has recently been passed by their state or local government. This action must be taken within a short time after the law has been passed. A certain percentage of eligible voters can sign a petition demanding that the measure be referred to them for approval or rejection. It is then placed on the ballot in the next general election. If a majority vote "no," it is no longer a law. For instance, voters in several states voted against proposals to stop the building of nuclear power plants.

In every state except Delaware, amendments to the state constitution must be approved by voters in a referendum. In some states, other types of measures must also be referred to the people. This is known as the *mandatory referendum*. For example, in 1976 a majority of Alaska voters approved a proposal to move the state capital from Juneau to Willow, a small town about 170 miles north of Anchorage.

A third type of referendum is the *optional referendum*. This appears on the ballot when a state legislature voluntarily refers legislation to the voters.

EXTENSION of the RIGHT to VOTE

LIMITATIONS ON VOTING RIGHTS	DATE CHANGED	METHOD OF CHANGE	GROUP WHICH GAINED THE VOTE
Property Ownership	Largely completed by 1828	Individual states eliminated the requirement	White males who did not own property
Race, color or previous condition of servitude	1870	15th amendment	Black men
Exclusion of women	1920	19th amendment Wyoming granted full suffrage to women for state elections in 1890	Women
Exclusion of residents of the District of Columbia from presidential elections	1961	23rd amendment	Residents of the District of Columbia
Poll tax	1964	24th amendment Harper vs. Virginia State Board of Elections	People unable or unwilling to pay a tax to vote
Residency requirement over 30 days	1970	Voting Rights Act of 1970	People who move frequently
Minimum age	1971	26th amendment	People who are 18, 19, and 20 years old

*Most states deny voting rights to those hospitalized for mental illness and those convicted of a felony or electoral corruption. Though before 1926 some states permitted aliens to vote, today all voters must be citizens of the U.S.

Figure 3-1

Initiative. The initiative permits citizens to propose laws to their state or local governments. The initiative exists in some but not all states. Citizens who want a particular issue on the ballot must first circulate a petition among registered voters. Under the *direct initiative,* if a certain percentage of voters sign the petition, then the proposal will be on the ballot in the next general election.

Some states have the *indirect initiative.* After the required number of people sign the petition, the proposal goes to the state legislature. If the legislature does not pass the proposal, then the measure is presented to the voters.

The referendum and initiative enable citizens to use the vote as a resource to propose, amend, and defeat laws made by governments. This type of voting is a powerful check on officials who have been elected. It also allows citizens to have a direct influence on legislation.

1. Describe the differences between open and closed primaries.
2. Compare the functions of primaries, general elections, special elections, and recall elections.
3. What are the differences between a referendum and an initiative?

VOTER REGISTRATION

In every state, voters must register to be eligible to vote. (To *register* means "to record or enroll your name officially.") Registration rules and procedures vary from state to state, but there are basic similarities. To be eligible to vote, a person must be a citizen of the United States, 18 years old or older, and a resident of the state, county, and precinct in which he or she plans to vote. (Cities and towns all over the United States are divided into voting areas called *precincts.* People vote in the precinct of their permanent residence.)

The requirements today allow many more people to vote than were allowed in the past. Figure 3–1 shows how the right to vote has been gradually extended since the early 1800s.

To register, a citizen must prove his or her identity and place of residence. Then he or she must complete a form. In the past, voter registration forms were usually filled out in person at the office of the local board of elections or the city or county clerk. Today, however, a number of states allow a voter to register by mail.

In most states, citizens must register from 20 to 30 days before the next election to be eligible to vote in that election. One result of this is that many people think about registering too late to qualify to vote. In these states, it is typical for less than 60 per-

cent of otherwise eligible voters to take part in an election.

In five states, voters can register as late as election day. These states are Minnesota, Wisconsin, North Dakota, Maine, and Oregon. In each of these states more than 60 percent of the potential voters actually voted in the 1976 presidential election. Over 70 percent turned out to vote in Minnesota, which had the highest percentage of any state in the country.

1. What are the basic requirements for registering to vote? Can you fulfill these requirements?
2. Describe the changes in voting requirements since the 1800s.

ELECTION-DAY PROCEDURES

The regulation of elections is the duty of state government. Thus, there are slight differences in the way elections are conducted from state to state. However, the similarities outweigh the differences. Following is a description of typical election-day procedures.

At the Polling Place. A *polling place,* where citizens go to vote, is located in each precinct in a community. Polling-place officials begin work very early in the morning on election day. These officials admit citizens to the voting booths or machines and watch to see that the rules are carried out properly. They keep records of who comes to the polling place to vote. There are also poll watchers from each party to guard against violations of the rules.

After the polling place is opened, voters may enter and cast ballots. (Although voting machines are used in most places today, the act of voting is sometimes called "casting a ballot.") As voters arrive at the polling place, they must check in with a clerk, who finds the voter's name in the list of registered voters. Voters whose names are on the list of eligible voters sign in by writing their names on a form kept by a clerk.

Polling-place officials may challenge any citizen who checks in if they think the person may not be eligible to vote. A challenged citizen must leave the polling place immediately. Challenged citizens who can prove that they have the right to vote, or who testify in writing that they are eligible, may proceed to vote. If a voter's testimony is later proved false, the person can be charged with vote fraud. This is a crime which may be punished with a fine and/or imprisonment.

After checking in with a clerk, the citizen is ready to vote. In some places, the citizen votes by marking a paper ballot. In other places, voters pull levers on a machine. In every state, voters have the right to vote in private. They can make their choices free from the pressure of others.

Polling-place officials close the polls at the end of the day (usually 6:00 or 7:00 p.m.). Vote totals for each candidate are tallied, or counted. Then the ballot boxes or voting machines are sealed and returned to local election-board officials.

Voting a Ticket. In every general election, many citizens are *straight-ticket* voters. This means that they vote only for the candidates of one party. Citizens will do this when they feel strong loyalty to their political party and believe that their party's candidates are the best people for office.

In contrast, many citizens vote a *split ticket* in general elections. This means that they vote for candidates of one party for some offices and candidates of other parties for other offices. For example, a voter may choose the Republican candidates for president and vice-president and the Democratic candidate for representative to Congress.

In every election, a few citizens choose to make a *"write-in"* vote. This means that the citizen votes for a person whose name is not on the ballot. This is done by writing this person's name on the ballot. Most "write-in" candidates do not win election to office.

Absentee Voting. In all states provision is made so that voters who must be away from their precincts on election day can vote by *absentee ballot*. Citizens in the armed forces, college students, and the seriously ill are among those who may vote by absentee ballot. In advance of the election, an application for absentee voting must be filed with election officials in the voter's home precinct.

1. Give a step-by-step description of election day procedures for a voter.
2. Distinguish between straight- and split-ticket voting.
3. How can citizens vote if they are not able to go to the polling place in their precinct?

Political Parties in Elections

As you read earlier, a political party is an organization whose main purpose is to win elections for the candidates it sponsors. Two major political parties in the United States—the Democratic and Republican parties—perform basic duties in carrying out the electoral process.

Within each party there is general agreement on various public questions involving the function of government and the programs it should sponsor. At times there is also much disagreement within each party. For example, Democrats often disagree with other Democrats on certain questions and may find themselves siding with Republicans in these matters.

Even when they disagree with one another, members of a political party are still united by one strong bond. That bond is the common desire for their party and its candidates to gain public office.

A TWO-PARTY SYSTEM

In some countries, such as France, Italy, and Israel, there are a number of political parties which compete through elections for control of the government. This situation is called a *multiparty system*.

In other countries, such as the Soviet Union, Cuba, and Yugoslavia, there is only one legal political party. This is a *one-party system*. In these countries there is no competition between political parties for control of the government. Rather, individuals within the one legal party compete for leadership positions.

Party Origins. The Constitution of the United States makes no mention of political parties. Therefore, there are no constitutional rules governing the function of political parties in this country. Through the years, though, a *two-party system* has developed. For more than a century the Democratic and Republican parties have been dominant in American politics.

The Democratic party traces its roots to Thomas Jefferson and the Democratic-Republican party, which was active from about 1791 to 1824. Jefferson and his supporters organized the party because of their opposition to the economic policies of Alexander Hamilton, secretary of the treasury under George Washington. The party began to disintegrate by the presidential election of 1824.

By about 1830 a new Democratic party was built around Andrew Jackson, who was elected president in 1828. Most historians point to the time of Andrew Jackson as the active beginning of today's Democratic party.

The origin of the Republican party dates back to 1854. The Republican party developed out of the slavery question. Republicans were against the spread of slavery into new territories. The Republican party built its strength from the decline of the Whig party, which had competed with the Democrats as a major party from the 1830s to the 1850s. By the mid-1850s, however, the Whig party had split over the slavery issue. Most Northern Whigs joined the New Republican party, while many Southern Whigs returned to the Democratic party. Abraham Lincoln was the first Republican to be elected president, in 1860.

Third Parties. A number of smaller, or minor, parties have taken part in American elections since the early 1800s. (See Figure 3–2.) However, these *third parties* usually do not win elections. Very few minor party candidates have won seats in Congress or in state governments. No minor party candidate has ever won the presidency. The best showing of a third-party presidential candidate took place in 1968 when George Wallace received 9.9 million votes as the American Independent Party candidate. He took 13.5% of the popular vote in the presidential election won by Republican Richard Nixon.

Earlier, in 1912, Theodore Roosevelt won 27.4% of the vote as a third party candidate. (This only amounted to about four million votes, however, because there were fewer voters in 1912 than in 1968.) The 1912 election was an unusual situation. Roosevelt had already served two terms as president, 1901–1909.

In 1912, however, he decided that he wanted to run for president again. When the Republicans nominated William Howard Taft, instead, Roosevelt and his followers founded their own party, popularly known as the Bull Moose party. Thus, Roosevelt was much better known than most third party candidates.

THIRD PARTIES, 1856 to the PRESENT

PARTY *dates	PLATFORM	PRESIDENTIAL CANDIDATES	FINAL STATUS OF PARTY
Constitutional Union 1860/1860	Wanted to promote a reconciliation between North and South over slavery and to preserve the Union.	1860 John Bell	Ended with the start of the Civil War.
Prohibition 1872/1976	Wants to eliminate manufacture and sale of intoxicating liquor.	1872 James A. Black (first presidential candidate)	Still exists.
Greenback 1876/1884	Wanted to retain inflationary paper money. Opposed a return to the gold standard.	1876 Peter Cooper 1880 James B. Weaver 1884 Benjamin F. Butler	Returning prosperity ended main issue and most members joined the Populist party.
Socialist Labor 1892/1976	Militant Marxist organization. Calls for a revolution of the working classes to take over control of production.	1892 Simon Wing (first presidential candidate)	Still exists.
Populist (People's Party) 1892/1908	Wanted government ownership of railroads, free coinage of silver, graduated income tax, direct election of senators, and other reforms.	1892 James B. Weaver 1900 Wharton Barker 1904 Thomas E. Watson 1908 Thomas E. Watson	After 1896 most joined the Democratic party.
Socialist 1900/1976	Wants collective ownership of the means of production and equal distribution of wealth.	1900 Eugene V. Debs (first presidential candidate)	Still exists.
Progressive ("Bull Moose") 1912/1916	Favored Women's suffrage, workers' compensation laws, and laws prohibiting child labor	1912 Theodore Roosevelt	Most members joined the Republican party in 1916.
Progressive 1924/1924	Supported various labor and farm reforms, chief being elimination of corporate monopolies.	1924 Robert M. LaFollette	Ended as national party with the death of LaFollette in 1925.
Worker's Party of America (Communist) 1924/1976	Goal is the overthrow of capitalism and the creation of a communist government ruled by the working classes.	1924 William Z. Foster (first presidential candidate)	Still exists.
Socialist Workers 1948/1976	A Marxist group expelled from the Communist party. Wants more radical change than the Communist party.	1948 Farrell Dobbs (first presidential candidate)	Still exists.
States' Rights Democratic Party 1948/1948	Opposed to civil rights.	1948 J. Strom Thurmond	Members returned to the Democratic party.
People's Progressive Party 1948/1952	Opposed Truman's handling of cold war diplomacy.	1948 Henry A. Wallace 1952 Vincent Hallinan	Ended after 1952 election.
American Independent 1968/1972	Opposed civil rights activism, urban riots, anti-Vietnam War demonstrations, and heavy spending on government programs to aid the poor.	1968 George C. Wallace	Ended with Wallace's return to the Democratic party.

*Dates of first/last time the party chose a presidential candidate.

Figure 3-2

Despite their poor electoral record, third parties have influenced American politics and government. Minor parties focus public attention on new issues or problems or on new ways of dealing with old issues or problems. They hope to educate as many citizens as possible about their beliefs. And, they try to persuade them to accept new ways of thinking. Some minor parties have been successful in persuading one or both of the major parties to accept some of their ideas. However, the Republican party is the only third party ever to graduate to the status of a major party.

1. What is the origin of the Republican party? of the Democratic party?
2. What is a third party? How have third parties influenced American politics?

PARTY STRUCTURE

The structures of the Republican and Democratic parties are very similar. As you can see in Figure 3-3, the two parties are structured similarly on the local, state, and national levels.

Party structure may appear tightly organized from the chart. However, political parties in the United States are actually very informal organizations. They are very loose in their authority structure, for there is no central party leadership. Each level—local, state, and national— operates independently of the others and selects its own leaders. In many cases, the local parties are not in communication with the state parties. The state parties are often only in loose communication with the national party office. The national committee itself often has very little communication with congressional party leaders.

One way to think about party structure is to picture a loose coalition of several groups. (Coalitions are groups of people with similar interests or goals.) These groups work together most often during presidential elections but otherwise follow their own paths. The coalition combines its efforts to win presidential elections. For local elections, however, usually only the local level of the party is involved. Likewise in state elections, the state level of the party will be most heavily involved in trying to win offices. Sometimes the national level may extend some help. For example, it is not uncommon for a president to campaign for a gubernatorial candidate of the same political party. (Gubernatorial means "of or relating to a governor.")

The effectiveness of a political party on any level depends upon resources. Some local officials, for example, have large amounts of money, support, and skills as resources. Richard J. Daley was mayor of Chicago for more than 20 years. For a number of years he was also chairperson of the Cook County Democratic party. With these two positions Daley had a great many resources at his command. Other mayors and other county chairpersons do not have as many resources as Daley had. Therefore they do not command as important a power position in helping candidates get elected.

Local Organizations. Each level of the party structure has its own method of organization. At the local level, there are several different groups. At the base are precinct workers. Above them are ward, city, and county committees. (A ward is an administrative area of a city, made up of several precincts.) The details of local party structures vary widely. For the most part, though, both the Democratic and the Republican parties have precinct leaders in each election precinct in the country. (There are more than 146,300 election precincts in the United States.)

Precinct leaders, sometimes called precinct captains, have a list of the names of voters in their precinct and the party—if any—they belong to. The basic tasks of precinct leaders are to know the voters in their district, to get the voters in the party to register to vote, and to encourage voters to actually vote on election day. In some states precinct leaders are chosen in primaries. In others, they are selected by the county committee.

Leaders of the ward and city political organizations also have close contact with voters. City and ward leaders are chosen at local conventions or primaries.

County committee members are usually elected, either by county conventions or in primaries. In most cases across the United States, county leaders tend to be very powerful figures in the party structure. Depending on the resources they exert, county leaders can be very influential in swaying the votes of party members at state and national primary conventions. They maintain contact

with the state party organization. However, these leaders are largely independent of state and national pressures.

State Committees. There are state committees for both the Democratic and Republican parties in each state. A chairperson officially heads the state party. Often the state chairperson is chosen by influential politicians in the state, although the committee conducts a formal election procedure. The committee itself can be chosen in several ways, varying from state to state. Usually, committee members are elected at party conventions or in primaries.

The state committee usually maintains a headquarters and does administrative work. In particular, state party leaders take a major role in fund raising. They raise money for state and national election cam-

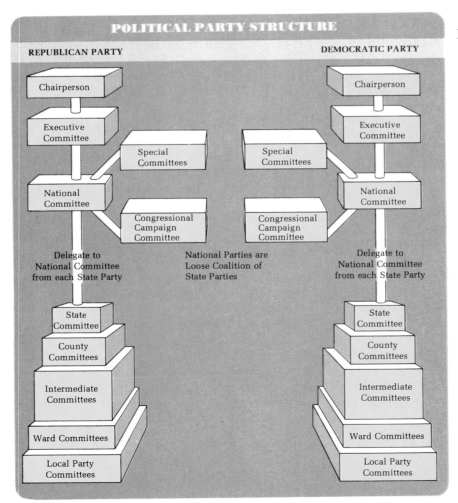

Figure 3-3

POLITICAL PARTY STRUCTURE

paigns. Often they aid in local elections as well. Fund raising takes up a major portion of the state committee's time.

The most pressing task of the state leaders is campaign management. State leaders manage the campaigns of national candidates in their states. They are also responsible for organizing the campaigns of state candidates. In addition, they give aid to local officeholders or candidates from their party. Generally, state leaders have advanced through the party ranks. They are skilled organizers who have the time, knowledge, skills, and status to organize statewide campaigns and fund-raising efforts.

It is at the state level that the looseness of the party structure is most evident. State leaders often do not know local chairpersons. Although they are supposed to serve as liaisons with the national party organization, many state leaders rarely communicate with the national party office, except in a presidential campaign. Often they do not know party leaders in other states. Therefore, there is a lack of communication both between and within levels in the party structure.

National Party Structure. The national committees for both the Democratic and Republican parties are loose federations of influential people from state parties. Neither committee is a centralized group which can pass down decisions authoritatively to the state and local levels. National committee members meet infrequently (one to three times a year). At these meetings their chief concern is planning the next national convention. It is at the national convention, held once every four years, that each major party chooses its nominees for president and vice-president.

The committees for the Democratic and Republican parties were created in the mid-nineteenth century. The Democratic National Committee was created at the National Democratic Convention in 1848, when it was mandated that one member be chosen from each state. The Republican National Committee was formed at its convention in 1856.

The most powerful party figure at the national level is the national chairperson. Generally, a chairperson is selected by the party's ranking candidate or the incumbent president. He or she is then formally elected by the national committee as a whole. The job is a reward for long service to the party. The national chairperson serves as spokesperson for the party. During presidential elections the national chairperson also acts as national campaign manager and fundraiser.

There are several problems in national committee organization which contribute to its weakness. First, the national committees do not have a firm base. They are only coordinating bodies for state representatives. They also have no working connection with Congress. Therefore, they cannot act to encourage party support on legislative issues.

The office of chairperson is rotated every few years, making continuity in the role impossible. Sometimes the change takes place even sooner than that. For example, in 1972, Mrs. Jean Westwood of Utah was selected by the Democratic party as its national chairperson. After the defeat of George McGovern that year, Mrs. Westwood was forced to resign. Changes in leadership such as this make it difficult to have a consistent focus for national attention in the national party structure.

Size also limits the effectiveness of the national committee of each political party. The national committees have grown in size over the years to include not only one committeeman and one committeewoman from each state, but also other influential party leaders at the state level. Such conditions have made it difficult for the group to act in a coordinated way.

1. How are the Democratic and Republican parties organized on the local, state, and national levels?
2. What resources would be valuable to people working in political parties?

Brendon Byrne and Ray Bateman ran for governor of New Jersey in 1977. Like all candidates they had to explain their positions so citizens could vote intelligently. Bateman and Byrne used a variety of methods to keep in touch with voters. They met with citizens personally, made speeches, talked with news reporters, participated in a television debate, and distributed campaign literature.

Brendan Byrne has delivered...

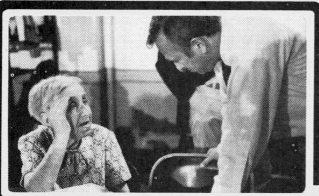

RAY BATEMAN

HE LISTENS . . .
HE UNDERSTANDS . . .
HE GETS THINGS DONE!!!

COMPARING DEMOCRATS and REPUBLICANS The Democratic and Republican parties share many basic beliefs. In general, both parties want to maintain a high standard of living for all Americans, to support the growth of business and industry, to keep our nation's armed forces strong, and to provide aid for needy people. Leaders of both parties support the goal of maintaining a strong nation which will hold a leadership role throughout the world.

Differences Between Parties. There are also major differences between the parties. Long-standing differences exist on both foreign and domestic issues. They range from defense spending to unemployment. Every four years at their presidential nominating conventions, the Democrats and Republicans write party platforms. A *platform* is a statement of beliefs for which the party's candidates stand during an election campaign. A comparison of the platforms of the two major parties can reveal similarities as well as differences.

The statements in Figure 3-4 are from the Democratic and Republican party platforms of 1976. Study the platforms carefully. Look for similarities as well as differences in the ideas of the two parties.

Differences Within Parties. There are many differences within the parties as well as between them. Often, some Democratic members of Congress will side with Republicans in voting on certain issues. Likewise, sometimes Republicans join with Democrats in supporting or rejecting a proposal. For example, a bill to provide money for jobs was being considered in the Senate in 1977. The Republicans were divided on

Figure 3-4

POLITICAL PARTY PLATFORMS	
SUMMARY OF SELECTED STATEMENTS FROM THE REPUBLICAN PARTY PLATFORM, 1976	**SUMMARY OF SELECTED STATEMENTS FROM THE DEMOCRATIC PARTY PLATFORM, 1976**
a. Oppose massive government spending programs to reduce unemployment.	a. Reduce adult unemployment to 3% within four years.
b. Solve unemployment and inflation through increased business expansion and controlled government spending.	b. Halt the steep increase in prices of consumer products.
c. Support amendment to the United States Constitution to make abortion illegal.	c. Oppose amendment to the United States Constitution to make abortions illegal.
d. Tighten rules governing welfare programs.	d. Support a federally financed national health insurance program and help reduce health costs for the elderly.
e. Oppose national health insurance. Oppose guaranteed annual income for Americans.	e. Provide a guaranteed minimum income for the poor.
f. Support passage of the Equal Rights Amendment banning discrimination on the basis of sex.	f. Support passage of the Equal Rights Amendment banning discrimination on the basis of sex.
g. Support spending on the development of up-to-date weapons.	g. Support restrictions of the right of major oil companies to own all phases of the petroleum industry. Purpose—to encourage competition between companies.
h. Increase the size of the armed forces.	h. Reduce defense spending.
i. Oppose federal registration of firearms.	i. Seek disarmament and arms control agreements with other nations.
j. Support heavy sentences for crimes involving the use of dangerous weapons.	j. Support strict controls over the manufacture, sale, and possession of handguns.

the issue. Milton R. Young, a Republican senator from North Dakota said, "I am deeply concerned about unemployment and economic growth in this country . . . [However] there is a real question as to whether providing public service jobs is the best way to ease our unemployment problem."

Republican Senator Edward William Brooke did not agree with his party colleague in the Senate. He said, "The purpose of these additional funds is to step up the efforts to deal with the continuing high rate of unemployment which affects our nation. . . . It is clear we must continue to stimulate the economy until unemployment is reduced substantially and the pace of recovery reaches more satisfactory levels." Brooke clearly supported federal spending for jobs, whereas Young was opposed to the particular proposal in question.

There are also differences among the Democrats in the Senate. Democrat John Durkin from New Hampshire agreed with Edward Brooke in the latter's statement about unemployment. Durkin said, "Government concern cannot be the total answer to this problem, but it can be an important beginning."

On the other hand, fellow Democrat John Little McClellan from Arkansas disagreed with Durkin. He said that federal spending " . . . may be one way of providing jobs temporarily, but it falls far short of reaching the goal that we need to seek to achieve today, and that is providing permanent employment."

The chart on page 96 shows how Democratic and Republican members of Congress lined up on several issues during one congressional session. Study the chart carefully.

1. What are main differences in the ideas of the Democratic and Republican parties?
2. With which platform statements do you agree? Disagree?
3. How can parties use ideas as resources in order to influence political decision-making?
4. Based on Figure 3-5, on what issues did Democrats and Republicans vote along party lines?
5. On what issues did party ranks divide?

WHAT PARTIES DO

The three main functions of political parties in elections are nominating candidates, influencing voters, and mobilizing voters. Both parties perform these jobs in similar ways.

Nominating Candidates. As discussed earlier, political parties nominate, or select, candidates to run for public offices in general elections. The two methods for selecting candidates are the direct primary and the nominating convention.

Direct primaries are discussed on pages 82–83. They are held in every state to nominate candidates for local government offices and to nominate candidates for Congress. They are also used in many states to nominate candidates for state office.

A *nominating convention* is a meeting of delegates who represent other party members from the area in which they live. At the nominating convention these delegates decide upon candidates to support as their party's choice for various offices. Indiana is one state which uses nominating conventions to select candidates for some statewide offices. (In Indiana, candidates for governor and lieutenant governor are selected in primary elections.)

Only rarely does a candidate campaign seriously or successfully for office without nomination and support by a political party. One recent example was former Democrat Harry F. Byrd, Jr., who ran successfully in 1976 as an Independent for United States senator from Virginia. Another example is James Longley. Longley ran for governor of Maine in 1974 as an Independent and won.

Independent candidates often lack the political resources needed for successful

UNITED STATES HOUSE OF REPRESENTATIVES

HR 7575. Agency for Consumer Protection.

Passage of the bill to create an independent Agency for Consumer Protection to coordinate federal consumer protection activities and represent consumer interests before other federal agencies and the courts.

	Yea	Nay
Rep.	20	119
Dem.	188	80

Passed 208-199, Nov. 6, 1975.

S 2662. Foreign Military Aid/Sales.

Adoption of the conference report on the bill to authorize $3,166,900,000 in foreign military assistance for fiscal 1976 and to provide new congressional controls on U.S. arms sales.

	Yea	Nay
Rep.	38	98
Dem.	177	87

Adopted 215-185, April 28, 1976.

HR 10210. Unemployment Compensation.

Adoption of the conference report on the bill to extend unemployment compensation coverage to state and local government employees and certain other workers not eligible.

	Yea	Nay
Rep.	70	56
Dem.	202	41

Adopted 272-97, October 1, 1976.

UNITED STATES SENATE

S 200. Agency for Consumer Advocacy.

Passage of the bill to set up an independent Agency for Consumer Advocacy (ACA) to represent consumer interests before other federal agencies and courts, and to gather and disseminate consumer information.

	Yea	Nay
Rep.	19	17
Dem.	42	11

Passed 61-28, May 15, 1975

S 2662. Foreign Military Aid/Sales.

Adoption of the conference report on the bill to authorize $3,166,900,000 in foreign military assistance for fiscal 1976 and to provide new congressional controls on U.S. arms sales.

	Yea	Nay
Rep.	13	21
Dem.	38	14

Adopted (and thus cleared for the President) 51-35, April 28, 1976.

HR 14232. Labor-HEW Appropriations, Fiscal 1977.

Passage, over the President's Sept. 29 veto, of the bill to appropriate $56,618,207,575 for the Departments of Labor and Health, Education and Welfare and related agencies for fiscal 1977.

	Yea	Nay
Rep.	19	11
Dem.	48	4

Passed (thus overriding the President's veto and enacting into law) 67-15, Sept. 30, 1976.

Figure 3-5

election campaigns. Political parties usually have the money and leaders with skills, information, ideas, and status needed to mount winning races for public office. Political parties also include large numbers of supporters willing and able to work in election campaigns.

Influencing Voters. Political parties exist to win elections. To achieve this goal, they must influence voters to back their candidates. Thus both during and between election campaigns, political parties work to persuade voters that the party's ideas and candidates are best for themselves, their communities, and their country.

Political parties often do many things to promote candidates. For example, they can buy advertising space on billboards. There they promote their candidate's name, image, and campaign stands. In some major cities as many as 50 to 100 billboards may appear for a particular candidate during an election campaign. These and other campaign expenses are supported by party contributions.

Other publicity methods include newspaper and television ads for a candidate. Having the candidate in the news brings him or her closer to the voter. Television campaigns are becoming increasingly popular with candidates. Many people watch television, a lot more than read the newspaper, so it is a very effective medium. However, television advertising is also expensive. Complaints have been raised that while some candidates can afford media spots, others cannot.

Parties often prepare brochures about candidates and newsletters which provide information about the candidate's accomplishments. These brochures and letters are written by campaign staff and distributed to voters. Campaign literature such as this is very important. It builds voter knowledge about party candidates and their stands on different issues.

Individual citizens can also do much to influence other voters. Sometimes when people are directly involved in their party, they will put bumper stickers on their cars. Or they will parade for a candidate to show support. Very often people discuss campaign issues and the merits of competing candidates with family, friends, and co-workers. As a result of these discussions, people can sway others to vote as they themselves intend to.

Mobilizing Voters. To win elections, each party tries to *mobilize* (or, make active) the largest possible number of voters on election day. Three main activities involved in motivating voters are *registration drives, canvassing,* and *voter round-up* on election day.

Political party leaders organize voter-registration drives. This aims to increase the number of those who might vote for their candidates. The party chairperson in each county of a state is responsible for organizing voter-registration activities. A risk of conducting voter-registration drives is mobilizing voters who prefer the other party. Thus, party workers tend to conduct voter-registration drives in concert with canvassing. A *canvass* of voters involves contacting citizens, either face to face or by telephone, to ask them their party and candidate preferences. Unregistered voters who seem willing to support the party's candidates are urged to register. Canvassers may provide forms in those states which permit registration by mail.

On election day, party workers try to round up as many supporters as possible and get them to the polls. Every vote counts in elections. There have been instances in which candidates for state and even national office have come within just several hundred votes of one another. In an effort to get as many voters to the polls as possible, campaign workers often offer services such as transportation and baby-sitting to supporters who need them.

1. Describe the three main functions of political parties in elections.
2. What advantages do major party candidates have that candidates running on an Independent ticket lack?
3. Which resources could you contribute to the party of your choice?

The Election of a President

Presidential elections are held once every four years, on the first Tuesday after the first Monday in November. They are the culmination of the years of hard work and excitement that go into waging a successful presidential campaign.

The road to election as president begins with seeking party nomination. This can be the most difficult step toward the presidency, for often there are many competitors vying to be their party's nominee. In seeking the presidential nomination, an individual must rely on his or her own resources. Political experience, wealth, status, and other resources discussed in Chapter 2 can be crucial in gaining party support.

Political party members are busy during an election campaign. They register voters, try to convince people to vote for their candidates, and work to get their supporters to the polls on election day.

Once candidates have announced that they intend to run for president, they plan strategies for winning delegate support at their party's national convention. It is at the national conventions that the Democrats and Republicans choose their presidential and vice-presidential nominees.

There are several different methods by which states choose delegates to the national party conventions. In many states, presidential primaries are held. In the other states, delegates are chosen at party conventions or by party committees.

PRESIDENTIAL PRIMARIES

In 1976, 30 states and the District of Columbia provided for presidential primaries. In a *presidential primary,* registered voters show their preference among the various contenders for their party's nomination by voting for the slate of delegates committed to the candidate they prefer. In a *presidential preference primary,* voters choose delegates to the national convention, but delegates are not bound to support the candidates they represent.

There are no federal rules on how or when a primary must be held. Each state determines these details for itself. For example, in 1976, the first primary was held on February 24th in New Hampshire. The last three were held on June 8th in Ohio, New Jersey, and California.

Until 1976, the "winner-take-all" rule was followed in several presidential primary states. According to this rule, the candidate who won the largest number of votes in a state primary was then assured all state delegate votes at the national convention. For example, in 1976 President Gerald Ford won the Republican presidential primary in Wisconsin. As a result, he was given the support of all 45 of that state's delegates at the Republican national convention. This was true even though other candidates had received portions of the Republican vote in Wisconsin.

In an effort to make the primary process more representative of voter preferences, the Democrats adopted reform rules for their 1976 convention. Their purpose was to do away with the "winner-take-all" system. According to the new rules, in a presidential primary each candidate will receive delegate support in direct relation to the candidate's share of the primary vote. It is no longer an all-or-nothing situation. Several states had to amend their laws to conform to this new rule.

About half the presidential primary states require that the names of all the recognized contenders for a party presidential nomination be entered on the primary ballot. This was done to give voters a wide range of choice. In most of these states, however, it is possible for a person entered as a primary candidate to have his or her name removed from the ballot. This might be done when a state loss could hurt a candidate's total campaign effort.

1. Describe the presidential primary system.
2. What are some advantages and disadvantages to a "winner-take-all" system?

CITIZENS in PARTY ACTIVITY

Citizens play key roles in all three major functions of political parties—nominating candidates, influencing voters, and mobilizing voters. Citizens often take leadership positions in local party activities. They also ring doorbells and lend financial support. They may encourage their friends to vote.

The following case describes George McGovern's effort to win the 1972 presidential primary in Wisconsin. As you read, think about the different ways in which citizens became involved in the McGovern

99

campaign. Also consider the types of political resources that were used.

★ Victory in Wisconsin

Senator George McGovern of South Dakota announced his candidacy for the presidency on January 18, 1971. Few dreamed that he would win the Wisconsin presidential primary fifteen months later, let alone the Democratic presidential nomination. Known mostly for his early opposition to the war in Vietnam, McGovern seemed to lack the qualities necessary for a successful Democratic candidacy—money, labor support, and big-city strength. His victory in Wisconsin was due primarily to two factors—(1) a broadly based local campaign organization and (2) his stands on the Vietnam War and taxes.

Even before McGovern's formal announcement, a young Nebraskan was at work creating a grass roots organization for him in Wisconsin. Gene Pokorny was a 25-year-old veteran of Eugene McCarthy's 1968 presidential bid. Pokorny was a talented political organizer. He possessed all the necessary characteristics outlined by Gary Hart, McGovern's campaign manager—"efficient, low-key, persistent, methodical, durable (mentally and physically), orderly to the point of compulsion."

Pokorny drove into Wisconsin in November 1970. He was armed with a road map, a supply of three-by-five cards, and a list of 50 contacts. Within a year and a half he had expanded that list to 10,000 names. And he had established campaign committees in all 72 Wisconsin counties and in every city and town in that state.

Upon his arrival, Pokorny's first task was to identify potential McGovern volunteers and supporters. These people were found in many places—among students and teachers on college campuses, in liberal Democratic organizations, and among former McCarthy workers. An important source which Pokorny wanted to tap was housewives. During the campaign many private homes became the headquarters for McGovern volunteer groups.

Once supporters were identified and contacted, Pokorny put them to work. They recruited new volunteers, canvassed every neighborhood to identify McGovern voters, registered voters, distributed literature. This operation was commanded from 39 official neighborhood centers around the state.

Person-to-person contacts were supplemented by direct mailings. Pokorny sent special letters to farmers, labor organiza-

Senator George McGovern talks with a factory worker during the 1972 presidential primary campaign in Wisconsin. Personal contact with the voters helped him win that primary election.

tions, and other groups which were potential sources of votes, funds, and volunteers. Finally, in February 1972 a special Sunday supplement was put in all major Wisconsin newspapers. It outlined McGovern's position on the Vietnam War and property taxes. And it appealed for funds and pledges of support. An envelope was attached to make it easier for people to reply. The response was substantial, and all the names were added to Pokorny's list. Then, at the end of February, Pokorny sent one final letter to everyone on his list. He asked all McGovern supporters and contributors to mobilize their friends and neighbors in the final four weeks of the campaign. They were given a task for each week:

Week 1 Collect a dollar apiece from ten friends.
Week 2 Place McGovern bumper stickers on the cars of ten friends.
Week 3 Recruit ten new McGovern voters in the neighborhood.
Week 4 Get these new voters to the polling place on primary election day.

Gene Pokorny was able to command over 10,000 volunteers because they all had a common goal. They wanted to elect George McGovern as president. Many people supported McGovern because of his early and vocal opposition to the war in Vietnam. In Wisconsin he also tapped widespread voter discontent with rising property taxes. This feeling was especially strong among blue-collar workers. McGovern had co-sponsored a tax reform bill in Congress for property tax relief. He campaigned heavily on that issue in Wisconsin.

McGovern's campaign swings through Wisconsin were coordinated by Pokorny. One of his concerns was that McGovern volunteers and Wisconsin supporters maintain their enthusiasm over the long campaign. Frequent visits by the candidate was one way of doing that. A second way was to keep in constant contact with volunteers and potential volunteers. This enabled Pokorny to offer encouragement and give instructions. It also gave him feedback from those in the field.

McGovern's campaign visits to Wisconsin served another purpose for Pokorny. He knew that many party regulars considered McGovern a radical because of his antiwar stance. McGovern met with county Democratic organizations all across the state, assuring them that he was in the mainstream of Democratic party traditions.

From McGovern's viewpoint, his personal contacts with the voter were even more important. As he later said,

"The whole theory is that the little guy standing there as a clerk or a machine-tool operator, or a farmer—he's just as important as the governor and he has just as many relatives and contacts. Let the frontrunner collect the endorsements. That little guy is the secret of my success."

McGovern traveled all over Wisconsin, stopping in almost every town, and visiting factories, stores, and bowling alleys. Gordon Weil, McGovern's executive assistant, called this the "blitz campaign of the bowling alleys." People were surprised and happy when McGovern would drop in to meet them. They told their friends. "Here's a man who really cares for the little people."

Pokorny's organization and McGovern's stand on property taxes reaped its reward. In the Wisconsin presidential primary McGovern won 30 percent of the popular vote, compared with George Wallace's 22 percent, Hubert Humphrey's 21 percent, and Edmund Muskie's 10 percent. Weil recalls the victory:

"The McGovern family and I left the Milwaukee Inn, where we had been staying, to await the returns at the Pfister Hotel where the victory celebration would take place. As we stepped into the elevator on our arrival there, a hotel man told McGovern: 'The television is projecting you as the winner.' That was the first news of the first McGovern victory. It was hard to believe."

As winner of the presidential primary in Wisconsin in 1972, George McGovern knew he could count on delegate support from Wisconsin at the 1972 Democratic National Convention. In the quest for the Democratic party nomination, McGovern faced Senators Hubert Humphrey, Edmund Muskie, and Henry Jackson, as well as Governor George Wallace, in primary after primary. McGovern was the winner of many of the primaries, which led to his nomination as the Democratic presidential candidate.

Despite the strong support McGovern had from several segments of the American population, the support was not broadly based enough. He was overwhelmingly defeated in the 1972 election by President Richard Nixon, the Republican incumbent.

1. What resources did Gene Pokorny use to build support for his candidate?
2. What resources did George McGovern himself have that contributed to his victory in Wisconsin?
3. How might you be involved in a primary campaign?
4. How did citizens take part in the Wisconsin primary campaign?

From NOMINATION *to ELECTION*

The Constitution contains no information on the nomination of presidential candidates. Much of this process has been established by tradition and party preferences. For example, there are no federal laws calling for or regulating national party conventions. This procedure was started by the parties in 1832.

National Conventions. The national conventions are held in the summer of election year. In both the Democratic and Republican parties, the national committee (discussed on page 91) has responsibility for planning the convention. Once a date and location are chosen, the national committee contacts the party organization in each state.

The state parties are then informed of how many convention votes they are entitled to. In 1976, the Democrats allowed 3,008 delegate votes, and the Republicans set their total at 2,259.

Delegates to the national conventions come from each of the fifty states, the District of Columbia, Guam, Puerto Rico, and the Virgin Islands. In past conventions, the Democrats also have had representatives from the Panama Canal Zone. As you have read, delegates are chosen in presidential primaries, at state party conventions, or by state party committees.

Petitions. Nomination at a national party convention is the main method by which presidential and vice-presidential nominees are entered on state election ballots. Independent and minor party candidates can also have their names placed on election ballots—by going through the petition process. A candidate may be placed in nomination for president if a specified number of qualified voters sign a petition. Regulations regarding nomination by petition vary among the states.

The Campaign. After a candidate has been nominated by the political party, the presidential campaign begins. For a period of about two months, usually beginning on Labor Day, the Democratic and Republican candidates seek to bring their views before the public through radio and television coverage, tours, press conferences, rallies, and dinners. In recent years, television debates have played an increasing role in presidential elections. The first was between John F. Kennedy and Richard M. Nixon in 1960. Most recently, another series was conducted in 1976 between Jimmy Carter and Gerald Ford.

The Electoral College. Presidential candidates conduct campaign activity right up until election day. Then it is up to voters to indicate their choice. When voters cast their ballots for presidential and vice-presidential candidates on election day, they are technically voting to elect members of the

Presidential candidates Jimmy Carter and Gerald Ford conducted a series of three debates on national television during the 1976 election campaign.

electoral college. The electoral college is not a college as we normally think of it. Rather, it is a body of people chosen to elect the president and vice-president of the United States.

In every state, each party selects a slate of electors. In most states the candidates for electors are not listed on the ballot. The voter sees only the names of the presidential and vice-presidential candidates on the ballot. This is why many people are unaware that they are not voting directly for president and vice-president. In reality, they are voting for a slate of electors, who in most instances cast their own ballots in accordance with the results of the popular vote in their state.

According to the Constitution, the electoral college today functions like this:

1. Each state is allotted as many presidential electors as the number of representatives and senators who represent the state in Congress.

2. The legislature in each state determines how that state's presidential electors are to be chosen.

3. Each elector casts one ballot for president and one for vice-president. The vot-

ing takes place in each state and in Washington, D.C., on a date set by Congress. (Congress has set the date as the Monday after the second Wednesday in December of election year.)

4. The votes are counted during a special meeting of both houses of Congress.

5. The person receiving a majority of the presidential votes becomes the president. The person receiving a majority of the vice-presidential votes becomes the vice-president.

6. If no one receives a majority of votes cast for president, the House of Representatives will select the president by a majority vote of the states. Each state will have one vote. If no one receives a majority of votes cast for vice-president, the Senate will select the vice-president by a majority vote of the whole number of senators.

Today, the electoral college has 538 members. To be elected president or vice-president, a candidate must receive a majority—at least 270—of the electoral votes. The electoral college operates under the "winner-take-all" system. This rule says that a state's electoral votes should be cast as a unit for the candidate receiving the largest

103

ELECTORAL VOTES, by STATE

State	Votes	State	Votes	State	Votes
Alabama	9	Louisiana	10	Ohio	25
Alaska	3	Maine	4	Oklahoma	8
Arizona	6	Maryland	10	Oregon	6
Arkansas	6	Massachusetts	14	Pennsylvania	27
California	45	Michigan	21	Rhode Island	4
Colorado	7	Minnesota	10	South Carolina	8
Connecticut	8	Mississippi	7	South Dakota	4
Delaware	3	Missouri	12	Tennessee	10
Florida	17	Montana	4	Texas	26
Georgia	12	Nebraska	5	Utah	4
Hawaii	4	Nevada	3	Vermont	3
Idaho	4	New Hampshire	4	Virginia	12
Illinois	26	New Jersey	17	Washington	9
Indiana	13	New Mexico	4	West Virginia	6
Iowa	8	New York	41	Wisconsin	11
Kansas	7	North Carolina	13	Wyoming	3
Kentucky	9	North Dakota	3		

Figure 3-6

number of popular votes in the state. If a state has ten electoral votes, then all votes should be cast for the candidate receiving the largest popular vote in that state. (See the list of electoral votes for each state in Figure 3-6.)

Under the electoral college system, it is possible for a candidate who has received fewer popular votes than the opponents to receive a majority of the electoral votes. The reason for this is the "winner-take-all" rule. In fact, two presidents were elected under these conditions—Rutherford B. Hayes in 1876 and Benjamin Harrison in 1888. This fact has led people to criticize the electoral college system. There are other weaknesses as well. For example, there is no law that requires electors to vote for the candidates who win the popular vote in their states.

Proposals have been suggested for doing away with the electoral college and instituting direct election of president by the people. There are pros and cons for direct election. Enthusiasm has been expressed for this idea, as well as objections. On balance, given the objections which have been raised, it seems unlikely that direct popular election will replace the electoral college system in the near future.

1. What are the steps involved in winning election as president?
2. What is the purpose of the electoral college?
3. How does the electoral college function?
4. What advantages would there be to instituting direct election of the president and doing away with the electoral college? What disadvantages can you think of?

Citizens in Election Activity

Some citizens are very active participants in electoral politics. They may be candidates for public office. Or they may play leading roles in managing election campaigns. Other citizens are less involved. Their participation may range from helping out in an election campaign to taking part in a rally or giving money to a campaign fund.

Many are hardly involved at all. They may watch television programs about candidates and their campaigns or perhaps read newspapers and magazine articles about elections. They may vote on election day.

Finally, some citizens tend to pay little or no attention to electoral politics. They do not even bother to vote.

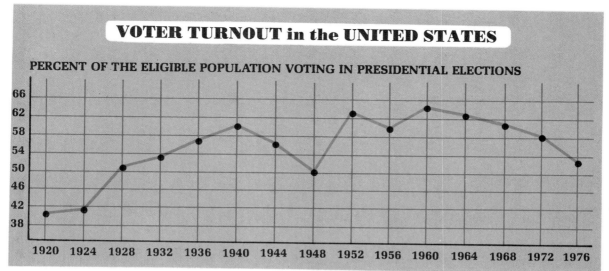

VOTER TURNOUT in the UNITED STATES

PERCENT OF THE ELIGIBLE POPULATION VOTING IN PRESIDENTIAL ELECTIONS

Figure 3-7

Source: Hart Research Associates, Inc.

HOW MUCH PARTICIPATION

Figures 3-7 and 3-8 contain information on how extensively citizens take part in elections. Figure 3-7 shows that since 1920 no more than 64 percent of the American population eligible to vote has ever turned out to vote in a presidential election. As Figure 3-8 shows, the turnout tends to be much less for state and local elections than it is for presidential elections.

Figure 3-7 reveals some interesting patterns. It shows that in 1976 almost one third of those eligible to vote did not even register to vote. Elections to choose representatives to Congress draw fewer than 50 percent of eligible voters when they are not held during a presidential election year. The local level suffers even more seriously. Less than 40 percent of the eligible voter population tends to turn out to vote in local elections. Therefore, there is a priority in voting. The largest turnout is for presidential elections. Other national races get the second largest turnout. The local level is left far behind in getting voters to the polls.

Figure 3-9 shows that political participation for most people does not extend much beyond voting. The most common political activity besides voting is to persuade

Figure 3-8

WHO PARTICIPATES?

1. In 1976, about 29% of those eligible to vote were not registered to vote.

2. In elections for Congress held in those years when there is no presidential election, voter turnout is often less than 60%. Over the last two decades, the percentage has been dropping.

3. Less than 60% of those eligible to vote in local and state elections voted on election day in November, 1976.

PARTICIPATION in ELECTORAL POLITICS

TYPE OF PARTICIPATION	1960	1964	1968	1972	1976
	BY PERCENT				
Worked for party or candidate	6	5	6	5	4
Attended rallies or meetings	8	9	9	9	5
Tried to persuade others how to vote	32	32	33	32	31
Wore campaign button, displayed bumper sticker	21	16	15	14	6

Source: Center for Political Studies, University of Michigan

Figure 3-9

others how to vote. Relatively few people actually work for party candidates. As the chart shows the political process is run by a small number of people. Those few people are absolutely key to the maintenance of a representative system of government.

1. What resources do you have that you might use to participate in electoral politics?
2. What are some reasons you can think of for participating in election activities?

Figure 3-10

PERCENTAGE of PERSONS REPORTING THEY VOTED in PRESIDENTIAL ELECTIONS, 1972 and 1976

GROUP	1972 %	1976 %
Sex		
Male	64	59
Female	62	59
Race		
White	65	61
Black	52	49
Spanish origin	52	49
Age		
18–20 years old	48	38
21–24 years old	51	46
25–34 years old	60	55
35–44 years old	66	63
45–54 years old	71	68
55–64 years old	68	66
65–74 years old	68	66
75 years old and over	56	55
Education		
8 years or less	47	Not available
12 years	65	
More than 12 years	79	

WHO PARTICIPATES Figures 3-10, 3-11, and 3-12 provide information about the participation in electoral politics of different groups in the American population. Use these data cards to decide which groups tend to take the most active part in electoral politics.

There are many reasons why people choose to vote or not to vote. Some of these reasons have to do with income and education. Other reasons include religion or ethnic or racial identification. Traditionally, Protestants and Catholics have voted for one party or the other in blocs, because of stands that particular candidates have taken on religious issues. There are also traditional votes by region. In the South people have tended to vote Democratic, although Southern Democrats often have different political ideas than Democrats from the northeastern states.

One of the single largest factors in voting is party identification. This means that people continue to vote for one party over a period of time. They identify with a party platform or a party stance in general over the years. In this case, the candidate can be less important than the party aims and goals which he or she represents.

Figure 3-13 shows what percentage of the voting-age population has identified with each major political party since 1937. Notice the advantage which the Democrats have had over the years in terms of numerical support. Note also that in 1976, 46 per-

Figure 3-11

PERCENTAGE of DIFFERENT GROUPS REGISTERED to VOTE, 1976

1. Between 50% and 60% of those black voters who were eligible to vote actually registered to vote.
2. Less than 50% of those Hispanic voters eligible to vote actually registered to vote.
3. Of those eligible voters between ages 18 and 29, 50% were registered.
4. Of those eligible voters between ages 30 and 44, 72% were registered.
5. Of those eligible voters age 50 or over, 85% were registered.

Figure 3-11

cent of eligible voters identified themselves with the Democratic party. Another 22 percent identified themselves with the Republican party. And 32 percent did not identify with either party. Most of the latter do not vote on the basis of party loyalty. They are political "independents."

Figure 3–14 shows party identifications of various sectors of the population from the period 1952 to 1972. Note, for example, that people in professions and business tended to vote for Republicans in each of the elections during this period. However, many voted for Lyndon Johnson against Barry Goldwater in 1964. It is important to know that for every generalization about party identification, there is an exception to the rule. Study the table carefully and answer the questions which follow.

1. Which groups tend to vote mostly Democratic? What resources do the Democrats have as a result?
2. Which groups tend to vote Republican? What resources do the Republicans have as a result? How are these resources different from those of the Democrats?
3. What resources could you bring to the Republican or Democratic parties?

CITIZENS in a PRESIDENTIAL ELECTION You have seen how citizens can take an active part in politics. The following case about Jimmy Carter's victory in the 1976 presidential election illustrates how resources were used by the

Figure 3-12

VOTER TURNOUT by INCOME and AGE, 1974 and 1976

1. Highest levels of voting occurred among college graduates with annual incomes of more than $25,000.
2. Lowest levels of voting occurred among those with less than an eighth grade education who had annual incomes of less than $5,000.
3. Less than one fourth of those between the ages of 18 and 21 voted in 1974 and 1976.
4. More than one half of those between the ages of 55 and 66 voted in 1974 and 1976.

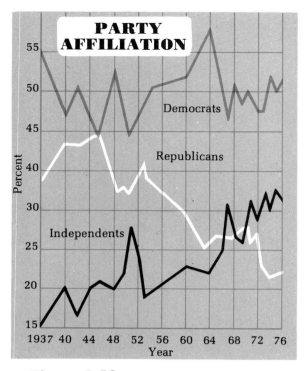

PARTY AFFILIATION

Percent

Democrats

Republicans

Independents

55
50
45
40
30
25
20
15

1937 40 44 48 52 56 60 64 68 72 76
Year

Figure 3-13

Democrats to win the election. It also shows citizen participation. As you read the case, think about what resources were used by whom.

★ **A Narrow Win for Carter**

In early 1976, James Earl Carter, former governor of Georgia, began his quest for the presidency. But few observers at the start of the race gave him much chance to win the Democratic party's nomination. The public did not initially believe that Jimmy Carter could win the nomination, since the Democratic race was filled with better-known candidates. Carter faced a tough challenge against these odds.

Carter's major challengers in the presidential primaries were Senator Henry Jackson of Washington, Senator Hubert Humphrey of Minnesota, Senator Birch Bayh of Indiana, Governor George Wallace of Alabama, Governor Jerry Brown of California, and Senator Frank Church of Idaho. These men competed for their party's nomination from January 1976 until the mid-July Democratic Party Convention in New York City.

However, by July Carter had all but won the nomination. He had impressive showings in various state presidential primary elections. (See page 99 for a discussion of the presidential primary system.) About three-fourths of the delegates to the Democratic Convention were chosen through the primary election process. Before the convention began, Carter had won the support of most of these delegates. Thus, he won nomination easily at the convention. He selected Senator Walter Mondale of Minnesota as his running mate.

In his acceptance speech, Carter said,

"Ours is the party that welcomed generations of immigrants—the Jews, the Irish, the Italians, the Poles, and all the others—enlisted them in its ranks, and fought the political battles that helped bring them into the American mainstream—and they have shaped the character of our party. . . . We *can* have an America that encourages and takes pride in our ethnic diversity, our religious diversity, and our cultural diversity. . . ."

Carter was making a bid to unite various ethnic and racial groups behind him, a main theme that became primary in his campaign.

At their convention in Kansas City in mid-August the Republicans nominated President Gerald R. Ford as their candidate. He had been challenged for the nomination by Ronald Reagan, former governor of California. Reagan had gathered considerable delegate strength by winning several primary elections. But he was not able to outdo Ford, whose position as president gave him the advantage. Ford selected Senator Robert Dole of Kansas as the Republican candidate for vice-president.

Former Minnesota Senator Eugene McCarthy also ran for president in this election on the Independent party ticket. McCarthy had made a bid for the Democratic presidential nomination in 1968. He was not successful in that attempt. However, he had built up a strong grass roots fol-

VOTE by GROUPS in PRESIDENTIAL ELECTIONS, 1952-1972

	1952 Stev.	1952 Ike	1956 Stev.	1956 Ike	1960 JFK	1960 Nixon	1964 LBJ	1964 Gold.	1968 HHH	1968 Nixon	1968 Wallace	1972 McG.	1972 Nixon
NATIONAL	44.6	55.4	42.2	57.8	50.1	49.9	61.3	38.7	43.0	43.4	13.6	38	62
Sex													
Men	47	53	45	55	52	48	60	40	41	43	16	37	63
Women	42	58	39	61	49	51	62	38	45	43	12	38	62
Race													
White	43	57	41	59	49	51	59	41	38	47	15	32	68
Non-white	79	21	61	39	68	32	94	6	85	12	3	87	13
Education													
College	34	66	31	69	39	61	52	48	37	54	9	37	63
High School	45	55	42	58	52	48	62	38	42	43	15	34	66
Grade School	52	48	50	50	55	45	66	34	52	33	15	49	51
Occupation													
Prof. & Business	36	64	32	68	42	58	54	46	34	56	10	31	69
White Collar	40	60	37	63	48	52	57	43	41	47	12	36	64
Manual	55	45	50	50	60	40	71	29	50	35	15	43	57
Members of labor union families	61	39	57	43	65	35	73	27	56	29	15	46	54
Age													
Under 30 years	51	49	43	57	54	46	64	36	47	38	15	48	52
30-49 years	47	53	45	55	54	46	63	37	44	41	15	33	67
50 years & older	39	61	39	61	46	54	59	41	41	47	12	36	64
Religion													
Protestants	37	63	37	63	38	62	55	45	35	49	16	30	70
Catholics	56	44	51	49	78	22	76	24	50	33	8	48	52
Party													
Republicans	8	92	4	96	5	95	20	80	9	86	5	5	95
Democrats	77	23	85	15	84	16	87	13	74	12	14	67	33
Independents	35	65	30	70	43	57	56	44	31	44	25	31	69

Figure 3-14

Stev. = Adlai E. Stevenson
Ike = Dwight D. Eisenhower
JFK = John F. Kennedy
LBJ = Lyndon B. Johnson
Gold. = Barry M. Goldwater
HHH = Hubert H. Humphrey
McG. = George S. McGovern

Survey by the American Institute of Public Opinion. The Gallup Poll, Princeton, N.J.

lowing in parts of the country. Eight years later, though, McCarthy found that as a third-party candidate he had neither the popular backing nor the resources to compete for the presidency on the same scale as the two major party candidates did.

Basically, the 1976 presidential election was a contest between two men—Gerald R. Ford and Jimmy Carter. The candidates competed for public support in a lively campaign. Featured were three nationally televised debates. Throughout his campaign, Ford stressed his experience. He asked the voters to return him to office so he could finish the job he had started. Ford hoped to benefit from holding the resources of the presidency, which included the vast com-

munications and transportation facilities of the federal government. He could move about the country on the presidential airplane, and his statements were always front page news. He also commanded a loyal and able White House staff which could help him campaign. Furthermore, Ford was buoyed by the knowledge that only eight incumbents had been defeated in 200 years. The last such defeat was in 1932.

In contrast to Ford, Carter stressed the need for change. He tried to associate Ford with the tarnished regime of former President Nixon. Carter also charged that the Republicans were mainly the party of the rich and the privileged. He claimed that the Democrats more adequately represented the

Jimmy Carter speaks to a group of citizens from the back of a campaign train, a popular technique used by many generations of presidential candidates.

different racial, ethnic, and income groups in the country.

Ford stressed the importance of solving problems through private enterprise and individual effort. Carter was more willing to use the federal government to help solve problems such as unemployment, high prices, poverty, and the need to provide medical services to the poor and elderly.

Owing to a new law on the financing of presidential election campaigns, both Carter and Ford had a spending limit of $21.8 million. Thus, the usual financial advantage of the Republicans was minimized. Although private individuals could still spend their own money to promote the cause of their preferred candidate, they could make only limited contributions to the election campaign funds.

A majority of newspaper editorials appealed to voters to back Ford. Thus, the Republicans retained their traditional advantage of widespread favorable press.

Throughout the campaign Ford and his backers tried to appeal to political independents, who outnumbered the Republicans in 1976. This strategy was based on the need to blunt the Democratic party's large numerical advantage. In 1976 this advantage was about 2 to 1 over the Republicans.

Ford also hoped for a low voter turnout on election day. This wish was based on the knowledge that Republicans tend to turn out in strong numbers on election day. In contrast, many who think of themselves as Democrats do not register or vote. If these Democrats remained on the sideline, then the more active Republicans might achieve victory, even though fewer in number.

Carter's strategy was to stress voter-registration drives and a large voter turnout. Thus, Democratic party workers mounted large-scale efforts to register as many voters as possible. On election day, they planned to get these voters to the polls. Both labor unions and black interest groups spent large sums of money. They involved many of their members in working to register potential Democratic voters. These groups ran advertising campaigns to influence their members and others to vote Democratic.

The AFL-CIO's Committee on Political Education (COPE) took an active part in the campaign for Jimmy Carter. (The American Federation of Labor-Congress of Industrial Organizations is an organization of labor unions which numbers about 17 million members.) AFL-CIO leaders believed Carter would do more to help labor unions than would Gerald Ford.

COPE mailed millions of letters to union members urging them to vote for Carter. COPE workers also conducted a telephone campaign in the five days before the election. This campaign tried to influence the voting decisions of AFL-CIO members. On election day, COPE workers provided free baby-sitting and transportation services to help voters get to the polls to vote for Carter and other candidates favored by the AFL-CIO leaders.

Figure 3–15 presents results of the 1976 election. Carter won a narrow victory over Ford, with only a 2 percent margin of victory in the popular vote. Support for Carter was strongest among blacks. Only 17 percent of black voters voted for Ford. Carter actually lost the white vote—48 percent for Carter, 52 percent for Ford. Strong support for Carter also came from labor-union members and blue-collar workers.

In contrast, Ford's strongest support came from high-income earners and those in professional and managerial occupations. People earning more than $20,000 a year gave Ford a 62-to-38-percent margin of votes. The bar graphs on page 112 give information about who supported which candidate.

Support by black people was particularly important to Carter. Carter won several states in the South because of black voters. For instance, Carter won Mississippi by fewer than 12,000 votes, but he had more than 134,000 black votes there. Carter won in Louisiana by 77,000 votes. This state

RESULTS of the 1976 PRESIDENTIAL ELECTION

CANDIDATE (PARTY)	POPULAR VOTE	PERCENT OF POPULAR VOTE
Jimmy Carter (Democrat)	40,828,587	50.1
Gerald Ford (Republican)	39,147,613	48.0
Eugene McCarthy (Ind)	745,042	less than 1 ★
*Minor party — small percentage of votes		

*Minor party candidates received a small percentage of votes.

Figure 3-15

would have gone to Ford without the 274,000 black votes which were cast for Carter. In Texas, blacks gave 276,000 votes to Carter, which enabled him to carry the state. Black votes also made the difference for Carter in New York, Pennsylvania, and Maryland. Without this overwhelming black voter support, Carter would have lost the election.

Citizens took many roles during the 1976 election. For example, Catherine Norris, a black woman, thought that blacks would get a better deal with Carter. She said the following about her participation:

"Mostly, I just talked for Carter. I held meetings and went door-to-door to tell people why I supported him. Never trying to persuade anyone, I talked about why I feel comfortable

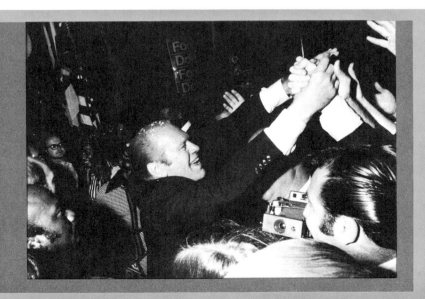

President Gerald Ford shakes hands with well-wishers at the Republican national convention in 1976.

HOW VARIOUS GROUPS VOTED in the 1976 PRESIDENTIAL ELECTION

Sex	Carter	Ford
Male	52	48
Female	52	48

Race	Carter	Ford
White	48	52
Black	83	17
Other	82	18

Occupation	Carter	Ford
Professional/Manager	43	57
Other white collar	51	49
Blue collar	59	41

Income	Carter	Ford
Under $8,000	62	38
$8,000-$12,000	57	43
$12,000-$20,000	50	50
Over $20,000	38	62

Age	Carter	Ford
18-21	49	51
22-29	56	44
30-44	52	48
45-59	48	52
60 and over	48	52

Religion	Carter	Ford
Protestant	46	54
Catholic	55	45
Jewish	68	32
Other	59	41

Party	Carter	Ford
Democratic	80	20
Independent	48	52
Republican	11	89

Ideology	Carter	Ford
Liberal	74	26
Moderate	53	47
Conservative	30	70

Presidential vote, 1972	Carter	Ford
Nixon	27	73
McGovern	83	17

Union membership	Carter	Ford
Yes	62	38
No	48	52

Size of community (more than 500,000)	Carter	Ford
Suburbs	53	47
Cities	60	40
(less than 5,000) Rural	47	53

Location	Carter	Ford
Farm areas	43	57
Nonfarm areas	53	47

Carter
Ford

Numbers in bars are percentages.

Figure 3-16

From CBS/New York Times Poll

with Carter. He seemed to be the man who would do the most for the poor people. He is the best for black and white, rich and poor. I also supervised meetings at which community people were asked to voice their opinions about what Carter should do on specific issues."

Other black citizens met in local, state, and national groups to plan black voter support for Carter.

Charlotte Zietlow from Bloomington, Indiana, said this about her involvement in the Carter campaign:

"I did several things for the Carter campaign. Position papers from Carter were secured by me to be available in the office so campaign workers would have accurate information. I also helped secure Barbara Jordan as a major speaker to build interest in the campaign locally. Many speaking appearances were scheduled by me for campaign workers to talk to any group, large or small, with whom we could get an appointment."

Ed and Barb Olson from Chicago were also active workers for Carter. They did the following:

"We had a list of all the voters. We called them on the phone and asked them what they thought the most important issue was in the campaign. Depending on how they answered, we put their names into one of four piles: definite Carter, leaning toward Carter, leaning toward Ford, definite Ford. Those leaning toward Carter and Ford were sent Carter's position on the issue they identified. On election day, definite Carter supporters and those leaning toward Carter were called and encouraged to vote."

A sixth-grader named Bill Peters talked about his work in the election.

"I helped out in the campaign office running the ditto machine, answering phone calls, licking stamps, whatever needed to be done. It was really exciting being part of politics. Meeting politicians, listening to them, and seeing what they do was really terrific."

Citizen efforts from the youngest to the oldest, across age groups, income categories, and race clearly contributed to Carter's victory. Even with this kind of citizen support, however, a large proportion of voters stayed home on election day. Only slightly more than 53 percent of the voters took part, which was the lowest turnout in a presidential election since 1948. Of all citizens over 18 years old, 27 percent voted for Carter and 26 percent for Ford, and 47 percent did not come to the polls at all.

Figure 3–16 shows that Carter won 297 (55 percent) of the electoral votes. (There is a discussion of the electoral college on pages 102–103.) A total of 270 electoral votes are needed to win the presidential election. If one more big state, such as New York, Pennsylvania, or Texas, had gone Republican, Ford would have been the winner.

1. How did groups such as labor unions and black political organizations contribute to Carter's victory?
2. Why did the Democrats stress voter registration drives more than the Republicans in the 1976 presidential election?
3. Why have the Republicans been able to compete successfully with the Democrats over the years, even though fewer people identify with their party?
4. How did individual citizens contribute to Carter's victory? What roles did they take?
5. How might you participate in a presidential election campaign?

Figure 3-17

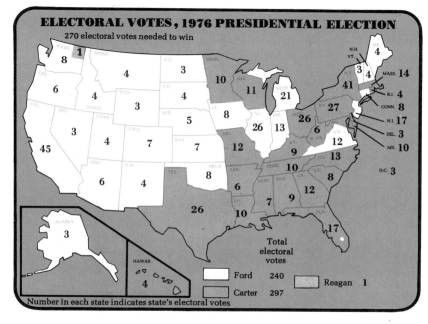

ELECTORAL VOTES, 1976 PRESIDENTIAL ELECTION

270 electoral votes needed to win

Total electoral votes

Ford 240
Carter 297
Reagan 1

Number in each state indicates state's electoral votes.

Chapter Review

1. What kinds of elections are held as part of public government in the United States? What are the functions of each kind?
2. What are the basic requirements for voting in public elections in the United States? How do these requirements vary among states?
3. Describe a typical election process from primary through election.
4. What third parties have influenced American politics and in what ways? Why have third party candidates seldom won major elections?
5. Describe the structure of the Republican and Democratic parties.
6. What are the main functions of political parties in the United States?
7. Summarize the similarities and differences between the Republican and Democratic parties.
8. What major steps must a candidate for president of the United States take in order to be elected to office?
9. How could a presidential candidate lose the popular vote but still win the presidency?
10. Describe the factors that affect voter participation.

Chapter Vocabulary

Define the following terms.

election	recall election	multi-party system
political party	referendum	third party
partisan	initiative	coalition
nonpartisan	precinct	gubernatorial
nominate	register	ward
primary election	polling place	party platform
closed primary	straight ticket	nominating convention
open primary	split ticket	mobilize
ballot	write-in vote	canvass
general election	one-party system	electoral college
special election	two-party system	elector

Chapter Analysis

1. In essay form, discuss the possible advantages and disadvantages of recall elections. Then form a point of view based on this analysis.
2. Analyze the advantages and disadvantages of registering as a member of a political party versus registering as an Independent. Based on this analysis, what do you expect to do? Explain.
3. List the ways in which a political party tries to influence voters to back its candidates. Then, in essay form, describe the techniques you would use if you were planning the campaign for a major political candidate. Explain why you would choose each tactic.

1. Research the arguments pro and con for eliminating national party conventions and replacing them with a national primary to nominate the presidential and vice-presidential candidates in both parties. Present these arguments in a short oral report.

2. Write a letter to your state senator or representative. Inquire whether or not citizens in your state have the right to an initiative. If so, propose a law that you would like to see enacted, detailing the steps necessary for its passage. If your state does not use the initiative, list alternative ways that a citizen might be able to recommend state laws.

3. Investigate the voter registration rules in your community. Inquire about the percentage of eligible voters that registered for the last election. Then suggest ways in which the rules might be reformed to encourage greater voter registration.

4. Interview members of your family who are registered voters. Determine if each is registered as a Democrat, Republican, Independent, or as a member of a third party. Ask the reasons for their decisions.

Chapter Bibliography

Dollar Politics: The Issue of Campaign Spending (Congressional Quarterly: Washington, DC), 1971.
Narrative description combined with charts and tables highlights key events involved in issue of campaign spending.

National Party Conventions (Congressional Quarterly: Washington, DC), 1976.
Presents a history of presidential nominating conventions from the Democratic Convention of 1837.

Choosing the President (League of Women Voters Education Fund: Washington, DC), 1976.
A short readable pamphlet that focuses on the role of political parties and voters in the election of the president.

Vote Power: How to Work for the Person You Want Elected, William T. Murphy, Jr. and Edward Schneier (Anchor Books: Garden City, NY), 1974.
Discusses effective roles for citizens in political campaigns.

A Campaign Album: A Case Study of the New Politics, Eric Rennie (United Church Press: Philadelphia, PA), 1973.
Chronicles the senatorial campaign of James Duffey of Connecticut.

Chapter Objectives

★ To learn the purpose and functions of interest groups in political activity

★ To identify different types of interest groups

★ To develop skills in working in political groups

chapter 4

CITIZENS in POLITICAL GROUPS

In most situations, an effective group of citizens has more power than does a citizen acting alone. An effective group can use the resources of all its individual members. In addition, it has group resources such as numbers and, frequently, status.

This chapter begins with a discussion of interest groups, one common type of political group. Citizen action in interest groups has a profound effect on American life. Interest groups promote the election of a specific person. They save forests from destruction and rivers from pollution. They organize workers. They influence legislation in areas such as education. The actions of interest groups affect your life in many ways.

An effective political group does not "just happen," however. To work well together to get something done, group members must have certain qualities. Group actions must follow certain steps. Working in groups is a skill you'll learn in this chapter. You can apply it to a variety of groups to which you belong.

Citizens in Interest Groups

One of the most effective groups in which citizens work together for common action is the interest group. An *interest group* acts in order to influence the distribution of resources in favor of its members. Its purpose is to express actively the interests of its members on specific issues. Interest-group members use their resources to gain goals which are important to the group.

Not all groups in which members share common interests and goals are interest groups. A key part of the definition of an interest group is the active expression of interests. An interest group is a mouthpiece for its members. It exists in order to affect action in favor of group interests. The science club at your school may be made up of students who share a common interest in science. It is not an interest group, however, unless members publicly express their opinions on issues and attempt to influence actions and outcomes in their favor. If, for example, the purpose of the science club is to try to persuade the school administration to improve the science facilities and expand the science course offerings, then the club is acting as an interest group.

There are hundreds of organized interest groups in our country. These organizations support the interests of groups such as labor and business; professional groups like teachers, lawyers, and doctors; students; religious groups; and ethnic groups like blacks, Hispanic Americans, and Native Americans.

Often, groups with opposing interests find themselves in conflict over an issue. For example, the Tobacco Institute is an interest group made up of tobacco companies. The members of this group want to increase the sale of tobacco products and the profits of their businesses. The Tobacco Institute wants to use its skills and money to influence governments to make laws which will help producers, sellers, and consumers of tobacco.

On the other hand, Action on Smoking and Health (ASH) is an interest group whose purpose is to protect nonsmokers. This group tries to influence government officials to pass laws banning smoking in public places. For example, ASH persuaded the Miami, Florida, city government to outlaw smoking in buses, elevators, department stores, and grocery stores. Many other cities and a few states have similar laws.

ASH does not always have its way, however. For instance, in North and South Carolina, pro-smoking groups such as the Tobacco Institute influenced a majority of government officials to vote "no" to "no smoking" laws.

Interest groups take many forms. Of these, three basic types are most important. The first can be called the *issue-oriented interest group*. ASH is such a group, focusing on the issue of smoking and attempting to ban smoking from as many public places as possible. There are many issue-oriented interest groups. Environmental interest groups are also examples of issue-oriented groups.

Government-oriented interest groups are another important type. These groups are also called *lobbies*, groups that promote their interest by influencing public government. Lobbies normally have headquarters in Washington, D.C., or in state capitals, where staff members spend most of their time trying to gain lawmakers' support on issues that are important to the interest group. Common Cause is a good example of a lobby that works to influence government on issues its members believe in. Sometimes called "the citizens" lobby, it has taken up causes such as election reform and the 18-year-old vote.

A third type of interest group is the *self-oriented interest groups*. In these, a specific group of people join forces to promote their own interests. Labor unions are perhaps the best example of self-oriented interest groups. The United Steel Workers, for instance, is a union that represents the interests of steelworkers in the United States. A wide range of interests may be important to the union, but all reflect the specific concerns of steelworkers. The National Association for the Advancement of Colored People (the NAACP) is also a self-oriented interest group. The NAACP seeks to represent blacks in the United States on various issues, especially those related to civil rights.

One interest group may act in different ways at different times. For example, the NAACP acts as an issue-oriented group when it focuses all its attentions and resources on an issue like civil rights.

In the same way, when any interest group promotes its interests by influencing public government, it is acting as a lobby. For example, many issue-oriented groups spend a great deal of effort attempting to influence government action in favor of interests they support. Labor unions like the United Steelworkers have groups within them that act as lobbies. They attempt to influence legislation so that it is favorable to the interests of workers.

ISSUE-ORIENTED GROUPS Wide-ranging in the interests they represent, issue-oriented groups can be found on every side of almost every issue. They seek the success or defeat of something members believe is important.

The issues that such groups back can be long-term or short-term issues. Peace is a good example of a long-term issue supported by many interest groups. There are well-established associations and research groups that promote peace year after year.

An election, on the other hand, often brings about many short-term issues around which interest groups form. Groups are put together to support the interests of a particular candidate or piece of legislation, and are disbanded when the election is over.

Generally, issue-oriented interest groups revolve around a single issue or topic. For example, the Sierra Club is a national group concerned with environmental issues. Members might agree that other issues are important, but their main desire in this group is to support conservation and environmental quality.

Representatives from many women's interest groups attended the National Women's Conference in Houston in 1977. They adopted a 26-point program to present to President Carter.

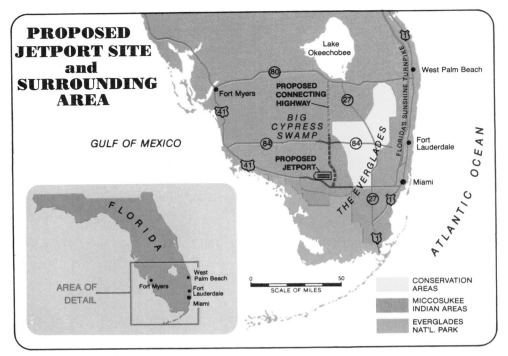

PROPOSED JETPORT SITE and SURROUNDING AREA

Lake Okeechobee

West Palm Beach

PROPOSED CONNECTING HIGHWAY

Fort Myers

BIG CYPRESS SWAMP

GULF OF MEXICO

Fort Lauderdale

PROPOSED JETPORT

THE EVERGLADES

FLORIDA'S SUNSHINE TURNPIKE

Miami

ATLANTIC OCEAN

FLORIDA

AREA OF DETAIL

Fort Myers

West Palm Beach

Fort Lauderdale

Miami

0   50
SCALE OF MILES

CONSERVATION AREAS

MICCOSUKEE INDIAN AREAS

EVERGLADES NAT'L. PARK

Figure 4-1

Following is a case about the activities of various issue-oriented groups, including the Sierra Club, in the Florida Everglades. As you read the case, determine what issues and interest groups were involved. Think about how those interest groups used resources, and what their impact was on the distribution of resources in south Florida.

★ Save the Everglades

Florida's most striking natural feature is the Everglades, a 1,719-square-mile swampland in the southern part of the peninsula. (See the map on this page.) Many people see the Everglades as a rich source of animal and plant life and of fresh water needed by the people of south Florida. They think it is a magnificent natural monument that should be kept as it is. Others, however, see the swamp as a vast wet wasteland. They believe it is an obstacle to progress that should be drained, cleared, and developed.

In 1968 bitter conflict erupted over the Everglades. The conflict was between those who wanted to develop the swampland and those who wanted to preserve it. The question was, Should a highway, an airport, and industries be built in the Everglades area?

Conflict over how to use the swamp began in the air. Residents of Dade County, near the site of Miami's huge international airport, had been complaining about excessive noise and commotion caused by jets and the traffic of their passengers. These complaints influenced the Dade County Port Authority to seek an out-of-the-way location for a new jetport to relieve the air-traffic congestion in Miami. The Port Authority asked the Federal Aviation Administration (FAA) for help. As a result, they received a $500,000 grant to support planning for a new airport.

After much study, the Port Authority officials decided that a small jetport should be built in eastern Collier County, at the edge of the Everglades. The Port Authority promised to try to protect the wildlife and water supply of the Everglades.

Early in 1968, however, Robert Padrick, Chairman of the Central and Southern Florida Flood Control District, discovered some alarming facts about the Port Authority's plans. He learned that they had decided to cut a four-lane super highway straight through the Everglades. The highway would run from Miami to the proposed airport. Also, various business leaders in south Florida had been working to persuade the Port

Authority officials to develop the Everglades area. The Port Authority had been buying land for a large jetport with motels and a shopping center.

Robert Padrick quickly told others about the Port Authority's plans. Leaders of several interest groups concluded that the Port Authority's decisions had doomed the Everglades. The bulldozers, concrete, and steel of the land developers would destroy the valuable natural resources of the swampland. Joseph Browder of the National Audobon Society, Gerri Souci of the Sierra Club, Superintendent Raferty of the Everglades National Park, and numerous other conservation leaders decided to pressure the Port Authority officials to change their plans.

The conservationists wrote questions about the possible outcomes of the new jetport. They sent the questions to local newspapers and television stations, and asked the Port Authority officials to answer the questions publicly. In this way they hoped to generate public pressure to block the Port Authority's plans. The results were disappointing. The Port Authority officials answered that the ideas of "alligator lovers and bird watchers" should not stand in the path of progress.

There was little public response to this first open clash between the Port Authority and the conservationists. So the Port Authority officials felt free to move forward with their plans. They influenced the Federal Department of Transportation to grant $200,000 in April of 1969 to start building a rapid transit system in the Everglades. By May, several businessmen had decided to start building shopping centers, motels, and industries near the proposed jetport.

In June, the conservationists appealed for help to Senator Henry Jackson, a leading member of the United States Senate Committee on Interior Affairs. Jackson's committee investigated the Everglades jetport issue. They urged the Secretary of the Interior, Walter Hickel, to order a study of the situation. Hickel followed this suggestion and asked Dr. L. B. Leopold, a noted ecologist, to determine the possible effects of the proposed jetport on the environment. The National Academy of Science also decided to look into this issue.

The studies of the National Academy of Science and the Department of the Interior

Opponents of the Everglades jetport wanted to preserve these undeveloped wetlands, but the Port Authority argued that building the jetport would make better use of the land.

were finished at the end of August 1969. Both studies concluded that if the Port Authority's plans were carried out, the Everglades would be damaged severely.

Despite the scientists' findings, the Dade County Port Authority officials decided to move ahead. They argued that the Federal Aviation Administration and the Federal Department of Transportation had approved their plans. They had already spent $13 million on this project and did not want the money to be wasted.

Important business, industrial, and labor union leaders were solidly behind the Port Authority. They argued that by developing the swampland they would generate jobs and money. Many jobs would be filled by people who had been out of work.

The conservationists responded by taking the issue to national newspapers and magazines. Articles about the threat to the Everglades appeared in *Life, Time, Newsweek, The New York Times,* and the *Christian Science Monitor.* Programs on radio and television proclaimed the dangers to the environment by the Port Authority plans. Throughout the nation, people were aroused. They wrote letters to their representatives in Congress, to Secretary of the Interior Hickel, and to President Nixon, urging the saving of the Everglades.

Secretary Hickel became opposed to the jetport development and prodded President Nixon to intervene. Governor Kirk of Florida and the Metro Commission of Dade County reportedly decided that the new jetport should be built elsewhere.

Officials of the Federal Aviation Administration and the Department of Transportation would no longer support the Port Authority's jetport plans. The bulldozers were stopped in their tracks. All building at the edge of the Everglades was halted. A short time later, the Port Authority agreed to search for another jetport site.

Through stubborn, skillful political action, several interest groups saved the Everglades. At the same time they gave the

American people a valuable lesson in ecology. Unfortunately, the tuition for this lesson was rather expensive—the $13 million that the Port Authority spent on an unfinished project.

Conflict over how to use natural resources has continued. Conservation groups have clashed with industrial, business, and labor leaders. The conflicts cannot be settled easily. Most people agree that a clean environment is good. People tend to agree that it is wise to conserve natural resources. Most people also agree that economic progress is good. The problem is how to balance the interests of conservationists and those seeking more industries, jobs, and income.

1. What issue was involved in the Everglades controversy? What interest groups were involved?

2. How did people, especially those in interest groups, use resources to oppose and to support the jetport?

3. What was the impact of interest-group activities on the distribution of resources in south Florida?

4. How might you use resources to make an impact in an issue-oriented interest group?

GOVERNMENT-ORIENTED GROUPS

As lobbies, government - oriented interest groups attempt to influence the government's distribution of resources. They do this by affecting government policies and decisions. The chart on page 123 lists the 25 major lobbies in the United States.

Lobbyists. In their effort to influence government, these interest groups employ men and women called *lobbyists.* Lobbyists represent their employers—interest groups—in Washington, D.C., and in state capitals. Essentially, the lobbyist's job is public relations. Lobbyists keep themselves informed

25 TOP LOBBIES

1. Common Cause
2. International Union, United Automobile, Aerospace and Agricultural Implement Workers
3. American Postal Workers Union (AFL-CIO)
4. American Federation of Labor-Congress of Industrial Organizations (AFL-CIO)
5. American Trucking Associations, Inc.
6. American Nurses Association, Inc.
7. United States Savings and Loan League
8. Gas Supply Committee
9. Disabled American Veterans
10. The Committee of Publicly Owned Companies
11. American Farm Bureau Federation
12. National Education Association
13. National Association of Letter Carriers
14. National Association of Home Builders of the U.S.
15. Recording Industry Association of America, Inc.
16. National Council of Farmer Cooperatives
17. American Insurance Association
18. The Farmers' Educational and Co-operative Union of America
19. Committee of Copyright Owners
20. National Housing Conference, Inc.
21. American Petroleum Institute
22. American Medical Association
23. Citizens for Control of Federal Spending
24. American Civil Liberties Union
25. National Association of Insurance Agents, Inc.

Based on 1973 expenditures.

Figure 4-2

Source: *Congressional Quarterly* July 27, 1974

of all government action that would affect the interests of the groups they represent. By presenting favorable arguments and information, they attempt to persuade officials to act in the best interests of their specific lobby.

Andrew Biemiller was a lobbyist in Washington, D.C., during the 1970s, representing the AFL-CIO labor union organization. He tried to influence members of Congress to pass laws which would give benefits to labor unions. He argued against laws which would take away benefits from his group. As a lobbyist for the AFL-CIO, he worked to promote the goals and programs of organized labor.

Fern Lapidus has also been a lobbyist. In 1977 she represented the New York City Board of Education. In Washington, Ms. Lapidus works to further the interests of education in general, and education in New York City in particular. Her job has been described like this:

"to keep an eye on education legislation as it winds its way through Congress; to make sure that Federal money is paid out on time . . . ; to discover the sources of grant money; to find out what types of proposals for existing programs are winning approval and what kinds are being rejected, and to

provide a wide variety of information to the Board of Education, its staff, and to the local school boards."

Lobbying for Education. As Figure 4–2 shows, there is a great variety in the interests for which lobbies seek to influence the government. Educators are one group of people whose lobbying activities especially affect you. Two organizations of teachers often act to influence the government in matters that affect the nation's schools, students, and teachers. These groups are the National Education Association (NEA) which has about 1.8 million members throughout the United States, and the American Federation of Teachers (AFT) which has a membership of about half a million. Since most education in the United States is financed with public funds, these two groups often act as government-oriented interest groups. They seek to influence local, state, and national government to distribute resources to education.

In 1976 NEA and the AFT successfully influenced Congress to support the 1977 education appropriations bill. This piece of legislation involved the amount of money the federal government would budget, or *appropriate,* for education in 1977.

When Congress sent the 1977 education

appropriations bill to President Ford for his approval, he vetoed it. The President thought that Congress had voted to spend more money on education than should be spent. In order to override a presidential veto, a two-thirds majority in Congress must vote to do so.

Both NEA and the AFT mobilized members to influence senators and representatives, urging them to override President Ford's veto. Each organization contacted state and local affiliates who in turn placed advertisements in local media and communicated with members of Congress.

NEA, with its large membership and great resources, was able to call on members all over the United States. This excerpt from an article in the NEA newsletter describes some of the group's active—and ultimately successful lobbying techniques.

"NEA Government Relations staff had notified state contacts a week early predicting the veto and warning that an override attempt might occur just hours later. Local association presidents and staff were alerted to be ready to activate telephone trees and other lines of communications at a moment's notice so that associations could generate as many telegrams to members of Congress as possible. Meanwhile, NEA

lobbyists, who had spent a week in a hotel adjacent to the Capitol, were aided in their effort by association leaders and staff in town for other meetings."

The following case describes the specific efforts made by the AFT as an example of the lobbying activities for the 1977 education appropriations bill. As you read the case, think about how the AFT worked with COPE (the AFL-CIO's lobby group), and what resources were used and distributed in this situation.

★ The AFT Goes to Congress

When AFT president Albert Shanker first heard that President Ford was expected to veto the 1977 Labor–Health, Education, and Welfare Appropriations Bill, he sent a letter to all AFT state federation presidents on September 21, 1976. The letter urged them to prepare for a strong effort to override President Ford's veto.

Shanker asked the state federations to have state labor groups pass resolutions urging the president to sign the bill. He also suggested that they urge their representa-

An NEA delegation from Ohio leaves the Capitol Building after a meeting with House and Senate members about proposed legislation.

tives in Congress to override the veto. Finally, and most important, Shanker asked state federation presidents to send representatives from AFT state groups to Washington. There, the AFT members could lobby their representatives and senators, if President Ford did veto the bill.

The AFT grassroots lobbyists first met in Washington, D.C., on September 26. Team members were given lists of senators and representatives. These lists were broken down by states and congressional districts. Press releases and news contacts back to the lobbyists' home states were arranged.

On Monday morning the Committee for Full Funding of Education Programs coordinated the first combined meeting of all grassroots education lobbyists. Carl Perkins, chairman of the House Education and Labor Committee, spoke. He explained the need for enacting an appropriations bill before the deadline of Friday, October 1. The deadline was less than four days away.

After the meeting, the AFT lobbyists split into two groups. One attended the weekly AFL-CIO legislative meeting. The other joined the AFL-CIO COPE operating committee meeting. Both groups sought and received the support of the highly skilled legislative representatives and COPE directors of affiliated ALF-CIO unions.

President Ford would not act for several days. However, AFT lobbying began in earnest after the completion of these meetings. For the next three days, AFT representatives contacted members of Congress and their staffs. They supplied them with information about the importance of this bill. Meetings were held day and night coordinating AFT activity with that of other labor and education lobbyists.

AFT's public relations staff assisted AFT members in generating press coverage at home. This coverage highlighted the real issues involved. By mid-week, the grassroots lobbyists had gained commitments to override the veto from enough senators and representatives to make up the needed two-thirds majority in the House and Senate.

By late Wednesday afternoon, September 29, all that remained was for the President to act. At 5:45 P.M. the White House announced the veto. With it was a message accusing Congress of inflationary spending and partisan action.

In Congress, however, the lobbyists' work paid off. On September 30, both houses voted to override the veto. The House acted first, voting against the veto by a margin of 312 to 92. In the Senate the vote was just as large, 67 to 15 in favor of overriding.

All in all, 37 AFT lobbyists had come to Washington from all over the country. Explaining their cause, they had contacted more than 300 House members and staff and more than 50 senators. The results speak for themselves: almost $6 billion appropriated for education in 1977.

1. What was the issue in this case?
2. Which interest groups were involved?
3. How did the AFT and COPE use resources in order to influence Congress? What impact did they have on the distribution of resources in the United States?
4. How might you use your resources in a government-oriented interest group to make an impact?

SELF-ORIENTED GROUPS

There are many categories of self-oriented interest groups. One category is made up of organizations that promote the interests of specific religious, racial, or ethnic groups—people who share a common heritage or set of beliefs. These organizations do important work to fight prejudice and discrimination against group members and to improve social conditions for members. They also seek to inform non-members about the group. Two groups in this category are B'nai Brith and the Indian Rights Association. B'nai B'rith is an organization of Jews who want to give service to their own people and "humanity at large." The Indian Rights Association is another self-oriented interest group, "dedicated to promoting the spiritual, moral, and material welfare of American Indians."

Many professional groups are self-oriented interest groups that work to promote the interests of specific professions. For example, the American Bar Association is an association of men and women who are lawyers, and the American Medical Association is an organization of doctors. The Association of Women in Architecture is a professional organization of female architects.

There are also many interest groups made up of people who share common interests in a sport or hobby. In this category are interest groups like the Sport Balloon Society of the U.S.A. and the American Snowmobile Association.

Labor unions are another type of self-oriented interest group. There are thousands of labor unions in the United States. These unions represent the interests of workers in almost every occupation. Some are made up of workers with specialized skills, such as the Amalgamated Ladies Garment Cutters Union. Others, like the United Mine Workers of America, represent many different kinds of workers in one area, such as coal mining.

Unions are formed by workers who believe that an organized group can have more power than unorganized individual workers. In an organized group, workers pool their resources to gain far more power than each worker could have alone. They use this power to gain benefits such as higher wages, safer working conditions, health care, and retirement pensions.

Organizing a union is often a difficult job. The story of the organization of the United Farm Workers union illustrates many of the problems, techniques, and benefits of forming a union. The United Farm Workers' Organizing Committee was organized by Cesar Chavez. It began in California in the 1960s. Its first members were a group of grape pickers who wanted to increase their strength in dealing with grape producers.

As you study the case on the UFWOC, think about how the union was organized, how it represented the interests of grape pickers, and what resources were used to influence growers.

★ The Birth of a Union

Like many other Mexican Americans, members of Cesar Chavez' family came to the United States as refugees from the Mexican Revolution of 1910–1920. Chavez was born in 1927 on his parents' farm in Yuma, Arizona. Ten years later, a depression forced his father to give up the farm to a bank. The family became migrant workers, moving from place to place, working on farms as the crops were ready to be harvested. The Chavez family moved over the southwest area from Arizona through southern California to work in the fields, picking crops.

As migrant workers, the Chavez family lived as many others did. They stayed year-round in tents without light or heat. Most of the winter they ate wild mustard greens and had no money for food or housing. Throughout this period, Cesar grew to know the migrant worker families and their way of life. He was one of them.

Chavez married young and moved into a *barrio* in San Jose, California. (A *barrio*, the Spanish name for a section of a city, is an area inhabited mainly by Spanish-speaking people.) This *barrio* was so poor it was called "Sal Si Puedes," or, "Get out if you can." Most of the Mexican Americans who lived in "Sal Si Puedes" had no way of improving their lives. They could not "get out."

In 1952 Chavez left farm work to become an organizer for the Community Service Organization. This group worked to involve farm workers in civic matters. In this job Chavez learned skills of organization and leadership. He also became known to Chicanos all over the state of California.

Cesar Chavez and his followers hold a meeting to build public support. This support was an important political resource during his efforts to organize the United Farm Workers union.

More and more, Chavez believed that farm workers needed to join forces to improve their economic condition. Only by solving economic problems could the farm workers improve their lives.

So, with $900 savings, Chavez set up headquarters in Delano, California. He began to build an organization that would represent farm workers. Chavez described the early days like this:

"By hand I drew a map of all the towns between Arvin and Stockton—86 of them, including farm camps—and decided to hit them all and to get a small nucleus of people working in each. For six months I travelled around planting an idea.

"We had a simple questionnaire, a little card with space for a name, address and how much the worker thought he ought to be paid. My wife, Helen, mimeographed them, and we took our kids for two or three day jaunts to these towns, distributing the cards door-to-door and to camps and groceries [stores].

"Some 80,000 cards were sent back from eight Valley counties. I got a lot of contacts that way, but I was shocked at the wages people were asking. The growers were paying $1.00 and $1.15, and maybe 95% of the people thought they should be getting only $1.25. Sometimes people scribbled messages on the cards: "I hope to God we win" or "Do you think we can win?" or "I'd like to know more." So, I separated the cards with the penciled notes, got in my car and went to see those people.

"We didn't have any money at all in those days, none for gas and hardly any for food. So I went to people and started asking for food. It turned out to be about the best thing I could have done, although at first it's hard on your pride. Some of our best members came in that way. If people give you their food, they'll give you their hearts. Several months and many weeks later we had a working organization and this time the leaders were the people."

After months of visiting and organizing, Chavez founded the National Farm Workers' Association in 1962. By 1964 the association had 1,000 member families. It was organized in 50 different groups in 7 southern California counties.

The NFWA served many functions for its members. The association represented workers in grievances against employers. It

127

also provided legal aid to members who had disability claims or other legal problems. The association managed a credit union through which members could obtain low-interest loans. There was a farm workers' press called *El Malcriado*.

Little by little, the association's strength increased. In 1965 the NFWA faced its first major test. In the process, a union was formed. The test came in the form of a strike called by members of the Agricultural Workers Organizing Committee. Filipino migrant workers who were members of the AWOC went out on strike, protesting low wages in the Delano grape harvest. Chavez and the NFWA members decided to support the AWOC workers. So, they joined the strike against Delano area grape producers. The workers demanded pay increases, safer transportation and working conditions, better housing, and accident insurance.

Before they were finished, Chavez and farm workers had cleared a strike zone that covered a 400-mile area. Workers without a cent to their names refused to work in the strike zone. More than 1,200 Mexican American and Puerto Rican workers from the NFWA joined the AWOC picketers. They threatened that strikebreakers would lose membership in their organizations forever.

The grape producers fought the strike by bringing in workers from other areas. As the strike was broken by the newcomers,

Chavez and the AWOC leaders realized that other tactics were needed. To attract widespread publicity and support, Chavez made national appearances on behalf of the farm workers. In addition, Chavez and members of the NFWA decided to join forces with the AWOC to form a union. The union was the United Farm Workers Organizing Committee (UFWOC).

With the strength of numbers, unity, and national publicity, Chavez and the farm workers called a national boycott of grapes produced by two of the largest grape growers. All over the country, concerned people stopped buying grapes produced by those companies.

Farm workers went on strike against the companies as well. To publicize the strike and boycott, Chavez and 57 workers marched the several hundred miles from Delano to the state capital at Sacramento. With 10,000 supporters, Chavez sat on the steps of the capital on Easter Sunday. The protestors wanted to encourage legislation that would bring higher wages and benefits to the grape pickers. They also wanted recognition of the union as the bargaining agent for farm workers, and public sympathy for the grape pickers.

At this point, a large national union, the Teamsters, refused to transport produce across the picket lines from the farms to the markets. Finally, one of the large grape

Gains made by the United Farm Workers in California helped migrant farm workers throughout the nation.

producers agreed to sign a contract with the UFWOC. The company recognized the UFWOC as the only bargaining agent for the grape pickers. Although other companies refused to sign and the strike continued, this contract was a major step in the direction of union strength. The strike and boycott continued until July 1970. By that time 85 percent of the grape growers in California had signed contracts with the farm workers' union.

1. What resources did Chavez use in organizing the NFWA?

2. What resources did the NFWA have? What resources did the UFWOC have? How would these resources help the workers?

3. How did the UFWOC represent the interests of farm workers?

4. How might you act in a self-oriented interest group to make an impact on issues that are important to you?

The Skill of Working in Groups

You have seen the power citizens can have when they join forces in effective groups to support common interests. Individuals acting alone could not have stopped the multimillion dollar jetport in the Everglades. Nor could they have changed the lives of grape pickers, or defeated a presidential veto. In order to achieve such goals, a group must be very strong and very effective. What are the qualities that make one group effective and another not?

Most of us have been part of successful group work in which people have had rewarding experiences. Note the following commentary from students:

"I really get a lot out of working in this group. I've made a lot of friends and we enjoy working together."

"I really learned a lot from working in this group. We studied issues that I didn't know before, and we took action that involved me in politics for the first time."

"We really showed 'em! We won our goals, against all odds. Success is great! And it's all because of this group."

Most people have also had bad experiences in groups. We have all heard the criticism, "That looks as if it were put together by a committee!" We also know of groups that have done nothing, groups that have fallen apart, or groups in which there has been a lot of conflict. Often we have very negative images of groups, and for good reason. Few groups really work effectively. It is a rare combination that puts people and tasks together in such a way that jobs are accomplished in harmony and mutual benefit.

Some of the problems of group work are illustrated by these student comments:

"I did all the work in the group. Everyone else just sat around while I did all the planning and spent hours getting things done. I don't like this situation. Somebody else is going to have to do the work the next time."

"If those two people don't stop arguing, we'll never get anything done."

"This group never gets anything done. We just meet and meet for hours and talk about trivia. We're more interested in how we *might* do something than in actually getting something done."

The reasons for success and failure of groups are sometimes hard to point out. However, there are some basic principles for putting together a group and for getting things done which will help the group be successful.

People in a group must think of it as a group effort rather than an individual effort. In any group there are leaders, followers, and necessary roles for people to take in order to get things done. However, group members must be willing and able to work together to achieve group goals.

ORGANIZING A GROUP

Your first step in working in a political group may actually be to form a group. Suppose you have a goal, something you want to accomplish. You realize that you cannot accomplish it alone. So, you decide to join forces with other people who share your goal.

In order to put together a group successfully, you must select people who have certain characteristics. The case that follows describes the creation and work of an effective political group. As you read, think about the characteristics of the group members. Also, identify ways in which the group reached its goals.

★ Caution—Marine Biologists at Work

In 1969 two New York City high school teachers designed a brand new biology course for students at their school. The school is John Dewey High School in Brooklyn. The teachers were Harold Silverstein and Lou Siegel. Little did the two men know that their course would train a dynamic group of high school ecologists.

Silverstein and Siegel began with a wish to teach marine biology to high school students. John Dewey is near Jamaica Bay and the Atlantic Ocean. The teachers wanted students to have a chance to study the biology of their environment. So, they planned a course that would include field trips to nearby beaches.

The marine biology classes began successfully. In the beginning, students approached their subject from a purely scientific angle. Then, in 1971 Lou Siegel became involved in a local environmental issue. He found out that the Army Corps of Engineers planned to build a wall around Coney Island. (See the map on page 131.) This wall was supposed to protect New York City from hurricanes. Siegel was very concerned. He was sure that the wall would hurt the marine life in the area. And, he felt certain that it would soon be covered with graffiti. (*The New York Times* also was worried about what the wall would look like. They published an editorial with the cartoon reprinted on page 131.) Finally, Siegel did not think that the wall was needed. There had been only four big hurricanes in the area in the last 200 years.

Siegel and Silverstein did a scientific report on the possible effects of the wall. Based on their research they showed that the wall would damage the marine food chain. In addition, they pointed out that the wall would soon become an eyesore.

The two teachers presented their report at a Corps of Engineers hearing. There was no response. The Corps decided not to build the wall after all, but their decision was based on lack of funds, not ecology. The Corps developed another plan. Again, Siegel and Silverstein believed the plan's proposals would damage the marine life at Coney Island. This time, they wrote a paper, which they sent to congressional representatives and newspapers. One congressman took up the cause, and the plan was defeated.

Harold Silverstein commented on these experiences. "We learned that you can go through the official channels, but unless you have some political or social input nothing happens." The men had learned that they needed to use their resources to get results.

Up to this time the marine biology students had not been involved in environmental issues. However, in 1972 the class began an ecological study of marshlands. About that time, they were contacted by someone

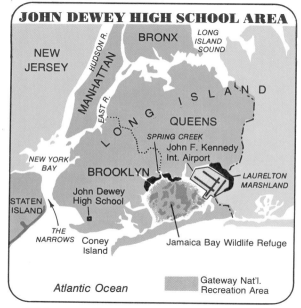

Figure 4-3

who wanted help. This person had heard about the work at John Dewey. He told the teachers and students that the New York City Environmental Protection Agency (EPA) wanted to fill in a nearby marshland. (The EPA is responsible for air and water facilities in New York City.) Many people in the community wanted to preserve the marshland, an area called Spring Creek.

A special group was formed to investigate the Spring Creek problem. Interested students worked with the two teachers to make an intensive study of the Spring Creek marshland. Tests and observations of the area were conducted and reported.

The group also decided to call in some special help. They asked the Sierra Club to work with them. The group respected the Sierra Club's record in protecting the environment. And, they realized that the Sierra Club had better contacts and more clout than their group did at that time. Also, Sierra Club lawyers had experience in the legal aspects of environmental issues. This was a specialized area in which the John Dewey group had little *expertise,* or knowledge and skill in a particular field.

The marine biology students, Harold Silverstein, a Sierra Club lawyer, a young law student, and an environmental group leader worked together. Each member of the

group had something to offer—scientific knowledge, legal experience, understanding of the workings of government agencies. And all had enthusiasm and commitment for the job they were doing.

Also, all members of the group shared a common goal. They wanted to stop the EPA from destroying the Spring Creek marshland. Together they had set out to reach that goal.

A public hearing on Spring Creek was scheduled by the EPA. At such a hearing, people who are concerned with the specific problem have a chance to present their views.

All of the John Dewey group worked to prepare a report on Spring Creek. Before the hearing, they sent a copy of the report to the EPA.

Two students, Harold Silverstein, his son who was a law student, the Sierra Club lawyer, and the environmental group leader represented the John Dewey group at the hearing. Facing them were 12 professionals—lawyers and biologists—from the EPA.

The John Dewey group expected to defend their position against these experts. To their surprise, however, they did not have to

The New York Times/Norm Doherty.

defend anything. EPA said that, after reading the report, they had sent their biologists out to Spring Creek. They agreed with the John Dewey report. Spring Creek would not be touched.

The students and teachers had become an effective environmental protection group. They had learned how to work together to produce impressive results. They had learned when to call in experts with needed experience. They had learned how to function in new ways in the environmental area. They had fought battles and won them.

Today, more than 300 students take part in the marine biology program at John Dewey High School. About 75 of these students work closely with Siegel and Silverstein on special environmental cases brought to them by the community. Since Spring Creek, the group has had many other significant victories.

The photographic feature on pages 136–137 will bring you up to date on John Dewey's marine biologists today.

> 1. What characteristics of these group members do you think made the group effective?
> 2. How did the group members accomplish their goal? What resources did they use?

Characteristics of Effective Groups. There are three important characteristics to consider in building any group. In an effective group, members must (1) have common goals, (2) possess key resources, and (3) be able to work together. Clearly, the John Dewey group had common goals and key resources. They also were able to work together.

A group can be organized successfully when there is a single goal or a set of goals on which most members can agree. For example, there were important *common goals* involved in the formation of the John Dewey

High School group. First, the two teachers wanted to form a marine biology class. As they pursued that goal, they developed a group around the issue of protecting the environment. This common goal helped group members organize and dedicate themselves to their task. A common goal allowed people to work together effectively with unity.

In a successful group, members also agree on *specific objectives* in order to achieve their goal. For example, the John Dewey group agreed to do an ecological study of Spring Creek. This was the objective which would help them achieve their goal of preserving the environment. The students and teachers in the group clearly agreed with one another on the plan. They then recruited the Sierra Club lawyer and the environmentalist who also shared their objectives. Whenever a group forms, it is important to have shared goals and objectives. For example, half of the John Dewey group might have believed in ecological studies and the other half only in protest movements. Then, the group would have had great difficulty working effectively.

Also essential in putting a group together is to have members with some *key resources* necessary for getting the job done. The group at John Dewey High had quite a few resources. First of all, they had the skills to do an environmental survey. From this study they gained valuable information for the EPA. Information was the key resource in this case. The lawyer and the environmental group leader also had special skills based on professional experience in environmental work. The John Dewey group had the resources necessary in order to make their voice heard by the EPA.

Without careful inventory and planning by an initial group of people who have the resources to get the job done, a group cannot function successfully. In forming a group, organizers must look for members who have these characteristics.

Goals and resources alone are not sufficient, however. People also need *to be able* to work together. Otherwise the group can be "all talk and no action." Two things are important in helping people in a group do things together. The first is the establishment of rules. Rules define what people can and can't do. Without some informal rules about who is in charge, the people in a group might not be able to accomplish something together. Rules, then, help to guide action so that people can work together effectively.

A second important part of doing something together is establishing roles. Deciding who will be responsible for various types of activities is important. It is not just a coincidence that most groups have either formal or informal officers. Even voluntary groups like the Sierra Club have them. This distinction of roles helps groups work smoothly.

1. Make a list of tasks that you would like to try to accomplish with a group of students. The tasks should involve school life. For example, you might want to raise money for the school library, or conduct a campaign for a candidate for student government, or plan a class function. Choose goals that could be achieved in a relatively short time (no more than a few weeks). Later, you might try to accomplish one of these tasks.

2. Share your ideas with your class and form a group with other students. Choose one task for the group to work on.

3. Using the principles of group formation that you have learned, prepare a summary of goals, resources, rules, and roles needed to do the job. Later you may act based on these plans.

GETTING THINGS DONE Once you have formed a group, your object is to get something done. This stage has its own problems and solutions. Groups can be well formed and

still fail to get things done because major steps in planning and acting are not carried out. The following case presents a hypothetical situation in which a group wants to "get something done."

★ **Traffic Lights in Hightown**

Hightown is a suburban community located in the heart of the Midwest. In the past, Hightown never had a traffic problem. It is "off the track" for most people who must enter and leave the suburbs. Now, however, an expressway has been built which passes through the edge of the community. Traffic on and off the expressway has clogged streets. As a result, many Hightown residents are unhappy.

The problem is particularly severe in front of Hightown High School. The high school is within walking distance for many students. Crossroads to the high school often are filled with students passing from the residential area of the community to the high school. Now, there is no traffic light in front of the high school. This bothers many people who drive automobiles, as well as the students who have to cross the road. They are sure that there will be an accident someday.

The City Council is considering putting traffic lights in the town but has not made a decision about the area around the school. Many of the students are anxious for the City Council to make this one of their high priorities. They are talking about the problem and trying to figure out a way that they can get the Council to consider putting a traffic light in front of the school. Aware that the city has limited funds to allocate, they want to present their case well.

1. If you were a student at Hightown High School, what would you do to have a traffic light installed in front of the school?

2. What resources would help you in your task?

These students are working as a group to produce a school newspaper. Their first two steps are to agree on a plan and to assign tasks (bottom photo). Individuals then write news stories (center photo). Others are responsible for doing the final layout (top photo).

Five Steps. It is possible to identify steps in getting something done in any group. If you recognize a problem and want to do something, one of the first things you should do is analyze the steps that might be followed in order to get the job done.

A group which wants to reach a goal (in this case the goal of influencing the City Council to approve a traffic light) needs to be able to *think out a plan* before anything else is done. A series of steps must be agreed upon.

The group also should think about the *time* that it will take in order to carry out the steps. For example, if the deadline is the next Council meeting, then the group must be sure that members can carry out their steps within that time limit. Often timing is crucial.

After a plan is developed, carrying out a task depends on people and the skills and resources they bring to the task. A group must think about *who will carry out various steps of the task and what special skills members can offer for achieving a goal*. At Hightown High School, the principal and teachers need to be brought into the plan. This action would show that the entire school is behind this particular issue. Also, the principal's status may be helpful in convincing city council members. Taking a poll or getting a petition signed might be part of the plan. If so, one might recruit a number of students who could perform this particular task more easily than teachers, administrators, or people in the community.

A third step in the process involves developing *alternative strategies*. People who are carrying out a task should always think about the fact that unexpected events or conditions may cause plans to take longer, or may make it impossible to carry out certain steps in the plan. So, in determining a plan for carrying out a task, a group should be sure their plan is feasible. For example, if the Hightown principal and teachers were unable to speak at the council meeting, students might suggest key community leaders who could address the meeting. These alter- natives should be made part of the original plan.

The fourth step involves *communication*. In any group activity in which several people are doing different things, communication is necessary. Initially, people must discuss ideas thoroughly. In this way they can understand the task as a whole and their particular role in it. Periodically, key group members should discuss progress of the task. They should make sure people have the resources they need, and act as central sources of information. Throughout the group work, people must be able to share problems and ideas.

The fifth step is *determining people and skills to act as backup*. More time or more people may be needed in order to reach the goal. Backup involves the kinds of resources that are necessary if some people fail to do their part or if the task itself takes longer or seems more complex. It is an important part of carrying out a task.

In summary, there are five major steps involved in successfully carrying out a task:

1. Plan the steps that will be necessary to carry out the activity. Also think about how much time it will take to carry out each of these steps.

2. Identify people and skills necessary to accomplish the task.

3. Create flexible alternatives for each step.

4. Provide for checks and communication among people working on the task.

5. Determine the people and skills necessary for back up.

1. Think about the five steps as they relate to objectives your group defined earlier.

2. Then, meet with your group again and discuss how to carry out the objectives.

3. Following the principles you have just learned about getting things done, prepare a "master plan" for working in a group to accomplish your task. Discuss with your teacher whether or not your group should actually attempt what you have planned.

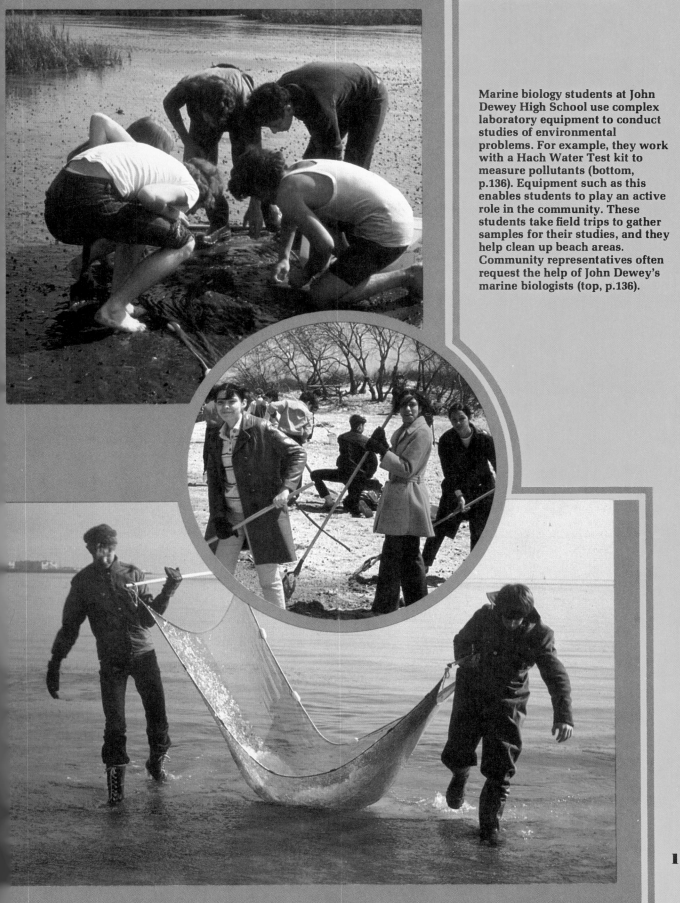

Marine biology students at John Dewey High School use complex laboratory equipment to conduct studies of environmental problems. For example, they work with a Hach Water Test kit to measure pollutants (bottom, p.136). Equipment such as this enables students to play an active role in the community. These students take field trips to gather samples for their studies, and they help clean up beach areas. Community representatives often request the help of John Dewey's marine biologists (top, p.136).

1. Describe the functions of an issue-oriented interest group.
2. Summarize the action of interest groups in the Everglades controversy. What resources were used and distributed?
3. Describe the functions of a government-oriented interest group.
4. Summarize the action of the AFT and the NEA in the education appropriations bill veto. What resources were used and distributed?
5. Describe the functions of a self-oriented interest group.
6. Summarize the actions involved in the formation of the UFWOC. What resources were used and distributed by the groups involved?
7. How do lobbyists engage in politics?
8. What are the important principles for working in groups?
9. What characteristics should group members have?
10. What steps are important for a group to take to accomplish its goals?

Chapter
Vocabulary

Define the following terms.

interest group	lobby	expertise
issue-oriented interest group	lobbyist	appropriate
government-oriented interest group	migrant worker	
self-oriented interest group	barrio	

Chapter
Analysis

1. Determine the criteria for an interest group. In other words, what makes an interest group different from other types of groups? Next, test your criteria by analyzing each of the student groups in your school. Which are interest groups and which are not?
2. In your opinion, what are some of the ways in which lobbies might affect the distribution of government resources? For example, do lobbies help ensure the equal distribution of federal funds? Do you think private citizens always should support lobbies? Explain.
3. Review the characteristics of an effective group. Then analyze the Everglades, AFT, and UFWOC case studies and determine how these features contributed to the success of each group. Do you think that any additional characteristics should be added? Explain.
4. To encourage people to work together in a group, roles and rules must be established. In your opinion, what are some of the most important rules and roles in any successful group? If possible, use examples from groups in which you have been involved.

1. Investigate the number and kinds of interest groups that function in your community. Identify each as an issue-oriented, self-oriented, or government-oriented interest group.

2. Choose an issue that you feel strongly about. It can be a school, community, state, national, or international issue. Find out what interest groups are involved on both sides of the issue. Plan ways in which you could participate in an interest group that is working on the issue.

3. List all the various groups that are associated with your school system. Include student, faculty, and parent organizations. Determine if each group is an example of an interest group, giving reasons why or why not. Then investigate the ways one of the groups attempts to achieve its goals.

4. Research one of the large national interest groups such as the Sierra Club, the NAACP, the United Farm Workers, or NOW. Identify specific examples when this group has acted as a self-oriented group. Determine other instances when it has acted as a government-oriented or an issue-oriented group. Record this information in chart form.

5. Imagine that you have been asked to help organize a group of students to work on a fund-raising project for the senior class. Describe how you would organize the group, following the steps outlined in this chapter. Be sure to consider how group members will be selected and how they will work together.

Chapter Bibliography

Corporate Ambassadors to Washington, Robert W. Miller and Jimmy D. Johnson (The American University: Washington, DC), 1970.
Focuses specifically on the Washington representatives of businesses, considering their personal qualifications, roles with Congress and the president, and relationships with their companies.

Pressures Upon Congress: Legislation by Lobby, Thomas P. Murphy (Barron's Educational Series, Inc.: New York, NY), 1973.
Highlights how various interest groups influence Congress.

Interest Group Politics in America, Robert H. Salisbury (Harper and Row: New York, NY), 1970.
Composed of many articles each of which considers a different aspect of interest group politics. The book also features specific interest groups.

Political Brokers: Money, Organizations, Power, and People, edited by Judith G. Smith (Liveright: New York, NY), 1972.
Case studies of groups such as the Americans for Democratic Action, Common Cause, The American Medical Political Action Committee, The Democratic National Committee and several others.

Chapter Objectives

★ To analyze how citizens participate in unions as interest groups

★ To apply knowledge of politics and interest groups to the United Mine Workers of America

★ To develop valuing skills

★ To apply knowledge and skills involved in interest-group politics to the study of a local interest group

5

CITIZEN PARTICIPATION in an INTEREST GROUP

As you learned in Chapter 4, a labor union is a type of interest group. Unions express the desires and needs of their members to management and to government. As a result, unions have had a major impact on people's lives. Unions are often responsible for the increased wages that their members receive. They speak up for improved working conditions, added benefits, and the right of workers to pursue grievances against employers.

Chapter 5 focuses on one union in particular—the United Mine Workers of America, or UMWA. The UMWA is an industrial trade union. It represents workers in most of the coal mines and coal-processing industries in the United States. The UMWA also has local unions in Canada. In addition to obtaining better wages for miners, the union has achieved other important gains as well. Chief among these are benefits which protect the health and safety of miners, give assistance to families when miners are injured, and provide pensions for retired miners.

Chapter 5 explores some basic questions about the UMWA: (1) How does the UMWA function as a political interest group? (2) What kinds of politics operate within the UMWA? (3) What type of influence does the UMWA have on government?

Unions as Interest Groups

Labor unions today are strong political forces. There are about 200 unions in the United States, made up of about 20 million members. (See Figure 5-1.) Most unions are affiliated with the AFL-CIO, a federation of national and international unions which represents about 17 million men and women.

One of the major activities of the AFL-CIO is to work for laws favorable to labor. As such, this organization has a great deal to

say about what happens to workers. The AFL-CIO has had successes over the years in influencing management and government on behalf of the nation's work force. (Study Figure 5-2 to see how the United States' labor force has grown in this century.)

Labor unions did not always enjoy a position of influence, however. The following chronology highlights the major developments in the history of the labor movement. As you read, look for turning points in the growth of labor unions as interest groups.

Figure 5-1

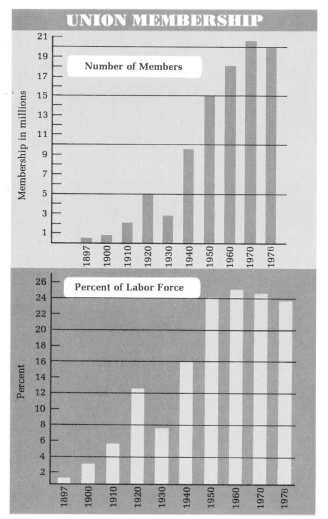

Source: Statistical Abstract of the U.S. 1978

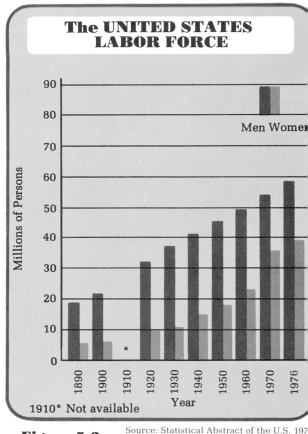

Figure 5-2

Source: Statistical Abstract of the U.S. 1978

142

Labor unions today represent a wide variety of people and occupations. Pictured here are miners, a garment worker, and a sheet metal worker.

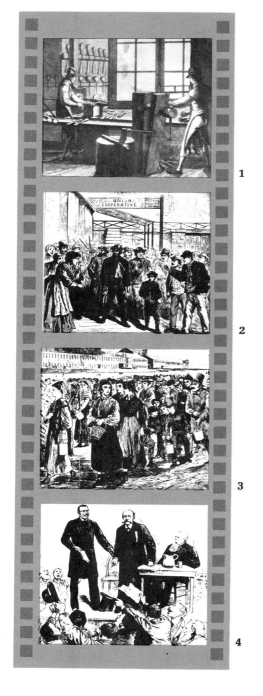

1. Many factories in the 1820's, like this one, relied on skilled workers.
2. Pennsylvania coal miners go on strike in 1871.
3. The work day begins at an early New England factory.
4. The Knights of Labor hold an annual convention in 1879.

A History of the Labor Movement

Local unions were first formed in this country in the 1790s and early 1800s. These early unions were *craft unions,* organized according to the type of job an individual performed. Workers such as bakers, shoemakers, and mechanics banded together in separate groups in order to get fair wages or fair prices. There was nothing known as a national union at this time.

People in these craft unions wanted many of the same things that unions seek today. High among their demands were increased wages and a shorter working day. (In the early 1800s, many people worked a 10-hour day or more.) To enforce their demands, these unions relied largely on strikes. In a *strike,* employees as a group refuse to work.

The early unions failed, however, for several reasons. They failed because workers were unorganized, separated by geographic area, and divided by job skills. The unions failed because they lacked money; surely the workers had none to spare. In addition, management clearly had the upper hand. Better organized than the workers, they formed employers' associations. They went to court to stop strikes. Ruling that striking was a form of conspiracy, the courts usually ordered strikers back to work. Unions were banned by law in many places.

The early unions also had to deal with economic conditions. In bad times, many people lost their jobs, and unions lost their power to bargain. In good times, when unions went on strike, management charged "conspiracy" and brought in strikebreakers to replace striking workers.

Despite problems faced by unions, labor groups continued their struggle to be recognized as legitimate interest groups. The major formation of national unions occurred in the years following the Civil War.

The year 1869 is a milestone in the history of the labor movement. This is when the organization known as the Knights of Labor was formed.

The Knights of Labor was the first major attempt in the United States to bring all workers, both skilled and unskilled, together in a union. The Knights took part in a number of railroad strikes, and workers won demands in one of them. Although the Knights of Labor was an important step forward in the labor movement, the organization declined in the late 1800s.

The AFL, organized in 1886, became the major representative of craft union interests. (A *craft* is an occupation requiring special skill and training.) The first AFL president was Samuel Gompers. Gompers was largely responsible for the swing toward organization and power in the labor movement. His organizational skill made the AFL a sound and lasting labor federation.

The organization of the AFL was mainly by craft units of skilled workers. The various units were held together through affiliation with the national association. When an issue concerned the economic interests of most or all the units, the AFL organization represented them as a whole. There was also a strong emphasis on craft autonomy. This meant that local units were independent from the larger organization in their internal affairs. The AFL was the first national association of craft unions to represent in an effective way the economic interests of its members.

Based on his experience with earlier unions, Gompers decided to focus on immediate economic gains for workers. These included higher wages and shorter working hours. In the late 1800s, workers in different industries shared the frustration of working long hours for little pay. Garment, steel, and

5. Women delegates attend a Knights of Labor convention in 1886.
6. Railroad strikers stop an express train.
7. Samuel Gompers meets with British labor leader at an AFL convention in 1894.
8. A family works together as garment workers.

9. These men work in a nineteenth century metal factory.
10. Violence breaks out at Homestead steel mills in 1892.
11. Secretary of Labor Frances E. Perkins (right), inspects a garment plant in 1933.
12. Silk workers check on the progress of a strike in 1934.

textile workers, among others, commonly worked 60-hour weeks, often with faulty equipment. Miners in particular suffered in dangerous jobs.

Gompers decided to focus on bread-and-butter wage and benefit issues around which workers could unite. He worked to keep the AFL out of political election campaigns which could divide the workers. Unity would make labor strong, he thought. And he was right. Labor finally had a leader who could begin to make unions work.

Even with the strength of Gompers' leadership, the first days of the AFL were still not very steady. A number of violent strikes and lockouts took place. (In a *lockout*, an employer refuses to allow employees to work.) For example, in 1892, strikers and private guards battled at steel mills near Homestead, Pennsylvania. And in the Pullman strike of 1894, troops were called out by the federal government to stop violence.

Despite difficulties, organized labor grew in the late nineteenth and early twentieth centuries. Workers continued to demand decent wages and working conditions. In the early 1930s, however, when the nation was in the middle of the Depression, the labor movement reached a low point. Then in 1933 Congress passed the National Recovery Act, and in 1935 it passed the National Labor Relations Act (Wagner Act). The purpose of these laws was to protect union rights. The Wagner Act guaranteed the right of workers to organize unions to bargain with their employers.

By the late 1930s, the nation had largely recovered from the Depression. Unions had the power of numbers, and they began to speak for a sizable portion of the work force. Also, they had legislation on their side, which made their voice at the bargaining table legitimate. Working conditions in most industries were improved by the bargaining process. Wages were increased, and jobs were awarded according to ability. Gompers and other labor leaders had done their work well.

A split occurred in the AFL in the late 1930s. At issue was whether mass-production workers should be organized by craft or by industry. Many AFL leaders believed that mass-production workers should be organized by craft, or job (welder, riveter, etc). Others, headed by John L. Lewis of the United Mine Workers of America, maintained workers should be organized by industry (steel, coal, automobile, etc). The people in favor of *industrial unions* instead of craft unions split off from the AFL. In 1938, they formed a new organization, the Congress of Industrial Organizations (CIO).

By 1940 the AFL had over 4 million members. The CIO had over 3 million members. The two associations disagreed on some basic issues. During the 1940s, however, they made great strides in organizing unions in industries that had never before had union protection.

During World War II, President Franklin D. Roosevelt established the National War Labor Board. This board helped to solidify bargaining and ease conflict relationships among unions and between unions and the government. In 1947 the Taft-Hartley Act was passed. This act continued the guarantees of workers' rights, but it also outlawed certain union practices. It forbade the *closed shop*, in which employers agree to hire only union members. And it gave states the power to restrict *union shops*, in which newly hired workers have to join the union.

Before the Taft-Hartley Act, 11 states had passed right-to-work laws. These laws guaranteed the right of a person to get and keep a job whether that person decided to join a union or not. The result was to protect both union and non-union members. The passage of the Taft-Hartley Act encouraged other states to pass right-to-work laws, since a provision of the act protected the worker from forced union membership. (Today, approximately 20 states have right-to-work laws in effect.)

In 1955, the AFL and CIO resolved their differences and formed one organization—

13. **John L. Lewis was one of the founders of the C.I.O.**
14. **The AFL and CIO disagreed about how to organize labor unions.**
15. **Steel workers join the CIO.**
16. **These women work in a modern garment factory.**

17. Assembly lines speed up factory work.
18. Steel workers are pleased about a new contract.
19. A union committee meets to discuss strategy.
20. Contract talks between the United Auto Workers and General Motors begin on friendly terms.

the AFL-CIO. A number of unions—such as the United Mine Workers of America, the United Auto Workers, and the Teamsters—do not belong to the AFL-CIO today. Nonetheless, the AFL-CIO has helped make unions a powerful force.

Unions today fight for economic issues with a great deal of political force. Members of Congress and the president pay attention to what labor leaders have to say on economic issues. Working people have solid, significant political support through the labor movement. They have a voice in passing bills into law and have formed lobbies to influence major legislation. They have hospitalization benefits, guaranteed vacation days, and rights to bring a grievance against a company if they believe their working conditions are unsafe.

Of course, there have been problems with unions. Some union leaders have been accused of taking union funds for their personal use. Fraud, and even violence, have been known to occur in union elections. Racial discrimination and the question of whether public employees should have the right to strike are other problems which have plagued unions. However, in spite of these difficulties, the labor movement has had a dramatic effect on the lives of millions of Americans. The work week has been shortened, workers' wages are among the highest in the world, and working conditions have improved greatly. Samuel Gompers and other early labor leaders would be gratified to see how many of their original goals have been accomplished.

1. What resources did the AFL have that earlier unions did not?
2. How did the AFL use its resources successfully?
3. Compare the resources of unions to those of other interest groups you know about. Which groups use resources in the same way as unions? Which use them differently? Explain.

GROWTH of the UMWA

The United Mine Workers of America is one of the most active labor unions in the United States. As of 1977, the UMWA represented about 200,000 miners and 70,000 retired miners on pension.

The health, safety, and welfare of coal miners is crucial to the normal operation of the coal industry. The coal industry in turn is crucial to the national economy. Coal is a valuable natural resource. It is used to heat homes and buildings and is the chief fuel in factories that generate electricity with steam. Coal is essential to steel-making. It is also used to manufacture products such as aluminum, cement, paper, and textiles. Thousands of people in the United States are employed in coal-related industries. Because it represents workers who supply the nation with a vital resource, the UMWA has particular significance as an interest group.

In this section you will read about the history and politics of the UMWA in depth. As a result of your study, you will see the role that resources and political activities have played in the growth of this interest group.

The section is divided into several case studies. Each deals with a period in UMWA history. As you read the material, think about the following questions: (1) How were resources used to build the UMWA? (2) What political activities have occurred within the UMWA? (3) What gains for miners have been achieved through the UMWA? (4) How did individual miners support the growth of the UMWA?

★ Organize!: 1860–1920

Conditions in the coal mines have always been dangerous. Since the early 1800s, miners have faced the hazards of cave-ins, gas explosions, and disease from breathing coal dust over a period of years. A coal miner named Caleb Leadbetter worked in the coal mines at the turn of the twentieth century. Following are his reflections on his mining experiences.

"A young boy first learned about the mines when he loaded coal with his daddy. The boy didn't have to have no physical examination or nothin' like that; he just went in and helped his dad shovel coal in that car.

"A boy's dad showed him all about the mine. He took more care of his son than he did himself in the

In the early 1900s, young boys commonly worked along with their fathers in the coal mines, where they faced the same hazards as grown men.

Coal miners head into the mines at the beginning of a long and difficult shift. They do not return to the surface until after dark.

safety category. His dad took care of him and learned the boy every hazard of the mines.

"A man had to take care of everything. You had to clean up rock and slate. You had to lay the track to get your cars up close. Lots of times, you had to bail water out. That's all for nothin'! Lots of times people worked a day or two for nothin', just tryin' to get a place to work. That's not only one miner; that's all of 'em.

"Seems like miners was lower than dogs to the company. You didn't have no voice. The company had all the voice. They gave you a place with water in it or bad top or somethin', and they said, 'You've got to work here.' You asked 'em, 'What about movin' this water out?' and they told you, 'That's your problem. You either work or we'll fire you.'

"I never got fired, but I know people that did. If the company didn't like a man, they called the other companies and told them not to hire that fella. You couldn't get a job nowhere.

"I worked in pillarin'. Pillarin' means to get the coal out that's left between the rooms. You started at the furthest point back so you could keep the hollow section behind you. Then the roof didn't hurt you when it fell.

"Now you gotta have that fall. See the top is always pressin' down on your mine. This big weight can ride to the other parts of your mine and ruin it, but when this big fall comes, it takes the pressure off the other parts and you can mine in there too.

"An old, experienced miner can tell just about the minute the roof is gonna fall. I've seen big falls come. You'd be away from that fall, but when it came, the wind from it would blow trap doors down. I've been knocked down many a time on a big fall. I'd be goin' away from it and that air would knock you down while you's runnin' from it.

"My God, one time this man was runnin' from one of these big falls, but he was late runnin'. He ran around a big mine car, and he had his hand over in the car as he was comin' along. That top broke and caught his arm, and he couldn't run. He hollered and prayed and everything else, his arm in that car. They called that company doctor, and he came to the mines. The doctor couldn't get him out. This mountain was sittin' right on that car, and he had his arm over in it. That doctor went in that mine and cut that man's arm off, brought him out of there, and he still lived. It was really somethin'."

Caleb Leadbetter's experiences were typical of mining conditions from the late 1800s into the early 1900s. Because of these conditions, coal miners began a struggle to unionize in the second half of the nineteenth century. Coal companies were against the formation of unions, so for years miners joined together in secret societies. Members kept their unions secret, because the companies would fire them if their union membership were discovered. Several attempts were made to unionize all miners in the 1860s and 1870s, but these efforts were unsuccessful.

The year 1890 marked a turning point for coal miners. In that year the United Mine Workers of America, or UMWA, was formed. The major goals of the union were to seek increased wages and improved safety conditions for coal miners. The UMWA pledged "[t]o reduce to the lowest possible minimum the awful catastrophies which have been sweeping our fellow craftsmen to untimely graves by the thousands." The UMWA also demanded a shorter work week. (Coal miners averaged a 60-hour work week before 1898.) In addition, the union worked for laws to prevent children under 14 years of age from working underground.

The union grew rapidly. In 1903, under the leadership of John Mitchell, it had 175,000 members and a million-dollar treasury. Despite its growth, the union had only limited success in its early years. At this point the coal companies had the upper hand. The companies hired professional detectives and amateur thugs to threaten union organizers with violence. In reaction to violent actions against them, miners claimed "an eye for an eye." The fighting between miners and the coal companies brought many deaths. Most of the dead were miners.

Many mines remained unorganized because of the threat of violence. Also, miners feared the loss of their jobs. They knew there were always other men ready and willing to take their places in the mines.

Even when miners managed to form unions, strikes were frequently lost. In addition, the early unions were not successful in gaining improved benefits as rapidly as miners had expected.

The man who most significantly affected the course of UMWA history was John L. Lewis. Early in his career Lewis was elected president of a small local union in Panama, Illinois. He had a knowledge of power, people, and language that enabled him to rise rapidly within the UMWA. Fol-

John L. Lewis was the person most responsible for making the UMWA a strong and powerful union.

lowing a short term as a local union president, John L. Lewis became a lobbyist for the mine workers in Springfield, Illinois.

Lewis soon came to the attention of Samuel Gompers. He served as a national legislative representative for the American Federation of Labor. In this job, Lewis learned about American industry, the process of influencing government, and the use of power.

In 1916, John L. Lewis returned to the UMWA and worked at its international headquarters in Washington, D.C. He learned the economics of the coal industry and built political strength inside the UMWA. In 1918, John L. Lewis was appointed to fill the union vice-presidential office. When high-ranking union leaders forced UMWA president Hayes to resign in 1919, the union's executive board appointed John L. Lewis to fill the remainder of Hayes' term in office.

Lewis thus became president of the UMWA without a single miner casting a ballot for him. As required by the UMWA's constitution, Lewis ran for office in the 1920 election and won a full term in office by a narrow margin.

John L. Lewis held the UMWA presidency for the next 40 years. During his years in office, Lewis created a solidarity among the membership that forced the coal companies to accept the union as a fact of life. More than any other individual, John L. Lewis shaped the structure and politics of the UMWA.

1. Why did coal miners want to unionize?
2. Why was the UMWA unable to achieve many gains in its early years?
3. Why couldn't individual coal miners do much to fight the coal companies?
4. What resources did Lewis bring to the union that made its future look brighter?

Figure 5-3

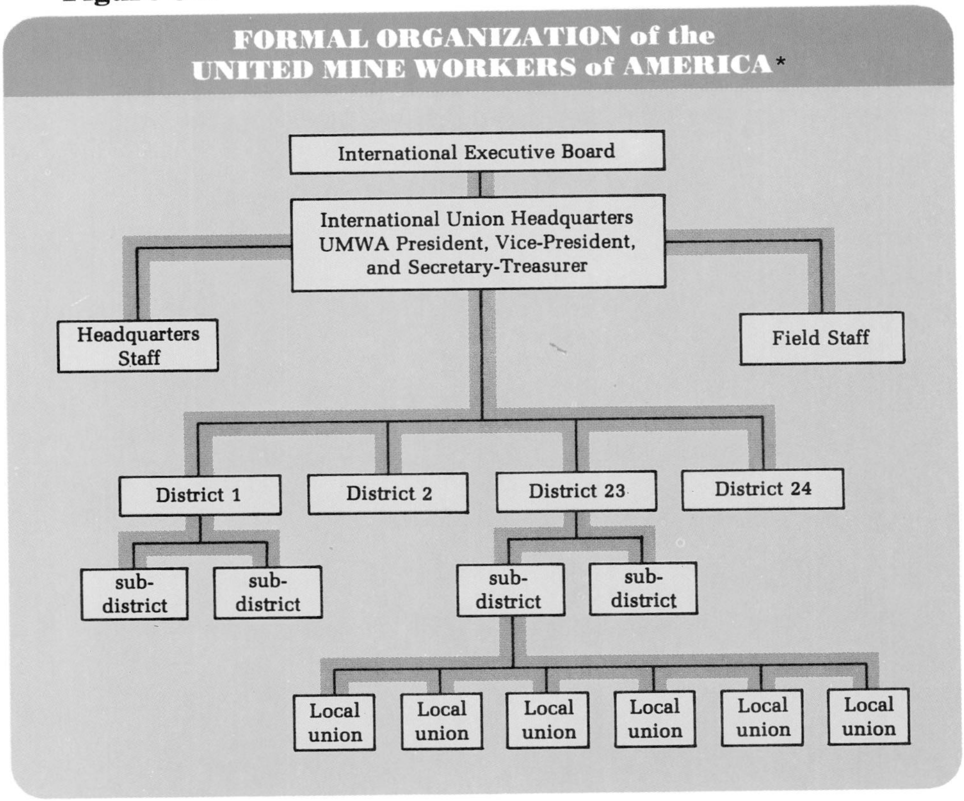

FORMAL ORGANIZATION of the UNITED MINE WORKERS of AMERICA*

*The UMWA has locals in Canada.

★ The Battle for Power: 1920–1950

John L. Lewis pictured the UMWA as an army locked in battle with the coal companies. He believed the union's success in the fight depended upon strong leadership at the top and unquestioned discipline below. Only then could the union fight management and win benefits for members.

Soon after he became president, Lewis moved to strengthen his leadership position. He had to have loyalty, he felt, to make the union strong. He made sure everyone at union headquarters would follow him without question. And he moved to consolidate his support at the district level. (Figure 5–3 shows the levels of the UMWA organization.)

Yet, not everyone thought that loyalty to Lewis was either needed or good for the union. One of these men was Alexander Howat. Howat was president of District 14 in Kansas. An aggressive leader, Howat was well known throughout the union. He did not want his district to be run by a dominating leader from the international organization. He would fight Lewis bitterly for many years. He would lose.

Lewis used Article III, Section 2 of the UMWA constitution to destroy Howat. Section 2 reads as follows: "Charters of Districts, Sub-Districts and Local Unions may be revoked by the International President, who shall have authority to create a provisional government for the subordinate branch whose charter has been revoked." The constitution gave complete power to the president. No charges had to be specified. No trial was required. Lewis could remove elected district officers who opposed him and replace them with appointed officials who supported him.

Shortly after the 1921 convention, Lewis used his authority against Howat. He suspended Alexander Howat and Howat's supporters. Howat appealed the suspension to the union's International Executive Board. Lewis defended his action, and he was upheld by a narrow vote.

Howat fought back. He appeared at one UMWA convention after another to argue for his restoration to union membership. Finally, Howat obtained a union card from his old Kansas local and had himself selected as a local delegate to the 1927 UMWA convention. But the credentials committee, which Lewis appointed, refused to admit Howat.

Howat then went to the convention floor to plead his case before the delegates. A friend of Howat's rose and asked why Howat was not accepted as a delegate.

John L. Lewis, chairperson of the convention, boomed out a reply to the question. "The credentials of Alexander Howat have not been reported to this convention because the International President returned his credentials to the local union in Kansas, which gave them to him. That action was taken because he is not a member of the United Mine Workers of America."

Another delegate challenged Lewis. The delegate argued that Howat's dues were accepted by the local Kansas union and so Howat must be a member.

Lewis roared back. "It does not make any difference what you think. The chair has ruled."

John L. Lewis was firmly in control. Throughout the 1920s and 1930s, Lewis fought internal battles in the union and built his power by crushing his opposition. By the 1940s Lewis had unquestioned control of the UMWA. No one within the ranks challenged his decisions.

This strong loyalty won miners many benefits. Solidly backed by the whole organization, Lewis led a series of strikes against the coal companies. His ability to mobilize hundreds of thousands of miners enabled Lewis to win the benefits that he desired.

Perhaps the most important victory occurred shortly after World War II ended. The nation was making a difficult transition from a war-time to a peace-time economy. The economy was booming, miners were making good wages, and the nation needed coal to run its factories and boost industrial progress. Lewis knew this, and used his

153

knowledge well in bargaining with management. At the contract bargaining session in 1946, Lewis opened the session by demanding that the coal companies pay a royalty on every ton of coal produced by union workers. The royalty payments would establish and maintain a welfare and retirement fund for miners and their families. Lewis told the coal operators,

> "If we must grind up human flesh and bones in an industrial machine—in the industrial machine that we call modern America—then, before God, I assert that those who consume coal, and you and I who benefit from that service, owe protection to those men and we owe security to their families. I say it! I voice it! I proclaim it! And I care not who . . . opposes it!"

The proposal was unheard of in American industry. The coal companies rejected it. On April 1, 1946, the union contract expired. In keeping with the UMWA tradition of "no contract, no work," the miners went out on strike. Ten days later the companies still refused to accept royalty payments in a new contract. Lewis and the union bargaining team walked out of the negotiations.

The strike continued. Despite economic hardship to their families, miners throughout the nation closed ranks behind Lewis. They did so not only because of his power, but because he was fighting hard for their interests. By late May, the coal fields were still closed, and the nation's energy supplies were so low that a general halt to industrial production seemed very likely.

Under President Truman's order, the federal government seized control of the coal mines. Lewis continued to keep the miners out. The government quickly negotiated a special contract with the union. Provisions for royalty payments were included in the agreement. Lewis ordered the miners back to work, and coal production resumed.

Many months later, the government still controlled the mines. The coal companies finally surrendered and signed a contract

The support of rank-and-file workers was one of the most important political resources for John L. Lewis while he was UMWA president.

with the UMWA that included royalty payments to the union's health and welfare fund. Lewis had won the greatest bargaining concession in the history of coal negotiations. Under Lewis, the UMWA had become one of the strongest labor interest groups in the United States.

1. What benefits did John L. Lewis seek for coal miners?
2. How did miners act to strengthen their union during this period?
3. Why did Lewis take the coal miners out on strike in 1946?
4. What gains did Lewis win?
5. How did Lewis use political skills to make these gains? What economic knowledge did he have that made his strike actions successful? What part did the miners' loyalty to Lewis play in union efforts to gain benefits?

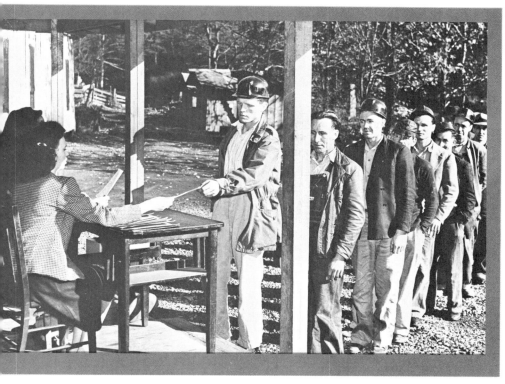

Miners from the Davidson Mine in Gintown, Alabama, line up to receive their last pay check before they go out on strike in 1946.

★ The Battle to Save the Coal Industry: 1950–1960

Strikes and hard, open bargaining characterized the relationship between miners and coal companies in the 1940s. The 1950s were different. A time of labor peace settled across the coal fields. John L. Lewis and the coal companies bargained quietly behind closed doors.

The change in relationship between the companies and the UMWA occurred because of the serious economic problems that confronted the coal industry. The demand for coal decreased dramatically in the 1950s. In homes everywhere, oil and gas replaced coal-burning furnaces. Railroads converted from coal to diesel locomotives. Steel companies still required coal, but that market alone was too small to support the entire industry.

The survival of the industry, and of the union, depended upon the sale of coal to electric generating plants. But these plants could burn either coal or oil, depending upon which fuel was cheaper. Thus, the fate of coal companies, miners, and the UMWA depended on cheap coal prices.

John L. Lewis decided on a plan to save his union and the coal industry from extinction. Like all important decisions in the UMWA, the choice was made by Lewis alone. And he had the power to enforce his decisions.

Cheap coal required modernization and consolidation of the industry. Early in 1951, Lewis negotiated a new contract with the coal companies. In private, he agreed to give the big companies a free hand to mechanize the mines without union interference. The National Bank of Washington, owned by the UMWA, loaned money to large companies to enable them to buy modern equipment. The machines permitted the companies to produce more coal with fewer miners. Thousands of small mines, unable to afford automation, closed down.

Lewis's decision affected hundreds of thousands of people. Jobs dwindled. Nearly 300,000 miners were laid off. Yet, he expected to restructure the coal industry with a minimum of pain to individuals. Lewis thought an expanding national economy would provide jobs to young people who might otherwise have gone underground. The UMWA's welfare fund would provide pensions for older miners who were forced to retire early.

Lewis's plan was disrupted by an unexpected economic recession that swept across the country in the mid-1950s. As other industries reduced production, the demand for coal fell lower. Layoffs increased. Other jobs became scarce.

Desperate for work, many unemployed UMWA miners took jobs in thousands of small non-union mines called "dog holes." The dog holes paid wages far below union scale. Thus, they were able to underprice the major coal companies that were required to pay union wages to their employees. Soon the dog holes captured a large share of the coal market. The major companies were forced to lay off even more union miners.

For both the UMWA and the big coal companies, the crisis became desperate. Lewis resorted to drastic action. He led the union into a series of "sweetheart" contracts. Sweetheart contracts were secret arrangements in which both sides agreed to ignore parts of the national contract. Wages were slashed in union mines throughout the coal fields. Companies withheld required payments into the UMWA's welfare fund.

Lewis was able to accept sweetheart contracts because they were negotiated in private. Only a few top union leaders knew that Lewis willingly accepted lost benefits, and these leaders were completely loyal to

him. Coal miners did not have the right to vote on contracts. Whatever John L. Lewis negotiated was binding on the entire membership.

Angry miners, unaware of the sweetheart deals, blamed their lost benefits on the companies. Bitterness spread through the coal fields and violence flared. Mines were dynamited and vandalized by roving bands of unemployed miners. A few people blamed their troubles on the union. But allegiance to Lewis and the miners' tradition of absolute solidarity prevented much criticism from being directed at the UMWA.

By 1960 the situation began to stabilize. The coal industry, given up for dead ten years earlier, came alive and looked ahead to better days. John L. Lewis had won another victory by saving the coal industry.

The price of victory was high. The number of coal miners working in the industry had decreased sharply. The UMWA had fewer members than at any time in its history since the early days. The union had loaned union money from miners' dues to

promote the mechanization that put hundreds of thousands of miners out of work. Sweetheart contracts had resulted in the loss of benefits for members who kept their jobs. And, the number of non-union mines had increased. The high accident rate for underground workers continued. The union had won no new safety laws since 1952. Black lung disease, which results from long inhalation of coal dust, continued to cripple and kill miners. However, the problem was ignored.

When Lewis retired in 1960, the coal industry had been saved. But the sacrifice had been great.

1. What did John L. Lewis hope to gain through sweetheart contracts? What gains did he win? What did he lose?
2. How did Lewis use his skills to save the coal industry? What information did Lewis have that others did not? How did the idea of loyalty help Lewis to get what he wanted?
3. How did miners act politically during this period?

★ **The Battle to Save the Union: 1960–1972**

When John L. Lewis retired in 1960, power was transferred to Thomas Kennedy, who had been vice-president under Lewis. Lewis picked Tony Boyle to fill the vice-presidency. Kennedy was 73 years old and in poor health when he became president. In 1962, he became seriously ill, and Boyle took over as acting president of the UMWA. When Kennedy died early in the next year, total authority passed to Boyle. Little had changed since Lewis had departed, and the smooth succession of Boyle to the top job in the union suggested the continuation of the political legacy that John L. Lewis had built.

Boyle continued a policy of complete cooperation with coal companies, a policy that John L. Lewis started when the industry was economically depressed. Boyle said, "The UMWA will not abridge the rights of mine operators in running the mines. We follow the judgment of coal operators, right or wrong." But many miners felt Boyle was wrong and refused to follow him.

Although working conditions have improved since the 1800's, the miner's job is still difficult and dangerous. At mines like these in Pennsylvania and Virginia, coal miners produce over 500 million tons of coal a year.

In the early 1960s, coal miners were among the highest paid workers in the country, but they lagged far behind in other benefits. For example, they lacked unemployment protection and job security. Companies routinely laid off older miners with only a few working years left. They replaced them with younger employees with a full career ahead. Also, there was no pay for sick or injured miners, although accidents and black lung disease made coal mining one of the most dangerous jobs in the country. Miners knew that workers in other industries were making tremendous gains. Soon, the coal fields rang with the voices of angry, dissatisfied union members.

The controls that John L. Lewis had established within the union were still well oiled. Years of work under Lewis had taught Boyle how to use them. District officers, representatives, and organizers were appointed by Boyle. Thus, he had control over them. Boyle had control over union money. He loaned money to districts in order to increase his influence over them. The union treasury paid the expenses of friendly delegates to attend conventions. Unfriendly miners had to pay their own way. The machinery worked well. Despite the bitterness in the union, Boyle was easily reelected to the presidency in 1964. His position at the top seemed secure.

However, anti-Boyle hostility increased in 1968. Boyle negotiated a new contract. He won a large wage increase but ignored the other interests of miners. Then came the Farmington disaster. A concentration of methane gas exploded at Consol No. 9 mine in Farmington, West Virginia. Seventy-eight miners were buried underground.

Rank and file members began to ask questions. Why had so many miners died at Farmington? Why was coal mining as an occupation the biggest killer of workers in the country? What was the union doing about it?

Believing that the union was deaf to their concerns, a small group of West Virginia miners formed the Black Lung Association. Black lung begins when miners breathe coal dust. After several years, the dust kills the hairs in their air passages. Tiny particles of coal collect in the small air sacs in a miner's lungs. Eventually the lungs collapse, and the afflicted miner begins a slow, painful death.

Since black lung is the enemy of every coal miner, membership in the association grew rapidly. A series of statewide wildcat strikes and demonstrations in Charleston, the state capital, forced the West Virginia legislature to pass a law in 1969 that provided compensation to black lung victims.

The black lung victory convinced many miners that the Boyle machine could be challenged. New leaders emerged. Joseph "Jock" Yablonski led the group that challenged Boyle. Yablonski was a member of the union's International Executive Board and was well known throughout the UMWA. After Yablonski announced his candidacy for the presidency, he was fired from his job by Boyle. Nevertheless, Yablonski continued to campaign and developed enough support to win a presidential nomination on the 1969 UMWA election ballot.

Boyle used every resource under his control to defeat Yablonski in the general election. UMWA staff employees, whose jobs depended on Boyle's reelection, campaigned full-time for him at union expense. Boyle used his control over district and subdistrict officials to influence miners. One local president told the membership, "I don't want a single Yablonski vote in this local." The union printed nearly 90,000 more ballots than there were voting members, more than enough extra votes to stuff ballot boxes in Boyle's favor. The election results showed Boyle with 81,056 votes and Yablonski with 45,870.

Yablonski and his supporters protested. They filed detailed charges of hundreds of election law violations with the United States Department of Labor. They demanded that the government set aside the election results and schedule a new election under federal supervision.

Two weeks after the election and before the government could act, Joseph Yablonski, his wife, and his daughter were shot to death in their home. The murder shocked the entire country. Public outrage forced an investigation by the government. In 1972, a federal judge ruled the 1969 UMWA election invalid and ordered the UMWA to hold a new election. This time Boyle lost to a man named Arnold Miller. Arnold Miller won the new election on the promise to improve benefits and give the miners a democratically run union. Shortly afterwards Boyle was convicted for his role in the Yablonski killings.

1. What were Tony Boyle's goals for the union?
2. What gains did he win?
3. How did Boyle use his skills to run the union? How did he use money?
4. How did union members oppose Boyle and change the course of the UMWA?

★ Union Democracy: 1972–1974

Arnold Miller's victory against Tony Boyle in the 1972 election was a result of a backlash against Boyle's leadership. It was also a result of Miller's belief that the UMWA should be run democratically.

Miller was a determined miner. There were other determined miners who decided to support him. They formed a group called The Miners for Democracy. They wanted a union which would take care of miners' interests and would be run by miners. Across 23 states they campaigned in every local for Arnold Miller.

Miller's election victory in 1972 was made possible in part by the federal government. When Joseph Yablonski was murdered, his two sons took their case to the district court. The court said that the election was invalid. In addition, the court said the United States Labor Department would supervise the next election. Miller was assured the right to station observers at union polls. There were more than 1,500 polling places and more than 1,000 poll watchers in that election. The federal government had helped to prevent the kind of tactics that had been used in the Yablonski case.

And Miller won "big." When the votes were counted in December 1972, he had a victory margin of almost 20,000 votes over Tony Boyle. He won by a vote of 70,373 to 56,334. He won because he campaigned actively among the miners. He won because the federal government enforced a fair election. He also won because of the hopes and aspirations of the Miners for Democracy.

The Miller administration then proceeded to make good on the platform of the Miners for Democracy. Miller reorganized the union, but his most important victories

Arnold Miller talks with miners during his campaign for president of the UMWA in 1972. His goal was to introduce democracy into the union organization.

were demonstrated in his negotiation of the 1974 contract. Miller had pledged to democratize the union. He intended to do it in its most serious set of negotiations—the contract under which every miner in the United Mine Workers would work.

Until 1974, many people felt that contracts had been trade-offs. The union had given in on something in order to get something else. They had obtained higher wages by giving in on sick leave; they had received more vacation time by giving in on grievances. This time the negotiating team was pledged to "stick to its guns" and get benefits.

At the union's international convention, miners rewrote the UMWA constitution to give themselves voting rights in the new contract. Miller would not sign the contract until it was ratified at every local union meeting throughout the UMWA.

Rank-and-file ratification was an important issue to Miller. (Rank-and-file means members of a group who are not leaders or officials.) He included every single miner in the ratification process. Local union meetings were held all across the districts of the UMWA. There were district representatives on the bargaining council. This made the council large, but gave representation to different points of view. In effect, the UMWA was, for the first time, going to sign a contract which reflected the will of the membership.

What did the miners gain as a result of the 1974 contract? A lot! Higher wages, paid sick leave, pension increases, hospital cards, grievance procedures, widows' benefits, and the right to a safe work place are only a few of the direct benefits they won.

These gains are very real for miners. Luther Stoner, a miner for over 25 years, talks about modern mining and the gains the union has made in the following way.

> "Minin's been good to me. I've got more than I've ever had in my life. My wife works, I work, and we make good money. We're not millionaires, but if

we want to pay two or three hundred dollars for something, we can go downtown and pay for it.

"Sure, there are some miners who only care about making the big buck. There are always people like that around. But most guys are interested in coming out of there in one piece, and seeing their friends and fellow workers come out in one piece. Just to be treated like a person, rather than a chunk of coal, is what we're after.

"Some people say that coal mining is just naturally dangerous and there isn't anything we can do to stop the deaths. Well, as far as a lot of us are concerned, coal is gonna be mined safely or it isn't gonna be mined at all."

1. What were the goals of the Miners for Democracy? What actions did they take to reach their goals?
2. What did miners gain in the 1974 contract negotiations?
3. Compare the views of Caleb Leadbetter and Luther Stoner.

★ **Problems of the UMWA: 1974—the Present**

Arnold Miller successfully negotiated a contract, but it takes more than contract negotiation to run a union. Throughout his first years as president, Miller effectively set in operation the apparatus for democratic procedures. Yet, there were individuals who did not believe in those procedures. There was also a lack of leadership ability among union workers who had never had to make decisions in the union before.

When UMWA elections were held in the spring of 1977, Miller was reelected to the union presidency by only a slight majority. It was a three-way race between Arnold Miller, Harry Patrick, and Lee Roy Patterson. Patrick and Patterson received 65 percent of the votes. Because of the way the votes were split, Miller won by a slim

By the 1970s, the United Mine Workers of America had won many victories for its members, including safer working conditions, higher wages, and more benefits. New problems are facing the union, however. Many young miners are not as willing as their fathers were to offer their complete support to the union. The union must also face wildcat strikes as well as a growing number of nonunion mines.

amount. He could say that he was the head of the union, yet the union members clearly had problems backing Miller as president.

One set of problems centered around union headquarters. Shortly after Miller was elected in 1972, the three officers—Miller, Mike Trbovich as vice-president, and Harry Patrick as secretary-treasurer—began to disagree. Miller sensed competition from Patrick, and Trbovich dropped out of headquarters activity. The league of bright, new, and able people who surrounded Miller at union headquarters at the beginning of his term began to leave. They quarreled with Miller's policies and began to dislike his increasingly strict leadership style. At the international headquarters in Washington, union democracy was, in effect, destroying the unity of the union's leaders.

There were also problems in the field. From local through state organizations, union members were having difficulty with leadership. The membership was worried about the new leadership and its ability to translate the contract into benefits that miners could see in their everyday lives. Many miners thought that the democracy was not working, and they blamed Arnold Miller.

In addition to these problems, UMWA leadership began to face a number of other challenges in the late 1970s. One challenge has come from the ranks of young miners. Many of today's miners are a new breed—young (in their 20s and 30s) and confident. Thousands of them served in combat in Vietnam and have had some college education. Many are far less intimidated by their employers than their fathers were in the 1950s and early 1960s, when work in the mines was hard to find. A number of these young miners have taken an active part in union politics. These young miners are not afraid to tell the UMWA leadership what they think. They have been among those who are concerned with the ability of leadership to serve miner interests.

Another challenge to the UMWA has been the growth of non-union-produced coal. With the opening of new, non-union mines in the western states, the once-powerful UMWA has been presented with a new threat. In 1977, the percentage of coal produced by UMWA miners was 52 percent. This means that almost half the nation's coal was coming from mines without a UMWA local. Many who work at non-union mines have earned wages significantly higher than the level set in the union contract. They have received medical benefits as well. This indicates the price coal operators are willing to pay to keep the UMWA from organizing in the new western mines.

The UMWA also faced waves of wildcat strikes in the second half of the 1970s. (*Wildcat strikes* are strikes not authorized by conditions of the contract.) A cutback in medical benefits was the cause of a number of these strikes. In December 1977, the UMWA contract expired. Negotiations between labor management and the coal companies for a new contract were not successful, and the union miners as a whole went on strike.

The disorder in the coal fields in the late 1970s was far different from the optimism that existed when Arnold Miller first took office in 1972. At that time, there was genuine hope for the restoration of UMWA strength. It was hoped that the union as an interest group could once again have serious impact on the coal companies, Congress, and state legislatures.

To his credit, Arnold Miller restored full democracy to the union for the first time in half a century. And the 1974 contract obtained under his leadership won unprecedented gains for the miners.

But disagreements within the union and a loss of faith in Miller's leadership seriously hampered the effectiveness of the UMWA. In the late 1970s, the UMWA reached a turning point. Some gains have been made as a result of Miller's actions, and participation in the union has been strong. However, the future of the UMWA remains to be seen.

1. What resources did Miller use? What skills did he have? How did he use the idea of democracy?
2. How did individual miners contribute to Miller's success?

VALUE ANALYSIS

You have just studied the history of the United Mine Workers in terms of gains and losses, resources and activities. There is another way to look at the growth of the United Mine Workers. This is through value analysis. The skill of value analysis involves determining the value or values in a given situation.

There are two ways in which values can be identified. One way is by asking whether an action or result is desirable, whether something "should be." In the case of the UMWA, it means asking, for example, "In the past, have miners acted for 'good' purposes and 'just' ends?" It might mean asking, "Should miners strike if a group of men in one mine have not been paid because of disagreement with management over the number of hours worked?" The answers to these questions reveal what is considered important, in other words, the values of those involved. The answers reveal what a person thinks is best in a situation.

Values can also be identified in terms of preferences. Values can be determined by the choice that a person or group makes between alternatives. Questions asked involve considering whether something is "better" than something else. For the UMWA, the alternatives may revolve around whom to support in a union election, how to campaign for mining legislation, and when to speak up about certain problems. None of the alternatives may be ideal, but some may be better than others. In any situation, the alternative chosen, in other words the preference expressed, reflects the values considered important. The preference reveals what a person thinks is better in a situation.

Determining the values in a situation often means probing until the fundamental values are revealed. For example, a hypothetical person named Mr. Clark thinks it is desirable for limits to be set on campaign spending in elections. He is reflecting a value having to do with moderation in spending. We can then ask, "What other reasons might Mr. Clark have for taking this position? Why does Mr. Clark consider limits on campaign spending to be important?" The answer might be that Mr. Clark believes that elections are fair only if there is financial equality among candidates. He might also believe that candidates should compete evenly on their merits. Equality, then, might be an important value in this situation. So might fair competition.

It is important for you to think about the values that underlie what people say and do. Value analysis will help you understand why people and groups act as they do. It will also help you decide if you agree with them.

1. Read the following statements. Which ones reflect values? Which do not? Explain.
    a. Resources should be used to benefit as many people as possible in a group.
    b. Many miners earn $60 a day in wages.
    c. In the 1930s, miners wanted benefits similar to those which workers in other industries were receiving.
    d. Some interest groups prefer to involve just a few people, instead of many, in their lobbying efforts.
    e. Coal is one of the nation's most valuable resources.
2. What are some fundamental values underlying each of the following statements? (You may find it helpful to begin your answers with the phrase, "It is important to—"
    a. Stand on your own two feet.
    b. Equal pay should be given for equal work.

c. Live and let live.

d. There's no time like the present.

e. Be a sport.

3. Review the history of the growth of the UMWA and answer the following questions:

    a. What values were important to miners in the years 1860 to 1920? What values do you think were important to the coal companies during this period?

    b. Do you think that the actions of John L. Lewis during the years between 1920 and 1950 were desirable? What fundamental values were behind his actions during that period?

    c. Do you think Lewis's actions in the years between 1950 and 1960 were justified? Why? What fundamental values are at the base of your position?

    d. Do you think opening up the UMWA to democratic procedures was a good thing for the UMWA in the early 1970s? Why? What values are at the base of your position?

    e. What are three fundamental values which can be traced through the history of the UMWA?

4. What fundamental values would be important to you if you were a miner? Which ones are important to you in a group to which you belong?

The UMWA and Government

Over time the UMWA has built its organization into a strong political interest group. As an interest group, the UMWA seeks to influence government at the state and national levels. Primarily a self-oriented interest group, the UMWA also acts as a government-oriented group.

There are two major ways that an interest group can affect the operations of government in its behalf. One way is through elections. In 1973, COMPAC, the Coal Miners' Political Action Committee, was formed. Since then, COMPAC has worked for a number of different candidates at various levels of government. COMPAC has worked for candidates who are sympathetic to the needs of coal miners. It does so in the hope that once elected to office, these people will promote miners' interests.

Another major way in which an interest group can influence government is through legislation. COMPAC has served as an interest lobby on legislation affecting black lung compensation, strip mining, and industrial safety. By lobbying for legislators to sponsor certain bills, UMWA benefits from legislation which helps all mine workers.

Union support for candidates and legislation has directly affected the health and life-style of miners. Without black lung legislation and without a mine safety bill, miners would be without important financial compensation and safety protection which they now have.

Influencing the government has another important result. It helps to standardize working conditions for miners throughout the country. Therefore, miners in West Virginia, Alabama, and Nevada all operate under the same safety standards and job qualifications. This equality is an important protection for the miner and the mining industry as a whole.

ORGANIZING COMPAC The UMWA organization COMPAC was formed at the 1973 International Convention, after Arnold Miller's election. The idea behind COMPAC was to provide coal miners with a strong political arm which would stretch across the local,

Gathering Information. Now, do your research. If you are dividing the project with classmates, use your knowledge of working in groups to work as efficiently and thoroughly as possible. Record your information accurately.

Choosing a Method of Presentation. Think about how you will present the results of your research to the class. You may choose to work directly from a written report; or you may wish to make a combined oral and visual presentation. Your teacher will help you decide on the method of presentation.

Presenting Your Findings. When you present your findings to your class, the following questions should be discussed about the interest group you've studied:

1. How does this group function as an interest group?
2. What resources does the group use in carrying out its activities?
3. What benefits do the members get from the interest group?
4. How might you participate in this interest group or in one like it in order to reach goals that you think are important?

---

1. In what ways are a union's activities political?
2. Outline the history of the labor movement in the United States.
3. In what ways did consolidation interests help the labor movement? Give examples in your answer.
4. Outline the history of the UMWA from its beginnings to the present. Include in your outline summaries of the people and actions important in each period of the history.
5. How did John L. Lewis strengthen the UMWA? What problems were created by his actions as a leader?
6. What effects has Arnold Miller had on the UMWA?
7. Describe the UMWA in its roles as a government-oriented interest group, as an issue-oriented interest group, and as a self-oriented interest group.
8. What are the results of COMPAC's activities?
9. What political resources do unions use? Give examples in your answer.
10. What resources might be distributed as a result of the UMWA's activities? Give examples in your answer.

Chapter Review

Chapter Vocabulary

Define the following terms.

craft	closed shop	rank-and-file
strike	union shop	wildcat strike
lockout	black lung disease	"sweetheart" contract
industrial union		monitor

Chapter Analysis

1. Why did the early unions fail? How were later labor movements able to successfully overcome these problems?

2. Review the activities of the major leaders in the labor movement such as Gompers and Lewis. What resources did each use to become an effective leader?

3. Analyze the positive and the negative effects of the American labor movement. Based on this analysis, form a point of view on the role that unions have played in the United States. For example, what effect have they had on American politics?

4. Based on the UMWA case study, how do citizens participate in union activity? For example, what can individual union members do to support the organization's growth?

5. Compare and contrast UMWA politics in the John L. Lewis, Tony Boyle, and Arnold Miller administrations. For example, how were decisions made? How were resources distributed? What was the role of the rank-and-file union member?

6. Research some of the efforts by business, industry, and government to control the power of unions. Do you think it is advisable or necessary to control union activities? Explain.

7. At the end of 1977, the UMWA went on strike. Investigate the reasons why the strike was called. In other words, what were the union's goals? Then examine the final settlement and determine whether or not the miners were able to achieve all their original goals, explaining why or why not. Compare and contrast this strike with those discussed in the case study.

Chapter Activities

1. Identify a union other than the UMWA which you would like to study. Choose an aspect of the union's activities and prepare an oral or written report on the topic. You might want to study the union's history and growth, or investigate the union's relation to government today.

2. Investigate the subject of coal. Do a project on the scientific aspects of coal, on the history of coal as a source of energy, the role of coal in the

present and future energy crises, or some other topic. Present your project to the rest of the class. After the reports are given, discuss with other students the reasons why coal is a valuable resource for the UMWA.

3. Read about a labor leader—past or present—who interests you. Write a biography of this man or woman.

4. Interview one or more union members in your community. Report on advantages and/or disadvantages they see in belonging to a union.

Chapter Bibliography

Labor On the March: The Story of America's Unions, Joseph L. Gardner (American Heritage Publishing Co., Inc.: New York, NY), 1969.
  A clearly written illustrated history of the labor movement in America.

The Autobiography of Mother Jones, edited by Mary Field Parton (Charles H. Kerr and Company: Chicago, IL), 1925.
  A fascinating account of the life and work of Mary Jones in which she tells of her efforts to support coal miners and describes her work with the UMWA.

American Labor: A Pictorial Social History, M. B. Schnapper (Public Affairs Press: Washington, DC), 1972.
  A unique presentation of pictures, cartoons, and advertisements which document the history of labor in America.

Working, Studs Terkel (Pantheon Books: New York, NY), 1972.
  Revealing interviews with American workers in many fields.

The United Mine Workers Journal (The United Mine Workers of America: Washington, DC).
  The official news magazine of the UMWA. Appears periodically, reporting on actions taken by and activities of interest to the UMWA.

State and Local
Political Activities

Chapter Objectives

★ To understand how constitutions affect
   your life

★ To analyze different plans for government
   that were important in the founding
   of the United States

★ To understand why and how the Constitution
   of the United States was created

★ To analyze state constitutions and
   compare state and national structures of government

★ To apply the idea of federalism to national-state
   relationships in the United States

chapter 6

STATES CREATE a NATION

Almost 200 years ago the 13 original states approved the first constitution that united them into the United States of America. That constitution was the Articles of Confederation. It was in effect from 1781 to 1789. By 1789 the 13 states had approved the Constitution of the United States of America. It is this structure of government that unifies the 50 states today.

When the states created a nation, they decided that it was necessary to give certain powers to the national government. They kept other powers for themselves. Their first effort at dividing powers—the Articles of Confederation—was not successful. Their second effort—the Constitution—provided a division of powers that has lasted for more than two centuries.

In order to understand national, state, and local government today, you must begin with the original divisions of power. These divisions reflected the states' ideas and needs.

In this chapter you will learn about the ways in which 13 states created one nation. You will analyze the important proposals that contributed to the development of the Constitution. And, you will learn about the relationship the states set up between themselves and the nation they created. (In Chapter 11 you will analyze the Constitution from the standpoint of the national government and its powers.)

Plans for National Government

In 1776 the English colonies declared their independence. Since then, constitutions have been made at the national, state, and local levels in this country. As you learned in Unit 1, constitutions, whether written or not, establish the basic rules and principles of a government. In a constitution a group sets forth what it expects its government to do and, to some extent, how it should do it.

The Constitution of the United States is probably the single most important factor in determining the kind of government the United States has today. Yet, this Constitution was created almost 200 years ago! It has survived through time because it is a "living" document. It is interpreted and amended to meet new needs.

The ARTICLES of CONFEDERATION

The first constitution of the United States was the Articles of Confederation. This plan was in effect from 1781 to 1789. The government established in this constitution was the first united government of the 13 newly independent states.

State Governments. The Declaration of Independence had not created one new government. Instead, it resulted in the creation of 13 new governments, one in each state. As the Declaration stated,

> " . . . these United Colonies are, and of right ought to be Free and Independent States . . . and that as Free and Independent States, they have full Power to levy War, conclude Peace, contract Alliances, establish Commerce, and to do all other Acts and Things which Independent States may of right do. . . . "

After the 13 colonies declared their independence, each new state set forth its plan for government in a state constitution. Some of the former colonies rewrote their colonial charters. Others drafted completely new state constitutions. Thomas Jefferson remarked that constitution-making was "a work of the most interesting nature and such as every individual would wish to have his voice in."

Creating a National Government. As early as 1777, while they were still at war with Great Britain, the new states began their efforts to link their separate governments. They worked through the Second Continental Congress. The First and Second Continental Congresses were assemblies of delegates from most of the colonies. They met first to try to deal with Great Britain and finally to declare independence from it. For more than a year after the Declaration of Independence, delegates to the Second Continental Congress debated different plans for government. On November 15, 1777, the Congress approved a plan, called the Articles of Confederation. It was not until March 1, 1781, that all 13 states *ratified,* or formally approved, the plan. It took effect as the new nation's first constitution.

The Articles of Confederation is a set of 13 articles. In a constitution, an *article* is one part or division of the document. Each article describes a specific part of the plan.

The main purpose of these 13 articles was *confederation,* or union, among the 13 states. Indeed, the preamble to the Articles speaks of "perpetual union" between the 13 states. The *framers* of the Articles knew that the separate states could not survive unless they were united. (To "*frame* a document" means to draw it up, or produce it.) So, the framers of the Articles tried to structure a government that would unify the states.

The Articles of Confederation set up a national political structure for the new United States of America. The 13 articles are summarized on page 177.

Two Principles of Government. Two important structural principles are reflected

The Articles of Confederation

Article I: Names new confederation "The United States of America."

Article II: States retain sovereignty and all powers not specifically given to Congress.

Article III: States enter into "League of Friendship" for common defense and general welfare.

Article IV: Unrestricted travel and exchange between states.

Article V: Establishes national Congress, in which each state has one vote.

Article VI: No state may sign treaties with other states or nations without permission of Congress.

Article VII: Rules for appointment of army officers.

Article VIII: Establishes a general treasury to pay for charges of war and expenses of general welfare. Money to come from taxes levied by authority of state legislatures.

Article IX: Specifies that Congress has power to:
  Declare war and make peace.*
  Send and receive ambassadors.
  Make foreign treaties and alliances.*
  Act as arbitrator in disputes between two or more states.
  Regulate the value of currency, and coin and borrow money.*
  Establish a postal system.
  Regulate Indian affairs.
  Regulate weights and measures.
  Raise a navy and maintain an army of troops requested from the states.*
  *To carry out these powers requires the agreement of at least nine states in the Congress. Other powers can be supported by a majority.

Article X: Committee of states should act if Congress is not assembled.

Article XI: Provides for entry of Canada into the confederation. No other colonies to be admitted without agreement by at least nine states.

Article XII: The United States assumes responsibility for debts incurred by the Continental Congresses before the establishment of this confederation.

Article XIII: Requires that all states abide by the decision of the thirteen states assembled in the national Congress.

in the Articles of Confederation—state sovereignty and national unity. Although the states wanted a national government, their strongest sentiments were in favor of state sovereignty. The word *sovereignty* is defined as "supreme and independent political authority." In other words, a sovereign state considers itself the highest political authority. No other government has power over the state without consent.

The 13 former colonies had experienced the control of a higher government—the British government. They were anxious not to put themselves in the same position again. They did not want to give great power to a national government that could in turn control them, taking away their sovereignty. Article II (page 177) of the Articles of Confederation points out: "Each state retains its sovereignty, freedom, and independence and every power, jurisdiction and right, which is not by this Constitution expressly delegated to the United States, in Congress assembled." Article III describes the union of states as "a firm league of friendship with each other for the common defense, security of their liberties, and their mutual and general welfare."

In the Articles of Confederation the states gave the national government, in the form of a congress, certain important powers. The powers of Congress are summarized in Article IX on page 177. However, most of the powers of government were retained by the individual states. Citizens thought of themselves first as citizens of their own states.

There were many important powers that were not given to the national government. First of all, Congress did not have the power to tax citizens. It could raise money only by asking the states to contribute money to the national government or by borrowing money. The states had heavy financial obligations of their own after the Revolution. They were unable and unwilling to contribute sufficient funds to the national government.

Congress had no power to enforce its rulings. It had no power to collect taxes. And it had no way to force the states to do anything that they did not want to do. As the summary of Article IX indicates, 9 out of the 13 states had to consent before Congress could even exercise most of its powers.

The 13 states were jealous of one another and frequently disagreed. It was almost impossible for Congress to reach the necessary 9-state vote on any controversial issue. In addition, all 13 states had to agree to any changes in the Articles themselves.

Under the Articles the United States was in a condition of extreme disorder and national weakness. The several states bickered among themselves,. However, there was no central power which could settle their conflicts. Trade broke down as each state continued to coin its own money and levy taxes against products coming in from other states. The weak union of states was vulnerable to the military might of other nations, since it was unable to maintain either an army or a navy. By 1785 the United States of America, which had just won its freedom from Britain, was near collapse.

1. Did the Articles of Confederation succeed in promoting its goal? Explain your answer.
2. What contradictions appear in the rules for government established in the Articles of Confederation?
3. Select an issue now being discussed in a school or community group. How would the issue be decided differently if the group were operating under the Articles of Confederation?

The VIRGINIA PLAN

In 1785, trade disputes between Virginia and Maryland led to a meeting between representatives of the two states. Based on the success of this meeting, another conference was held in Annapolis,

The Virginia Plan

1. Articles of Confederation should be corrected and enlarged to accomplish the objectives of common defense, security of liberty, and general welfare.

2. Representation in the national legislature should be proportional to financial contribution or to the number of free inhabitants of the given state.

3. The national legislature should consist of two branches.

4. The members of the first branch should be elected by the people of the states.

5. The members of the second branch should be elected by the members of the first branch.

6. Each branch should possess the right to originate laws and to legislate in cases where states are incompetent or in violation of national harmony or existing laws.

7. A national executive should be instituted to be chosen by the national legislature.

8. The executive and some members of the national judiciary should form a council to examine every act of the national legislature and shall have the power to reject those acts.

9. A national judiciary should be established to be chosen by the national legislature.

10. Provides for admitting new states to the union.

11. The United States should guarantee a republican form of government to each state.

12. A provision should be made to continue the Congress (as organized under the Articles of Confederation) until after the reform of the union has been completed.

13. Provides for amendments to these articles of union.

14. The legislative, executive, and judicial powers within each individual state should support these articles of union.

15. These amendments to the Confederation should be presented to an assembly or assemblies of representatives from individual states.

Maryland, in September 1786. When the meeting opened, only five states had sent representatives. So, another meeting was agreed upon for the following year "for the sole and express purpose of revising the Articles of Confederation...."

The Constitutional Convention. This second meeting began on May 25, 1787. It became the Constitutional Convention. Out of this meeting, which lasted less than four months, came the Constitution.

Concerned leaders had called upon each state to send representatives to the convention in order to make revisions in the Articles of Confederation. Thereby they hoped to create a stronger central government. Every state except Rhode Island sent delegates to the convention. (Rhode Island's state legislature was controlled by citizens who were very opposed to stronger central government.)

Fifty-five delegates from the other 12 states attended convention sessions. Among the delegates were outstanding American leaders, including Benjamin Franklin, James Madison, Alexander Hamilton, and George Washington. All the delegates were men, and many of them were young. Although Benjamin Franklin was 81, the average age of delegates was 42–43. Fifteen of the 39 who eventually signed the Constitution were in their 20s or early 30s.

Less than a month after the convention opened in Philadelphia, two new plans for government had been presented by delegates. Of these plans, one—the Virginia Plan—represented a replacement for the Articles of Confederation. The other—the New Jersey Plan—aimed simply to revise the Articles.

Virginia's Proposal. The Virginia Plan was the first submitted to the convention. It was also the plan which most closely resembles the Constitution finally adopted. Proposed by the delegates of the state of Virginia, this plan represented a clear break from the old Articles of Confederation. The Virginia Plan is outlined on page 179.

The alternative presented by the Virginia Plan is clearly stated in its first article. This article says that the Articles of Confederation should be improved and expanded. Like the Articles, this plan's goals were to promote the common defense, the security of liberty, and the general welfare of the states. However, the Virginia Plan set out to do what the Articles had not done to accomplish these objectives. The Articles had unified the states in a formal sense, but not in a real way. Therefore, the Virginia Plan was designed, not only to unify, but to deal specifically with workable solutions to problems of defense, liberty, and general welfare.

The Virginia Plan set out three important principles or rules for government which were different from those in the Articles of Confederation. First, it divided and specified the powers of the national government. Three departments were developed to replace the single department—Congress—established under the Articles. The Virginia Plan proposed a national legislature, a national executive, and a national judiciary. This structure spread the power of government among the different branches. It also balanced power so that it would not be concentrated in a single branch. The "cross-checking" specified in Article 8 is an example of this balance and diffusion. The Virginia Plan suggested expanding government powers. But, by separating government functions, the supporters hoped central government could be more responsive to a diverse set of needs for governing the United States.

In addition to the principle of division of powers, a second structural principle was important. In Article 6 of the Virginia Plan, power was given to the national legislature over the states. In other words, the states would no longer retain complete sovereignty. The national legislature would have the power to legislate in cases where states were unable to act. When problems arose over taxes or postal services, for example,

The Constitution, part of which is reproduced here, evolved from weeks of debate and compromise among state delegates to the Constitutional Convention. The historical painting, below, shows George Washington presiding over one of the Convention sessions.

the national legislature could step in to regulate these activities.

The plan also indicated that the national legislature could pass laws to bring states into harmony with the national interest. The national legislature would also be able to veto any state laws that violated national interests. In this way, the national government would be given some clout over the states. The national government would not be given complete supremacy. However, in cases of incompetence or national interest it was given power to do something to try to make the situation workable for the nation as a whole. Under the Articles of Confederation this kind of solution was impossible because the states were sovereign.

The Virginia Plan had an important "twist" to it, however, which caused a great deal of discussion and debate. Article 2 of the Plan calls for representation on the basis of either financial contribution or population. Larger states, like Virginia, had more money and more people than the smaller states. Under this plan for representation in the national legislature, larger states would have more representatives. Thus, they would be more powerful than the smaller states.

As you can see from the map on page 183, there were differences in the populations of the states. The Virginia Plan immediately drew the support of the large states—like Massachusetts and Pennsylvania. Generally, the small states opposed this plan for representation. Luther Martin, a delegate from Maryland, sent a letter to the Maryland legislature in which he expressed his opinion about the Virginia Plan. He said, "The object of Virginia and the other large states to increase their power and influence over the others did not escape observation. . . ."

The Virginia Plan was the source of great controversy, especially between large and small states. Assume, for example, the following situation involving five states. Virginia and New York were large states. Rhode Island, Delaware, and Georgia were small states. The issue is whether or not to increase taxes.

Under the Articles of Confederation, Congress had no power of taxation. Virginia and New York might choose not to increase taxes. Delaware, Rhode Island, and Georgia might choose to increase them. Each state could make its own decision about taxes.

Under another plan, that did not allow total state sovereignty, each state might have one vote in Congress on the subject of taxation. Suppose Virginia and New York are against new taxes. Rhode Island, Georgia, and Delaware are in favor of them. In this case, a majority would rule because the vote would be 3 to 2. New taxes would be imposed because the decision of the majority would hold for all states.

The voting system under the Virginia Plan would be quite different. In this case, Virginia might have 11 votes and New York 5. Rhode Island and Delaware might have 1 vote each, and Georgia 3. This would mean that as long as Virginia voted for an issue, the resolution would be resolved in Virginia's favor. This would give the big states a great deal of power in the national legislature. It would allow them to make laws which could apply to the small states, because, under the Virginia Plan, national laws were applicable to all 13 states.

The Virginia Plan clearly posed an alternative to the Articles of Confederation. It also produced controversy. Think about the Virginia Plan and answer the following questions.

1. How were the goals of the Virginia Plan different from those of the Articles of Confederation?

2. Describe the basic principles or rules for government in the Virginia Plan. How were they different from those in the Articles of Confederation?

3. How might you as a citizen in 1787 have been affected differently by the Virginia Plan and by the Articles of Confederation?

The ***NEW JERSEY*** ***PLAN*** Those states that opposed the Virginia Plan formulated their own ideas for revision of the Articles of Confederation. Chief among these planners were delegates from Delaware, Maryland, New Jersey, and some of the New York delegation. On June 14, William Paterson, a delegate from New Jersey, presented to the convention an alternative scheme that reflected the concerns of these delegates. It came to be known as the New Jersey Plan.

The Small States' Proposal. The plan submitted by William Paterson differed from the Virginia Plan in several major ways. It was a revision rather than a total replacement of the Articles of Confederation. Its primary goal, as stated in Article 1, was "that the Articles of Confederation ought to be so revised, corrected and enlarged as to render the federal Constitution adequate to the exigencies [requirements] of Government, and the preservation of the union." The New Jersey Plan sought to correct the weaknesses of the Articles of Confederation. Its aim was to give appropriate power to the federal government in order to overcome these weaknesses. Its nine articles are outlined on page 185.

In the New Jersey Plan, the national Congress established under the Articles of Confederation was retained. Furthermore, each state was to have one vote in the national Congress, as had always been the case.

Unlike the Articles, however, the New Jersey Plan proposed a three-part government. It would contain legislative, executive, and judicial branches. The legislature would elect an executive to be composed of several persons. This executive branch would have no veto power. The federal judiciary would be appointed by the executive. In this way, the New Jersey Plan shared an important principle with the Virginia Plan. Both specified powers and divided responsibility in order for government to

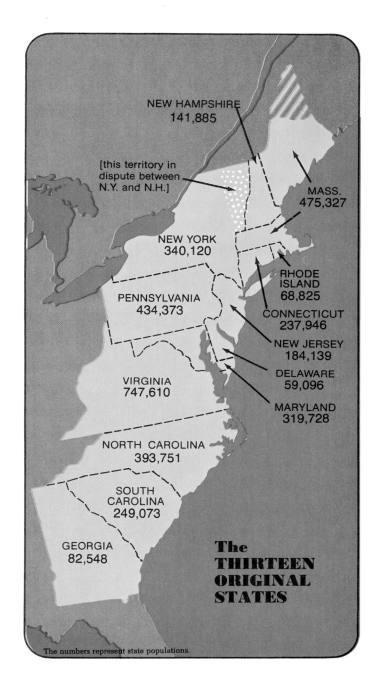

Figure 6-1

function more effectively. Both outlined three separate but interrelated branches of government.

In Article 6, the New Jersey Plan made one of the most important contributions of either of the plans. This article proposed that all acts of the United States should be

183

William Paterson

considered the supreme law of the land. If the national government made a law, it automatically applied to the states. The concept of the supremacy of the national constitution is the central article from the New Jersey Plan which has been carried forth into the Constitution.

In another difference from the Virginia Plan, the New Jersey Plan provided for equal representation of states. In other words, each of the states would have an equal number of votes in the legislature. Majority rule would determine policy. Thus, a majority of the states, rather than a minority of the large states, would have to agree.

Controversy. The existence of the two plans divided delegates of the Con-

stitutional Convention into two camps. Those who favored the Virginia Plan included most of the large states. They would probably gain more influence at the national level if that plan were adopted. Also favoring the Virginia Plan were those delegates who felt that the old Articles of Confederation should be completely replaced with a new plan for government.

Favoring the New Jersey Plan were the small states. They felt that they could be best represented at the national level if all the states had one vote in Congress as under the old Articles of Confederation. Also supporting the New Jersey Plan were those people who felt that the Articles of Confederation should be revised and expanded but not completely discarded and replaced.

1. Which goals of the New Jersey and Virginia plans were similar? Which were different?

2. How did the structure proposed in the New Jersey Plan differ from that of the Virginia Plan?

3. How do you think the conflict in representation between the New Jersey Plan and the Virginia Plan could best be resolved? What impact would that resolution have on citizens?

The Constitution of the United States

The delegates to the Constitutional Convention had come to the meetings with certain basic principles of government in common and yet with certain major disagreements. As you have seen in the New Jersey and Virginia plans, delegates shared a desire to create a functional central government. All wanted this government to represent the people. And all believed that the basic power of government rested with the people. This principle, called *popular sover-*

eignty, is the essence of democracy (See page 190).

It is important to note, however, that the "people" in whom power rested were free, white men. At that time in American society, black slaves, women, and Native Americans had no political power. None of these groups would be allowed to vote, nor otherwise participate in the political process. This situation did not change for many years.

The New Jersey Plan

1. The Articles of Confederation should be revised, corrected, and enlarged to suit the needs of the union.

2. The Congress should have the power to pass acts for raising revenue and regulating trade and commerce.

3. The states should be taxed according to their population.

4. The states and Congress should be authorized to elect a federal executive.

5. A federal judiciary should be established, appointed by the executive.

6. All acts of the United States Congress should be the supreme law of the land.

7. A provision should be made for the admission of new states into the union.

8. The same rule for becoming a citizen should exist in every state.

9. Laws for prosecuting crimes should be applied equally in all states.

The COMPROMISES

In spite of the common goals of the states at the convention, there were major conflicts that had to be settled. This was necessary before a workable plan for government could be established. Most of the conflicts were the result of differing interests of large states vs. small states, of agriculture vs. business, of North vs. South. These conflicts were resolved in a series of compromises. (A *compromise* is a mutual agreement. Usually, a compromise involves each side giving in on some points and winning on others.)

The Great Compromise. The most important conflict concerned representation in the legislature, as you have read. Benjamin Franklin observed, "til this point . . . came before us, our delegates carried on with great coolness and temper."

As you saw in the two plans, the large states wanted representation in the national legislature to be based upon population. They realized this would give them more political resources. The small states argued for equal representation among all the states. After heated debate a compromise was reached. Today it is often called "The Great Compromise," for without it the convention was deadlocked. The compromise, proposed by Roger Sherman of Connecticut, was this: The new government would have a Congress made up of two separate houses. In the upper house, to be called the Senate, each state would be represented by two elected senators. The lower house, called the House of Representatives, would base its membership on the population of each state. Therefore, larger states would have more members in the House of Representatives than smaller states would. Legislation would have to be approved by a majority vote in both houses of Congress.

The vote on the Great Compromise was extremely close. Out of the nine voting states, only Connecticut, New Jersey, Delaware, Maryland, and North Carolina were in favor of the compromise. Pennsylvania, Virginia, South Carolina, and Georgia voted against the compromise. The delegation from Massachusetts was divided among its own members and therefore did not vote. The delegates from New York had returned home and were not present for the vote. The delegates from New Hampshire had not yet arrived at the Constitutional Convention. And Rhode Island had never sent delegates to the convention at all.

After the Great Compromise, the convention had less difficulty in completing its business. There were important matters to be considered, but these were more easily resolved than the issue of representation in the legislature.

The Three-Fifths Compromise. If representation in the House of Representatives was to be based on population, a decision was needed on how population would be counted. Southern states had large populations of slaves who were not to be part of the voting population. However, the southern states argued that slaves should be included in the state population used to determine the number of representatives in the House. States without large slave populations disagreed. Finally, a compromise was reached. It was decided that a state's representation would be based on a count of all free persons and "three fifths of all other persons." This inequity was changed by constitutional amendments in the 1860s.

Other Compromises. Other important compromises were required between factions at the convention. Several of these involved commerce. Some federal regulation of trade was required, but many states worried that a central government would have too much power over trade. So, it was decided that Congress could regulate commerce between states (interstate commerce). However, states would retain control of commerce within their borders. In addition, Congress was not allowed to regulate the slave trade until 1808.

There was also great disagreement over how the president—the executive—should be selected. Various methods were proposed, such as selection by Congress, by state legislatures, or by the people. The electoral college, which you read about in Chapter 3, was the final solution to the debate.

States disagreed on the question of who should be allowed to vote. Finally, this was left up to the decision of each individual state. Today, constitutional amendments have placed federal controls on who is allowed to vote. For example, the Twenty-sixth Amendment states that no citizen 18 years old or older can be denied the right to vote because of age.

Another area of disagreement involved the method of selecting justices for the Supreme Court. One proposal urged that judges be chosen by the Senate. Another argued that judges should be chosen by the executive. A compromise was reached, whereby federal judges are selected by the executive but approved by the Senate.

1. What conflict was resolved by the Great Compromise? How was it resolved?
2. What was the "three-fifths compromise"? Is its solution in effect today?
3. How do the constitutional compromises affect you today?

CREATING the DOCUMENT At the end of July the delegates had resolved their differences. They had come to agreement on the plan for government they wanted to establish in the nation's new constitution. Now it was necessary to put their proposals in a formal document. A committee of five delegates was appointed by the convention to draft a Constitution. The committee included James Rutledge from South Carolina, Edmund Randolph from Virginia, Nathaniel Gorham from Massachusetts, Oliver Ellsworth from Connecticut, and James Wilson from Pennsylvania.

186

In early September the draft was completed. A committee headed by Gouverneur Morris of Pennsylvania wrote the final document. On September 17 the Constitution of the United States of America was officially signed by 39 delegates.

The document signed on that September day in Philadelphia consisted of seven articles outlining a federal government. A summary of the articles appears on page 188. The complete document can be found beginning on page 616.

Principles of Government. The goals of the Constitution are stated in its preamble:

"We, the People of the United States, in order to form a more perfect Union, establish Justice, insure domestic Tranquility, provide for the common defence, promote the general Welfare, and secure the Blessings of Liberty to ourselves and our Posterity, do ordain and establish this Constitution for the United States of America."

These goals are more clearly stated in this constitution than in any previous document or plan.

The principles of government stated in the Constitution are a combination of ideas incorporated in the Articles of Confederation, state constitutions, the Declaration of Independence, and the New Jersey and Virginia plans. They also are part of a long tradition of democracy (See page 190).

In this constitution, tasks and powers were much more clearly specified than in previous documents. For example, the president has the power to enforce the Constitution and the laws made by Congress as well as to enforce treaties. The president can veto legislation, recommend measures to Congress, call special sessions of Congress, and recommend Supreme Court appointments. The president also serves as commander in chief of the armed forces. The office of president represents one of the most important changes in the new constitution. Neither the Articles of Confederation nor any of the state constitutions had provided for a strong executive.

The principle of national supremacy is asserted to its fullest extent in the Constitution. Taking its ideas and wording from the New Jersey Plan, Article VI of the Constitution specifies that its rules and those laws made by Congress will be "the supreme law of the land." At the same time, the Constitution is based on the principle of *limited government*. The national government is limited to those powers it is given by the states in the Constitution. Delegates at the Constitutional Convention knew well the dangers of unlimited power.

Ratification. The last article of the new constitution provided for ratification—formal approval—of the document by the states. Before the Constitution could go into effect, 9 of the 13 states had to ratify it. A convention was called in each state for the purpose of deciding whether or not to ratify the document. Figure 6-2 on page 189 lists the dates on which each state ratified the Constitution.

Although all 13 states eventually voted for ratification, approval was not accomplished easily. Mainly, people objected to the amount of power the new plan gave to a central government. Those who supported the Constitution were called *Federalists*. Those who opposed it were known as *Anti-Federalists*.

Following are some of the arguments against the new Constitution. Read the arguments carefully. Try to determine why the writers objected to the new plan for government.

Letter from Samuel Adams
to Richard Henry Lee
3 December, 1787

"If the several states in the union are to become one entire nation, under one legislation, and its laws be supreme and control the whole, the Idea of Sovereignty in these States must be lost."

The Constitution of the United States

Preamble: States that the people of the United States are setting up this constitution in order to form a better union, establish justice, insure domestic peace, provide for common defense, and guarantee liberty for themselves and their descendants.

Article I: Establishes legislative powers vested in a Congress composed of a Senate and a House of Representatives. Sets rules for membership and representation in each house. Powers of Congress are listed. These include collecting taxes, coining money, and declaring war. Congress is given the power to make all laws required to carry out its responsibilities.

Article II: Establishes executive powers vested in a president. Sets rules for eligibility and election of president. Presidential powers are listed. These include enforcing the Constitution, the laws made by Congress, and treaties, appointing high officials such as ambassadors and Supreme Court judges, and acting as commander in chief of the armed forces.

Article III: Establishes judicial powers vested in a Supreme Court and in lower courts set up by Congress. Powers of the judiciary are listed. These include explaining the meaning of the Constitution, settling legal disputes between states, settling legal disputes between states or citizens and foreign governments.

Article IV: Defines relations of states to one another. Specifies that they must honor each other's laws.

Article V: Defines process for amending the Constitution.

Article VI: Establishes that the Constitution is the supreme law of the land.

Article VII: Establishes ratification procedures (nine of the thirteen states must give their approval).

The full text of the Constitution appears on pages 616–625.

James Winthrop
3 December, 1787

"It is impossible for one code of laws to suit Georgia and Massachusetts. They must, therefore, legislate for themselves. . . . The idea of [a country] on an average of one thousand miles in length and eight hundred in breadth, and containing six millions of white inhabitants all reduced to the same standard of morals, of habits and of laws is in itself an absurdity, and contrary to the whole experience of mankind."

George Clinton to
the Citizens of New York
11 October, 1787

"This convention has exceeded the authority given to them, and has transmitted to Congress a new political fabric...."

George Mason in the
Ratifying Convention
of Virginia
4–12 June, 1788

"Mr. Chairman, whether the Constitution be good or bad, the present clause clearly discovers that it is a national government, and no longer a confederation. I mean that clause which gives the first hint of the general government laying direct taxes. The assumption of this power of laying direct taxes . . . is calculated to annihilate totally the state governments."

Patrick Henry

"I look upon that paper [the Constitution] as the most fatal plan that could possibly be conceived to enslave a free people."

This is just a small sample of the arguments against the plan for government developed in the Constitutional Convention. However, these statements contain some of the major reasons why so many people opposed the new Constitution.

There seemed to be just as many people arguing in favor of the Constitution as there were those who argued against it. Many people felt that the Constitution established a workable plan for government which was appropriate to the needs of the new and growing nation. Of those who favored the Constitution, many worked together to urge its ratification. They tried to show that people had nothing to fear from the new plan for government.

Three leaders—Alexander Hamilton, James Madison, and John Jay—wrote numerous essays in favor of the new Constitution. A series of 85 essays written in defense of the Constitution are known as *The Federalist Papers*. Excerpts from Federalist Paper 45 are reproduced on page 191. They illustrate some of the arguments that the Federalists used in favor of the new Constitution. Try to identify how James Madison refuted the charges of the Anti-Federalists.

Figure 6-2

RATIFICATION of the CONSTITUTION

STATE	ORDER OF RATIFICATION	DATE OF RATIFICATION	VOTE IN STATE CONVENTIONS
Delaware	1	December 7, 1787	30–0
Pennsylvania	2	December 12, 1787	46–23
New Jersey	3	December 18, 1787	38–0
Georgia	4	January 2, 1788	26–0
Connecticut	5	January 9, 1788	128–40
Massachusetts	6	February 6, 1788	187–168
Maryland	7	April 28, 1788	63–11
South Carolina	8	May 23, 1788	149–73
New Hampshire	9	June 21, 1788	57–47
Virginia	10	June 25, 1788	89–79
New York	11	July 26, 1788	30–27
North Carolina	12	November 21, 1789	194–77
Rhode Island	13	May 29, 1790	34–32

History of Democracy

The word "democracy" comes from the Greek words *demos* (meaning "people") and *kratos* (meaning "rule or authority"). The simplest definition of "democracy" is rule by the people. Today, the word refers to a government in which final authority is vested in the people. This power is exercised either directly by the people or indirectly through representatives who are freely elected.

Democracy in Ancient Greece. The origins of democracy, like the word itself, go back to ancient Greece. As early as the seventh century B.C., Athens and other city-states were practicing simple forms of democracy. These early democracies were direct, not representative. All free male citizens were eligible to become permanent members of the local assembly. This entitled them to vote directly on important matters.

Democracy During the Middle Ages. The Middle Ages saw the rise of *feudalism* as a social and economic system in Europe. Under the feudal system, a group of people pledged their loyalty and service to a lord, who owned a large piece of land called a *fief*. In return for this pledge, the lord guaranteed certain rights and protections to his subjects called *vassals*. Out of the need to control these complex relations grew the feudal court system. It eventually led to the development of other types of representative bodies such as councils and assemblies.

In 1215, King John of England was forced by his nobles to sign the Magna Carta, one of the most important documents in the history of democracy. The Magna Carta granted the nobles historic civil liberties and served as the basis for winning other personal freedoms. With the signing of this document, the seeds of English democracy were planted. However, its growth was slow and often painful.

Democracy During the Renaissance. The European Renaissance during the fourteenth to sixteenth centuries helped to spread democratic ideals throughout the Western world. The spirit of individuality reborn during this period of history caused many people to demand greater personal freedoms. The Protestant revolution of the sixteenth century also fostered democratic processes. Some of the newly formed Protestant groups had democratic structures.

Democracy in England. Conflict between the British people and the crown eventually erupted into Civil War. In 1688, the supremacy of the British Parliament over the crown was finally secured. The next year, Parliament passed the Bill of Rights, which guaranteed fundamental civil liberties to all British citizens. During the next three centuries, these rights were slowly expanded. By 1928, all adult British citizens had the right to vote.

Democracy in France. Seventeenth- and eighteenth-century French political thinkers such as Montesquieu, Voltaire, and Rousseau furthered the cause of democracy in their writings. Their outspoken criticism of the abuses of the French monarchy and their support of important democratic ideals helped to spark the French Revolution in 1789. Although the revolution failed to establish a democracy in France, its ideals of "Liberty, Equality, and Fraternity" had a strong influence on the American democratic experience.

James Madison—Federalist Paper 45

"Was, then, the American Revolution effected, was the American Confederation formed, was the previous blood of thousands spilt, and the hard-earned substance of millions lavished, not that the people of America should enjoy peace, liberty, and safety, but that the government of the individual States might enjoy a certain extent of power . . .?"

"The powers delegated by the proposed Constitution to the federal government are few and defined. Those which are to remain in the State government are numerous and indefinite. [The federal government will use its powers on] external objects, as war, peace, negotiation, and foreign commerce. . . . The powers reserved to the several states will extend to all the objects which, in the ordinary course of affairs, concern the lives, liberties, and properties of the people. . . ."

The conventions in some states ratified the new Constitution within three months. Others argued for eight or nine months before accepting it. However, by July 26, 1788, 11 states had ratified the new plan. In 1789, George Washington was elected as the first president and a new government was organized. North Carolina finally ratified the Constitution in November 1789, but Rhode Island refused to ratify it until May 1790.

1. Compare the goals stated in the Constitution with those in the Declaration of Independence and the Articles of Confederation.

2. What rules or principles of government are stated in each of the articles of the Constitution?

3. How would the removal of any one of the articles of the Constitution affect the work of government? Are there any articles you think should be added?

4. How might the lives of citizens be different if the New Jersey or the Virginia Plan had been adopted instead of the Constitution?

The BILL of RIGHTS

One argument often heard against the Constitution was that it did not insure the basic and fundamental rights of American citizens. Many felt that the new plan provided for a government that could be insensitive to the needs of individual citizens. These Americans urged that a "bill of rights" be added to the Constitution. Most state constitutions had such bills, or lists, of rights to ensure such basic freedoms as freedom of speech and assembly for their citizens. In order to assure ratification, supporters of the Constitution promised to push for a bill of rights in the first session of Congress.

At its first meeting, Congress passed 12 amendments to the Constitution. Of these, 10 amendments, comprising the Bill of Rights, were ratified by enough states to become a part of the Constitution in 1791. A summary of the Bill of Rights appears on page 192. Since 1791, 16 other amendments have been added to the Constitution.

The Bill of Rights affects citizens as much as any other single part of the Constitution. It provides them with such freedoms as the right to peaceable assembly, the right to a jury trial, and protection against cruel and unusual punishments.

1. List the rights and freedoms guaranteed in the Bill of Rights.

2. Choose two rights in the Bill of Rights and describe how they affect you.

CONSTITUTIONS and YOU

Every one of the 50 states in the United States today has its own constitution. In these documents, all the states have organized their governments in ways fairly similar to the structure established in the national Constitution. For example, each state has an executive, legislative, and judicial branch of government.

The Bill of Rights

1st Amendment: Freedom of religion, speech, and press. Right of assembly and petition.

2nd Amendment: Right to keep and bear arms.

3rd Amendment: Freedom from the arbitrary occupation of one's home by the military.

4th Amendment: Freedom from unreasonable search and seizure.

5th Amendment: Protection from arbitrary indictment, double jeopardy, and self-indictment. Right to due process of the law with respect to life, liberty, or property. (*Due process of the law* is a series of legal proceedings carried out according to established rules.)

6th Amendment: In criminal cases, right to counsel and to a speedy and public trial by jury, with all accusations and witnesses made known.

7th Amendment: Right to a trial by jury in civil cases.

8th Amendment: Protection from cruel and unusual punishments and excessive bail.

9th Amendment: Delegation to the people of all rights not specifically listed or described in the Constitution.

10th Amendment: Reserves for the states or the people all rights not delegated to the federal government.

You are affected by constitutional rules and structures every day. The following case is an example of a state constitution as it influences the lives of citizens. It shows the impact of New Jersey's constitution on education in the state.

As you read the case, think about how branches of state government interact. And, think about constitutions' impact on citizens.

★ Who Will Support the Schools?

On July 1, 1976, a historic decision was made by the State Supreme Court in New Jersey. By a 9 to 2 decision, schools were shut down throughout the entire state. The 88,000 students who were in summer school programs had to change their plans. School administrators struggled with the chaos. Taxpayers were aroused. Legislators were frustrated.

The case began in the courts in 1970. At that time the mother of Kenneth Robinson, age 7, charged that her son was not receiving a good education. She argued that he was not learning to read. Therefore, she said, he would be disadvantaged throughout his entire life. Mrs. Robinson's lawyers took the case to the Hudson County Superior Court. There, in 1972, Judge Botter ruled that Mrs. Robinson was right. He decided Kenneth was not receiving equal educational opportunity under the law. In his opinion the state of New Jersey was not providing "quality" education in Kenneth Robinson's school.

The history behind the case began in 1817. In that year New Jersey established a school fund in order to pay for public education. In 1828 a property tax was instituted which would allow the state to distribute money to local communities to support public school facilities.

By 1875, some state legislators were worried about the quality of education. They passed an amendment to the constitution which stated that all youth in New Jersey should have a "thorough and efficient education." It is through this constitutional amendment that the 1970s controversy arose.

In the Kenneth Robinson case, the Hudson County Superior Court concluded that the amendment to the constitution was intended to provide equal educational opportunity for New Jersey children. In April 1973 the State Court said that the amendment "can have no other import." The court also added, "if local government fails, the state government must compel it to act, and if the local government cannot carry the burden, the state must itself meet its continuing obligation." In other words, communities that could not or would not provide high-quality education must have state help.

The court's decision was upheld by the New Jersey State Supreme Court. Indirectly, the state supreme court passed the whole question of school financing to the state legislature. If the state were to step in and make changes, the legislature would have to raise the funds.

For a long time the New Jersey legislature had not voted sufficient money for the school fund. The funds simply were not enough to finance education in the state. Some communities had more money to spend on education than others did. And the state school fund was not able to provide sufficient money to needy communities.

There were additional problems the legislature had to consider. New Jersey did not have a state income tax. Funds for the running of the state were financed through a sales tax. Most legislators did not want to increase the sales tax, which had already become a burden to citizens. They were also afraid of citizen outcry if they increased property taxes.

The court had ordered the legislature to raise $378 million. This would balance the school budget. There was no existing source through which the funds could be gained. Adding a new state income tax seemed to be the only alternative.

At six different times, however, the Assembly tried to put through an income tax bill. (The New Jersey legislature is made up of the Assembly and the Senate.) Assembly members generally were deeply divided over the tax. However six different versions of an income tax bill were sent to the Senate. And six times the Senate rejected the income tax. The legislature appeared to be deadlocked.

Governor Byrne entered the situation. He said he would veto any tax package that relied primarily on a sales tax increase. On television and radio the governor urged citizens to write letters to their legislators to convince them to support an income tax. The response was immediate.

There was a flood of mail from taxpayers. But, it had exactly the opposite effect the governor desired. Many New Jersey taxpayers were tired of paying high taxes. They did not want more. In letters to their legislators they protested the income tax. Interest groups such as the Federation of New Jersey Taxpayers came out vocally against the tax. According to Bernadine Silver, a vice-president of the group, "we are determined and unalterably opposed to the addition of any new or higher tax on residents of the state, particularly an income tax."

Other groups, such as the School Board Association, also entered into the battle. They asked the state supreme court to take back its threat to close the public schools on July 1. The groups said that the closing of the schools was itself a threat to equal educational opportunity.

193

Finally, as a result of the conflict and the closing of the schools, New Jersey did pass an income tax resolution. The tax provided funds to be distributed to school districts on the basis of need. This redistribution was designed to equalize the quality of education throughout the state since school districts no longer had to rely so heavily on local property taxes.

1. What might have happened if the New Jersey Constitution had set up only a legislature? What if it had not set up a state judiciary? What might have happened if the legislature had been structured differently?

2. How did this issue affect citizens of the state of New Jersey? How did it influence the average taxpayer? What might its impact be on students?

A Federal System of Government

In the Constitution of the United States, the power of government is divided between the national government and the state governments. This is a form of government called *federalism*. A *federal system* of government divides powers between a central government and a number of regional governments.

DIVISION of POWERS

The Constitution outlines a federal division of powers. Certain powers are *delegated,* or assigned, to the national government. Other powers are *reserved,* or kept, by the state governments. And some powers are *concurrent* or shared; that is, the powers are exercised by both the national and the state governments. Finally, certain powers are *denied* to the national government and certain powers are denied to state governments.

Use the Constitution reprinted on pages 616–626 to check the specific articles and sections described in this discussion.

Delegated Powers. In creating the Constitution the 13 states delegated certain powers to their national government. The powers are divided among the three branches of government, some held by each branch and some shared.

Articles I, II, and III list most of the specific powers of the national government. In addition, Congress is given the power to "make all laws which shall be necessary and proper for carrying into execution the foregoing powers." This is sometimes called the "*elastic clause.*" In other words, Congress has the right to pass whatever legislation is necessary to enforce the powers delegated to it. For example, Congress is given the power to regulate naturalization. To do this, Congress passes laws concerning ways of becoming a citizen.

In Unit 3 you will study the powers of the national government in greater detail.

Reserved Powers. Although the main body of the Constitution prohibits the states from exercising certain powers, it does not specifically grant any powers to the states. The framers of the Constitution had set out only to define a national government, not to define state governments. However, many people were afraid that a national government would take advantage of the omission of state powers. So, Amendment 10 in the Bill of Rights states: "The powers not delegated to the United States by the Constitution, nor prohibited by it to the States, are reserved to the States respectively, or to the people."

By including Amendment 10 in the Constitution, the citizens of the United States

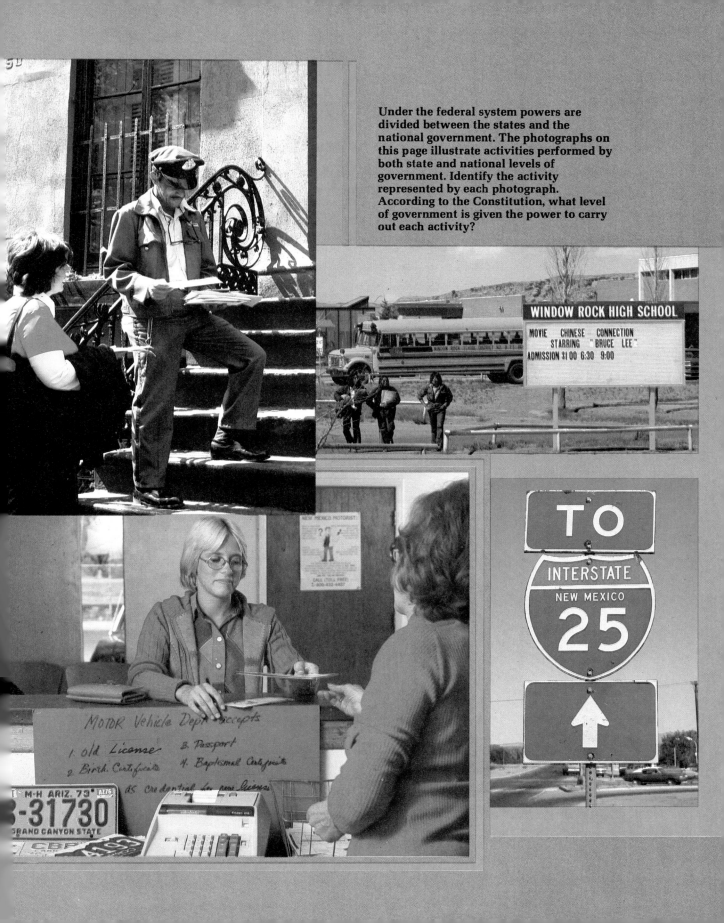

Under the federal system powers are divided between the states and the national government. The photographs on this page illustrate activities performed by both state and national levels of government. Identify the activity represented by each photograph. According to the Constitution, what level of government is given the power to carry out each activity?

made it clear that the states would have many powers of government. For example, the power to establish schools is not given to the national government in the Constitution. And the Constitution does not deny this power to the states. Therefore, the establishing and running of schools and other educational institutions are controlled by each state for its own citizens. States also make rules about marriage and divorce, about the operation of motor vehicles, about elections for state and local offices, and about many other aspects of our lives.

The Constitution does not discuss local government, nor does it prohibit states from controlling local governments. Therefore, states have established rules within which local governments operate.

Concurrent Powers. Many powers of government are shared by the national government and the 50 state governments. For example, both the national government and the states have the power to collect taxes on personal incomes. (In turn, some states allow certain cities to tax personal income.) Both state and national governments have the power to set up courts to maintain and interpret laws. Both have the power to define crimes and their punishment. These and other powers are shared by both state and national governments.

Denied Powers. In addition to delegating and reserving powers, the Constitution also denies powers to both national and state governments. These prohibitions are expressed or implied in the Constitution and its amendments.

The national government is specifically prohibited from certain actions, particularly in Article I, Section 9. In addition, the amendments prohibit certain actions on the part of the national government. For example, the First Amendment specifically prohibits Congress from making any laws that would deny citizens freedom of religion, speech, press, assembly, or petition.

In addition, by not delegating a power to the national government, the Constitution

reserves it for the states. Thus, those powers reserved for the states are denied to the federal government. For example, the power of regulating marriage is a power denied to the federal government by the Constitution's silence.

State governments are also denied certain powers by the Constitution. Article I, Section 10, lists powers which no states may exercise. For example, states may not enter into treaties, coin money, or engage in war. In addition, the Tenth Amendment specifies that no state may have powers delegated only to the national government by the Constitution.

Finally, neither the national nor the state governments may exercise any power that would contradict the powers of the other. In other words, the national government cannot exercise any power that would threaten the very existence of a state government, and vice versa.

1. Describe the division of powers defined in the Constitution and its amendments. Explain delegated, reserved, concurrent, and denied powers.
2. How does this division of powers affect you?
3. Study the photographs on page 195. Which photographs picture activities that are the responsibility of the states and which show activities that are carried out by the federal government? Do any photographs depict activities carried out at both state and federal levels?

RIGHTS and RESPONSIBILITIES The national government has certain constitutional rights and responsibilities. These are in addition to the delegated powers that the national government possesses.

The Supreme Law of the Land. Article VI, Section 2, states: "This Constitution, and the laws of the United States which shall be

4. Delegates to the Constitutional Convention wanted to make government responsible to the people; however, their definition of the "people" was limited. Explain why.

5. Summarize the compromises that resolved major conflicts at the Constitutional Convention. How did each compromise affect the final governmental plan?

6. Some people trace the beginning of American political parties back to the Federalists and the Anti-Federalists. How did these two groups differ in their attitudes toward government?

7. Why was the Bill of Rights important in setting up a new national government?

8. In your opinion, what are the most important powers reserved to state governments? Explain.

9. How do the rights and responsibilities of the federal government reinforce the concept of federalism?

10. To understand American government, you must be aware of the relationships among national, state, and local governments. Explain why.

Chapter Vocabulary

Define the following terms.

article	compromise	reserved powers
confederation	Federalist	concurrent powers
sovereignty	Anti-Federalist	denied powers
ratification	delegated powers	"elastic clause"
federalism		

Chapter Analysis

1. Construct a chart in which you compare and/or contrast the plans of government proposed in the Articles of Confederation, the Virginia Plan, the New Jersey Plan, and the Constitution. Consider such information as goals, division of powers, structure of government, and any other data that you think are important.

2. Using the Constitution (pages 616–625), summarize the division of powers set forth in that document. In your opinion, has the separation

of powers strengthened or weakened the national government? Support your position.

3. In essay form, respond to the following question: "How do the goals stated in the preamble to the Constitution reflect the basic functions of American government?"

Chapter Activities

1. In diary form, record your activities for one week. Then review the rights and freedoms guaranteed in the Bill of Rights. How does each right or freedom affect your daily life?

2. Investigate the arguments of one of the Federalists or Anti-Federalists who led debates over ratification of the Constitution. Then, with the rest of the class, recreate these debates. You should be prepared to play the part of the individual that you choose to research.

3. Obtain a copy of your state's constitution. Study the document, comparing and/or contrasting it to the Constitution of the United States. Find out how many constitutions your state has had, how old this one is, and whether or not there are any proposals for a new constitution. Also, study the amendments to your state constitution.

4. Prepare a biography of one of the outstanding individuals who took part in the Constitutional Convention. Consider the resources that this person brought to the convention and the role that he played in the final drafting of the Constitution.

5. Investigate the ways in which the Constitution affects your life as a student. Prepare an oral report on this topic, demonstrating what parts of the Constitution have an impact on your educational experience.

Chapter Bibliography

Miracle at Philadelphia, Catherine Drinker Bowen (Bantam Books, Inc.: New York), 1966.

An account of the Constitutional Convention, highlighting the drama which surrounded that meeting, presented in great detail and in a readable style.

The Federalist Papers, Alexander Hamilton, James Madison, John Jay (New American Library: New York), 1961.

A reprinting of the Federalist papers, in which the authors presented their arguments in favor of a strong central government.

Framers of the Constitution, Dorothy Horton McGee (Dodd, Mead and Company: New York), 1968.
>   Biographies of those men present at the Constitutional Convention in Philadelphia.

Notes on Debates in the Federal Convention of 1787, James Madison (Ohio University Press: Athens, Ohio), 1969.
>   A complete set of the notes which James Madison took at the Constitutional Convention in Philadelphia. Provides insights available in no other source.

The Convention and the Constitution: The Political Idea of the Founding Fathers, David G. Smith (St. Martin's Press: New York), 1965.
>   An informative account of basic principles of the American government, focusing on the activity surrounding the drafting of the United States Constitution. Contains a large section on federalism.

Chapter Objectives

★ To learn the meaning of political activity
★ To apply the concepts of leadership, decision-making, communication, and participation
★ To analyze political life in terms of political activity and political resources
★ To develop skills in using concepts

chapter 7

POLITICAL ACTIVITIES of CITIZENS

You learned in Chapter 2 that politics is activity in which resources are used and distributed. Chapter 2 examined resources—what they are, how they are used, who has them. In this chapter you will study those activities in which resources are used and distributed.

Acting as a member of your student council is an example of political activity. The decisions that council members make affect the distribution of many resources. And members are using resources like skills and knowledge as they make their decisions.

You can identify many more political activities. And, you can see that some of these activities are familiar to you. You see them in action and may even take part in them. Political activity is not something conducted only by "politicians in Washington." You are a political actor too.

In order to analyze these political activities, it is useful to divide them into categories. For example, many political activities can be grouped under the heading "Participation." Identifying categories of ideas is an important skill, one which you will learn in this chapter.

What Is Political Activity?

Political activity is action in which citizens use and distribute resources in a group. An essential part of politics, political activity runs both public and private governments. As political actors, all citizens engage in political activity. You will see in this chapter that often political activities are actions you take for granted. You may not have thought of them as political before.

The many kinds of political activity can be grouped under large headings. In our discussion we will focus on four general areas. These are decision-making, communication, participation, and leadership.

The MEANING of DECISION-MAKING An essential part of the political process, decision-making occurs in any political situation. *Decision-making* is an activity through which choices are made from two or more alternatives. Political decisions involve the giving or withholding of resources in a group. State legislatures, for example, are constantly involved in decision-making. When legislatures meet, one of their main responsibilities is to decide how the state will spend its money on services such as education, health, and transportation. As a result of their decisions, the resources of the state are distributed to specific groups and institutions.

Choices, Alternatives, and Outcomes. Decision-making involves three fundamental ideas: choices, alternatives, and outcomes.

First, each political decision begins with a choice situation. You may have decided to vote Republican rather than Democratic, to raise money for the United Way instead of for the March of Dimes, or to participate in a letter-writing campaign instead of a strike or public demonstration. The existence of a choice is a fundamental aspect of decision-making.

Closely related to choice is the idea of alternatives. (An *alternative* is one of two or more things to be chosen.) Whenever an individual or group is confronted with a choice, there are two or more alternatives from which to choose.

When a decision is made, the result, or outcome, must be considered. With each alternative there is a desired outcome. The outcome in decision-making reflects a redistribution of resources. For example, think about your decision to vote for one candidate rather than another. The desired outcome of your decision is to give more resources to the winning candidate.

So, when you identify a decision-making situation you should analyze the choice involved, the alternatives that are available, and the outcome that is desired. The following case describes a decision-making situation. As you read, identify the choice, the alternatives, and the outcome.

★ **A Decision at Oceanside**

At Oceanside High School, the principal, Malcom Warren, worked closely with members of his administration and with students to decide upon the location of a school smoking area. Smoking in schools had been illegal in Oceanside. Thus there had been no need for an official smoking area. Despite the illegality, however, a great deal of smoking did occur at the school. Most of it took place in school restrooms and in the school parking lot.

School administrators attempted to keep the smoking situation under control. Students were penalized in several ways if they were caught smoking.

Then smoking was legalized in the schools of Oceanside. This happened when

An important part of decision-making is choosing among alternatives. Students at Oceanside had to consider possible outcomes before deciding on the site for the smoking area.

the governor of the state decided that each local school board could determine smoking rules in its community schools. Oceanside's school board voted to allow smoking in specified areas within each high school. It was up to individual high schools to select the smoking areas in their schools.

Principal Malcolm Warren called a meeting of the students to identify one area on the school grounds where students could legally smoke cigarettes. He said that students caught smoking outside of this area would be penalized as before.

Various locations were proposed by students. Some favored establishing a smoking area just outside the cafeteria. They felt this location would allow them to smoke during their lunch hour. Other students felt that the smoking area should be established in front of the school. However, most students felt that the smoking area should be officially established in the parking lot behind the school.

The primary argument against the parking lot was its size. It was a large area that would be difficult for the school to keep clean. However, any official smoking area would require daily maintenance by school personnel.

Mr. Warren discussed these three alternatives with his administration. He also discussed them with the student council and the remainder of the student body. He also made a point of talking with students on an informal basis, so that he could hear their opinions. After hearing the ideas of teachers, administrators, and students, Mr. Warren believed that a majority wanted the official smoking area to be in the parking lot behind the school. He decided to establish the smoking area there.

1. Identify the choice, alternatives, and outcome at Oceanside High School.
2. What resources might have been redistributed as a result of the decision?

The MEANING of COMMUNICATION Communication is the exchange of ideas or information. Political communication affects the use and distribution of resources in a group. Through political communication, people try to influence each other's opinions and actions in order to achieve a political goal.

For example, a citizen might send a telegram to a state representative. The telegram urges the representative to vote for a law providing more money for the public schools in the state. Writing and sending this telegram is a political activity. The communicator is trying to influence the distribution of resources.

Another citizen might telegraph the same representative. This message contains information about a social event that the sender thinks would be interesting to the representative. Because it does not result in or involve the distribution of political resources, the telegram is not a political communication.

Three processes are essential to communication: sending information, receiving information, and having channels through which information can pass. One way to understand these ideas is to think about a television set. A television set acts as a channel of information. When you turn on your television set and get a picture, a television station is transmitting, or sending, information. The viewer is receiving that information.

Sending Information. In politics, individuals or groups send information in a variety of ways. For example, different interest groups regularly send messages to government leaders to influence their decisions. Interest groups sometimes "flood" public officials with letters that advocate the interest group's point of view about some public issue or problem.

The petition is another technique citizens use to communicate their views to leaders. (A *petition* is a formal, written request. Often a petition is signed by many people who support the request.) Groups often write their proposals in the form of public petitions. They try to obtain as many signatures as possible on the petition. Then, the group sends the petition to public officials whom they want to influence. During the Vietnam War, for example, many antiwar groups wrote petitions asking for an end to the war. They obtained thousands of signa-

tures on the petitions. Then, they sent them to the president and to members of Congress. Those who supported the war also used petitions to express their views to government leaders.

Massive public demonstrations and rallies are another means of political communication. (They are also examples of participation.) During the 1960s many civil rights organizations expressed their views to government officials through marches and rallies. Citizens against the war in Vietnam also communicated their opposition by mass demonstrations. On November 15, 1969, an estimated 250,000 people gathered in Washington, D.C. to protest U.S. involvement in Vietnam.

Individuals or groups often engage in activities in order to "make news." They hope this news will be reported on the front pages of newspapers and by television news programs. Sometimes interest groups arrange press conferences at which they can communicate their ideas to news reporters. Or, they send press releases to newspapers. By "making news" about themselves, people can communicate their ideas both to public officials and to the general public. In this way they hope to win support for their ideas.

Newspapers, television, and radio report on the activities of important government officials and communicate these ideas to the public. Sometimes public leaders make special use of the media in order to communicate more directly with the people. Presidents, for example, hold "fireside chats," make public statements, conduct press conferences, and appear on radio and television.

Receiving Information. People send information with the expectation that it will be received. However, no form of communication is always effective. Information that is sent is not always received. Or, it is not received by the correct audience. If you want to change government policy on employment, for example, it may not be effective to communicate your ideas only to your friends.

Channels of Information. In order to communicate effectively you must decide the best way to send information to be sure that it is received. To do this, you must clarify what you want to communicate, to whom, and how. For example, consider the question of employment again. Suppose you are seriously concerned about the unemployment rate among young adults. You want to try to do something about it. After some careful thought, you come up with several ideas you think could help solve the problem. What do you do now?

First, you must carefully outline just what you want to say. You must be sure that your ideas are well thought out and developed.

Then, you should figure out to whom you want to communicate your ideas. In the case of unemployment, you want to communicate your ideas to those people who can do something to solve the problem. Find out who in your community controls jobs. What companies hire young people? What public officials work in human resources training programs? What other citizens would be helpful in supporting ideas and solving problems?

Having determined the audience, you must decide how best to reach that audience. What channels of information would be best to use? Should you make appointments to talk to people? Should you circulate petitions? Should you write letters? Should you place an advertisement in the newspaper?

Usually, several different channels of information are appropriate. For example, you may not be able to talk to those in charge of human resources in your community. But you could write them a letter or send a petition. On the other hand, you may know someone in a company who hires young adults. The best way to "send" your ideas to that person might be in a face-to-face conversation. And if you want to tell many other citizens about your ideas, you might do it best with a petition or a newspaper advertisement.

When you identify channels, the main question you are concerned with is determining the access which a person or group has in sending information to another person or group. Some people can communicate their views directly to one another while others do not have such direct access.

Some people can easily send messages because they occupy an important office. The news media report their activities because of the positions they hold. In this instance status becomes a valuable political resource which allows a person to communicate. The following case is an example of such communication.

★ **A Trip to the South**

Just six months after his election as president, Jimmy Carter traveled to several southern states to talk with citizens. He wanted to inform them in detail of basic policies of his administration. Carter also wanted citizens' advice about policies which affected them. During his trip he spoke with thousands of people. Because many of his activities were carried on television, he frequently reached millions of Americans.

One of his stops was Yazoo City, Mississippi, population 12,000. There, in a school gym, he met with a large number of community residents. In responding to their questions he spoke about the federal budget, complained about high steel prices, and comforted citizens about soaring utility rates. The President engaged in this communication in order to affect the distribution of political resources. By meeting with the citizens of Yazoo City, he was able to communicate knowledge about the policies of his administration. As a result, he hoped to win popular support for his actions.

Sometimes individuals do not have resources such as status or wealth. For these citizens, effective communication involves working together with large numbers of individuals. Through this cooperation, communication can affect the distribution of resources. The following case describes such cooperation.

★ Clean Air Now

On January 7, 1970, citizens of Riverside, Redlands, and San Bernardino, California, delivered petitions to the California state legislature. The petitions contained 140,000 signatures. The purpose of this action was to call attention to the problem of smog in southern California. Citizens were angered by the lack of government action.

Part of the text of one petition read: "The pollution of our air continues year after year with no signs that smog control programs are clearing the air. . . . We want nothing less than clean air now." Placed end-to-end the petitions would have stretched a mile and a half. They were accepted on behalf of the then governor Ronald Reagan and the California legislature. The presentation of the petitions received news coverage on both radio and television at the local, state, and national levels.

The petition drive was co-sponsored by radio station KRNO, San Bernardino, and Clean Air Now, a citizen group in Riverside. Following the presentation the Clean Air Now newsletter stated: "The ultimate success of this effort . . . must be measured in the results which flow from this new public awareness."

This citizen action spread knowledge about problems of air pollution to many people. As a result of this and other efforts of southern California citizens the federal Environmental Protection Agency was pressured to investigate the problem and propose a solution.

1. Describe the process of communication reflected in the cases you have just read.
2. What resources might be used in political communication? What resources might be redistributed?

The MEANING of PARTICIPATION

Participation, or taking part, is one of the most frequent experiences in politics. Political participation is activity in which interests are organized in common action which involves the use and distribution of political resources in a group. For example, members of the Sierra Club are involved in political participation. They organize themselves in this group because they all have a common interest, which is to protect and preserve the environment. Through this organization, the members attempt to influence the distribution of resources to protect nature.

An election is another kind of political participation. In an election, voters take part in an organized activity. By voting they are affecting the distribution of resources like status, wealth, and support.

By participating politically, people organize their interests. Voters organize their interests to support a candidate. Club members organize around common interests. The case that follows describes participation in one group called Operation PUSH. As you read, identify the interests that are organized.

★ People United to Save Humanity

In Chicago, black leaders led by the Reverend Jesse L. Jackson have organized a national group called Operation PUSH. PUSH stands for "People United to Save Humanity." PUSH was formed to confront the problems of black Americans. It began by dealing with the question of employment. In April of 1974, Reverend Jackson said, "The threefold goal of our movement at this point . . . is to secure the jobs of those already working . . . , to get the unemployed employed, and to get those working but not making a livable wage organized."

From its Chicago base, PUSH coordinates its work with "satellites" in cities throughout the country. In doing so, it works closely with educators, ministers, and local leaders.

Operation PUSH is not a one-issue organization. As problems of blacks are identified, PUSH tries to solve them by organizing people throughout the country.

One important program sponsored by PUSH is called PUSH for Excellence. The program focuses on education for black Americans. Local government leaders and school officials from around the country are participating in PUSH for Excellence because of their interest in improving the quality of education for black Americans. The program opposes drugs and violence. It is against racism in schools.

In addition, PUSH proposes school-wide meetings to be held three times a year. At these meetings academic excellence would be honored just as athletic excellence is now recognized. PUSH for Excellence urges the mass media to give students awards for their cultural and academic achievements, just as they nominate students to all-city and all-state athletic teams. PUSH also backs city-wide study hours from 7:00 P.M. to 9:00 P.M. each night.

Reverend Jackson thinks that people can be more effective citizens if they acquire as much knowledge as possible while they are in school. He believes this knowledge will aid students as they seek employment after high school or if they decide to pursue a college education. Jackson has said: "I believe we need to give the people a vision. We need to tell our young people: . . . 'first and foremost we need to put your hands and your bodies and your minds to work building our communities.' What we must do for our young people is challenge them to put hope in their brains . . . ."

1. How has Jesse Jackson organized interests for participation in PUSH for Excellence?
2. In what ways could you participate in a program like PUSH?

Degree of Involvement. Jesse Jackson has organized individuals and groups with a similar interest. Not all of these people participate in the same ways, however. Participation involves taking roles. Unit 1 introduced you to these roles—observer, supporter, advocate, and organizer.

At a rally in Los Angeles, California, the Reverend Jesse Jackson asks students to pledge involvement in PUSH for Excellence.

In any political group, people participate in different ways all the time. For example, in PUSH for Excellence a variety of people and groups have become involved in the activities of the organization—community members, students, civic leaders, school administrators, and others. Some of these groups and individuals are more intensely involved than others are.

Some citizens act as observers of the PUSH for Excellence program. These people live in the communities where the program has become active. However, they have no direct and continuing involvement. Rather, they watch what is happening in the schools.

Parents often serve as supporters of PUSH for Excellence. Many of them work more closely with teachers than they have in the past. In addition, they come to school so that they can pick up their children's report cards. These parents who support the program do other things such as arrange evening study hours for their children.

In addition to those who observe and support PUSH for Excellence, there are also people who serve as advocates of the program. These people include both civic leaders and school administrators. They often speak out publicly about their experiences with PUSH for Excellence in the hopes that their views will persuade others to join.

Finally, participation in PUSH for Excellence involves organizers. In this case, Reverend Jackson and his Chicago-based staff match people with resources in order to effectively organize the program. Their participation is essential to the successful operation of PUSH for Excellence.

When participating in groups, people do not necessarily fill the same role all the time. For example, Reverend Jackson might serve as an organizer at one point from his Chicago-based headquarters. However, in speaking to students in a school in Hartford, Connecticut, he is serving as an advocate for his PUSH for Excellence program. When he watches others speak in support of his program, he is an observer. Jackson also acts as a supporter when he works to further the goals of PUSH for Excellence.

Observers, supporters, advocates, and organizers do different things when they participate in groups. For any group to make progress in organizing its interests, all these people are needed.

1. What resources do you think are redistributed because of participation in PUSH for Excellence?
2. What roles might you take in political participation? Describe a situation involving each role.

The MEANING of LEADERSHIP

Leadership exists in any group. Either one person or a group of people take the responsibility for organizing and directing members of a group. Political leadership is activity which organizes and directs people to affect the distribution of resources in a group. This definition is similar to the definition of participation. However, leadership involves the direction of those people who take part. It focuses on how these people are organized and directed toward a goal.

Reciprocity. Leadership concerns a relationship between leaders and followers called reciprocity. (*Reciprocity* means "mutual exchange.") Followers are those people who are being organized. They might be students of a school, residents of a community, citizens of a state, or members of any other group. Followers carry out the work and get things done. They interact regularly with leaders.

Several kinds of relationships exist between leaders and followers. Some relationships are *formal*. That is, they are based on established rules or laws. For example, a president has a formal relationship with Congress. It is outlined in the Constitution.

Other relationships may be *informal*. Citizens carrying out leadership activities may not have formal power. They must rely on their superior political skills, personal wealth, or access to important information in relating to followers.

Resources. Resources are redistributed as a result of political leadership. For example, suppose your community wants to make better use of the magazines and newspapers that citizens throw away. First, the goal must be identified and agreed upon. In this case, citizens might set a goal of developing a paper recycling program. Then, some person or group of people must take responsibility for organizing and directing the citizens of the community to save old paper and take it to a recycling center. The recycling center itself would have to be set up and organized.

As a result of organizing people for this purpose, knowledge about conservation will be spread throughout the community. Wealth may also be redistributed as the city spends less money on paper products. Money is saved because paper is reused. And money may be spent to set up and run the recycling center. Time is also used in different ways by citizens as they collect papers, and perhaps work in the center. In addition, status may also be redistributed to those who run the recycling center.

Trustee Leadership. Three types or styles of leadership are most common. Each involves a different amount of reciprocity, or a different relationship between leaders and followers. The term "trustee" describes one type of leadership. A person or a group who engages in this type of leadership believes that superior skills give them the authority to lead as they wish. People who lead as trustees feel they know what is in the best interests of their followers. They act accordingly. In a trustee relationship, followers often give their loyalty to leaders because the leaders are able to make things "work."

Former Mayor Richard Daley of Chicago related to citizens of the city as a trustee. Daley ran a tightly controlled city government in which he held tremendous authority. He controlled key political resources which gave him power in local, state, and national politics. For many people, Daley made Chicago "work." Because of what he was able to accomplish, many citizens put their trust in him. They gave him a free hand to do what he thought was best. Therefore, he frequently carried out tasks consulting only those individuals and groups he chose to consult.

Broker Leadership. The term "broker" describes a second type of leadership. This type involves a great deal of interaction between leaders and followers. People or groups are able to lead as brokers both because they control key political resources, and because they interact frequently with their followers.

Many governors who engage in effective leadership relate to their followers as brokers. They often have a good understanding of the political structure of their state, a necessity for their election to office. This knowledge is also essential if they are to work successfully with the variety of political groups in their state.

For some governors, meetings with citizens of the state provide an opportunity to learn of public opinion and to share views about important issues. This interaction is an effective way of gaining popular support.

Certainly, all governors are not the same. However, throughout the 1970s many of them have found it valuable to increase their interaction with the citizens of their states. Often this helps identify problems which are of importance to the people. It also helps outline solutions.

In 1975, for example, Governor Jerry Apodaca of New Mexico began setting up five Citizens' Service Centers. These centers were located away from Santa Fe, the capital of New Mexico. They provided a place where Governor Apodaca could interact

Governor Jerry Apodaca of New Mexico believes that a governor should discuss issues with citizens to stimulate the exchange of views.

with many of the citizens of New Mexico on a regular basis.

Delegate Leadership. The term "delegate" reflects a third style of leadership. In a delegate relationship, leaders often respond directly to the desires of their followers. People and groups who lead as delegates listen as carefully as possible to followers. Then they act in strict accordance with followers' goals. For example, elected representatives may feel that their job is to carry out the views of their constituents. (Of course, elected representatives may also lead as trustees or brokers.) Many political leaders believe what this state legislator said: "My job is to act exactly as I think my constituents would act if they were here. Someone has to represent the views of our district in the state legislature. That's what I was elected to do."

As you analyze politics, remember to look for different ways in which leaders relate to their followers. The style of leadership you find in a particular situation may depend on the issue involved. A president of the United States, for example, acts in all three leadership styles. A president may act as a trustee leader when he or she has clear constitutional authority. On the other hand, a president who needs congressional approval acts as a broker. Then, the president needs to make his or her views known and to hear the views of others. And, a president acts as a delegate, following the wishes of the American people.

1. Distinguish differences among delegate, trustee, and broker styles of leadership.
2. For each of these categories, name one leader you know who exemplifies that style.

The Skill of Identifying Concepts

You have studied four important categories of political activities—decision-making, communication, participation, and leadership. Each of these categories represents what is called a *concept*. Understanding concepts and how to identify them is a valuable skill. With it you can better study and understand political life.

WHAT IS a CONCEPT?

A *concept* is a name or idea that describes all of the objects or activities that share essential qualities. "Table," for example, is a concept. This is not a concept: "a 6-foot-long piece of mahogany with four legs." Neither is this: "the place where we eat breakfast every morning." Those are specific descriptions. However, both of those descriptions are part of the concept "table." The concept "table" means "a flat slab held up by legs or some other support." Coffee tables, operating tables, card tables—all are included in the concept "table."

"Table" is a category of objects that share certain qualities. The essential qualities of tables are these: flat, slab, held up by some support. A human body has two legs but is not a flat slab. A road may be flat but it is not a supported slab. Human bodies and roads lack qualities that are essential to the idea of "table."

```
1. (a) Describe three things, beings, or activi-
   ties that could be included in each of
   these concepts: bird, human being, paint-
   ing. (b) What qualities are shared by the
   items you listed for each concept?
2. (a) What concept includes all of the fol-
   lowing activities: football, swimming, jog-
   ging, tennis? (b) What qualities are shared
   by these activities? (c) Write a definition
   of the concept.
```

Some concepts are as clear-cut as "table." Others are more complex. Political concepts like power or democracy are more abstract than "table" or "fruit" or "weather." Nonetheless, these political concepts are general ideas that describe activities that share essential qualities.

Examine the concept "participation," for example. It is a general idea that includes all activities in which people take part in a common action. Participation is political when the activities result in the distribution of political resources in a group.

Based on this definition of the concept "political participation," you can classify activities. Working for a mayoral candidate is part of the concept "political participation," for example. Your interests in a candidate and what he or she stands for are organized in campaign work. As a result of your taking part, your candidate has more resources like time and loyalty. If the candidate wins, your participation will have helped. Thus your participation will have distributed power to your candidate instead of to another. On the other hand, participating in a tennis match is not part of the concept "political participation." Why not?

```
1. List five activities that are part of the con-
   cept "political participation."
2. What qualities do these five activities
   share?
```

USING CONCEPTS

The use of concepts allows us to identify and describe objects, types of behavior, and events in the world around us. When the labels and definitions that constitute concepts are commonly understood, they allow us to communicate better with each other. They enable us to sort what we see and feel into categories that other people can also understand.

For example, the concept "political leadership" allows us to *identify* and *describe* an important relationship between people. We can use the concept to describe the relationships between governmental leaders and their constituents, between the principal and the students at a high school, or between any leaders and followers. Political leadership is a useful concept because it permits us to *distinguish* what is going on from some other possible activity.

213

Some concepts are more useful than others because they have more meaning or *significance*. The concepts "decision-making," "communication," "participation," and "leadership" are significant political concepts. They allow us to identify and describe political life. They aid us in understanding how and why things happen the way they do.

As you use concepts, remember that they are valuable tools for the study of politics. These rules will help you use concepts most effectively:

1. Use concepts to identify and describe.
2. Use concepts to distinguish.
3. Use concepts that are significant.

> 1. Use a concept to identify two activities you performed today.
> 2. Use a concept to describe three people whom you know.
> 3. Use two concepts to distinguish between different activities you perform every day.

The following case describes recent efforts of citizens who have taken an interest in television for children. The case illustrates the variety in political activity presented in this chapter. By working with this case, you can practice skills in using the concepts you have learned in the chapter.

Read the case carefully, then identify examples of the four kinds of political activity you have learned about in this chapter. For instance, make a list noting all of the examples of decision-making, communication, leadership, and participation you read about. Then, identify other concepts described in the case.

★ **Speaking for Children**

"[You] should be able to let a child watch a child's program without constantly looking over his shoulder . . . TV is a stranger in everybody's living room, talking to their children . . . [To put] a child of 2 to 11 to an intellectual contest with an American advertising agency is about as fair as putting a grade-school boxer into the ring with George Foreman."

Peggy Charren
President, Action for
Children's Television

At the time of this statement, in 1974, it was estimated that more than 96% of all American households had at least one television set. It was estimated that 45% had two sets.

The television programs which enter homes through these sets are created by three major television networks, as well as the public broadcasting system (PBS). While PBS receives funds through the government and gifts, the three networks are supported by the sale of advertising time. Large companies spend millions of dollars a year to buy such advertising time. One minute of commercial time can cost well over $25,000.

In 1976 the sale of time to advertise children's products made $400 million for the three networks. Major cereal and toy

treat TV with T.L.C.

LOOK AT TV WITH YOUR CHILD!

LOOK OUT FOR TV BEHAVIOR YOUR CHILD MIGHT IMITATE

LOOK FOR TV CHARACTERS WHO CARE ABOUT OTHERS

LOOK FOR WOMEN WHO ARE COMPETENT IN A VARIETY OF JOBS

LOOK FOR PEOPLE FROM A VARIETY OF CULTURAL & ETHNIC GROUPS

LOOK FOR HEALTHY SNACKS IN THE KITCHEN INSTEAD OF ON TV

LOOK FOR IDEAS FOR WHAT TO DO WHEN YOU SWITCH OFF THE SET...

READ A BOOK...DRAW A PICTURE ...PLAY A GAME

This excerpt from a pamphlet illustrates how Action for Children's Television uses communication as a political activity to promote its views.

companies, for example, each year spend more than $10 million apiece to advertise their products. Much of this money is spent for commercials on children's television programs.

Many of these programs are shown on Saturday morning. Some parents think that Saturday morning television provides their children with entertainment and keeps them busy. Some parents say that their children learn important information from watching these shows. Others, however, believe that many Saturday morning programs are of little value to children. What is more, they say, the commercials with these programs lead children to nag their parents to buy a particular product. Parents feel that, often, these products are not beneficial.

Like many others, Peggy Charren of Newtonville, Massachusetts, objected strongly to some of the programs her children watched. She particularly disliked the commercials that appeared with the shows. Instead of turning her television off, Ms. Charren decided to do something about the problem. In 1968 she and four other parents founded an organization they called Action for Children's Television (ACT).

ACT focused first on the content of children's programs. Then, in an important decision, the group chose another alternative. It decided to focus its efforts on commercials aimed at children. Members thought this was the best way to have a long-term impact on children's television. ACT believes that young children should be protected from advertisements they cannot fully understand or evaluate. The group argues that being subjected to professional advertising on television makes unfair use of children.

During its early years ACT became involved in several activities. It published a newsletter to inform people of its actions and purposes.

In 1970 several ACT members traveled to Washington to petition the Federal Communications Commission. They asked the commission to stop commercials on children's television and to stop hosts of these shows from advertising products for children.

By Christmas 1971 ACT had filed another petition. This one was filed with the Federal Trade Commission. ACT asked the commission to prevent the selling of toys to children via television. And in the spring of 1972 ACT asked the Federal Trade Commission to stop drug companies from advertising vitamins in ads directed toward children.

In 1972, in response to pressure by ACT and other parents, three drug companies voluntarily withdrew ads for their products. The next year the National Association of Broadcasters said that hosts of children's shows could not participate in selling products to children via television. ACT was not responsible alone for the action of the drug companies and the National Association of Broadcasters. However, it provided necessary citizen input on these important issues.

Today, ACT has more than 9,000 members. The organization reaches people in many ways. Members have given testimony before congressional committees investigating broadcast practices. As you read, it has petitioned several commissions to take specific action regarding advertising on children's television.

There are more than 100 "ACT contacts" in more than 100 cities across the nation. These people are available to speak to various groups and to provide information to anyone who asks. "ACT contacts" also organize their own meetings of local parent-teacher association groups. Furthermore, ACT develops books and pamphlets to help citizens learn how they can become active in support of better children's television.

1. What political activities are carried out by ACT? Give examples.
2. What political concepts could you use to describe ACT's activities? Give examples.
3. What other concepts are illustrated in the case?

The North Valley Community Center in Albuquerque, New Mexico, is a multi-purpose neighborhood center. Among its services are health care and recreation for the elderly.

Citizens are involved in many political activities through the center. For example, Maria Martinez helps a welfare client decide the best way to solve his problems through existing government channels (bottom left photo). In the top right photo a staff member is helping a local resident write a letter to the city council to complain about the lack of plumbing in her neighborhood.

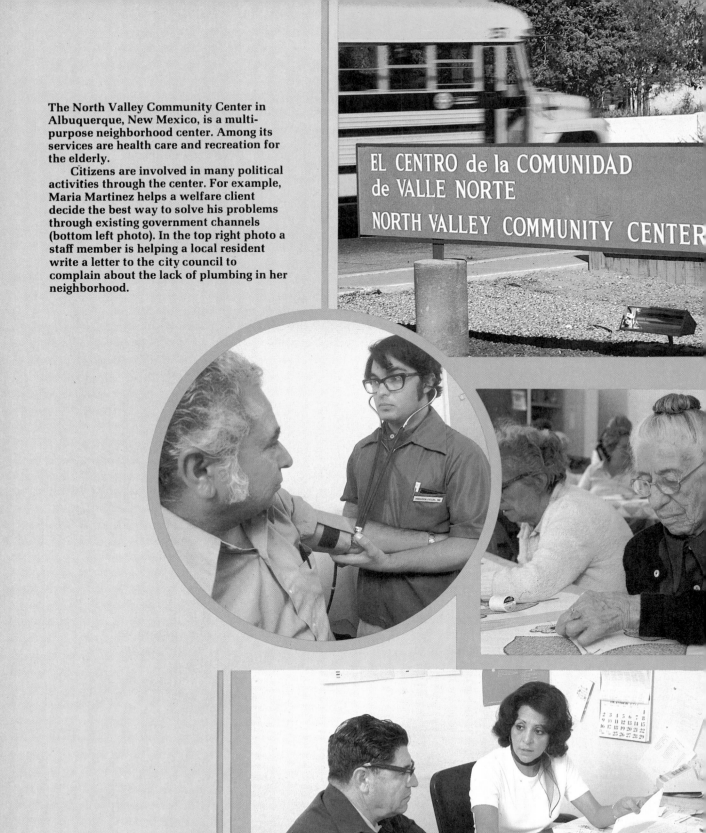

The Center also directs the participation of local citizens as they repair a home for winter (far right photo). The director of the Center works closely with the city government (bottom right photo).

Chapter Review

1. Define *political activity,* and describe examples of activities which you consider to be political.

2. List the four main categories of political activities, with examples of each. Check any specific activities in which you can or do take part.

3. Review the three fundamental elements in decision-making. Then describe a real or hypothetical decision-making situation in your school or community. Identify each element in the decision-making process.

4. How does leadership affect the distribution of political resources?

5. How does communication affect the distribution of political resources?

6. What are some of the various ways of sending information? In your opinion, which are the most effective politically? Explain.

7. "In order for information to be an effective political resource, the proper channels of communication first must be determined." Explain the meaning of this statement.

8. How can citizen participation influence the distribution of resources within a political system?

9. Summarize the three types of political leadership. If you were an elected leader, which style would you adopt? Explain.

10. What important functions do concepts serve? What are the main political concepts discussed in this chapter?

Chapter Vocabulary

Define the following terms.

political activity	leadership	trustee
decision-making	alternative	broker
communication	petition	delegate
participation	reciprocity	concept

Chapter Analysis

1. Establish criteria for determining whether or not an activity is political. Test your criteria through an examination of your own daily activities. Are your activities political? Why or why not?

2. In the past 20 years, television has become an important means of communication. In essay form, discuss the ways in which the use of television can be an important and an effective political activity. Consider the question from the following viewpoints: the news broadcaster, the political candidate, the private citizen, the elected official, and the interest group.

3. If you want to write a letter to your representative, what factors make it most successful as a political activity? Write such a letter on an issue of importance to you.

4. Explain the ways in which politics and political resources are concepts. In other words, what qualities are shared by all activities, objects, or ideas that make up each of these concepts?

1. Plan ways in which you could engage in decision-making, communication, participation, and leadership in your school or community. Write proposals for political activity in these areas. Describe resources you would use and distribute through your activities.

2. Investigate an important local, state, national, or international leader. Be prepared to give an oral report analyzing the leadership style, activities, and traits that have made this person successful.

3. With other class members, identify important decisions that have been made in your school or community in the last few months. Then analyze the process by which these decisions were made.

Chapter Activities

The Political Image Merchants: Strategies in the New Politics, edited by Ray Hiebert, Robert Jones, Ernest Lotito and John Lorenz (Acropolis Books: Washington, D.C.), 1971.
> A clearly written discussion of various aspects of politics, in many short articles by different authors. Includes numerous concrete examples of political activity.

Practical Political Action: A Guide for Young Citizens, The Lincoln Filene Center for Citizenship and Public Affairs (Houghton Mifflin Company: Boston, MA).
> Discusses ways of participating in electoral politics with special attention to the precinct level.

Presidential Television, Newton N. Minow, John B. Martin, Lee M. Mitchell (Basic Books, Inc.: New York, NY), 1973.
> Presents an account of the role of television communication in presidential politics.

Decision-Making in the White House: The Olive Branch or the Olives, Theodore C. Sorenson (Columbia University Press: New York, NY), 1963.
> An inside look at the process of decision-making in the White House of President John F. Kennedy, written by a man who served as Special Counsel to President Kennedy.

Chapter Bibliography

Chapter Objectives

★ **To analyze how state governments function**

★ **To apply the concepts of leadership, decision-making, communication, and participation to state political activity**

★ **To develop skills in participating as a supporter**

★ **To develop the skill of interpreting evidence**

STATE POLITICAL ACTIVITIES

Chapter 8 introduces you to political activity at the state level. It describes the role of states in our federal system. It also discusses the powers exercised by the branches of state government.

By examining state government, you will realize the impact that it has on your daily life. For example, the law that requires you to attend school is a state law. It is the state that decides on standards and requirements for all students in your state. Also, think of the driver's test that you have taken or may be planning to take. This test is prepared and given by your state. Each state passes its own traffic laws and establishes speed limits. It also uses state funds to build and maintain state highways.

In this chapter you will continue your study of the roles which people play as members of groups. Chapter 8 focuses on the supporter role, which was first presented on page 37 and which you will now study in greater detail. In addition, the skill of interpreting evidence is introduced. This instruction will build on the other skills that you have been developing throughout this program.

States in the Federal System

As you learned in Chapter 6, when the first 13 states approved the Constitution, they agreed to give up certain powers that they had enjoyed under the Articles of Confederation. They gave some important powers to the national government. The powers that were given to the national government are referred to as *delegated powers*. Some of these delegated powers are ones with which you are probably quite familiar. The powers to coin and print money, regulate trade between states, and conduct foreign relations are examples of delegated powers.

The states also set aside, or *reserved*, important powers for themselves. The Tenth Amendment to the Constitution outlines this division of powers.

"The powers not delegated to the United States by the Constitution, nor prohibited by it to the states, are reserved to the states respectively, or to the people."

(There is an earlier discussion of delegated and reserved powers in Chapter 6 on pages 194 and 196.)

Before examining the reserved powers of the states, first consider what states are not allowed to do. Article I, Section 10, of the Constitution and the Fourteenth Amendment present restrictions upon the states. According to the Constitution, states shall not do the following:

1. Make treaties or alliances. (An *alliance* is an agreement made among people or groups to further common interests.)
2. Coin money.
3. Use anything but gold or silver in payment of debts.
4. Impair the obligations of contracts.
5. Grant any title of nobility.
6. Pass any laws that deny "due process' or "equal protection" under the law.

In addition, states shall not, without the consent of Congress,

7. Tax imports or exports.
8. Tax vessels.
9. Keep armed forces in time of peace.
10. Enter into any agreement with a foreign power.
11. Engage in war, unless invaded or presented with immediate danger.

The Constitution also places obligations on the states in their relations with each other. Each state must give "full faith and credit" to the laws of other states. No state can favor its own citizens over people from other states. Finally, states cannot settle disputes between themselves by contract. Rather, disagreements should be submitted to the Supreme Court of the United States.

In addition to these formal prohibitions, states may not interfere with interstate commerce or with the exercise of national powers. Beyond these restrictions, there are no formal limits on the powers of state governments other than those set in individual state constitutions.

RESERVED POWERS It is impossible to detail all the powers reserved to the states. None of the state constitutions provides an all-inclusive list specifying state authority. However, certain powers are commonly stated in most state constitutions. In general, states are empowered to carry out the following activities.

Conduct Elections. All state governments conduct and monitor elections for local, state, and national offices. They decide most of the qualifications that citizens must meet in order to vote. However, state voting requirements must be in accordance with

From Territory to Statehood

You've learned about the first 13 states, which were organized after the American colonies declared independence from Great Britain in 1776. Each of these 13 states officially became a part of the United States upon ratifying the Constitution, written in 1787.

Several states (Kentucky, Vermont, Tennessee) were carved out of territories in the 1790s. The United States acquired vast amounts of new land in the 1800s. As a result, new states were formed from these lands. Most of today's states were originally part of these territories.

Alaska and Hawaii are the most recent admissions to statehood. They became states in 1959. Alaska was purchased from Russia in 1867, and Hawaii was annexed (added) to the United States in 1898. American territories today include American Samoa, Guam, and the Virgin Islands. Puerto Rico is considered a self-governing commonwealth.

Article IV, Section 3 of the Constitution provides that new states may be admitted by Congress. Specific rules have been set to define the procedure for becoming a state. To become a state, people of a territory must petition Congress for statehood. If Congress agrees to this petition, the people then elect delegates, who draw up a state constitution. The constitution must be approved by the people of the territory and by Congress. Congress then votes to admit the territory as a state.

Territories have sought statehood for some of the following reasons:

Representation at the National Level. Statehood allows people to have representatives in the United States Congress. For example, before it became a state, the territory of Hawaii had one nonvoting delegate to represent its citizens in the United States Congress. While this person could observe activities at the national level and report them back to the citizens of Hawaii, the delegate had no power in Congress. Once it became a state, Hawaii was immediately represented by two senators. In addition, it elected members to the United States House of Representatives.

Vote for National Leaders. Before gaining statehood, the citizens of a territory cannot participate in voting for either president or vice-president of the United States. Yet, the president is the person who chooses the territorial governor as well as most territorial judges. Upon gaining statehood, citizens can participate in national elections.

Self-Government. Statehood also enables citizens to have control over the election of their state and local leaders. They can elect leaders without seeking approval from anyone outside the state. Also, states can pass their own legislation. For example, before Hawaii became a state, it had a constitution called the Organic Act. Under this act, a territorial legislature was established. While this legislature had the power to pass laws, the Congress of the United States had the authority to change or declare invalid any law passed by the legislature. As a result of statehood, Hawaii has a legislature whose actions are no longer subject to approval by the United States Congress.

Constitutional provisions, national laws, and Supreme Court decisions.

Congress determines when national elections are held. It is up to the states, however, to decide when elections in their state will be held for the governorship and the legislature. States also decide whether an open or closed primary system will operate, and what kind of balloting procedures will be followed.

Establish and Maintain Public Schools. The federal government does not have the power to enact educational laws. This power is reserved to the states. State legislatures pass laws regarding instructional and teaching requirements. Through the State Department of Education, local school systems are supervised by the state.

Within state guidelines, local communities are allowed to run their own school systems. For example, the school board in your area makes important decisions regarding the number of schools in a district, the hiring of teachers, and the range of courses offered to students. However, these decisions cannot be contrary to established state policies.

Exercise Policing Power. In addition to supervising elections and education, state legislatures exercise *policing power*. This means that legislators act to protect and to promote public safety, health, and welfare. As a result, states may enact child labor laws, set traffic speed limits, and prohibit gambling. For example, in Maine it is illegal to sell liquor to anyone under the age of 20. And in Kansas state inspectors can conduct unannounced inspections of adult home-care facilities.

Establish Local Governments. One of the main powers of state governments is the establishment of local governments within the state. Local governments of all types—counties, cities, towns, townships, villages, etc.—receive their powers from state government. The constitution of each state describes the organization and powers that

levels of government in that state are to have.

Other Powers. Most state governments also have many other important powers. States determine laws for marriage and divorce, corporation charters, and professional licenses. They also are responsible for trade, highways, utilities, and construction within their borders. Laws vary among the 50 states. For example, in Alabama persons under 21 cannot marry without parental consent. In New York, however, parental consent to marriage is not necessary for anyone over 18.

In exercising their powers, states may not pass laws or take actions that conflict with the Constitution or federal laws. As the Constitution states, national laws are the "supreme law of the land."

1. Explain the concept of reserved powers.
2. Choose one of the reserved powers described in this section. From what you know, how is that power carried out in your state?

CONCURRENT POWERS In addition to reserved powers, states also share powers with the federal government. Certain powers have been granted in the Constitution to the federal government. Unless any of these powers are forbidden to the states, the states may exercise them concurrently, or along with, the federal government. As you learned in Chapter 6, these are called *concurrent powers*.

Examples of concurrent powers are the authority to raise money, spend money, and set minimum wage standards. The federal and state governments can also enforce laws, punish lawbreakers, and provide for the health, safety, and welfare of citizens.

Hawaii Becomes a State

Hawaii became the fiftieth state of the union on August 21, 1959. The Hawaiian Islands had been annexed to the United States in 1898 and given territorial status in 1900.

As a territory, Hawaii was headed by a territorial governor, appointed by the president of the United States. The heads of various government departments were appointed by the territorial governor. Justices on the territorial Supreme Court as well as other judges were appointed by the president of the United States.

A legislature was established. It was composed of 2 houses—a senate containing 15 members and a house of representatives containing 30 members. While the territorial legislature had the power to pass laws, the Congress of the United States had the authority to change or to declare invalid any law passed by the legislature. Hawaiians also had one non-voting delegate to the United States Congress.

As a territory, Hawaii received federal aid from the United States government. It also had the protection of the United States armed forces and enjoyed trade advantages. Despite these advantages, there were those in Hawaii, who as early as 1900 suggested that Hawaii become a state, not merely a territory. Statehood would give Hawaiians representation in Congress. It would also enable citizens to vote for the president of the United States and for officials on the state and local levels. Both these rights were denied them as long as Hawaii remained a territory.

Until the 1930s, many influential Hawaiians in the sugar and pineapple industries opposed statehood. In the 1930s, sugar exports began to decline. At this time, sugar interests decided to favor a "closer relationship" with the United States.

A 1940 vote authorized by the territorial legislature showed that a majority of Hawaiians favored statehood. The statehood movement was interrupted by World War II. On December 7, 1941, United States ships stationed at Pearl Harbor were attacked by the Japanese air force. As a result of this attack, the United States entered World War II. The war was an opportunity for many Hawaiians to demonstrate their loyalty to the United States. Citizens of the territory carried out their military duties with great distinction, and many were honored following the war.

The movement for statehood gained strength after the war. In 1959, Congress approved legislation granting statehood to Hawaii. The bill was passed by Congress and signed by President Eisenhower in March of that year. Three months later, the people of Hawaii indicated their desire for statehood by voting overwhelmingly in favor of becoming the fiftieth state of the United States.

Raise and Spend Money. The power to raise and spend money is important to states. It is up to each state to decide how funds will be spent on the many services that it provides. (Figure 8-1 shows how state revenues were divided among major services in 1974.)

Approximately 80 percent of the money that states spend comes from state taxes of one kind or another. Property taxes, sales taxes, income taxes, and taxes on business corporations represent the four largest sources. Revenues from various utilities and from state-operated liquor stores provide a smaller amount.

In 1974, states received 17.6 percent of their income from the federal government.

One way the federal government has provided this assistance is through *grants-in-aid* programs. Through these programs, the federal government has made money available in the areas of employment and training, human resources, and highways. This type of aid was used widely in the 1960s. States and communities applied to the federal government to obtain money for a specific purpose. When the money was granted, guidelines were set over how the money was used. As of 1975, more than 500 major grant-in-aid programs had been offered to states.

President Nixon began *revenue sharing.* (*Revenue* is income produced by a given source.) A revenue sharing law, known as the State and Local Fiscal Assistance Act, was passed in 1972. It provided for the federal government to return to the states a percentage of the money it collected from them in federal income taxes. The states could then determine how to use the money. With the establishment of the act, there were cutbacks in the grants-in-aid programs to the states. In recent years, through both grants-in-aid and revenue sharing, more than one fifth of all state revenues have come from the federal government.

Set Minimum Wage Standards. The power to set guidelines for minimum wages is shared by state and federal governments. (*Minimum wages* are the base salary which employers must pay employees.) For example, in 1977 the federal government legislated the minimum wage to be $3.10 by January 1980. However, federal minimum wage standards apply only to categories of workers such as those employed by large interstate corporations. (*Interstate corporations* are companies that do business in several states.) All other employee categories fall under state minimum wage laws. For example, individuals are subject to state laws if they work for a retail business that makes an annual profit less than a minimum set by the federal government.

As a result of this concurrent power, wage standards vary within states. They also differ from state to state. For example, in New York the industrial commissioner assembles a wage board that issues orders. These orders regulate the wages of workers not included in the federal law. In some cases the New York laws allow higher hourly wages than federal standards. This is not always the case. For example, in 1977

Figure 8-1

HOW STATES SPENT THEIR MONEY, 1976

ITEM	PERCENT OF TOTAL EXPENDITURES
Education	38.0
Public Welfare	12.3
Highways	9.4
Health and Hospitals	8.1
Police Protection and Correction	5.2
Sanitation and Sewage	3.2
Natural Resources	1.8
Housing and Urban Renewal	1.2
All Other	16.8

Source: Statistical Abstract of the U.S. 1978

Oklahoma raised the minimum state wage to $2.00. This was lower than the $2.30 minimum wage established by the federal government for employees of large interstate corporations.

Establish Courts and Correctional Facilities. The federal government has its own court and penal systems. (*Penal* means relating to or involving punishment.) These facilities are used for cases that involve federal laws. Cases that involve a state law are tried in state courts. Each state has the power to establish a court system to interpret the laws of the state. Each state can also build a prison system to provide correctional facilities for those who break the laws. The state judicial systems handle about 90 percent of the civil and criminal court cases in the United States.

Provide Health, Safety, and Welfare. Both the state and federal governments are concerned with providing services to the American people. Both levels of government have established programs to aid the unemployed, the handicapped, the elderly, and the poor. Sometimes state and federal governments work together to administer these programs. For example, although the federal government has provided a food stamp program, the states often set guidelines on who is eligible for program benefits.

1. Explain the concept of concurrent powers.
2. Choose one of the concurrent powers described in this section. From what you know, explain how that power is carried out in your state.

STRUCTURE of STATE GOVERNMENT

The 50 states which make up the United States range in size from Alaska, which is the largest state in area, to Rhode Island, the smallest state. Twelve states have populations of over five million people. Four states have populations of less than half a million people.

The states vary greatly in geography, climate, and natural resources. The jobs that people have and the ways they live are very different as a result.

Although there is great diversity among the states, there are also a number of important similarities. Many of these similarities stem from the common powers and organization of state government.

As you read in Chapter 6, each state has its own constitution, or plan for government. State constitutions differ in many ways. They are alike, however, in that each contains the rules of how state government is to be organized and how it is to function.

The constitutions in each of our 50 states provide for three separate branches, or areas, of government. These are the legislative, executive, and judicial branches. Each branch has separate powers defined by the state constitution. As in the federal government, state government is organized in a system of checks and balances.

1. List at least five questions that you have about the structure and function of state government.
2. Look for answers to these questions as you learn about the three branches of state government in the following pages.

The State Legislative Branch

The legislative branch of state government is responsible for making state laws. The law-making body is called the state legislature in 26 states, the general assembly in 19, the legislative assembly in 3, and the general court in 2. Members of the state legislature, referred to as *legislators,* are elected by the people of the state.

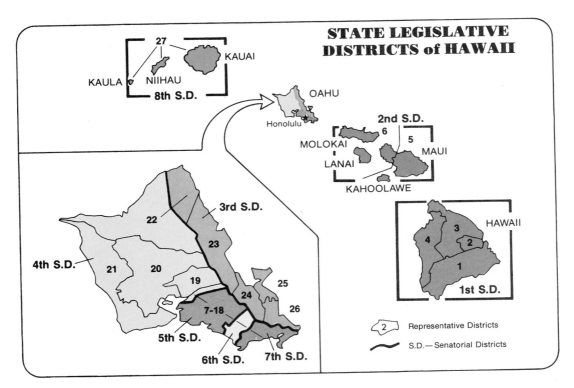

Figure 8-2

As you read in Chapter 6, in 49 states the legislature is composed of two houses—an upper house and a lower house. This is known as a *bicameral,* or two-chamber, system. While names differ from state to state, the upper house is usually called the state senate. The lower house is usually called the state house of representatives. Nebraska is the only state which has a *unicameral* legislature, consisting of one body of representatives.

In bicameral legislatures, there are more members in the house of representatives than in the senate. However, members of the senate represent larger districts than do members of the house. Therefore, each senator has many more constituents than each house member. (A *constituent* is one of a group who elects another person to represent him or her in a public office.) Figure 8-2 shows an example of legislative districts.

The way in which seats in the state legislature are *apportioned,* or distributed, is an important decision. In the past, many districts were determined on the basis of geography. In other words, legislative seats were distributed among districts of similar size.

However, the population size was often different from one district to another. As a result, people in rural areas often had proportionately greater representation in the state legislature than those in urban areas.

In 1964, the Supreme Court of the United States issued a decision that gave equal representation to citizens in the state legislatures. In the ruling *Reynolds* v. *Sims,* the Supreme Court decided "the size in *both* houses of a bicameral state legislature must be apportioned on a population basis."

In upholding the decision of the Court, Chief Justice Earl Warren said the following. "Legislators represent people, not trees or acres. Legislators are elected by voters, not farms or cities or economic interests."

As a result of this ruling, state legislatures periodically *reapportion,* or adjust, the distribution of legislative seats. They do this to account for changes in population. The effect has been to shift political influence from rural areas to suburban and urban areas. Therefore, as more people move to metropolitan regions, increased attention is given to problems associated with urban development.

The legislature provides citizens with their most direct representation in state government. By communicating with state legislators, citizens can actively participate in state politics.

LEGISLATORS To become a member of a state legislature, a person must be a United States citizen. In addition, most states have set the age of 21 as the minimum age for members of the state house of representatives and 25 as the minimum age for members of the state senate. Another requirement for election to a state legislature is residence in the state for a given period of time. This amount of time varies from state to state.

The salaries received by state legislators vary also. In 1977–8, a legislator in the state of California received $61,599 for a two-year term of office. This was the highest pay of any state in the country. The lowest pay was received by New Hampshire legislators, who received $200 for a two-year term of office.

Term length varies. In most states, the term for a member of the house of representatives is two years. The term for a member of the senate is four years in most states. In some states, however, senators serve two-year terms.

In most states, membership in the house or the senate is a part-time job. Depending on the state, legislatures meet either each year or every other year. The length of each legislative session varies, but it is usually 120 days or less. If an urgent matter develops between regular sessions, the state governor has the power to call the legislature into *special session.*

When the legislature is in regular session, legislators either live in or commute to the state capital. When the legislature is not in session, most legislators occupy other jobs, although they are always available to their constituents.

1. What are the basic qualifications to be a member of a state legislature?
2. What effect can state legislators have on the distribution of resources in their state?

THE COMMITTEE SYSTEM Figure 8–3 provides a list of committees organized in the Texas legislature. These committees are typical of those found in other state legislatures. Permanent committees are referred to

The lower houses of bicameral legislatures are known by a variety of names. The one in Virginia, shown here, is called the House of Delegates.

COMMITTEES in the TEXAS LEGISLATURE

SENATE STANDING COMMITTEES		
Administration	Appropriations	Human Resources
Economic Development	Business and Industry	Insurance
Education	Calendars	Intergovernmental Affairs
Finance	Constitutional Amendments	Judiciary
Human Resources	Criminal Jurisprudence	Judicial Affairs
Intergovernmental Relations	Elections	Liquor Regulation
Jurisprudence	Employment Practices	Local and Consent Calendars
Natural Resources	Energy Resources	Natural Resources
State Affairs	Environmental Affairs	Public Education
HOUSE STANDING COMMITTEES	Financial Institutions	Regents, Compacts, and Districts
Agriculture and Livestock	Government Organization	Rules
	Health Services	Security and Sanctions
	Higher Education	State Affairs
	House Administration	Transportation
		Ways and Means

Figure 8-3   Source: *Chief Elected and Administrative Officials.* Legislative Reference Library, 1979

as *standing committees.* The number of committees in state legislatures is usually not less than 20 and not more than 60. Those committees that meet between legislative sessions are referred to as *interim committees.* In most states, both houses of the legislature have their own committees. The exceptions are those few states where members of both houses work together on *joint committees.*

Committees in the state legislature are important for several reasons. First, most legislatures are too large to work effectively as one group. Therefore, members are assigned to smaller committees. Here most of the real work is done. Members of committees become especially knowledgeable in their field. Members often have a special interest in the area for which the committee is responsible. Committees play an important role in making laws.

1. Explain the difference between a standing committee, an interim committee, and a joint committee.

2. What is the function of the committee system in state legislatures?

3. How can the committee system affect legislative decisions regarding who gets what in the state?

HOW a BILL BECOMES a LAW

There are several basic steps in the creation of a state law. In the first stages of the legislative process, a bill is written. (A *bill* is a draft of a law presented to the state legislature for enactment.) A bill can be drafted by an individual legislator, a group of legislators, a lobbyist, or an attorney representing an interest group. In several states, citizens can propose bills through an initiative or a referendum. (See pages 83–85.) In some instances, bills are submitted to the state legislature by the office of the state attorney general. This office customarily drafts proposals for the state governor and other state agencies. A bill may be introduced in either house of a state legislature.

After legislation is submitted, it is usually referred to a *legislative reference service.* This is commonly a division of the state library or a part of the legislature itself. Specialists employed by the service do research to ensure that there is no conflict between the proposed state law and any federal laws. They also help in final drafting of a bill.

Once prepared, a bill is read before the house in which it has been introduced—the house of representatives, for example. Members make a second reading to determine which standing committee will work on it.

While a bill is in committee, open hearings are held. At these hearings, citizens can offer their views to the legislators. Based upon these hearings and their own careful study, committees often add amendments.

The bill plus amendments in the committee report is then submitted to the entire house for a third and final reading and a vote. At this point, all the legislators have to decide whether or not they will vote in favor of the bill.

Voting can occur in a number of ways. A *voice vote* can be taken in which the volume of responses for or against an issue determines the outcome. The presiding officer can ask for a *division of the house*. In this instance, members register their responses on a bill by standing. If a *roll call vote* is called, legislators record their votes by saying "yea" or "nay" as their names are read.

In order for a bill to be passed by the house, it must be approved by a majority of all members of the house (not just those present for the vote). A bill may be referred back to committee for further study, approved by the entire house, or rejected.

If passed by the house, a bill then goes through a similar process in the state senate. If passed there, some states provide that any differences between the house and senate versions of the bill be ironed out in a *conference committee*. Representatives from the house and senate work jointly on conference committees. In states without conference committees, the senate version of the bill goes back to the house for approval.

Once a bill has passed in both the state house and senate, the bill is sent to the governor's office. If signed, the bill becomes a part of state law. The governor can also veto, or reject, the bill. If this happens, the bill can become law only if a majority of both houses vote to override the governor's veto.

1. Outline the steps involved for a bill to become a law.
2. Based on what you've read about state legislatures, identify the variety of political activities which occurs in them.
3. What political activities are reflected in the lawmaking process?
4. In what ways can citizens try to influence state legislative activity?

ACTIVITY in a STATE LEGISLATURE The material presented up to this point has given you an overview of state legislatures in the United States. The case study which follows describes activity in one particular legislature. The case focuses on the Oregon legislature and a law it passed in 1971.

As you read the case, identify examples of political activity. Think in terms of leadership, decision-making, communication, and participation. Also think about the resources which were used and distributed as a result of each activity.

During debates on bills, legislators have the opportunity to communicate their views to others. They often make speeches on the floor of the state house or senate.

231

★ The Bottle Bill

"NO DEPOSIT. NO RETURN. BORN AROUND 1935. DIED IN OREGON SEPT. 30, 1972. MAY IT RUST IN PEACE."

These words were engraved in a tombstone found behind a house in Portland, Oregon, in 1972. The tombstone was dedicated to a new law passed by the state legislature in Oregon. The law banned the use of pull-tab beverage cans and nonreturnable soft drink and beer containers. It required a five-cent refundable deposit on most beer and soft-drink containers. It required a two-cent refundable deposit on beer bottles that could be reused by bottling companies.

Hoping to rid the state's highways and parks of empty nonreturnable cans and bottles, a "bottle bill" was introduced into the 55th session of the Oregon legislature in 1969. However, it was defeated in the Oregon House of Representatives. This was a victory for can and bottle representatives, who had appealed for more time to deal with the litter problem. They opposed the bottle bill. They claimed that many people employed in the manufacture of nonreturnable cans and bottles would lose their jobs. Grocery representatives from around the state also opposed the bill. They said it would be difficult for grocers to handle the large number of returned cans and bottles.

Both groups said that the problem involved more than cans and bottles. According to them, all containers were concerned, not just those which held soft drinks and beer. They urged a massive public education campaign to teach people how to properly dispose of their refuse.

Between 1969 and 1971, the industry took very little action to educate the public about throwing away refuse. Therefore, at the 56th session of the Oregon legislature in 1971, several legislators introduced another bottle bill. The first reading of the bill occurred on February 9. The new proposal, known as House Bill 1036, aimed to curb the production and use of pull-tab cans and nonreturnable containers for beer and soft drinks. The bill had the strong backing of Governor Tom McCall. In addition, environmental groups, led chiefly by the People's Lobby Against Nonreturnables, had built support for such a law throughout the state.

The bill required a deposit of from two cents to five cents on most beer and soft drink containers. The new law aimed to help beer and soft drink manufacturers recycle their containers.

The day after it was introduced, House Bill 1036 was referred to the House State and Federal Affairs Committee. This committee studied the bill carefully.

The committee received intense pressure from various groups. First, representatives of the United States Brewers Association, the Brewers Institute of Oregon, United Grocers, the Carbonated Beverage Container Manufacturers Association, the American Can Company, and Safeway Stores all argued against the bill. Many of these representatives spoke in the open hearings held by the committee. Others attempted to contact legislators individually. They did so in an effort to persuade them to vote against the bill in committee. If the committee voted against the bill, it would never reach the House floor for a vote by the full House.

Opponents of the bill argued that it would cause a severe loss of jobs in the beverage industry in Oregon. They also claimed it would place an extra load on grocers. (Grocers would have to handle the many thousands of returned bottles.) In short, they felt that it would be an economic disaster for Oregon.

Some of the local news media also opposed the bill. On March 29, 1971, the *Oregonian,* a local newspaper, urged that the problem of waste be handled "without throwing large numbers of glass workers and can makers out of work, upsetting the container industry or destroying segments of the beverage industry."

Some committee members wanted to keep the bill from going to the House floor.

Litter was one problem noted by persons who favored passage of the bottle bill in Oregon. How could a photograph be used as evidence to support the need for the bill?

They urged that the bill be referred again to a subcommittee which had studied the bill previously. According to one of the bill's sponsors, this was "an attempt to kill the bill." Fortunately for its supporters, the motion was defeated by a vote of 9 to 5.

Roger Martin was a committee member who supported the bill. He argued that opponents of the bill had been given two years to try other means of controlling litter. He did not feel they should be given another chance. Martin wanted the committee and the entire legislature to act immediately. Another committee member who supported the bill, Al Densmore, also felt it was time to act. "We have become in the last decade largely a throwaway society without determining where to throw [our refuse] away."

Despite the opposition of can manufacturers, labor groups, and grocers, the bottle bill finally reached the house floor. It did so on April 7, 1971, by a final committee vote of 12 to 1.

A motion to return the bill to the House State and Federal Affairs Committee was defeated 52 to 8. House Bill 1036 then easily passed the entire House by a vote of 54 to 6.

The bottle bill was immediately introduced into the Oregon Senate. There it encountered serious opposition by the same groups which had opposed it in the House. The bill was immediately referred to the five-member Consumer Affairs Committee. The committee held hearings throughout May. At these hearings, the committee heard arguments for and against the bill. These arguments were much the same as those which had been heard in the House State and Federal Affairs Committee.

A member of the Glass Bottle Blowers' Association remarked,

> "No organization or body of citizens has been more active and more concerned about our state's solid waste management problem than the members of the Glass Bottle Blowers' Association. . . . I do not believe we should use economic injury to a substantial number of citizens for the sake of an experiment. House Bill 1036 if enacted into law will cost several of our members their jobs!"

Other people in opposition to the bill used statistics. A vice-president of the Portland Bottling Company asserted that 80 percent of the litter was not related to beer and soft drinks. Furthermore, he claimed that only 1 percent of all solid waste was related

233

to soft drinks. He said, "The bill is not workable. It will only make a supermarket into a garbage dump."

The director of the Washington office of the American Can Company also opposed the bill. He took a different approach. In asserting that the bill would cause a loss of jobs in his industry he said the following. "We are not asking for justice, but for mercy."

On April 28, 1971, the Senate Consumer Affairs Committee held a three-hour hearing before an enormous crowd. Both supporters and opponents of the bottle bill were present. Many had testified before the House State and Federal Affairs Committee. During this hearing, a compromise was reached which led to final passage of the bill.

With the help of State Attorney General Lee Johnson, the amount of deposit required on some bottles was reduced. Under the compromise, beer bottles which could be reused would require a deposit of only two cents. As a result of this compromise, the bill emerged from the Consumer Affairs Committee by a vote of 4 to 1.

After the bill was reviewed by the entire Oregon Senate, it was re-referred to committee. Attempts at re-referral to committee in the Oregon House had been designed to kill the bill. The purpose of re-referring the bill to the Senate committee, however, was to clarify some of its terms.

After it was amended, the bill was voted out of committee to the Senate floor.

The amended bill passed by a vote of 28 to 8 on May 27. The House passed the amended version of the bill on June 1. On June 2, House Bill 1036 was signed by Oregon Governor Tom McCall. It became law on October 1, 1972. Oregon was the first state to pass a bottle bill. Similar legislation has since been introduced in over 25 states.

Laws passed by state legislatures are sometimes challenged by their opponents in the state courts. The Oregon bottle bill faced such a challenge. Local industries, claiming that the law discriminated against them, filed suit in Marion County Circuit Court. However, the judge found the new law to be "valid in every respect."

The judge went on to say that the action by Oregon's 56th legislative session reflected a major response to citizen concern about the environment. In his opinion, "The Court would be ill-advised to interfere in any manner in this timely and necessary endeavor."

Governor McCall endorsed the decision of the court saying "It is heartening to know that implementation of this law will occur on October 1 as scheduled."

1. What types of political activity can you identify in the Oregon case?
2. What kinds of political resources were used? Who used them? How were they used?
3. How were resources distributed as a result of political activities in this case?

The Skill of Interpreting Evidence

In Unit 1 you learned the skill of gathering evidence. Once evidence is obtained, it is important to know how to interpret it. Information is of little value unless you understand it and can relate it to other knowledge you have.

This section on interpreting evidence is divided into two sections. First, you will apply skills in interpreting evidence in forms such as graphs, charts, and tables. Second, you will be introduced to skills in detecting and explaining bias in evidence. To learn

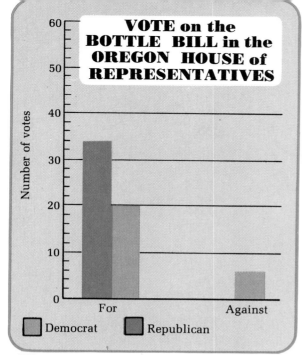

Figure 8-4

and apply skills in interpreting evidence, you will use data from the Oregon case.

GRAPHS, CHARTS, and TABLES

As you learned in Chapter 2, graphs, charts, and tables can provide a great deal of important information. For example, the bar graphs in Figure 8-4 reveal interesting facts. They show the support which members of the Oregon House of Representatives gave to House Bill 1036 (the bottle bill). Study the graph. What conclusions can you draw from this graph?

Given the following information about the bottle bill vote in the Oregon Senate, prepare your own graphs. Be sure to show the relationship between party affiliation and vote. Choose the graph format which you think works best—bar graph, line graph, or pie graph. Review pages 62, 64, and 70–71 for information on how to prepare graphs.

Figure 8-5

| VOTE on the BOTTLE BILL in the OREGON SENATE | |
REPUBLICANS	DEMOCRATS
11 votes yea 3 votes nay	11 votes yea 5 votes nay

The graph you have worked with in Figure 8-4 is a bar graph. Line graphs are another useful way to present information. Look at the line graph in Figure 8-6. It contains information offered during the bottle bill debate. This graph shows the growth in usage of nonreturnable cans and bottles.

Figure 8-6 can help you identify the market share of nonreturnable containers in a given year (in relation to returnable containers). In this case, market refers to all manufactured cans and bottles. *Market share* means "portion of the market."

In addition to relating two sets of information, line graphs can also reveal trends. By looking at the entire period 1960–1969, a trend can be identified in the use of nonreturnable containers.

1. What was the market share of nonreturnable containers in 1960? 1965? 1969?
2. Based upon the information in the graph, how would you expect the 1960–1969 trend to have gone in the 1970s?

Figure 8-6

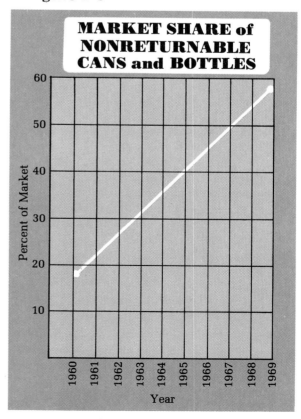

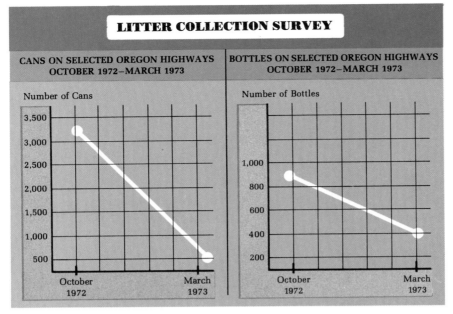

CANS ON SELECTED OREGON HIGHWAYS
OCTOBER 1972–MARCH 1973

Number of Cans

3,500
3,000
2,500
2,000
1,500
1,000
500

October 1972   March 1973

BOTTLES ON SELECTED OREGON HIGHWAYS
OCTOBER 1972–MARCH 1973

Number of Bottles

1,000
800
600
400
200

October 1972   March 1973

Figure 8-7

The line graphs in Figure 8–7 show the results of an Oregon State Highway Department survey. This survey was undertaken to assess the impact of the bottle bill legislation. Twenty-five highway sites were randomly selected. In October 1972 and again in March 1973, cans and bottles littered in these areas were collected.

> 1. Based on the information in these graphs, how would you judge the effect of the bottle bill?
> 2. What do the graphs indicate about a future trend regarding the number of cans and bottles littered on Oregon's highways?

The table in Figure 8–8 reveals which members of the Oregon legislature voted against the bottle bill. The table also indicates the party affiliation of these members, as well as the general area which each represents. The table on page 237 gives information about major bottling firms in Oregon before the bottle bill was passed. Study these tables as well as the map of Oregon in Figure 8–10. Then follow these steps:

> 1. Identify the area represented by each person who voted against the bottle bill.
> 2. List the locations of the major bottlers in Oregon.

> 3. Find them on the map on page 238.
> 4. Of those legislators who voted against the bottle bill, list those from cities where major bottling companies are located.
> 5. Answer the following questions:
>   a. If the bottle bill posed a threat to jobs, which cities had the most to lose?
>   b. Based on the data provided, what relationship does there appear to be between the "nay" votes and the location of major bottling companies?
>   c. What conclusions might you draw about the reasons for the negative votes?
> 6. Consider the following additional data:
>   Of the 32 representatives from Portland, Salem, and Eugene, 22 voted in favor of the bill.
>   Of the 11 senators from those three cities, 9 voted in favor of the bill.
> 7. What impact does this data have on your answer to question 5c? (Figure 8–8 only presented part of the data, which led you to a biased conclusion. You will study bias below.)

DETECTING BIAS Bias involves the selective use of evidence to tell one side of a story. Many people used bias when they reported the initial effect of the bottle bill.

LEGISLATORS WHO VOTED AGAINST the BOTTLE BILL

STATE SENATORS

Name	Political Designation	Home City
Keith A. Burbidge	Democrat	Salem
L.W. "Lynn" Newbry	Republican	Talent
E.D. "Debbs" Potts	Democrat	Grants Pass
Dick Groener	Democrat	Milwaukie
Tom R. Mahoney	Democrat	Portland
Wm. H. "Bill" Holmstrom	Democrat	Gearhart
Anthony "Tony" Yturri	Republican	Ontario
Kenneth A. Jernstedt	Republican	Hood River

STATE REPRESENTATIVES

Name	Political Designation	Home City
Harvey Akeson	Democrat	Portland
Howard L. Cherry	Democrat	Portland
Ken Maher	Democrat	Portland
Grace Olivier Peck	Democrat	Portland
Norman R. Howard	Democrat	Portland
Bernard Byers	Democrat	Albany

Figure 8-8

Those who favored the bill pointed out that the number of cans and bottles littering the highways of Oregon decreased sharply following the enactment of the bill. The graphs on page 236 point this out.

Those who opposed the bill also were biased in their explanation of its effects. These people pointed out that between September 1972 and December 1972, beverage containers increased as a percentage of all litter from 17 to 24 percent.

Those who favored the bill said the number of cans and bottles collected dropped. Those who opposed the bill said cans and bottles represented an increased percentage of total litter. Who was right? Both groups were. The sample numbers which follow illustrate this point. Suppose that in the first three months after passage of the bottle bill, supporters of the law found that the number of bottles collected on state highways had dropped from 1,000 to 100. They could use this information to show how effective the bill had been.

Let's say the opponents collected 1,000 pieces of litter at the same time the bill was passed. Assume that of the 1,000 pieces, 100 (or 10 percent) were bottles. Also imagine that three months later, the opponents collected only 400 pieces, of which 60 (or 15 percent) were bottles. They could report that the percentage of bottles littering the highways had actually risen after passage of the bill.

Figure 8-9

MAJOR BOTTLING FIRMS in OREGON

NAME OF FIRM	LOCATION
Coca Cola Bottling Co.	Portland
Gamble, Inc.	Portland
Pacific Coca Cola Co.	Portland
Pepsi-Cola Bottling Co.	Portland
Portland Bottling Co.	Portland
Seven-Up Bottling Co.	Salem
Dad's Root Beer — Canada	Portland
Cascade Beverage Co.	Salem
Shasta Beverages	Portland
Willamette Beverage Co.	Eugene
Blitz-Weinhard	Portland

Source: Directory of Oregon Manufacturers, 1972

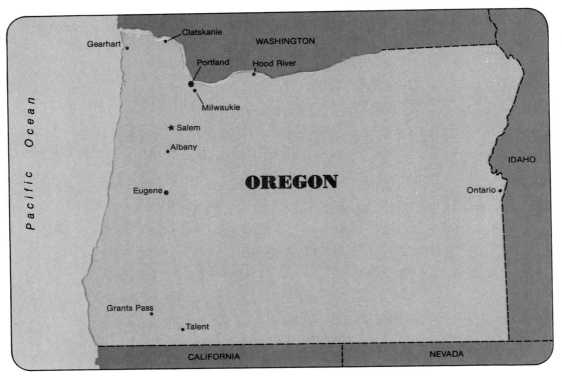

Figure 8-10

The crucial point here is that each group chose its method of selection and reporting because it wanted to make a certain point. It is clear that in this case both groups used facts, but each tailored them to support a different point of view.

When people have strong opinions about issues, they often use only those facts which support their opinions. This happened in Oregon. It probably happens among people you know all the time.

It is important to be able to detect bias in order to wisely interpret evidence. Remember: Bias is the selective use of evidence to support a particular point of view. To identify bias, always ask yourself the following:

1. What opinion is being supported by the facts?
2. What else could be interpreted from the facts?

3. How might the facts be arranged differently to say something else?

1. Describe three instances you know of in which bias has been used. Discuss how the evidence was selectively used to tell just one side of a story.
2. On these two pages are cartoons which appeared in newspapers. Study them carefully. Ask the previous three questions about each one. Describe the nature of bias in each cartoon.

"YOU DON'T UNDERSTAND, SON. WHEN DEMOCRATS GO THERE, IT'S A SELLOUT— WHEN WE GO, IT'S A JOURNEY FOR PEACE."

The State Executive Branch

The executive branch of state government is responsible for enforcing state laws. The executive branch in each of the 50 states is headed by a governor, who is in charge of the activities of this branch.

In addition to the governor, a number of other officials help run the state government. A lieutenant governor (second in line to the governor), secretary of state, attorney general, treasurer, auditor, and commissioner of public education are found in most states. Usually they are elected by the people. In some states, though, they are appointed by the governor.

The executive branch of state government also consists of a number of agencies and departments. These have been established to provide services and administer programs for citizens of the state. Each agency or department is headed by an official, appointed either by the governor or the legislature. Figure 8-11 presents some departments which are typically found in state governments.

Thousands of people are employed by the executive branch in each state. Most obtain their positions after passing a *state civil service test*. This test is given to determine if applicants are qualified to fill state jobs. Large numbers of state employees have jobs

Figure 8-11

DEPARTMENTS in TEXAS STATE GOVERNMENT

Department of Agriculture
Department of Banking
Department of Community Affairs
Department of Corrections
Credit Union Department
State Department of Health
Department of Highways and Public Transportation
Department of Human Resources
Texas Department of Labor and Standards
Department of Mental Health & Mental Retardation
Parks and Wildlife Department
Department of Public Safety
Savings and Loan Department
Treasury Department
Texas Department of Water Resources

Heads of these departments are either appointed by the governor or elected by the people.

Source: *Chief Elected and Administrative Officials.* Legislative Reference Library. 1979

as typists, safety inspectors, clerks, chemists, stenographers, lawyers, social workers, and accountants. Many others work on road construction and repair for the state highway department. This is only a sample of the types of jobs held by state employees.

The OFFICE of GOVERNOR

To be eligible for governor, a person must be a citizen of the United States, a resident of the state for a certain number of years, and fulfill an age requirement. Most states require a candidate for governor to be at least 30 years old. Several states have a minimum age of 25.

The governor is elected by the people of the state. In most states, a governor is elected to serve a four-year term of office. In other states, the governor's term of office is two years. In some states, the governor cannot serve two terms in a row.

Governors have important powers and duties within the structure of state government. The most basic duty is to see that laws passed by the state legislature are carried out. This is often done by issuing orders which describe how a new law is to be enforced. These orders are called *executive ordinances.*

Governors are also important as legislative leaders. They outline legislation which they would like to see passed during their administration. They regularly present these proposals to their state legislatures. At the beginning of each legislative session, it is customary for governors to address the legislature in a state of the state message. In this message, governors specify those programs which they will propose during the upcoming legislative session.

The veto has become increasingly important to governors. In most states, acts passed by the legislature are submitted to the governor. Based upon review of the legislation, he or she either accepts or rejects each act. The governor's signature on a piece of legislation is all that is required for it to become law. However, most governors have the power to veto legislation if they do not favor its implementation.

There are several different types of vetos. Some states have provisions for a *pocket veto.* This provision requires that any act passed at the end of a legislative session must be signed before it can go into effect. If the legislation is not signed, it is automatically vetoed.

More than half the states grant the governor the power of the *item veto.* This provision allows the governor to reject specific items within bills. For example, a state legislature might pass a bill allowing a total of $2 million for the construction of highways throughout the state. A governor can reject specific items in the bill which seem either inappropriate or too costly.

The following is a summary of powers and duties of the governor. The governor

1. Enforces state laws.
2. Proposes state legislation.
3. Prepares the state budget.
4. Calls special sessions of the state legislature.
5. May call upon the state police force or the state militia (to keep order in times of emergency).
6. May pardon criminals.
7. Represents the state at ceremonies.
8. Appoints administrators.
9. Fills vacancies that occur in elected office.
10. May remove certain officials.
11. Heads his or her state political party.

In addition to these duties, the governor is often busy voicing the needs of the state at the national level and communicating with the people of the state.

1. What is the most basic duty of governors?
2. How do governors function as legislative leaders?

3. Explain the veto power. Describe the different types of vetos.

4. Based upon the responsibilities you have read about, in what ways do you think governors can affect the distribution of resources in their states?

ACTIVITY in the GOVERNOR'S OFFICE

The following case is about Governor Ella Grasso of Connecticut. Mrs. Grasso was elected governor of Connecticut in 1974. She is one of the few women to serve as governor in this nation's history. Like the governors of other states, Governor Grasso faced major problems upon assuming office. The measure of her success has largely been judged by the way she handled those problems.

The case which follows describes events which occurred soon after Governor Grasso took office. It serves as an example of how a governor interacts with other political actors in state government. As you read the case, identify as many examples of political activity as you can.

★ Leadership under Ella Grasso

In November 1974, Ella Grasso was elected governor of Connecticut. She was inaugurated in January 1975, succeeding former Republican Governor Thomas J. Meskill. Her victory over her Republican opponent Robert Steel was convincing. The total was 631,382 votes for Grasso to 431,142 votes for Steel.

Governor Grasso is a Roman Catholic whose parents came to this country from Italy. The large Catholic population in Connecticut combined with the great number of Americans of Italian descent helped to make her a popular political candidate. This popularity proved to be an asset.

In 1943 she began working with the Connecticut League of Women Voters. In 1952 she ran for and won a seat in the Connecticut General Assembly. (The General Assembly is the lower house of Connecticut's legislature.) Through this position, she established herself as a leader in the state Democratic party.

From 1959 until 1970, she served as Connecticut's secretary of state. In these years she developed a style of leadership that helped her when she became governor. One Connecticut Democrat said, "It was all those years as secretary of state, talking with the town committees and the people who vote. . . . Everyone knows Ella, from one end of the state to the other. They know she's smart and they know they can trust her."

Governor Grasso has reflected on her years as secretary of state. She feels that she was able to build support among the state's citizens by being available to them. "Everybody who wanted to have a meeting place and didn't know where to go came to my office. . . . The job opened a large window for me on the world of Connecticut."

Ella Grasso also gained experience at the national level. She represented Connecticut's Sixth District in the United States House of Representatives from 1970 to 1974. However, when she learned that Thomas Meskill would not run for reelection as the governor of Connecticut, she set her sights on that office.

During her election campaign she won widespread support from groups throughout the state. Clearly, her long experience in the state Democratic party was a major asset in winning election as governor.

When she began her term in office, Governor Grasso discovered that the state of Connecticut was over $80 million in debt. As governor, she was determined to eliminate the debt. At the same time, she also promised not to impose an income tax on the citizens of Connecticut. She once said, "An income tax is not a good idea for Connecticut. The people of the state have said time and time again that this is a tax program that is not acceptable."

To help raise state revenues, Governor Grasso worked to increase the state sales tax. Taxes on businesses and real estate also were raised. Even with these increases, it was difficult to remove the debt. In a frustrated remark about the budget she declared, "Here I am—governor—with not a penny to spend."

Early in 1975, the legislature proposed a solution to the problem. Each year people who work for the state of Connecticut are guaranteed a salary raise. In order to gain additional revenue for the state, the legislature decided to cancel the raise.

The proposal angered the unions which represented the state's workers. They urged the governor to work with legislative leaders to compromise and save some of the salary increase.

Rather than their normal raise, Governor Grasso proposed a salary increase which was three quarters of the original amount. She proposed that the money be obtained from the state's annual contributions to the employees' retirement fund.

While the unions supported this proposal, it received mixed reaction in the legislature. Some legislators argued that problems in the economy made it impossible for many people to obtain any raises at all. Why, they wondered, should Governor Grasso make it possible for state employees to get even three quarters of their expected raises?

The labor unions wanted Governor Grasso to continue urging legislative leaders to reconsider her compromise. She agreed. During the spring and early summer of 1975, she worked closely with members of the legislature. As a result, Governor Grasso was able to help resolve the conflict. In early June, when only one week remained in the state legislative session, both houses agreed to her proposal.

This incident demonstrated the Governor's ability to work with the legislature. When she was pressured by the unions to support their salary increase, she suggested a compromise. Many people believe she learned this skill during her long years of service in the state Democratic party.

Governor Grasso demonstrated a willingness to communicate openly with the citizens of Connecticut. Upon entering office, she held a news conference nearly every day. She also presented and worked to pass a freedom of information act for Connecticut. This law ensures public access to meetings and the work of state agencies.

On important issues such as the budget, she seeks the input of citizens throughout the state. In her first year in office, Governor Grasso called four public meetings on the budget. Each was held in a different city. In this way she was able to share important information with people around the state. She was also able to sample their opinion regarding the budget.

Governor Grasso's attitude of openness in government was not limited to a specific issue such as the budget. As the Governor has said, "It's important for me to keep my curbside office that allows me to walk down the street and do business."

The case above illustrates how one governor carries out the major responsibility of dealing with the state budget. Review the case carefully. Then answer the following questions.

1. What examples of leadership can you identify in this case? Does Governor Grasso relate to her followers more like a broker, a trustee, or a delegate?
2. What examples of decision-making can you identify in this case?
3. What examples of communication can you find in this case?
4. How did citizens try to influence Ella Grasso as a state leader?
5. How was resource distribution affected in the case you just read?
6. In your own state government, what examples of political activity and resource distribution can you identify?

During a typical day, Governor Grasso performs many duties. Her heavy schedule usually requires that she arrive at work early (middle photo). One part of the day is taken up by meetings with state department heads (top photo). Ceremonial duties include presenting certificates at an official reception at the governor's residence (bottom photo).

The State Judicial Branch

In the United States there are two court systems—the federal court system and the state court system. The federal courts are discussed in Chapter 14.

The judicial branch of state government is responsible for interpreting state laws. This includes determining whether laws have been violated and the extent of the violation. The judicial branch also decides the punishment to be carried out against people who break the law.

In general, state courts are concerned with two different kinds of legal proceedings—civil and criminal. A *civil suit* involves an argument between individuals or groups concerning their respective rights. The state itself can be involved as a party to a civil suit. A civil suit might involve one party suing another for damages to property.

A *criminal case* involves a violation of the state's criminal code. Crimes fall into two categories—felonies and misdemeanors. *Felonies* include major crimes such as murder, nighttime burglary, and arson. *Misdemeanors* include less serious crimes such as shoplifting and trespassing.

STATE COURT STRUCTURE

In order to settle the many civil and criminal suits brought to their attention, most states have established state court systems organized on several levels. Court organization varies from state to state; however, general types of courts can be described. (See Figure 8–12.)

Justices of the Peace. At the base of the ladder in the state judicial system are justices of the peace. These officials usually preside in small towns and rural areas. Most justices of the peace deal with misdemeanors and minor legal matters. For example, they hear cases involving traffic violations, drunkenness, and loitering. They can issue warrants for arrest, and they also perform marriage ceremonies. They generally deal with civil cases amounting to less than $100. They do not deal with criminal cases at all.

Like most local officials, justices of the peace are elected. They do not hold their terms for life, but have specified terms.

Police Courts. Justices of the peace are not found in urban areas. Police courts, also known as magistrates' courts, operate in urban areas instead. Judges in these courts are usually elected. Often they do not have legal training. The matters they deal with are similar to those handled by justices of the peace.

Municipal Courts. Municipal courts are on the second rung of the state judicial ladder. Municipal courts are found in our nation's larger cities. Judges with legal training handle civil as well as minor criminal cases on a city-wide basis.

There are frequently divisions within the municipal court system. For example, traffic courts, small claims courts, domestic relations courts, and juvenile courts are municipal courts which exist independently in many areas.

County Courts. Above the municipal courts are the county courts, which exist in some, but not all, states. They deal with more serious civil and criminal cases. Generally, they deal with probate and inheritance cases in their civil jurisdiction. (*Probate* means to certify the authority of a will.) They also deal with criminal cases that are not handled by municipal courts.

In more than half the states, county courts are staffed by a single judge, who serves the courts of several counties. This judge is often called a circuit judge, or a district judge. The judge travels from county to county on given days of the week.

State Trial Courts. The state trial courts rank above the local courts previously described. The trial courts often serve several

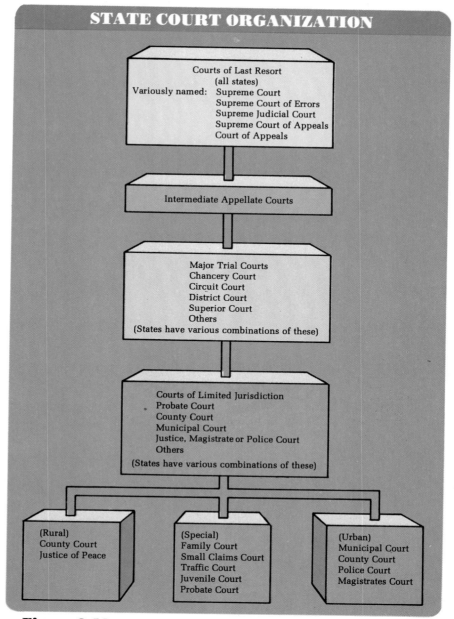

STATE COURT ORGANIZATION

Courts of Last Resort
(all states)
Variously named: Supreme Court
Supreme Court of Errors
Supreme Judicial Court
Supreme Court of Appeals
Court of Appeals

Intermediate Appellate Courts

Major Trial Courts
Chancery Court
Circuit Court
District Court
Superior Court
Others
(States have various combinations of these)

Courts of Limited Jurisdiction
Probate Court
County Court
Municipal Court
Justice, Magistrate or Police Court
Others
(States have various combinations of these)

(Rural)
County Court
Justice of Peace

(Special)
Family Court
Small Claims Court
Traffic Court
Juvenile Court
Probate Court

(Urban)
Municipal Court
County Court
Police Court
Magistrates Court

Figure 8-12

counties. It is through these courts that cases involving constitutional rights, sizable money in civil cases, and major criminal offenses are handled.

States differ in the formal name given to their trial courts. Some states call them district courts, others call them circuit courts, and some refer to them as superior courts.

Trial courts serve as the first forum where legal argument is heard in criminal cases. The state brings charges against people accused of crimes. *Defendants,* people who have been accused of a crime, are given the right to present their legal defense before a jury of 12 people. In our legal system, every defendant is entitled to legal counsel. If a person cannot afford to hire a lawyer, defense counsel will be supplied free of charge by the state. A state prosecutor, representing the people of the state, presents evidence in an effort to prove the defendant's guilt.

A Legal Word List

Arraignment: A process by which the accused, in court, is presented with the charges prepared by the grand jury or prosecutor. The accused then enters a plea of guilty or not guilty.

Arrest: Being taken into custody by authority of the law.

Beyond a reasonable doubt: A standard for judging an accused person's guilt or innocence. The jury must be convinced that the proof offered against the accused included every fact necessary to constitute the crime with which the accused is charged.

Defendant: The accused person, whose case is defended in a trial.

Defense attorney: Lawyer for the accused (the defendant).

Evidence: Testimony or an object presented in court that establishes or proves a point.

Grand jury: A group of 12 to 23 people who listen to charges brought by prosecutors against persons suspected of breaking the law. Grand jurors decide whether or not there is enough evidence to indict the accused, thereby bringing him or her to trial.

Indictment: The formal, written accusation charging a person with a crime. An indictment is proposed by a prosecutor and presented to a grand jury. The grand jury decides whether or not to present the indictment to the court.

Interrogation: The questioning of the accused or a witness.

Petit jury: A trial jury of 12 citizens, chosen with the approval of the defense and prosecution. The petit jury decides by unanimous vote the accused person's guilt or innocence.

Plaintiff: A person who brings a law suit into court. The plaintiff accuses the defendant of illegal action.

Prosecutor: A government lawyer, either elected or appointed, who investigates and brings to trial violators of the law.

Right to counsel: A defendant's right to have an attorney. If the defendant cannot afford a lawyer, one must be appointed by the court.

Right to remain silent: Accused persons are guaranteed the right to consult their attorney during interrogation. They must be told that they can remain silent, warned that what they say may be used against them, provided with a lawyer before questioning, questioned in the presence of their lawyer, permitted to consult with their lawyer during interrogation, and given an attorney if they cannot afford one.

Speedy trial: Within a reasonable amount of time of indictment, an accused person must have a trial to prove guilt or innocence.

Subpoena: A written legal order, ordering a witness to appear in court.

Trial by jury: A public, formal examination of evidence in court before an impartial judge and an impartial group of citizens. Its purpose is to determine the guilt or innocence of the accused. The trial jury usually consists of 12 persons from the community who have been fairly selected and approved by both the prosecution and defense.

Verdict. In a trial, the decision reached by a unanimous vote of a jury.

It is the responsibility of the jury to decide whether a defendant is guilty of the crime for which he or she is charged. Jurors base their decision on the evidence presented during the course of the trial. In order for a defendant to be found guilty, jurors must believe the defendant is guilty *beyond a reasonable doubt.* The verdict must be unanimous. In other words, all jurors must agree in their decision.

Higher Courts. Each level of the state court system is designed to give fair and impartial trials. However, if a person convicted of a crime feels the court has misinterpreted or misapplied a state law, or feels there has been an error in proper legal procedure, an attempt may be made to appeal to a higher court. The same right holds for the losing party in a civil suit. In some cases, decisions reached at one court are overturned by a higher court.

Higher courts include the appellate and state supreme court in each state. Appellate courts have *appellate* jurisdiction. In other words, they hear appeals from lower courts. Appellate courts have been established in nearly half the states. Like the trial courts, they too are known by different names in different states. There are typically between three and nine justices on an appellate court. To decide upon a ruling, a majority of the justices must agree.

Appellate courts were originally established to reduce the number of appeals which were made directly to the state supreme courts. While appellate courts can hear an original trial, generally they review the decisions of lower courts.

If a citizen or group is not satisfied with the ruling of an appellate court, their case may be appealed further. They may attempt to appeal to the state supreme court. There are from five to nine justices on a supreme court, depending on the state. If a citizen or group is still not satisfied with the ruling of a state supreme court, an attempt can be made to appeal the case to the Supreme Court of the United States. The Supreme

Court will review a state supreme court ruling only under certain conditions. A case must deal with the meaning of a provision in the national Constitution or a federal statute or treaty for the Supreme Court to become involved. Otherwise, the state supreme court is the final resort. (You will learn more about the United States Supreme Court in Chapter 14.)

Remember that court organization is different among the states, and so are court procedures. There are also great differences in the laws passed in the states. Laws governing divorce and taxes, for example, may vary to a great extent even among neighboring states.

1. Describe the different levels of state court organization.
2. What does it mean to appeal a case?
3. Under what conditions will the Supreme Court of the United States review a case from the state courts?
4. How can state courts affect the distribution of resources in state politics?
5. How can citizens make use of state courts?

CITIZENS TAKE a CASE to COURT

Courts can be an effective arena for citizen participation. When citizens object to state laws, they may challenge them in the state courts. As the following case shows, citizens can be successful when they bring a case to court. Read the case carefully and identify examples of political activity.

★ The Indiana License Law

In 1977, Indiana enacted a law requiring that a driver's photograph appear on his or her driver's license. This new law went unnoticed by most citizens in Indiana. Until

Judges in the state court system have many duties. In addition to presiding at trials (top right photo), they also hear motions and arguments in chambers (top left photo). Other duties may include verifying the results in a contested election (middle right photo) and giving the oath of office to state officials (bottom photo).

they had to obtain or renew their licenses, most people were not even aware of the new requirement.

However, several religious sects in Indiana objected to the law. In particular, the Pentecostalists and the Amish were disturbed by it. They claimed that having their pictures taken would violate biblical restrictions against "graven images."

Approximately 350 Amish operate cars in Indiana. The cars are black and quite simple. The Amish want to continue to operate their cars. However, the new license law violated their religious beliefs.

Dr. Joseph Willmer, co-chairman of the National Committee for Amish Religious Freedom, expressed his views through the following statement.

> "The Constitution permits groups such as the Amish and Pentecostalists to practice their religions as they please so long as they are not harmful to themselves, or to the state. . . . The Amish would not consider violating the law if the photograph requirement ultimately has to be enforced against them. However, they would probably feel compelled to move to one of the states which already grant religious exemptions to drivers license photographing."

There are several states which offer such exemptions. These include Kansas, New Mexico, Minnesota, North Carolina, Iowa, Missouri, Alabama, New York, Oklahoma, and Alaska.

In order to seek an exemption from the new law, the Amish filed a suit against the state of Indiana. The suit was filed in Vigo County Superior Court, Division 2, in Terre Haute, Indiana.

The issue was clear. Indiana had passed a law which some of its citizens found unacceptable. The Amish had two alternatives—either move to another state or challenge the law in the Indiana state courts.

On September 16, 1977, Judge Charles McCrory ordered the state to exempt the Amish and Pentecostalists from the photo requirement. The judge said,

> "This court can find no interests of the 'highest order' on the part of the State of Indiana which overbalances the constitutional right of these petitioners to freely practice their religious beliefs.
>
> "It appears a hollow argument that a required picture upon an automobile license 'for the purpose of identification' suddenly becomes a necessary state interest that overrides deep-seated, sincere religious constitutional guarantees. . . ."

1. What kind of case is this—civil or criminal? Explain.
2. At what level of the court system was this case initiated?
3. According to Indiana, what law has been called into question?
4. According to the Amish, which of their rights would the law violate?

Citizens in State Political Activity

As you have learned, the operation of state government involves many people working together. Legislators, judges, the governor, and other people in the executive branch are all important in making state government work for you. These people can be thought of as *formal* political actors. They have been elected or appointed to office.

There are also many *informal* political actors active in state politics. These are individuals and groups who do not hold formal position in state government but who take part in state political activities in numerous other ways.

Many people evaluate state politics by thinking of the policies that are made for them by the state. However, there are many opportunities for citizens to participate directly in state politics. It is possible for citizens to make the three branches of state government responsive to them and their interests.

As you recall, in the Oregon bottle bill case, organized business and industry groups attempted to influence the Oregon legislature in its 55th and 56th sessions. Interest groups of many other types have also worked to influence the actions of state government in their behalf. For example, through state offices of the American Federation of Teachers and the National Education Association, teachers work to influence legislation which is of interest to them. The medical and legal professions are examples of other groups which are well represented through local and state groups (as well as through national organizations).

To participate in state politics, citizens don't have to belong to an established professional organization or interest group. If a particular issue becomes important to them, citizens can band together with others to work either for or against that issue, as you will see in the following case.

PARTICIPAT-ING in STATE POLITICS

The following case describes how different people and groups interacted in California politics. As you will read, the safety of nuclear power plants was at issue.

As you read the case, think about how informal political actors can become involved in state political activities. Identify examples of political activity. Also, describe the resources that enabled people to act effectively.

★ California and Proposition 15

On June 8, 1976, California held state primary elections. Citizens nominated party candidates to run for local, state, and national offices. On that day, California citizens also voted on 15 proposed plans, referred to as *propositions*. The most controversial proposition by far was the last one—Proposition 15.

Proposition 15 focused on the safety of nuclear power plants in California. The proposition aimed to restrict further development of nuclear reactors until strict safety requirements were met. Until June 8, the Nuclear Regulatory Commission in Washington, D.C., alone had decided the safety standards for nuclear plants. They did this for every state throughout the country. Proposition 15 required that the California legislature pass judgment on the safety of all nuclear reactors in that state. A two-thirds vote of both houses of the legislature would be needed for such approval. Proposition 15 also required that public utility companies and nuclear reactor manufacturers accept full responsibility for any accident at a nuclear plant.

A vote to support the proposition would slow nuclear plant construction in California. It would also lend moral support to similar efforts. Such efforts were under way in Oregon, Colorado, Arizona, Maine, Michigan, North Dakota, Ohio, Oklahoma, and Washington.

A vote against the proposition would support existing state and federal nuclear policy. Utility companies could continue to build more nuclear plants to meet the state's demands for energy.

By obtaining more than 200,000 signatures on a petition, citizens in California can have a proposition placed on the ballot during a general election. Proposition 15 qualified for the June 8 ballot with 500,000 signatures.

Californians for Nuclear Safeguards, the People's Lobby, Project Survival, The

Sierra Club, and Friends of the Earth took active roles in organizing people throughout the state in support of Proposition 15. These groups emphasized the potential danger of an accident in a nuclear power plant. They pointed out the dangerous effects of radioactivity. They noted the lack of knowledge then available on nuclear power. All these things, they argued, meant that the future construction of nuclear power plants in California should be restricted with special safeguards.

Supporters of Proposition 15 raised $1 million. They relied most heavily on small donations from individuals to support their cause. In addition, they organized a variety of fund-raising activities. These included bike-a-thons, boutique sales, pizza dinners, picnics, garage sales, and frequent passing of the hat.

Supporters, or proponents, of Proposition 15 set up 46 regional headquarters throughout California. They established additional headquarters on college campuses throughout the state. From these headquarters, the proponents provided information to the citizens of California and answered questions regarding Proposition 15.

Proposition 15 supporters also organized more than 4,000 people to go from door to door in cities throughout the state. Their goal was to convince citizens to vote "yes" on the initiative. Well-known, popular personalities were asked to speak to California voters in support of Proposition 15. A former San Francisco 49er quarterback appeared in one advertisement. In the ad he said "Do you want the safest nuclear power possible? If your answer is yes, your vote is 'yes' on 15."

The opponents of Proposition 15 were also well organized. The No on 15 Committee was set up. The skills of a California public relations firm were enlisted. Opponents of Proposition 15 raised well over $3 million in an effort to defeat the initiative.

People were opposed to Proposition 15 for several reasons. Many feared that addi-tional restrictions on nuclear plants would effectively put an end to nuclear energy in the state. They pointed to the possible loss of jobs should nuclear power plants be shut down. Opponents of Proposition 15 also claimed that nuclear power plants were safe. They said the citizens of California should not worry because the chance of a nuclear accident was very slight.

Some opponents were concerned with the Proposition 15 requirement that a two-thirds majority of the state legislature approve new safety standards. To those familiar with the operation of the California state legislature, this two-thirds restriction seemed severe.

A citizen who opposed Proposition 15 wrote the following letter to the editor of the *Los Angeles Times*.

"I am opposed to Proposition 15 not because I have 'sold out,' but because I believe in democracy by majority rule.

The initiative requires . . . a two-thirds vote by the California legislature to continue nuclear power in our state. It is virtually impossible to achieve a two-thirds vote on most major issues coming before the legislature. It means that only 14 state senators, either by voting No or simply not showing up to vote at all, can block legislation. That is not majority rule, but minority rule."

The opponents of Proposition 15 presented their views in newspaper advertisements. (Supporters of Proposition 15 also took out newspaper advertisements. However, with only $1 million raised, this group could not afford as much advertising as the No on 15 Committee.) Two groups—the California Council for Environmental and Economic Balance and the Citizens for Jobs and Energy—worked with the No on 15 Committee. These groups obtained the support of well-known scientists who testified to the safety of nuclear power. These groups also received the support of influential newspapers, such as the *Los Angeles Times*.

Of the $3.5 million spent by the No on 15 Committee, $296,000 was donated by Pacific Gas and Electric Company (PG&E). PG&E is the largest utility company in California. In addition to PG&E, the San Francisco-based Bechtel Corporation, then the nation's leading builder of nuclear plants, donated $231,000 to the No on 15 Committee. Smaller amounts were given by Westinghouse Electric ($88,895), General Electric ($50,000), Bobcock and Wilcox ($35,000), Combustion Engineering ($35,000), and U.S. Steel ($25,000).

Opponents of Proposition 15 received further support from out-of-state groups. These organizations feared that if Proposition 15 were passed in California, similar action might be taken in their states.

The media campaign over Proposition 15 was waged intensely for several months. Supporters and opponents of the proposition advertised extensively. The mass media, posters, t-shirts, bumper stickers, and billboard signs were all used in an attempt to swing the uncommitted voters. In May, 1976, about one third of the California voters favored the proposition. One third opposed it. And one third were still undecided. Despite all the information made available to them, some Californians were not yet sure how they would vote on June 8.

At the same time that California voters were being bombarded with information, the state legislature attempted to take a firm stance on nuclear power. In early May, assemblymen Charles Warren (D-Los Angeles), Terry Goggin (D-San Bernardino), and Bruce Nestande (R-Orange) introduced three bills. The first two called for a legislative review of methods of nuclear waste disposal and nuclear fuel reprocessing. The third bill called for a one-year study on the possibility of locating nuclear plants underground.

These three bills narrowly cleared the California Assembly in April 1976. In the Senate they were referred to the Senate Public Utilities, Transit and Energy Committee. Here they ran into stiff opposition by opponents of Proposition 15. However, many people, including Governor Jerry Brown, felt that these bills represented a good compromise to Proposition 15. The bills imposed new restrictions on the use of nuclear power in California. These were restrictions, however, which the utility companies could accept. Therefore, Governor Brown decided to take action in order to move the bills through the Senate.

The governor told the press, "I am very concerned about the dangers of nuclear energy production and I will work hard to get these bills out. . . ." In addition to his public support of the three bills, Governor Brown also made several private telephone calls to key legislative leaders. He urged them to work for quick passage of the bills.

The bills passed the California Senate by early June. Governor Brown's support had been crucial. At the signing ceremonies, Assemblyman Warren, chief sponsor of the bills, praised the governor's actions.

A poll taken on June 7 showed a plurality of Californians leaning against Proposition 15. There were still a large number of people who wanted more information about the issue. Passage of the proposition seemed doubtful, however. The action taken by the legislature may well have decided the issue for many California voters. The three bills passed by the legislature seemed to have assured many Californians that their state government would act to protect them against potential dangers posed by nuclear power.

On June 8, the citizens of California voted down Proposition 15 by a 2 to 1 margin. Even though they lost, some of the supporters of Proposition 15 were pleased with the outcome. After the June 8 decision, Ms. Shirley Wilkerson, executive director of Project Survival said, "More and more people are showing concern. The bills passed by the state legislature were a big step. The largest state in the country is saying they are concerned about nuclear power. Isn't that a victory?"

The Proposition 15 case provides several examples of how resources were used in political activities. As discussed in Chapter 2, the effectiveness of political activity often depends largely on the kind and amount of resources which political actors have. Those who can use resources effectively can then have a greater impact on the distribution of other resources to other people.

Analyze the relationship between resources and activities in the Proposition 15 case by answering the following questions:

1. What resources did the various political actors in this case use?
2. What political activities were they involved in?
3. What political resources were distributed as a result of the political activities you listed above?

CITIZENS as SUPPORTERS

In the Proposition 15 case, many concerned people worked to persuade the citizens of California to vote one way or the other regarding the initiative. People on both sides of the issue spent a great deal of time and money to build voter support for their position. For example, those who favored Proposition 15 worked through the People's Lobby and Project Survival to set up regional headquarters in California. These groups enlisted the volunteer help of hundreds of citizens. Without these volunteers, the groups would not have been able to communicate their message effectively to citizens of the state.

The volunteers participated as supporters in the group effort. As discussed in Chapter 1 (page 37), supporters are necessary for groups to achieve their goals. Supporters carry out the tasks once decisions are made. A good supporter:

1. Is reliable.
2. Follows directions.
3. Works hard.
4. Works well with others.

Many of the citizens working through groups both for and against Proposition 15 carried out these criteria. Think back again about the volunteers who participated in the battle over Proposition 15. In going door-to-door to persuade people to vote for the initiative, members of the People's Lobby and Project Survival demonstrated they could work hard and well with others.

The exercise on the following two pages will help you develop skills in acting as a supporter. An imaginary situation involving recreation facilities for senior citizens is presented in this exercise. Be prepared to place yourself in the supporter role in the situation described.

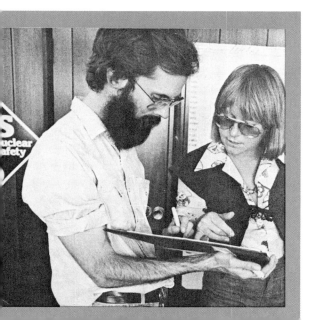

Volunteers were an important political resource for those who favored Proposition 15. They worked as supporters to help make the group's message known to people throughout the state.

★ The Supporter Role

Recreation for Senior Citizens

Imagine the following situation: A number of citizens in your state want state funds to be provided for recreation facilities for senior citizens. A group called Recreation for Senior Citizens (RSC) is formed. The group will work to influence the legislature to pass a new law authorizing the money.

Many citizens in the state have joined RSC. However, not many have had experience in working to influence the state legislature. The leaders of the group, however, have worked extensively with the legislature before. Their organizational skills and legislative experience represent important political resources.

Thousands of high school students are in support of this effort. They feel it is important to provide recreation facilities for senior citizens, just as there are recreation facilities for teenagers. Like most other members, very few of the student supporters have ever been involved in political activity at the state level. Therefore, most of them follow directions from the RSC organizers.

This newly formed interest group will soon have a meeting to discuss the last round of strategy. The group has a limited amount of money to spend on advertising. However, its greatest strength lies in the number of people who have volunteered their help. High school students from various parts of the state are among those who will attend this meeting.

Profile: Mr. / Mrs. Nathan

Mr./Mrs. Nathan is the Director of Information Activities for Recreation for Senior Citizens. A major responsibility of this job is to see that information about the group's goal is spread throughout the state. The group does not have much money. Therefore volunteer help is extremely important.

There are a great many things which adult and student volunteers can do. Small groups of volunteers can be organized to talk to people about state support for senior citizen recreation facilities. This can be done either at community meetings or by volunteers going door to door. Volunteers can also write leaflets and paint posters as another means of informing the citizens of their communities about the need for the recreation facilities.

Profile: Mr. / Miss Frankel

Mr./Miss Frankel is the Director of Fund Raising for Recreation for Senior Citizens. The major responsibility of this job is to plan fund-raising activities. Money is needed to place advertisements in newspapers, purchase radio and television time, maintain needed office supplies, pay for telephone charges, and meet a variety of other expenses. It has been difficult to raise the money to pay for these expenses. New ideas and new activities are needed.

Student volunteers could be particularly helpful in the fund-raising effort. There are a number of activities they could arrange—car washes, baby-sitting services, bake sales, and auctions, for instance.

Profile: The Supporter

Imagine the following: As head of the student council in your high school, you have a great deal of status among the students and faculty. They respect your opinions and judgments. Although busy with homework and a part-time job, you have decided to join the Recreation for Senior Citizens effort. You intend to go to the upcoming planning meeting and to offer your help in either public relations or fund-raising activities.

Review the material you have just read and then do one of the following assignments. Your teacher will tell you which assignment to follow.

Assignment 1

a. Imagine yourself a member of Recreation for Senior Citizens, one who is assuming the supporter profile. Decide whether you would like to volunteer to work with Mr./Mrs. Nathan in information activities, or with Mr./Miss Frankel in fund-raising activity.

b. Write a paper in which you describe the activities you'd like to become involved in as a supporter. Also describe how you will perform these activities, and how your efforts will be of help to the goals of Recreation for Senior Citizens. Be certain to identify the resources you plan to use.

Assignment 2

a. With two of your classmates, form a group of three for discussion of plans for Recreation for Senior Citizens. One person should play the part of Mr./Mrs. Nathan, a second person should play the part of Mr./Miss Frankel, and the third person should play the part of a supporter of Recreation for Senior Citizens.

b. In your group of three, Mr./Mrs. Nathan and Mr./Miss Frankel should present their ideas. The supporter should then choose one or perhaps several activities to work on. The supporter should carry out the criteria for the supporter role.

c. Each person in your group should answer these questions:

1. What are the qualities of a good supporter?
2. In what way was the supporter in your group most helpful?

Chapter Review

1. Discuss the restrictions that regulate interstate and state-federal relationships.
2. Summarize the powers reserved to the states.
3. In chart form, describe the powers and responsibilities of each branch in state government. Based on this information, prove that state government is based on a system of checks and balances.
4. Review the Supreme Court ruling in *Reynolds* v. *Sims*. How did this decision affect political activities and resource distribution in state legislatures?
5. How can citizen communication play an important role in the state legislative process?
6. Review the Oregon bottle case, and determine the role(s) that committees play in the legislative process.
7. What are some of the political activities of state governors? Of these, which do you think are the most important? Explain.
8. Review the duties of and restrictions on each level of the state court system. How do these protect the rights of individual citizens?
9. Analyze how citizens can affect political decision-making in each of the three branches of state government.
10. Describe some ways in which you might participate in state politics.

Chapter Vocabulary

Define the following terms.

bicameral	joint committee	item veto
constituent	bill	pocket veto
unicameral	voice vote	civil suit
apportion	roll call vote	criminal case
special session	conference committee	felony
standing committee	veto	misdemeanor
interim committee	civil service	appellate

Chapter Analysis

1. In recent years, Americans have become increasingly mobile. About one fifth of the population change their residences at least once a year. Given this figure, do you think that state laws, such as those on education, should be more uniform? Explain why or why not.
2. Based on Chapter 8, how do the three branches of state government interact to set state policy? What is the role of citizens in this process?

3. If you wanted to influence politics within your state, for which office or branch of government would you seek election or appointment? Explain the reasons for your choice.

Chapter Activities

1. Using past copies of state newspapers, determine key state legislation and policies during the last year. Select one bill or issue, and investigate the role played by interest groups, political parties, state officials, and individual citizens.

2. Review the general discussion of the duties of state governments. Then get a copy of your state constitution, and describe the duties outlined in it.

3. Reread the analysis of bias on pages 236–239. Then pick several editorials or letters to the editor, and underline statements of bias.

4. Identify a civil or criminal case that has been brought to trial in a state court in your area. Then write a report describing the nature of the case, its outcome, and any efforts to appeal the verdict.

Chapter Bibliography

Governing Our Fifty States and Their Communities, Charles Adrian (McGraw-Hill Book Company: New York, NY), 1972.
   A brief but thorough introduction to the responsibilities of the branches of government at the state and local levels.

The Book of the States, Council of State Governments, Lexington, KY.
   A biannual catalogue of information on all aspects of state government, including detailed information on the function of state government in each state.

State Government News, Council of State Governments, Lexington, KY.
   A publication of the Council of State Governments which appears periodically throughout the year. Usually about 30 pages long, the magazine reports recent actions of states in key areas such as tax reform, education, and health.

The Fifty States and Their Local Governments, edited by James W. Fesler (Alfred Knopf: New York, NY), 1967.
   One of the best sources available on all aspects of state and local government.

Government by the States: A History, D. S. Halacy, Jr. (The Bobbs-Merrill Company, Inc.: Indianapolis, IN) 1973.
   A simple history of state government, filled with drawings, pictures, tables, charts, and other information.

Chapter Objectives

★ To learn the form and function of different units of local government

★ To analyze how local government affects citizens and how citizens can influence local government

★ To apply the concepts of decision-making, communication, participation, and leadership to local government

★ To develop skills in interviewing

★ To develop skills in making decisions

Help hire a Mayor. Vote.

On November 8th there is an election for Mayor, President of the City Council, Comptroller, Borough President and Councilmembers. For information contact The League of Women Voters (674-8484) 817 Broadway, New York, New York 10003.

chapter 9

LOCAL POLITICAL ACTIVITIES

Of all governments, the level that is closest to you is local government. The structure of local government and the political activities carried out on the local level affect your life every day.

There are several units of local government. These include municipalities, counties, townships, and special districts. All these governments overlap one another. Yet each has different responsibilities and provides some different services.

No government exists in a vacuum. Local governments are involved in many ways with state and national governments. State and national laws and financial aid, as well as social and economic conditions, affect local governments more and more. As you read in Chapter 8, all local governments are established by state governments. According to state constitutions, each state legislature has the power to set up governments in localities within the state.

The local level of government is also the level at which you as a citizen can participate most easily and most often. In this chapter you will learn about some of the activities and roles you can take part in at the local level.

You will also learn several valuable skills that will aid you in participating as a citizen. The first of these is interviewing as a way to collect evidence, especially about your own community. The other is the skill of making decisions.

Forms and Functions of Local Government

As you can see in Figure 9–1, local governments far outnumber any other type of government in the United States. At the local level, these governments can be divided into two categories. The first of these is the municipality. A *municipality* is an incorporated unit of government in a given geographic area. (The process by which states officially organize local governments is called *incorporation*.) Cities, villages, and towns are three kinds of municipalities.

On a larger scale are counties, townships, and special districts. Often these units of government include municipalities within their boundaries.

CITIES, VILLAGES, and TOWNS

The differences among cities, villages, and towns are based on population and on government organization. Most states, for example, have rules stating that a municipality must contain a certain number of people before it can be a city.

Cities. The majority of all municipalities are classified as cities. However, the number of cities in each state varies. Hawaii has only one urban area. (*Urban* means related to, or part of, a city.) Illinois, on the other hand, has more than 1,200 cities.

Today, most Americans live in cities. If you look at a population distribution map of the United States, you can see that the densest population is concentrated in the major urban areas of the nation.

Forms of City Government. Three forms of government are found in the cities of the United States. They are the mayor/council form, the commission form, and the council/manager form.

The *mayor/council* is the most traditional form of municipal government in the United States. It consists of an elected executive called a *mayor* and an elected legislature called a *city council*.

Originally a mayor's power was very limited. Voters directly elected many of the city's officials, who were then independent of the mayor. This structure still operates today. It is called the weak-mayor/council form. In this form the mayor has little influence over the city budget. Usually, he or

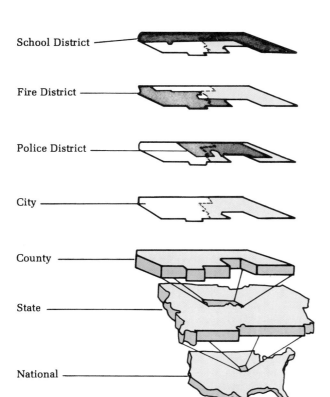

School District

Fire District

Police District

City

County

State

National

Figure 9-1

GOVERNMENTS in the UNITED STATES	
Type of Government	Number of Units
National	1
State	50
Local	79,826
Counties	3,042
Municipalities	18,862
Townships	16,822
School Districts	15,174
Special Districts	25,962

Source: Statistical Abstract of the U.S. 19

The MAYOR/COUNCIL FORMS of LOCAL GOVERNMENT

WEAK MAYOR FORM

Voters

Elect — Elect — Elect

Mayor — Council — Other Elected Executives

Appoints — Appoints — Appoints

Department Heads — Department Heads — Department Heads

STRONG MAYOR FORM

Voters

Elect — Elect

Mayor — Council

Appoints

Chief Administrator

Department Heads

Figure 9-2

she is unable to veto the council's actions. This type of government reflects citizens' reluctance to allow any single person or office to become too powerful.

In the late 1800s city problems became more complex. At that time many cities adopted a strong-mayor/council form of government. The mayor became an active and powerful administrator. Many cities today operate with a strong-mayor/council government.

Strong mayors appoint department heads and members of boards and commissions. They prepare the budget for the council's consideration and usually have the power to veto measures passed by the council.

Figure 9–2 outlines the two kinds of mayor/council government. Today, more than 50 percent of the municipal governments in the United States are either a weak- or a strong-mayor/council form.

The *commission* form of municipal government operates in only 3 percent of the nation's municipalities. This form of city government began when a tidal wave and flood devastated Galveston, Texas, in 1901.

The weak-mayor/council government was handicapped by the lack of strong executive leadership. As a result, recovery was extremely slow. Leading citizens then proposed a commission form of government as an alternative.

Voters elected five commissioners who served as a board that set the city's policy. In addition, each commissioner was in charge of a city department. Figure 9–3 outlines a typical commission form of government today.

Figure 9-3

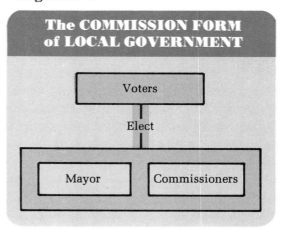

The COMMISSION FORM of LOCAL GOVERNMENT

Voters

Elect

Mayor — Commissioners

261

The commission form was very popular at first because it was simpler and less expensive than the mayor/council form. Today, however, a small board is seldom able to deal with complex urban problems.

The *council/manager* form grew out of a reform movement in the early 1900s. Reformers wanted city government to be efficient, businesslike, and not "political."

Under this system, voters elect a small council. The council hires a professional manager to serve as the city's administrator. The city manager appoints city department heads and carries out the council's policies. Since the city manager is not elected, he or she does not have to worry about "politics." The manager can devote full time to conducting city business.

Today about 40 percent of the nation's cities use a council/manager type of organization. Figure 9-4 outlines the organizational structure.

1. What are the differences among the three forms of city government described?
2. If you live in a city, what form of government does your city have?

Size. Most municipal government in the United States is organized in one of these three forms. Some forms tend to fit certain types of communities better than others. For example, the mayor/council form is the most popular in both the largest and the smallest cities. The reasons for this differ, however. Small cities usually have fewer complex problems that would require a professional manager. The largest cities, on the other hand, are more likely to need strong political leadership. This can come from a mayor who is able to work with many diverse groups.

In a middle-sized city, political conflict is not usually the most important problem. Rather, the city government needs to provide services such as paved streets and lighting. Thus, a professional manager is most often found in these cities.

1. What form of city government is most likely to be found in large communities? in medium-sized communities? in small communities?
2. Why do you think size affects the form a city government has?

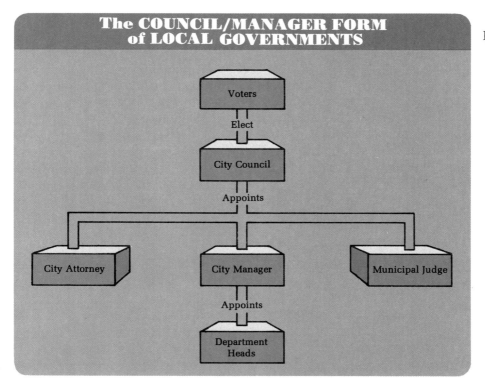

The COUNCIL/MANAGER FORM of LOCAL GOVERNMENTS

Figure 9-4

3. Does your community fit these characteristics? Explain.

Municipal Charters. As you know, local governments are organized and their plans for government are approved by the state in the process called incorporation.

An incorporated unit of government has an official plan for government. In a municipality this plan is called a *charter*. There are a number of different kinds of municipal charters in the United States today. In each case, the state has the authority to alter the charter. The state can change the powers, the officers, and the territorial jurisdiction of the municipality.

City Government in Action. The forms of municipal government described here reflect formal patterns of organization. Do governments based on these forms always work that way in practice? The following cases will help you answer that question. The first is about the weak-mayor/council system in Belleville, Illinois. The second describes how the council/manager government of Beloit, Wisconsin, handled a local problem.

★ The Mayor of Belleville

Belleville, Illinois, is a medium-sized city with a weak-mayor/council form of city government. The mayor has little formal power. In fact, until the early 1960s, being mayor was not even a full-time job.

Beginning in 1947, however, Belleville's mayor, M. V. Calhoun, made a series of important changes in the city. These included a merit system for the police department, a community planning program, a traffic control plan, sewer expansion, and the annexation of suburban areas.

Calhoun's ability to act forcefully was not based on his formal powers. Rather, it was due to his personal prestige and political ability. Before Calhoun was elected, there were serious problems in Belleville's government. A committee of leading citizens asked Calhoun to run for mayor because he was known to be a person of great honesty and strength. As a former school superintendent he had gained the respect and trust of local citizens.

Once he became mayor, Calhoun revealed his political ability. The strongest political forces in Belleville were labor unions, which had dominated the city council, and the business interests belonging to the Chamber of Commerce. For years they had opposed one another. Mayor Calhoun, however, was able to work with both groups. And he convinced the city council and the Chamber of Commerce to cooperate.

One of Mayor Calhoun's greatest achievements was that his successors were able to continue many of his strong policies. This was possible because Calhoun had built such a sound political base.

★ Traffic Jam in Beloit

On June 27, 1959, there was an enormous traffic jam in the Wisconsin city of Beloit. Because a section of the nearby interstate highway was unfinished, traffic was routed right through Beloit's business district. Many vacationers followed this route to resort areas. In addition, local weekend shoppers and many traffic lights contributed to the problem.

During the previous summer, Beloit city council members had worried that traffic jams would become a serious problem. Heavy traffic was dangerous if it interfered with emergency vehicles. Heavy traffic also might convince people not to use facilities in downtown Beloit.

The council took no official action, however. There was a general-feeling that traffic problems were an administrative matter. They were the concern of the city manager, Archie Telfer. Most council members felt that Telfer should "work something out" with the State Highway Department. Therefore, Telfer, city engineer Ed Bennet, police traffic lieutenant Donald Lightfoot, and experts from the Wisconsin Highway Department worked on a plan. They proposed that their plan be used if traffic became a problem during the summer of 1959. The plan would reroute northbound traffic through a residential part of the town. This would reduce downtown congestion.

The traffic jam of June 27, 1959, convinced Lieutenant Lightfoot that traffic needed to be rerouted. So, on July 2, rerouting signs were put up. The plan seemed to work well. However, gas station operators and restaurant owners along the original route were unhappy. The increased flow of traffic had brought them business. Now, business was suffering. So they complained to city council members.

When the council met on the evening of July 6, 35 citizens attended the meeting. This was an unusually large number. George Denison, owner of a cafe on the old route, spoke strongly against the rerouting. So did the manager of Beloit's best hotel and the operator of a large gas station. A lawyer for Beloit businessmen also presented a petition signed by 45 citizens who opposed the re-

routing. No one spoke in favor of the rerouting. The council was impressed and voted unanimously to restore traffic to its original route.

The city manager and traffic officials were disappointed. As experts they had prepared a careful plan that solved a serious problem. The city council's decision to throw out the plan appeared to them to be unwise. However, the council had the power to make that decision.

1. How well did political activity in Belleville fit the formal pattern of a weak-mayor/council organization?
2. How well did political activity in Beloit fit the formal pattern of the council/manager organization?

Villages. Another unit of local government is the village. Villages are small municipalities. Usually, they have a population of a few hundred people. Villages are formed when population in a rural area becomes large enough so that people feel the need to organize a government.

In order to set up a village government, people in an area must request permission

from the state legislature. Each state has its own requirements that must be met in order for a village government to be established. The legislature gives the village government specific powers. Usually, these include the right to maintain fire and police departments and the right to provide other services for citizens.

Most villages are governed by a board or council and an executive. These men and women are elected by village residents.

If a village's population grows greatly, village residents may feel the need for a more complex government. They may apply to the state legislature to give the village the legal status of a city. Each state has a certain population which it requires before a municipality can have the status of a city. Usually a population of several thousand people is required. Villages with increased populations want to become cities because state laws permit city governments to do more than village governments. A larger population requires more services.

Towns. The town is the oldest kind of municipality in America. English colonists in America called their settlements "towns."

A town consisted of a group of houses, with farms in outlying areas. As population grew, people settled further and further from the central section of the town. However, as long as they were within the geographical boundaries of the town, people were considered town members.

The colonists ran their town governments as direct democracies. *Town meetings* were held regularly. At these meetings, all town members decided together how to run the local government.

Today, many rural areas in New England and in some parts of the Midwest have town governments. The rights and responsibilities of these governments are set up by state legislatures.

Usually, a town meeting is held once a year. At the meeting, all town business is discussed. Officials are also elected. These officials include a small board of men and women called *selectmen*. They manage town affairs between town meetings. In addition, voters elect officials who manage schools, roads, taxes, and other town responsibilities.

Town governments function well in areas where the population is small. Then,

Population and physical size are key factors in the governmental needs of municipalities. A village requires very different government services than a city does.

all citizens can take part in running their community. However, town governments are limited. When a municipality has a large population, many government functions are required. It would be impossible to run the government of a large modern city at an annual town meeting.

1. Compare the size and functions of city, village, and town governments.
2. How does size of population relate to functions of government?
3. What kind of municipality do you live in or near?

OTHER LOCAL GOVERNMENTS

In addition to their municipalities, states are divided into other units of local government. These include counties, townships, and special districts.

Counties. Every state is divided into units of government that correspond to counties. (In Alaska these units are called "election districts." In Louisiana they are called "parishes.")

The size and number of counties in a state vary tremendously. For example, in 1970 there were only 150 people living in Loving County, Texas. At the same time there were more than 7 million people living in Los Angeles County, California. Texas has more than 250 counties. Delaware has only 3. In 1977 there were about 3,044 counties in the United States.

Counties were originally established in the southern colonies. There, population was spread out in agricultural areas. There were few central towns. County government was a way of centralizing government services for a large rural area.

Today, county governments still serve rural areas. However, many counties are made up largely of cities. Cook County, Illinois, for example, is composed entirely of Chicago and its surrounding urban area.

County governments, like municipalities, are structured by state legislatures. As a level of government between municipal and state, counties help centralize certain functions. For example, they often provide county libraries, schools, highways, and law enforcement. Counties also can collect certain taxes and supervise some elections. County government is centered in the county's principal city, the *county seat.*

Forms of County Government. The vast majority of county governments are run by commissions. Commissions have anywhere from 3 to 50 elected members. These governing groups are called "county boards," "county commissioners," or something similar. Voters also elect other officials, such as sheriffs, judges, coroners, treasurers, and clerks. Figure 9–5 shows the organization of county government in Iowa.

A growing number of counties are adopting structures that include an executive or manager. These resemble the council/manager and mayor/council forms of municipal government. These changes are occurring mostly in urban areas. County governments in these areas have to provide more services for more people. Thus, they often need a more streamlined form of government.

Townships. Townships are another form of local government covering a larger area than a municipality. Townships began in colonial times, when counties in some states were divided into smaller units, called "townships."

Today, rural areas in 16 states can be governed by township governments. As in colonial times, townships exist within counties. At the same time, there may be towns or villages within townships. Town or village governments administer the municipalities, while the township government administers the rural areas.

Township governments usually consist of an executive and a board of commissioners. These officials are elected by township

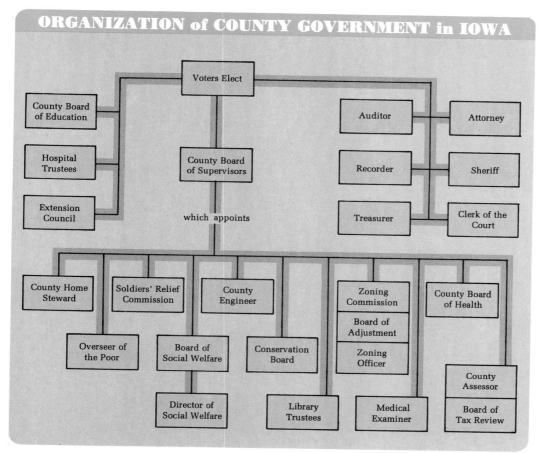

ORGANIZATION of COUNTY GOVERNMENT in IOWA

Voters Elect

County Board of Education

Hospital Trustees

Extension Council

County Board of Supervisors

which appoints

Auditor

Attorney

Recorder

Sheriff

Treasurer

Clerk of the Court

County Home Steward

Soldiers' Relief Commission

County Engineer

Zoning Commission

County Board of Health

Overseer of the Poor

Board of Social Welfare

Conservation Board

Board of Adjustment

Zoning Officer

County Assessor

Director of Social Welfare

Library Trustees

Medical Examiner

Board of Tax Review

Figure 9-5

voters. Like county governments, townships also include other elected officials. These men and women supervise schools, roads, and other areas of government.

Special Districts. Special districts are formed when people have a common need not provided for by other units of government. For example, people in one part of a county may need special sewage services. A special sewage district may be set up to serve them. Or, people in two cities may have a common need for water from one lake. A special water district might be set up by the state government. This special district would oversee the water supply for the two communities. Generally, special districts are set up to oversee education, fire protection, soil conservation, water supply, drainage, and public housing.

The largest single service for which special districts are set up is education. About one third of all local expenditure is spent on public education. School districts are set up to administer all the schools in a given area.

1. Compare county and township governments.
2. How does county government affect you?
3. Find out whether or not you live in any special districts.

PROVIDING SERVICES Local governments provide a wide range of services for citizens. The type and variety of services vary from area to area, depending on size and needs. There are certain services, however, which are offered by the vast majority of local governments.

Most communities, for example, provide police and fire protection, garbage collection, and health services such as hospitals and inoculation programs. They also sponsor recreational programs and facilities. They build libraries, civic centers, tennis courts, and sponsor programs in public parks. They operate public transportation systems and control local water supplies. If streets in your area need repair, or if you feel new street lighting systems should be installed, local government would be the level of government for you to contact.

These are just a sample of the services offered by local governments. If you were to consider just one community and review the services it offers, your list would be quite long. Think of your own community, for example. How does it perform the services just described? What other services does it offer?

Following is a case which illustrates how one community in California developed a comprehensive service system. As you read, think about how local governments provide important services and about the political activities that are involved.

★ Building a Human Services Program

In 1969, eleven youths in a California community died from drug abuse. Everyone in the community was shocked and upset. As one effort to prevent future tragedies of this sort, a citizen's advisory board was set up. Citizens wanted to help those in trouble to solve their problems. In addition, an expert was hired to improve human services in the community. General discussions were held in community groups, schools, churches, and public meetings throughout the city.

The city council helped to support meetings of the citizenry. They also gave funds to the Teen Post. This local hotline was organized as a communication center for people who were in trouble. A group of youths organized a self-help organization, so that peers would be available to counsel those who needed them. The city hired several para-professional community workers in an effort to make contacts across all age and ethnic groups in the city.

After these programs had been organized and underway for two years, the city reorganized the services into a Human Services Department. The city council allocated $200,000 per year to support the department. It grew to include a Youth Services Department, a Family Services Department, and Senior Citizens bureaus.

The community had organized to solve the problem. In doing so, it had developed one of the most comprehensive human services delivery systems in the United States. They could not have done it without city council support, the creation of a city de-

At city council meetings like this session, in Miami, Florida, citizens participate in their local government. The citizens who have been elected as council members represent the community in decision-making. Other citizens attend open meetings of the council.

partment, and dealings with all organizations that were trying to provide services. Mutual cooperation and citizen involvement had enabled the city government to provide new services and to function in ways that it had not before.

> 1. What new services were gained for citizens?
>
> 2. What political activities were carried out in order to build the program?
>
> 3. What resources were offered by the city council?

Citizens and Their Local Governments

You are a part of local government by the very fact that you live in a county, a city, a village, a township, or a special district. Your opinions and your actions affect local government. Some citizens, however, take part in local government more actively than others do.

Have you ever been to your city hall or municipal building? What was your reason for going? Have you ever spoken with a city or county official? Why? In what ways do you think you and your family have ever influenced local policies?

Individual citizens can have more influence on government at the local level than at any other level. City council and school board meetings often are open to the public. City Hall is nearby. Citizens can complain directly about holes in the roads, an unsafe intersection, or an abandoned house. Actions taken by a city council or any local agency directly affect people in the community.

CITIZEN ACTION Four ways that citizens can be involved in local government include learning about local issues, trying to influence policies, voting, and serving in the government.

Learning about Local Issues. This is the first step in becoming actively involved in local government. Local radio, television, and newspapers provide news and background on important local issues. Citizens also can attend public meetings of the city council, school board, or other agencies. Public hearings on controversial issues are common. In many communities, a person can talk directly with local government officials about an issue.

Influencing Policies. Think back to the case study on Beloit, Wisconsin. How did George Denison and other business owners try to influence city government? Why do you think they were successful?

Speaking at a city council meeting or public hearing can be an effective way to influence local policies. In Beloit, for example, local citizens seldom attended city council meetings. At the most, two or three people might come to watch. So, when 35 people came to the July 6 meeting, several speaking forcefully against rerouting, the council listened. Many Beloit shoppers and other residents may have been happy that traffic had improved. However, they did not attend the meeting. As a result, the speeches against rerouting had an even greater impact.

Another common way to try to influence local policies is to write letters to officials or to newspapers. Does a newspaper in your community print letters expressing citizens' views? What local policies or problems are people writing about?

Local citizens may also join with others to form an interest group that tries to influence local government. Or, existing interest groups may be affected by an issue and may actively try to influence policies.

Voting. Voting is one common way for citizens to participate in local government. Yet often as few as one fourth of the eligible voters actually vote in a local election. People are more likely to vote if state and national elections are held at the same time as local elections. Statistically the people most likely to vote are those who live in large eastern cities that have a strong mayor form of government. The smallest number of people voting in elections occurs in cities with a council/manager form.

Electing government officials is only one way citizen votes count in local government. Citizens also may vote on local bond issues, to approve tax increases, or to express their opinions on an issue.

Serving in the Government. Citizens also serve in local government. They may run for an elected office or be appointed to a local job. Although only a small percentage of citizens hold local office, it is an important way to influence public policies.

1. Describe four ways citizens can actively participate in local government.
2. What ways have you and your family participated in local government?

LOCAL POLITICAL ACTORS Whenever you participate in local political activity, you are a political actor. Remember if you do not have elected or appointed status in local government, you are an *informal political actor.* On the other hand, if you have an elected or appointed job in local government or local politics, you could be called a *formal political actor.*

Statistically, most formal political actors at the local level have been white males. Out of 5,733 mayors in 1976, for example, 239 were women. More than 4,600 were white. On the other hand, in 1977 there were more than 150 black mayors.

Few local officials have served in government before their election. Usually, they do not plan to make politics a career.

Most local officials spend only part of their time carrying out political duties. In large cities there are full-time jobs in government. But this is not the case in most smaller communities.

The following profiles describe two people who are involved in formal political activity. Think about their resources and the political activities they carry out.

★ **Profile: Jessie M. Rattley**

Jessie Rattley directs the Peninsula Business College in Newport News, Virginia, and serves on the city council. She is not a typical city council member. When elected in 1970, she was the first woman and the first black to serve on the Newport News council.

Blacks make up one third of Newport News' population. Rattley decided to run for office because she felt blacks needed better representation.

She was particularly concerned about the need for good communication in the narrow, 22-mile-long city. To improve communication between people and their government, Rattley holds a public meeting once a month. For two hours in the evening she is available to answer citizens' questions. She says, "I've enjoyed it and I think I've been able to accomplish something."

★ **Profile: Ron Stephenson**

"One of the duties I assumed when becoming a county commissioner was to serve on the Pennington County-Rapid City [South Dakota] Civil Defense Board. I attended most of the meetings, but I admit, not with a great deal of fervor. It seemed that we went over the same subject matter—routine plans for possible disasters—and that the main thrust of civil defense was an attempt to secure excess equipment from the federal government for our fire departments and other local agencies. When it came to expending county funds for civil defense matters, ... I had mixed emotions as to whether that money was being properly spent. Then came June 9, 1972!"

That evening heavy rain in the Black Hills produced the danger of flash floods in canyon areas. When Commissioner Stephenson learned of the danger, he acted.

First, Stephenson warned the people who lived in areas that might be flooded. Then, the Civil Defense Emergency Operations Center was set up at the Court House. Stephenson met there with the county sheriff, the county coroner, the mayor of Rapid City, the chief of police, and the city public works director. They agreed that the sheriff would take command and Stephenson would assist him.

The flood was the worst in the history of South Dakota. More than 200 people were killed. Property damage amounted to more than $100 million. Stephenson said this about his experience:

"The main problem, I suppose, is to get people excited about disaster preparation in areas where nothing has happened. Programs must be developed in those areas—through civil defense, school systems, and other organizations—to insure that the public is aware of possible danger, and that they know how to cope with disasters that will occur."

1. What resources do Rattley and Stephenson use? What activities do they carry out?

2. Compare them with local government officials you know. What resources do your local officials have? What roles—observer, supporter, advocate, organizer—do they carry out? What activities do they carry out?

3. How might you act to support your local government officials?

LOCAL CITIZEN GROUPS

As you have learned, citizens often have their greatest influence by working in organized groups. Public employee organizations, church groups, labor unions, neighborhood associations, political parties, citizen leagues, business organizations, service clubs, and other groups of citizens often participate in local political activity. Government officials, as well as the public, are more likely to pay attention to a spokesperson for the chamber of commerce or community service council than to a single individual.

Some citizen groups are directly involved with local government. The League of Women Voters, for example, provides voters with information about the structure and function of local government and about candidates for local office. The League also conducts study programs on local issues and suggests ways of making government more responsive to citizens.

Political parties are important political actors in communities where mayors and other officials run as Democrats or Republicans. However, in about 75 percent of the nation's municipalities elections are nonpartisan. As a result, political parties generally play a much smaller role in local politics than in state and national politics. In Chapter 2, for example, you read about Los Angeles Mayor Tom Bradley's election in nonpartisan politics.

Many citizen groups do not have political participation as their primary goal. Service clubs are one example. Lions, Kiwanis, and Rotary clubs sponsor service projects in the local community. Service club members are mostly business men and women. They often act as interest groups on issues that affect local business interests.

Neighborhood associations are citizen groups that can directly affect the lives of citizens in the neighborhood. Traditionally, these associations have been concerned with issues that could threaten the health

By working together in groups, members of neighborhood associations can change their neighborhood—and their own lives. This building had deteriorated so badly that it was abandoned. Neighbors in the People's Development Corporation worked to restore it. Now some group members live in it.

and safety of residents. Issues might include potholes in the roads, poor lighting, or bad storm sewers. Suburban neighborhood associations, for example, often support zoning laws to keep "fast-food" restaurants out of the neighborhood because they fear the increased litter and traffic.

Another type of neighborhood association is being organized in large cities like New York. These organizations attempt to restore their neighborhoods physically. They see this as a first step toward improved community life.

One of the most successful of these groups is the People's Development Corporation (PDC) in the South Bronx. The South Bronx is a neighborhood in New York City. It is in an advanced state of urban decay. Many of its buildings are abandoned and burned out, and poverty and unemployment are high.

As you read this case, think about the resources PDC members used, and in what ways their actions will affect the community in which they live.

★ New Homes in the South Bronx

The People's Development Corporation was organized in December 1974 by a young man named Ramon Rueda. More than half of the PDC's 40 members are Hispanic Americans and most of the others are black. Women comprise about one third of the members.

Ramon Rueda first became interested in community organization in high school. Later, he took a course in urban housing at New York University. This gave him important insights into housing practices in New York City.

Rueda's leadership ability is responsible for much of the PDC's success. A Bronx political observer noted,

> "I call this 'housing by charisma.' Its success depends on a leader and the group's willingness to follow him. The leader doesn't have to be authoritarian—in fact he probably couldn't get away with that—but he has to be someone who can set the pace."

By mid 1977 the PDC had completely restored one 70-year-old abandoned building. PDC members themselves did almost all the work on the building—much of it backbreaking demolition and difficult renovation. (They did hire skilled craftsmen to train them in the beginning.) To finance the reconstruction, the PDC acquired a state grant and city loans. They also had the assistance of a team of high school dropouts organized in a city youth program.

When the first building was completed, the PDC began work to restore five other buildings in the neighborhood. They also built a park, which they called Unity Park.

Neighborhood organizations like the PDC cannot singlehandedly revive inner cities. But they can revive people's pride in themselves and in their neighborhood. Such efforts also serve as models for other communities.

1. What political resources do citizen groups have that individuals do not?
2. What activities can citizen groups carry out?
3. Are you or your family a member of a citizen group? How do its activities compare with those of the PDC?

Debbie Stabenow, chairperson of the Ingham County Board of Commissioners in Michigan, is involved in many areas of local politics. She delivers a county newsletter and makes many phone calls to keep in touch with her constituents. She presides at regular Board meetings and supervises various county projects. These include building an animal shelter, renovating the county jail, and discussing county services for older residents. She plans her busy schedule so that she has time to spend with her husband and son.

Government in Metropolitan Areas

In 1800, about 5 percent of the nation's population lived in cities. By 1970 almost 75 percent of the people in the United States were urban dwellers, living in densely populated areas.

Since World War II the regions surrounding cities have grown into satellite communities called *suburbs*. In recent times, inner-city crime, pollution, and decay have increased middle-class migration to these communities.

Often suburban towns are so closely tied to a central city that they form what is termed a *metropolitan area*. As these regions expand, they merge into "strip cities" or "megalopolises." (A *megalopolis* is a heavily populated region, including several cities and their surrounding suburbs.) As a result, the problems faced by American central cities are no longer confined within their political boundaries.

COPING with the METROPOLIS

Many problems confront metropolitan governments. Within urban centers, diverse groups of people have varying needs and interests. City and county governments are not always able to meet the demands of these groups. One consequence of this has been a growth in federal spending at the state and local levels, as you can see in Figure 9–6.

As metropolitan areas expand, it becomes more difficult to service the populace. Sometimes, residents begin to believe that they have little impact on city hall decisions.

The suburban migration of many industries and middle-class residents complicates the situation. Often a majority of urban dwellers are those who cannot afford to leave. Moreover, the taxes and jobs needed to support these groups decline as industries relocate.

Local governments must attempt to solve these problems. Yet the large number of governments in metropolitan areas makes this difficult. In addition to the city government, each surrounding suburban town or community has a government, as do the counties in the area. Special districts, such as school districts, add to the confusion.

No single government has the resources or the authority to deal with metropolitan problems. However, cooperation between governments is often very difficult.

There is no single solution to all metropolitan problems. However, several communities have developed programs to handle some of the difficulties associated with urban growth. In this section you will examine three such efforts. As you read each case study, think about the specific plans implemented in each city. Begin to consider how these programs have affected the distribution of resources within each community.

★ Limiting Growth in Boulder, Colorado

Citizens in Boulder have witnessed the effects of uncontrolled growth in other western states. They are determined to prevent similar situations from occurring in Boulder.

In November 1976, voters approved a one-half reduction in housing construction. Currently, only 415 new homes can be built each year. The allocation of these building permits is strictly regulated.

To limit growth further, Boulder has initiated an Open Space Program. The city is purchasing land in Boulder Valley to be used only for recreational purposes.

Some city leaders fear that limiting Boulder's growth will make housing too expensive for middle- and low-income families. Boulder's City Planning Director admitted that this had been the effect of some of the programs, although this was not the original intent.

276

FEDERAL SPENDING at STATE and LOCAL LEVELS

Transfer Payments		Grants-in-Aid	
Total	180.7	Total	80.2
Income security	129.1	Income security	13.9
Social security	90.3	Public assistance cash	6.7
Railroad retirement	4.9	Child nutrition and	2.8
Civil service retirement	10.8	related programs	
Unemployment benefits	11.3	Other	4.3
Benefits for coal miners	1.0	Health	12.9
Food and nutrition	4.8	Education	20.8
Other	6.9	Veterans benefits	.9
Health	25.1	Other	31.9
Education	3.6	(1978 est.)	
Veterans benefits	13.2		
Retired pay for military	9.1		
Other	.6		

Figure 9-6

Source: Statistical Abstract of the U.S. 1978

★ Dayton's Neighborhood Priority Boards

The city of Dayton, Ohio, has made a major effort to increase citizen participation in government. Voters in each of Dayton's six neighborhoods elect 25 to 35 representatives to serve on a neighborhood priority board. These boards meet weekly to discuss community needs. Each month board chairpersons present neighborhood problems and goals to the city manager. Appropriate government policies and actions are then reported back to the community.

The neighborhood priority boards alert officials to specific issues. Therefore, although their role is advisory, the boards have a direct effect on the appropriation of city funds. Because citizens are aware of their influence on government decisions, participation in local government has increased.

★ Metro Government in the Twin Cities

One of the most successful metro governments in the United States is the Metropolitan Council of Minneapolis—St. Paul. It is essentially a regional planning agency superimposed by the state over hundreds of municipal governments. Its purpose is to contain suburban sprawl and urban decay in the Twin Cities area.

The main plan proposed by the council is to retain future development within an 800-square-mile perimeter in which sewers and other facilities already exist. Services will not be extended outside of this area. In this way, the council hopes to discourage future urban development and to promote agricultural activities.

To enforce this plan, the state legislature passed the Metropolitan Planning Act. Under it, the Metropolitan Council will provide local towns with detailed plans for sewers, highways, parks, and mass transit until 1990. By 1980 each locality must provide a land-use plan that fits the regional plan.

The council also is currently at the head of a movement to deal with pollution, water supply, waste disposal, and health care on a regional level. Metro already has created a sewer system based on regional needs. It is attempting to extend its authority over other services, such as mass transit.

Urban experts admit that the Twin Cities plan cannot be directly applied to other large cities such as New York or Newark. However, they advocate the principle of regional planning as a solution to urban decay and the middle-class exodus to the suburbs.

1. Compare the plans made by the three metropolitan areas described. How does each depend on citizen cooperation and action?

2. What are the major problems in the metropolitan area nearest to you?

3. Why do governments have problems distributing resources and making effective decisions in metropolitan areas?

The Skill of Generating Evidence: Interviewing

Who participates in local political activities in your community? How do these people communicate with other decision-makers and with other citizens? Why do they take part in local politics? You would not be likely to find the answers to questions like these in a book or magazine. However, you could begin to answer some of the questions by interviewing local political actors. Interviews are one valuable way to obtain information. They are especially useful when that information is not otherwise available.

You have already learned about the values and uses of evidence. You have practiced the skills of gathering and interpreting evidence. People interested in their own community often must create or generate evidence. Evidence can be important for describing a community, explaining trends, influencing others to support your position, and many other activities.

No one else may have recorded the information that you need. However, there may be people in the community who have that information. Their knowledge or opinions can provide the evidence you are seeking.

There are several ways to obtain information, to generate evidence that has not been recorded. One of these is to conduct interviews. Interviews have some important advantages over other ways of generating evidence:

1. Interviews are *flexible* ways of generating evidence. You can find out about ideas you hadn't thought about before.

2. Interviews provide ways to *probe* into topics when someone has important information.

3. Interviews allow people to talk about topics in their own way with *their own words.*

4. Interviews allow *interaction* between the interviewer and the respondent. (The

person being interviewed is called a *respondent*.) By making sure that other people understand your questions, you can get better evidence.

In extended interviews, you can gather a great deal of information. Thus, interviews can be very useful if you want to learn about a person or topic in depth.

USING INTERVIEWS Marlene wants to know when her favorite TV program starts. Should she interview the station manager? Clearly, an interview would not be the best way to get this information. Marlene could easily find the answer to her question in a published television schedule. Interviews are not the best way to gather evidence in the following cases.

1. Do not conduct interviews when you need evidence which is already *available* in books, manuals, or charts.

2. Do not conduct interviews when you want to find information which can, without very much difficulty, be gathered by a written questionnaire.

3. Do not conduct interviews when you need to *observe* someone's behavior rather than find out their opinions about what is happening.

Before you can conduct an interview, two tasks must be completed: (1) You need to construct an interview schedule, and (2) you need to decide which people to interview.

INTERVIEW SCHEDULES An *interview schedule* is a list of questions you will use to guide your interview. By constructing a schedule before the interview, you can think carefully and thoroughly about what you want to find out. You can construct questions that are directly related to what you want to learn. If you will be interviewing more than

Open-ended Interview Schedule

Interviewer _____

Person Interviewed _____

Date _____

Subject: _____

1. What are your opinions about the high bus fare in our community?
_____
_____
_____

2. Do you have any suggestions for lowering the fare? _____
_____
_____
_____

3. Do you think citizens should push to get the fare lowered? Why or why not? _____
_____
_____
_____

4. How old are you?_____

5. How *far from* the center city do you live?
_____

6. How many times a week do you use a bus?
_____

Forced-choice Interview Schedule

Interviewer _____

Person Interviewed _____

Date _____

Subject:_____

1. Are you in favor or opposed to the current bus fare in our community?
_____ In Favor _____Opposed

2. Would you support any of the following proposals to lower the fare?
_____Boycott the city bus service.
_____Use car pools.
_____Develop more forms of transportation including a subway system.

3. Do you think citizens should push to lower the bus fare?
Yes_____ No _____

4. How old are you?
under 20 _____ 20–40_____
40–60 _____ over 60_____

5. How *far from* the center city do you live?
0–1 mile_____ 1–5 miles____
more than 5 miles_____

6. How many times a week do you use a bus?
0 _____ 1–2 _____ 2–5 _____
more than 5_____

Figure 9-7

one person, a schedule also assures that you will ask each person the same questions.

Questions on an interview schedule may be either *open-ended* or *forced-choice* questions. When answering an open-ended question, a person may give any response that he or she thinks is appropriate. Forced-choice questions ask people to choose among various answers that the interviewer has already developed. The sample interview schedules on page 279 illustrate the difference between open-ended and forced-choice questions.

When you design questions for an interview schedule, you should follow four basic principles of asking questions.

1. Questions should be clear.
2. Questions should be related to a specific topic.
3. Questions should be unbiased.
4. Questions should be properly sequenced.

At this point, you may want to review the section on asking questions in *The Skill of Gathering Evidence* (pages 72–77).

Questions on an interview schedule are usually divided into three parts. The first part introduces people to the topic of the interview. This helps them think about the remaining questions. The next part of the schedule is the body of the interview. These questions are directly related to the evidence you are trying to generate. The final section normally includes brief questions about the background of the respondent. These might focus on age, sex, religion, income, or occupation. Good background questions help you interpret and evaluate the respondent's answers. They provide information about the perspective or position from which the person is answering the questions. Find these three parts on the interview schedules on page 279.

> 1. Choose a topic about which you would like to generate evidence by interviews.
> 2. Make up a brief interview schedule on your topic. (Save your schedule for further use.)

CHOOSING RESPONDENTS

An important part of successful interviewing is the wise selection of people to interview. The quality of the evidence you collect will be determined, in part, by your respondents.

The first step in the selection process is to analyze *what kind of people* could best provide the information you need. In other words, who can give useful answers to your questions. In part, this depends on the kind of information you are seeking. If, for example, you want to find out how the city council members feel about a local issue, you only want to interview city council members. On the other hand, if you want to know how citizens in the entire community feel about that issue, you should interview a cross section of the local population.

The second step in the selection process is to decide *how many people* you can and should interview. Several factors are important. First, how many people can conduct interviews? Are you the only interviewer, or are you part of a team? Second, how much time do you have in which to collect your evidence? Third, how many people are accessible to you?

Also, deciding how many people to interview is directly related to your analysis of what kind of people you should interview. Assume you had decided to interview city council members. If there are only six members of the council, it may be possible and reasonable for you to interview all of them. On the other hand, if you had decided to interview a cross section of the local population, you must make a selection within that group.

Samples. There are a number of ways in which to choose a sample within a large group. (A portion of a group can be called a *sample*.) You can make a *random sample*. In a random sample, people are chosen at random, without regard for their special qualifications. You might, for example, call every thousandth person listed in the telephone directory. Random samples are useful when you want to interview a general group, and when you are able to interview a great many people. The larger a random sample is, the more likely it is to be representative of the total group.

In general, a *systematic sample* is more practical for interviewing. A systematic sample is based on specific criteria or rules of selection. When it is necessary for you to interview only a sample of a group, it is probably important for your sample to be representative of the entire group.

In order to make a systematic sample, you must set up criteria for selection. For example, for a cross section of your local population, you might want to interview a certain number of people in each of these categories: young people under 18, voters 18 to 30, voters 31 to 50, voters 51 to 65, voters over 65. In addition, among the adults you would include a representative distribution of men and women who are blue-collar and white-collar workers, unemployed workers and high-level executives, housewives and working mothers.

By carefully choosing respondents in this way, your sample should reflect the whole. Then, answers to your interview questions can produce valuable evidence.

1. Using the topic and questions you developed earlier, decide what kind of people you want to interview. Describe the reasons for your choices.
2. Decide how many people you want to interview. Describe the reasons for your choices.
3. Describe the selection process you would use to choose respondents.

CONDUCTING an INTERVIEW

Once you have constructed an interview schedule and chosen respondents, you are ready to conduct your interviews. The following checklist of interview techniques will help you.

1. Develop a standard introduction to use when you approach a respondent.
2. Test your interview schedule by conducting some interviews with people not in your sample.
3. Make sure everyone involved in interviewing others has similar instructions and some experience in carrying out the interview.
4. Be friendly and impartial when you conduct your interview.
5. Read your questions as they are written, in the order they appear on the schedule. Ask all the questions, and discuss any answers that seem unclear.
6. Try not to make your note-taking obvious.
7. Whenever possible, interview people alone, in as comfortable a setting as possible.
8. Be sure to thank the people you interview for their cooperation.

1. Using the interview schedule you constructed earlier, practice interviewing another person.
2. How successful do you think your interview was?

COMPILING and ANALYZING EVIDENCE

When you have completed all the interviews, it is necessary to compile, or put together, the data you have collected. You should do this in a very systematic way. For this discussion assume you or your team have interviewed 10 respondents, using the interview schedule on page 282 (Figure 9–8).

Beginning with your first question, tally and compare all the answers you received. For example, list all the issues or concerns mentioned in response to Question 1. (It would also be useful to note by each item the number of times it was mentioned.) Then, record the number of persons who

```
                          Interviewer _____
                     Person
                     Interviewed _____

                     Organization or
                     government position _____


                          Date _____


Subject: Participating in Local Politics

1.  What local issues or concerns are most important to your organi-
    zation or government office? _____
    _____

2.  Which of the following statements best describes your political
    activities.

          a.  I often propose an activity or position on an issue and
    _____    try to convince others to accept it.

          b.  I usually support an action or position suggested by
    _____    someone else.

          c.  I mostly watch and listen in order to learn more about
    _____    the topic.

          d.  I am usually involved in organizing the activity after the
    _____    group has decided on it.

3.  How many community groups do you belong to?

    _____ 0 _____ 1-2 _____ 3-4 _____ more than 4

4.  What is your age? _____

5.  How long have you held your present position (office)? _____
```

Figure 9-8

answers in each. For example, you could set up these age categories for Question 4: 18 to 21, 22 to 31, 32 to 45, 46 to 65, over 65.

After you have compiled the data in this way, you may want to compare responses on another level. Still using the interview schedule on page 282, you could compile data based on the positions held by respondents. For example, how many people who are over 45 years old selected answer 2a, how many selected 2b, and so on? Or, you might want to look at all the respondents who listed a certain issue in response to Question 1. How many community groups does each of those respondents belong to?

Careful study and analysis of interview responses is an important part of interpreting evidence you have generated. The more accurate your interpretation is, the more accurate your conclusions based on that evidence will be.

chose each of the statements in Question 2. And record the number of people who selected each of the categories in Question 3.

Answers to questions like Questions 4 and 5 on this interview schedule are compiled slightly differently. It probably would not be practicable to list every age given in answer to Question 4 or every amount of time answered in Question 5. The most sensible procedure would be to set up your own categories. Then, record the number of

1. Construct a new interview schedule on a topic about which you would like to generate evidence.
2. Using this schedule, interview someone in your school or community. Discuss with your teacher the possibility of interviewing additional respondents.
3. Based on the same interview schedule, describe how you would conduct a series of interviews. Indicate how you would compile and analyze responses.

The Skill of Making Decisions

In this chapter you have read several cases that show citizens making decisions which had important effects on their local governments. Understanding how they made those decisions is important if you want to influence the activities of your own local government.

You need to know how to make decisions in order to make wise choices among alternatives and in order to bring about the outcomes that you prefer. To do this, you must design a decision-making strategy. In this section you will learn important decision-making skills, such as planning a strategy, determining alternatives, delegating responsibilities within a group, and determining the information needed to reach a decision.

IDENTIFYING a STRATEGY

A decision-making strategy can be defined as a plan of action through which individuals try to reach their goals. As a plan of action, every strategy has stages or steps. People must figure out with whom they will talk, what information they need to know, and how they will act to promote their goal.

An example of a strategy is outlined in the following case study, a hypothetical decision-making situation. As you read, try to determine the major steps included in the strategy. You may want to list the steps on a separate sheet of paper.

★ Marsha's Defeat

Marsha Barton had joined the Riverdale Citizens League because she believed citizens could make a difference. Now, however, she was discouraged. The League never seemed to do anything Marsha thought was important.

Finally, Marsha decided to do something about her annoyance. She decided to propose a League activity that would make a difference. Marsha's idea was for League members to help the Riverdale City Council plan long-range community activities.

A good part of that night, Marsha thought about her idea. She made a list of reasons why the Citizen League could aid city council members in planning for the future of the community. She even staged arguments with herself over the objections she had heard all day.

The next day Marsha presented her idea to her friends again. They liked it better this time and offered to help her work it out. Sara, Angelo, Kathy, Jim, and Bob agreed to meet with Marsha the next evening.

Marsha also asked Alfred Palmer, her representative on the city council, what he thought. He encouraged her to go ahead with her idea.

Feeling very successful, Marsha met the next evening with people who wanted to help her. The group agreed that city planning was important, but they had several different opinions about how the idea should be carried out.

After a long discussion, the group decided that Marsha's plan was the best. However, they thought they needed more information about whether or not the plan would work before they presented it to officials. Kathy was elected to poll city council members on their views of the plan. She was also to ask them if the citizens' committee might have facilities in City Hall. And, she was to ask Mayor Alice Whitehouse how she felt about the plan.

On Monday afternoon, the group met again. Kathy reported that everyone she had talked to was in favor of the plan.

The group thought more about how the plan could be carried out. They agreed that the Citizen League should sponsor the proposal as a League activity. The League could canvass citizens to find out what their needs were and who could work with the council. Certain evenings during the week could be scheduled when they would meet at the city council building.

Marsha and her friends decided that the plan would work. All agreed to take major roles in helping to get it started. The group then decided how to move. Marsha, Angelo, and Kathy would draw up a plan. Then, Marsha would introduce it at the next Citizen League meeting. Other members of the group agreed to come and vote in favor of the proposal. Each decided to contact at least one League member to get his or her support for the plan.

At the Tuesday meeting of the Citizen League, the president began by discussing car pools that were needed for the next week. Marsha raised her hand and was given the floor to introduce her proposal. She spent about 20 minutes talking about her idea. When she sat down, the League president said that the group should think about the plan. He then continued to ask for volunteers for the car pool.

When the president finished the assignments, Marsha again brought up the issue of the planning committee. But the president said that the meeting had run too long already and should be adjourned. Marsha tried to argue for a vote on the plan. However, the president insisted on adjourning the meeting. No one in the group felt they could oppose the president. So, the meeting was adjourned.

The Citizen League met the next Tuesday, and the next, and the next. The president never let Marsha's plan come up again. Finally, the whole issue was dropped.

1. What are the steps in Marsha's decision-making strategy?
2. In your opinion, what did Marsha do wrong?

STEPS in DECISION-MAKING

What had Marsha done wrong? She certainly knew what a strategy was. She knew that *a strategy is a plan of action through which individuals try to reach their goals*. She had a goal, and she tried to reach it.

Marsha began on the right track. She thought hard about the problem that she was interested in. She even wrote it down and thought of arguments and counterarguments. During this time she was engaging in the first step of any decision-making activity. She was *developing a clear statement of the problem*.

"How can we make Riverdale a better place to live?" is not a clearly stated problem. It is vague. People would be confused about Marsha's plan of action. Examples of clearly stated problems are "How can we increase the membership in the Citizen League?" or "How can citizens contribute to plans for the community?" In each case,

there is a clear object—increased membership, citizen planning—that someone is trying to achieve. Marsha did this. She knew that she wanted the Citizen League to sponsor a meaningful citizen contribution by setting up a planning committee to promote the quality of life in Riverdale.

Next, Marsha met with a group of supporters to talk about plans and alternative suggestions. This discussion helped to make the issue clearer. The group developed arguments for and against different proposals. Finally they decided that Marsha's plan was best. In doing this, Marsha and the group took another step correctly. They *determined important alternative ways of solving the problem*. This is a key step in any strategy. It makes people aware of the counterarguments to their position.

Next, the group asked relevant community and council members about the plan. They did this to find out whether it was workable. At this stage of their work, the group was *seeking information relevant to the policy alternative that they favored*. Without this type of information, the feasibility of the proposal would always be questionable.

The group then planned how they would move to introduce and gain support for their proposal. They decided that Marsha would introduce the decision. They also decided that each of them would call one member of the Citizen League to get that person to vote for their idea. They were *determining the sequence of moves they would make in order to gain support for their proposal*.

Group members were also *delegating roles*. This too is an important part of carrying out a plan. In this case, Marsha was taking an organizer role by introducing the decision and beginning to move the Citizen League to act. Other members were taking advocate roles by agreeing to telephone other Citizen League members.

Finally, Marsha's group decided that they would have the Citizen League take the proposal to the city council for its support. In doing this, they were *deciding a way of carrying out their proposal if the group voted for it*. This is an important part of any strategy. Many decisions are made without ever being carried out because no plans were made to see the decision through.

If Marsha did all of these things, what went wrong? What did she leave out?

It's clear that Marsha's plan was frustrated by the club president. Marsha was cut off, and the president controlled the vote. Why did this happen? It happened because Marsha failed to do one very important thing. She forgot to look at the Citizen League itself as a group. She did not question what group characteristics were important to the success of her plan. In this case, the Citizen League was run by one person— the president. Marsha could do all she wanted to influence League members to support her, but she would always fail without the president's support.

Whatever strategy Marsha planned should have been based on sound knowledge of the group that was to make the decision. If she had figured out that a club was run by one person, she should have known that the president would be the key person to talk with. She could have determined why the president opposed her plan. Then she could have developed a different strategy.

Marsha's mistake is a common one. Always remember to have a *sound knowledge of the operation of any group in which you work*.

In review, these steps are important in successfully making decisions in any group:

1. Make a clear statement of the problem that you want to solve.
2. Determine the important characteristics of the group in which the problem is to be raised.
3. Make a statement of important alternative ways of solving the problem. Decide which one you favor most.
4. Determine the information that is relevant to supporting the policy alternative that you favor.
5. Determine the sequence of moves you will make in order to gather support behind the alternative you favor.
6. Make a list of roles that individuals will take in making these moves.
7. Determine a way of carrying out the policy if the decision is made in your favor.

1. Devise a decision-making strategy for a decision to be made in your class, school, or community. Use the seven steps in making a decision.
2. Report on and discuss the results of your decision-making.

---

1. Explain the relationship between state and local governments.
2. In chart form, outline the main features of the three forms of city government. Assess the strengths and weaknesses of each.
3. Review the features of county government.
4. What services are provided by local governments? In your opinion, which are the most important? Explain.
5. Why do individual citizens have more influence at the local level of government than at any other level?

Chapter Review

6. Summarize the differences between a formal and an informal political actor in local politics.

7. Why do citizen groups usually have a greater influence on local politics than political parties?

8. Review the instances in which you would use interviews to generate evidence. Summarize the main steps in the interviewing process.

9. List some of the most critical problems facing metropolitan governments today. Propose possible solutions to these problems.

10. Summarize the steps in effective decision-making. What are some issues on which you might have to make decisions?

Chapter Vocabulary

Define the following terms.

municipality	town meeting	open-ended question
incorporation	selectmen	forced-choice question
urban	county	sample
mayor	parish	random sample
city council	county seat	systematic sample
commission	township	suburb
charter	special district	metropolitan area
city	generate	megalopolis
village	respondent	
town	interview schedule	

Chapter Analysis

1. Construct a chart, detailing the form, functions, and responsibilities of each of the following units of local government: cities, towns, villages, counties, townships, and special districts.

2. If you were to seek an elected office or appointed job at the local level, which would you choose? What qualifications and resources would you need to obtain this position? Explain.

3. Review the interviewing process. As a participant in local politics, why is this an important skill to have? Discuss instances in your community in which evidence generated by interviews might influence decision-making.

4. In recent years, some metropolitan areas have merged into "strip cities" or megalopolises. If this trend continues, what might be the effects on local government? What new forms of government might be necessitated?

1. Using your local newspaper as a source, cut out articles that describe different kinds of political activity in your community. Classify these articles as examples of decision-making, communication, participation, or leadership.

2. Obtain a copy of the government charter for your community. Study this document, and write a short report on the form and functions of your local government. Conclude your report by deciding whether or not any revisions should be made in the charter.

3. Work out a plan to interview a famous political person. Then write a hypothetical interview with this individual. If possible, with another student, present your interview to the class.

4. Draw graphs depicting the population growth in your county during the past 100 years. Then invite a local county official to talk about the problems and benefits that this growth has caused. Ask the speaker to discuss the ways in which county government has changed to meet the demands of an expanding population.

5. Investigate the various citizen groups in your community. Select one of these, and study the ways in which it influences local government.

6. Prepare a map of the nearest metropolitan area, showing all the towns, villages, cities, and counties within that area. Determine the number and types of local governments represented in your map.

7. Devise a decision-making strategy about an issue that is important to you. Carry out each of the steps in decision-making and report the results to your class.

Chapter Bibliography

Reshaping Government in Metropolitan Areas, Committee for Economic Development, New York, NY, 1970.

An overview of metropolitan trends, highlighting issues such as education, welfare, crime, and transportation.

America's 50 Safest Cities, David Franke (Arlington House Publications: New Rochelle, NY), 1974.

Lively descriptive case studies of 50 American cities, including interviews with citizens of the various communities.

The Municipal Yearbook, International City Management Association, Washington, DC, 1977.

Includes a wealth of graphically presented information about cities in the United States, especially data on city finances and population.

From America's Counties Today: 1973, National Association of Counties, Washington, D.C., 1973.

Contains useful information on county government, including the structure of county government, its programs and personnel. Includes material on modern and innovative county governments.

Chapter Objectives

★ To analyze how citizens participate in community life

★ To apply the concepts of political resources and political activities to the study of a specific community

★ To apply skills of interpreting evidence

★ To develop skills in valuing

chapter 10

CITIZEN PARTICIPATION in COMMUNITY LIFE

By applying the concepts leadership, decision-making, communication, and participation, you have learned a great deal about state and local political activities. You have also seen that citizen involvement can make government more responsive to the needs of people.

Chapter 10 presents an in-depth look at politics in a specially selected community—Santa Barbara, California. You will be asked to apply the concepts and skills learned in this unit to local politics in Santa Barbara. This community has experienced active citizen involvement in recent years. The activity is largely a result of an oil spill which occurred off the Santa Barbara shore in 1969. (An oil spill is a patch of oil accidentally discharged into a body of water.) Quality of life has long been a major issue in Santa Barbara. The oil spill served to intensify citizen concern.

As you read the material, try to identify similar examples of political activity in your city or town. Also think about these questions: Has your community ever experienced a major disaster? If so, what kinds of citizen activity occurred after the disaster? How did such activity affect community life?

Background for Political Activity

This chapter focuses on Santa Barbara, California, and the political activity engaged in by its citizens. (The map on this page shows Santa Barbara and other California cities.) Over the years, people living in the area have shown a desire to take part in making decisions for their community. Today, many citizen groups are active in Santa Barbara's political life. These groups have a great deal of influence upon the policies made by the city government.

Citizens of Santa Barbara feel strongly about their community. They treasure the natural beauty of the Santa Barbara area. They want to preserve this beauty. In addition, many citizens enjoy the "small town" feeling in Santa Barbara. Residents also appreciate the opportunities they have to influence the quality of life in their community.

Citizen involvement in Santa Barbara did not just "happen." The city has a history of active citizen participation. This history, combined with reaction to the 1969 oil spill, accounts for active political participation.

Figure 10-1

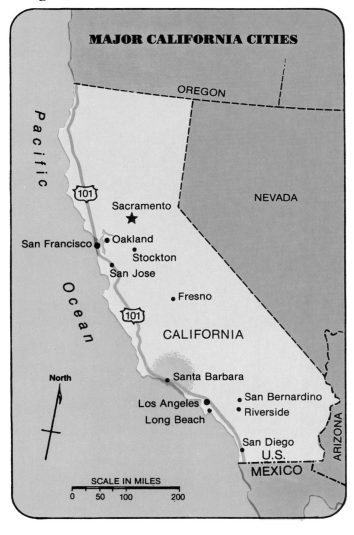

A HISTORY of SANTA BARBARA Until the late 1500s, Native Americans were the only people living in the Santa Barbara area. In the late 1500s, this situation changed. White settlers, mostly Spaniards, entered the area. These people brought with them diseases unknown to the Native American population. As a result, many Native Americans died.

Spaniards occupied the Santa Barbara area throughout the 1600s and 1700s. During the late 1700s they built the Santa Barbara Mission. This mission has been reconstructed over the years, and it still stands today. In the 1800s, settlers continued to move into the Santa Barbara area as well as into other parts of California. California became a state in 1850, and Santa Barbara became incorporated as a city in that same year.

Hot springs were discovered in Santa Barbara in the 1870s. These springs lured many people to the area. The city grew quickly and took on an image as a residence for health-seekers. In addition to its reputation as a health center, many people considered Santa Barbara an ideal vacation spot. Its year-round moderate temperatures, as

290

well as its access to both beaches and mountains, made it extremely attractive.

Furthermore, Santa Barbara possessed a natural harbor. Stearns Wharf, built in 1868, made the harbor usable by ocean vessels. In 1887, the first train arrived in Santa Barbara. The city then became even more accessible to the rest of America.

In the 1890s, an oil boom occurred in suburban Summerland. There the first off shore oil wells were drilled from rigs erected on wharves. Attempts were made to develop oil fields in other parts of Santa Barbara. One derrick erected at Miramar Beach was destroyed, however, in the late 1890s. The destruction was caused by a group of people led by the publisher of a local newspaper. This group felt that oil exploration would ultimately mar the beauty of Santa Barbara. The group's action showed the extent to which some Santa Barbarans would go to protect their community.

In June 1925, a major earthquake occurred in Santa Barbara. In 19 seconds, the mission towers toppled, business buildings collapsed, hotels crumbled, churches were shattered, and railroad rails became twisted. The city was left without communication of any kind. Property damage extended to $15 million. Thirteen lives were lost.

After the earthquake, the city council appointed architectural review committees to set rules for rebuilding destroyed structures. These groups said that no new buildings could be constructed unless they had low-pitched red tile roofs, plaster walls, and arched fronts. This meant that most of the downtown area that had been destroyed by the earthquake would be rebuilt in a Spanish style. Also, the new groups recommended that no signs or billboards be used anywhere in the city.

The population boom following World War II brought other matters to the attention of Santa Barbara's citizens. In 1948 there was a severe water shortage in the city. Water was rationed for the first time in the city's history. It was apparent to many people in Santa Barbara that the area's limited natural resources should be guarded closely. For the first time, citizens began to consider limiting the city's population growth.

Also after World War II, major oil fields were discovered in the Santa Barbara Channel. During the 1950s, huge elevated oil platforms were constructed in the Santa Barbara Channel. The building of these oil platforms outraged many citizens of Santa Barbara. Oil exploration touched off a serious conflict which continues to this day.

The first oil discoveries in Santa Barbara were on land. The shore area shown here was developed in the late 1920s. Notice the tall rigs, or derricks, which support drilling machinery.

Buildings destroyed by the 1925 earthquake are shown in this photograph, taken shortly after the disaster. Decisions made by city planners in the 1920s influenced the way Santa Barbara looks today.

1. What are some of Santa Barbara's important natural resources? How did they affect the development of Santa Barbara?
2. What kinds of citizen action have taken place in Santa Barbara in the past?

BLOWOUT at PLATFORM A

The controversy behind the oil platforms set the scene for politics in Santa Barbara in the 1970s. From the time they were built, many citizens found these platforms unacceptable. One civic leader summarized his feelings this way:

"Back in the early 60s, I couldn't believe what was happening off shore. All of a sudden there was a platform one day. It rose up out of the ocean. I couldn't believe we would allow a platform to obstruct the horizon. Every time I drove to work from my house, I'd see this object on the horizon that wasn't meant to be there. It scared me. What would happen if a ship ran into it? Or what if something went wrong with it technically? Something could happen."

Something did happen on January 28, 1969. Of the three platforms located in federal waters, two were operated by Union Oil Company. These platforms were called platform A and platform B. From its platform A, Union Oil Company drilled more than 20 oil wells.

Drilling for oil beneath the ocean poses a potential hazard for marine life. Therefore, oil companies are supposed to follow strict safety standards. These standards help reduce the possibility of a drilling accident. Despite attempts to follow these standards, Union's well A-21 had a blowout on January 28. (A *blowout* is an uncontrolled eruption of gas or oil from a well.)

Gas and oil erupted from the well, reaching skyward 20 stories to the top of platform A. People working on the platform rushed to seal the well, for they knew that a spark could ignite the entire platform. Despite their attempts, oil began leaking rapidly.

The results of the spill were staggering. Some people estimate that more than 6,000 birds were killed in the initial days of the spill period. In addition to the loss of birds and other animal life, the financial cost was high. Expenses approached $100 million approximately one year after the spill! These costs did not include the multimillion-dollar lawsuits which followed.

The spill touched off a wave of citizen outrage in Santa Barbara. Individuals and groups in the community quickly took sides.

The 1969 oil spill resulted from a blowout at an offshore oil platform like the one shown here (top photo). Oil pollution damaged offshore waters and recreational areas such as this marina (bottom photo).

Citizens of Santa Barbara took action in reaction to the oil spill. They formed environmental groups, held rallies (center photo), and testified at Congressional hearings in Santa Barbara and in Washington, D.C. They even petitioned the president of the United States to stop oil development in the Santa Barbara Channel.

Some people wanted to limit future oil exploration and drilling in the Santa Barbara Channel. Some people even wanted to limit the growth of the community in areas such as housing, transportation, and population. Other people felt that despite the oil spill, Santa Barbara should continue its growth.

As a result of the 1969 oil spill, the 1970s saw increased political activity in Santa Barbara. Individuals and groups became determined to protect the quality of life in their community.

1. What damages resulted from the blowout at platform A?
2. What were citizen reactions to the oil spill?
3. How might citizens participate to prevent another disaster? How could they communicate opinions to officials?

Citizen Groups Form in Santa Barbara

Throughout Santa Barbara history, citizens have been active in community life. In 1920, for example, citizens formed the Santa Barbara Community Arts Association. The Association was organized to promote music, art, drama, and architectural planning. One of the group's organizers was Dr. Pearl Chase. Pearl Chase based her actions on the belief that only through citizen groups can community members influence the way their community is run.

Pearl Chase summarized her belief in citizen action in this way:

"Government officials are temporary. They come and go. This constant turnover means that many citizen organizations have far greater importance in community affairs. Don't assume leadership will come from the professions. . . . If you are to succeed, you must be led by *citizens* and *citizen groups,* with the interest and support of key public agencies."

Citizen groups acted according to this belief after the 1969 oil spill. Several groups formed to reassert public control over actions taken by the city. The type of action taken by these groups is not unique to Santa Barbara. It can occur in any city as long as citizens are willing to put in the necessary time and effort. Politics requires continual work. This commitment is illustrated by the following two Santa Barbara organizations.

Dr. Pearl Chase

GET OIL OUT! The day after the spill, James "Bud" Bottoms began working to form the first of many new citizen groups. The oil spill motivated him and many others to protest oil company activities in the Santa Barbara Channel.

In the following selection, Mr. Bottoms describes the formation of Get Oil Out. This organization is popularly known as GOO! The selection is from an interview conducted with Mr. Bottoms. As you read, think about the political resources which GOO used and the types of political activities it took part in.

★ The Formation of GOO

A friend and I worked together to organize GOO. We realized from the start that GOO needed to take the issues to state government. Therefore, we called an ex-state senator. We thought that he could tell us how to contact the governor and work with others at the state level.

Our next step was to set up an office and to become incorporated. Many, many people wanted to help. Lawyers gave their time to GOO, and artists sent in poems and pictures for our newsletters. The Santa Barbara *News-Press,* our local newspaper, was with us 100 percent.

The newspaper was very important, because we did not have the support of local television. The local paper did not try to cover up the oil spill. It was big news. Moreover, almost daily something was printed about GOO. The local newspaper is probably half the reason for our success.

Once established, we came up with the idea of a membership and yearly dues. We selected a board of 12 directors and hired a secretary.

We had to be sure that environmental issues were brought before the public. We just couldn't wait for something to develop. GOO was formed because of the oil disaster. But since the oil spill we have had to create special events or issues.

A year after GOO was founded we held an Earth Day. This event was in recognition of the oil spill. Earth Day was on January 28, 1970. Therefore, we called ourselves the January 28th Committee. As a result of this ac-

tivity, other groups, such as the Community Ecology Center and the Community Environmental Council, were organized.

The Citizens Planning Association, which was established before the spill, is taking a more critical look at things now. This citizen group reviews city planning proposals and makes recommendations as to their merits.

I think we showed people that they should speak up and express their views on community issues. Many did express their opinions. Thousands of letters went to newspapers. Many people were interviewed over radio and television. People began attending hearings and giving their opinions on issues.

As a citizen group, GOO has worked to influence the future of Santa Barbara. Every time there's a city election we write a questionnaire and send it to the people who are running for office. This way we learn their views on issues of concern to us. GOO has served as an information center, also. GOO is the best source of information on oil spills in the country. Letters come in every day from schools all over the nation asking for information about the effects of oil on the environment.

In general, GOO has helped raise community consciousness. I could probably mention a dozen organizations that have come about in the last seven years that have something to do with the environment. What's happened is that people are now aware that they can do something. A large number of these organizations have come about because of this awareness.

As you have just read, GOO has been very active in community politics. Through the Santa Barbara *News-Press* and its own newsletter, GOO has regularly publicized oil activities in the Santa Barbara Channel. It has organized rallies and public demonstrations. Legal battles have been conducted against some of the country's biggest oil companies. As a result, GOO has reached a large number of citizens in the community with its message.

THE COMMUNITY ENVIRONMENTAL COUNCIL

As Bud Bottoms pointed out, a number of environmental groups have formed in Santa Barbara in recent years. One of these groups is the Community Environmental Council (CEC). Since 1970, this group has sponsored one special project each year. One of its earliest projects, as well as its most successful, was the Community Ecology Center. Hal Conklin was a leader in starting both the Community Environmental Council and its Center. In the following selection he describes the differences between these organizations and GOO.

★ Activities of the Community Environmental Council

We are not an advocacy group. (An *advocacy group* supports a particular issue or program.) We are a non-profit educational institution. Therefore, we do not take positions for or against issues. Our main task is to point out the issues and to ask questions. It is our belief that the only way you can bring about change is through open public forums. We try to provide the opportunities where people can discuss the issues. CEC trusts that the public will make the right decisions.

Because of our approach, the Ecology Center has had a low profile in terms of fighting specific issues. This is different than GOO, which is an activist group. GOO fights the problems, such as the oil spill, that are a result of the oil rigs. The Ecology Center would never be seen in this light. That is not the kind of center we started nor is it the kind that we are now. This doesn't mean that we don't make ourselves known. However, in doing so we use a much more subtle approach than GOO.

Our financial base comes from a variety of sources. About 600 people in the community have memberships in the Community Environmental Council. We use that money to support each of our projects.

We advertise our services and information. For example, information is posted around the public library. Also, announcements are sent to the local schools and colleges. The biggest newspaper in town is very supportive of us. The alternative newspaper, with 10,000 subscribers, also promotes the CEC and the Ecology Center.

Besides media contacts, we have contacts among the concerned citizens in our community. There are many community organizations in this town. Everybody who has any concern for the community is involved in one of these organizations. We know many of these people, so we can get news out through them. Santa Barbara is a relatively small town of 70,000 people—150,000 if you count the surrounding community. Therefore, a lot of information about our organization is spread by word-of-mouth. In 48 hours, everybody in town can know that something is going to happen.

The number of members in the CEC has remained stable. We have about 600 active members. However, the membership changes from year to year. We lose 50–75 members a year, but that many new people join each year. Therefore, many people know of our work and support us.

There is no way to know if we will continue to be influential. All we can do is to stand on our track record and say, "Based upon what we have done so far, we will probably be influential." I think our process has worked well. We try to be honest. We try to encourage positive thinking among community members.

1. Under what style of leadership does the CEC operate?
2. What political resources have been used by the CEC?
3. What political activities has CEC become involved in? How could this involvement affect the distribution of resources in Santa Barbara?
4. How can people act in each of the four participant roles through organizations like GOO or the CEC?
5. List five ways in which you might act as a supporter in either GOO or the CEC.

Changes in City Government

Get Oil Out, the Community Environmental Council, and other environmental groups worked to make citizens aware of oil company activities. (Because of their concern with the environment, these groups are referred to as environmental groups.) They also tried to prevent uncontrolled urban planning in the Santa Barbara area. They held rallies and demonstrations. They published newsletters, wrote articles, and took out advertisements in the local newspaper. Through these methods, citizen groups urged the city government to carefully consider any activities that might damage the local environment.

In addition to these methods of putting pressure on city government, the environmental groups worked to elect their slate of candidates to local office. The city council election of 1973 provided such an opportunity for the environmental groups. As the following material shows, these groups worked to unseat city council members who were more responsive to business interests than to environmental concerns. Their goal was to achieve an environmental majority on the city council. As you read the following section, think about the form of city govern-

ment in Santa Barbara, the activities of the Citizens Coalition, and how the environmental groups tried to achieve their goals.

FROM OUTSIDERS to INSIDERS Santa Barbara is governed by a city council, a city administrator, and several city commissions. There are seven voting members on the city council, one of whom is elected as the mayor. The council makes most major decisions, and the city administrator implements them. All seven council members are elected. The city administrator is appointed by the Santa Barbara City Council.

The job of city administrator is much the same as the job of city manager. John Scott, city administrator for Santa Barbara during much of the 1970s, described his job this way: "My job [was] to carry out policy set by the city council, to administer the business of the city, and to recommend policies to the city council for adoption."

Before 1973, the council did not take a consistent position regarding the environment. For example, in 1967 it voted to ban all oil-related activities from Stearns Wharf. However, the same council voted to enlarge the Santa Barbara portion of U.S. Highway 101. This highway runs up and down the state of California. It has several traffic lights—in the middle of Santa Barbara. The council wanted to redesign this portion of U.S. Highway 101 to allow more traffic to travel on it at a higher rate of speed.

Also, in 1972 the city council decided to consider a $75 million development project. This project aimed to build large commercial facilities across from the beach. Some people objected vigorously to the plan. To create alternatives to it, they formed a citizens' committee—the Committee for Santa Barbara. They asked architects, designers, economists, scientists, and environmentalists to help them in their work. A scaled-down version of this plan was later considered.

By 1973, many citizen groups felt it was crucial to have an environmental majority on the city council. This meant selecting and supporting four candidates in the 1973 city council election. To achieve their goal, the groups banded together in what became known as the Citizens Coalition. Any citizen of Santa Barbara who wanted to could join the Citizens Coalition. The group held open meetings throughout the community. It attempted to interview every potential candidate for city council. The coalition met weekly to evaluate candidate interviews.

Based on these evaluations, the Citizens Coalition chose four people to support in the 1973 city council election. Each was prepared to speak up and act on behalf of environmental concerns. These four candidates became known as the reform slate. It was their desire to change the course of urban growth that Santa Barbara was following.

Through hard work and financial support, the Citizens Coalition helped to elect all four of their candidates. An observer of political life in Santa Barbara described the significance of the 1973 city council election in the following way.

"One direct result of the oil spill was the election of the reform slate of council members. They composed a majority of the new government.

These people were different from previous council members, mostly because they were not business people. The reform slate consisted of one woman and three men. The woman was a housewife. One of the three men was steward and business manager of a small labor union. Another was a college administrator who also held a divinity degree. The third man was a young physicist.

"These people ran on an anti-oil, pro-environment program. They wanted oil and oil-related activities controlled. If possible, oil was to be kept out of the channel and off the city-owned wharf.

"The new council members also wanted to discourage overuse and overgrowth. Up until that time most of us had been led to believe that bigger was better. The new members initiated a study to determine the ideal population for Santa Barbara, given its resources. Nothing quite like this had ever been done before. A private firm estimated that it could do the study for $240,000. However, the new reform members of the city council felt the study could be done by volunteer experts for much less. As a result, the study was conducted by people who volunteered their time. The total cost was about $40,000, far less than would have been paid to a private firm! They got a milestone report for the money."

1. Describe Santa Barbara's form of government.
2. Why did many citizens want an environmental majority on the Santa Barbara City Council?
3. Describe the activities of the Citizens Coalition.
4. What kinds of programs would you expect the four new city council members to sponsor?

PROFILE of a CITY COUNCIL MEMBER

What type of person was elected to the city council in 1973? Consider carefully the concerns of Leo Martinez, for example.

Before 1973, there had never been a Chicano elected to the city council in Santa Barbara. (Mexican Americans comprised 26 percent of the city's population.) Some people felt that the city could not be responsive to the needs of Mexican Americans without a Chicano on the city council. This situation was remedied when Leo Martinez became a city council member in 1973.

Martinez was one of the four Citizens Coalition candidates. He was thus supported by a broad range of groups in the city.

Martinez's victory enabled him to be responsive to different needs. He was concerned with environmental issues. He also intended to deal with the needs of the city's Chicano population. Below are comments by Martinez about his role on the city council.

"When I got on the council, there was only one minority member on the city commissions. That was a Mexican American on the police-fire commission. Since I have been on the city council, we have nominated sixteen Spanish surnamed commissioners to different commissions. We also put the first black person on the police-fire commission.

"Part of my role in city government is ensuring fair laws for the minority community. In the past, the laws often have not meant the same thing for everyone. Allocations of money never got down to all the people. I've been making sure that this does not continue."

Martinez had been active in Santa Barbara politics even before his election to the city council. He had taken an active interest in Casa de la Raza, founded by Chicano groups in 1971. Casa de la Raza was formed to provide services for the Chicano population. It organized a children's medical clinic, a day care center, a meeting place for organizations, a dance hall, and a theater group. It also had free legal services for minority groups.

Martinez feels strongly that concerned people like him must remain active in politics. He believes there must always be some individual or group to see that resources are equally distributed among city residents. In his opinion,

"Policies change with the people who hold office. Therefore, if programs are not carried out to ensure equality, things can return to the way they were. In the 70s we were able to win election because 'the giant was sleeping.' Now it's awake and angry. Therefore, if we are to achieve our goals, the next elections are also very important."

1. What were the major concerns of Leo Martinez as a member of the city council?
2. In what ways did Martinez want to help the Chicanos of Santa Barbara?

GROWTH CONTROL in SANTA BARBARA

In the city council election of 1973, environmental groups proved they were a strong political force. Their concerns received attention through the efforts of the reform city council members. The new members of the city council worked to curb the rapid growth and development of Santa Barbara.

In the early 1970s, the planning commission recommended that a study be conducted to evaluate the impact of growth in Santa Barbara. As pointed out earlier, this task was undertaken by various citizens in

Located between the coast and the mountains, Santa Barbara offers its residents scenic views and a pleasant climate. It is also noted for its Spanish architecture. A good example is the courthouse. Today the beaches have been restored and are once again an appealing part of the Santa Barbara scene.

the community. Experts from all fields formed a task force.

The task force study was released in 1974. It contained an important conclusion. The study concluded that the city could support a population of up to 85,000 citizens without straining its resources. With a population of over 70,000 in 1974, this meant that the city could support only 15,000 more people. This meant in turn that construction and the development of business and industry might have to be curbed so that Santa Barbara would not grow beyond the identified limits.

Based upon the study, the city adopted a growth control *ordinance* (law) in 1975. This ordinance affected new zoning regulations throughout the city. Under an old general plan written in 1964, it was possible to build 43 small living units on an acre of land zoned for residential housing. Under the 1975 ordinance, zoning changes reduced the number of such units from 43 to 12 per acre. This was a reduction of 72 percent. Critics of the plan charged that it increased unemployment among the members of the building trades. They also claimed that it increased the costs of housing in the community, and that it discouraged business investment throughout the Santa Barbara area.

In order to meet the goals of the new law, the number of annual building permits had to be drastically reduced. Furthermore, strict conservation measures began to be observed in all areas of city life.

Many people were not happy with the new plan. More than any other single action, the 1975 growth control ordinance made people question the activities of citizen groups and the city council. Just as the oil spill mobilized one set of interests in 1969, the new plan mobilized an opposing set of interests in 1975.

1. What effect did the 1974 study results have on the 1975 growth control plan in Santa Barbara?

2. Are there growth control laws in your community? If so, describe them. If not, do you think such laws are necessary? Explain.

THE OPPOSITION ORGANIZES

In reaction to the growth control ordinance, other Santa Barbara citizens organized to make their voices heard. A variety of people were opposed to the ordinance. They included people in the construction industry, business leaders, small business owners, some unions, and other interested citizens.

Arguments against the ordinance were varied. Some people were afraid that Santa Barbara would lose important businesses, which would increase property taxes and unemployment. Others pointed to problems caused by restrictions on building homes. They argued that existing housing would become too expensive. This, in turn, would mean that middle- and low-income people could not move to Santa Barbara.

Some opponents of the ordinance feared that restricting growth in the city would mean that the surrounding areas would grow even larger. In their opinion, this would increase pollution, traffic congestion, and energy use.

Opponents of growth control focused on the 1977 city council election. Since 1973, the council had generally voted in favor of strict environmental controls by a 4 to 3 majority. To change this, the opponents would need to gain a majority on the city council. The sides quickly formed for the upcoming election.

1. How do the concerns of the opponents of growth control differ from the concerns of the environmental groups?
2. How can people act in each of the four participant roles in a local political dispute such as this one?

People on both sides of the growth control question in Santa Barbara have been concerned with striking a balance between economic and environmental needs. They want to preserve Santa Barbara's natural beauty, as this photograph shows, as well as to maintain its spirit of vitality.

ANOTHER CITY COUNCIL CONTEST

The 1977 city council election in Santa Barbara was a bitter campaign. Business and environmental interests vied for control of the city council.

Prior to the election, the city council consisted of the following people: Sheila Lodge, Bud Eyman, Gus Chavalas, Leo Martinez, Nyle Utterback, Lawrence Schatz, and Mayor David Shiffman.

Martinez, Utterback, and Schatz had won their council seats in 1973 with strong support from the Citizens Coalition. Together with Sheila Lodge, they represented a majority of council members who favored strict control over the city's growth. (Sheila Lodge had replaced the fourth Citizens Coalition candidate when that candidate gave up her council seat.) The outcome of many council votes reflected a difference in viewpoint between these four and Eyman, Chavalas, and Shiffman.

Lodge, Eyman, and Chavalas were not up for reelection until 1979. Therefore, the city council election of 1977 focused on four positions—the mayor's office and those of three council members. Mayor Shiffman was challenged by only one person. Whichever candidate of the two received a majority of votes would become the next mayor of Santa Barbara.

Utterback and Schatz decided not to run for reelection. Martinez, however, decided to defend his city council seat. He was joined by 12 other people seeking membership on the city council. Of the 13 candidates on the ballot, the three who received the most votes would become new members of the Santa Barbara City Council.

Filing for the March 8, 1977, election began on December 9, 1976. On that same day, a group called Citizens for a Responsible City Government met to screen possible candidates. Most of the members at the meeting had been part of the Citizens Coalition, which had been active in the 1973 election. These new groups received support from national environmental organizations like the Sierra Club.

Citizens for a Responsible Government decided to support three candidates. These candidates became known as the United Santa Barbara Slate. The slate consisted of two council candidates—Joanne Miller and Hal Conklin. Joanne Miller was head of the City Planning Commission. Hal Conklin was co-director of the Community Environmental Council. The third member of the slate was Lyle Reynolds, a retired dean of students at the University of California campus in Santa Barbara. Reynolds was a candidate for mayor. While not officially a part of the United Santa Barbara Slate, Leo Martinez clearly shared its views on important issues.

In campaign literature, the United Santa Barbara Slate declared, "Fine old neighborhoods are being destroyed by traffic jams, smog and neglect. The City must encourage the renovation and rehabilitation of these areas. We can prevent the construction of ugly, high density buildings which violate the traditional character of Santa Barbara." Working to "keep Santa Barbara beautiful" was a major goal of the United Santa Barbara Slate.

Another important group also met in December. This group, the Good Government League, was headed by a chairman and a board of 35 directors. Thomas Brash-ers, then head of the Good Government League, said its members wanted to "help elect people who favor a balance between the environment and the economy."

The Good Government League endorsed three candidates for city council and one for mayor. Its council candidates were Jeff Cain, Patricia Fillippini, and Francis Lopez. David Shiffman was supported as the mayoral candidate.

During the campaign, one of the Good Government League candidates said, "We need a good balance between economy and environment, and right now the economic side is hurting. Let's run the city like a business, the way businesspeople run their operations. Let's bring common sense and a business-like approach to local government." Another candidate stated, "There is a need for essential growth if we are to survive. I believe that without some growth, anything will eventually die."

The campaign was bitter, and the results were extremely close. Figure 10-2 details the outcome.

As the results show, three of the four candidates supported by the Good Government League were elected. These three were David Shiffman, Pat Fillippini, and Francis Lopez. Jeff Cain was defeated.

Figure 10-2

RESULTS of the 1977 CITY COUNCIL ELECTION in SANTA BARBARA	
Candidates for City Council	Votes Received
Shiffman } Mayoral Candidates	10,013
Reynolds	9,917
Lopez	10,373
Fillipini	9,263
Conklin	8,232
Cain	7,634
Miller	7,518
Martinez	6,917
Alexiades	2,211
Brilliant	1,974
Trubilles	1,726
Handy	1,463
Atkins	770

Hal Conklin was the only member of the United Santa Barbara Slate to win office. Both Joanne Miller and Lyle Reynolds were defeated. Leo Martinez lost his council seat.

Therefore, what had been a 4 to 3 environmental majority on the council changed drastically to a 5 to 2 business and labor majority. The city council elected in 1977 consisted of Sheila Lodge, Bud Eyman, Gus Chavalas, Francis Lopez, Patricia Fillippini, Hal Conklin, and Mayor David Shiffman.

As is customary in Santa Barbara, the new government did not go unchallenged. Concerned citizens continued to be active in seeking a healthy quality of life for Santa Barbara.

1. Describe the position of the Good Government League.
2. Describe the position of the United Santa Barbara Slate.
3. What resources do you think were available to each side?
4. How could you become involved in a city council campaign in your town?

VALUES in COMMUNITY LIFE Several important propositions were placed on the March 8, 1977, ballot in Santa Barbara. Perhaps the most controversial of these was Proposition A.

This proposition was divided into two sections—A-1 and A-2. Section A-1 asked the voters whether or not they supported the zoning changes adopted by the Santa Barbara City Council. Section A-2 asked the voters if they wanted to limit the population size of the city.

Proposition A had been placed on the ballot to see whether citizens were still in favor of the 1975 growth control ordinance. The results from Proposition A would not be legally binding. However, they would indicate how the citizens felt about the growth control plan.

The Good Government League helped organize the opposition to Proposition A. Section A-2 received a great deal of attention. League members believed that limiting the population would negatively affect future employment and prosperity in Santa Barbara. Other opponents of Proposition A insisted that Santa Barbara was not growing too fast. Furthermore, they argued, it was unfair to limit the size of any community. People should be able to live where they want.

Supporters of Proposition A urged the city to limit growth. In their estimation, if this were not done, Santa Barbara's population would soon grow from 70,000 to 100,000 people. Supporters believed that there were just not enough natural resources, such as water, to service 100,000 people. Moreover, if the city were forced to use water from another part of the state, the cost would be enormous. The United Santa Barbara Slate adopted these arguments and vigorously supported Proposition A.

The advertisement on page 305 was used to influence voters on Proposition A. Study the ad carefully. Then answer the following questions:

1. What ideas are presented in this ad to influence voters to vote yes on Proposition A?
2. What factors can create bias in an ad?
3. Do you think there is bias in this ad?
4. How is bias used in political ads in your town?

PROPOSITION A as a VALUE ISSUE As you learned in Unit I, a value issue can be looked at in either of two ways. It can involve those things that a person desires. Or, it can involve those things that a person considers to be good or bad, right or wrong, just or unjust.

By this definition, the battle over Proposition A was clearly an important value issue. It involved plans for community development. It asked citizens to think what they wanted Santa Barbara to be like in the future. At the same time, it raised serious questions about what is right and what is wrong.

For example, is it right to place a limit on the number of people who can live in a city? Should people be able to move where they want? Is it fair for a community to say that it will not borrow other resources if and when they are needed? If these questions have not already been asked in your community, they may soon be.

In Unit I you also learned that certain fundamental values are at the roots of most value issues. In the battle over Proposition A, several fundamental values were involved. These included truth, trust, liberty, and personal freedom.

Identifying value issues and determining fundamental values are two important skills. In considering value issues, other skills are also important.

In order to successfully confront a value issue, you need to determine alternative ways of dealing with it. For example, one issue addressed by Proposition A was how Santa Barbara should ensure that its natural resources would meet future community needs. One solution was proposed by the supporters of Proposition A. These people believed that the best way to handle the issue would be to limit the population. In this way, available resources could meet future needs. However, this was not the only possible solution. For any value issue there is usually more than one alternative. Before taking action, all alternatives should be considered.

To identify alternatives, the facts must be studied. Then various proposals can be made. Assume, for example, that you had been asked to study the alternatives to Proposition A. The alternatives could have been made based on a study of natural resources in Santa Barbara, in the rest of California, and in the surrounding states. From this investigation, you might have suggested that to meet demands on the water supply, it would be possible for Santa Barbara to seek new dams or perhaps desalinate (remove salt from) ocean water. Or, you might have suggested that the problem take care of itself. This could be a workable approach. It would simply involve letting the citizens of

305

Santa Barbara use the resources available to them until the resources ran out. Part of suggesting this alternative would be a belief that strict conservation measures could be followed to avoid running out of resources.

Once you have considered alternatives to a value issue, it is important to think about the consequences of each proposal. For example, some alternatives to population growth in Santa Barbara are the following:

1. Limiting the population.
2. Allowing the population to grow and borrowing resources from a nearby city or state.
3. Doing nothing until the city runs out of resources.

For each of these alternatives, there are important consequences for the citizens of Santa Barbara.

1. Assume that you were living in Santa Barbara at the time that Proposition A was placed on the ballot. Write a paragraph describing the consequences of each alternative way of handling the issue of population growth. Then, based upon these paragraphs, determine which alternative is most acceptable.
2. Think carefully about a value issue that you have been involved in recently. At the time you may not have thought about all possible alternatives. Make a list of the alternative ways to deal with this value issue. Remember, even if you do not agree with a particular alternative, place it on your list anyway. Then, outline the consequences of each alternative. Based upon the consequences, choose the alternative most acceptable to you.

As you deal with value issues in political life, be certain to follow the rules introduced thus far:

1. Clearly identify the value issue
2. Identify the fundamental values behind the value issue
3. Identify alternative courses of actions for dealing with the value issue
4. Determine the consequences of each alternative.

In choosing an alternative upon which to act, certainly your own preferences will motivate you. However, you should also be fully aware of the way in which each alternative will affect the lives of other people in the situation. This may cause you to think differently about an issue.

You will have opportunities to use these skills at other points throughout this course. By paying careful attention to them, you will be able to make informed judgments about important value issues.

 ## *Participation Project: The Quality of Life*

In this chapter you have seen how concern for the quality of life can motivate people to become involved in local politics. Now you can construct your own study on a quality-of-life issue. In doing the study, you should apply the skills learned in this unit—making decisions, interviewing, interpreting evidence.

The steps involved in preparing your study are the same as those used in the participation project for Unit I.

Choosing a Topic. Think of several quality-of-life issues that affect you and your community. Select one issue around which citizen groups have formed. Through a study of this issue you should be able to analyze the activities of citizen groups, the resources they use, and how they use them.

Choosing a Method of Working. This study can be done by you working alone or with other people in a group. If your teacher decides on group work, he or she will be in charge of breaking the class into groups. If you are doing group work, think about the people you will be working with. Determine the kinds of resources you need to do your study and think what resources each person in your group can contribute to the project.

Stating Objectives. You need to formulate carefully objectives for your case study. For example, if you focus on the issue of noise control, state an objective such as "The purpose of this study is to explore how the city government deals with noise control." Or another objective might be stated as "The purpose of this study is to determine whether the new expressway is a cause of excessive noise."

Choosing Sources. Use a wide variety of sources in preparing this study. Research newspaper materials, magazines, minutes from meetings, and films, for example. The more lively the study is the better it will be. One valuable source of information could be interviews with members of your community. Be sure to prepare interview questions that will yield information about the quality-of-life issue chosen. Be certain to choose sources that enable you to deal with your objections. Your skills in interpreting evidence will help you analyze source materials.

Gathering Information. If you are working with others, divide the study into tasks. Each person should be responsible for completing a part of the assignment. It might be best to divide the work among the group members according to objectives (third step above).

Choosing a Method of Presentation. In sharing your case study with the class, you may choose to make either an oral or a written report. You also may want to use an entirely visual presentation. Decisions must be made about how your study is to be presented. Share these ideas with your teacher.

Presenting Your Findings. When you present your study, the following questions should be discussed:

1. What quality-of-life issue is involved?
2. What groups are involved?
3. What resources does each group have? How does it use these resources?
4. What activities does each group carry out?
5. What conclusions resulted from the interviews carried out in the community?
6. What are opinions of class members on this issue? How did they arrive at their opinions?

1. What historical evidence proves that Santa Barbara has a long history of citizen involvement?
2. How did the blowout at well A–21 set the stage for politics in Santa Barbara during the 1970s?
3. Contrast the political activities and resources of the groups known as GOO and CEC.
4. Summarize the ways in which the environmentalists became formal political actors in Santa Barbara politics.
5. Reread the profile of Leo Martinez. How did his background compare to the typical local officials described in Chapter 9? What resources did Martinez bring to his job as city council member?
6. Why did the Santa Barbara business community organize to oppose environmental groups? In your opinion, were business people equally concerned with the quality of life in Santa Barbara? Explain.
7. Summarize the arguments for and against the 1975 growth control ordinance in Santa Barbara. If a similar issue were raised in your community, what position would you support? Explain.
8. Review the 1977 city council election in Santa Barbara. In your opinion, why was the United Santa Barbara Slate largely unsuccessful?
9. Explain the reasons why Proposition A was a value issue.
10. What skills are important in making a decision on a value issue? List several issues in your community that might require the use of such skills.

Chapter Vocabulary

Define the following terms.

quality of life	blowout	advocacy group
oil spill	environmental group	ordinance

Chapter Analysis

1. In essay form, discuss ways in which the Santa Barbara study proves that citizens can be active in local governmental decision-making.
2. Select an issue of concern in your community. Then based on the studies of various Santa Barbara citizen groups, plan a strategy for making your local government responsive to your views.
3. Analyze the different kinds of political activities in the Santa Barbara study.
4. Explain the meaning of a value issue. Analyze why the abilities to determine and to evaluate a value issue are important political skills.

1. Investigate the general question of quality of life. What issues—such as pollution and community growth—are involved in quality-of-life controversies?

2. With a group of other students, prepare a pictorial history of your community, illustrating the groups of people and activities that have influenced its development. Highlight any instances of citizen involvement. Be prepared to present your photographs, line drawings, and graphics to the rest of the class.

3. Make a timeline of events in the quality-of-life issue in Santa Barbara. Begin your timeline with the blowout at Platform A, and go up to the city council election. Be sure to use equal intervals of time appropriate to the period being studied.

4. Investigate what the city council does in your community. Think about how you could become involved in a city council election. If possible, invite a member of the council to speak to your class about his or her role in local government.

5. If you wanted to protest an environmental issue or disaster, such as the Santa Barbara oil spill, how would you go about it? Develop a plan for constructively expressing your views.

**Chapter
Bibliography**

Black Tide: The Santa Barbara Oil Spill and Its Consequences, Robert Easton (Delacorte Press: New York), 1972.
　　A thorough and readable account of the Santa Barbara oil spill and its political consequences.

Pollution, Prices, and Public Policy, Allen V. Kneese and Charles L. Schultze (The Brookings Institution, Washington, DC), 1975.
　　Looks at the background behind various pollution problems confronted by the United States, then focuses on federal legislation designed to solve the problems and difficulties in enforcing that legislation.

Your Environment and What You Can Do About It: A Citizen's Guide, Richard Saltonstall, Jr. (Walker and Company: New York), 1970.
　　Describes different types of pollution and contains a set of actions citizens can take to improve their environment. Also in this work is a section on environmental law.

The Sierra Club Bulletin, published by the Sierra Club, San Francisco, California.
　　A periodical featuring articles that discuss important and current environmental issues.

Santa Barbara Past and Present: An Illustrated History, Walker A. Tompkins (Tecolote Books, Santa Barbara), 1975.
　　A fascinating illustrated history, highlighting the major events in the city's past.

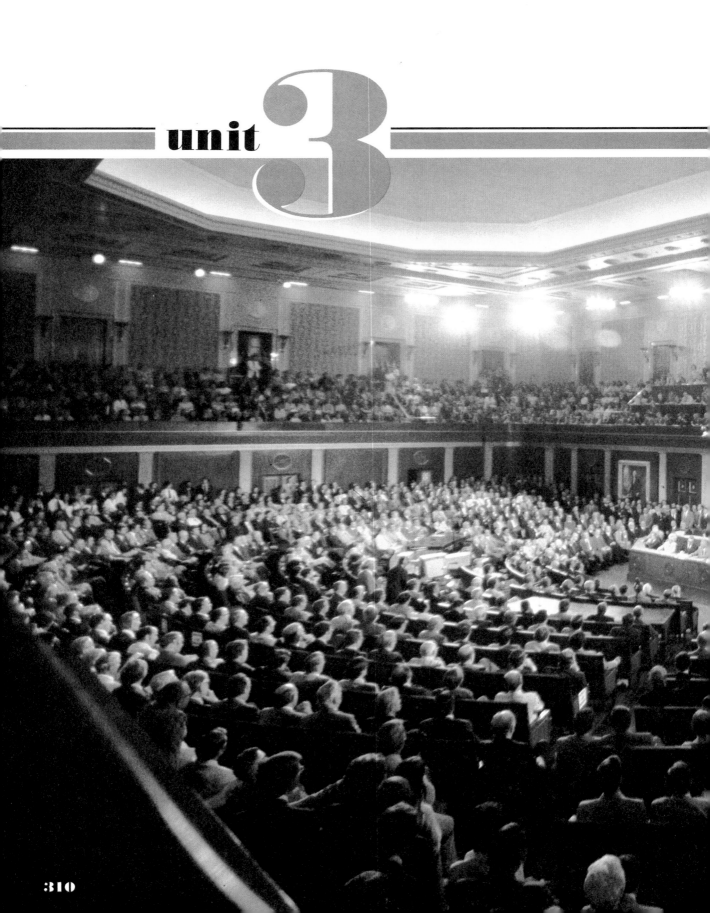

unit 3

National Political Systems

Chapter Objectives

★ To identify and analyze basic principles in the constitutional plan for government

★ To learn the meaning of political systems

★ To analyze and compare basic types of political systems

★ To develop skills in acting as an advocate

★ To develop skills in making comparisons

chapter 11

The CONSTITUTION and POLITICAL SYSTEMS

In Unit 2 you examined the development of plans for government in the United States, from the Articles of Confederation to the Constitution. In this unit you will investigate the national government outlined by that Constitution.

The Constitution determines the overall ways in which the national government can use and distribute resources. The Constitution also describes the general activities of the national government. The relationships of political resources and activities within a group form a political system. In this chapter you will learn how to identify systems, especially political systems. And you will learn about four basic types of political systems. All these systems exist in governments in the United States. By developing the skill of making intelligent comparisons, you will be able to identify and compare these political systems.

This national government, set up in a constitution ratified almost 200 years ago, may seem distant from your life. However, it is a government made up of citizens. And it is a government structured in such a way that citizens can affect its functioning. Throughout this unit you will see ways in which citizens acting as advocates have an impact on their national government.

A Plan for National Government

You have studied the Constitution as it reflects the goals of the states that created it. The states ratified a plan for government that was based on the important concepts of *popular sovereignty, limited government,* and *federalism.* These basic principles define the states' relationship to the national government they created.

Other principles define that national government. Most important among these are *separation of powers, checks and balances,* and *constitutional change.* As you study these principles, refer to the Constitution on pages 616–626.

SEPARATION of POWERS

As you have learned, the framers of the Constitution divided power in the national government among three different branches, or parts. These are the legislative branch, the executive branch, and the judicial branch. The rights and responsibilities of each branch are carefully described in the Constitution. This division or separation of powers prevents any one person or part of government from controlling the entire government—or the entire nation. It also enables the government to function more efficiently.

The Legislative Branch. The first article in the Constitution sets up the legislative branch. The branch is called the Congress of the United States. The Constitution divides the branch into two parts, the House of Representatives and the Senate.

The legislative branch is designed to make laws for the nation. Article I, Section 1, of the Constitution says, "All legislative powers herein granted shall be vested in a Congress of the United States. . . . " The Constitutional powers of Congress are summarized on page 315.

The key to Congress' power is found in the last item of Article I, Section 8. There, it says that Congress has the power "to make all laws which shall be necessary and proper for carrying into execution the foregoing powers, and all other powers vested by this Constitution in the Government of the United States, or in any department or office thereof." This statement is called the *"elastic clause."* It allows Congress to make all laws necessary for the functioning of government.

The "elastic clause" stretches Congressional powers. Because of it, the powers of Congress today are not limited to those specified almost 200 years ago in Article I, Section 8. For example, today Congress makes laws about pollution, air travel, and the use of radio and television. None of these is mentioned in the Constitution.

As you know, the Great Compromise decided the rules for representation in Congress. (See page 185.) Men and women may exercise the power of Congress by being elected as representatives or senators. The rules of eligibility for election are described in Article I, Sections 2 and 3.

In Chapter 12 you will study the way the legislative branch functions today.

The Executive Branch. The second article in the Constitution sets up the executive branch. Article II, Section 1, says, "The executive power shall be vested in a President of the United States of America. . . . " The basic responsibility of this part of the national government is to defend the Constitution and to execute the laws made by the legislative branch. (To *execute* a law means to carry out the instructions of the law, to see that it is done.)

The specific constitutional powers of the executive are described on page 316. Study this page carefully. The Constitution does not specify many ways in which the president is supposed to execute laws and defend the Constitution. Because of this lack of specificity, presidential powers have grown and developed from those first exercised by George Washington. Today, for example, the president has become the chief initiator of legislation. The president not only executes the laws but, in fact, he or she also recommends extensive programs of legislation to Congress.

In order to exercise presidential powers, presidents have the assistance of a vice-president. Also, Article II, Section 2, mentions "executive departments." The Constitution does not further describe departments or agencies within the executive branch. Over the years, however, the executive branch has grown tremendously. Today, it consists of the Executive Office and the federal bureaucracy. Altogether, the executive branch consists of about 3 million people.

Men and women may exercise the powers of the executive branch by being elected president or vice-president. The rules of eligibility for election are described in Article II, Section 1. Also, men and women can

Powers Granted to Congress in the Constitution

1. To impose and collect taxes uniformly throughout the United States.
2. To borrow money.
3. To regulate commerce with foreign nations, among states, and with Indian tribes.
4. To establish rules for naturalization and bankruptcies.
5. To coin money, set the value of money, and set standards of weights and measures.
6. To punish those who counterfeit federal money or securities.
7. To establish a postal service and roads.
8. To establish patent and copyright laws.
9. To create federal courts below the Supreme Court.
10. To define and punish maritime crimes (that is, crimes relating to the sea and ships).
11. To declare war and make laws concerning captures during wartime.
12. To create and support armies.
13. To create and support navies.
14. To make rules for the regulation of armed forces.
15. To call forth a militia (National Guard) to carry out federal laws, put down rebellion, and fight invasion.
16. To organize and regulate that militia.
17. To govern the district in which the seat of government is located (Washington, DC) and other federal properties such as forts.
18. To make all laws necessary to carry out the above powers and all other powers granted to the federal government (the "elastic clause").
19. To impeach government officials (House of Representatives) and to try impeached officials (Senate).
20. To declare the punishment for an act of treason against the United States.

Powers Granted to the President in the Constitution

1. To be commander in chief of the armed forces.
2. To grant pardons for federal offenses, except in cases of impeachment.
3. To make treaties, with the advice and consent of the Senate.
4. To nominate ambassadors and other representatives to foreign governments, federal judges, and other federal officers, with the advice and consent of the Senate.
5. To inform Congress on the state of the Union.
6. To recommend legislation to Congress.
7. To call special sessions of Congress.
8. To receive ambassadors and other representatives of foreign governments.
9. To be responsible for the faithful execution of all laws.
10. To commission all officers of the United States.
11. To veto bills passed by Congress.

serve in one of the departments or agencies in the executive branch.

Chapter 13 of this book covers the work of the executive branch.

> 1. What are differences and similarities in the powers given to the president and the Congress?
> 2. How are the powers of these two institutions "separate"?

The Judicial Branch. The Constitution also designates a judicial department. Article III, Section 1, says "The judicial power of the United States shall be vested in one Supreme Court, and in such inferior courts as the Congress may from time to time ordain and establish. . . . " Today the judicial branch consists of the Supreme Court and 105 lower federal courts. (There are 11 circuit courts and 94 district courts.)

As in the description of the executive departments, the Constitution does not specify the work of the lower courts. Article III concentrates on the Supreme Court. The Constitutional powers of the federal courts are summarized on page 317.

The federal courts have the power to decide whether or not the behavior of citizens and policy-makers in the United States is lawful or not. In the end, the entire legal system of the United States finally rests on the decision of the nine justices of the Supreme Court.

Men and women can exercise the power of the judicial branch by being judges in the federal judicial system. Article II, Section 2, states that the president shall appoint federal judges. These appointments must be confirmed by a majority vote in the Senate.

In Chapter 14 you will study the judicial branch and the development of its powers in greater detail.

1. Compare the powers of the judicial branch with those of the legislative and executive branches.
2. In your opinion, is the separation of powers an effective way to structure government? Explain your answer.

Resources and Activities. The Constitution never uses the words "resources" or "activities." However, by the separation of powers, it does distribute resources and activities in relatively equal ways. Resources may be different, but they are equalized by the separation of powers in the Constitution. And, all three branches of our national government share equally in many political activities.

There is no pinnacle of power which holds all the resources and carries out most of the activities in the government in the United States. Separation of powers contributes to this equalization of resources and political activities. The limits on the accumulation of resources and the execution of activities are carefully set out and defined in the Constitution.

Use the descriptions of powers on pages 315, 316, and 317 to answer these questions.

1. What political resources do you think each branch has? Give specific examples.
2. What political activities do you think each branch performs? Give specific examples.
3. There are four problems listed below. Which branch of government would hold major responsibility for resolving each situation?
   a. A new energy plan needs to be approved. Otherwise, resources will be wasted and the country will be without needed energy in a short time.
   b. A decision needs to be made about whether or not a law passed by Congress is constitutional. The law involves the federal government's right to make transportation plans for the nation as a whole.
   c. A decision needs to be made on whether to send military aid to a gov-

Powers Granted to the Federal Courts in the Constitution

1. To settle all legal disputes involving federal laws, federal treaties, and the Constitution.
2. To settle all legal disputes involving ambassadors or other representatives of foreign governments.
3. To settle all legal disputes involving maritime jurisdiction.
4. To settle all legal disputes involving the national government.
5. To settle all legal disputes among states.
6. To settle all legal disputes between a state and citizens of another state.
7. To settle all legal disputes among citizens of different states.
8. To settle all legal disputes between a state and/or its citizens and a foreign government and/or its citizens.

Through the use of the "elastic clause," Congress is able to make laws covering circumstances that did not exist when the Constitution was written. It has, for example, empowered the Environmental Protection Agency (EPA) to control the pollution of our air and water. The establishment of waste treatment facilities and the monitoring of air quality are some ways in which the EPA has worked to control pollution.

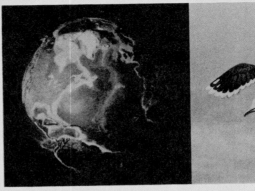

SAVE OUR AIR

UNITED STATES · SIX CENTS

AN EQUAL EMPLOYMENT OPPORTUNITY PROJECT

POLLUTION CONTROL PROJECT

ENVIRONMENTAL PROTECTION FOR CITY OF ALBUQUERQUE
NEW 4.5 MILLION DOLLAR WASTE TREATMENT FACILITIES
$ 3.525 FEDERAL DOLLARS $ .587 STATE DOLLARS

ernment threatened by attack. Military aid would certainly help the other government to win the war. However, it might involve the United States in the war.

d. Money needs to be appropriated for older people to receive more medical and welfare benefits.

CHECKS and BALANCES

Another important influence on how government works is the principle called "checks and balances." To *check* something can mean to stop it or control it. Checks and balances in government refer to power. The framers of the Constitution set up ways for each branch to check or stop the actions of the other branches. These checks help balance power among the three branches.

The chart on page 320 (Figure 11–1) shows the basic system of checks and balances written into the Constitution. These checks and balances apply to six general authorities. They are veto power, appropriation, appointment and treaty-making, judicial review, impeachment, and amendment.

Veto Power. All legislation passed by Congress goes to the president for approval. A bill can become law if the president signs it or if the president allows 10 days (excluding Sundays) to pass without acting on it.

Article I, Section 7, of the Constitution gives the president the power to veto, or reject, a bill. If the president vetoes a bill, he must send a message to Congress explaining the reasons. If a bill reaches the president fewer than 10 days (excluding Sundays) before Congress adjourns, the bill cannot become law unless the president signs it. If he does not sign the bill, it is defeated. This procedure is called a *pocket veto.*

Article I, Section 7, also gives the Congress a way to check the president's veto power. According to the Constitution, Con-gress can override a president's veto if two thirds of the members vote to do so.

In the spring of 1976, for example, the majority of Congress voted for a bill to provide $125 million to improve the staffing of federally funded day-care centers serving low-income families. To become a law, this bill had to be signed by President Ford. However, on April 6, President Ford vetoed this bill. He explained that he thought the states, not the federal government, should set standards for day-care-center staff. The states, Ford argued, knew their own needs better than the federal government did.

On May 5, 1976, the House of Representatives responded to the President's veto of the Day Care Standards Bill. A two-thirds majority of the members voted to override Ford's veto. If the Senate also voted by a two-thirds majority to override the veto, the bill would have become a law. However, the Senate voted 60 to 34 (with 6 abstentions) to sustain the President's veto. The Senate used its power to support the President on this legislation.

Appropriation. The House of Representatives must introduce, and the Senate must approve, any laws providing money which the executive branch needs in order to manage the government. By refusing to vote money for certain activities, Congress can handicap activities. Senators and representatives can express their opinion on the president's plans and provide a serious check on the power of the presidency.

Appointment and Treaty-making. The president has the power to appoint federal judges, ambassadors, and heads of various government departments. But the Senate must approve these appointments by a majority vote. Those who cannot win approval of the Senate do not take office.

The president also has the authority to make treaties with foreign governments. But, treaties with foreign nations cannot take effect unless they are approved by a two-thirds vote in the Senate. For a nuclear test-

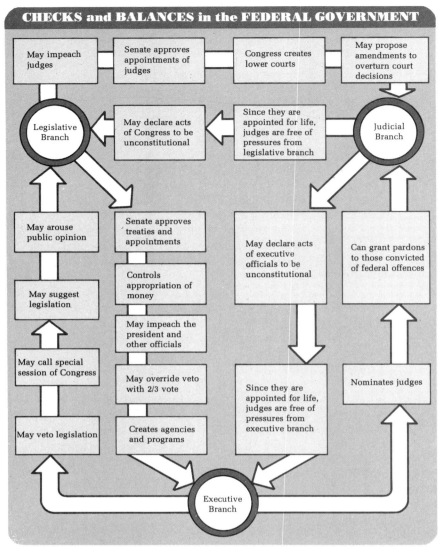

CHECKS and BALANCES in the FEDERAL GOVERNMENT

May impeach judges

Senate approves appointments of judges

Congress creates lower courts

May propose amendments to overturn court decisions

Legislative Branch

May declare acts of Congress to be unconstitutional

Since they are appointed for life, judges are free of pressures from legislative branch

Judicial Branch

May arouse public opinion

Senate approves treaties and appointments

May declare acts of executive officials to be unconstitutional

Can grant pardons to those convicted of federal offences

May suggest legislation

Controls appropriation of money

May impeach the president and other officials

May call special session of Congress

May override veto with 2/3 vote

Since they are appointed for life, judges are free of pressures from executive branch

Nominates judges

May veto legislation

Creates agencies and programs

Executive Branch

Figure 11-1

ban treaty to be approved, for example, the president and the secretary of state will negotiate the treaty with foreign governments. But the treaty cannot take effect unless the Senate approves it.

Judicial Review. The federal courts have a powerful means of checking the executive and legislative branches. In the early years of the nation's history the federal judiciary established its authority to veto laws or actions of the legislative and executive branches by declaring them "unconstitutional." A law or action is unconstitutional if somehow it violates or contradicts the Constitution. This veto

power is called judicial review. In other words, judges review laws or actions and accept or reject them. If the judicial branch decides a law or action is unconstitutional, that law or action becomes illegal.

Federal judges can use the power of judicial review only in cases brought before them in court. If someone believes that a law or action is unconstitutional, he or she must challenge its legality or constitutionality and bring the case to court.

For example, in 1962 Congress passed the Cunningham Amendment to the postal services bill. Under this amendment the Post Office Department was directed to hold all mail, except sealed letters, that they would classify as communist propaganda. The department would then notify the addressee, who would have 20 days in which to respond in order to receive the mail. In New York, Corliss Lamont challenged the legality of the Cunningham law. Lamont said that the law inhibited his right to receive publications, a guarantee falling under the First Amendment to the Constitution. The Supreme Court supported Lamont and declared the amendment unconstitutional.

Other Supreme Court cases on Congressional legislation, especially those involving activities considered to be subversive, have been decided in favor of protesting citizens. One of the most famous was the decision on the McCarran Act. This act was passed by Congress in 1950, requiring the registration of Communist party members. The Court ruled that the law was unconstitutional because it violated citizens' rights against self-incrimination.

In addition, several executive actions have been ruled unconstitutional. These include President Truman's seizure of the steel mills during the Korean War and several parts of President Roosevelt's "New Deal" proposals after World War II.

These powers of judicial review have been used by the Court fewer than 100 times. Yet they present a very real check on both the legislative and the executive branches.

Impeachment. Another check of one branch on another involves the congressional power of impeachment. To *impeach* officials is to accuse them of wrong conduct in doing their job. The Constitution gives to the House of Representatives the power to impeach a president, federal judge, or other civil officer of the federal government. The Senate sits as a court to try the accused official. If convicted, the official is removed from office. See Article I, Section 3, of the Constitution.

The Watergate affair is an example of the start of the impeachment process. The House of Representatives checked the ac-
tions of President Nixon by beginning impeachment proceedings. Rather than face the possibility of impeachment and then trial before the Senate, Nixon resigned his office.

Amendment. Congress may use its power to propose constitutional amendments as a way to check the federal courts. If Congress opposes a court ruling that a law or action is unconstitutional, then Congress may try to amend the Constitution.

The Sixteenth Amendment to the Constitution is an example of this aspect of checks and balances. In 1895 Congress had passed a law giving the federal government the right to tax citizens' incomes. A year later the Supreme Court ruled that income taxes were unconstitutional, stating that any direct tax must be divided among the states on the basis of population (see Article I, Section 9, in the Constitution). Congress and the president felt, however, that the federal government could not function without the revenue it would gain from income taxes. As a result, the Sixteenth Amendment was added to the Constitution in 1913, giving Congress the right to tax income directly.

Following are examples of actions which could be taken by the national government. In each case, explain how one branch might check action by other branches.

1. The Congress passes a bill which gives the United States Commissioner of Education the power to decide what textbooks may or may not be used in public schools throughout the country. The president signs the bill, making it a law. Many citizens are unhappy. They believe that the national government should not have the power to tell school officials what textbooks can or cannot be used. What can be done to check the president and the Congress?

2. The president signs a treaty with another nation which gives up United States control of a major seaway in that nation. Some members of Congress support the president because they believe the other

nation's sovereignty is violated by U.S. ownership. But many representatives are unhappy because they believe the foreign government is unstable and U.S. defenses would be threatened without control of the waterway. A few senators doubt the constitutionality of some aspects of the treaty. What can Congress and the Courts do to check the action of the president?

3. Congress passes an energy bill which would increase taxes for citizens who drive large automobiles, but would not place direct controls on major corporate consumers. The president is unhappy with the bill, saying that it does not "go far enough." Many citizens believe that they would be denied equal protection by the new tax, and question its constitutionality. What can the president, citizens, and the courts do to check the Congress?

4. Think of a hypothetical case in which checks and balances would affect your everyday life. Show how the three branches could check each other in this situation. As a citizen, how could you influence what happens?

CONSTITUTIONAL CHANGE

All the rules established in the Constitution are designed to help government serve citizens. The United States was founded with the idea that government should be by and for the people. The rules about constitutional change especially give citizens a continuing "say" in the structure and function of their government.

Citizens can change the plan for government by several processes. They can formally change the Constitution by amending it. Or, they can make changes in a number of other ways, such as laws or changes in interpretation.

The Amendment Process. The process for changing the Constitution by amendment is stated in Article V. This article describes two different ways in which amendments can be proposed to the states. It also outlines two different ways in which states can ratify amendments and make them part of the Constitution. These four ways are

1. Congress can propose amendments by a two-thirds vote in both houses. The amendments take effect when ratified by the legislatures of three fourths of all the states. (Today, 38 states make up three fourths of the total.)

2. Amendments proposed by Congress can take effect when ratified by special state conventions in three fourths of all the states.

3. If two thirds of the state legislatures request it, a national convention can be called by Congress to propose amendments.

4. Amendments proposed by a national convention may take effect when special state conventions in three fourths of the states ratify them.

Between 1791 and 1971, 26 amendments were added to the Constitution. All but one amendment, the twenty-first, were proposed by Congress and adopted by three fourths of the state legislatures. (The Twenty-first Amendment was proposed by Congress and ratified by state conventions.)

As you read in Chapter 6, the first 10 amendments were added to the Constitution soon after it was ratified. These amendments, called the Bill of Rights, protect the rights of citizens. (See a summary of the Bill of Rights on page 192.)

Since 1791, 16 other amendments have been ratified and added to the Constitution. These amendments are summarized on page 323. Like the first 10 amendments, many of these extend the civil rights of citizens. Amendments which are particularly relevant to citizens rights are the Fourteenth, Fifteenth, Nineteenth, and Twenty-sixth Amendments. In addition, other amendments make necessary changes or clarifications that are designed to make government function more effectively.

The amendment process has had a powerful effect on American citizens and their

Amendments Passed After the Bill of Rights

Eleventh Amendment (1795): Declares that the judiciary of the United States does not have authority to hear a suit against a state if brought by a citizen of another state or a foreigner.

Twelfth Amendment (1804): Provides a better way of electing the president and vice-president.

Thirteenth Amendment (1865): Puts an end to slavery.

Fourteenth Amendment (1868): Defines citizenship of the United States and of a state, prohibits states from taking away the rights of citizens unlawfully, defines the basis of representation in the House of Representatives, states certain disqualifications from holding public office, and confirms certain Civil War debts and disclaims others.

Fifteenth Amendment (1870): Declares that no citizen shall lose the right to vote because of race, color, or previous condition of servitude.

Sixteenth Amendment (1913): Gives Congress power to enact federal income-tax laws.

Seventeenth Amendment (1913): Provides that United States senators shall be elected by the people.

Eighteenth Amendment (1919): Prohibited the manufacture, sale, or transportation of alcoholic beverages. (Repealed in 1933.)

Nineteenth Amendment (1920): Provides that no citizen shall be refused the right to vote because of being a woman.

Twentieth Amendment (1933): Changes the date of the inauguration of the president and of the opening of the Congress, and provides for filling the presidency and vice-presidency under certain conditions.

Twenty-first Amendment (1933): Repeals the Eighteenth Amendment and forbids the carrying of alcoholic liquors into any state, territory, or possession of the United States in violation of its laws.

Twenty-second Amendment (1951): Limits the number of times anyone may be elected to the office of president.

Twenty-third Amendment (1961): Gives citizen residents of the District of Columbia the right to vote for the president and vice-president.

Twenty-fourth Amendment (1964): Declares that no citizen shall be prevented from voting for the president, the vice-president, or members of the Congress because he [or she] has not paid a tax.

Twenty-fifth Amendment (1967): Sets forth the method of determining presidential disability, and provides a plan for filling a vacancy in the office of vice-president.

Twenty-sixth Amendment (1971): Provides that no citizen, who is 18 years of age or older, shall be denied the right to vote in federal or state elections because of age.

Source: Catheryn Seckler-Hudson, *Federal Textbook on Citizenship.*

government. It has guaranteed the individual rights of citizens and forbidden the government to abridge those rights. It has also been the basis for the extension of citizens' rights through constitutional means.

Informal Change. The amendment process is a formal process for change. However, there are other informal ways in which the Constitution has been changed over time. In each of these ways, citizens and government have responded to new times. They have acted to protect citizens' needs and citizen participation.

One way in which the Constitution has been changed is by *laws* passed by Congress. Through the "elastic clause" Congress has the flexibility to pass laws needed to carry out its duties. As times change, so do the laws passed by Congress. For example, Congress was given the power to regulate commerce between states. Interstate commerce today is very different than it was in 1800 and present laws reflect those changes. The interstate commerce laws passed by Congress over the years have expanded congressional powers.

Congress has also passed laws to establish federal courts. As states have come into the union and as population has increased, the judiciary has grown in size and in complexity.

Congress has passed laws creating executive departments for the president. As you know, these were not specified in the Constitution. All the cabinet departments have been developed because of laws passed by Congress.

Treaties have also added to or changed the Constitution. For example, the president is commander in chief of the armed forces, with the power to direct those forces in certain ways. However, a nuclear test-ban treaty changes the president's power to direct the armed forces in nuclear tests.

Through *judicial review,* the federal courts function to expand the meaning of the Constitution. The courts interpret what the Constitution says. By their interpretations, they can change citizens' understanding of the Constitution. For example, the Fourteenth Amendment prohibits discrimination. In 1896 the Supreme Court ruled that racially segregated facilities were constitutional if all facilities were equal. (This is the "separate but equal" ruling made in *Plessy* v. *Ferguson.*) In 1954, however, the Court changed its interpretation of the Fourteenth Amendment. In the land-

The busing of elementary school students to achieve racial balance in schools is one example of how judicial review has expanded the meaning of the Constitution.

mark *Brown v. Board of Education of Topeka* case, the Court ruled that "separate but equal" was not constitutional. In other words, the Court acted to change citizens' understanding of what the Fourteenth Amendment means.

The *practices of political parties* have also expanded the Constitution. The Constitution calls for the election of officials. But it does not specify the way in which candidates for office are to be chosen. It does not mention political parties. Today, however, political parties play a central role in the election of government officials. They affect citizens' participation in ways not outlined in the Constitution.

All these processes make the Constitution a living plan for government. They allow it to be adaptable to twentieth-century needs. However, these changes have not altered the basic distribution of resources and activities in the three branches of government.

1. Describe the amendment process.
2. Describe other ways of changing the Constitution.
3. How might such changes affect you?

Systems in Government

You have begun to learn about the structure of government set up by the Constitution. You have seen that constitutional principles such as separation of powers define how resources are used and distributed and how activities are carried out in a government.

This structure determines how government functions. According to constitutional rules, for example, no one person or group could say "Now, people who are 18 years old can vote!" Instead, a specific amendment process had to take place in order to bring about that change.

In Chapters 12, 13, and 14 you will study the working of the national government in depth. Before you do, it will be useful for you to see the ways in which the Constitution has set up different systems in the national government. Government operates within these systems.

WHAT IS a SYSTEM? The concept "system" is a familiar one. You talk about stereo systems, grading systems, communications systems, solar systems, digestive systems. You may also want to "beat the system." What do all these systems have in common? What rules govern their operation?

Characteristics of Systems. Three general characteristics define any system. First, a system has parts. Second, the parts of a system are related to one another. Third, changes in the relationships among parts affect the system. Any system has all three characteristics.

A single object is not a system. In your stereo system, for example, the turntable alone does not make up a system. The turntable and the receiver and the speakers and whatever other components you have work together as a system. This is true of any system.

In addition to objects, processes can be parts of systems. In a communications system, for example, a television set, an announcer, and a television station are some parts of the system. The process by which the sounds and pictures are transmitted to your TV set is also part of the system.

The second essential quality of a system is the relationship among its parts. If a number of objects do not have a relationship, then they do not form a system. For example, 10 marbles do not form a system. The pieces and board of a chess or checkers set and the rules of the game do form a system, however, when you are playing the game. Each part has a relationship to each other in the game. What happens to one piece, or part, affects the other parts of the system.

The third essential quality in a system is the effect of change. Think again about a chess or checkers game. A change in the position of one piece affects the relationship among the other pieces in the game. It also affects the power relationship between the two players.

1. Analyze your school as a system. What are the parts of the system? What relationships exist among the parts? What kinds of changes would affect the system?
2. What other systems do you come in contact with? Name three.

Political Systems. In a study of politics and government, you can make use of the concept "system." In any government there are a number of political systems. An understanding of these systems will help you analyze the government and the political activity within that government.

Like any system, a political system is made up of related parts that are affected by change. People, resources, and activities are the basic parts of any political system. First of all, a political system exists within a group of people such as a nation or a community. Within a political system people can also be thought of in smaller groups such as voters, the executive branch, the legislative branch, the judicial branch.

Political resources are also important parts of any political system. Votes, for example, are an integral part of the representative democracy in the United States. Wealth is a vital part of any political system. It is used by campaign managers to finance political campaigns. It is used by governments to support the running of the government. It is used to pay for all the services governments provide for citizens. In what other ways are resources parts of political systems?

Political activities are parts of any political system. Without congressional decision-making, for example, we would not have federal laws. Without communication and participation, a representative democracy could not exist. And leadership is an ingredient in any political system.

National, state, and local constitutions determine the basic relationships among the parts of political systems in the United States. In addition, the ways in which resources are used and distributed and the ways in which activities are carried out produce certain relationships among people, resources, and activities.

1. Describe the relationship among these parts of a system of local government: mayor, city council, voters, elections, school board, schools.
2. How would the principle of separation of powers affect relationships among parts of the national political system in the United States?

As in any system, a change in one part of a political system can affect relationships among all the other parts. For example, a change in the ratio of Democrats to Republicans in Congress can affect the relationships between the executive and legislative branches. The appointment of new Supreme Court justices can change the judicial branch's relationship to all other parts of the system.

The development of television is a good example of a change which affected many relationships among resources, activities, and people in a political system. Television has become a very important part of political campaigning. Its existence changes activities in communication between candidates and voters. Its value as a campaign tool changes the use and distribution of resources by candidates who can afford to use television advertising. Its use by candidates can greatly affect their relationship with voters. Candidates can turn personal attractiveness and skill in the use of media into resources they can use to persuade millions of voters over a broad geographic area within a short period of time.

A Political System in Action. Within each of the branches of government—major parts of the system—there are other systems at work. These can be called *sub-systems,* systems within a system. Congress, for example, has its own political system, with parts and relationships affected by change. The following case study describes an incident which reflects the working of our national political system, as well as the political system within the Senate. As you read, identify parts, relationships, and the effects of change within the national political system. Also identify examples of these within the Senate as a political system.

★ With Advice and Consent

Article II, Section 2, of the Constitution says: "The President . . . shall nominate and by and with the advice and consent of the Senate shall appoint . . . judges of the Supreme Court." The Senate must approve the president's nomination by a majority vote. Thus, the power to select Supreme Court justices is divided between the president and the 100 senators.

In mid-January 1970, President Richard M. Nixon nominated George Harrold Carswell to fill a vacancy on the Supreme Court. Carswell, who lived in Florida, was a federal judge of the Fifth Circuit Court of Appeals.

At first, observers believed the Senate would approve Carswell's nomination. The mood of the Senate was expressed by the attitude of Birch Bayh, Democratic Senator from Indiana. He believed that the President was strongly in favor of having Carswell on the Supreme Court. He also thought that the President had the power to influence a majority of senators to go along with him. Even though Senator Bayh himself opposed Cars-

swell's nomination, he believed he could do little to stop this appointment to the Supreme Court.

In time, however, Birch Bayh became a leader of a group of Democrats and Republicans who wanted the Carswell nomination defeated. Bayh's decision to oppose Carswell was made on February 25. On that day he heard Senator Edward W. Brooke, Republican of Massachusetts, declare on the Senate floor: "I will vote against confirmation of Judge Carswell."

Brooke, the Republican Senator from Massachusetts, gave three main reasons for opposing his Republican president. First, Brooke claimed that Carswell believed in segregation of whites from blacks. He quoted from a 1948 Carswell speech: "I believe that segregation of the races is proper. . . . I have always so believed and I shall always so act. . . . " Brooke gave several other examples of Carswell's support of racial segregation and white supremacy. As a black man, Brooke found these actions unfitting for a Supreme Court justice.

Brooke's second reason for opposing Carswell was his poor record of handling civil rights cases as a federal judge. Carswell

"YOU CAN'T HAVE A BALANCED COURT IF THEY *ALL* BELIEVE IN CIVIL RIGHTS."

From Herblock's *State of the Union* (Simon & Schuster. 1972).

had a reputation for consistently making judgments against black people and their causes and for treating civil rights lawyers rudely.

Brooke's third reason for opposing Carswell was his poor record as a legal scholar and clear thinker. Brooke argued that Carswell did not have the ability to be a Supreme Court justice.

Brooke's speech impressed Birch Bayh. He began to consider how he might oppose Carswell and what the chances were for success. Bayh realized that the prospects for defeating Carswell were dim. The American Bar Association's Committee on the Federal Judiciary had endorsed the Carswell nomination unanimously. The Senate Judiciary Committee had voted 13 to 4 in favor of Carswell. Finally, only 19 senators had declared opposition to Carswell. To defeat the nomination, 51 votes were needed.

Carswell's support in the Senate came mainly from three groups. A bloc of conservative Republican senators believed that Carswell shared their beliefs about law and government. A bloc of southern Democrats and Republicans believed that Carswell, a fellow southerner, would represent their regional interests on the Supreme Court. Finally, a group of moderate and liberal Republicans supported Carswell primarily because they felt the need to be loyal to their Republican president, Richard Nixon.

The first senators to oppose Carswell were a few Democrats and Republicans who disagreed with Carswell's ideas about the Constitution or government. Some of the Democrats in this group were also motivated by their dislike of the Republican president.

On March 2, an Associated Press poll reported that 37 senators were for Carswell, 20 against, and 43 were undecided. To capture the votes of these 43 "undecided" senators became the objective of those who opposed Carswell.

President Nixon had been putting as much pressure as possible on wavering senators, urging them to support Carswell. Several senators were up for reelection in 1970. Nixon indicated that those who supported Carswell would receive strong support from him and the vice-president and that those who opposed Carswell would face the president's opposition in their bids for reelection. In return for their support of Carswell, President Nixon also offered to help some senators obtain needed public works projects for their states.

President Nixon informed the two Republican party leaders in the Senate that he would not support their party leadership positions unless they were completely loyal to him on the Carswell issue. Both men had misgivings about Carswell, but the President influenced them to support the nomination.

Groups outside the Senate began to work to defeat the Carswell nomination. For example, several national labor unions and civil rights organizations launched campaigns to influence public opinion against the Carswell nomination. The AFL-CIO, the United Auto Workers, the NAACP, and the Americans for Democratic Action (ADA) were prominent in this anti-Carswell campaign. Their tactics included letter writing to senators, letter writing to newspapers, and personal contact, when possible, with "undecided" senators.

The letter-writing campaigns against Carswell had a strong impact on some senators. Senators Thomas Eagleton of Missouri and Hiram Fong of Hawaii, for example, had declared support of Carswell. Both changed their positions as a result of mail overwhelmingly against the nomination.

Prominent newspapers published articles and editorials about the weaknesses of Judge Carswell. These articles in newspapers such as the *Washington Post* and *The New York Times* helped to influence a few senators to oppose Carswell. For example, Republican Senator Margaret Chase Smith of Maine was swayed to vote against Carswell by a well-written article in the *Boston Globe*.

Thomas Dodd, a Democrat from Connecticut, changed his position. He said "...I shall vote against confirmation of Judge Carswell. Most black people and many working people do not feel that they will get a fair shake if Judge Carswell is on the Supreme Court.... If the people of this country are to have faith in our system, we must put men on the Court in whom they can have confidence."

Perhaps the most significant efforts to influence the senators were those of lawyers' groups around the country. Some influential lawyers had initially endorsed Carswell. However, as the anti-Carswell campaigns developed, numerous lawyers' groups strongly opposed the nomination. They showed that more than 40 percent of Carswell's decisions as a federal judge had been reversed by higher courts. This suggested that Carswell lacked knowledge and skill as a judge. When Gale McGee, a Democrat from Wyoming, changed his vote, he said, "I think the real issue here was that it was felt there were stronger judges who met the criteria in the South than this particular nominee—a very fine man, but not of the stature that the times would seem to require."

Louis Pollak, Dean of the Yale University Law School, declared that Carswell was not capable of being a Supreme Court justice. William Van Alstyne, Professor of Law at Duke University, agreed with Pollak. Criticisms such as these from prominent lawyers swayed the votes of several senators. Others opposed Carswell when his colleagues on the circuit court would not voice their support.

The Senate vote on the Carswell nomination was scheduled for April 8. A large, excited crowd packed the Senate gallery. At one o'clock, a single buzzer sounded to signal the start of the roll-call vote. The first four votes were for Carswell. Then Birch Bayh cast the first "no" vote. The final vote was 51 "no" and 45 "yes." Among the opponents were 12 Republicans.

1. What parts of the national political system are described in the Carswell case? What parts of the Senate's political system are described?
2. What are the relationships between the parts of the systems?
3. How did changes in some relationships influence others in the Carswell nomination?

CITIZENS as ADVOCATES

In every political system, citizens acting as advocates can play an important role. Advocates influence resources and activities within the system, whether in public or in private government. Birch Bayh, for example, acted as an advocate in the rejection of the Carswell nomination. So did those editors who published editorials opposing the nomination. Think about advocates in the political system of your school. In what ways are they able to influence resources and activities?

As you read in Chapter 1 (page 39), advocates advocate one idea, position, or course of action. They try to influence others to agree with them. To participate successfully as an advocate, you should follow these guidelines. A successful advocate:

1. Knows the general feelings of the group about an issue.
2. States a clear position on an issue.
3. Presents reasons for his or her position.
4. Knows how to use political resources to influence others.

The exercise in the following two pages will help you develop skills in acting as an advocate. A hypothetical situation involving a student newspaper editor's right to express dissent is the focus of the exercise. Read the material carefully and be prepared to place yourself in the advocate role in the situation described.

★ *The Advocate Role*

Conflict at the Eagleton Express

Eagleton High School is a large city high school. Basketball is a strong tradition at Eagleton, and the Eagleton Eagles are among the best basketball players in the state. The school has become proud of its reputation.

Eagleton is run directly by the principal, Mr. Whitmore, who makes most decisions about school affairs. Eagleton students and teachers have learned that it's important to talk with the principal in order to get anything done in the school. Mr Whitmore has the full backing of the city school board.

Recently, the school board has decided to consolidate Eagleton High School and nearby Welch High School, which serves a suburban area. The principal, teachers, and students are in favor of the consolidation. However, there is considerable disagreement on the issue of school name. The school board and the principal claim that the consolidated school should have a new name. After all, they say, Welch High School had its own traditions, pride, and reputation. Welch students might not feel comfortable with the Eagleton name.

The decision will be made by Mr. Whitmore, with the approval of the school board.

Students in both schools have strong opinions on the issue. Students at Eagleton have been divided over the issue. Many students want to retain Eagleton High School's name. They're proud of their traditions and their basketball team's statewide reputation. They want the students from Welch to take on the Eagleton school name.

The students at Welch are also very proud of their school. They have been famous for 4-H activities, winning many state and national prizes. They want their high school name to be recognized also.

Ed Greenberg, editor of Eagleton's school newspaper, wants to publish editorials that oppose changing the Eagleton name. He knows that the editorials will anger those students who are in favor of the name change. However, he believes that student protest against the change might influence the principal's decision. He wants to use the newspaper editorials to express his views on the change in an effort to persuade students to oppose it actively. However, as the following profiles show, other students are opposed to Ed Greenberg's idea. Read them carefully.

Profile: Jean / John Rose

You, a junior at Eagleton High, strongly believe that editorials in the school newspaper are not a good way to solve the problem. You think they will upset students on both sides and in both schools. You also see the principal as the key person in the situation.

In your opinion, students should find a way to express their opinions to Mr. Whitmore without creating bad feelings on the part of other students. Also, you suggest that a survey of student opinion be made so that people could speak from evidence.

Profile: Sally / Pete Wharton

You are a senior at Eagleton High School and are upset by the idea that the school newspaper would publish editorials opposing the name change. As a senior, you have seen conflict before and think that it is very

bad for the school. You fear that the entire school community would become involved, which would be bad for students and their education. As a senior, you want to complete your last year without major conflicts.

Profile: The Advocate

A junior at Eagleton High School, you are strongly in favor of Ed Greenberg's right to publish editorials opposing a change in Eagleton High School's name. Although you accept Mr. Whitmore's decision to change the school name, you believe that students have a right and responsibility to express their opinions in an orderly fashion.

Review the material you have just read and then do one of the following assignments. Your teacher will tell you which assignment to follow.

Assignment 1

a. Assuming the advocate profile, write a letter to Mr. Whitmore. Advocate Ed Greenberg's right to publish an editorial opposing a change in the school name.

b. Again acting as an advocate, outline the ways in which you would attempt to influence Jean/John Rose and Sally/Pete Wharton to agree with your position.

Assignment 2

a. With two of your classmates, form a group of three to discuss the issue of the newspaper editorials. One person should play the role of Jean/John Rose. Another should play the role of Sally/Pete Wharton, the third should play the advocate.

b. The advocate should listen to the positions of the other two group members. Then, he or she should attempt to influence and change their positions.

c. At the end of the discussion, the other two group members should reevaluate their positions and decide whether or not the advocate had persuaded them to change their minds. The advocate should describe any other plans or arguments that might have been used to advocate publishing the editorials.

d. Finally, the group should answer the following questions:

1. What were the group's general feelings about the issue?
2. What was the advocate's position on the issue? Did he or she state it clearly? Did the advocate convince others?

Four Political Systems

Not all political systems are the same. The parts of the systems, the relationships among the parts, and the effect of change may differ from one system to another. For example, think about the political systems described in the Carswell case, in the UMWA under John L. Lewis, and in Santa Barbara, California. In what ways do they seem different from one another?

In spite of variations, there are certain important similarities that allow you to group political systems. For example, it may seem to you that the political systems in your school club and in your community are not at all alike. But closer examination might show that the president of the club and the mayor of the community have the same resources and carry out political activites in the same ways. So, those two political systems might be grouped in the same category of political systems. In this course you will categorize political systems into four types. These are

1. *Elite* political systems
2. *Bureaucratic* political systems
3. *Coalitional* political systems
4. *Participant* political systems

As you will learn, each of these types represents a certain pattern of resources and activities. In any elite political system, for example, resources are used and distributed and activities are carried out quite differently than they are in any coalitional system.

In discussing different types of political systems, it is helpful to think about a *continuum,* or a scale. For example, if you are discussing the political resources of a system, you could label one end of a continuum *concentrated resources* and label the other end *shared resources.* (The two ends of a continuum represent opposite degrees of a given quality.)

In the following discussion and cases you will examine some of the similarities and differences among the four different types of political systems.

ELITE POLITICAL SYSTEMS An elite system is a "top-down" organization in which the "top" is responsible for the operation of the system. One person or small group controls the system, and makes all important decisions.

In an elite system resources are concentrated at the top. The controlling person or group has more resources to use and distribute than anyone else in the system. In such a system, knowledge is an important political resource, often possessed by only the top decision-makers. When national security is at stake, or when secret information is kept, then top decision-makers have a significant advantage over others. They have a knowledge resource which others do not have. This is also true of wealth, skill, and status resources.

There is very little reciprocity, or give and take, in the activities in an elite political system. Decisions are made at the top and handed down. A leader commands a follower to make a decision. Communication is largely "top down" and participation is restricted to a small group.

The most positive characteristic of elite systems is their efficiency. Since they do not allow much participation in decision-making, decisions can be made quickly.

Of course, not all elite political systems are alike. The description you have just read could be called a *model* of an elite political system. Both a dictatorship and a monarchy are elite political systems. So was the UMWA under John L. Lewis. All these may have important differences in the ways in which resources are used and distributed, for example. But in all of them, basic control of that use and distribution is in the hands of a limited number of people.

In the same way, the Constitution structures the presidency as an elite political system. The president of the United States is the nation's chief decision-maker. Within the executive office, the president is in control. He or she has more resources to use and distribute than anyone else has. To a great extent the president determines the kind of activities that are carried out and the ways in which they are accomplished by the executive office.

The following case describes an example of presidential decision-making. As you read, think about President Nixon's responsibility in making this decision. Also, note the roles others played in the decision-making process.

★ President Nixon Decides

Throughout the 1960s the United States involvement in the Vietnam War had caused distress and controversy. President Nixon had campaigned for the 1968 election, promising that he would withdraw U.S. troops from Southeast Asia. He wanted to "Vietnamize" the war, leaving the Vietnamese in charge of the war in their country.

By 1970, however, serious problems in the nation of Cambodia—adjacent to Vietnam—threatened the "Vietnamization" policy. Since Cambodia was not at war with the United States, Communists established strongholds there, along the Cambodian-Vietnamese border. They attacked South Vietnam from those sanctuaries. As commander in chief of the armed forces, President Nixon felt that he must reconsider the United States' relationship to Cambodia. During a 10-day period between April 20 and April 30, 1970, he made his decision.

The President had several alternatives in this situation. The United States could do nothing, allowing the Communists to build strength in Cambodia. Or the United States could give air support to the Vietnamese, bombing Communist strongholds in Cambodia in the hope of reducing their forces. However, air support alone had been unsuccessful in many similar situations in this war. The President could also supplement the air support with ground support (land troops). However, this would mean greatly increased involvement in Southeast Asia. Nixon had promised the American people that this would not be the case.

On April 20, 1970, the President announced the withdrawal of an additional 150,000 U.S. troops from Vietnam over the next year. By April 30, however, both ground and air troops had been committed in Cambodia. The war had been widened, and the hopes for immediate troop withdrawals had been dashed. What happened during those 10 days that caused such a reversal in policy?

On April 21, Communist troops had taken over two provincial capitals in Cambodia. Cambodian General Lon Nol made an explicit and extensive request for arms from the United States. President Nixon, who was not pleased with the request, called an emergency meeting of the National Security Council for the next afternoon. (The National Security Council is a group of people who advise the President on all matters involving the nation's security.)

By the time of the meeting on April 22, the President had thought through his alternatives. He strongly believed that the United States should provide air and ground support to the Vietnamese so that they could fight the Communists from Cambodia. For one reason, Nixon was worried that other Communist nations such as the Soviet Union might think that the United States was a "paper tiger" if it backed down on support because of the promises of troop withdrawals from Southeast Asia.

The Council discussed many alternatives. One was proposed by General Creighton Abrams, the U.S. commander in South Vietnam. Abrams' proposal, endorsed by the U.S. ambassador to South Vietnam, was to make limited air strikes against Cambodia.

Abrams believed this might keep the Communists from tightening their grip on the border areas and threatening the "Vietnamization" program. A preliminary decision was made by the Security Council to take action if, upon analysis, it was true that the Cambodian Communists were a threat to the "Vietnamization" program.

On April 23 the President called a meeting of the Washington Special Action group. This group consisted of special advisor Henry Kissinger, the director of the CIA, the chairman of the Joint Chiefs of Staff, the deputy defense secretary, and the undersecretary of state. Nixon asked this group to draw up several options for action. At this point, some form of action was clearly confirmed.

On April 24, the President left for his retreat at Camp David, where he thought long and hard about the Cambodian situation. The next day he called and spoke with Henry Kissinger, who had prepared a thick notebook of options as had been requested in previous meetings. For two hours the two men discussed various proposals and their probable consequences.

On Sunday, President Nixon again met in secret with the National Security Council. The President was leaning heavily toward the commitment of U.S. ground troops as well as air support for the Vietnamese. Secretary of State Rogers stated his doubts about this policy. Attorney General John Mitchell said there could be "political difficulties" at home if this policy were undertaken. It was felt then that U.S. troop commitments would not be necessary.

On April 27 the President met independently with everyone involved. Secretary Rogers was called in, as were White House aides H. R. Haldemann and John Ehrlichman. Nixon talked many times with Henry Kissinger and other members of the Security Council. That night, by himself, he read through the entire "options book" cover to cover. Then the President made his decision.

On April 28, Nixon informed Henry Kissinger that as commander in chief he was going to commit full air and ground support to fight the Cambodian Communists. Secretaries Rogers and Laird were informed of the decision.

On April 30 at 6:00 P.M. the White House staff was assembled and told about the decision to commit full troops in Cambodia. At 7:00 the President briefed members of Congress and the Cabinet. He then made a speech to the American people announcing the commitment of troops.

By making his decision in this way the President had overruled his own secretary of state. He had worked with the same information held by many of his advisers and had come to far different conclusions. Said one high administration official, "It was the President's personal decision. Some say it was a lonely decision. . . . "

1. Based on this case, in what ways is the executive branch an elite political system?
2. What influence did advisers have on President Nixon's decision?
3. What resources did Nixon use in making his decision?

BUREAUCRATIC POLITICAL SYSTEMS Unlike elite political systems, bureaucratic systems have many different levels of authority. Usually, a *bureaucracy* is a system of government that operates through appointed officials. No one person has the power to make all decisions. Instead, decision-making takes place at many levels, according to official rules. However, people at higher levels have more power than those at lower levels do. In order to carry out their important policies, leaders must allow subordinates to make many decisions. (A *subordinate* is a person who has less power than, and is under the authority of, another person.) Subordinates carry out those decisions by mobilizing their own subordinates. There is, in effect, a chain of command.

Most large corporations, for example, have bureaucratic government. Decisions are made at many levels within the company. However, the president has more power than the vice-presidents have, and the vice-presidents have more power than the department heads have, and so on.

Resources in a bureaucratic system are distributed throughout. People at the top have the most resources, but those at other levels also have resources. Status, for example, usually increases the higher one rises in a bureaucracy. Most bureaucracies, in fact, use status as an incentive for people to "move up the ladder." As people rise in level, they gain more resources and participate more in the policy decisions of the organization.

Political activities in a bureaucracy are also stratified, or layered, in the same way that resources are. Decision-making is generally by a *plurality rule;* that is, a group, but not a majority, makes most decisions. Usually this includes top and middle leaders in the system.

Leadership in a bureaucracy is based on merit and status. People move up as they work longer for the organization and as they develop more skills. People are promoted according to how well they work in the system.

Communication generally runs through channels. Often one must fill out form after form in order for approvals to be gained at each level of the system before a final decision is made. This process is sometimes called "bureaucratic red tape."

Participation takes place according to position or level. There is more participation at the top of the system, but many different people carry out varied roles and functions within the system. Therefore, an individual's role may be important, although not a top decision-making role.

Bureaucracies work well when many interests must be satisfied, for levels of a bureaucracy provide checks on how the policy is carried out. However, those checks can create snags when every step of a process must go through many already set-up procedures on its way to completion. When this happens, bureaucratic systems are not efficient.

All public governments at the national, state, and local levels include bureaucratic systems. Bureaucracies are necessary for governments, especially large governments, to function. As you read the following case about how New York City's government distributes its money, think about what characteristics make it a bureaucratic system. Consider how you might operate differently in this type of system than you would in an elite system.

★ **Managing New York City's Money**

When New York City faced a major financial crisis in the mid-1970s, many agencies were set up to monitor the city's budget and spending. In 1975, the federal government gave New York City a loan to help the city through its problems. Because of this the federal government wanted the city to restructure its financial organization and to be responsive to the need for austerity. As a result, three of the most important men in finance in New York City began to work together. Together, these three held primary responsibility for the city's money.

Harrison J. Goldin was the comptroller for the City of New York. (A *comptroller* is a government or corporate official who is responsible for auditing financial records. In an *audit,* trained people examine and verify the accuracy of financial records.) When Goldin came into office, he hired three accouting firms, which audited the accounts of New York City. Goldin's goal was to redesign the city's accounting system and to have the Municipal Assistance Corporation and the Control Board, two of the city's main financial organizations, integrate their budgeting.

According to Goldin, this revitalization and reorganization of the accounting would put the city back on its feet. It would streamline the bureaucratic procedures so that financial recording could be consistent and accountable to the public.

Goldin had the power to restructure the accounting system in New York. However, he was responsible to many organizations. He had to send reports to the Control Board, the secretary of the treasury of the United States, the General Accounting Office for the City of New York, and the state comptroller. According to Mr. Goldin, working with all these agencies can be summed up in the following words: "It requires a special type of tolerance."

Another man in the "hot seat" in the financial crisis was the director of the Office of Management and Budget, Donald D. Kummerfeld. Kummerfeld worked with the mayor and helped to decide "who got what." Because he prepared the budget for New York City, he influenced the distribution of resources. Thus, he had considerable clout in financial circles in New York City. Kummerfeld worked with both agencies within the New York City financial struc-ture and agencies outside, including those of the federal government. Kummerfeld and Goldin worked together to set straight the city's finances.

John C. Burton was New York City's deputy mayor for finance, the third of the big three who controlled the city's finances. Representing the mayor in financial deal-ings, he was also in charge of all public re-porting of the city's resources. As Burton de-scribed his job, "I represent the Mayor with the varied financial groups with whom we must retain relationships. . . . I also deal with specific problems such as transit and pen-sions. Kummerfeld and I and the comptrol-ler will be involved in such problems, but I don't think we trip over one another. We share responsibility."

Goldin, Kummerfeld, and Burton were each responsible for large bureaucracies within the New York City financial system. Hundreds of men and women worked with them at various levels of responsibility in the city departments related to finances.

The three men and their departments were under the direction of, and reported to, the Emergency Financial Control Board at the state level. The Board has the ultimate financial power. It is able to establish the minimum amount of money from which Kummerfeld prepared his budget. Burton

Citizens wait to testify at budget hearings of the New York City Council.

then announced the choices to the public, and Goldin was responsible for the accounting. Initial policy decisions are made by the Emergency Financial Control Board. Goldin, Kummerfeld, and Burton could advise and make suggestions to the Control Board, but it has ultimate policy-setting responsibility. The Board is also in charge of monitoring spending patterns for the city.

Perhaps Kummerfeld best summed up the tangle of relationships and levels of the bureaucracy. He said, "It drives me crazy."

1. How do New York City's finances illustrate the workings of a bureaucratic system?
2. If you were in the position of Goldin, Kummerfeld, or Burton, how would you act differently in this system than you would in an elite system?

COALITIONAL POLITICAL SYSTEMS

A coalitional political system does not have the same kind of structure for the levels of power that a bureaucratic system has. In a coalitional system the majority usually rules, with each person having an equal vote. In order to form a majority, members must cooperate. Thus, they form *coalitions*—alliances among people or groups that have similar interests and goals.

The Carswell case (pages 327–329) is an example of a coalitional political system in action. On a broad level, the Senate's Democrats and Republicans each represented a coalition. In addition, within each party coalition there were smaller groups for or against the nomination. Republicans and Democrats for the nomination formed a coalition across party lines. A similar coalition existed among Republicans and Democrats opposed to the nomination. Also, the American Bar Association and other special interest groups formed coalitions for or against Carswell. Eventually, the decision not to appoint Carswell was decided by a majority.

Often in a coalitional system political resources are fairly equally distributed. Not every group has the same resources, but groups can compete on a relatively equal basis. Both the Democrats and Republicans had resources to use in the Carswell case. Republicans had the backing of President Nixon, whose support gave a certain status to those who were in favor of Carswell's nomination. This status was not shared by the Democrats. On the other hand, Birch Bayh and the Democrats who led the fight against Carswell had important bargaining skills that helped them defeat many Republicans and fellow Democrats who favored the nomination.

Members of the American Bar Association, Supreme Court justices, and local bar associations had greater legal expertise than most other people. They were able to use this knowledge to influence people both in favor of and against the nomination.

Political activities in a coalitional system are carried out by many people. As noted, decision-making is based on majority rule. Leadership is often based on advocacy, as well as the control of resources. As described previously in the Carswell case study, people such as Birch Bayh advocated a position around which they could mobilize groups and form coalitions. Usually, reciprocity in coalitional leadership is great, for it takes a convincing leader and a genuinely supportive following in order for coalitions to work. Leaders cannot force followers to make a decision. Therefore, they must interact to convince other people that their position is correct.

Resources such as status and skills are important aspects of leadership in a coalitional system. A leader who is highly respected and has excellent bargaining skills will have greater success in forming a coalition than a person with neither status nor skills will have.

Communication is a necessary ingredient in the formation of coalitions. People must share their interests and goals in order to work together in a coalition. By communicating his disapproval of the Carswell nomination, Senator Edward Brooke started a movement that led to the further expression of disagreement on the part of other senators.

In forming coalitions, senators like Birch Bayh communicated to others their reasons for rejection of the Carswell nomination. By this communication they persuaded others to join them.

Because all members of coalitional systems have a say in decisions, there is some participation by all. Every senator who voted on the Carswell nomination participated in that decision.

> 1. Analyze the formation of the coalition against the Carswell nomination.
> 2. What coalitions supported the Carswell nomination?
> 3. In your opinion, could individuals like Birch Bayh have stopped the nomination without joining or forming coalitions? Explain.

The hypothetical front page of a school newspaper reproduced on page 339 provides examples of political systems and sub-systems in a high school.

> 1. What coalitional systems are described?
> 2. What other kinds of systems are described?

PARTICIPANT POLITICAL SYSTEMS

In a participant political system, each member of the system has equal power. Any group decision must be unanimous, and any person can veto the actions or votes of other group members.

In order for this distribution of power to be effective, a participant system is usually small and must be composed of people who agree on basic issues. The Organization of Petroleum Exporting Countries (OPEC) was originally a participant system. Made up of oil-producing nations, the group agreed to meet and unanimously decide on questions such as the price of oil. As the organization grew and world conditions changed, however, it became apparent that some member nations wanted to increase the price of oil dramatically, while others did not. It was no longer possible to make decisions unanimously. Rather than destroy the basic political system, members changed it to a coalitional system.

In a participant political system, all members have an equal share of political resources. This situation enables everyone to have equal power.

Activities in a participant political system are undertaken by everyone. Decisions are made by a *consensus*, or unanimous rule, by which everyone must give his or her opinion and agree. Compromise is a necessary part of a participant system. Technically, there are no leaders in such a system. Everyone is an equal participant, and the give-and-take and sharing of resources and responsibilities are the operating rules for the system.

In its ideal type, as defined above, a participant political system really does not exist in any public government today. In the United States the institution most like a participant system was the New England town meeting of the past. However, political systems are now operating which are more participant than coalitional and which come close to the ideal type.

One example of a somewhat participant political system is found in the 44th Ward Assembly in the city of Chicago. Chicago is a vast, heterogeneous, and complex city. Its wards are normally run by powerful individuals who most often make their own decisions. When Dick Simpson was elected to the 44th Ward, he decided to change all that. So, a truly participant system on the model

THE MARTIN LUTHER KING JOURNAL

VENDING MACHINE CONTROVERSY SETTLED

by Samantha Fox

The issue which embroiled Martin Luther King High in controversy for two months has been settled. A final decision was achieved at yesterday's All-School Council meeting. The soft-drink machine will stay in the student lounge. The candy machine, however, will be removed from the school early next week. "It was difficult to find a solution that a majority could agree on," said Principal Jacob Robinson. Many groups and individuals have been involved since the issue first developed.

Sarah Vanderstal, home economics teacher, initially raised the subject at a faculty meeting. She voiced concern that students were filling up on candy and soda, causing them to skip lunch. Citing the low nutritional value of candy, Mrs. Vanderstal argued that the school contributed to lowering health standards by allowing the vending machines on school property.

The issue ballooned quickly. Custodians grumbled about candy wrappers in the halls and on school grounds. Teachers complained about students eating candy in class. Dr. Robinson reported receiving calls from parents who supported Mrs. Vanderstal's position. Members of the Home Economics Club thought good nutrition was very important and wanted the candy out of the school. They spread the issue among students.

Support for the vending machines was organized by the Junior Class. Their class treasury has received 25 percent of the profits from candy and soft-drink sales. Juniors encouraged students, teachers, and the vice-principal to support them in keeping the machines.

Finally, a vote on the issue was taken yesterday by the All-School Council. In addition to regular student and faculty delegates, other interested parties were present. These included

representatives from the Home Ec Club and the Junior Class Committee. After debate on the question of whether the candy machine and soft-drink machine should be removed, the council voted separately on the status of each machine. The result was 7 to 4 in favor of removing the candy machine and 9 to 2 against removing the soft-drink machine.

During the heated debate preceding the first vote, the Junior Class Committee and junior class members of the council argued in favor of continuing their class's source of revenue. "How can we pay for the Junior Festival without the money from the vending machines?" argued Lucille Washington, representative of Junior homeroom 203.

Josepha Blanca, president of the Home Ec Club suggested that the council give juniors permission to sponsor noontime dances every other Friday. Revenue from the dances could be used to finance the Junior Festival. This suggestion persuaded a number of council members to join the anti-candy machine forces!

Arguments against the soft-drink machine were weak, however. Juniors were able to rally support to their side by presenting a report from the Acme Vending Company. Acme stated that bottled orange juice could be substituted for one of the soft drinks in the machine.

NEW PRINCIPAL-STUDENT DIALOGUE

by Fred Laster

After eating in the student cafeteria last Tuesday, Dr. Robinson has decided to make it a habit. He plans to lunch with students every Tuesday and Thursday.

The principal found the informal conversation valuable. "It gave me a chance to hear from a lot of students. I also had a chance to explain the problems with which the administration is faced," he said. Students brought up a particular problem with the principal. They were concerned about teachers monitoring the cafeteria before school. The students agreed that they wanted to have order in the cafeteria, because it was the only place where people could stay before school. But, they preferred to form a committee to organize activities and to monitor their own pre-school activity. The principal and the students both thought this was a good idea.

The principal decided that this was a good idea. He told the students that he would instruct the All-School Council to plan the committee and work out the details. He hopes that lunches with students will result in more good ideas.

Any student is invited to join Dr. Robinson for an informal exchange of ideas over the lunch table.

of the New England town meeting was developed in the center of one of the largest cities in the United States.

As you read this case about the 44th Ward Assembly, think about why the system is a participant and not a coalitional one. Analyze how people acted differently than they did during the Carswell hearings.

★ The 44th Ward Assembly

"I . . . do hereby pledge that I will be bound by the decisions of the 44th Ward Assembly on important issues before the City Council and on projects undertaken to promote the welfare of the citizens of this ward and of this city, provided that those decisions are either unanimous or approved by a two-thirds vote as outlined in the Assembly's charter. . . . "

This was the statement made by Dick Simpson when he was elected as alderman to the Chicago City Council from the 44th Ward. It fulfilled a campaign promise that he would bring government by the people to the 44th Ward.

During the first year after his election, Simpson began holding meetings of the 44th Ward Assembly. He said, "When I first ran for the post of 44th Ward Alderman in the winter of 1970–71, one of the three basic issues I campaigned on was involvement of citizens in government policy-making. I pledged, if elected, to create a 44th Ward Assembly with delegates from precincts and community organizations to consult with me (and to direct me on important issues) in governing the ward and in representing my constituency in the City Council." In January 1972, Simpson held the first Ward Assembly meeting. Elections took place for representatives in all 63 precincts in the ward. In addition, provision was made for about 50 representatives from community organizations. Anyone in the ward could come to assembly meetings. Voting members, however, would be elected by precincts and by responsible organizations.

The first meeting of the Ward Assembly showed that participation by the community would not be a "rubber-stamp" process. The first thing that the 44th Ward Assembly did was to tell their alderman what they did or did not want done in the meetings. A charter was constructed, establishing rules for procedures. Then, Simpson began to introduce some of the local politicians who were running for elected office. At that point in the meeting, the assembly protested. Members said that they were not interested in watching politicians at these meetings. It was their meeting and they were going to make policy. According to Simpson, "They told me: 'This is a policy-making body and it doesn't waste time on electioneering.' Well, I asked them to make my aldermanic decisions for me, and they didn't lose any time doing it!" From the first meeting, the 44th Ward Assembly has initiated legislation for their alderman to take to the city council and has developed workable ward policy.

When controversial issues arise in assembly meetings, positions are often taken on both sides. However, most issues are decided by consensus. When a consensus of the entire assembly cannot be reached, a vote is taken by the elected members and a two-thirds majority vote instructs the alderman or decides policy in the ward. As Simpson told a newspaper in 1971, "We'll try to work by consensus, we'll try to agree. I think this will happen at least 90% of the time. But if two thirds of the voting assembly disagrees with me, I will vote their way." He strongly wanted the people to participate in making policy about their districts.

A great many important decisions have been made during the first two years of the Ward Assembly. In the first year of its life, the assembly collaborated with other community groups in convincing the Chicago Transit Authority to extend the number of reduced-fare hours for senior citizens. The assembly also located possible sites for additional parks and play lots in the ward. It was responsible for the introduction to the city council of a new ordinance prohibiting trucks with oversized loads from operating on the ward streets. And, it sponsored a ward fair, which more than 3,000 citizens attended.

The second year the Ward Assembly created standing committees to focus on projects in the community. One of the most important of these projects involved the prohibition of red-lining by ward banks. (Red-lining is a process by which a bank or loan company decides that certain areas of a city are poor risks in which to grant loans.) If banks would not give loans to people living in a poor neighborhoods, they would not have the money to rebuild, and indeed the neighborhood would go downhill. The Ward Assembly believed that Chicago banks were refusing loans on the basis of physical location rather than on a person's real ability to repay.

In February 1974, the assembly passed a unanimous resolution directing their alderman to introduce legislation into the city council to prevent such red-lining policies. Dick Simpson introduced such a bill in the city council, and meanwhile assembly members tried to persuade local banks to state that they were against red-lining. By April 1974, seven banks had vowed not to make rules for any city area in connection with home or business loans.

This work is typical of the 44th Ward Assembly. There is now more capital invested in the ward than ever before. Citizens feel less discriminated against. The 44th Ward in Chicago, a large, sprawling part of a major city, has brought democracy home to the people. Participation by hundreds of individuals has improved not only the ward itself but the entire city through the policies of the Ward Assembly.

1. What resources do citizens in the 44th Ward Assembly have? What activities do they carry out?

2. In what ways is the 44th Ward Assembly a participant political system? How does the assembly operate differently than the coalitional system in Congress?

3. How might you operate differently in a participant political system than you would in a coalitional one?

The Skill of Making Comparisons

You have just learned about four different types of political systems. In order to understand each one, you have compared it to the others. An ability to make comparisons is a useful and important skill for a student of government and politics. By comparing the resources and activities within political systems, for example, you can identify types of political systems and you can better understand how to function within those systems.

THREE STEPS Making comparisons is a process of identifying similarities and differences. For example, look at the two shapes in Figure 11–2 on page 342. In what ways are the figures similar? In what ways are they different?

You have undoubtedly heard the expression "comparing apples and oranges." It says that a specific comparison is not valid or reasonable. In order to make valid, reasonable comparisons, you should follow three useful steps.

1. Determine what you want to compare.

2. Make sure the objects, ideas, or processes you want to compare are comparable.

3. Make sure your comparisons are significant.

First, you must decide what you want to compare. Suppose you are comparing the two shapes in Figure 11–2. Your first step is

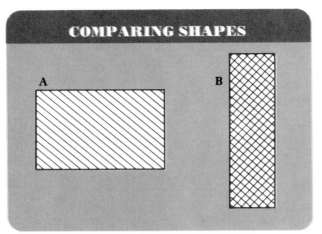

Figure 11-2

to decide whether you want to compare them in size, shape, color, design, or all of these characteristics. You cannot make a good comparison by comparing the size of one shape to the color of the other. This fact is very obvious in the comparison of two simple shapes. When you compare more complex things, however, it is even more important to identify exactly what you want to compare. For example, if you want to compare political systems, you must carefully decide what about them you want to compare. You cannot make a good comparison of the resources in one system with the activities in another.

These characteristics, such as size, shape, and resources, are concepts. (See

Figure 11-3

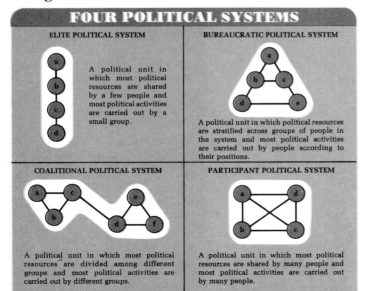

pages 212–215 to review the skill of identifying concepts.) "Umbrella ideas" like concepts are useful in making comparisons. They enable you to focus on one central idea which you can use to examine similarities and differences in several things.

Your second step is to be sure that it is possible to compare whatever you want to compare. You can, for example, compare the color or the size or the shape of a building and an apple. You cannot, on the other hand, make an intelligent comparison of their taste! On a more complex level, you can compare the distribution of resources in elite and coalitional political systems. You cannot compare President Ford's use of the veto with the number of members in the House of Representatives.

The third step in making intelligent comparisons is to make comparisons that are significant. Suppose you want to make an overall comparison of the political system in your school and the political system in your community. A comparison of the time school begins with the time city hall offices open probably is not a very significant comparison for your understanding of the two systems. On the other hand, a comparison of the resources used and distributed by the school principal and the community mayor can provide significant understanding of the similarities and differences between the two systems. This comparison is significant because resources affect political activity throughout a political system. They have an impact or a consequence. Significance can be equated to having an impact or a consequence. In your study of school and community political systems, comparisons should show you what has an impact or consequence on political life.

The four diagrams in Figure 11–3 on this page outline the four types of political systems you have studied in this chapter. Study the structure outlined in each diagram and statement. Make intelligent and significant comparisons of the four systems, based on the diagrams and statements.

1. Describe the principle of separation of powers as it operates in the federal government. In what ways are the three branches of government both separate and interrelated?

2. Describe the principle of checks and balances as it operates in the federal government. What checks are provided against the power of each branch? What is the balance of power among the branches?

3. What are the powers of Congress? of the President? of the federal courts?

4. Describe the principle of constitutional change as it operates in the federal government. Give examples of formal and informal change processes.

5. How have constitutional amendments affected citizens' rights? Give examples of amendments involving those rights.

6. What three characteristics are essential in any system? Describe a system, identifying and explaining those characteristics in the specific system.

7. What is a political system? What are the similarities and differences among the four basic types of political systems?

8. Describe examples of an elite, a bureaucratic, a coalitional, and a participant political system.

9. What are the essential steps in making good comparisons? Compare two things using those steps.

10. What are the important characteristics of a successful advocate?

Define the following terms.

separation of powers	advocate	continuum
"elastic clause"	comparison	plurality rule
to execute laws	elite system	bureaucratic red tape
checks and balances	bureaucratic system	comptroller
judicial review	coalitional system	audit
impeach	participant system	consensus

1. The powers of Congress and the president have greatly increased over the years. Explain how this has happened. What checks prevent either of these branches from becoming too strong?

2. Enumerate some of the ways in which the Constitution can change. In your opinion, do these procedures strengthen or weaken the federal government? Explain.

3. In what ways does the Carswell case illustrate the system of checks and balances? How did citizens affect the operation of this system?

4. Review the role of an advocate. In your opinion, why are advocates essential in any political system? Support your answer with examples from the news, your school, or your community.

5. Summarize the main features of an elite, a bureaucratic, a coalitional, and a participant system. Which system best describes each branch of the federal government? Explain. Which system best describes the total federal system? Explain.

6. Study the four types of political systems in Figure 11–3. State the most significant differences and similarities.

Chapter Activities

1. Investigate the local government in your community and determine its main parts. Compare your findings with other students, and compile a general profile of the local political system. Discuss the ways in which these parts are related. Consider factors that could change these relationships.

2. During the Vietnam War, the state of Massachusetts petitioned the Supreme Court to review the constitutionality of the war. In a 6–3 vote, the motion was denied. Research the background to this case. What parts of the political system were involved? What effect did the Supreme Court decision have on the relationship between these parts? How might a decision to try the case have affected the American political system? Explain.

3. Briefly describe how the television media has affected the American political system. For example, has it become a part of the political process? Then study either the Nixon-Kennedy or Ford-Carter television debates. Determine whether or not it supports your analysis, explaining why or why not.

4. Select a country other than the United States. Study its government, and position it on a continuum similar to the one described on page 332. Be prepared to defend your decision in a class discussion.

5. Make a study of your school as a political system. Investigate what type of political system governs the school as a whole. In addition, examine the sub-systems that govern smaller groups such as a school club. In your study, use the skills of gathering evidence and interviewing.

6. If you belong to a political group, choose an issue which has currently created differences of opinion among group members. Play the advocate role in regard to this issue. Keep a diary of your activities and share it with your teacher or class.

Edwin S. Corwin's The Constitution and What It Means Today, revised edition, Harold W. Chase and Craig R. Ducat (Princeton University Press: Princeton, NJ), 1973.

> Focuses in detail on the articles and amendments of the Constitution of the United States. Discusses each and highlights the significance of articles and amendments for citizens today. An excellent source for students who desire an in-depth understanding of any portion of the Constitution.

The Meaning of the Constitution, Angela Roddey Holder (Barrons Educational Series, Inc.: New York, NY), 1974.

> Another excellent discussion of the articles and amendments to the Constitution. Contains many examples of everyday application of the Constitution.

Inside the System, edited by Charles Peters and Timothy J. Adams (Praeger Publishers: New York, NY), 1970.

> Composed of articles by different authors, highlighting subjects such as the White House Staff and Cabinet, the day of a Senator, and activity within various agencies and departments of the national government.

Winning Elections: A Handbook in Participatory Politics, Dick Simpson (The Swallow Press, Inc.: Chicago, IL), 1972.

> The Chicago alderman highlighted in one of this chapter's case studies (pages 340–341) discusses effective citizen participation in elections.

Chapter Objectives

- ★ To learn how Congress operates as a coalitional political system
- ★ To learn how congressional decisions are made
- ★ To analyze the limits on congressional activities
- ★ To analyze how citizens can influence Congress
- ★ To develop skills in bargaining

chapter 12

The LEGISLATIVE BRANCH

Congress is often called "the people's branch" of the national government since all its members are elected by the voters. This is not true of either the executive or the judicial branch. In the executive branch, only the president and vice-president are elected; all other officials are appointed. Federal judges are also appointed.

Of the three branches of the national government, the legislative branch is closest to individual citizens. You have a greater chance of influencing your representatives or senators than of influencing the president or the Supreme Court. At the same time, actions taken by Congress directly affect your life. For example, Congress sets minimum wages and taxes your income.

Because of the close relationship between citizens and Congress, understanding the nature of Congress is important. The United States Congress operates as a coalitional political system. Members represent a variety of people, and they must compromise and form coalitions with those who have similar interests. Skills in bargaining are essential for this process. In this chapter you will learn bargaining skills which will enable you to work more effectively in political groups.

Congress as a Coalitional System

To understand the legislative branch of the federal government, you must examine its structure, the functions it performs in the federal system, and the people who perform those functions. As you investigate the resources used and distributed by members of Congress and the activities they carry out, you will see how Congress functions as a coalitional political system.

STRUCTURE and FUNCTIONS The United States Congress is a *bicameral,* or two-chamber legislature, composed of the Senate and the House of Representatives. The Senate has 100 members, two from each of the 50 states. The House of Representatives has 435 members.

Representation. Representation in the House is based on state population. The more populous a state is, the more representatives it has in the House. For example, Arizona, a state with less than 2 million people, has 4 representatives. California, a state with more than 20 million people, has 43 representatives. Each state is guaranteed at least 1 representative, no matter how small the state's population. Vermont, for example, has 1 representative. The map on this page (Figure 12-1) shows how the 435 seats in the House of Representatives are divided among the 50 states.

United States senators are elected "at large." In other words, all voters in the state vote for senators. In turn, a senator represents all citizens in his or her state.

Each member of the House in contrast, is elected by voters of a certain district within the state. For example, the state of Indiana has 11 congressional districts, as Figure 12-2 shows. In 1976 voters in Indiana's third district elected John Brademas, a Democrat, as their representative, while voters in the seventh district elected John Myers, a Republican.

Qualifications. Article I, Sections 2 and 3, of the Constitution describe the require-

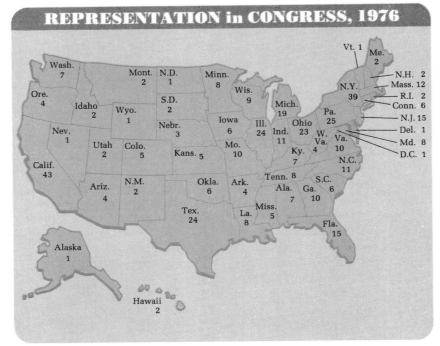

Figure 12-1

REPRESENTATION in CONGRESS, 1976

ments for membership in Congress. To be eligible for the Senate, a person must be at least 30 years of age, a citizen of the United States for nine years, and a resident of the state to be represented in Congress. To qualify for the House of Representatives, a person must be at least 25 years old, a citizen of the United States for at least seven years, and a resident of the state to be represented in Congress.

Terms. Members of the House of Representatives serve two-year terms, and senators serve six-year terms. One third of the Senate seats are on the ballot, or "up for election," every two years. For example, in 1972 one third of the Senate seats were on the ballot. A second third were on the ballot in 1974, and another third in 1976. To continue serving as a senator, a person elected in 1972 would have had to run again and have been reelected in 1978.

Corresponding to the two-year terms in the House of Representatives, each two-year span is considered as a separate Congress. For example, the 1st Congress extended from March 4, 1789, to March 4, 1791. The Congress whose representatives were elected in 1976 was the 95th Congress. Its life span extended from January 4, 1977, to January 4, 1979. Within the period of each Congress there are two regular sessions, one held each year.

Congressional Functions. The Constitution grants the Congress extensive legislative powers. In addition, each house of Congress has certain unique responsibilities.

All tax bills must originate in the House of Representatives. The House also has the power to impeach the president, federal judges, and other federal officials. The Senate has the power to try impeachments, confirm many presidential appointments, and approve treaties. The constitutional powers of Congress are summarized in Chapter 11, on page 315.

The structure and powers of Congress, as described in the Constitution, include several important congressional functions.

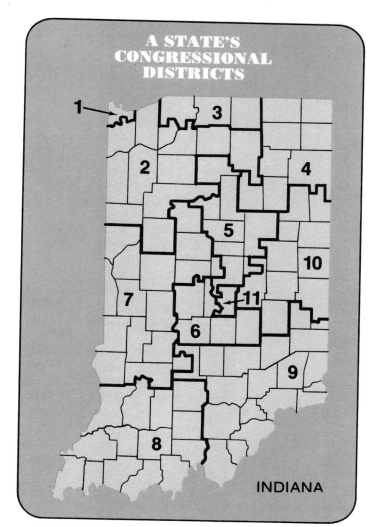

Figure 12-2

Among these are law-making, investigating, and representing constituents. (A *constituent* is a voter represented by an elected official.)

Law-making is the best known congressional function. In a two-year term as many as 700 laws may be passed by Congress and signed by the president. Congress, by a two-thirds vote, may also propose amendments to the Constitution. As you know, these become law when ratified by three fourths of the states. You will examine the law-making function of Congress in greater detail later in this chapter.

Congress conducts many investigations. Committees and subcommittees hold hearings on legislation that is before Congress.

Committee members invite experts, administration officials, or interested citizens to testify at these hearings. In addition, individual citizens may ask to speak at congressional hearings.

Hearings also help Congress oversee the operations of the national government. Officials of government agencies are frequently asked to appear before congressional committees to discuss the activities of their agencies. Through such hearings, Congress can determine whether laws are being applied as it intended.

Members of both the House and Senate are elected as representatives of their constituencies. Voters expect their senators and representatives to promote and protect their interests in the national government.

Members of Congress also provide other services to their constituents. These include face-to-face meetings, answering letters, and keeping citizens informed through newsletters or press releases. In addition senators and representatives are often asked to help local citizens deal with governmental agencies.

In his book *You and Your Congressman,* Representative Jim Wright describes some typical problems which a member of Congress might be asked to solve for constituents:

"—A serviceman, stationed in Greenland, has learned that his father has died and that his mother is on the verge of nervous collapse. He needs help in getting compassionate leave.

—A small industrial firm wants to offer its products to the federal government but doesn't know which agency to deal with or the proper form in which to prepare its bids.

—A disabled veteran needs hospitalization in a hurry. The nearest Veterans' Administration Hospital is overcrowded and cannot possibly admit him. Arrangements must be made to get him into another one.

—An inventor is certain that he has come up with something which will transform the whole technological future of the world. Unfortunately, he can't get anyone to listen to him.

—A homeowner with a Federal Housing Authority loan has made payments regularly for eight years. However, because of illness, he has missed the last two payments and the mortgage company has issued instructions for foreclosure. The congressman will try to get the FHA to intercede.

—A student preparing a thesis needs some information from the Library of Congress.

—A local manufacturer is in trouble with the Federal Trade Commission because of an advertisement. He feels he is being discriminated against and that the FTC is treating him more harshly than it is treating his competition. He wants a top-level interview with officials."

The variety of congressional functions means that the work day of members is busy and long. According to a task force of the House Commission on Administrative Review, the typical work day in the House of Representatives lasts from 8:30 A.M. to 7:30 P.M. A representative spends about four and one-half hours with work on the floor of the House or in committees. He or she devotes another three hours to work in the office—seeing constituents, reading mail, reviewing legislation with staff members, or planning meetings.

Luncheons, meetings, and discussions with other legislators can account for another three to four hours of the day. In addition, many representatives take work home during the evening.

Think about the structure and functions of Congress and answer the following questions:

1. How do the two houses of Congress differ in representation and function?
2. Which function of Congress do you think is most important for the nation as a whole? Which function is most important to you?

PROFILE of the 95th CONGRESS

HOUSE		SENATE	HOUSE		SENATE
PARTY			**PROFESSION**		
289	Democrats	61	215	Lawyers	65
144	Republicans	38	81	Businessmen and bankers	13
0	Independent	1	45	Educators	6
SEX			14	Farmers and ranchers	6
418	Men	100	22	Career government officials	0
17	Women	0	24	Journalists, communications executives	4
AGE			2	Physicians	0
27	Youngest	34	1	Veterinarians	1
77	Oldest	80	0	Geologists	2
49	Average	54	6	Workers and skilled tradesmen	0
RELIGION			25	Others	3
255	Protestants	69	**ETHNIC MINORITIES**		
107	Catholics	12	17	Blacks	1
18	Jewish	5	2	Orientals	3
4	Mormons	3	4	Spanish	0
51	Others	11			

Figure 12-3

From: U.S. News & World Report
Sources: "Congressional Directory," National Democratic and Republican Congressional Committees, Associated Press

SERVING in CONGRESS What types of people are elected to Congress? Do they reflect the social characteristics of the voters who elect them? How do members of Congress view their role as leaders?

Social Characteristics. Figure 12-3 illustrates some social characteristics of the members of the 95th Congress (1977–1978). The typical member of Congress in 1977, as in previous years, was a white, middle-aged, Protestant male. He was likely to have had a college education and a high-status occupation before becoming a congressman.

Some segments of the population have fewer representatives in Congress than their size would indicate. For example, women made up only 3 percent of the 95th Congress, even though more than 50 percent of the American population is female. Black representatives made up another 3 percent of the 95th Congress, but more than 11 percent of the American population is black. Judging from the chart, what other general statements can you make about the social composition of the 95th Congress?

Leadership. All members of Congress exercise leadership in some way. They are leaders in the sense that they represent their constituents. Many also act in leadership roles among their peers in Congress.

Following are profiles of several senators and representatives who were members of the 95th Congress. As you read the profiles, think about how each member viewed his or her role as a leader. Which style of leadership (trustee, broker, delegate) seemed most important to each person? Also think about the personal resources which these senators and representatives brought to Congress.

★ **Profile: Senator Edward W. Brooke**

Edward W. Brooke of Massachusetts was first elected to the United States Senate in 1966. The only black to serve in the Senate since Reconstruction, Brooke was elected to a second term in 1972. But Republican Brooke was defeated in a stunning upset in the fall elections of 1978.

Edward Brooke grew up in Washington, D.C., graduated from Howard University, and

351

**Senator
Edward W. Brooke**

served in the army during World War II. After the war he attended Boston University Law School, graduating in 1948. Brooke then opened a private law practice in Boston.

By 1962 Brooke was politically strong enough to challenge Elliott Richardson, then a Boston lawyer, for the Republican nomination for Massachusetts attorney general. Brooke won this primary and defeated the Democratic challenger in the election.

As Massachusetts attorney general Brooke was criticized by some blacks for his decision declaring a student strike against desegregation illegal. He defended himself, saying:

> "I am not a civil rights leader, and I don't profess to be. . . . I am a lawyer and . . . the attorney general of Massachusetts. I can't serve just the Negro cause. I've got to serve all the people of Massachusetts."

Since his election to the Senate in 1966, Edward Brooke has supported anti-poverty legislation, tax reform, better government planning, and truth-in-lending laws. Brooke introduced an open-housing amendment to the Senate's 1968 civil rights legislation. He was also a member of President Johnson's Advisory Commission on Civil Disorders. Brooke was a leader of the vigorous fight in opposition to President Nixon's Supreme Court nominees, Clement Haynsworth and G. Harrold Carswell, whom he considered to be unqualified and to be opponents of civil rights. Senator Brooke was a member of the Banking and Currency and the Aeronautical and Space Sciences Committees.

Brooke has taken a strong stand in favor of busing for school desegregation, even though it is not very popular with his constituents. He notes:

> "I have always believed that those of us who serve in public life have a responsibility to inform and promote leadership for our constituents. If we were going to have government by consensus, they really wouldn't need us in Congress at all."

★ Profile: Congresswoman Elizabeth Holtzman

A native New Yorker, Elizabeth Holtzman has represented the Sixteenth Congressional District from Brooklyn since 1972. As a relative newcomer, she won the Democratic nomination over Emanuel Celler, a man who had served the district for 50 years. Many considered him unbeatable. When Holtzman declared her intentions to challenge the aging Democrat in the primary, Celler is said to have commented that her effort was like trying to topple the Washington Monument with a toothpick.

Holtzman has solid credentials, a Phi Beta Kappa graduate of Radcliffe College and a 1965 graduate of Harvard Law School. She practiced law in New York both before and after becoming a mayoral assistant to New York Mayor John V. Lindsay.

**Congresswoman
Elizabeth Holtzman**

Senator Birch Bayh

In November the heavily Democratic and liberal Sixteenth District sent Elizabeth Holtzman to Washington. She set up offices in Washington and Brooklyn, chose independent non-party people for her staff, and promised to publish her financial records regularly. "My victory," she declared, "says that no political figure, no matter how powerful, can forget the people he was elected to serve."

In Congress Holtzman has supported legislation for women's rights, federal aid for low-income housing, wage-price controls, aid to mass transit, and environmental protection. She also actively opposed the Nixon policies regarding the Vietnam War.

As a member of the House Judiciary Committee, Representative Holtzman considered articles of impeachment against President Richard Nixon. She saw parallels between this experience and that of the Founding Fathers.

> "The Founding Fathers," she explained, "had a very direct experience with tyrannical government, . . . with abuse of power and the deprivation of individual liberties. . . . They created a democracy. We came into a situation that was so inconsistent with a democratic system. . . . The majority of the committee clearly came down and reasserted their commitment to the values of the Founding Fathers. They said, 'This is what we stand for, this is what this country is about.'"

To Elizabeth Holtzman, casting her "yea" vote for impeachment was not vindictively destroying a president, but upholding the values of a democratic system.

★ **Profile: Senator Birch Bayh**

Birch E. Bayh, Jr., was born on an Indiana farm in 1928. A 1951 graduate of Purdue University, with a degree in agriculture, Bayh moved from farming to a political career in 1954 when he was elected to the Indiana House of Representatives. While a full-time legislator he earned a law degree and was admitted to the bar.

In 1962 Bayh ran for and won a seat in the United States Senate. When no one wanted the chairmanship of the Senate Judiciary subcommittee on constitutional amendments, Birch Bayh volunteered for the job. He evaluated his achievements by observing:

> "We've had only 26 constitutional amendments in the history of our country, and I was author and floor manager of two, and a third is before the states for ratification. Sometimes we wonder whether our lives make any difference to the world or not. I think mine has."

Senator Bayh favors legislation to abolish the electoral college. (He is in favor, instead, of a system of direct election of the president.) He also has supported civil rights legislation, agricultural price supports, effective crime control with respect for civil liberties, as well as cuts in military spending and stricter controls on multinational oil companies. With Senator Brooke, Bayh led the Senate fight against President Nixon's nominations of Clement Haynsworth and G. Harrold Carswell to the Supreme Court.

Bayh campaigned for the 1972 and 1976 Democratic presidential nomination. He explained his views of the presidency and his hopes for creating good and responsive government to the people this way.

> "I think I could reestablish standards of excellence in this country, get

the best minds and keenest intellects back into the government, and create a problem-solving team that would make government believable again. That's what my life is all about, the use of governmental power to solve the problems of the people."

★ Profile: Congressman Manuel Lujan, Jr.

The 95th Congress is the fifth Congress in which Republican Manuel Lujan, Jr. has represented citizens of Albuquerque, New Mexico. The son of a three-term mayor of Santa Fe, Lujan is a graduate of the College of Santa Fe. After graduation he joined his family's insurance and real estate business.

In the 95th Congress Lujan was a member of the Interior and Insular Affairs Committee and the Science and Technology Committee. He was also active in Republican Party affairs in New Mexico and on Capitol Hill.

Congressman Lujan's support for reduced government spending, a balanced budget, a smaller national debt, and lower taxes earned him the "Watchdog of the Treasury" award from the National Alliance of Businessmen. Lujan has taken a stand that jobs are needed to fight poverty but that they must come from a partnership of government and private enterprise. To this end he introduced in the House the Rural Job

Opportunity Act to encourage industry to expand into non-urban areas. Lujan also favors setting aside more government contracts for smaller and medium sized businesses. Congressman Lujan also has supported increased federal aid to education and the development of new, non-polluting sources of energy.

Manuel Lujan has described his role as a Congressman both as a strong leader and as a reflector of his constituents' views.

"I generally perceive the role of Congressman to be a 'carrier out' of the will of the people in his district. Of course, there will be times when a Congressman will have to rely more on his personal judgment and less on trying to vote the way 'folks back home' would, because [the Congressman] often has information at hand which is not available to the general public."

★ Profile: Senator John C. Stennis.

John Stennis was born in Mississippi in 1901. He received a B.S. degree from Mississippi State College and earned a law degree and Phi Beta Kappa key at the University of Virginia in 1928. Stennis returned to Mississippi where he set up a law practice and was elected to the Mississippi House of Representatives. He also served as a district attorney and circuit judge from the 16th judicial district of his state. In 1947 John Stennis was elected to the United States Senate. The Senate has often turned to John Stennis to investigate and mediate. He was a member of the Senate committee that investigated the conduct of Senator Joseph McCarthy. Until 1974 he headed the Senate Select Committee on Standards and Conduct, which reviewed accusations of misconduct against Senate members.

Senator Stennis has advocated electoral college reform, federal funds for medical research, housing, and rural development. He was active in Senate filibusters against civil

Congressman Manuel Lujan, Jr.

Senator
John C. Stennis

rights legislation and is a strong supporter of states' rights. Senator Stennis voted for the War Powers Act of 1972 limiting the President's war-making powers. He believed this new limitation would help restore the balance of power between the Executive and Congress.

As chairman of the Senate Armed Services Committee since 1969, John Stennis could be labeled one of the most powerful people in the Senate. It is this committee that approves all military appropriations before they are sent to the floor. (In 1976 one-quarter of the U.S. budget was spent on defense.) Stennis believes the military must justify its financial requests. "I've told the Department of Defense the burden of proof is on them. There is no assumption of need." Stennis sees his responsibility to the military and the Senate clearly.

> "They [the military] are entitled to a chairman who understands their problems and is highly considerate of those problems. The chairman ought to see they're not knocked around—and I do. But so far as being obliged to do what they want done, I'm a Senator first. My obligation is not principally to the military; [the institution which] gave me this power is the Senate."

★ Profile: Senator S. I. (Samuel Ichiye) Hayakawa

Several weeks before the November 1976 elections, a political observer said the following of S. I. Hayakawa's remarkable Sen-

ate campaign in California. "There's no way for Hayakawa to win this election, but he's going to." And he did, defeating Democratic incumbent John Tunney.

Senator Hayakawa was elected to the United States Senate from California at age 70. He came to the Senate after a 30-year career in college teaching and administration. Born in Canada of Japanese parents, Hayakawa earned degrees in English from the University of Manitoba (B.A. 1927), McGill University (M.A. 1930), and the University of Wisconsin (Ph.D. 1935).

From 1955 to 1968, Hayakawa was a professor at San Francisco State College. In November 1968, he was appointed president of the college by Governor Ronald Reagan. At that time the students at San Francisco State were involved in protest demonstrations. Hayakawa took strong measures to quell student protests on the campus.

As college president, Hayakawa, a life-long Democrat, began to feel ideologically closer to the Republican party than to the Democratic party. He changed his political affiliation to the Republican party soon after retiring from San Francisco State in 1973.

During his first six months in office Hayakawa voted with the Republican party's positions 85 percent of the time and with conservative positions 90 percent of the time. Senator Hayakawa believes in less, but more efficient, government. He voted in

Senator
S. I. Hayakawa

favor of eliminating the Senate Select Committee on Aging on the grounds that its work could easily be done by another committee. He has supported a bill to allow young people to work for below the minimum wage as a way to reduce youth unemployment. The Senator also berates politicians for not working harder to appeal to young voters, particularly those under 21.

Some of the Senator's friends describe him as an enormously disciplined man. He sets out to do a job and sticks with it until it is complete. Hayakawa believes that hard work and sacrifice will help a person get ahead. He believes that it was his support of the traditional work ethic that helped him be elected to the Senate.

Hayakawa enjoys being senator and has expressed hopes for accomplishment.

"I'd like to be a . . . good senator . . . to have my personal philosophy about government and people . . . have an impact on the country."

1. What styles of leadership are represented by these members of Congress?
2. What personal resources do these people bring to Congress?
3. What are some of their important goals? Which ones do you share with them?
4. In what ways do the profiled members of Congress reflect the dominant social characteristics of the 95th Congress? (See Figure 12–3.) In what ways are they different?
5. How do the leadership roles taken by congressional representatives compare with those you have studied in communities? in interest groups? in schools?

A COALITIONAL SYSTEM

Five factors contribute most significantly to the coalitional nature of Congress. These are majority decision-making, variety of interests, high participation, bloc voting, and the sharing of resources.

Majority decision-making is practiced in both the House of Representatives and the Senate. This means that when more than half of those voting agree on a position, it becomes the position of the whole body. Majorities in both the House and the Senate must approve a piece of legislation before it can be sent to the president for action. Coalitional political systems traditionally have a majority decision-making rule.

Members of Congress, elected by voters within a single state or district, represent a *variety of regional, ethnic, and economic interests.* Thus, they must form coalitions with other members who have similar interests in order to pass bills they favor and defeat bills they oppose. These coalitions may change frequently as the Congress considers different issues.

A *high rate of participation* is characteristic of a coalitional system, and exists in Congress. Every senator and representative has an equal vote in their respective chambers, and most do vote on important issues. Members also serve on committees and respond to requests from citizens in their state or district.

Bloc voting further illustrates the coalitional nature of Congress. *Blocs* are coalitions of senators or representatives who tend to vote the same way on many issues.

Traditionally, there have been three major blocs in both the House and the Senate. The first is composed of northern Democrats who represent mostly the urban and industrial areas of the northern and eastern parts of the country. The second bloc consists of southern Democrats who try to protect the rights of individual states and promote agricultural interests. A third bloc is formed by Republicans, who tend to vote together as members of the same party.

None of these blocs is rigid, and bipartisan support is common on many bills. Yet, regional and party loyalties can have an impact on votes in Congress.

Finally, *political resources are shared* by many individuals in a coalitional system

The opening of each new Congress marks the beginning of a busy schedule for senators and representatives (bottom photo). Most members of Congress, like Romano Mazzoli of Kentucky, have aides to help them review and research the huge volume of proposed legislation (center photo). Committee work occupies several hours of a day. Some hearings receive wide spread public attention. This was especially true of the Watergate hearings (top photo).

like Congress. In a majority rule situation, for example, each member who has a vote possesses an equally powerful resource. In addition, as a participant in a coalition or regional bloc, each senator or representative shares its resources. All members do not have equal amounts of wealth, knowledge, skills, and status. For example, as you will learn, party leaders and committee chairpersons have greater resources than other members of Congress do. However, resources are spread among various groups.

The following case will help you understand how Congress operates as a coalitional system. As you study it, think about the ways in which Congress is shown functioning as a coalitional system. What blocs are evident in this case? What resources do you think you would need in order to operate effectively in such a system?

★ The 18-Year-Old Vote

The Voting Rights Act of 1965 was a historic document which extended the right to vote to blacks in many states by restricting the use of devices such as literacy tests. According to the Voting Rights Act, the national government was to enforce the law. This provision was intended to prevent state or local governments from imposing illegal restrictions on voting.

In 1970 the Voting Rights Act was due to be renewed. The House of Representatives passed a new bill that basically extended the original provisions of the 1965 act.

When the bill reached the Senate, however, Senator Mike Mansfield, a Democrat from Montana, proposed an amendment to it. The amendment would lower the voting age from 21 and extend the right to vote in national, state, and local elections to all citizens 18 years of age and older.

The amendment provoked an active debate. Senator Edward Kennedy, a Democrat from Massachusetts, quickly came to the support of the amendment. He said, "I believe the time has come to lower the voting age and to bring American youth into the mainstream of the political process."

Other Northern Democrats and some Republicans also offered their support for the amended bill. Senator Barry Goldwater, a Republican from Arizona, concluded:

> "I support extending the vote to young citizens because I know it is right. Young Americans can raise families, hold jobs, be taxed, be tried in adult courts, and be trusted on the public highways, and yet they are not allowed to vote. Youth today is better informed than any previous generation. I hold that there is no sensible reason for denying the vote to 18-year-olds."

Some conservative Republicans opposed the amendment. However, the strongest opposition came from Southern Democrats. Sam Ervin, a Democrat from North Carolina, led the opposition. He argued that the Constitution gives state legislatures, not Congress, the power to establish the qualifications of voters.

In spite of the arguments of Southern Democrats, the Senate passed the new Voting Rights Act with the amendment extending the vote to 18-year-olds. The chart on page 359 shows how different groups voted. As you can see, a large majority of both Republicans and Democrats voted in favor of the bill.

Before the bill could be sent to President Nixon, the House had to pass it with the amendment added. Again, in the House, Southern Democrats opposed the amendment. Their case was presented by George W. Andrews, a Democrat from Alabama, who said, "The Senate amendment lowering the voting age to 18 shares a common evil with the Voting Rights Act: both trample on the rights of the states."

Speaker of the House, John W. McCormack, a Democrat from Massachusetts, and majority leader, Carl Albert, a Democrat

CONGRESSIONAL VOTES on the VOTING RIGHTS ACT of 1970

	Senate		House of Representatives	
	In Favor	Opposed	In Favor	Opposed
Republicans	26	8	100	76
Democrats	38	9	172	56
Northern Democrats	32	0	138	6
Southern Democrats	6	9	34	50

Figure 12-4

from Oklahoma, led the fight for approval of the amended bill. Representative Albert noted that if the House did not accept the bill with the Senate amendment, it would be telling both young people and blacks that there was no place for them in the orderly political process.

The amended bill passed the House by a vote of 272 in favor and 132 against. Figure 12-4 shows how the vote breaks down. As in the Senate vote, the split between Northern and Southern Democrats is clear.

Several states refused to enforce the new Voting Rights Act because it included the 18-year-old vote provision. The issue was then brought to the Supreme Court.

In a 5 to 4 decision, the Supreme Court ruled that Congress had the authority to regulate federal elections, but it could not regulate state and local elections. In response to the Court's action, both houses of Congress passed a resolution, proposing a constitutional amendment to extend the voting age to 18. In 1971 the Twenty-Sixth Amendment was ratified by three fourths of the states.

1. How does this case illustrate the operation of a coalitional system?
2. What coalitions were involved? What were the bases for these coalitions?
3. How did members of the coalitions use political resources?
4. How might you use similar resources in a school, community, or interest group in which you are involved?

Congressional Decision-Making

How does the decision-making process work in Congress? How does a bill become a law? The activities involved in congressional decision-making and legislation are among the most fascinating in national politics.

Decision-making in Congress depends on two factors. One is the decision-making structure. By studying this structure, you learn who has the greatest influence over decisions and the process by which decisions are made. A second factor involved in congressional decision-making is the way the decision-making structure actually functions in reality.

The internal structure and rules of Congress have a direct impact on its decision-making activities. Leaders of the Democratic and Republican parties in Congress manage the day-to-day operations on the floors of the House and Senate. Their activities can influence actions taken in Congress.

Committees are a second major part of the congressional structure. Thousands of bills are introduced in Congress every year, and members of Congress cannot be expert on all of them. To handle this problem, Congress has created committees that study each bill and make reports and recommendations. These committees usually decide which measures the House and Senate will consider.

The rules that regulate its activities also influence decision-making in Congress. In order to gain approval, a measure must follow an established procedure. The process by which a bill becomes a law illustrates one example of this procedure.

As you read about the decision-making structure, think about how this structure affects congressional decisions. Which members have more resources within the structure?

PARTY LEADERS

Every two years, at the start of a new Congress, the congressional members of the Democratic and Republican parties meet to select *floor leaders*. These are the people who organize and manage activities for each party.

In the House of Representatives the *majority party* (the party with more than half the members) chooses a *majority leader* and a *majority whip*. The selection takes place in the *caucus*, or meeting, of the representatives belonging to the majority party.

The majority leader is the chief spokesperson of the majority party. He or she also arranges the day-to-day House schedule. The majority whip keeps party members informed about measures before the House, polls them on how they plan to vote, and tries to make sure that members are present for important votes.

The *minority party* also selects a *minority leader* and a *minority whip*. They perform similar tasks to those of their majority counterparts. However, they have less power, since their party is in a minority.

The most powerful leader in the House is the *Speaker of the House*. Members of the majority party select a candidate for Speaker in their caucus. All members of the House vote in the selection of the Speaker. However, since all majority members are pledged to vote for the candidate selected in the party caucus, the majority candidate is guaranteed election.

The Speaker of the House has sometimes been called the second most powerful elected position in the nation. The Speaker sets the agenda (the order of business) in the House, grants members permission to speak on the floor, and decides when a vote will be taken. In addition, he or she assigns bills to appropriate committees.

In the Senate, majority and minority party members also elect leaders and whips. However, the majority party caucus does not choose the Senate's presiding officer. According to the Constitution, the vice-president of the United States presides over the Senate. Senators do elect a *president pro tempore,* but that position is largely ceremonial. The president pro tem presides over the Senate in the absence of the vice-president.

In the House, the jobs of party floor leaders are powerful and demanding. The party floor leaders in the Senate generally have less influence. The Senate is a much smaller body, and the task of co-ordinating its activities is less complicated. As a result, the job of floor leaders tends to be less important.

Party floor leaders in both the House and the Senate need strong negotiating and bargaining skills. They cannot order party members to vote for or against a specific bill. Therefore, they must use their knowledge, status, and skills to persuade others. Floor leaders often take the lead in forming coalitions.

Congressional party leaders also serve as links between Congress and the president. If the president belongs to the same party as the majority in Congress, majority floor leaders can help promote presidential programs. In addition, presidents often seek advice from congressional leaders.

Selecting leaders is a top agenda item at the beginning of each new two-year term of Congress. At times, the decisions are almost automatic. Leaders in the previous session of Congress are maintained with little or no opposition. However, as the 95th Session of Congress convened in 1977, the top jobs in both the House and Senate were open. The following case describes the selection process by which Democratic party leaders were chosen. As you read, analyze the process as a coalitional one.

★ "Tip" Comes Out on Top

During January 1977 the Democrats, as the majority party in both the House and the Senate, faced the task of picking a House Speaker, a House majority leader and whip, and a Senate majority leader and whip.

In the Senate, Robert Byrd of West Virginia was selected unanimously to be the Democratic majority leader. He had been opposed briefly by Hubert Humphrey of Minnesota, who withdrew when he realized he could not defeat Byrd. Alan Cranston was selected, without opposition, as the whip, the number two leader.

In the House of Representatives, the top job, Speaker of the House, was filled rather easily. Thomas "Tip" O'Neill, from the Eighth Congressional District in Massachusetts, won all his party's votes.

O'Neill's move toward the powerful office really began in 1971. Morris Udall of Arizona and Hale Boggs of Louisiana were locked in a tight contest to become House majority leader. In working to line up support, both courted "Tip" O'Neill, a popular, trusted, respected member of the House since 1952. O'Neill's strong support of Boggs influenced several others to back him. When Boggs won, he used his influence to help O'Neill gain the position of majority whip.

When Boggs died in a plane crash, O'Neill succeeded him as majority leader. In this position he did numerous favors for important Democratic members of the House. When they needed help in pushing a bill, O'Neill was there with strong support. In

As Speaker of the House, Thomas "Tip" O'Neill has important political resources. How can he use these resources during sessions of Congress?

this manner, he built a loyal following in the House.

In 1976, Speaker of the House Carl Albert of Oklahoma announced he was retiring from politics. Albert did O'Neill the favor of telling him his plans before making them public, thus giving O'Neill a head start in campaigning for the Speaker's job. O'Neill quietly started rounding up votes by reminding House members of the favors he had done for them. When it was time to hold the election for Speaker, "Tip" O'Neill had no opponents.

Selecting a House majority leader was much livelier. There were four contenders, each of whom appeared to have a chance to win: John McFall of California, Philip Burton of California, Richard Bolling of Missouri, and Jim Wright of Texas.

John McFall had held the position of majority whip in the previous session of Congress. However, he had lost favor with some party leaders and was unable to rally the entire California delegation behind him.

Philip Burton seemed to have more support from fellow Democrats than the other candidates did. However, he had served in the House for only 12 years, far less time than any of his competitors. Furthermore, "Tip" O'Neill was against him.

Richard Bolling was a veteran member of the House who had served there since 1948. He was well respected, but had run for majority leader once before and had lost. Bolling had pushed hard for congressional reforms, making a few enemies in the process.

Jim Wright was also a veteran member of Congress, with 22 years of service. Generally well liked, Wright was considered cooperative, loyal, and trustworthy. "Tip" O'Neill's behind-the-scenes support of Wright's candidacy was his greatest asset.

In the first round, the voting was as follows: Burton—106, Bolling—81, Wright—77, McFall—31. Since no candidate had a majority of the votes cast, there was a second round of voting, without including McFall.

The second round score was Burton—107, Wright—95, Bolling—93. Again, no candidate had a majority. However, Bolling was eliminated from the running. Burton still seemed to be the favorite, however O'Neill's support of Wright was a strong influence in his favor.

In the third vote, Jim Wright won 148 votes to Philip Burton's 147. Jim Wright of Texas was the new House majority leader.

1. In what ways did the selection of leaders reflect a coalitional political process?

2. How are party leaders chosen in each house?

3. What is the power of the Speaker of the House?

4. Why do senatorial floor leaders have less influence in general than those in the House?

The COMMITTEE SYSTEM

The task faced by members of Congress is a large one. More than 25,000 bills may be introduced in a two-year term. As many as 700 bills are eventually passed by both houses. Congress copes with this heavy work load by dividing work among committees.

Each member of the House and Senate is assigned to one or more *standing* (permanent) *committees*. These committees specialize in different types of legislation. For example, the House Armed Services Committee works only on business related to the military.

The House has 22 standing committees, and the Senate has 15. The congressional committees of the 95th Congress are listed in Figure 12–5.

In addition to the standing committees, Congress creates special temporary committees to deal with specific problems. Ordinarily, these do not have the power or importance of a standing committee. *Select*

CONGRESSIONAL COMMITTEES in the 95th CONGRESS

HOUSE COMMITTEES	SENATE COMMITTEES
Standing Committees	**Standing Committees**
Agriculture	Agriculture, Nutrition and Forestry
Appropriations	Appropriations
Armed Services	Armed Services
Banking, Finance and Urban Affairs	Banking, Housing and Urban Affairs
Budget	Budget
District of Columbia	Commerce, Science and Transportation
Education and Labor	Energy and Natural Resources
Government Operations	Environment and Public Works
House Administration	Finance
Interior and Insular Affairs	Foreign Relations
International Relations	Governmental Affairs
Interstate and Foreign Commerce	Human Resources
Judiciary	Judiciary
Merchant Marine and Fisheries	Rules and Administration
Post Office and Civil Service	Veterans' Affairs
Public Works and Transportation	
Rules	**Select and Special Committees,**
Science and Technology	**95th Congress, First Session**
Small Business	Democratic Policy Committee
Standards of Official Conduct	Legislative Review Committee
Veterans' Affairs	Democratic Senatorial Campaign
Ways and Means	Committee
	National Republic Senatorial Committee
Select and Special Committees,	Republican Policy Committee
95th Congress, First Session	Special Committee on Ethics
Ad Hoc Select Committee on	Special Committee on Indian Affairs
Outer Continental Shelf	Special Committee on Intelligence
Democratic National Congressional	Special Committee on Nutrition and
Committee	Human Need
Democratic Steering and Policy Committee	Special Committee on Small Business
Republican National Congressional	Special Committee on Aging
Committee	
Republican Policy Committee	
House Recording Studio	
Select Committee on Aging	
Select Committee on Assassinations	
Select Committee on Ethics	
Select Committee on Narcotics Abuse	
and Control	
Select Committee on Modernization of	
House Gallery Facilities	

Figure 12-5

committees examine matters that do not fall within the exact area of any standing committee. For example, the Watergate Committee was a select committee in the Senate—the Select Committee on Presidential Campaign Activities. *Joint committees* are composed of members of both houses and act as a single body. *Conference committees* are made up of some members from each house and meet to work out differences between Senate and House versions of a piece of legislation.

Most congressional committees are further divided into several subcommittees.

The Senate Human Resources Committee, for example, has eight subcommittees. Each subcommittee specializes in one part of the overall subject area of the committee, as you can see in Figure 12–6.

Committees do most of the daily work of the Congress. When a bill is introduced in either the House or the Senate, it is assigned to a committee for study. If a majority of the committee members oppose the measure, they can "kill" it by not reporting on it.

When a committee does report a bill to the floor, it can also recommend a vote for or against the measure. Such reports can

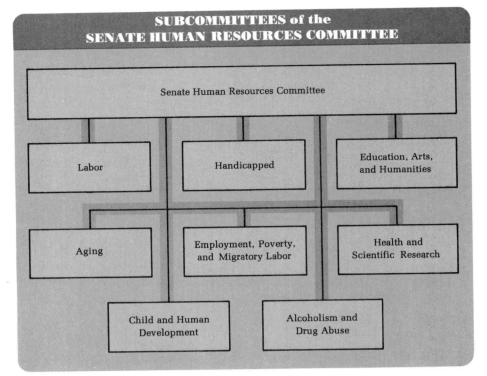

SUBCOMMITTEES of the SENATE HUMAN RESOURCES COMMITTEE

Senate Human Resources Committee

Labor

Handicapped

Education, Arts, and Humanities

Aging

Employment, Poverty, and Migratory Labor

Health and Scientific Research

Child and Human Development

Alcoholism and Drug Abuse

Figure 12-6

have a great influence on other members who cannot study each bill in detail. In this way congressional committees control the future of most legislation.

Some committees have more power and prestige than others because they handle bills that are important to a large number of people. In the Senate these include Appropriations, Foreign Relations, Finance, Armed Services, Judiciary, Agriculture, and Commerce. Among the most influential committees in the House of Representatives are Rules, Appropriations, Ways and Means, Armed Services, Judiciary, Agriculture, and Interstate and Foreign Commerce.

In the House, one committee has more power than all the others. The Rules Committee has the authority to decide when a bill will be considered on the floor of the House. It can also set limits on the length of debate and decide whether anyone may add amendments. If the Rules Committee favors a bill, it can pass special resolutions to speed its passage. However, if it opposes a measure, it can also withold it from floor action.

Committee Assignments. All members of Congress serve on committees. In the House of Representatives each member serves on one standing committee. Senators have two or three committee assignments.

The party composition of committees reflects overall party strength in the House or Senate. For example, if one third of all Senators are Republicans, then about one third of the members of each Senate committee will belong to the Republican party.

The caucuses of party members at the beginning of each congressional term make committee assignments. Many factors may influence these decisions; however the most important one is a member's own interests, knowledge, and skills. Thus, a person who studied agriculture in college and represents a district or state where farming is important would probably be assigned to the Agriculture Committee.

The most important member of any committee is the *chairperson*. The status of the chairperson gives him or her authority over other committee members. A chairperson appoints subcommittee members, hires staff assistants, calls committee meetings, controls their agendas, and presides over them. He or she also represents the committee to other members of Congress and to the executive branch.

Skilled committee chairpersons can use their resources to influence other committee members to support or oppose bills. In addition, a chairperson can personally kill a bill by not putting it on the agenda. If the committee does not consider a bill, it cannot report it to the floor.

The chairperson of a committee is nearly always the member of the majority party who has the most seniority. *Seniority* is a high status based on number of years of service. A person who has been on the House Appropriations Committee for ten years has more seniority than a person who has served on it for four years.

The caucus of the majority party must approve the appointment of committee chairpersons. Although party caucuses have voted against senior committee members, this happens only rarely.

1. What is the function of the standing committees in Congress?
2. Why is the House Rules Committee particularly powerful?
3. How are members of Congress assigned to committees?

HOW a BILL BECOMES a LAW

A bill becomes a law when it is passed by a majority vote in both houses of Congress and signed by the president. How does this happen? What procedure is followed? Who influences the decisions that are made?

To answer these questions, we will follow the course of one fictional bill through Congress. It is a bill that would provide new health benefits to elderly veterans of the armed forces. We will call it the Veterans' Bill. Before it becomes law, this bill will pass through eight stages.

Stage one is its introduction. Most bills may be introduced in either house of Congress. Representative Brown introduces the Veterans' Bill in the House of Representatives. The Speaker of the House then assigns it to the Veterans' Affairs Committee for study and recommendation.

Committee deliberations and action are *stage two.* The chairperson of the Veterans' Affairs Committee assigns the bill to the subcommittee on Medical Facilities and Benefits.

Next, the subcommittee conducts public hearings. Among those it invites are an official from the Veterans' Administration, representatives of veterans groups, administrators from leading veterans' hospitals, and several veterans.

Finally, the members of the subcommittee "mark up" the bill. That is, they go through it line by line and make changes they believe are necessary on the basis of the hearings, staff research reports, and their own judgment. The subcommittee recommends to the whole committee that the "marked up" version of the bill be approved.

The Veterans' Affairs Committee can decide to kill the bill by not acting on it or it can report it to the House floor. After a discussion, the committee votes to report it out of committee; in other words, they vote to speed the bill to the House floor for voting. They recommend House approval.

In *stage three* the Veterans' Bill is sent to the House Rules Committee. The Rules Committee holds a hearing to decide when and how to schedule the bill for action on the floor of the House. It decides by a majority vote to report the Veterans' Bill to the House for immediate consideration with the possibility of amending it.

Stage four is consideration by the House. The Speaker of the House and the majority leader confer with influential House members about when to schedule the

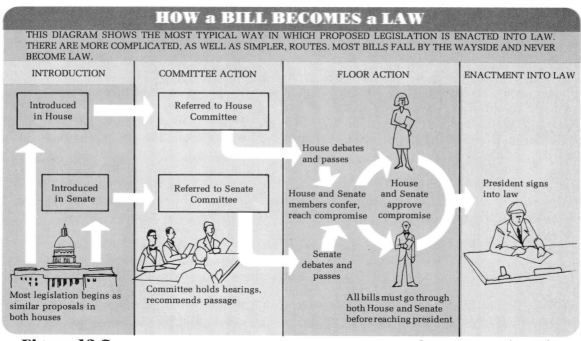

HOW a BILL BECOMES a LAW

THIS DIAGRAM SHOWS THE MOST TYPICAL WAY IN WHICH PROPOSED LEGISLATION IS ENACTED INTO LAW. THERE ARE MORE COMPLICATED, AS WELL AS SIMPLER, ROUTES. MOST BILLS FALL BY THE WAYSIDE AND NEVER BECOME LAW.

INTRODUCTION	COMMITTEE ACTION	FLOOR ACTION	ENACTMENT INTO LAW

Introduced in House → Referred to House Committee

Introduced in Senate → Referred to Senate Committee

House debates and passes

House and Senate members confer, reach compromise

House and Senate approve compromise

Senate debates and passes

President signs into law

Most legislation begins as similar proposals in both houses

Committee holds hearings, recommends passage

All bills must go through both House and Senate before reaching president

Figure 12-7

Source: Congressional Quarterly

bill for debate. Then the majority leader puts it on the calendar.

When the Veterans' Bill reaches the floor, the members debate it. One representative proposes an amendment that would set limits on the new benefits. The House members reject the amendment. They vote, instead, to accept the bill as it was reported from the Veterans' Affairs Committee.

Next the Senate must consider the bill. We will call its path through the Senate, *stage five*. The Senate follows the same basic steps as the House except that the Senate's rules committee does not function in the same way as its House counterpart. When the Senate Veterans' Affairs Committee reports on the bill, it goes directly to the Senate floor. The Senate passes the Veterans' Bill, but it also approves an amendment that limits its benefits.

The House and Senate versions of the bill are different, but they must be identical before the bill can be sent to the president. This problem will be resolved in *stage six*, the conference committee.

The party leadership of each house appoints a small number of senators and representatives to a conference committee. Some of the toughest bargaining in Congress takes place in conference committees. The members must agree on a single version of the Veterans' Bill. They must compromise so that both the House and the Senate can accept the new version.

Once the conference committee agrees on the contents of the Veterans' Bill, the bill enters *stage seven*. The House and Senate each vote on the compromise bill. A majority of both houses approve the new version of the bill and send it to the president.

Presidential action is *stage eight*. The president may veto the bill, let it become law without his or her signature, or sign it. The president signs the Veterans' Bill and it becomes a law.

Figure 12–7 shows a summary of the steps by which a bill becomes a law. Both the chart and the example of the Veterans' Bill illustrate the strong position held by committees in the pathway of any bill introduced in Congress.

Think about how the internal structure and rules of Congress influence its decision-making process and answer the questions:

1. What are the stages by which a bill becomes a law?
2. Which members of Congress have more political resources than others? Which resources are most important to them?
3. How does the committee system affect the decision-making process in Congress?

CONGRESS ACTS

You have seen that party leadership, the committee system, and congressional rules affect how Congress makes decisions. Because of this decision-making structure, certain individuals and groups have more political resources than others. As a result, they have more influence over congressional decisions.

The cases which follow describe two types of congressional decision-making activities. The first concerns a proposal for a constitutional amendment. The second involves a bill about highway spending. As you read the cases, think about how the decision-making process in them is different or similar. Also consider the types of activities undertaken by members of Congress.

★ The Equal Rights Amendment

A constitutional amendment that would guarantee equal rights for all persons regardless of sex was first proposed in Congress in 1923. The idea was then introduced in every term of Congress for the next 49 years. The House of Representatives passed such a resolution several times, but the Senate never passed it until 1972.

In 1971 Martha W. Griffiths, a Democrat from Michigan, introduced a resolution, again proposing an equal rights amendment, in the House of Representatives. When introducing the resolution, she said:

"Women have lagged behind Negroes in coverage by existing equal laws because the Supreme Court has refused to apply the equal protection clause of the 14th Amendment to women as it has to minority groups. The women's rights amendment would not affect areas of privacy such as separate washrooms for men and women, but it would outlaw discriminatory actions by government agencies...."

She presented the following examples of discrimination against women:

"The Air Force requires female enlistees, but not men, to be high school graduates and unmarried. It requires only women to submit photographs with their applications. For what purpose? The FBI refuses to hire women as special agents. Many schools expel unwed mothers, but take no action against unwed fathers."

The Equal Rights Amendment (ERA) resolution was assigned to the House Judiciary Committee which debated it for many weeks. Committee chairperson Emanuel Celler of New York opposed any constitutional amendment. He agreed that discrimination against women did exist, but he felt that this could best be corrected by specific laws.

Some committee members, such as Don Edwards, a Democrat from California, strongly supported the resolution as it had been introduced. Others, however, hesitated. They did not want women to be drafted into the armed forces. They also felt that women needed special protection in some occupations.

Representative Charles Wiggins, a Republican of California, proposed two amendments to the ERA resolution. One exempted, or excused, women from the draft. The second permitted Congress or individual states to enact laws allowing different labor standards for men and women. Such laws might forbid women to work on certain hazardous jobs.

With these compromise amendments attached, the House Judiciary Committee approved the resolution and recommended that the House pass it. The debate on the House floor centered around Wiggins' amendments.

Bella Abzug, a Democrat from New York, said that protective labor laws would "protect women from only one thing—from participating effectively in society, despite the fact that many are compelled by economic conditions to work."

Martha Griffiths, the original sponsor of the bill, added, "If this [change] is added to the resolution, then I must in all good conscience ask you to vote against [it]."

Representative Wiggins argued that to reject his amendments would be to "turn away from common sense and accept the consequences of identical treatment of men and women in all cases." Emmanuel Cellar added, "War is death's feast. It is enough that men can attend."

The House rejected the Wiggins amendments. By a vote of 453 to 24, it passed the original ERA resolution. The resolution said that an amendment would be added to the Constitution which stated, "Equality of rights under the law shall not be denied or abridged by the United States or by any state on account of sex."

Nine of the eleven women representatives voted for the resolution. One was absent, and Lenore Sullivan, a Democrat from Missouri, voted against the measure.

The ERA resolution was next introduced in the Senate and was assigned to the Judiciary Committee. The Judiciary Committee, by a vote of 15 to 1, reported the resolution to the floor and recommended approval. Its report stated:

> "There is overwhelming evidence that persistent patterns of sex discrimination permeate our social, cultural and economic life. . . . We cannot afford to wait any longer for Congress and each of the fifty state legislatures to find the time to debate and revise their laws. There is an imperative for immediate action."

On the other hand, Senator Sam Ervin, Democrat for North Carolina, said:

> "[T]raditional customs and usages of society undoubtedly subject women to many discriminations . . . In as much as they are not created by law, they cannot be abolished by law. They can only be altered by changed attitudes in the society which imposes them."

Senator John Stennis, Democrat from Mississippi, argued that "a very grave question [was proposed] from the standpoint of national security as well as the treatment of womanhood."

Senator Birch Bayh, Democrat from Indiana, was Senate floor manager for the resolution. Speaking in favor of an Equal Rights Amendment, he said

> "We have, it is true, eliminated some forms of . . . discrimination from our midst, but despite our past efforts, our system is flawed by shameful . . . and socially outmoded discrimination against the women of this country. .·. . I believe—and I am sure the men and women of America believe—that equality of rights must mean equality of responsibilities, or else it is a charade."

Marlow Cook, a Republican from Kentucky, also spoke in support of the ERA resolution. He said,

> "It should be emphasized that this amendment provides for equality of both men and women. While the major result of the amendment will apply to the end of established discriminary practices against women, it will also affect statutes which discriminate against men."

The ERA resolution received widespread support in the Senate. In the final vote on March 22, 1972, only six Republicans and two Democrats voted against it. If legislatures in three fourths of the states have ratified it within seven years, it will become an amendment to the Constitution.

★ A Ceiling on Highway Spending

In June 1976 a transportation appropriations bill was introduced in the House of Representatives and was assigned to the Appropriations Committee. Part of the bill appropriated money for highway construction.

President Gerald Ford and budget leaders in Congress wanted the bill to set a ceiling, or top limit, on the money that could be spent for highway construction. This was part of a move to cut back federal spending and control inflation.

In an effort to do this, the House Appropriations Committee imposed a $7.2 billion ceiling on highway construction as part of the transportation bill. Then it reported the bill to the House floor.

Opposition to the ceiling was strong. James Howard, Democrat of New Jersey, argued that such a limit on highway construction "would create an immediate and long term damage to our highway programs." He noted that unemployment in the transportation industry was already 14 percent. The proposed ceiling on spending, he argued, would make conditions even worse.

Howard proposed adding to the bill a series of four amendments that would remove the ceiling on highway spending. Silvio Conte, a Republican from Massachusetts, warned that President Ford would veto the entire transportation bill if it did not contain the ceiling.

House members accepted Howard's amendments by a vote of 251 to 146. Even a majority of Republicans (74 of 145) voted in favor of the amendments, in spite of President Ford's opposition. The House passed the transportation bill with the amendments attached and sent it to the Senate.

The Senate Appropriations Committee approved a version of the bill that included the original ceilings on highway spending. When it was reported to the floor, the Senate passed it easily by a vote of 74 to 6. Few senators expressed any opposition to the ceiling.

Thus, the Senate version of the transportation bill imposed a ceiling on spending for highway construction, but the House version did not. Congressional leaders appointed a conference committee to resolve the differences.

On July 22 the conference committee approved the Senate version of the bill. They noted that President Ford had threatened to veto the transportation appropriations bill if it did not impose ceilings on highway spending.

The Senate version of the bill was then sent back to the House for repassage. Many representatives were uncertain about how they would vote.

James Howard, however, remained vocal in his opposition to any ceilings on highway spending. He stated: "What is at stake here is whether highway money is going to be spent according to the will of the House and the people of the United States, or whether control is going to be transferred downtown to the bureaucracy."

In spite of Howard's efforts, the House passed the Senate version of the bill by a surprisingly large margin, 226 to 167. One representative noted, "The vote was much closer than it looked. Up until the last three minutes, it could have gone either way." A number of members voted to support the bill after it became apparent that it would pass.

The Senate then repassed the bill by voice vote. President Ford signed it into law.

1. How does the decision-making process differ in these two cases? What role did the president play?

2. What political resources were used in each of these situations? Who had the most resources?

3. What political activities were undertaken? What resources were redistributed as a result of these activities?

4. How is the decision-making process in Congress comparable to that of a school, community, or interest group you have studied?

About 100 high school students, chosen from many different states, work as pages in Congress. The pages shown here work in the House of Representatives. They attend school early in the morning, then report to the House Doorkeeper's office at the Capitol. Some pages receive assignments directly from the Speaker of the House. Others pick up flags that members of Congress will present to constituents.

One of the pages' most important duties is providing members of Congress with documents. Some material is picked up at the House Document Room. Pages use carts to deliver large numbers of documents to the House floor. They also prepare packets of material which party floor leaders will distribute to members. When the House adjourns for the day, pages leave for other duties.

The Skill of Bargaining

You have read three cases about congressional activity—the 18-year-old vote, the Equal Rights Amendment, and the highway bill. In each, senators and representatives used important resources to make their positions known. They were advocates for or against bills. and they used skills in bargaining to influence others to support them.

Bargaining is very important in a coalitional political system. In a coalitional system you have to gain the support of a majority for your position. This requires good bargaining skills.

Bargaining can be defined as a political activity in which two or more individuals attempt to influence each other to support different decision alternatives. To bargain requires at least two people who have different interests and goals and who want to reach a common decision. This does not mean that in large groups everyone must agree with the decision that is made in the name of the group.

For example, every member of the Senate Agricultural Committee might not agree with a resolution. Yet they must agree that if a majority of the committee reaches a decision, it will become the position of the whole committee.

Bargaining is crucial in group decision-making. For example, suppose a fictional senator Arnold Smith has $500 to spend. He could buy something for his home or perhaps take a vacation. He might ask friends for advice, but as long as it is his money, he alone will make the final decision. It is an individual decision.

Senator Smith also takes part in group decision-making as a member of the Senate Judiciary Committee. The committee has $50,000 to spend for a study of the enforcement of the Voting Rights Act. Senator Smith wants the committee to pay a commercial firm to conduct a survey. However, other committee members prefer a study done by the committee's staff.

Senator Smith cannot make this decision alone. A majority of the Judiciary Committee must agree. Therefore, Senator Smith must gain support for his position from others. In short, he must bargain to have his position accepted by members of the group who may hold different opinions.

To bargain effectively you must know two things about the people you want to influence. First, you need to know *where they stand* on the issue. What is their preference? Secondly, you need to know the *interests they have* in supporting their position. Why do they take that position? This knowledge gives you a basis for bargaining with others.

WAYS of BARGAINING

If you can identify the alternative positions that people in a group hold and the interests they have, then you are in a good position to begin bargaining effectively. The methods you use to bargain with another person depend on the particular person and the group you are in.

In some cases you may know people in a group very well and you may try to bargain with them by seeking common ground on which all can agree. In other cases, there may be strongly opposing viewpoints among group members. You may find that you need to bargain with them on different grounds using different methods.

No training given in this material will replace your capacity to be sensitive to the type of people and the group context in which you are working. However, in this section we will outline some different bargaining methods. These will give you some alternatives to think about when you work within a group.

There are three basic methods you could use to bargain effectively with others: convincing, trading, and confronting.

Effective bargaining is an important part of decision-making in many different groups. The people shown here are taking part in a bargaining session between labor and management.

Convincing Others. You might bargain by trying to convince others to accept your position. If you feel strongly that your position is best, you can try to change other people's minds so they will support you.

You could do this in several ways. You could show them that your goal is more important or more *significant* than other goals. Secondly, you might argue that your plan would be more *effective*—that it is more likely to succeed. You could also try to convince others that your position is more *sound* by offering solid evidence or logical arguments in favor of it.

Trying to convince others to accept your position is most appropriate if you believe that your goals are very important and if you think others can be influenced by your statements. This method of bargaining is most likely to be effective if others share goals that are similar to yours. You also have a better chance of convincing others if you are in an influential position based on your authority, experience, or knowledge.

Trading with Others. Convincing another person of your position may not be possible. People may refuse to accept the arguments you make in support of your position. In such a circumstance, you could bargain by trading.

You might offer others something they want in exchange for their support. In this case they do not agree with your position, but they are willing to support you because of something you can give them.

Secondly, you could offer to support a person on another issue if he or she supports you on this one. You might also agree to make other compromises for support from others.

Trading usually works best as a bargaining method when you are willing to give up something in order to gain support. One method of trading is to develop a compromise position. Such a position would have some elements of your original position and some elements proposed by others.

Confronting Others. Convincing or trading may not work in all situations. If you cannot convince others or trade with them, you might want to confront those who oppose your position.

In this case, you would take a stand against another person's position which could help you gain support from others. These people may not be entirely convinced that your position is best; however, you may convince them that they should not support someone else. Thus, you may increase support for your position by pointing out the negative consequences of other actions.

Confronting others is an appropriate bargaining method when you know you cannot make the most of your own position.

Yet, you don't want the group to make a decision which will be in direct contradiction with what you believe. In this situation you are trying to minimize your losses.

None of these three ways of bargaining—convincing, trading, or confronting—works in every decision situation. Whether or not they are effective depends upon the people involved in the situation. It depends on the interests and personalities of the people who are bargaining and on their relationship with one another. It also depends on the general composition of the group.

1. What are three basic methods of bargaining?
2. Think about an issue in your school or community in which a group is trying to reach a common decision. What is your position on the issue? How might you use the different bargaining methods in this situation? In your opinion, which method would probably work best?

Influences and Limits on Congress

Congress has the power to make laws for the people of the United States. This power is not limitless, however. As you know, the Constitution establishes a formal system of checks and balances to prevent any one branch of national government from becoming too powerful.

Many informal limits on congressional power also exist. Lobbies and interest groups, citizen advocates, public opinion, party and regional loyalties all influence actions taken by Congress. You will learn about both the formal and informal limits on Congress in the following material.

FORMAL LIMITS on CONGRESS The United States Constitution grants extensive legislative powers to the Congress, but it also sets limits on that power. Both the president and the Supreme Court can limit the power of Congress.

The president checks congressional actions in three ways. First, the president has the power to veto legislation passed by Congress. As you know, Congress may override a veto with a two-thirds vote in each house, but this does not happen often. For example, Congress was able to override only 12 of 59 vetoes by President Gerald Ford.

Most presidents have used the veto power sparingly. Often a president can convince Congress to change the contents of a bill by only threatening to veto it.

A second presidential check on Congress is the power to call special sessions of Congress. If Congress has failed to act on an important issue, the president may call it into session until it resolves the issue.

From Herblock's State of the Union (Simon & Schuster, 1972).

"LET ME MAKE TWO THINGS CLEAR. FIRST: THE COUNTRY IS IN FINE SHAPE. AND SECOND: CONGRESS IS TO BLAME FOR THE MESS WE'RE IN."

The president also influences Congress by his or her power to suggest its agenda. In the State of the Union address and in many other statements, presidents outline legislative programs that they want Congress to consider.

Although only a member of Congress may formally introduce a bill, the bills themselves are frequently suggested by the president or an adviser. Once one of these bills is introduced, presidents use their status and other resources to convince members of Congress to vote for it. In fact, we often judge the effectiveness of a president by noting how many of his or her programs were passed by Congress.

The Supreme Court of the United States has the power of judicial review as you learned in Chapter 11. It can rule whether laws passed by Congress are constitutional when a case is brought before it. The Supreme Court has only declared about 100 such laws unconstitutional in the history of the United States. The possibility of a Supreme Court ruling, however, serves as an effective check on congressional power.

1. What formal limits affect congressional power?
2. What examples can you find of the president or Supreme Court using their powers to limit the actions of Congress in any of the case studies you have read in this chapter?

INFORMAL INFLUENCES

The very nature of Congress sets limits on its activity, for the members of Congress represent a wide variety of people who have different needs and interests. Members of Congress, who must periodically face reelection, cannot ignore the opinions of their constituents.

The necessity for a majority vote is another limiting factor. Forming a coalition of a majority of members is often a difficult task. You have seen that only about one fourth of the bills introduced are ever passed by both houses. In addition, the need to compromise and bargain means that bills which do pass may be "watered down." Such conditions can effectively prevent Congress from becoming too powerful.

Other informal limits on congressional activities include party and regional loyalties, public opinion, interest groups and lobbies.

Party and Regional Loyalty. You saw earlier in this chapter that voting blocs in Congress are often based on party or regional loyalties. These loyalties can act as a limit on members of Congress. A senator, for example, might personally believe in the need for mass transportation but vote for a highway bill because other senators from his or her region strongly support it.

Political parties provide an important source of identification for members of Congress. For example, you saw in Chapter 11 that Senator Birch Bayh was able to mobilize Democrats against the nomination of G. Harrold Carswell to the Supreme Court. At the same time Republicans mobilized behind President Nixon.

Party loyalty is a result of the strength of the two-party system in the United States. Democrats and Republicans oppose each other in most elections across the country. The two parties also hold different philosophical positions on many issues. You have seen in Unit I how party ideology can operate to split the two parties further apart.

Regional loyalties can also affect congressional actions. Since the end of the Civil War, a major regional split has existed between Southern and Northern Democrats. Southern Democrats have usually been concerned with protecting the rights and power of individual states. Northern Democrats, in contrast, have been more concerned about big city problems and urban growth. Further, Northern Democrats are more likely than Southern Democrats to want the national government rather than state governments to provide important services.

Regional loyalties may also split the Republican party. Western Republicans tend to be more conservative than those from eastern states. However, because Republicans have often been the minority party, they are more likely to put aside regional loyalties in favor of party loyalty.

Public Opinion. Members of Congress are directly responsible to the citizens who elect them. Voters expect them to represent their interests in the national government. As a result, public opinion is very important for most senators and representatives.

Many members of Congress conduct regular polls or surveys of voter opinion in their district or state. Letters and telephone calls from constituents can also help legislators judge public opinion.

The importance of public opinion for an individual representative or senator depends largely on his or her leadership role as well as the issue facing Congress. A broker or delegate style of leadership depends more on public opinion than a trustee style.

A broker relies on interaction with constituents so he or she is in frequent contact with the public. Delegates must be informed about the concerns and opinions of constituents so that they can effectively represent them in Congress.

In many cases, however, voters are content to leave issues in the hands of their legislator as a trustee. They may have little interest in the issue or they may feel that their senator or representative is more qualified to handle governmental problems.

Interest Groups and Lobbies. You saw in Unit I how interest groups, such as the AFT and the NEA, can influence public policy. Such groups carefully monitor the activities of Congress. In addition, they usually have direct access to members of Congress and often have an impact on their actions and decisions.

Access to representatives and senators is very important to interest groups and lob-

bies. They need the opportunity to talk with a legislator in order to try to convince him or her to support their position. Interest groups use two major political resources to gain access to members of Congress. These are knowledge and wealth.

Lobbyists are expert in many subjects which are considered in Congress. For example, lobbyists from the American Farmers' Union usually know more about agricultural problems than members of congressional agricultural committees. Members of these committees can use expert information and advice from lobbyists to help them reach a decision.

The American Farmers' Union also provides information about the opinions of farm leaders and individuals. This type of information can help members of Congress judge public reaction to their decisions.

Lobbyists provide a service to members of Congress when they furnish accurate information. Those who are reliable sources of information usually have the most influence in Congress. Legislators are more likely to consider their viewpoint.

According to Representative Jim Wright, Democrat from Texas, the effective lobbyist:

"Attempts to persuade by fact and logic that there is merit on his side of the issue. . . . Whatever influence these individuals and groups which they represent have on members of Congress almost always exists in direct proportion to the reputation for truthfulness and objectivity which they individually have earned."

Contributing to election campaigns is a second way lobbyists and interest groups try to gain access to members of Congress. According to a Federal Election Commission report, special interest groups donated more than $22 million to campaign funds of Congressional candidates during the 1976 election campaign.

Committee chairpersons received the largest sums because of their influential positions in Congress. Almost 60 percent of the total, more than $13 million, was contributed to the chairpersons of 15 major House committees. The heads of the most prestigious committees received the most money.

1. Which of the formal limits on Congress do you think is most important? Why?
2. Which of the informal limits on Congress do you think is most important? Why?
3. What pressures do you think you would feel as a member of Congress?

CITIZEN ADVOCATES Citizen advocates can have an important impact on Congress. They may write letters or perhaps contact their senators or representatives personally. Those who work in groups, however, usually have the most influence.

Below is a case which illustrates how citizen advocates can affect actions by Congress. As you read the case, think about the role played by advocates in a coalitional system.

★ **Saving the Veterans' Affairs Committee**

During the 94th Congress (1975–1977), some senators felt that the cumbersome committee structure of the Senate should be reorganized. They argued that the Senate did not need 31 committees and 176 subcommittees and that senators had to spend too much time on committee work.

In response to these criticisms, the Senate created a select committee to study the committee system. It appointed Senator Adlai Stevenson, a Democrat from Illinois, as chairperson. The committee's task was to trim the number of Senate committees.

Stevenson's committee presented its report at the beginning of the 95th Congress. It proposed that the number of Senate committees be reduced from 31 to 15, and that the number of subcommittees be reduced from 176 to 100.

The chairpersons of the committees to be eliminated protested vigorously. They did not want to lose their positions of influence.

As senators debated the report on committee reorganization, several interest groups became involved in the dispute.

A group of older Americans lobby to convince Senator Don Riegle of Michigan to vote for a national health insurance bill.

They feared that Stevenson's plan would threaten their access to senators and would reduce their ability to influence congressional decisions.

The case of the Veterans' Affairs Committee is a good example. The select committee recommended that it be abolished. Business concerning veterans of the armed forces would then be handled by the Armed Services Committee.

Citizen groups such as the American Legion and the Veterans of Foreign Wars (VFW) strongly objected to this move. Veterans had been treated favorably by the Senate Veterans' Affairs Committee, and they did not want to risk losing their privileges. They decided to fight against the proposal to reform the committee system.

Veterans groups used a variety of tactics to convince senators to support their position. An open letter in support of the Veterans' Affairs Committee was published in the VFW magazine. VFW leaders appointed two top members from each state to meet with their senators to try to persuade them to save the committee.

Leaders also urged members of the VFW and American Legion to write letters to their senators. Thousands of letters, advocating maintenance of the Veterans' Affairs Committee, were sent.

Several state commanders of the VFW and the American Legion went to Washington, D.C., to meet personally with senators. When senators returned to their home states for visits, they were often met by local members of the VFW and the American Legion who urged them to vote against the elimination of the Veterans' Affairs Committee.

Finally, leaders of the VFW and American Legion appeared before the Senate Rules and Administration Committee which was conducting hearings on the reform plan. They spoke persuasively about the need to retain the Veterans' Affairs Committee.

During the floor debate, Senator James Allen of Alabama moved that the Veterans' Affairs Committee be reinstated. Senator Dick Clark, a Democrat from Iowa, supported him.

Allen and Clark have very different political ideas and rarely agree on issues before the Senate, but in this case they joined forces. Allen, a member of the VFW and the American Legion, shared the concerns of the veterans groups. He wanted to protect their special access to Senate leaders. Clark is a liberal who often disagrees with leaders of veterans groups. However, Senator Clark would be running for reelection in 1978. He did not want the powerful veterans groups to work against him in that election.

Senator Clark's situation shows one reason why senators who often opposed each other joined a coalition to retain the Veterans' Affairs Committee. Some senators approved of keeping this committee because they wanted to see their favorite committee retained. Others were convinced by the veterans groups that the Veterans' Affairs Committee was necessary.

When the vote was called, an overwhelming majority of senators voted not to abolish the committee. The veterans had mounted a successful campaign. Senator Claiborne Pell of Rhode Island, who had served in the Senate for 16 years, said, "I've never seen anything like the campaign that the veterans have organized."

1. Who were the advocates in this case? Why were they successful?

2. What bargaining skills and tactics did the advocates use?

3. What political resources did the citizen advocates and senators use? Which do you think were most important?

4. What political activities were undertaken? What resources were redistributed as a result of these activities?

5. Who does a citizen advocate try to influence in a coalitional system?

6. On what basis was a coalition formed in this case?

7. How might you act as an advocate in a coalition system?

Writing to Members of Congress

Citizens act as advocates when they communicate with members of Congress to influence their decisions. By playing the advocate role skillfully, citizens increase their chances of having influence. Here are some suggestions for applying advocate guidelines to writing letters to members of Congress.

WRITING TIPS

1. Find out where your representatives stand on the issue with which you're concerned. This knowledge will guide what you write to them. For instance, suppose there is a bill before the Senate to provide increased federal aid to assist unemployed people to train for new jobs. You want the bill to be passed. You find out that one of your senators is for the bill and the other is against it. Thus, you should write a letter in support of the senator who is for the bill. You agree with his or her stand; there is no need for persuasion. You should write a different kind of letter to the other senator, in an effort to convince him or her of the merits of your position.

2. To advocate a position successfully, letter writers should state their position about an issue clearly and should present reasons for it. Emotional appeals are less likely to be convincing than a clear, concise discussion of evidence which supports your position.

3. It helps to discuss the likely consequences of voting "yes" or "no" on the issue. For example, you might use evidence to show that a new law to train unemployed people for new jobs could save money on welfare payments in the long run. Or you might use facts to show that job training problems are linked to a reduced rate of petty crime.

4. Know when to write a letter. For example, it is inefficient to write if the issue about which you are concerned is not before Congress. If a final vote is to be taken immediately, it may be too late to have any influence. A good time to communicate is when a bill is being studied by committees. If your representatives are not members of the appropriate committees, you may want to write to other members who do belong to these committees.

---

1. Explain why the Congress is the branch closest to individual citizens. In what ways can you influence your congressional representative?

2. How does Congress function as a coalitional political system?

3. Compare and/or contrast the qualifications, terms, and representative districts of a senator and a member of the House.

Chapter Review

4. What powers are shared by both the House and the Senate? What distinct powers are delegated to each?

5. What is the typical social profile of a member of Congress? What factors might change the social composition of future Congresses?

6. How do party leaders, committees, and committee chairpersons exert an important influence on legislative decision-making? What important resources does each use?

7. Review the eight stages through which a bill must pass before it becomes a law. At what points might a citizen advocate be able to influence the legislative process? Explain.

8. How does the passage of a Constitutional amendment differ from the passage of other bills?

9. What are the principles of good bargaining? Why are bargaining skills especially important in a coalitional political system?

10. In chart form, outline the formal and informal limits on Congress.

Chapter Vocabulary

Define the following terms.

bicameral	majority leader	chairperson
constituent	minority party	seniority
majority decision-making	minority leader	bargaining
bloc voting	standing committee	
majority party	select committee	

Chapter Analysis

1. If you were a member of Congress, what would you consider to be your most important activities? What resources would you need to conduct these activities successfully?

2. "Congress is truly representative of the American people." In essay form, agree or disagree with the above statement. Support your answer with evidence from the textbook, class discussions, and/or outside readings.

3. Suppose that you plan on running for the House of Representatives when you turn 25. What things would you do in the next years to prepare for the campaign?

4. Review the three different types of bargaining. Then propose a law you would like enacted, describing the bargaining techniques that you think would be most effective in securing its passage. Explain the reasons for your choices of bargaining strategy.

5. One of the informal limits on the power of Congress is citizen advocates. What tactics can citizens use to ensure that their interests are represented in Congress?

1. On a map of your state, draw in the Congressional districts. Identify the members of the House that represent each of these districts. Then write to your own representative, inquiring about how he or she stays in contact with the district's electorate.

2. Prepare a diary that you think represents the typical week of a senator or a House representative. If possible, send the diary to your own senator or representative, asking how it compares to his or her own weekly schedule.

3. Prepare a profile of one of your senators or representatives. Include information such as the following: years of service, personal resources he or she brought to Congress, style of leadership, important goals, committee assignments, and achievements as a member of Congress.

4. In a group in which you participate, practice bargaining skills. Report to the class on your activities.

How a Bill Becomes a Law: Congress Enacts Civil Rights Legislation, David M. Berman (The Macmillan Company: New York, NY), 1966.
> Shows the law-making process by highlighting the drafting and passage of the Civil Rights Act of 1960 and the Civil Rights Act of 1964.

The Role of the Congressman, Roger H. Davidson (Pegasis: New York, NY), 1969.
> Considers the jobs of members of Congress, discussing their jobs in Washington as well as the way in which they relate to their constituents.

The Senate's War Powers: Debate on Cambodia from the Congressional Record, edited by Eugene P. Dvorin (Markham Publishing Company: Chicago, IL), 1971.
> Relying on the transcripts of the Congressional Record, this book illustrates how the United States Senate debated U.S. military involvement in Cambodia in 1970. Clarifies the Senate's role in making foreign policy.

Congressional Reform in the Seventies, Leroy N. Rieselbach (General Learning Press: Morristown, NJ), 1977.
> An up-to-date work focusing on efforts toward congressional reform, such as redistributing committee power, reducing secrecy, and becoming more accountable.

Chapter Objectives

★ To analyze the roles, resources, and
  activities of the president
★ To identify the limits on the office of
  president
★ To understand how the Executive Office
  works
★ To learn the functions of the federal
  bureaucracy
★ To see how citizens can influence the
  activities of the executive branch
★ To develop skills in generating evidence

chapter 13

The EXECUTIVE BRANCH

The Constitution of the United States identifies only two positions in the executive branch of the national government—a president and a vice-president. Yet in 1978 almost 3 million people worked in this branch of the national government.

A large and complex organization has developed to help the president administer the laws. It includes an Executive Office with more than a dozen special councils that advise the president, 12 executive departments—whose heads form the president's cabinet—and nearly 60 independent agencies. Some government bureaus employ only a few people, while the postal service has more than half a million.

The president has the power to make final decisions and to establish policies. But the people who work in the offices and agencies of the executive branch are able to influence its activities. The public at large can also have an impact, whether as individuals or when organized in interest groups.

In this chapter you will see how the executive branch of the national government functions. You will also read how ordinary citizens can influence its policies and activities. Finally, you will learn additional skills in generating evidence. Techniques for conducting surveys and useful observation are tools used frequently by members of the executive branch. They can also be functional for you as a citizen.

The Presidency as an Elite Political System

An organizational chart of the executive branch is shown in Figure 13–1. As you can see, the president is at the top. As head of the executive branch, the president is responsible for administering the laws. He or she does this with the help of the many agencies represented on the chart and the millions of people they employ.

Studying an organizational chart is a quick way to review the basic structure of a branch of government. But it doesn't tell the whole story. For example, the president is responsible for American activities in more than 80 international organizations. These include not only the United Nations and North Atlantic Treaty Organization (NATO) but also groups such as the International Commission for the Conservation of Atlantic Tunas and the International Union of Radio Science.

Nor can a chart tell you much about how the president functions. What powers does a president have? What is his or her relationship with the Executive Office and the federal bureaucracy? What are the limits on presidential authority? What can citizens do to influence the chief executive?

PRESIDENTIAL ROLES

There are six basic roles played by the president of the United States. The main source for presidential authority in most of these roles is the Constitution. (The constitutional powers of the president are outlined on page 316.) But the roles have grown enormously in scope since the time of the Founders.

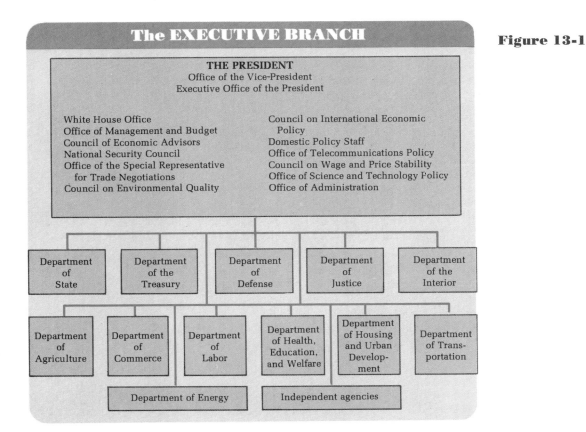

The EXECUTIVE BRANCH

Figure 13-1

THE PRESIDENT
Office of the Vice-President
Executive Office of the President

White House Office
Office of Management and Budget
Council of Economic Advisors
National Security Council
Office of the Special Representative for Trade Negotiations
Council on Environmental Quality

Council on International Economic Policy
Domestic Policy Staff
Office of Telecommunications Policy
Council on Wage and Price Stability
Office of Science and Technology Policy
Office of Administration

Department of State

Department of the Treasury

Department of Defense

Department of Justice

Department of the Interior

Department of Agriculture

Department of Commerce

Department of Labor

Department of Health, Education, and Welfare

Department of Housing and Urban Development

Department of Transportation

Department of Energy

Independent agencies

Chief of State. In this role the president carries out the ceremonial functions of the office. The president greets foreign visitors and entertains them and other special guests at the White House. He or she may also represent the United States on formal occasions abroad such as a coronation or a funeral.

As chief of state, the president issues proclamations, officially sponsors various charity drives, and signs documents. In one week, for example, the president may proclaim Mother's Day, buy the first Easter seals, and spend four hours signing bills and treaties.

Chief Executive. The Constitution gives the president the power to enforce the laws and to make important appointments. This is the basis for the role as chief executive. The president alone is responsible for appointing members of the White House Office. With the consent of the Senate, he or she appoints the members of other special offices in the Executive Office, the heads of the executive departments, and the directors of the independent agencies. The president establishes basic policy in the executive branch, and oversees how it is carried out.

Commander in Chief. The president, as commander in chief of the armed forces, has the ultimate authority over military operations. The framers of the Constitution made this provision in order to place the military under civilian control, and also because the executive branch can act more quickly than the legislature in time of emergency.

Presidents have not hesitated to use this power when they felt it necessary. President Harry Truman relied on it when he dismissed General Douglas MacArthur, a popular war hero, as commander of American forces in the Korean War. And it was this power that enabled President Nixon to give the order for full ground and air support against Communist forces in Cambodia.

Chief Diplomat. The president has the constitutional power to make treaties, with the consent of the Senate. The president is also given the authority to nominate ambassadors and receive foreign ambassadors. Over the years these provisions have served to give the president wide scope in determining foreign policy. The president alone, for instance, can *recognize* a foreign government—that is, formally acknowledge that it is valid and independent. President Nixon took an important step toward recognizing the People's Republic of China when he visited there in 1972.

In the twentieth century, presidents have made increasing use of the *executive agreement*—a kind of treaty that does not require Senate approval—in conducting foreign affairs. For example, an arrangement with the Soviet Union to limit intercontinental missiles may well be formalized in an executive agreement rather than in a treaty.

Chief Legislator. According to the Constitution, Congress has the power to make laws. However, Article II, Section 3, gives the president the right to recommend "such Measures as he shall judge necessary and expedient." On the basis of this clause, presidents since Franklin D. Roosevelt have taken an increasingly active part in proposing legislation to Congress.

The president usually outlines a broad program of legislative action in the State of the Union message, which is delivered to Congress every January. Then he or she fills in the details with messages on more specific topics as the year progresses.

Party Chief. Whether or not a president enjoys politics, presidents are head of their own parties. This is not a constitutional authority, of course, since the Constitution makes no mention of political parties.

In order to accomplish goals, especially getting laws through Congress, a president has to be a good politician. He or she needs to consult with party leaders, reward party members with jobs whenever possible, and help party candidates be elected to political office. As President Kennedy put it: "No president can escape politics. He has not only been chosen by the nation—he has been chosen by his party."

RESOURCES and ACTIVITIES

The president's job is difficult and complex. He or she must draw upon many political resources every day, such as status, wealth, knowledge, and skills.

Presidential Resources. Presidents hold the top status in the executive branch of the government, in the government as a whole, and in the country at large. They also have a high status among leaders of other nations. The Constitution confers most of this status. But it is reinforced by the position of the United States in the world.

The president controls much of the political wealth of the national government. The Office of Management and Budget (OMB), an agency in the Executive Office, helps the president prepare the national budget for congressional approval. Once Congress appropriates the money, OMB supervises its administration, deciding when and how to release funds for government programs and agencies.

The president can control wealth not only by spending it but also by refusing to spend it. In some cases, presidents have resorted to *impoundment*—holding back appropriated funds—when they have opposed programs for which the money was intended.

In addition to personal knowledge, presidents can call on a large number of experts for help. Among the more than 1,000 people who work in the Executive Office are hundreds of advisers who are specialists in a wide variety of areas, from missile systems to marijuana. White House aides often summarize important information provided by the specialists and present it to the president. The president has better access than any other single individual in government to the knowledge and information needed for making policy and conducting government business.

Presidents use many skills. They must be able to process the large amount of information they receive from advisers and others. It is also helpful if they are good at communicating and bargaining. President Franklin Roosevelt, for example, was noted for his ability—through radio "fireside chats" and other means—to make ordinary Americans feel that he understood their problems and could solve them. President Lyndon B. Johnson was a masterful negotiator with Congress. This skill was useful in winning passage of the Civil Rights Act of 1964 and the Voting Rights Act of 1965.

A president also has other important resources. Ideas such as citizens' loyalty to and respect for the office of president can give presidents invaluable support in their policies. Strong public support is a resource that can give presidents great leverage when dealing with other branches of government or with leaders of other nations.

Presidential Activities. When we think of presidential activities, we most often think of leadership. As chief of state, the president represents all the American people. As chief executive, he or she sets national policy and decides how vigorously laws will be enforced. In fact, leadership is an important activity of each role played by the president.

Decision-making is another presidential activity with which we are familiar. We are apt to think most readily of major decisions—for example, ordering a blockade or sending in the national guard. But a president may make a dozen decisions in a single hour that will also affect our lives. Such decisions vary from the appointment of a new agency head to an order limiting foreign imports.

We often think of the president as operating alone, sitting alone in the Oval Office announcing policies on television. Most of the time, however, presidents seek advice and opinions from many sources. Therefore, decision-making by the president is usually group decision-making, even though the president has the final word.

Communication activities are very important for presidents. They may take the form of private conversations with aides or world leaders, or they may be major public speeches or policy statements. With the growth of television since World War II, this medium has vastly increased the scope of presidential communication. It is estimated that between 10,000 and 15,000 people were present when President Lincoln gave the Gettysburg Address. Almost 59 million people watched President Carter's State of the Union message on television in January 1978.

> 1. What are the major presidential resources?
> 2. Which activities do you think are most important for the president today?

The EXECUTIVE OFFICE

Closely associated with the president in the executive branch are various organizations that make up the Executive Office of the president. The White House Office consists of the president's personal staff of aides, assistants, and clerical workers. Some White House aides advise the president on domestic and foreign policy issues. Others arrange appointments, organize trips, write speeches, make reports, talk with the press, and serve as liaisons with other government offices.

The other offices and councils in the Executive Office advise the president on a full range of domestic and international issues. Experts research problems and prepare reports that help the president establish policies.

The National Security Council, for example, debates military and security policy and advises the president on foreign relations. This council is made up of the president, the vice-president, the secretary of state, and the secretary of defense. In addition there are two advisers to the council (the director of the CIA and the chairman of the joint chiefs of staff) and one official (the assistant to the president for national security affairs).

The Council of Economic Advisers, a group of three economists, advises the president on overall policy issues. How can inflation be stemmed? Should taxes be cut? What level of unemployment can the country tolerate?

The office of the vice-president is also part of the Executive Office. The vice-president has little constitutional power. He or she presides over the Senate and becomes president if that office is vacant. Traditionally vice-presidents have had little to do. John Nance Garner, vice-president under FDR, spoke of the vice-presidency as "a spare tire on the automobile of government." Under President Jimmy Carter, however, Vice-President Walter Mondale became an influential adviser.

A direct line of authority exists between the president and each organization in the Executive Office. Presidents guide the activities of each office, and all the offices are directly responsible to the president. This kind of arrangement characterizes an elite political system as you learned in Chapter 11.

Even people who work in the White House Office, though they provide many services for the president, act as advisers and facilitators rather then policy makers.

One presidential aide gave the following advice to those who recruit people for positions in the White House Office:

Presidents of the United States

	NATIVE STATE	POLITICAL PARTY	SERVED
1. George Washington	Virginia	None	1789-1797
2. John Adams	Massachusetts	Federalist	1797-1801
3. Thomas Jefferson	Virginia	Democratic-Republican	1801-1809
4. James Madison	Virginia	Democratic-Republican	1809-1817
5. James Monroe	Virginia	Democratic-Republican	1817-1825
6. John Quincy Adams	Massachusetts	Democratic-Republican	1825-1829
7. Andrew Jackson	South Carolina	Democrat	1829-1837
8. Martin Van Buren	New York	Democrat	1837-1841
9. William H. Harrison	Virginia	Whig	1841
10. John Tyler	Virginia	Whig	1841-1845
11. James K. Polk	North Carolina	Democrat	1845-1849
12. Zachary Taylor	Virginia	Whig	1849-1850
13. Millard Fillmore	New York	Whig	1850-1853
14. Franklin Pierce	New Hampshire	Democrat	1853-1857
15. James Buchanan	Pennsylvania	Democrat	1857-1861
16. Abraham Lincoln	Kentucky	Republican	1861-1865
17. Andrew Johnson	North Carolina	Democrat	1865-1869
18. Ulysses S. Grant	Ohio	Republican	1869-1877
19. Rutherford B. Hayes	Ohio	Republican	1877-1881
20. James A. Garfield	Ohio	Republican	1881
21. Chester A. Arthur	Vermont	Republican	1881-1885
22. Grover Cleveland	New Jersey	Democrat	1885-1889
23. Benjamin Harrison	Ohio	Republican	1889-1893
24. Grover Cleveland	New Jersey	Democrat	1893-1897
25. William McKinley	Ohio	Republican	1897-1901
26. Theodore Roosevelt	New York	Republican	1901-1909
27. William H. Taft	Ohio	Republican	1909-1913
28. Woodrow Wilson	Virginia	Democrat	1913-1921
29. Warren G. Harding	Ohio	Republican	1921-1923
30. Calvin Coolidge	Vermont	Republican	1923-1929
31. Herbert C. Hoover	Iowa	Republican	1929-1933
32. Franklin D. Roosevelt	New York	Democrat	1933-1945
33. Harry S. Truman	Missouri	Democrat	1945-1953
34. Dwight D. Eisenhower	Texas	Republican	1953-1961
35. John F. Kennedy	Massachusetts	Democrat	1961-1963
36. Lyndon B. Johnson	Texas	Democrat	1963-1969
37. Richard M. Nixon	California	Republican	1969-1974
38. Gerald R. Ford	Nebraska	Republican	1974-1977
39. Jimmy Carter	Georgia	Democrat	1977-

Figure 13-2

"I would urge those who are in the appointing business to really pay an awful lot of attention to ability. I refer to ability in terms not only of natural intellectual equipment, but experience and judgment and personality characteristics that permit a man to serve in a staff role and to recognize his function is to serve the principal [the president] and not necessarily to establish his own individual identity and become a force in his own right."

1. What is the Executive Office of the president?
2. In what way is the Executive Office an elite political system?

LIMITS and INFLUENCES The president has enormous power, but it is far from complete. The limits on presidential authority are both formal and informal.

Formal Limits. According to the Constitution, the president must be a natural-born citizen of the United States. He or she must be at least 35 years old and must have lived in the United States for at least 14 years before being elected. The framers felt that setting these personal qualifications would ensure the loyalty and experience necessary for the office. There is nothing in the Constitution to prohibit the election of a woman to the presidency, but none has yet served.

The 22nd Amendment to the Constitution limits a president to two terms. Another amendment, the 25th, deals with presidential disability. If a president judges him- or herself "unable to discharge the powers and duties of his office," or is so judged by the vice-president and cabinet, the vice-president takes over as acting president. This amendment, ratified in 1967, was designed to prevent lengthy periods when the president is in office but is incapable of carrying out duties. This situation occurred during the presidencies of Woodrow Wilson and Dwight Eisenhower.

The 25th Amendment also makes it possible for the president to nominate a vice-president if the office becomes vacant, as it did after Gerald Ford took over from Richard Nixon. The remainder of *presidential succession*—the order in which the office is filled—is fixed by law. After the vice-president, next in line are the Speaker of the House and the president pro tempore of the Senate. The cabinet officers, in the order in which their departments were originally created, complete the order of presidential succession.

Other clauses in the Constitution establish a system of checks and balances to limit the power of the president, as you learned in Chapter 11. The Supreme Court, for instance, has the power to decide whether a president's actions have violated the Constitution—if cases involving alleged violations are brought before it. In 1935, for example, in the case of *Humphrey's Executor v. United States*, the Court ruled that the president does not have the power to remove a member of an independent regulatory commission.

Most checks on presidential power come from Congress, however. As you read in Chapter 11, these restraints may take the form of veto overrides, authorization (or not) of funds, refusal to approve appointments or treaties, and impeachment.

Congress has overridden only a small number of presidential vetoes. Similarly, the Senate confirms most presidential appointments and approves most treaties. The power to impeach and convict a president has also been used rarely.

When Congress does exercise its restraining powers, however, it can have a major impact on presidential policies. During Lyndon Johnson's presidency, for example, Congress forced the President to cut spending by $6 billion in exchange for its agreement on an increase in the federal income tax.

The threat of impeachment by the House of Representatives was also influential in President Richard Nixon's decision to resign in 1974. The events which led to his resignation are described on pages 391–392.

Informal Influences. Public opinion, interest group pressure, party loyalty, and the behavior of subordinates are among the informal limits on the presidency.

Since presidents are elected by the people, they need popular support in order to be effective leaders. When the public clearly supports the president's position, he or she can act decisively. If public opinion is strongly opposed to a particular action, however, the president may decide not to act, or to act more cautiously.

Lincoln summarized the power of public opinion this way: "Public opinion is everything. With it nothing can fail. Without it nothing can succeed."

One of the most dramatic examples of how public opinion limits the presidency took place during the Vietnam War. By early 1968 public opposition to the war had become so strong that President Johnson decided not to run for a second term.

Interest groups try to influence government policy by building public support for their causes. One goal of the American Jewish Committee, for example, is to promote good relations between the United States and Israel. Its leaders feel that presidents

The vice-president may substitute for the president in many of his or her roles, including chief diplomat. Here, Vice-President Mondale arrives in Rome to meet with Italian President Andreotti.

will support this goal if public opinion is favorable. Therefore, they try to promote a positive attitude toward Israel among the public.

The president may welcome interest-group support. For example, organized labor, through the AFL-CIO, may back a president's plan to raise the minimum wage. It may endorse and support specific presidential candidates when they run for election. But such help can itself limit a president's freedom of action. When a president needs support, he or she does not want to offend those who have offered or may offer it.

As you read, one of the president's roles is party chief. As such, he or she has certain obligations to the party that place some limits on choices. For instance, party members and leaders expect their president to try to carry out campaign pledges included in the party's platform. A president is also expected to consult with party leaders in Congress when making appointments and forming policies. The president cannot afford to ignore the party if he or she wants support in Congress or wants to run for reelection.

Presidents' relationships with their subordinates also tend to set informal limits on their actions. Theoretically, nearly everyone who works in the executive branch of the national government is responsible to the president. In practice, though, presidents have direct control over very few subordinates. The president appoints the top people in the executive departments and the members of most boards and commissions. The staff employees of these agencies, however, do not owe their positions to the president. They hold their jobs through the civil service system (see page 404). Civil Service job holders cannot be hired or fired by the president.

Presidential influence over subordinates is further limited by the large size of the executive branch. No single person can be aware of the activities of 3 million individuals. It is even possible for subordinates to work *against* the president's policies without his or her knowledge.

President Harry Truman summed up the problem presidents have with subordinates when he commented about his successor, General Dwight Eisenhower: "Poor Ike. It won't be a bit like the army. He'll sit there and say, 'Do this'—and nothing will happen. He'll find it very frustrating."

1. What are the major formal limits on the power of the president?
2. How is presidential authority limited by interest groups? By subordinates in the executive branch?
3. Describe three examples of situations reflecting formal limits on the president. Describe three examples of situations reflecting informal limits.

The Events of Watergate

June 17, 1972: Five men break in and are arrested at the Democratic National Committee headquarters in the Watergate apartment complex in Washington, D.C.

June 28, 1972—March 21, 1973: Unknown to the American people, the Watergate burglars are paid to keep silent.

November 1972—August 1974: Begun by the *Washington Post,* major American newspapers report White House involvement in the break-in and in a plan to cover it up.

August 1972—April 1973: Throughout the summer, fall, and following winter, President Richard Nixon says his staff has investigated and has found no involvement on the part of the White House staff in the Watergate affair. Nixon reelected president with 60.7% of the vote.

January 1973—March 1973: Watergate burglars plead guilty but presiding Judge John Sirica is not convinced the entire story is known. In March James McCord, one of the Watergate burglars, tells Sirica that all the defendants were under pressure to plead guilty and remain silent.

April 30, 1973: President Nixon tells the American people there has been no "whitewash" of Watergate. He accepts the responsibility for the incident, but he denies any personal involvement in the break-in and cover-up. He then announces the resignation of 4 top officials—H. R. Haldeman, Chief of Staff; John D. Ehrlichman, Chief Domestic Affairs Advisor; John Dean, Presidential Counsel; and Richard Kleindienst, Attorney General. Nixon appoints Elliot Richardson Attorney General and gives him the authority to appoint a special prosecutor to investigate charges of a Watergate cover-up.

May 1973: Harvard Law professor Archibald Cox is appointed Special Prosecutor. Richardson pledges complete independence for Cox and promises Cox he will not be fired except for "extraordinary improprieties."

A Senate select committee headed by Senator Sam Ervin (D.-N.C.) is created to investigate all aspects of Watergate, and begins televised hearings on May 17. Between May and September major Presidential aides, Republican party election officials, and Watergate conspirators testify. John Dean reveals details of a White House cover-up. Haldeman, Ehrlichman and others dispute Dean. For a while the hearings are rated as one of the most watched daytime television programs. In July a presidential aide reveals the existence of a taping system recording presidential conversations and telephone calls.

July 23—October 18, 1973: Cox subpoenas several presidential tapes bearing on the Watergate investigation. The President refuses to turn over the tapes even under court order. He claims throughout that this request violates his right of executive privilege.

October 19, 1973: The President proposes a compromise. He suggests he prepare and provide Cox with a verified summary of the tapes. Cox rejects the offer.

October 20, 1973: The President tells Richardson to fire Cox. Richardson refuses saying this would violate his pledge to Cox, and he resigns. When Deputy Assistant Attorney General William Ruckelshaus refuses to fire Cox, Nixon fires him. Finally the Solicitor General agrees to carry out the presidential order.

October 21–December 1973: Many in Congress, the media, and across the nation call for Nixon's impeachment or resignation. The House Judiciary Committee begins considering possible impeachment proceedings. Nixon appoints a new Special Prosecutor—Leon Jaworski, a Houston lawyer.

February–June 1974: The House Judiciary Committee begins to meet in closed session. The committee requests and subpoenas presidential tapes and papers but the President refuses to turn over the materials. Finally the committee receives tapes, documents, and a special grand jury report from the Special Prosecutor who obtained most of his material through hard-fought court battles. The committee then examines the evidence. Meanwhile Jaworski finds the President will not provide him with all the material he needs for his investigation and must appeal his request for presidential tapes to the Supreme Court.

April 30, 1974: Nixon makes public the edited, printed versions of a selection of presidential tapes. Within a short time a comparison of Nixon's edited version with the transcriptions prepared by Jaworski and the House Judiciary Committee reveals significant deletions and changes.

July 23–30, 1974: The House Judiciary Committee opens its final hearings and debate to television. Between July 27 and 30 the committee votes three articles of impeachment to be turned over for a vote by the entire House. The charges against the President are obstructions of justice, failure to uphold the Constitution, and defiance of the committee subpoenas.

July 24, 1974: The Supreme Court unanimously orders the President to turn over the tapes to Jaworski.

August 5, 1974: Nixon makes public a tape which he has been ordered to turn over to Jaworski. The tape shows that six days after the break-in he tried to impede the Watergate investigation. Calls for Nixon's resignation are very strong.

August 9, 1974: President Richard Nixon resigns from office.

A PRESIDENT'S DAY

The following case describes the events of one day during the presidency of Jimmy Carter. Of course, every day is different, but looking at one day in depth will help you understand how the presidency functions. As you read the case, consider the following questions. What resources does President Carter use? What political activities does he carry out? How are the various parts of the government interacting? What impact might these interactions have on American citizens?

★ A Day in the White House

Wednesday, April 6, 1977, is the middle of a typical busy week for President Jimmy Carter. On Sunday and Monday Carter had met with President Anwar Sadat of Egypt to discuss peace proposals for the Middle East. On Tuesday the two men held a joint news conference. Carter and his secretary of state, Cyrus Vance, also held a news conference about recent arms talks with the Soviet Union. And the President has made three appointments. He has named Abe Goodpaster superintendent of the United States Military Academy at West Point and Richard Ellis as head of the Strategic Air Command. (Both these positions are in the Department of Defense.) In addition he has appointed A. Daniel O'Neal as a commissioner of the Interstate Commerce Commission.

On this Wednesday Jimmy Carter gets up early. About 6:45 in the morning he takes the White House elevator from the family living quarters down to the Oval Office. Actually he will spend most of his working day in a study that is adjacent to the Oval Office. The study is a small room, simply furnished with a desk, a white couch, long curtains, a gold carpet, and two green easy chairs. Carter's personal secretary, Susan Clough, works in an office next to it.

When Carter enters his study he first takes off his suit jacket and puts on a gray cardigan sweater, which he keeps in a small closet. With a fire blazing in the fireplace, he settles down to work, sipping his morning coffee. As he works he listens to classical music and occasionally looks at the tulips and crabapple trees blooming on the White House lawn.

Carter's first meeting—with Zbigniew Brzezinski, his adviser on foreign affairs—begins at 8:30 A.M. Brzezinski briefs the President about problems in Africa. He also gives the President a long memo about relations with African nations that are in severe economic need.

After this meeting, Carter telephones Vice-President Walter Mondale and tells him, "I want you to tell Cy Vance [secretary of state] and Zbig [Brzezinski] that I want them to move in every possible way to get Somalia to be our friend." Mondale agrees.

At 9:45 two members of the President's White House Office, Hamilton Jordan and Frank Moore, arrive to talk with the President. They discuss the administration's foreign aid request, which is now before Congress. The two men believe that if the United States does not do more to help African nations, Soviet influence will increase there. Moore tells Carter that Senate Majority Leader Robert Byrd has been trying to convince other legislators that more aid to Africa is needed. He suggests that the President might give Byrd a call. "I will," Carter replies. "Any time you detect a subcommittee member who is willing to help us, just let me know. I'll be glad to give them a call."

Jordan and Moore also discuss domestic issues, especially the development of the administration's energy policy. The three men review documents and memos that present arguments for and against proposed points. Both the chairman of the Council of Economic Advisers and the secretary of the treasury have criticized these proposals, which were developed by James Schlesinger, the President's energy adviser. The two have asked to participate in any discussions about the proposal. Carter assures Jordan that both will be consulted.

After Jordan and Moore leave, the President meets in the nearby Cabinet Room with Senators John Glenn, Abraham Ribicoff, and Charles Percy, two Democrats and a Republican. They present a report to him about the spread of nuclear fuel. Carter informs the senators that he will cancel two breeder reactor projects in order to stop the production of plutonium, a dangerous nuclear fuel.

Next the President goes to the Oval Office, where he signs a bill that gives him authority to begin to reorganize the federal bureaucracy. The measure had a difficult time in Congress, but now Carter hopes that he

Communication is a very important political activity in the executive branch of the federal government. Like previous presidential press secretaries, Jody Powell (top photo) holds regular briefings for reporters. Some citizens may meet personally with the President during his trips around the country (center photo); however, most citizens communicate with him by sending letters or telegrams. Telegrams to the White House are received on the machines shown in the bottom photo.

will be able to make the bureaucracy more efficient.

It is now 10:45 A.M. President Carter returns to his study for a meeting with two other White House Office staff members, press aides Jody Powell and Rex Granum. He instructs them to brief reporters about his decision to cancel the breeder reactor projects. He also asks them to reassure the Japanese and the West Germans that the United States does not expect their nations to do the same because they do not have enough coal and oil reserves to replace nuclear fuel.

The aides remind Carter that he is scheduled to have lunch with George Meany and other labor leaders in about an hour. According to some critics, Carter hasn't kept his promises to the "working people." He is a bit worried about the meeting, but intends to take a low-key and firm line with the labor leaders.

Before lunch, the President meets with the union representatives in the Cabinet Room. Vice-President Mondale is there, too. Meany and the other union leaders urge Carter to protect the American television, textile, and footwear industries by placing higher tariffs on foreign imports. Carter opposes this policy because he wants foreign nations to invest in the United States and thus create new jobs. His position gives the labor leaders little comfort.

Back in the Cabinet Room after lunch, Carter meets with a group of Japanese businessmen and encourages them to invest more in the United States. He tells them that if Japan continues to sell many more products in the United States than it buys, it will be hard for him to avoid stricter restrictions on Japanese imports. He hopes that such a step will not be necessary.

So far the President has had very little leisure. He has been known to say, "I've reserved for myself only the things I have to do." In other words, he will be responsible for actions taken and will make final decisions, but will delegate as many tasks as

possible. Even so, it is hard to get everything done.

It is clear on this Wednesday that the President's energy policy is near a crisis point. Staff members have quickly organized a meeting, and now most of the Presidential advisers and aides gather with Carter. The meeting lasts for three and a half hours. "It was very tough," Carter says later. "They really took a lot of shots at Schlesinger, but he defended himself well. He is a very smart man. There was a lot of very strong give-and-take. I was proud of everyone."

As a result of the meeting, the advisers have agreed on about 85 percent of the energy plan. They have also explored ways in which the President might win support for his policy in Congress and from the public. How about a "fireside chat," where Carter would explain his plan on television? Other possibilities are a presidential speech before a joint session of Congress, and a televised press conference. Another energy meeting is planned for tomorrow.

At 7:00 daughter Amy arrives in the Oval Office to ask her father to come to dinner. By now Jimmy Carter is tired. He has had a long day, and is glad to take a break. After dinner, though, Carter returns to his study. His secretary has gone home, but Frank Moore and Hamilton Jordan are still in the White House discussing the energy meeting. Shortly after midnight the President finally leaves his study. In a few short hours another presidential day will begin.

1. What presidential roles did Carter play on this day?
2. What political activities did he carry out?
3. What resources did the President use?
4. Make a list of the persons with whom Carter interacted on this day. What are their positions in the government?
5. What evidence can you find that the Executive Office is an elite political system?
6. How do you think the President's activity affects you?

ADVOCATES and the PRESIDENCY In the preceding section you read about some general circumstances in which the public can limit the power of the president. Citizens can also work in a number of ways to influence specific presidential decisions and actions.

A few citizens have direct access to the president. Leaders of powerful interest groups, for example, may meet frequently with administration officials. Of course, most citizens can't meet personally with the president. But they can make their views known by working together with other people who have a similar interest. One single letter requesting pardon for an alleged war criminal would have little influence. But a citizen group that organized a letter-writing campaign resulting in thousands of letters would make a difference. Such an action requires a response from the president.

Another method of advocacy is petitioning. Petitions usually consist of one or more points on which the signers agree. For instance, thousands of Americans have gone on record as opposing the killing of whales.

Public demonstrations, or rallies, are a more visible means of political communication than letters or petitions. During the 1960s many civil rights organizations used this method to advocate an end to discrimination against black Americans. The largest and most publicized demonstration of this era was the "March on Washington" of August 28, 1963. Under the leadership of Martin Luther King, Jr., nearly 250,000 people traveled to the nation's capital to dramatize their support for the passage of a new civil rights law. The civil rights march made a strong impression on President John Kennedy, and was instrumental in the passage of civil rights legislation.

Publicity is a valuable resource for citizen advocates. Demonstrations are one way to achieve it, because they are usually covered by the news media. Press conferences, press releases, and advertisements are also used to make citizen demands known.

The following case study shows how citizens, acting as advocates, may influence presidential decisions and actions. As you read it, think about who the advocates were and how they influenced the president's choice among alternatives

★ **The 1973 Meat Boycott**

In 1973 food prices in the United States were rising rapidly. In February alone both the cost of living and the price of food had a greater monthly increase than at any time in the preceding 20 years. A pound of hamburger had risen 26 cents in price since 1969, and the price of sirloin steak had increased by 44 cents per pound.

People began to demand that President Nixon do something to stop the upward spiral of food prices. They were especially concerned about the cost of meat, which had become so expensive that many Americans could not afford it.

Nixon urged store owners to hold down their prices, but he took no steps to force them to do so by law. Food prices continued to rise.

Consumers soon began to organize. Four women in southern California formed a group called Fighting Inflation Together (FIT). Its aim was a meat boycott. FIT members felt that if Americans stopped buying meat, the supply would increase and thus the price would go down.

By the middle of March, many people in southern California were supporting FIT's efforts. National television news broadcasts in both the United States and Canada reported their success. June Donovan, one of FIT's organizers, described another way in which the group told people about the meat boycott: "We have passed out 18,000 letters and the recipients have mimeographed them in turn. We now have thousands and thousands of persons in this."

As people learned of FIT, they formed other protest groups. They included the All-People's Coalition in California, Families United Against Inflation in Michigan, the Long Island Meat Boycott Association in New York, Consumers on the Warpath in North Carolina, and Housewives for Collective Action in Texas.

These consumer groups planned a nationwide boycott of meat for the week beginning April 1 to demonstrate their concern and try to force prices down.

On March 15, President Nixon held a press conference. During the conference, he addressed the subject of meat prices. Nixon suggested that shoppers buy more carefully and that they try eating fish if meat was too expensive. And he commented: "You can be very sure that if I thought that price controls on farm products and on food prices would work, I would impose them instantly." Asked if he supported the proposed nationwide boycott of meat, the President responded cautiously: "I am not going to suggest to American housewives or to any group of Americans to join in boycotts and so forth. I generally do not feel that this is an effective use of what we call 'people power.'"

As April neared, popular support for the national boycott grew. Several members of Congress spoke out in support of a limit on food prices. So did George Meany, president of the AFL-CIO. "If food prices aren't brought down," said Meany, "there is no way union members are going to let their unions settle for a wage increase that won't even pay for their increased food bill. That's not a threat, that's a fact of life."

By March 29 Nixon had changed his mind about price ceilings for meat. In a nationally televised speech the President declared that future prices of beef, pork, and lamb were not to exceed their price on March 29. In effect, he wanted to put a ceiling on meat prices.

He instructed all retail food stores to post their meat prices on large signs to enable the public, as well as government inspectors, to check prices quickly. The price limitation would remain as long as necessary to bring prices under control. In concluding his statement, Nixon said, "Meat prices must not go higher and, with the help of the housewife and the farmer, they can and should go down."

The national meat boycott was held as scheduled in spite of Nixon's action. Organizers wanted to persuade the president to go further and actually lower meat prices. Although Nixon did not order such a reduction, the boycott did have some results. On the first day, many stores reported meat sales down by as much as 40 percent. By the

The idea of a meat boycott began in California and spread rapidly nationwide. These New Hampshire citizens picket in front of a local supermarket in support of the boycott.

fifth day, wholesale beef prices in Chicago fell from $70.25 to $67 per 100 pounds. Retail prices on some cuts of beef began to decline.

1. Who were the advocates in this case?
2. What did the advocates do to communicate their ideas to the President?

3. What alternatives did the President have in this case? Did the citizen advocates influence the President's choice among alternatives?
4. What would you have done in this situation if you were to take an advocate role?
5. Review the criteria for a successful advocate role. Did members of the meat boycott fulfill these criteria?

The Federal Bureaucracy

You have already read about a small segment of the federal bureaucracy—the Executive Office of the president. It is one part of the vast organization, outlined on page 384, that has developed to help the president see that the laws are "faithfully executed."

HOW the BUREAUCRACY OPERATES Actions taken by the federal bureaucracy have a direct impact on all of us. The purity of the air we breathe, the safety of our highways, the price of our food, and the kinds of medicines we take are just a few of the things in our lives that depend on some part of the federal bureaucracy. You have probably heard complaints that bureaucrats control too much of our lives. Understanding how the bureaucracy operates will help you evaluate criticisms of this sort.

Structure. The 12 executive departments form the largest part of the federal bureaucracy. Each one employs thousands of people and spends billions of dollars every year. For example, in 1977 the Department of Health, Education, and Welfare employed 157,000 people and spent $148 billion.

During his campaign for president in 1976, Jimmy Carter announced that he in-

tended to make the huge bureaucracy more efficient. Congress gave him the power to do this in 1977. He cut out some agencies and streamlined the organization of others. Yet, as the cartoon on page 399 indicates, he found the task to be a large and difficult one.

One important group that does not appear on the chart of the executive branch is the *cabinet*, which consists of the heads of all the executive departments (plus the vice-president). Neither the Constitution nor Congress created the cabinet. Instead it evolved since the time of Washington as a way for the president to consult with key persons in the executive branch of the government. As cabinet members, heads of the executive departments make proposals to the president and offer advice. Their most important function, however, is administering their departments.

Another important part of the federal bureaucracy consists of the nearly 60 independent agencies. Congress created these agencies and appropriates money for them. The president appoints their commissioners and directors, with the consent of the Senate.

Some independent agencies administer large government programs. For example, the National Aeronautics and Space Administration (NASA) directs space missions and conducts space-related research. Other independent agencies, such as the Environ-

" FIRST OF ALL, YOU NEED TO SET UP A DEPARTMENT OF PAPERWORK..."

mental Protection Agency, are regulatory commissions or boards. Their purpose is to enforce government regulations. The major independent agencies of the federal government are listed in Figure 13-3.

People. The average bureaucrat working for the federal government is a white, middle-class male with some college education. As of 1975, fewer than 25 percent of federal bureaucrats were black or Hispanic. Less than half were women, though this percentage had increased in recent years.

Because of civil service, most bureaucrats can be fairly certain of holding their jobs from one administration to the next. And, on the whole, the pay is good. For the majority of positions at lower and intermediate levels, government employees make as much as, if not more than, private employees doing the same type of work.

Another advantage of government work is the feeling of being involved in something important. One lawyer noted that, although he might earn more money in private practice, in no other job would he be likely to

INDEPENDENT AGENCIES of the FEDERAL GOVERNMENT

Figure 13-3

ACTION
Administrative Conference of the U.S.
Board for International Broadcasting
Civil Aeronautics Board
Commission on Civil Rights
Commodity Futures Trading Commission
Community Services Administration
Consumer Product Safety Commission
Environmental Protection Agency
Equal Employment Opportunity
    Commission
Export Import Bank of the U.S.
Farm Credit Administration
Federal Communications Commission
Federal Deposit Insurance Corporation
Federal Election Commission
Federal Home Loan Bank Board
Federal Maritime Commission
Federal Mediation and Conciliation
    Service
Federal Reserve System, Board
    of Governors
Federal Trade Commission
General Services Administration

Interstate Commerce Commission
National Aeronautics and Space
    Administration
National Foundation on the Arts and
    the Humanities
National Labor Relations Board
National Mediation Board
National Science Foundation
National Transportation Safety Board
Nuclear Regulatory Commission
Pennsylvania Avenue Development
    Corporation
Pension Benefit Guaranty Corporation
Railroad Retirement Board
Securities and Exchange Commission
Selection Service Commission
Small Business Administration
Tennessee Valley Authority
U.S. Civil Service Commission
U.S. Information Agency
U.S. International Trade Commission
U.S. Postal Service
Veterans Administration

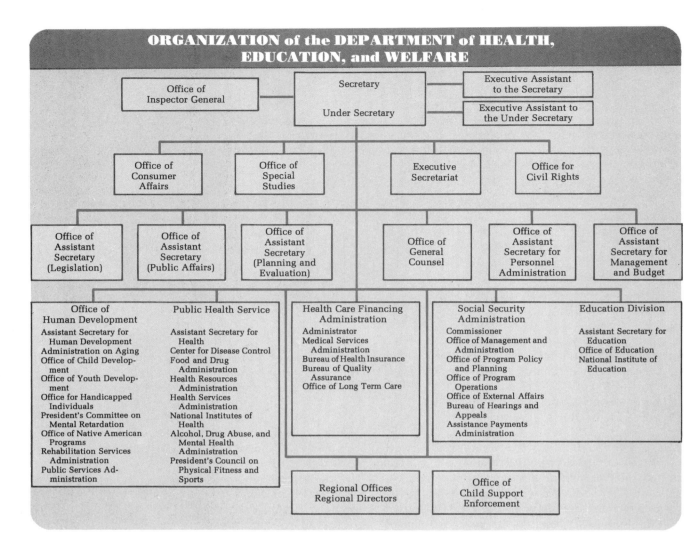

ORGANIZATION of the DEPARTMENT of HEALTH, EDUCATION, and WELFARE

Figure 13-4

On October 17, 1979, President Carter signed a bill creating the Department of Education. The health and welfare functions of the old Department of Health, Education and Welfare will be assumed by the newly named Department of Health and Human Services.

play a role in decisions affecting millions of people.

System. The departments and agencies of the federal bureaucracy are divided into many offices, administrations, and divisions. The organizational chart of the Department of Health, Education and Welfare in Figure 13–4 shows the complex organization of this one department. Each subsidiary office is administered by numerous *bureaucrats,* that is, people who work in a bureaucracy.

One way to look at this huge complex organization is to think of it, appropriately enough, as a bureaucratic system. Many layers of individuals and organizations are arranged in a pyramid of power and control.

At the top of the pyramid is the president. At the bottom are thousands of office workers in the departments and agencies. In between are various levels of administrators.

A bureaucratic pyramid has two major characteristics: strata and channels of communication and control. *Strata* are bands across the pyramid. Each stratum represents a different level of power and responsibility.

The federal bureaucracy has many strata. For example, suppose the president were to sign a bill providing money for local public school districts. The Department of Health, Education and Welfare (HEW) would administer the new law. The secretary of HEW would then allocate the money according to legal guidelines.

400

Once the basic policies had been established, the assistant secretary for education would pass the instructions on to the appropriate commissioner or deputy commissioner. He or she, in turn, would instruct an associate commissioner or program director to allocate the funds to the schools that fit the established guidelines. (See Figure 13–5.)

In a bureaucracy, individuals in one stratum usually interact only with persons in the stratum immediately above or below theirs. Thus, the president meets frequently with the Secretary of HEW, but he would probably never interact with an Associate Commissioner for State and Local Educational Programs.

You learned about channels of communication and control in Chapter 7. Just as the strata give the pyramid stripes horizontally, the channels of communication and control give it vertical lines. Instructions and other messages flow through the channels. Most flow from the top down, as in the example of the education bill. Sometimes, however, the channels work in reverse. A complaint may travel up the bureaucracy and eventually reach the ears of the president.

Figure 13-5

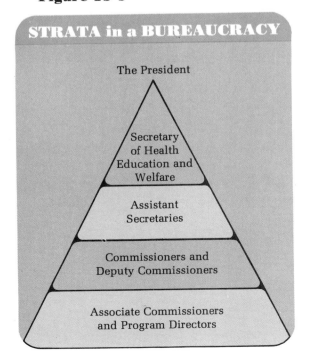

STRATA in a BUREAUCRACY

The President

Secretary of Health Education and Welfare

Assistant Secretaries

Commissioners and Deputy Commissioners

Associate Commissioners and Program Directors

Resources and Activities. Resources and activities in a bureaucracy are distributed by strata. Generally, the number of resources grows as one goes up the pyramid.

Those near the top of the pyramid have more status resources than those near the bottom. The secretary of state, for example, carries out policies made by the president. The secretary, however, also issues instructions to those in the next stratum below.

Skills and knowledge also distinguish different strata of the bureaucracy. Strata close to the top of the pyramid usually require more skills and knowledge than those near the bottom. As noted earlier, the president appoints the top officials of the departments and agencies, but other positions in the federal bureaucracy are filled through the civil service system. When individuals want to move up in the bureaucracy, they have to pass an examination indicating they have the necessary skills and knowledge.

Wealth is shared unequally in the bureaucracy as well. People at the higher levels have greater control over budgets with which to implement policies, as well as earning higher salaries. This control, combined with their other resources, gives them more influence over the political process than those below them in the bureaucracy.

Political activities follow the same pattern as the distribution of resources. For example, the most important decisions are made at the top. Individuals in the lower strata usually carry out the decisions of those above.

Communication runs through channels up and down the bureaucratic chain. Generally, however, communication is from the superior to the subordinate in order to carry out a given policy.

1. How does the relationship between the president and his or her press secretary differ from the relationship between the president and a deputy commissioner in the Department of Health, Education, and Welfare?
2. How would the federal bureaucracy function if it were an elite political system?

Mark Walther studies political science at a college in Iowa. In order to gain experience in government, he worked as an intern at the Department of State, Washington, D.C. He was assigned to the Bureau of African Affairs, where he assisted foreign service officers. As part of his job, Mark answered questions posed by American citizens about life in Africa and researched topics for the American embassies there.

Mark, like other interns, spent many hours in the State Department Library (top photo). He enjoyed official functions, such as receptions for visiting African heads of state (bottom photo).

The Civil Service

In George Washington's time, the federal government employed fewer than 800 people. By the late 1820s this total had increased to about 20,000. This was not a large number by today's standards, but it was big enough to concern Andrew Jackson when he became president in 1829.

Many people had held their federal jobs for years, growing old—and, some said, corrupt—in office. Jackson felt that such employees no longer served the interests of the people. A position should not be held too long by any one person. Official duties, Jackson said, ought to be made "so plain and simple that men of intelligence may readily qualify for their performance." This way there could be *rotation in office*—a fairly regular job turnover. And why not give positions to deserving members of one's own party? As one of Jackson's supporters put it, "To the victors belong the spoils." Thus arose the *spoils system*, whereby a new administration was expected to "clean house" and install the party faithful in government jobs.

Jackson meant to strengthen democracy by preventing jobholders from getting entrenched in office. But the spoils system led to serious abuses. The number of federal workers grew steadily. With each change of administration, office seekers swarmed into Washington, D.C., looking for jobs. Official duties, not always "plain and simple," were bungled by officeholders who were not always "men of intelligence."

By the 1870s the situation had become so disgraceful that reformers launched a program of civil service reform. (It was around this time that the term *civil service*—meaning civilians working for the government—came into general use.) Reformers wanted a *merit system*, with job appointments based on fitness, as determined by competitive examinations. Competent people would get and keep jobs, no matter what their party.

President Hayes favored the merit system and tried to persuade the executive branch to use it, but with little success. Only after President Garfield was assassinated by a disappointed job seeker did the government take firm action.

In 1883 Congress passed the Pendleton Act. It placed certain jobs on the "classified" list (meaning that they were to be filled by the merit system) and set up a Civil Service Commission to administer the program. Over the years the classified list grew. In the 1880s it included only about 10 percent of all federal employees. By the 1970s it covered over 75 percent of federal workers.

The Civil Service Commission itself employs some 7,000 people to recruit, examine, and assign employees. It administers examinations to applicants seeking civil service jobs. Those who pass are put on a list of eligibles in the order of their test scores. When a federal agency wants to hire someone, an administrator is given three names from the top of the list of those qualified. Though there are criticisms of this bureaucratic procedure, few today would want to return to the spoils system.

An AGENCY at WORK

One way to learn more about the federal bureaucracy is to examine how an actual agency works. In this section you'll take a closer look at the Federal Trade Commission (FTC).

The Federal Trade Commission is an independent regulatory agency that was created by Congress in 1914. A chairperson and four commissioners head the FTC, with a staff of more than 1600 employees. The agency's 1978 budget was $62.5 million.

The FTC enforces numerous government regulations that are intended to "promote free and fair competition" in business. FTC regulations, among other things, forbid false advertising and deceptive packaging.

The FTC may receive complaints about unfair or deceptive business practices from consumers, competitors, Congress, or federal, state, or local agencies. If the commissioners decide to consider a complaint, they order the staff to conduct an initial investigation.

The staff then recommends one of three actions: (1) an informal settlement; (2) a formal complaint by the FTC; or (3) dropping the matter.

Once the FTC makes a formal complaint against a company, the case is heard by one of the administrative law judges within the FTC. These judges are employed by the FTC but operate independently of the commission's control. They conduct public hearings and issue a decision in a case.

A judge can dismiss a case. Or, if the judge finds that a company's actions have violated the law, he or she orders it to "cease and desist"—that is, to stop that practice. The company may then either accept the decision or appeal to the commissioners for a review. The commissioners themselves can dismiss the case on review. However, if they uphold the judge's decision, that decision goes into effect within 30 days unless the company further appeals its case to a federal court of appeals.

The case that follows concerns a complaint made to the FTC about advertisements for Listerine mouthwash. As you read, think about how the FTC operates and what the case tells you about the federal bureaucracy.

★ What Listerine Can Do

The Warner-Lambert Company has made a mouthwash called Listerine since 1879. Like most mouthwashes, Listerine was designed to do away with unpleasant odors—as the ads put it, to "fight bad breath." However, advertisements for Listerine since 1921 also claimed that it helped cure colds and sore throats.

The package label stated: "Listerine Antiseptic Kills Germs By Millions On Contact For Bad Breath, Colds and Resultant Sore Throats."

In magazines the company used advertisements like this one:

"Nothing can cold-proof Johnny, but for fewer colds, milder colds, have him try this: Get plenty of rest, the right diet, gargle twice a day with full strength Listerine. Tests over a twelve year period proved that people who gargle with Listerine twice a day had fewer colds, milder colds than those who did not. Have your family try it."

Similar advertisements on television reached millions of viewers. The message was the same: while Listerine could not prevent all colds, it could help reduce the number of colds a person caught and make them milder. The ads were quite successful. Thousands of people believed the claims, and Listerine sold well.

In 1972 a group of citizens from New Jersey complained to the Federal Trade Commission that Warner-Lambert's advertising claims about Listerine were not true. After an initial investigation, the commission issued a formal complaint against Warner-Lambert.

An administrative law judge then conducted public hearings on the case. Physicians and other experts testified that Listerine could not prevent or cure colds. It might indeed kill germs, but it had no effect on viruses—and it is viruses that cause colds, they said.

As a result of the hearings, the judge ruled that Warner-Lambert's claims about Listerine constituted false advertising. He ordered the company to remove statements in Listerine advertisements that claimed it could cure or prevent colds.

The judge also ruled on December 9, 1975, that Warner-Lambert must inform the public that its former claims about Listerine were not true. The company was ordered to insert the following corrective statement in Listerine advertisements:

> "Contrary to prior advertising, Listerine will not help or prevent colds or sore throats or lessen their severity."

Warner-Lambert appealed this decision to the federal court of appeals. In August 1977, the appeals court ruled that the FTC had acted within its jurisdiction in this case. However, the court struck the phrase "contrary to prior advertising" from the required statement.

Warner-Lambert then took the case to the Supreme Court. In April 1978 the justices declined to review the lower court decision. This action upheld that court's decision requiring Listerine to correct past advertising claims.

1. How is the FTC operating as a bureaucratic system in this case?
2. How might the case have developed differently if the FTC were an elite system?
3. How does this case illustrate how citizens can influence the federal bureaucracy?
4. Do you think the activities of the FTC help you as a citizen? Why or why not?

The Skill of Generating Evidence: Surveys and Observation

Information is a vital resource used in all parts of the executive branch. The president, for example, needs information about the economy before making a recommendation that Congress cut taxes. The Department of Health, Education, and Welfare needs information about the courses taught in the nation's schools before funding a new curriculum development project. The Federal Trade Commission needs information about how a product is advertised in order to make a decision on a company's trade practices.

Much of this information is not available in newspapers, magazines, documents, or other published sources. The people who want it must generate the information, or evidence, themselves. In Chapter 9 you learned the skill of interviewing, an important technique in generating evidence. Two other techniques—conducting surveys and making observations—are also essential skills for generating evidence.

Surveys especially are used in the executive branch. In the Federal Trade Commission's investigation of Warner-Lambert's advertising of Listerine, surveys also provided important evidence about the effect of the advertising on consumers. That evidence played a major part in the commission's decision in the case.

Surveys of public opinion can also be important to the president in determining citizens' reactions to presidential policies. A president who wants to be reelected may rely heavily on public opinion polls.

Generating evidence by asking people questions or by observing their actions are

Surveying the opinions of others will help these students generate useful and important evidence.

skills which can be valuable to any citizen. They are especially valuable to the advocate, who needs sound information in order to convince others of his or her position.

CONDUCTING SURVEYS

Before you begin learning how to conduct surveys, review the skill of interviewing on pages 278–282.

The word "survey" comes originally from words meaning "to look over." Today, a survey is a "look over" of the opinions or behavior of a number of people. Surveys are conducted by asking many people the same questions and then systematically compiling the results.

The number of people whom you want to question is probably the most important factor in deciding whether to conduct interviews or a survey. When it is useful to gather information from a large number of people, a survey should be used. Suppose, for example, you want to answer the question "What proportion of the citizens in the state of Texas believe they can influence the decisions of the state legislature?" It would be almost impossible to interview enough people to generate accurate evidence to an-

swer this question. However, one could develop a set series of questions which could be printed and mailed to people throughout the state. Such a set of questions is called a *questionnaire*. The questions on a questionnaire can also be asked over the telephone, and many surveys are conducted in this way.

Asking Questions. Obviously, it is extremely important for the questions on a questionnaire to be the right questions. As you have learned, if your questions don't make sense, your answers won't make sense. The rules for asking good questions that you learned for gathering evidence apply as well to the asking of good survey questions. Review those rules on pages 72–74.

In a survey, a questionnaire can be thought of as an instrument to be used to gather evidence. Just as the thermometer measures body heat, so questionnaires can be used to measure people's opinions. Unlike an interview, in which the interviewer can probe the ideas of the person being interviewed, a survey depends totally on the specific questions on the questionnaire.

It is essential that each question on a questionnaire means the same thing to everyone who answers it. A question like "How many hours each day do you watch

Time started_____

Time finished_____

Total minutes_____ 14/15

I'm from The Roper Organization and we're conducting a survey about things that are happening today.

1. Three things that President Carter has talked a lot about that need attention in this country are reducing the level of unemployment, tax reform and simplification, and reorganizing the government bureaus and departments. Which one of those things do you think is the most important right now--reducing unemployment, tax reform and simplification, or government reorganization?

    Reducing unemployment..... 1   16/

    Tax reform and simplification........... 2

    Reorganizing government... 3

    Don't know.............. 4

2. We'd like to talk to you about the income tax system. How do you feel about the present federal income tax system--do you feel it is <u>quite</u> fair to most people, or <u>reasonably</u> fair, or somewhat <u>unfair</u>, or <u>quite</u> unfair to most people?

    Quite fair........... 1   17/

    Reasonably fair....... 2

    Somewhat unfair....... 3

    Quite unfair......... 4

    Don't know........... 5

37. Do you feel quite certain you paid neither more nor less federal income tax than the law calls for, or reasonably sure that you paid the right amount, or not very sure, or not at all sure whether you paid too much or too little?

    Quite certain......... 1   56/

    Reasonably sure....... 2

    Not very sure......... 3

    Not at all sure....... 4

    Don't know............ 5

38. About what percent of your <u>total</u> income would you say you paid in federal income taxes this year?

    _____ %   57/58
    (write in percent)

    Don't know........... Y

39. No matter how careful one is about preparing an income tax return that is correct and proper, there is always the possibility that you can be called in by the IRS for a tax audit and required to bring documents that prove your tax return is correct. At income tax time, does the possibility of being audited concern or worry you, or doesn't it bother you much?

    Concerns or worries.. 1 (ASK 40) 59/

    Doesn't bother much.. 2

    Don't know.......... 3 (SKIP TO 41)

40. What about being audited concerns you?

Figure 13-6

---

television?" is clear and direct. It will mean the same thing to anyone who answers it.

Good questions on a questionnaire are also relevant and valid. They relate directly to whatever you want to find out, they measure what you want to measure. If the object of your survey is to generate evidence on the television-watching habits of young people in your city, your questions must relate directly to that point. A question about what kind of programs the person watches most often is directly related. A question about the brand name of the person's television set is not to the point and will not yield information that can be used as evidence about television-watching habits.

> 1. What are the basic rules for asking good questions?
>
> 2. Using those rules, make up a series of questions you could use to survey people in your community on a topic of your choice. Save your questions.

Most questionnaires include three parts: background questions, main questions, and concluding questions. In the body of the questionnaire belong the main questions relating to your survey topic. Like the questions on an interview schedule, these main questions can be forced-choice or open-ended questions. Most surveys, however, concentrate on forced-choice questions. (Remember that these are questions for which the respondent is forced to choose an answer from among those provided.) In a survey, in-depth discussion does not take place as it can in an interview. Open-ended survey questions can produce confusing answers, and there is no opportunity to clarify them as there might be in an interview. Therefore, forced-choice questions are used to obtain uniformity in the kind of answers. If you ask a question about how often people vote, for example, an open-ended response might be "a lot." What does that mean? A forced-choice question, on the

```
61. Do you now happen to have any children in private
    school or college?

            Yes........ 1  (SKIP TO 63)       68/

            No......... 2  (ASK 62)

62. Did you ever send any of your children to private
    school or college in the past?

            Yes........ 1                      69/

            No......... 2

63. What was the last grade of regular school that
    you completed--not counting specialized schools
    like secretarial, art or trade schools?

            No school............. 1           70/

            Grade school (1 - 8).. 2

            High school (9 - 12).. 3

            College (13 - 16+).... 4

              F A C T U A L

Sex                       Economic level
Male.... 1    75/            A...  1      77/

Female.. 2                   A-..  2

                            B+..  3
Race
White... 1    76/            B...  4

Black... 2                   B-..  5

Other... 3                   C+..  6

                            C....  7

                            C-..  8

                            D+..  9

                            D....  0
```

other hand, will produce answers in given
categories like "once a year," or "only in
presidential elections." The answers of
many people are then comparable.

Background questions provide relevant
information about age, sex, political affilia-
tions, residence, or other areas that characterize the respondent. (As in an interview,
the person answering the questions is called
a *respondent*.) Background questions should
be developed on the basis of what specific
information about a person will be relevant
in interpreting his or her answers. Is it
important, for example, to distinguish between male and female opinions on a subject? If so, you must identify the sex of the
respondent.

Finally, many questionnaires include
concluding questions that give the respondent an opportunity to expand on previous
answers or express additional opinions.
Generally these are open-ended questions
like "Other than the responses you have

given on this questionnaire, do you have
any other opinions about this issue?"

Figure 13–6 shows part of an actual
questionnaire used by the Roper Poll organization. Identify the different kinds of questions and their functions.

1. What are the functions of the different
   kinds of questions on a survey questionnaire?
2. Add background and concluding questions to the series of main questions you
   developed earlier.

Selecting Respondents. A crucial part
of conducting a good survey is the selection
of the specific individuals to be questioned.
The total number of people whom you want
to measure in your survey is called the *population*. A population can refer to units of
many different kinds and quantities. It can
be all the teachers in your school, all the
adults in your state, all the students in your
class. It can be all the corn in a railroad car,
all the cats in your neighborhood, all the nations in Western Europe. What makes up the
population for your survey depends on the
topic questions you want to answer. If you
want to find out whether a majority of students believe they are well informed about
activities in your school, then the entire student body of your school is the population.
On the other hand, if you want to measure
citizens' opinions about the president of the
United States, then all citizens in the United
States are your population.

Usually, it is impractical to survey the
entire population in question. Therefore, as
you learned in interviewing, it is necessary
to select a sample of the population. Review
the discussion of random and systematic
samples on pages 280–281 in Chapter 9.

Random sampling is used much more
frequently in surveying than in interviewing. Surveys often cover very large
populations, such as all voters in the nation
or all citizens of a given community. With a

large population a random sample is more apt to reflect accurately the total population of the survey. In addition, random sampling is best used when the population is a general one, such as the entire student body of your school, rather than a specific group, such as all students who have held office in the student council.

Suppose you found yourself in the following situation. What kind of sample would you select for your survey?

You are a reporter on your school newspaper, assigned to find out student opinion about new lunch period rules. There are 2,000 students in your school. Since you do not have time to interview every student, you consider ways of selecting a sample of students to survey.

First, you think about walking around the cafeteria during lunch period and giving three people at each table a copy of the questionnaire. In this way you might survey about 300 students.

Second, you consider giving a questionnaire to each of the 50 members of the Student Council. After all, you reason, students selected these people to represent them. Therefore, their opinions should be representative of the opinions of all students.

Third, you could obtain from the office a list of the names of all students in the school. After placing each name on an index card in a container, you could blindly select 250 cards. The 250 students whose names were selected could be given questionnaires to fill out.

> 1. Decide whether each of the three methods is random or systematic sampling.
> 2. What are the advantages and disadvantages of each of the three alternatives?
> 3. Which method would you use?

Compiling and Analyzing the Evidence.
As you learned in compiling interview data, the systematic analysis of results is essen-tial. Review the steps for compiling and analyzing evidence on pages 281–282.

Remember that the information you generate by means of a survey will provide useful evidence only if it is carefully analyzed. You must count and classify responses and examine the patterns that they show. You must look for trends and draw relationships among answers. When you have finished with your analysis, you should be able to make several general statements about your findings. For example, suppose you have surveyed student opinion on whether or not students feel they can "make a difference" in school policies. At the end of your survey you might be able to make generalizations like these: A majority of students in this school believe that they can make a difference in school policies. This belief increases with class year (i.e., seniors believe this more strongly than freshmen). This belief is more prevalent now.

> 1. Describe the process of compiling and analyzing information generated by a survey.
> 2. Make up three generalizations that you might be able to make as a result of the survey you designed earlier. With the aid of your teacher determine how your survey might be carried out in your school or community.

OBSERVATION While interviews and surveys are good tools for generating evidence on people's ideas and opinions, observation is useful for finding out how people behave in certain situations. Evidence created by observation helps the advocate understand how people interact, in addition to what they say. As a group member you can also use evidence gained by observation to analyze characteristics of the group. This can help the group operate more effectively.

Observation allows you to obtain first-hand information, without relying on the reports and remembrances of other people. A good example of the benefits of observation can be seen in the experiences of one researcher who studied school groups. In an interview with a club chairperson, the researcher was told that decisions in that club were made by consensus. However, when the researcher observed the group, he discovered a different situation. In reality, the chairperson made all the decisions, and the other students went along because they felt they had no real choice.

Observation also allows the person generating evidence to use his or her own judgment about what is necessary information. By being present, the observer can note every piece of important information.

Like questions and answers, however, observation is only as good as the observer. A biased observer will not observe accurately. An unobservant person will not produce good evidence. The following hypothetical case illustrates what can happen as a result of observation.

★ News at Lakeville

Recently, the Lakeville School Board held a very important meeting to consider whether or not to build a new high school gymnasium. More than 500 citizens attended the meeting, held in the Lakeville High School assembly room. Among the spectators was Rick Carson, a reporter for the local *Lakeville Sentinel*. Following is part of Carson's newspaper article about the meeting.

SCHOOL BOARD FORCES DECISION

The Lakeville School Board voted unanimously last night to build a new high school gym. Once again, board members disregarded public opinion.

Many people in the audience were opposed to the new gym. The few who spoke against it were ignored by the board members. Board chairman Sam Gibbons prevented anyone from speaking for more than three minutes.

Also in the audience was Marty Murphy, a reporter for the *Splash*, a student newspaper at Lakeville High. The following is part of Murphy's newspaper article about the meeting.

LAKERS GET NEW GYM

On Monday night, the School Board voted to build a new gym for our high school. Basketball fans, including Mayor Kilburg, are very pleased by the decision.

A few people at the meeting spoke against the gym, but their opinions had little effect. Many people spoke very strongly in favor of the gym. Mr. Gibbons, the School Board chairman, was very fair in giving everyone an equal amount of time to express their views.

A few days later, Rick Carson and Marty Murphy discussed their different observations of the meeting.

Marty: I really disagree with your article about the School Board meeting. I think the people of this community are all for the new gym. Mr. Gibbons ran the meeting fairly.

Rick: That's not the way I saw it, Marty. Gibbons could have let the opponents of the gym speak more freely.

Marty: But Mr. Gibbons treated everyone equally. No one could speak longer than three minutes.

Rick: But three minutes wasn't enough time to present complete arguments. It was important for the anti-gym forces to have more time to talk, since the board members were already biased in favor of the new gym.

Marty: Mr. Gibbons is a very democratic School Board chairman. He conducts the meetings according to the rules. Everyone is treated equally.

Rick: Gibbons uses the rules to ram his decisions down the throats of people. He may

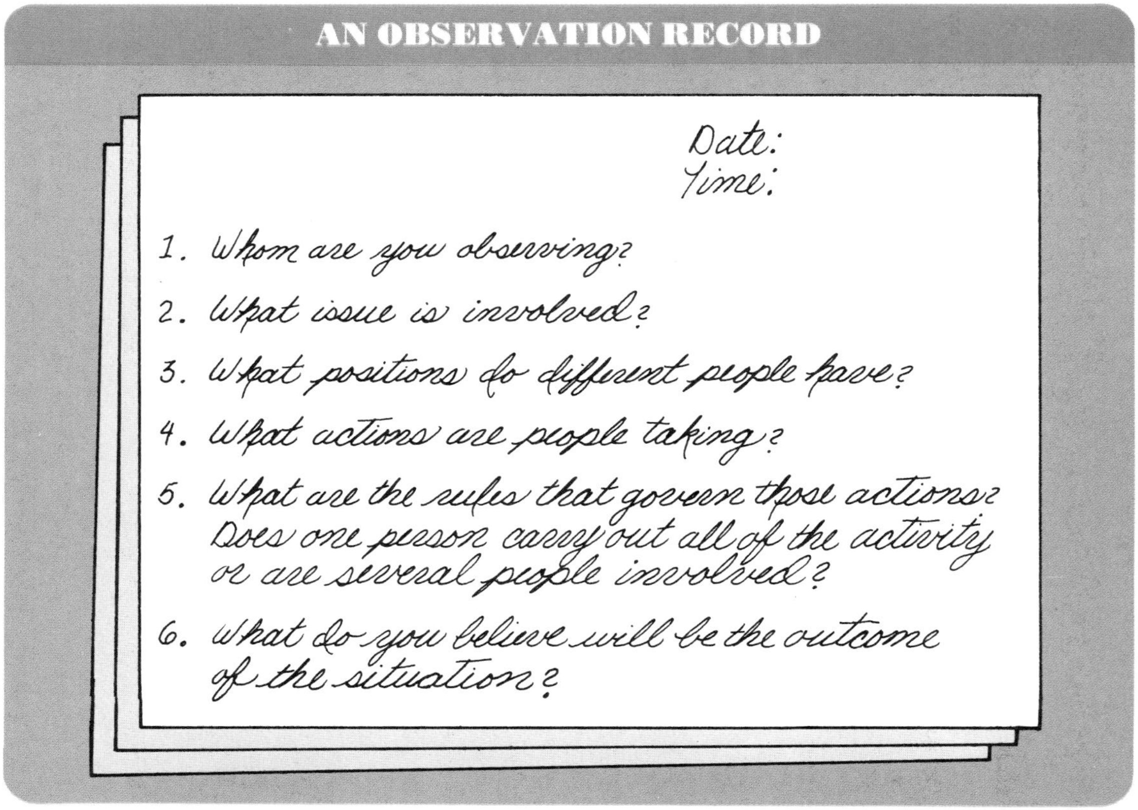

AN OBSERVATION RECORD

Date:
Time:

1. Whom are you observing?

2. What issue is involved?

3. What positions do different people have?

4. What actions are people taking?

5. What are the rules that govern those actions? Does one person carry out all of the activity or are several people involved?

6. What do you believe will be the outcome of the situation?

Figure 13-7

look like a fair leader, but he always seems to get his way.

As you can see, the two reporters interpreted their observations very differently. Each undoubtedly came to the meeting with his own bias toward the School Board, a bias which colored subsequent observation.

Using an Observation Record. One tool that will help produce good observation is an *observation record*. Similar in function to an interview schedule, an observation record sets up ahead of time the general questions to be answered during the observation. Figure 13-7 is a sample observation record.

Such a set series of questions has several advantages. First, it allows the observer

to think out in advance what to look for. Second, if you are observing more than one situation and wish to compare them, a single observation record ensures that you will be able to make valid comparisons. (See pages 341–342 on making comparisons.) Also, different observers should be able to use the same observation record and produce comparable results.

1. Identify a group you would like to observe in your school, and decide what aspect of the group you would like to observe.
2. Make up an observation record to use in your observation of that group.

1. What are the two major parts of the executive branch? How does each one limit the other?

2. Which of the president's roles have grown out of constitutional provisions? What other roles does the president have, and why?

3. Describe, with specific examples, the types of resources that are available to a president.

4. How is the president's power limited by Amendment 22? by Amendment 25?

5. How can a president use communications activities to counteract informal limits on his power?

6. Summarize the chief ways in which ordinary citizens can influence the president.

7. What is the cabinet? What functions do its members perform?

8. What is the difference between an organization like the National Aeronautics and Space Administration and a body like the Federal Trade Commission?

9. How does the federal bureaucracy operate as a bureaucratic system?

10. What are important points to remember in conducting a survey or in doing an observation?

Define the following terms.

executive agreement	impoundment	population
presidential succession	respondent	observation record
strata	questionnaire	sample
survey		

1. In several countries, a prime minister governs, while a monarch or president handles ceremonial duties. Do you think it would be a good idea to relieve the president of the chief of state role? Can you think of any disadvantages to this plan?

2. Many critics argue that the presidency has grown too powerful in recent decades. From what you have read, do you agree or disagree? Give reasons for your answer.

3. In your opinion, which is stronger—the influence of public opinion on the president, or the president's influence on public opinion?

4. During the 1970s, some people—among them President Nixon—wanted to combine executive departments (for example, housing and transportation) so that there would be fewer. Others wanted to add new ones, such as a Department for Women. Which do you think is a better solution for the problems of a complex modern society? Why?

5. The federal bureaucracy has been called a "fourth branch" of government. Why do you think this term arose? Does it seem correct to you?

Chapter Activities

1. Check newspapers or magazines for a recent decision made by the president or part of the federal bureaucracy. Then outline the steps that you as a citizen advocate might take in getting the decision reversed. Show how you might generate evidence in order to be more effective.

2. Many people in the United States today feel that the bureaucracy has grown too big and has too much control over our lives. Develop a questionnaire around this theme and survey opinion among 10 adults. What conclusions can you draw from this survey? Compare and/or contrast your findings with those of other students.

3. In 1977, Jimmy Carter presented a package of energy legislation to the Congress. At this time, he was acting as chief legislator. Investigate the proposed legislation, the actions taken by Congress, and the final bills passed. Based on this analysis, assess the legislative power of the president.

4. Select one of the past American presidents. Write a monologue in which the president presents a short biography, a statement of how he won election, and his major achievements as president of the United States. Be prepared to read your monologue to the class.

5. Select a topic on which you would like to generate evidence. Conduct a survey and/or observation. Report your methods and results to your class.

Chapter Bibliography

The Bureau of the Budget, Percival Flack Brundage (Praeger Publishers: New York), 1970.

A former Budget Director describes the Bureau of the Budget, revealing the budget-making process by focusing on specific cases.

Candidates '76, published by Congressional Quarterly, Washington, D.C., 1976.

Features informative political portraits of the major Presidential contenders in the election of 1976.

Unchosen Presidents: The Vice President and Other Frustrations of Presidential Succession, Allan P. Sindler (University of California Press: Berkeley), 1976.

Focuses on the vice-presidency, viewing this office from the point of view of the Constitution and also from the Congress. Also considers possible alternative processes of succession to the presidency.

Obtaining Citizen Feedback: The Application of Citizen Surveys to Local Governments, Kenneth Webb and Harry P. Hatry, (The Urban Institute, Washington, D.C.), 1973.

Focuses on the topics of the uses of citizen surveys, the dangers in citizen surveys, survey procedures, funding a survey, and organizing a citizen survey.

Chapter Objectives

★ To learn how the federal courts are
  organized

★ To understand how the Supreme Court
  operates

★ To analyze the federal judiciary as a
  bureaucratic system and the Supreme Court
  as a type of coalitional system

★ To analyze formal and informal limits on
  the federal courts

★ To make comparisons of resources,
  activities, and advocacy in the three
  branches of government

chapter 14

The JUDICIAL BRANCH

The federal court system seems rather distant from most of us. Occasionally, citizens serve on federal juries or become aware of Supreme Court cases. In general, we feel uninvolved. Actually, however, the federal court system, like our local and state systems, affects us every day. Federal court decisions directly affect our rights as well as our responsibilities.

The federal judiciary is a large bureaucratic political system. At the top is the Supreme Court, with nine justices. We are inclined to think of these justices with considerable awe. They make decisions for the national political system as a whole, decisions that are important for all of us. There are other types of federal courts and judges at lower levels. These courts hand down decisions that are also a vital part of the system.

In this chapter you will learn how the federal judiciary is organized and how it functions, with special emphasis on the Supreme Court.

The Federal Judiciary as a Bureaucratic System

The Constitution provides for a federal judiciary that consists of a Supreme Court and "such inferior courts as the Congress may from time to time ordain and establish." Throughout the years since 1788, that court system has developed into a fairly large bureaucracy.

ESTABLISHING JUDICIAL POWER The Constitution established the judicial branch of the federal government in 1787. Article III, Section 1, of the Constitution places the judicial power of the United States in the Supreme Court and in inferior courts. It is Section 2, however, which lists the jurisdiction of the courts. (*Jurisdiction* is the authority to interpret and apply the law.) Section 2 indicates that the powers of the federal judiciary will include the duty to settle legal disputes between citizens of different states, between two or more states, or between states and the federal government. It establishes the power to support citizens' rights to a trial by jury and extends the powers of the federal judiciary to include cases involving foreign governments and their representatives. (The powers of the judicial branch are summarized on page 317.)

All these powers are important and bear heavily on the conduct of law in the United States. However, the full definition of these powers took many years after the Constitution was ratified. To do so, the judiciary needed to establish three principles. First, it had to ensure its *right to decide.* The judicial branch had to be sure that it was indeed independent from political pressure on the part of the president and the Congress.

The judiciary also had to establish its *right to judicial review.* In other words, it needed to ensure its right to declare acts of Congress or other laws unconstitutional.

Finally, it had to establish its *right to judicial sovereignty.* This is the federal courts' right to make decisions which overrule decisions of state courts.

In 1789 the Judiciary Act passed by Congress established some principles for how the courts would be run. It gave the Supreme Court power over the state courts and

This engraving shows the Supreme Court of 1888 hearing oral arguments. Under Chief Justice Morrison R. Waite (center), the Supreme Court strengthened the states' regulatory powers.

418

defined the jurisdiction of each level of courts. In 1790, six justices were appointed to make up the first Supreme Court. In addition, two lower levels of courts were created. Included were 13 *district courts,* one in each of the states. The Judiciary Act set up the court system, but it did not define many of its powers.

Judicial independence was established as the federal court began to make decisions about the constitutionality of acts of Congress and the acts of the president. It was clear from the beginning that the justices were not going to take their cues from particular political factions, from party alignments in the Congress, or from the president.

The establishment of the Supreme Court's right to decide is often linked to a single case—*Marbury* v. *Madison*—and to the leadership of one justice—Chief Justice John Marshall. The case was heard in the Supreme Court in 1803.

Marshall dominated the Supreme Court for 34 years. A brilliant and logical justice, he established the court as a coequal with other branches of government. The Marbury case was the key case among Marshall's decisions.

★ **Marbury v. Madison**

The situation which provoked the case began as Federalist John Adams left the presidency in March 1801. In the last week of his term, Adams appointed 42 men to serve as justices of the peace. The Senate confirmed the commissions, and the President signed them. In the closing days of his term, however, Adams was very rushed, and not all the commissions were delivered.

When Democrat Thomas Jefferson took office as President, he refused to deliver some of the commissions which the Federalist Adams administration had processed. Instead, Jefferson wanted people of his own party to have the commissions. The Federalists protested strongly.

William Marbury and three other men whom Adams had commissioned complained to the Supreme Court about Jefferson's refusal to deliver their appointments. They wanted the Court to issue an order compelling the President to carry out a given duty, claiming that the Supreme Court had the right to try this case and to issue a writ of mandamus. (A writ of mandamus is a court order that commands a public official to perform an official act.)

There were three important questions in this case. The first one was whether Marbury had a legal right to his commission as a federal justice of the peace. The Court concluded that, yes, Marbury did have that right. The second question was that if he had a right, had that right been violated. This answer also was "yes." Finally, the crucial question of whether there was a legal remedy for the violation also received an answer of "yes."

In reaching his conclusion, the Chief Justice first declared the Court's right to interpret the laws. He said "It is emphatically the province of the judicial department to say what the law is."

Chief Justice Marshall did not issue the writ that Marbury requested, however. Instead, the Supreme Court declared a section of the 1789 Judiciary Act unconstitutional. The act added to the Court's original jurisdiction by giving it the power to issue writs of mandamus. But the Court ruled that its original jurisdiction could not be changed by Congress. Marshall declared, "All those who have framed written constitutions contemplate them as forming the fundamental and [supreme] law of the nation, and consequently the theory of every such government must be that an act of the legislature repugnant to the Constitution is void." With this statement the Court established its right to review a federal law and declare it unconstitutional.

It was not until 1810, in *Fletcher v. Peck,* that the Court ruled a state law unconstitutional. Marshall held that Georgia's legislature violated the Constitution's contract clause when it nullified a law providing for the sale of state land. The Constitution, Marshall ruled, "imposes limits to the state legislatures."

---

1. Where did the federal judiciary gain its powers of judicial independence, review, and sovereignty?
2. What was the impact of *Marbury v. Madison* on the powers of the federal judiciary?

The **JUDICIAL BUREAUCRACY** The judicial branch can be viewed as a bureaucratic political system. A stratified system of courts exists, with the Supreme Court at the head. As you study the court system, compare this judicial bureaucracy with the federal bureaucracy in the executive branch.

The judicial branch of the federal government includes three main levels of courts—the district level, the appellate level, and the Supreme Court. The diagram in Figure 14-1 outlines the court structure today.

District Courts. The first or lowest level consists of the federal district courts. Each state has at least one, and large states have several. New York, for instance, has four district courts. In 1977, there were a total of 94 federal district courts.

Federal district courts have *original jurisdiction*. In other words, a case involving federal laws could be heard, or tried, for the first time in a federal district court.

Two kinds of cases are tried in federal district courts—*criminal* cases and *civil* cases. As you learned in Chapter 8, a criminal case involves a charge that someone has violated a law. The defendant is prosecuted by the government—local, state, or national. For example, suppose a citizen refuses to pay income taxes to the federal government. This citizen has violated a federal law, thus he or she may be arrested and charged with this crime. The case is tried in federal district court to decide whether the person is guilty or innocent and what the punishment shall be. All criminal cases that involve the breaking of federal laws are tried in federal courts, except in instances in which state and federal courts share jurisdiction.

As you know, a civil case does not involve the violation of a criminal statute. A civil case involves legal action between two

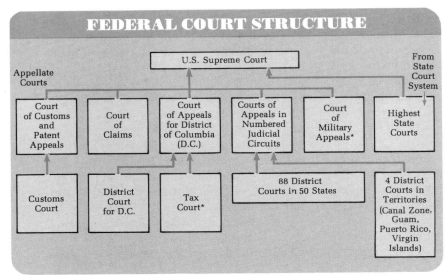

FEDERAL COURT STRUCTURE   **Figure 14-1**

Appellate Courts

U.S. Supreme Court

From State Court System

Court of Customs and Patent Appeals | Court of Claims | Court of Appeals for District of Columbia (D.C.) | Courts of Appeals in Numbered Judicial Circuits | Court of Military Appeals* | Highest State Courts

Customs Court | District Court for D.C. | Tax Court* | 88 District Courts in 50 States | 4 District Courts in Territories (Canal Zone, Guam, Puerto Rico, Virgin Islands)

*Neither the Tax Court nor the Court of Military Appeals is part of the federal judicial system. The Tax Court is an administrative agency and is part of the executive branch. The Court of Military Appeals is part of the government of the armed forces.

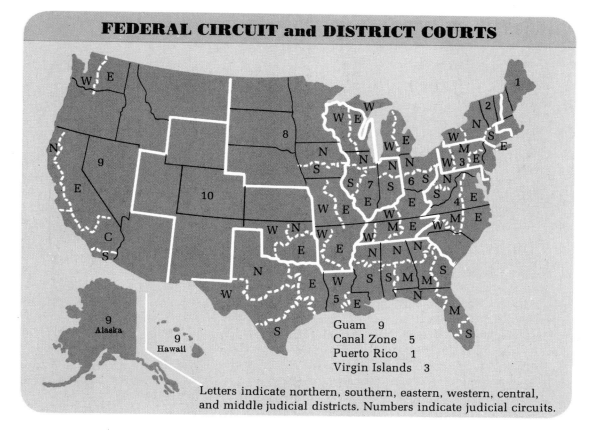

FEDERAL CIRCUIT and DISTRICT COURTS

Guam 9
Canal Zone 5
Puerto Rico 1
Virgin Islands 3

Letters indicate northern, southern, eastern, western, central, and middle judicial districts. Numbers indicate judicial circuits.

Figure 14-2

parties. The parties can be private citizens, corporations, or governments. For example, a businessman may charge that a competitor has spread false stories about his business practices. These stories, the businessman claims, have hurt his reputation and have driven customers away. So he sues his competitor for hurting his business.

In a civil case, the court first examines the evidence presented by the defendant and the *plaintiff* (the party which made the original complaint and brought the case to court). The court decides whether there is an issue of fact or law to be determined. If so, the case will go to trial. The result of the judge's decision in a civil suit is not a verdict of guilty or not guilty. Instead, there is a determination in favor of one side or another. Many decisions involve payment of money for "damages." Others involve the enforcement of contracts or regulations or the demand that one party cease or undertake some specific action.

Civil cases between two parties from different states or between U.S. citizens and foreign citizens are tried in federal courts. In addition any civil case involving damages of $10,000 or more can be tried in federal court.

The vast majority of criminal cases tried in federal district courts are heard before a single judge, with a jury. Civil cases are almost always heard by a single judge without a jury. A small percentage of cases, however, must be heard before a panel of three judges. They are cases that challenge the constitutionality of a state or federal law. These cases can be appealed directly to the Supreme Court; they do not go to a federal Court of Appeals.

Appellate Courts. The United States is divided into 10 geographical areas called *circuits,* each of which has one appellate court. (An eleventh court operates in the District of Columbia.) For example, the third circuit court deals with cases in the federal districts in Pennsylvania, New Jersey, and Delaware. The seventh circuit court covers the federal districts in Wisconsin, Illinois, and Indiana. Figure 14-2 shows the areas covered by district and appellate courts.

The 11 federal circuit courts have *appellate jurisdiction.* That is, these are courts in which a party who loses a lower court case may appeal to have the legal issue of a case reviewed.

If you lose a case in federal district court, you may appeal to a circuit court for a review of the decision. But, if you lose a case in a state court of appeal and that case involves a constitutional issue, you should appeal to the Supreme Court. Criminal cases in which the government is the losing party are the exception to this rule. The Fifth Amendment guarantees citizen protection from "double jeopardy"—that is, from being tried more than once for the same charge. Therefore, the government cannot appeal a criminal case, thus in effect retrying a citizen for the same crime.

A lawyer files an appeal with the court, on behalf of his or her client. The court must hear the appeal and give a decision. (As you will learn, only the Supreme Court has the right not to hear an appeal.) A majority of cases in which citizens are the losing party are appealed to circuit courts.

The following description of the work of the sixth circuit court explains the basic procedure that operates in a federal court of appeals. The sixth circuit court has its headquarters in Cincinnati, which is near the center of the area it serves—Michigan, Ohio, Kentucky, and Tennessee. In 1977, the sixth circuit court had eight judges: one chief judge, Harry Phillips, and seven associates.

The eight judges work in groups of three in order to divide the heavy load of work. The chief judge decides which associate judges are to work together on which days. He makes sure that each judge spends some time working with every other judge.

Lawyers on both sides of each case submit *briefs,* or written arguments, to a three-judge panel. After reading the briefs, the judges are ready to listen to arguments from the lawyers. Usually each lawyer has 15 minutes to speak, although in special cases, lawyers may be allowed up to 45 minutes. After the three-judge panel has heard its last case of the day, it meets in private to discuss all the cases. Then the three judges write a report about the cases and their decisions, which is sent to the other five judges of the sixth circuit court. If a majority of the eight judges do not agree with a given decision, then the chief judge requires that the case be heard again before all eight members of the court. The eight judges then make a final decision. Once the case is decided, one judge writes an opinion to represent the thinking of the court.

In a circuit court case the losing party—unless it is the government in a criminal case—has the right to try to appeal the decision to the *court of last resort,* the Supreme Court. However, only about 13 percent of the cases tried in circuit courts ever reach the Supreme Court. For most people, a district or a circuit court gives a final decision.

The Supreme Court. The highest level of the judicial branch in the United States is the Supreme Court. Since 1869, this court has been made up of nine members—one chief justice and eight associate justices. Like all federal judges, Supreme Court justices are appointed for life by the president, with the advice and consent of the Senate. (The Carswell case, pages 327–329, described the process through which federal judges are appointed.)

The Supreme Court accepts for hearing only those cases which the judges consider to be of major importance. At least four judges must agree to accept a case before it can be heard by the Court.

Most cases heard before the Supreme Court are appeals from lower courts. These include

1. Federal district courts
2. Federal circuit courts

3. Special federal courts like the Court of Claims (The material on page 423 describes these courts.)

4. Highest-level state courts

In an appeal, the Supreme Court acts as the final *arbiter,* or decision-maker. Like other court decisions, Supreme Court rulings become *precedents* in the United States; that is, they have the authority of established law.

Although the Supreme Court hears many appeals, most cases are taken care of in the lower courts. (As you read, only a small percentage of the cases heard in federal district courts ever reach the Supreme Court.) It costs a citizen an average of $10,000 in legal fees to take a case from a local court all the way to the Supreme Court. And often it takes the Supreme Court from two to five years to reach a decision on an important case. Since the process is both slow and costly, few citizens try to appeal a case in the Supreme Court unless they believe that it involves legal principle important for national justice. (And, as you will learn, the Court itself does not have the capacity to hear cases other than those they feel involve landmark decisions.)

In addition to appeals, a small percentage of cases heard before the Court are cases of original jurisdiction, as defined in the Constitution. The Court's original jurisdiction includes cases between

1. The United States and one or more states

2. Two or more states

3. Foreign citizens (including ambassadors) and either the United States or one or more states

4. A state government official and the federal government.

Of the almost 200 cases decided by the Court in 1977–78, only 13 were cases of original jurisdiction.

Special Courts in the Federal Judiciary System

NAME OF COURT (date established)	NUMBER OF JUDGES JURISDICTION	FUNCTION
Court of Claims (1855)	5 judges Nationwide jurisdiction; sits in Washington, D.C.	At times overlaps with federal district courts; hears cases of disputes involving government contracts; hears other cases, such as those involving patents and copyrights, claims, unjust conviction and imprisonment.
Customs Court (1926)	9 judges Nationwide jurisdiction; officially located in New York City, but may go to any U.S. port to hear a case	Reviews appraisals of imported goods, classification, rates and amount of duties; reviews customs laws that exclude certain imported goods
Court of Customs and Patent Appeals (1909)	5 judges Nationwide jurisdiction; decides when and where to meet, though officially located in Washington, D.C.	Reviews decisions of Customs Court, appeals on violations of patent laws, decisions on trademark applications, cases regarding unfair import trade practices

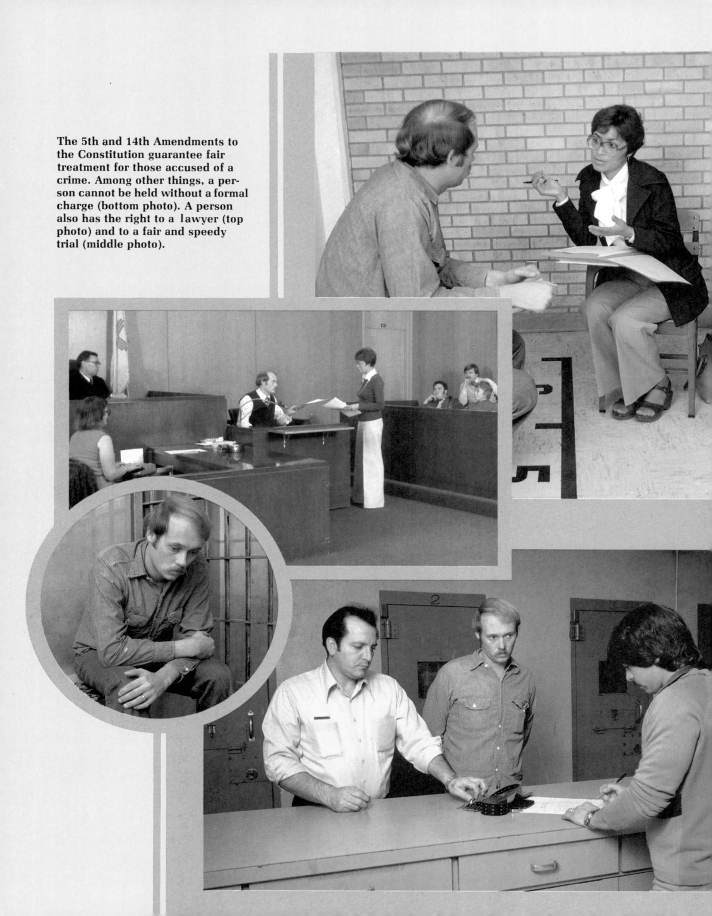

The 5th and 14th Amendments to the Constitution guarantee fair treatment for those accused of a crime. Among other things, a person cannot be held without a formal charge (bottom photo). A person also has the right to a lawyer (top photo) and to a fair and speedy trial (middle photo).

1. What is the jurisdiction of federal district courts? of circuit courts? of the Supreme Court?
2. How are federal judges appointed to office and how are they removed?

A Bureaucractic System. As you can see, the federal judicial system is a system of stratified authority, with increased authority at each higher level. Three basic strata exist, with the Supreme Court at the top, the appellate courts in the middle, and the district courts at the base.

Bureaucratic channels of communication and control also exist in this system. Written decisions and information on cases are passed through the system as cases proceed from one level to another. Higher courts have the authority to reverse the decisions of lower courts.

The following cases demonstrate the federal judiciary's operation as a bureaucratic system. One is the *Miranda* v. *Arizona* decision, which shows how a case proceeds from a state court directly to the Supreme Court. The second case, *Brown* v. *Board of Education of Topeka* demonstrates how a case moves from the federal district court directly to the Supreme Court. As you study the two cases, think about how the judiciary operates as a bureaucratic system, how the different levels of the bureaucracy interact, and how this bureaucratic system differs from the one in the executive branch. Also consider the constitutional issues involved in each case.

★ **The Miranda Decision**

On March 3, 1963, an angry family in Phoenix, Arizona, telephoned the local police department. They reported that their 18-year-old daughter had been picked up on the street as she walked home from her job at a local movie theater. She had been kidnapped, attacked, and then returned to the street, and had just come home. The family wanted the guilty person to be tried and convicted.

Ten days later the police picked up 23-year-old Ernesto Miranda. After the 18-year-old girl identified Miranda in a police line-up, he was taken into the interrogation room. There, police questioned Miranda for more than two hours. In the end they obtained from him a written confession that he had picked up the girl and had attacked her. At no time did the police inform Ernesto Miranda that he had a right to have an attorney (even if he could not pay the legal fees) or that he had the right to remain silent during questioning.

At his trial in the county superior court, an attorney was appointed by the court to defend Ernesto Miranda. During the trial, the police officers testified that Miranda made his confession voluntarily. Finding Miranda guilty of charges against him, the court sentenced him to 20 to 30 years in prison.

Miranda's attorney, Alvin Moore, appealed the case to the Arizona Supreme Court. Moore pointed out, in the appeal, that Miranda had not been informed, during questioning by the police, that he did not have to answer any questions and that he had a right to consult an attorney even if he could not afford to pay the lawyer's fees. (Legally, a court is required to appoint a lawyer if the defendant wishes to have one but cannot afford the fees.) The appeal claimed that the deprivation of Miranda's right to remain silent violated the Fifth Amendment to the Constitution. And his right to counsel was, the lawyer said, specifically expressed in the Sixth Amendment.

The Arizona Supreme Court ruled that Miranda need not have been informed by the police of his specific rights. Pointing out that Miranda did not specifically request a lawyer, the court claimed that he understood his legal rights and made a voluntary statement. Therefore, the court said, it was proper to admit the statement as evidence and to find Miranda guilty.

Ernesto Miranda and his attorneys decided to appeal the case before the U.S. Supreme Court. In a 5 to 4 decision in 1966, the majority of the justices ruled that Miranda's confession was not admissible in court because he had not been warned of his right to remain silent nor told that he could hire an attorney or an attorney would be provided for him. According to the Court, these omissions violated Miranda's rights, as guaranteed in the Fifth and Sixth Amendments to the Constitution.

Expressing the majority opinion, Chief Justice Earl Warren said:

> "He [suspect] must be warned prior to any questioning that he has the right to remain silent, that anything he says can be used against him in a court of law, that he has the right to the presence of an attorney, and that if he cannot afford an attorney, one will be appointed for him prior to any questioning if he so desires."

The minority opinion expressed a concern that the decision in favor of Miranda placed the rights of the individual suspect above the rights of society.

The Miranda decision has had important implications for criminal law in the United States. The decision made it clear that suspects must be told they have the right to remain silent before questioning begins and that anything they say may be used against them. Suspects also must be told that they have the right to the presence of a lawyer at questioning and that, if they cannot afford to hire an attorney, one will be provided free by the state. Suspects can waive, or give up, their constitutional rights, but only if they do so voluntarily, knowingly, and intelligently after all these things have been explained to them. Also, the court ruled that the police must stop questioning a suspect whenever a suspect requests it. All these criteria have become known as the *Miranda* rule.

Miranda v. *Arizona* was a landmark decision. The rights of the accused as ex-

pressed in the Fifth and Sixth Amendments to the Constitution were upheld.

1. What levels of the judicial bureaucracy did this case go through?
2. How does the judicial bureaucracy shown in this case differ from the operation of the federal bureaucracy and the executive branch?
3. What rights of citizens were upheld by *Miranda* v. *Arizona*?

One of the most famous cases of the twentieth century, *Brown* v. *Board of Education of Topeka*, reversed a lower court ruling. It was a unanimous Court decision, with one opinion.

★ Brown v. Board of Education of Topeka 1954

The case began in Topeka, Kansas. Oliver Brown, a black man, watched his children ride a bus to an elementary school more than 20 blocks away. He also watched his neighbor's children, who were white, walk to an elementary school only a few blocks from their home. Brown did not think this situation was fair. It resulted from the fact that there were separate schools for black and white children.

The state of Kansas had a law allowing cities to establish separate schools for whites and blacks, and many cities had done so. Topeka had 18 schools for whites and 4 for blacks. Oliver Brown and his wife thought that the schools for blacks were inferior. And they argued that racial separation deprived their children of the "equal protection of the laws" that is guaranteed by the Fourteenth Amendment to the Constitution.

Since 1948 the local Topeka chapter of the NAACP had tried to convince Topeka's board of education to end segregation in the schools. Kansas law gave the board the power to do this. By the summer of 1950, when no action had been taken by the board, the NAACP decided it was ready to make a test case out of the Topeka situation. (A *test case* is one which tests a law, established practice, or constitutional principle for the first time.)

Topeka NAACP officials wrote to the head of the NAACP, presenting their idea. Soon, the organization's legal office in New York, then headed by Thurgood Marshall, began to research and organize the case.

A black parent whose children were in a segregated Topeka school was needed to bring charges against the board of education. The NAACP chose Oliver Brown for several reasons. He was a veteran and was assistant pastor of his church. He also was a union member who would not be fired when the case was publicized. And Brown was a lifelong resident of Topeka who was a respected citizen who was not considered militant or radical.

With the help of the NAACP, the Browns took their case to the federal district court, where a three-judge panel decided against them. The court argued that there was substantial equality between white and black schools in Topeka. The buildings were of the same quality, the court said. The programs of study were roughly the same, and the qualifications and salaries of teachers were within the same range. Therefore, the court held, the Browns were not denied equal protection.

However, the Browns and the NAACP were not satisfied. They took their case to the Supreme Court. In a historic decision, delivered in May 1954, the Court unanimously ruled in favor of the Browns. Chief Justice Warren, who wrote the opinion, argued that separate facilities were "inherently unequal"—that is, unequal by their very nature. The opinion also stated that:

> "To separate Negro students from others of similar age and qualifications solely because of their race generates a feeling of inferiority as to their status in the community that may affect their hearts and minds in a way unlikely ever to be undone."

In other words, the psychological effects of separating the races were preventing black children from having equal protection under the law.

The Supreme Court also took this opportunity to assert the importance of education and of equal educational opportunity. Just as important as physical facilities, such as buildings, were intangible values, such as the ability to study with other students and exchange views with them. The opinion was summed up in these words:

The Brown decision meant that black students had the right to attend any public school. National, state, and local governments acted to put the decision into effect. In 1957, for example, President Eisenhower ordered the National Guard to escort black students attending Central High School in Little Rock, Arkansas.

"Today, education is perhaps the most important function of state and local government. Compulsory school attendance laws and the great expenditures for education both demonstrate our recognition of the importance of education to our democratic society. It is required in the performance of our most basic public responsibilities, even service in the armed forces. It is the very foundation of good citizenship. Today it is the principal instrument in awakening the child to cultural values, in preparing him for later professional training, and in helping him to adjust normally to his environment. In these days, it is doubtful that any child may responsibly be expected to succeed in life if he is denied the opportunity of an education. Such an opportunity, where the state has undertaken to provide it, is a right which must be available to all on equal terms."

1. What constitutional principle was involved in this case?
2. What do you think the impact of this decision was on the political system of the United States?

Federal Judges: Who Are They?

In the United States there are about 526 federal judges. How are they selected? What are their qualifications? What kinds of people are they?

SELECTION and QUALIFICATIONS Federal judges in the United States are appointed. Names submitted by the president are first reviewed by the Senate Judiciary Committee. The suggestions that it approves are sent to the Senate floor where they are voted on. A simple majority is required for approval. The important principle of independence applies in this case. The framers of the Constitution believed that federal judges should not be pressured by public opinion, and thus elections are avoided.

This is not to say that the president must personally select nominees for all federal judgeships. Instead, the president relies on the attorney general to make recommendations.

The attorney general in turn consults with senators, especially on lower-level federal appointments. Since judges in district and appellate courts serve specific geographic areas, it is important to consult with senators from those areas. This is true both because the Senate must confirm the appointments and because of an unwritten rule known as *senatorial courtesy.* According to this custom, if a senator is of the same party as the president, he or she is consulted on federal judgeships in his or her state. If the senator objects to the choice, the nominee's name is usually dropped.

The attorney general also relies on the Federal Judiciary Committee of the American Bar Association for recommendations. In fact, the ABA provides a list of names whenever federal judges are to be appointed. Members of the Supreme Court, especially the chief justice, also play a role in selecting judicial candidates, especially for positions on the Court itself.

As you know, all federal judges hold their office for life during "good behavior." They can be removed only by impeachment and conviction of "high crimes and misdemeanors," which has seldom happened. Clearly, once federal judges have been appointed, their tenure is largely assured. This lifetime appointment further adds to their independence from public pressures.

Judge Constance Baker Motley has served for over 10 years on a U.S. District Court in New York. She is one of the few women and blacks in the federal judiciary.

Qualifications. Most, though not all, federal judges have law degrees. However, they need not have had a great deal of experience in the federal judiciary in order to be selected. Most Supreme Court justices have been employees of the executive branch before their appointment. A few chief justices have been law professors. District and circuit court judges come to their jobs from various backgrounds: state court judgeships, federal court judgeships at other levels, private law practice, Congress, and governorships. Generally, district and circuit court judges come from the area of their judgeship.

As of 1978, there have been no women on the Supreme Court. The average Supreme Court justice has been white, Protestant, 55 years old at appointment, of Anglo-Saxon background, and from a socioeconomic group of high status. In the entire history of the Court, there have been only six Catholic and five Jewish justices. The first black, Thurgood Marshall, was appointed in 1967.

Federal judges at lower levels tend to fit this same pattern, although in 1977, 21 federal judges were black and 6 were women.

An additional factor of importance at this level is the individual's contribution to the local community. This involvement includes political party activity. Presidents almost always select district and circuit judges from their own political party.

Of course, the Supreme Court is not immune from political considerations. Presidents want justices who will make decisions in keeping with their own goals and positions. Even if presidents can select only one justice during their term in office—and this is the pattern—that ninth justice can make a significant difference in the balance of the Court.

1. How does the selection of federal judges illustrate the operation of checks and balances in the federal government?
2. What are the advantages of lifetime appointment of federal judges? Can you think of any disadvantages?

PROFILES of JUDGES The names of few federal judges are familiar to the average citizen. However, all the men and women who serve in the federal judiciary have affected your life.

The table on page 437 describes briefly general characteristics of the terms of each of the chief justices from John Jay through Warren Burger. Chief Justices of the early Courts, through the time of John Marshall, were most interested in strengthening the position of the Court to give it a strong place in running the national government. Later chief justices were able to be more concerned with constitutional freedoms of individuals. Beginning with the tenure of Charles Evans Hughes in 1930, the Court tried to ensure equal protection under the law for citizens and to uphold their fundamental constitutional rights. Recently, the Court has been most concerned with balancing the rights of the accused against the rights of society as a whole.

The following profiles describe three federal judges. As you read them, think about the resources of the judges, their activities on the bench, and the impact they have had on the political system.

★ Profile: Chief Justice Warren E. Burger

Chief Justice Warren E. Burger was confirmed as the fifteenth Chief Justice of the United States on June 23, 1969. His nomination redeemed President Nixon's campaign promise to appoint a strict constructionist to the Supreme Court. (*Strict construction* of the Constitution is a literal, close interpretation of the document.) Burger is a conservative jurist and a lifelong Republican. Born in Minnesota in 1907, he attended the University of Minnesota and earned his law degree *magna cum laude*. Burger then joined and later became a partner at a St. Paul law firm. In 1934, he helped organize the Young Republicans in Minnesota. Over the years he was involved in many ways in the activities of Minnesota's Republican party.

In 1953, President Eisenhower appointed Burger assistant attorney general in charge of the Civil Division of the Department of Justice. Two years later, Eisenhower

Chief Justice Warren E. Burger

appointed him to the U.S. Court of Appeals for the District of Columbia.

As a member of the Court of Appeals, Burger became known as a judicial conservative. He has maintained his conservative philosophy as Chief Justice. For example, in contrast to his predecessor, Chief Justice Earl Warren, Burger believes that Supreme Court decisions that provide additional protection to the accused have made it more difficult for the courts to carry out justice. He wrote: "The seeming anxiety of judges to protect every accused person from every consequence of his voluntary utterances is giving rise to myriad rules, sub-rules, variations, and exceptions, which even the most sophisticated lawyers and judges are taxed to follow.... Guilt or innocence becomes irrelevant in the criminal trial as we flounder in a morass of artificial rules poorly conceived and often impossible of application."

As Chief Justice, Burger hopes to streamline the administration of the courts and reform the American prison system. He urges judicial restraint and reform. He has traveled to several countries to observe and learn from other judicial systems. Burger has cautioned Congress about passing laws that will tax the already overburdened federal judicial system. He supports special training for trial lawyers, the creation of additional federal judgeships, and lighter workloads and higher salaries for overworked federal judges.

Newsweek reports that the Chief Justice works about 77 hours a week and is known to keep track of even hundreds of nonjudicial details. Some people have criticized the quality of Burger's opinions and his emphasis on administrative details. His supporters feel he is providing much-needed help to federal judges.

Warren Burger explains his conservative philosophy and emphasis on reform quite simply. "For fifteen years the activism around here [the Supreme Court] was judicial. Now it's time for the activism in looking over the entire system, for thinking through the whole administration of justice."

★ Profile: Justice Hugo Black

Hugo Black served for 34 years on the Supreme Court, from 1937 until two weeks before his death in 1971 when poor health forced him to retire. During his tenure, he participated in one fourth of all the decisions the Supreme Court had ever made and sat with one quarter of all the justices who had ever been on the Court.

Black, a native of Alabama, attended the University of Alabama Law School. He practiced law in Birmingham after graduation and in 1910 was appointed police court magistrate. Three years later he was elected county prosecutor. Black resigned this post to serve in World War I and then resumed private law practice in 1919.

Black represented the United Mine Workers and other unions and became well known for the high damages he won for his clients. In 1926 and again in 1932 Black was elected to the United States Senate. As senator he supported practically all of Franklin D. Roosevelt's New Deal measures.

When Roosevelt appointed Black to the Supreme Court, he was described as "an intellectual leftist liberal from below the Mason and Dixon line." His opposition to the existing Supreme Court was well known, but he easily won Senate confirmation. Within a month, however, a reporter for a Pittsburgh newspaper wrote, "Hugo L. Black, Associate Justice of the United States Supreme Court, is a member of the hooded brotherhood that for 10 long, blood-drenched years ruled the Southland with lash and noose and torch, the Invisible Empire, Knights of the Ku Klux Klan. . . . " Justice Black requested and got free radio time to reply. He explained that between 1923 and 1925 he was a member of the Klan but resigned when he became a senator. He was not presently a member as the newspaper charged. He denied being prejudiced and pointed to his unblemished Senate record as proof.

As a Supreme Court Justice, Black was totally committed to upholding the Bill of Rights. " . . . the Constitution was his bible. A well thumbed copy was always in his pocket . . . " noted an obituary for Black. Black considered the First Amendment the cornerstone of liberty. "My view is, without deviation, without any ifs, buts, or whereases, that freedom of speech means that you shall not do something to people for the views they have or the views they express or the words they speak or write." He believed the entire Bill of Rights applied to state government as well as to the federal government. Though many on the court disagreed with him on this issue, by the time Black died his dissenting views had been accepted in decisions such as the right to free counsel to the poor tried at the state level and the right to remain silent during police interrogation.

Black's literal interpretations also led him to uphold poll taxes and eavesdropping. He felt judges did not have a right to rule a thing unconstitutional if they considered it bad. "When the judges here begin to say

Justice Hugo Black

that a thing is so bad it has to be unconstitutional, that's when I leave 'em. I've been against poll taxes all my life but they're not unconstitutional. . . . Same with eavesdropping. I know about all the public furor and I don't favor eavesdroppers but it's not forbidden in the Constitution." He opposed some forms of demonstrations as a tactic, citing a literal interpretation of the Constitution. "The First Amendment protects speech. And it protects writing. And it protects assembly. But it doesn't have anything that protects a man's right to walk around and around and around my house, if he wants to, to fasten my people—my family—up into the house, make them afraid to go out of doors. . . ."

Throughout his long career Hugo Black shunned the label "judicial activist" many pinned on him. He simply saw himself as preserving the basic freedoms established by the nation's founders.

★ Profile: Judge Frank Minis Johnson

Frank Minis Johnson is a *federal* district judge for 23 southeastern counties in Alabama. He grew up in Winston County, Alabama, most famous for its refusal to secede during the Civil War. Judge Johnson earned his law degree in 1943 from the University of Alabama Law School. He served with the United States infantry in Europe from 1943 to 1946 and then practiced law for seven years in Alabama.

Judge Johnson is a third-generation Republican and public servant. His great-grandfather was the first Republican sheriff in Winston County. His father was once elected probate judge in that county. In 1952, Johnson was one of Dwight D. Eisenhower's campaign managers in Alabama. After the election Eisenhower appointed him U.S. Attorney for northern Alabama. Johnson created an impressive record for himself in this job, and in 1955 Eisenhower appointed him U.S. District Judge for Alabama's Middle District.

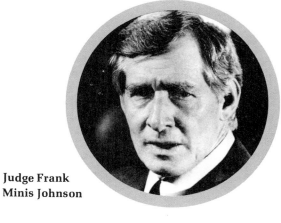

Judge Frank
Minis Johnson

Johnson soon became the center of national attention when he found himself ruling on dozens of civil rights cases that affected segregation in Alabama. His decisions shaped the extension of equal rights throughout the South and eventually the entire nation. As district judge, Johnson found himself opposing his old law school classmate George C. Wallace, who was then governor of Alabama. Johnson ordered Alabama schools, buses, parks, libraries, and museums desegregated. He ordered the end of the Alabama poll tax. He supported equal voting rights. He handed down the first order requiring states to reapportion their voting districts, an issue that finally won Supreme Court approval (*Baker* v. *Carr*). He also ordered many Alabama state prisons and mental institutions to bring conditions up to minimum constitutional standards.

Judge Johnson's reputation for fairness has been, for the most part, undisputed. He is reported to discuss pre-sentencing reports in private with defendants and their families before handing out the sentence in open court. A former law clerk for Johnson commented on the judge's fairness and his ability to mete out punishment when necessary. "If I were a criminal and I had some legal points—some mitigating factors—on my side, I'd want to go before Judge Johnson. If I deserved a heavy sentence, I wouldn't want to go before him." Johnson has even ordered prison terms for state legislators and officials found guilty in his courtroom.

Judge Johnson defends activism on the bench. He feels federal courts may act to protect a citizen's constitutional rights on the state level. In such cases, he says, judges have two choices. They can find solutions " . . . to fit the necessities of a particular case . . . [or] they can throw up their hands in frustration . . . [which would be] judicial abdication and make a mockery of the Bill of Rights."

Judge Johnson does not see himself as a lawmaker, despite his many historic decisions. His prime function is interpreting the law. "I don't make the law. I don't create the facts. I interpret the law," he says.

In 1977 Frank Johnson was nominated by President Jimmy Carter to become the new Director of the Federal Bureau of Investigation. Johnson declined the nomination, citing reasons of health.

1. What resources do these judges have?
2. What impact do you see that they could have on the United States political system?
3. What impact might they have on the lives of citizens?

The Supreme Court in Operation

Supreme Court decisions have an impact on many aspects of your life. If you have a job, for instance, your right to equal pay for equal work has been upheld by Supreme Court decisions. Supreme Court decisions have also affected what movies may be shown and what books may be sold in your community. Supreme Court decisions about equal educational opportunity affect the kind of school you go to, and who your schoolmates are.

The table on the following pages lists some of the landmark cases decided by the Supreme Court. The summaries of these important cases will give you an idea of the impact of the Court on the American political system.

INFLUENCE of the COURT The Court has influenced the United States as a political system in several ways. First, as you have read, the Court has solidified and extended its own powers within the system. As you know, the case of *Marbury* v. *Madison* established judicial review and the right to decide as principles for Supreme Court actions. Later, the Court established its right to overrule state court decisions, that is, its right to judicial sovereignty. Everyone of the landmark decisions—and many more as well—strengthened the Court's right and ability to interpret the Constitution and to act as the highest court in the land.

The Court has also acted to make the central government of the United States stronger. When the Constitution was written, no one could envision a society as big and complex as the one we have today. Many Supreme Court decisions—among them the decisions in *McCulloch* v. *Maryland* and *Munn* v. *Illinois*—broadened the power of the federal government so it could govern effectively.

The Court has also made important decisions regarding civil rights. *Plessy* v. *Ferguson* and *Brown* v. *Topeka Board of Education* involved the rights of minority groups. Citizen rights to fair procedures in arrests and trials were upheld by the *Miranda* decision, among others.

The Supreme Court has strengthened the separation of powers and the system of checks and balances among the president, Congress, and the courts. In *Schechter* v. *United States* the Court helped control the President and maintain the power of Congress. In *United States* v. *Richard Nixon* the

Landmark Supreme Court Cases

CASE (date)	SITUATION	DECISION	IMPORTANCE
Marbury v. *Madison* (1803)	President Jefferson withheld the commission of a justice of the peace, an appointment made just before President Adams left office.	The Court ruled that the man did have a right to the commission but that the law giving the court authority over the cases was unconstitutional.	Established the right of judicial review.
Dartmouth College v. *Woodward* (1819)	The state of New Hampshire attempted to alter the charter of Dartmouth College, which was chartered by the English Crown in 1769.	The Court ruled the original charter was valid and voided the state law.	Contracts were strengthened by protecting them against unreasonable government influence.
McCulloch v. *Maryland* (1819)	The Baltimore branch of the Bank of the U.S. refused to pay a tax placed on it by the state of Maryland.	The Court ruled that Maryland could not tax a branch of the Bank of the U.S. in Maryland. The Court upheld the implied power of Congress to create a bank.	Strengthened the federal system of government. It established the supremacy of federal over state government.
Gibbons v. *Ogden* (1824)	The state of New York gave exclusive navigation rights between New York and New Jersey to Ogden, while the federal government gave the same to Gibbons.	The Court ruled that a state cannot grant exclusive navigation rights for interstate commerce.	Further established the supremacy of federal over state law in matters of interstate commerce. Expanded the meaning of the commerce clause.
Dred Scott v. *Sanford* (1857)	Dred Scott, a slave, had been taken by his master to free territory and then returned to slave territory. Scott sued for his freedom, arguing that residence in free territory made him free.	The Court ruled that Scott could not be a citizen. It also ruled that since slaves were property, Congress could not prohibit slavery without violating due process.	Annulled the concept of free territory regarding slavery. Added to grievances that brought about the Civil War.
Plessy v. *Ferguson* (1896)	Plessy, who was 1/8 black, was arrested in Louisiana for riding in and refusing to leave the white-only car of a train.	The Court ruled that separate but equal facilities do not violate equal protection of the law.	Made the separation of races legal.
Schenck v. *United States* (1919)	Schenck, a socialist, was arrested for mailing flyers urging men to resist military service during World War I.	The Court ruled that the government could restrict Schenck's freedom of speech in a war situation because of the "clear and present danger" of violence.	Helped establish "clear and present" danger as a test for judging when freedom of speech can be limited.

CASE (date)	SITUATION	DECISION	IMPORTANCE
Schechter v. *United States* (1935)	The National Industrial Recovery Act (NIRA) gave the president power to set up codes of fair competition for business and industry.	The Court ruled that Congress had delegated too much power to the president, and that the federal government could not regulate intrastate commerce.	Helped maintain separation of powers and made Congress become more specific when delegating regulatory powers.
Brown v. *Board of Education of Topeka* (1954)	Black and white children were forced to go to separate, racially segregated schools.	The Court ruled that separation of races is discrimination even if facilities are equal.	Eliminated "separate but equal" doctrine established in Plessy v. Ferguson and marked the end of segregation in the South.
Gideon v. *Wainwright* (1963)	Gideon's request for a court-appointed lawyer was denied because he was charged with a misdemeanor, not a felony.	The Court ruled that defense counsel must be guaranteed to all defendants, regardless of their ability to pay.	Extended right to lawyer in all criminal state cases.
Miranda v. *Arizona* (1966)	After arrest Miranda was questioned by police and signed a confession which was used as evidence at his trial. Police never told him of his rights to remain silent and consult a lawyer.	The Court ruled that statements made by individuals who have not been informed of their rights are not admissible as evidence at their trial.	Required police to inform suspects of their rights.
Furman v. *Georgia* (1972)	Furman, a black man, was given the death sentence for an accidental shooting during a burglary.	The Court ruled that the death sentence in most instances is cruel punishment, violating the 8th Amendment.	Death sentences were eliminated until they could be written in such a way as to not discriminate.
United States v. *Richard M. Nixon* (1974)	President Nixon refused to release tape recordings of presidential conversations for the trial of Watergate defendants, claiming that they were protected by executive privilege.	The president must cooperate with the court by providing the necessary evidence needed for a criminal trial.	Executive privilege was narrowly defined and the entire Watergate scandal was revealed, leading to Nixon's resignation.
Regents of the University of California v. *Bakke* (1978)	When the Davis Medical School twice rejected Allan Bakke's application, Bakke, a white man, charged that the school's policy of reserving 16 out of the 100 positions for racial minorities was unconstitutional.	The Court ruled that Bakke must be admitted to the Davis Medical School, but while the Davis policy was unconstitutional, race may be used in other ways as a consideration in determining admissions.	Provided limits to the practice of affirmative action, preventing it from becoming reverse-discrimination.

Court's decision made it absolutely clear that the president is not above the law, but is subject to judicial procedures.

> 1. How has the Supreme Court made an impact on the American political system?
> 2. Which of the landmark cases has had the most effect on your own everyday life? Why?

COURT PROCEDURE

In the 1977–78 term about 4,000 cases were submitted to the Supreme Court. The Court made decisions in about 180 of these cases. How did the justices handle this overwhelming case load?

Supreme Court procedure for most cases follows four main stages. First, the justices hear oral arguments in public. Second, they hold private conferences to discuss the cases and decide them. Third, they write one or more opinions on each case. Finally, decisions are announced and become law in hearings open to the public.

Hearing Oral Arguments. The Supreme Court is in session for 36 weeks from October to June of every year. It meets in its own building, not far from the Capitol, in Washington, D.C. The public chamber where cases are heard seats close to 300 people. About 90 of the seats are reserved for the press and members of the bar; the remaining seats are reserved for the public. As a citizen you can visit the Supreme Court building, and, if there is space available, you can hear cases debated in oral arguments.

The justices, robed in black, sit behind a raised table (the "bench"), in order of their length of service. In the center is the chief justice. The most senior associate justice sits to his or her right, the next most senior to the chief justice's left. The justices then alternate from right to left along the table, with the most junior at the chief justice's far left.

Justices listen to oral arguments on Monday through Thursday in the first two weeks of each month. Normally, each lawyer is limited to one hour, although arguments have been known to last as long as four hours. After listening to the lawyers' arguments, the justices ask them questions.

Lawyers who try cases in the Supreme Court must have been admitted to practice before the Court. In order to qualify, a lawyer must have practiced for three years in his or her own state and must file an application accompanied by references from two lawyers who practice before the Supreme Court.

About half the cases argued before the Supreme Court are brought by or against the federal government. In all of these, the government is represented by the office of the solicitor general—a division of about 20 people within the Justice Department. The solicitor general is the fourth-ranking member of the Justice Department after the attorney general, the deputy attorney general, and the associate attorney general. The office of solicitor general not only presents oral arguments before the Supreme Court but must also approve all government cases that go before the Court.

Conferences. On each Friday during the weeks it is hearing oral arguments, the Court holds a conference. The justices meet in secret, discuss the cases before them, and make preliminary decisions. Usually, the Court has an agenda of about 75 items, or cases, each Friday.

The chief justice, who presides at conferences, first summarizes a case that has come before the Court. Then the other justices speak in order of seniority, the most senior justice speaking first and the least senior speaking last. In most conference sessions, a tentative voice or written vote is taken after discussion. At this time the least senior justice votes first. This principle has been established so that the opinions of more senior justices will not influence those with less seniority.

Chief Justices of the United States

John Jay (1789–1795): Helped set up Supreme Court procedure in formative period.

John Rutledge (1795): Appointed by Washington but not confirmed.

Oliver Ellsworth (1796–1800): Witnessed only a few decisions.

John Marshall (1801–1835): Greatly expanded authority of national government by broadening powers granted it by Constitution and by emphasizing limits on states. Strengthened judicial branch.

Roger B. Taney (1836–1864): Reversed trend of Marshall Court by stressing protection of states' rights. A Southerner and slaveowner, aroused storm of criticism with decision in *Dred Scott* v. *Sandford* (1857).

Salmon P. Chase (1864–1873): A Republican who favored most postwar aims of his party and thus evaded ruling on constitutionality of Radical Reconstruction. Attempted with limited success to maintain correct trial procedure in Johnson impeachment.

Morrison R. Waite (1874–1888): Through various decisions, strengthened the regulatory power of states.

Melville W. Fuller (1888–1910): Upheld traditional property rights, thus fostering growth of large corporations and restricting unions.

Edward D. White (1910–1921): First chief justice to have served first as associate justice. Established "rule of reason" for regulating business.

William H. Taft (1921–1930): Only former president to serve as chief justice. Instituted changes so Supreme Court could handle case load better. Ruled against curbs on business and child labor.

Charles E. Hughes (1930–1941): Though ruling against the NRA in *Schechter* v. *United States* (1935), upheld most New Deal legislation. Successfully opposed Franklin Roosevelt's 1937 plan to "pack" Supreme Court by adding up to six new justices.

Harlan F. Stone (1941–1946): As associate justice (1925–1941), noted for dissents, along with Justices Holmes and Brandeis, taking liberal stand on social issues. Upheld New Deal measures such as social security.

Frederick M. Vinson (1946–1953): In era of many split decisions, aimed to minimize controversy. Thus postponed hearings on education cases that might have reversed *Plessy*.

Earl Warren (1953–1969): Presided over Supreme Court in time of its greatest influence in changing society. Believed in "judicial activism," with Court moving aggressively against racial discrimination and in favor of legislative reapportionment and rights of accused.

Warren E. Burger (1969–   ): More inclined to "judicial restraint" than his predecessor. Believed in strengthening law enforcement and limiting rights of accused. However, voted with liberals on such issues as legalizing abortion and limiting wiretapping. Urged judicial reforms to ease case load and improve quality of judiciary.

Most of a Supreme Court justice's time is spent outside of the courtroom, as can be seen in these photos. Justice Blackmun, at his desk, considers a pending case (top photo). Law clerks work with Justice Stevens in his chambers (middle photo). In the bottom photo, Chief Justice Burger is presiding at a judicial conference.

Writing Opinions. A case is decided by majority rule, and the decision of those five or more justices who form the majority is known as the Court's decision. Usually, but not always, the decision is accompanied by a written opinion. If the chief justice has voted with the majority, he or she decides who will write the majority opinion of the Court. If not, the opinion is assigned by the senior justice on the majority side.

The selection process for writing a majority opinion is a political one. Generally, a chief justice will select someone who is closest to the opposition (the dissenters) so that conflict between the two sides can be minimized. If the chief justice considers the case to be a landmark, he or she will generally write the opinion.

There may be more than one opinion on the majority side. This happens when one or more justices agree with the Court's decision but not its reasoning. Written views of this type are known as *concurring opinions*.

Most Supreme Court decisions do not represent a consensus, but are split decisions. The Court agrees unanimously only about a third of the time. Thus, there is frequently at least one opinion representing the dissent.

Dissents are important in the judicial process. In time they may come to represent a majority rather than a minority position. One famous dissent was that by Justice John Harlan in the case of *Plessy* v. *Ferguson* in 1896. Justice Harlan objected to the doctrine of "separate but equal" that underlay the majority decision. His dissent—stating that "our Constitution is colorblind"—became the majority opinion in the *Brown* v. *Board of Education of Topeka* case in 1954.

Although one justice writes the first draft of an opinion, it is always collectively revised. All drafts are written out and then circulated to all nine justices, who comment on them.

A draft may go through many revisions. In the *Brown* case it took almost two years to reach the decision and there were more than 10 drafts of the majority opinion. Chief Justice Earl Warren, who wrote the opinion, wanted it to be unanimous, with no dissents. In order to achieve this, he had to bargain a great deal with other justices over the contents of his majority opinion.

Decision Days. On three consecutive Mondays of each month, the Court announces its decisions to the public. Not only are decisions announced, but all written opinions are published in order to make the logic of the court available to the public. On decision day, the Court's decisions become binding and the law of the land. They are then recorded and published by the federal government.

1. What are the four main steps in Supreme Court procedure?
2. Which of these steps do you think is most important? Why?

A Coalitional System. Supreme Court decisions are the product of many minds. They involve a lot of give-and-take. Each justice participates in every stage of decision-making, including the writing of opinions. As you have seen, many opinions undergo numerous changes before they reach their final form.

Just as the Executive Office forms a subsystem at the top of the executive bureaucracy, so the Supreme Court forms its own subsystem at the top of the judicial bureaucracy. But, while the Executive Office is an elite system, the Supreme Court may be thought of as coalitional.

The Supreme Court has many of the same coalitional characteristics that you have studied in the Congress. It exemplifies a system which is characterized by majority rule, bloc voting, shared resources, and high participation.

Majority Rule. The Supreme Court decides every case by majority rule. Unanimous decisions, such as that in *Brown* v.

The Board of Education, are rare. Most cases end in *split decisions;* that is, one or more justices vote in an opposite direction from the majority opinion. The *Miranda* decision and the *Ingraham* case which appears later in this chapter (444–445) are examples of split decisions.

Justices on the Supreme Court can exercise important influence over one another. Through formal office appointments and written notes to each other, justices attempt to influence each other on key segments of judicial decisions. Majorities in the Court are not automatic. They must be built through a process of interplay which is more formal than in other national political systems, but nevertheless is equally important and significant in Court decisions.

Justices are not totally independent from their own backgrounds and experience. Nor are they independent of politics. They are chosen by presidents to represent points of view on the court, even though a justice's judicial point of view may change.

These points of view are often considered to be conservative or liberal. A judicial conservative is not quite like a political conservative. A judicial conservative is a strict constructionist, one who believes in a strict, or narrow, interpretation of the Constitution. To a judicial conservative the actual words in the Constitution are the bases for law. Judicial conservatives in general believe strongly in the rights of governments in the administration of justice. A judicial liberal, on the other hand, believes in a wider, looser interpretation. He or she tends to consider in interpretation societal characteristics and inequalities. Therefore, a judicial liberal tends to interpret the Constitution's words according to social and political needs. Judicial liberals tend to stress individual rights, including "fundamental rights" not enumerated in the Constitution.

Bloc Voting. In the 1970s, the Supreme Court headed by Chief Justice Warren Burger has been characterized by bloc voting. Judicial conservatives on the Court are Chief Justice Burger and Justice William Rehnquist. Both of these men were appointed by President Nixon. They are often joined in the conservative camp by Justices Harry Blackmun and Lewis Powell, Jr., also Nixon appointees.

A judicially liberal bloc is made up of Justice William Brennan and Justice Thurgood Marshall. Before his retirement in 1975, Justice William O. Douglas usually joined Brennan and Marshall in a liberal coalition. Others on the court—Justices Stewart, White, and Stevens—vote sometimes with the conservative and sometimes with the liberal factions.

During the 1972–73 term, Burger, Blackmun, Powell, and Rehnquist voted together 70% of the time, voting in a conservative direction on opinions. They almost always voted in the majority. Justices Brennan, Douglas, and Marshall banded together on almost the same percentage of issues. Most often they were the dissenters on cases.

Because neither the conservative nor the liberal bloc forms the needed 5-vote majority, each must work to sway other members to vote according to their views. This is a classical characteristic of a coalitional system.

As you can see in Figure 14-3 on page 441, justices' rulings during the 1976–77 Supreme Court term followed classic conservative-liberal lines. Justices Brennan and Marshall were joined by Justice Stewart and Justice Stevens (William Douglas' replacement) in the liberal camp. These four men voted in a liberal direction on cases in which the ruling was in favor of the defendants. Justices Burger and Rehnquist were joined on some cases by Justices White, Blackmun, and Powell. On other cases, White, Blackmun, and Powell voted with Brennan and Marshall. All of the cases in this table were decided in favor of the liberals on the court.

However, in the second table (Figure 14-4) you see how in voting for rulings on

SUPREME COURT VOTING on RULINGS in FAVOR of DEFENDANTS, 1976-1977

CASE	Roberts v. Louisiana	Coker v. Georgia	Brewer v. Williams	GM Leasing v. U.S.	U.S. v. Chadwick
JUSTICES					
Burger	C	C	C	L	L
Rehnquist	C	C	C	L	C
Stewart	L	L	L	L	L
White	C	L	C	L	L
Blackmun	C	L	C	L	L
Powell	L	C	L	L	C
Stevens	L	L	L	L	L
Brennan	L	L	L	L	L
Marshall	L	L	L	L	L
	(5-4, liberal)	(6-3, liberal)	(5-4, liberal)	(9-0, liberal)	(7-2, liberal)

L = voted liberal   C = voted conservative

Figure 14-3

the prosecution, the conservatives dominated. Burger and Rehnquist were joined consistently by Blackmun and Powell. Brennan and Marshall broke their liberal pattern on two votes, yet were joined by Stevens and Stewart on some important issues. Therefore, considerable bloc voting with the need to influence those in the middle of the spectrum is evidenced by the 1976–77 rulings of the Supreme Court under Chief Justice Burger.

Shared Resources. All justices who are appointed to the Court share certain valuable resources. They should have outstanding legal skills and excellent judicial knowledge. All have had vast experience in gathering evidence and making decisions.

In their work on the Court all justices have the invaluable resource of immunity from political pressure, enabling them to make decisions on their judicial merit alone. In addition, all justices have the use of the highly knowledgeable Court staff of judicial assistants and clerks.

One of the greatest resources any Supreme Court justice brings to the Court is his or her past experience. Justices come to the Court with different backgrounds in judicial proceedings and different types of experience. Justice Thurgood Marshall, for example, came to the Court as an expert on civil rights and the rights of minorities and lower socioeconomic status groups. His skills in dealing with civil rights issues have contributed to the decisions of the court.

Figure 14-4

SUPREME COURT VOTING on RULINGS in FAVOR of the PROSECUTION, 1976-1977

CASE	Weatherford v. Bursey	Smith v. U.S.	U.S. v. Ramsey	U.S. v. Lovasco	U.S. v. Washington	Manson v. Brathwaite
JUSTICES						
Burger	C	C	C	C	C	C
Rehnquist	C	C	C	C	C	C
Stewart	C	L	C	C	C	C
White	C	C	C	C	C	C
Blackmun	C	C	C	C	C	C
Powell	C	C	C	C	C	C
Stevens	C	L	L	L	C	C
Brennan	L	L	L	C	C	L
Marshall	L	L	L	C	C	L
	(7-2, conservative)	(5-4, conservative)	(6-3, conservative)	(8-1, conservative)	(9-0, conservative)	(7-2, conservative)

L = voted liberal   C = voted conservative

Justice Rehnquist, on the other hand, came to the Court as a law and order advocate, who had made rulings in favor of the prosecution in many cases. His special skills are in both criminal and civil cases dealing with the rights of those who administer and uphold the law. He also is a strong advocate of presidential power.

In making any decision of the Court, justices rely on the particular expertise of other justices. Especially within blocs, opinions and experiences are shared. These shared resources contribute to both majority decisions and dissents which are made by justices.

Participation. There is also high participation by all justices on the Court. In any decision all justices consider all possible positions and all of the evidence regarding a case. In some cases there may be as many as nine separate opinions given by the Supreme Court. Therefore, in the deliberation of decisions, the voting on decisions, and often the writing of majority opinions or dissents, all justices participate highly in the full process of decision-making.

1. In what ways is the Supreme Court a coalitional political system?
2. How does it compare with the coalitional system you studied in Congress?
3. Which of the systems do you think citizens can influence the most?

LIMITS and INFLUENCES

The judicial branch is affected by both formal and informal influences. The Constitution sets up a number of formal limits on the power and function of the judiciary. In addition, citizens acting as advocates can have important influence on the courts.

Formal Limits. In your study of the Constitution you have learned about the powers granted to the judicial branch of the federal government. By describing the jurisdiction of the federal courts, the Constitution imposes a limit on their powers. The federal courts are limited to the powers described in the Constitution.

In addition, the Constitution gives the executive and legislative branches the power to limit the judicial branch in certain specified ways. As you know, the president is given the power to appoint all federal judges, and the Senate is given the power to approve or reject those appointments. By setting up this procedure, the Constitution gives both the president and the senators influence over what kind of men and women are federal judges, and thus gives them power to affect how the law will be interpreted.

The legislative branch also has the power to remove a federal judge from office. Judges are appointed for a term of "good behavior" (Article III, Section 1) and can be removed only by impeachment (Article II, Section 4). Like the impeachment process for a president, the impeachment of a federal judge is an act of the House of Representatives. The impeached official is then tried in the Senate. Few federal judges have been impeached.

The Constitution gives the legislative branch further influence over the judicial branch by giving Congress the power to create lower courts. This process began with the Judiciary Act of 1789.

Finally, the judicial branch can be limited by Constitutional amendments, which change the body of constitutional law on which the federal courts base their decisions. For example, as you read in Chapter 12, the Supreme Court declared the 1970 Voting Rights Act unconstitutional. Subsequently, the Twenty-Sixth Amendment was adopted in order to guarantee 18-year-olds the right to vote.

Informal Influence. Although the Constitution does not define the role of advocates in the court system, citizens are able to influence the courts in several ways.

The Supreme Court justices find some time to relax after a morning session in the East Court Room.

Generally, citizens are best able to advocate positions and influence the courts by action in interest groups. Interest groups often have the resources to act in ways that individuals cannot. For example, an interest group may have the money and expertise to make it possible for a case to be tried and appealed. The NAACP was able to do this with many civil rights cases. Citizens like Mr. Brown (*Brown* v. *Topeka Board of Education*) feel that a violation of rights has taken place. An organization like the NAACP uses its resources to take the case to court and use it to test a principle they advocate, such as equal educational opportunity. In the *Brown* case and many others, the NAACP financed the legal costs and provided expert lawyers to work on the case. Few individual citizens can afford the cost of seeing a case all the way up to the Supreme Court. By providing the opportunity for judicial decision, the interest group is affecting the course of justice.

A second way in which interest groups can influence the courts is by submitting *amicus curiae* briefs to the court. (*Amicus curiae* means "friend of the court." A *brief* is a detailed, written legal argument on one side of a case.) In this process an interested party, who is neither plaintiff nor defendant in a case, develops a brief providing factual information and legal precedents surrounding one side of the case. *Amicus curiae* briefs have been known to be very helpful in determining the outcome of cases. The NAACP, for example, filed an influential *amicus* brief in the *Brown* decision.

Interest groups also provide expert testimony for cases in which they have expertise on complex issues. Often in labor disputes, for example, union members provide expert testimony before federal courts. Environmental experts from organizations like the Sierra Club also are called upon to testify in federal courts.

In addition, the advice of legal interest groups like the American Bar Association can influence the appointment of federal judges. You saw this in operation in the Carswell case.

The following case illustrates how citizen advocates influence Supreme Court decision-making. It involves the case of *Ingraham* v. *Wright*. In this case, the Supreme Court upheld the right of school authorities to punish students for disciplinary reasons using the method of paddling. As you read the case, think about how interest groups and citizen advocates can affect decisions of the Supreme Court.

★ Ingraham v. Wright

Questions of school discipline have become important ones in the 1970s. Recent surveys of public opinion have shown that most parents of youth in schools rate discipline as the number one problem with which they are concerned.

In response to these kinds of concerns, the state of Florida formulated a law regarding school discipline. The law indicates that a teacher or an administrator in the school can inflict corporal punishment, or physical punishment, on a student, as long as it is not "degrading or unduly severe." For school administrators, this law seemed to provide for important disciplinary sanctions on the part of administrators and teachers while protecting students from punishment which would be in excess of their constitutional rights as citizens under the Eighth Amendment. They felt that the law would provide for punishment and at the same time would protect students from the cruel and unusual punishment prohibited by the Eighth Amendment to the U.S. Constitution.

The law, then, seems to protect both school administrators and students. In January 1971, two students at Charles R. Drew Junior High School in Miami decided that they did not think they were protected by such regulations. The students claimed that they had been excessively paddled by their school officials on repeated occasions. Specifically, James Ingraham, in the eighth grade, had been paddled for responding too slowly to a teacher and as a result had remained out of school for eleven days because of a hemotoma he incurred as a result of the paddling. Ingraham was joined by Roosevelt Andrews, who also claimed that on repeated occasions he had been severely paddled. At one point, he was struck so severely on the arm that he could not use it for several days.

The students were upset, and in the name of their parents and their lawyers, they took their case to court. Their purpose was to test their rights under the Eighth Amendment to the Constitution against cruel and unusual punishment. They also wished to test the due process clause of the Fourteenth Amendment, which grants citizens the right to know the punishments which will be used.

The students' parents and their lawyers were joined by the National Education Association. Briefs of amicus curiae were filed by the National Education Association supporting the contention that there is a constitutional claim that students have against the infliction of cruel and unusual punishment. They believed strongly that students should be able to be informed about their rights as citizens before such a punishment would occur, and that excessive punishment violated the Eighth Amendment.

Expert testimony and briefs were written against the students and in support of corporal punishment by the National School Boards Association and by the United Teachers of Dade County, local 1974. The United Teachers group claimed that teachers were continuously being oppressed by students who committed violent acts against them. Assaults were common and teachers needed a means of discipline which could counteract students' behavior. The need for discipline, they said, did not involve cruel and unusual punishment. However, it did involve punishment that could support teachers' rights as citizens to respond to misbehavior in meaningful and direct ways.

Both groups took their testimony and their cases to the Supreme Court. The cases were upheld. The defendants in the case consisted of the principal, the superintendent, and several assistant principals in the school system. In the District Court and the Court of Appeals, the case of the school authorities was upheld. In the Supreme Court, the Supreme Court ruled by a 5 to 4 majority to support the decisions of the District Court and the Appeals Court.

In writing the decision for the Court, Justice Lewis Powell was joined by Chief

Justice Burger and Justices Blackmun, Rehnquist, and Stewart in saying:

"The use of corporal punishment in this country as a means of disciplining school children dates back to the colonial period. It has survived the transformation of primary and secondary education from the colonials reliance on optional private arrangements to our present system of compulsory education and dependence on public schools."

In short, the majority of the Court felt that corporal punishment was part of the tradition of the schools. Students were not criminals. They were youth who were attending an educational function. Therefore, they did not fall under the Eighth Amendment to the U.S. Constitution.

In arguing in a dissent, Justice White was joined by Justices Brennan, Marshall, and Stevens in his dissent. He said:

"The Eighth Amendment places a flat prohibition against the infliction of 'cruel and unusual punishments'. This reflects a societal judgment that there are some punishments that are so barbaric and inhumane that we will not permit them to be imposed on anyone, no matter how opprovrious the offense. If there are some punishments that are so barbaric that they may not be imposed for the commission of crimes, designated by our social system as the most thoroughly reprehensible acts an individual can commit, then . . . similar punishments may not be imposed on persons for less culpible acts, such as breaches of school discipline. Thus, if it is constitutionally impermissible to cut off someone's ear for the commission of a murder, it must be unconstitutional to cut off a child's ear for being late to class. Although there were no ears cut off in this case, the record reveals beatings so severe that if they were inflicted on a hardened criminal for the commission of a serious crime, they might not pass constitutional muster."

Therefore, the Supreme Court upheld the right of the Florida school officials and the Florida legislature to provide for corporal punishment of students for serious offenses in schools. All states in the United States do not support such laws. New York City and the state of New Jersey, for example, specifically prohibit corporal punishment. However, the Supreme Court ruling means that corporal punishment is legal throughout the United States.

1. How can the president influence the federal courts? How can Congress influence them?

2. In what ways can interest groups affect federal court decisions?

3. How did citizen advocates participate in the *Ingraham* case?

COMPARING POLITICAL SYSTEMS In Chapters 12, 13, and 14 you have analyzed political systems in the three branches of government. You have identified the Executive Office as a basically elite system and the federal bureaucracy as a bureacratic system. Both Congress and the Supreme Court have been analyzed as variations of coalitional systems, while the federal judiciary has been seen as a bureaucratic system.

To make good comparisons among the branches of the national government, you can compare the various systems within the branches. To do this you must synthesize your understanding of the resources and activities within each of the systems, or subsystems, in the national political system. In addition, you should consider the ways in which citizens can act to influence each of these systems.

Make your own copy of a chart like the one shown in Figure 14–5. Based on what you have read and classroom discussions that have taken place, you can analyze each category—resources, activities, and citizen advocacy—in each of the systems shown on the chart. Fill in the appropriate general statements and specific examples in each category, for each system.

For example, in the Resources category, you can compare decision-making in each of the systems. You have seen that in the Executive Office the president makes most of the decisions. You can cite examples such as President Nixon's decision in Cambodia and President Carter's decision to cancel nuclear reactor projects.

In Congress, on the other hand, you have seen an example of an almost model coalitional system. Cases such as the ERA amendment and the highway bill provide innumerable specific examples of coalitional decision-making.

By synthesizing on the chart the information you have learned, you should be able to answer these questions:

1. What general statements can you make about the use and distribution of resources in each of the five systems on the chart? Give specific examples to illustrate your statements.

2. What general statements can you make about how political activities are carried out in each of the five systems on the chart? Give specific examples to illustrate your statements.

3. What general statements can you make about how citizen advocates can influence each of the five systems on the chart? Give specific examples to illustrate your statements.

Figure 14-5

A MODEL for COMPARING POLITICAL SYSTEMS					
	EXECUTIVE OFFICE (ELITE SYSTEM)	FEDERAL BUREAUCRACY (BUREAUCRATIC SYSTEM)	CONGRESS (COALITIONAL SYSTEM)	FEDERAL JUDICIARY (BUREAUCRATIC SYSTEM)	SUPREME COURT (COALITIONAL SYSTEM)
Political Resources Status Wealth Information Ideas Skills Other					
Political Activities Decision-making Leadership Participation Communication					
Citizen Advocacy					

1. What is the jurisdiction of the federal judicial system?
2. Summarize the principles upon which Supreme Court power is based. Briefly describe how these principles were established.
3. In what ways is the federal judicial branch a bureacratic system? How does this compare and/or contrast with the organization of the executive branch?
4. Outline the steps that a case must take before reaching the Supreme Court.
5. What are the formal limits and informal influences on Supreme Court power?
6. Review some of the ways in which the Court has influenced the United States as a political system.
7. What are the four main stages in which Supreme Court justices review cases?
8. The federal judiciary is a bureaucratic political system, but the Supreme Court itself is a coalitional system. Explain what this means.
9. What are the qualifications of most federal judges? How are judges selected?
10. Reexamine the following Supreme Court cases: *Miranda* v. *Arizona, Brown* v. *Board of Education of Topeka,* and *Ingraham* v. *Wright.* Identify the constitutional issue(s) in each case.

Define the following terms.

jurisdiction	circuits	concurring opinions
judicial review	appellate jurisdiction	arbiter
writ	brief	*amicus curiae*
original jurisdiction	court of last resort	senatorial courtesy
plaintiff	precedent	split decisions

1. Review the duties of state judiciaries in Chapter 8. How does the role of the federal judicial system compare and/or contrast with state courts?
2. List the powers of the Supreme Court. Compare this list with those powers enumerated in the Constitution. Which powers are not guaranteed by the Constitution? Explain how the Supreme Court has gained these rights.

3. Interest groups are not a formal part of federal government, yet they influence the decisions of each branch of government. In what ways can interest groups affect the federal judicial system? In your opinion, are interest groups a positive or a negative influence on the federal judiciary? Explain.

4. Summarize the ways in which the federal executive and legislative branches check the power of the federal judiciary. How does the judiciary check the power of these two branches of government?

Chapter Activities

1. Reread the description of the basic procedures that operate in a federal court (see pages 420–423). Next, working with another student, select an issue that might be heard in a federal appellate court. Prepare a brief for each side in the case. Be prepared to present these two briefs to the class.

2. Investigate a recent Supreme Court case that has not yet been decided by the Court. Write up a brief on one side of the issue while others in your class write up a brief on the opposite side. Have a debate in class and advocate your case. Be sure that you use evidence properly in order to build your case.

3. Write a biography of one of the current Supreme Court justices. Consider his background and how he was selected. Also, note important concurring or dissenting decisions made by this judge.

4. Make a list of your major weekly activities. Indicate how past Supreme Court decisions affect those activities.

Chapter Bibliography

Yankee from Olympus, Catherine Drinker Bowen (Little, Brown & Co: Boston), 1944.
    A fascinating biography of Oliver Wendell Holmes, Supreme Court Justice.

The Supreme Court: Justice and the Law, published by Congressional Quarterly, Inc., Washington, D.C., 1973.
    A look at the history of the Supreme Court, highlighting its actions between 1969 and 1973 and including biographies of the justices. Also features issues such as court reform, the jury system, and grand juries. Contains an appendix filled with a variety of information on recent court action.

Court In Session, Jethro Koller Lieberman (Sterling Publishing Company, Inc.: New York), 1966.

A very good overview and background to the court system at all levels of government. Contains useful explanations of legal terms and processes.

Federal Courts in the Political Process, Jack W. Peltason (Random House: New York), 1964.

A broad overview of the role of the federal courts, highlighting federal judges and their jobs, methods of recruiting judges, and how federal judges make decisions.

Chapter Objectives

★ To learn how civil rights have been
  guaranteed and expanded
★ To understand how conflict promotes
  change in political systems
★ To analyze the role of citizens' groups in
  advocating changes in civil rights
★ To extend and apply valuing skills

chapter 15

CITIZEN PARTICIPATION in CIVIL RIGHTS

Throughout this book you have seen how issues involving civil rights have played an important part in the American political system. Civil rights are guaranteed in the United States Constitution. They are a major concern of the Supreme Court, of Congress, and of the president. Each of these three branches of government works to protect the civil rights of Americans. Citizens themselves, alone and organized in interest groups, have labored to extend these rights—the essence of our representative democracy.

In this chapter, you will review the rights that Americans have as citizens. Then, through a historical perspective, you will see how conflict has produced change in our national political system, with special reference to the civil rights of women and black Americans, and to basic liberties such as First Amendment freedoms. An in-depth study of the Montgomery bus boycott, a protest action by blacks in the 1950s, will dramatize how citizen participation can affect civil rights at the national level.

How Rights Are Protected

A man mails out several thousand pamphlets attacking the federal government's foreign policy. A political group requests permission to hold a rally in a city park. Their request is denied, and group leaders appeal to higher authorities to reverse the community's decision. A woman leaves her job temporarily to have a baby. When she returns to work and finds that she has lost her seniority rights, she sues her employer.

What do these three very different incidents have in common? All of them involve civil rights. Civil rights are those rights and freedoms guaranteed to every American citizen. What are the most important of these rights, and where do they come from?

PROTECTORS of OUR RIGHTS Both the Constitution and the three branches of national government provide powerful protection of citizens' rights.

Constitutional Protection. The most fundamental guarantee of our civil rights is provided by the Bill of Rights, the first ten amendments to the Constitution. The First Amendment protects freedom of speech, freedom of the press, freedom of religion, and the right to assembly. These freedoms are often called "First Amendment rights."

Provisions in the Fourth Amendment through the Eighth Amendment in the Bill of Rights protect persons accused of crime. The Fourth Amendment guarantees our rights against "unreasonable searches and seizures." The Fifth Amendment guarantees that no one "shall be compelled in any criminal case to be a witness against himself." In the *Miranda* decision (pages 425–426) you saw that the Supreme Court upheld an accused person's right to remain silent. In the 1963 case of *Gideon* v. *Wainwright,* which you will read about later in this chapter, judges took into account the Sixth Amendment's assurance that an accused person should have "the Assistance of Counsel for his defence." The Seventh Amendment guarantees a trial by jury. The Supreme Court's 1972 ruling in *Roberts* v. *Louisiana* (that capital punishment as then administered was unconstitutional) was based partly on the Eighth Amendment's prohibition against "cruel and unusual" punishment.

Further amendments to the Constitution also protect our civil rights. The most

Among the basic civil rights guaranteed by the Bill of Rights are freedom of speech and freedom of assembly.

important is the Fourteenth Amendment, which specifies that no one shall be deprived of "life, liberty, or property without due process of law." It also states that no one shall be denied "equal protection of the laws." This promise of equality has been the basis for many actions extending civil rights to black Americans and other minority groups.

Other constitutional amendments have extended the vote—one of the principal rights of citizens in a representative democracy. Suffrage was granted to blacks by the Fifteenth Amendment, to women by the Nineteenth Amendment, and to 18-year-olds by the Twenty-sixth Amendment.

Protection by the Courts. The Constitution is not the only protector of our civil rights. As you can tell by the number of legal cases already discussed, the courts—especially the Supreme Court—play a vital role in interpreting what the Constitution means. In fact, the Supreme Court has usually been more liberal than the other branches of the national government in applying the language of the Constitution to extend civil rights.

Protection by Congress. Congress too has supported civil rights. It has done so partly by initiating amendments to the Constitution, such as the Equal Rights Amendment. It has done so partly by passing laws that broadened citizens' rights. One of these was the 1966 Freedom of Information Act, which extended freedom of the press by making various government records available to the public.

Protection by the Executive Branch. The executive branch has also acted to protect Americans' civil rights. A president may take a strong position on a bill or amendment. President Nixon, for instance, was very much in favor of the 18-year-old vote. The president may go even further. An executive order of Franklin D. Roosevelt in 1941 ruled that firms with defense contracts could not discriminate in hiring. This action

helped strengthen equality of opportunity for black workers.

Protection Through Citizen Involvement. Citizens themselves have worked to support civil rights. Acting in groups such as the NAACP and the American Civil Liberties Union, for example, citizens advocate the protection of individual liberties.

It has often been said that eternal vigilance is the price of liberty. This is especially true where civil rights are concerned. The very institutions that can protect our liberties can also limit them. The Supreme Court has handed down many decisions furthering civil rights, but it also ruled that relocation of Japanese American citizens during World War II was constitutional. Congress may liberalize our access to government documents, but it has also broadened the powers of the police to search citizens and listen to their conversations. President Abraham Lincoln signed the Emancipation Proclamation to free the slaves, but he also curtailed the civil liberties of northern dissidents during the Civil War.

Clearly, our rights are protected by the national government. And as citizens, we must exercise these rights in order to remain free.

1. What civil rights are protected by the Bill of Rights?
2. What role do the courts play in protecting our civil rights?
3. What part do Congress and the president play in supporting civil rights?
4. What can citizens do to protect their freedoms?

POLITICAL CONFLICT and CHANGE The history of civil rights in the United States is the story of many separate struggles. Some have involved heroic leaders who worked for years to accomplish noble goals. Many struggles were won because ordinary citizens were determined to be treated fairly.

A study of civil rights makes it clear that the American political system is not static but dynamic. Fundamental changes in civil rights lead to changes in the political system itself.

Political change is a result of activities which result in a different distribution of resources over time. To study change we need to block out two points in time. The next step is to determine the activities which produce differences in resources held by groups in the political system.

The growth of equal educational opportunity is an example of change. From the time of the *Plessy* v. *Ferguson* "separate but equal decision" in 1896 to the *Brown* v. *Board of Education* decision in 1954, there was a fundamental change in the civil rights of citizens in regard to equal educational opportunity. This change made a major impact on activities in the national political system. The change created new rules which determined where students would go to school and how school funds would be spent in providing students an education. The basic guidelines set by the 1954 Court decision regarding civil rights changed major federal policies and the distribution of resources and activities in the nation's schools.

When we look at changes that have been produced in the American political system, most have one central cause—conflict brought about by inequality in resources or activities. Most social changes begin because people become aware of inequalities in their treatment or in the resources they have. They then organize to improve their conditions. Their interests may clash with those who have the favored treatment or the larger share of resources, and conflict may result.

Conflict, which occurs when there is a confrontation in opposing interests, is a key factor in promoting change. For instance, before women gained the right to vote, they did not have resources that were equal to the resources of their male counterparts. Inequality produced conflict. *Suffragists*—advocates of the right to vote—campaigned for women's suffrage, and the confrontation produced a constitutional change. Resources were then distributed more equally.

For the sake of simplicity, we shall concentrate in this chapter on three key aspects of civil rights in the United States: the women's movement, the struggle of black Americans for equality, and changes in some of the basic liberties of all citizens. In each instance you will see how the president, Congress, and the courts interacted to bring about changes in civil rights, and how these affected the national political system. You will also see how citizen action has led to alterations in the political system.

1. How did the *Brown* v. *Board of Education* decision create change in our national political system?
2. In this chapter, you will read examples of how conflict can produce change. Describe several experiences of your own in which conflict produced change.

The Women's Movement

From the time of the first English settlements in the New World, American women were treated as second-class citizens. A woman could not vote, own property, sign a contract, or make a will. Women did not even have a right to custody of their own children in case of divorce. A married woman's legal status was chillingly summed up in the phrase applied to her—"civil death."

In the early decades of settlement—and for years after that in frontier communities—women worked at many different kinds of demanding jobs. They ran businesses, managed big farms, and practiced medicine. But when towns grew and men prospered, middle- and upper-class women were expected to remain at home, concentrating their attention on the "feminine" pursuits of child rearing and household management. (Black women, immigrants, and working-class women went right on working as hard as before.) As a group all women were regarded as weak, emotional, and inferior to men in intelligence.

From the early days of settlement until today, tremendous changes have been made in the rights and status of women. The following section traces the growth of gains for women. As you'll read, the women's movement of today has its roots in the first half of the 1800s.

FEMINISTS ORGANIZE

Feminism — the movement to gain equal rights for women—began in the reform era of the 1830s and 1840s. Women who took an active role in the abolitionist crusade realized how much discrimination they themselves suffered. In 1848, Lucretia Mott and Elizabeth Cady Stanton organized the Seneca Falls Convention. At that convention, delegates asserted, in a paraphrase of the Declaration of Independence, that "all men and women are created equal." They resolved that women should "have immediate admission to all the rights and privileges which belong to them as citizens of the United States."

The Struggle for Suffrage. Gains did come, but slowly. Several states granted women control over their own property. In New York, women also gained the right to sue in court. By the late 1800s, the efforts of most American feminists were directed toward securing *suffrage,* the right to vote. In 1869, Stanton and Susan B. Anthony organized the National Woman Suffrage Association, which worked to gain the vote and other reforms as well. That same year Lucy Stone and her husband, Henry Blackwell, founded the more conservative American Woman Suffrage Association, which concentrated all its efforts on winning voting rights for women. Both organizations were hampered by ridicule, lack of funds, and the fact that it was difficult for women—without the vote—to exercise meaningful pressure on elected representatives. (The two organizations united in 1890 to form the National American Woman Suffrage Association.)

New territories and states in the West were the first to grant women the vote—Wyoming in 1869; Colorado, Idaho, and

On October 23, 1915, over 20,000 women marched in New York City, demanding the right to vote.

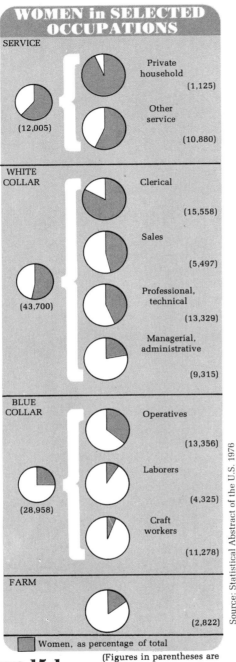

WOMEN in SELECTED OCCUPATIONS

SERVICE

Private household (1,125)

Other service (10,880)

(12,005)

WHITE COLLAR

Clerical (15,558)

Sales (5,497)

Professional, technical (13,329)

Managerial, administrative (9,315)

(43,700)

BLUE COLLAR

Operatives (13,356)

Laborers (4,325)

Craft workers (11,278)

(28,958)

FARM

(2,822)

☐ Women, as percentage of total

(Figures in parentheses are numbers of such workers, in thousands.)

Source: Statistical Abstract of the U.S. 1976

Figure 15-1

activity in the women's rights movement. But discrimination was far from over. Women were still expected to be subservient to men. If they worked away from home (and many did), they filled menial and service jobs and were paid less than men.

The Great Depression and World War II focused attention on economic problems and on the war effort. Only in the 1960s, with renewed civil rights activity on behalf of minorities, was there increased interest in extending the rights of women. This effort became known as the women's liberation movement.

The new phase of feminism was signaled by President Kennedy's appointment in 1960 of a Commission on the Status of Women. It recommended equal job opportunities, equal pay, and an end to legal discrimination. These goals were aided when the Civil Rights Act of 1964 prohibited discrimination, not only on the basis of race, but also on the basis of sex.

By the mid-1970s, women were entering politics and the professions in greater numbers. They had succeeded in liberalizing laws dealing with areas like credit and insurance. They were also working to end *sexism* (discrimination based on sex) in such areas as education and the mass media.

In 1973 Congress passed the Equal Rights Amendment. Hopeful of quick ratification by the states, feminists were disappointed when this did not happen. Many Americans—women's groups among them—opposed the amendment as unnecessary if not harmful.

Events of the 1970s showed that great progress had been made. However, for women and men committed to complete equality, there were still many barriers to overcome.

1. How were women discriminated against in the early decades of American history?
2. What are some gains which have been made in the 1900s?

Utah in the 1890s. Suffragists gradually won more followers to their cause until they gained victory with the ratification of the Nineteenth Amendment in 1920.

The Women's Liberation Movement. The period after 1920 was one of lessened

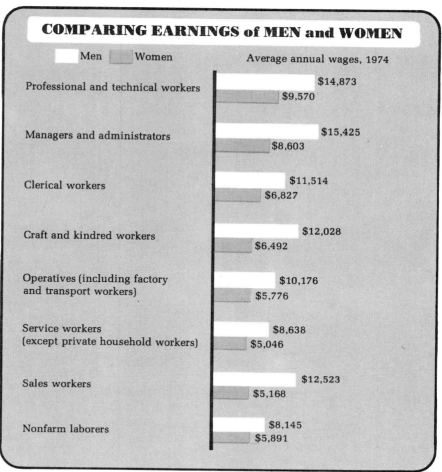

Figure 15-2

Source: U.S. Department of Labor, Women's Bureau 1976

CHANGE THROUGH the COURTS Some significant changes in the rights of citizens have been made as a result of legal actions, such as legislation or court decisions.

In the course of United States history, a number of civil rights have been expanded and broadened to include more people through the passage of constitutional amendments. The Thirteenth, Fourteenth, and Fifteenth Amendments are examples of such change. Congressional legislation has been another means by which civil rights guarantees have been extended. The Voting Rights Act of 1965 (page 464) is an example of this.

As you have read, people and groups can question the interpretation and applicability of laws by taking cases to court, usually starting at the state level. Court decisions can have a tremendous impact. Decisions made at the state level affect not only the people who are directly involved in the case but also all others in the state who are or who eventually will be in the situation under question in the courts. When cases are appealed to the Supreme Court, and when this Court hands down a ruling, the decision applies nationwide.

The following case study is an example of a case which began in the Idaho court system and was appealed to the United States Supreme Court. As you read, think about the implications this case could have beyond the immediate question it answered. How did the Court's decision affect the rights of women in general? How does the case demonstrate political change?

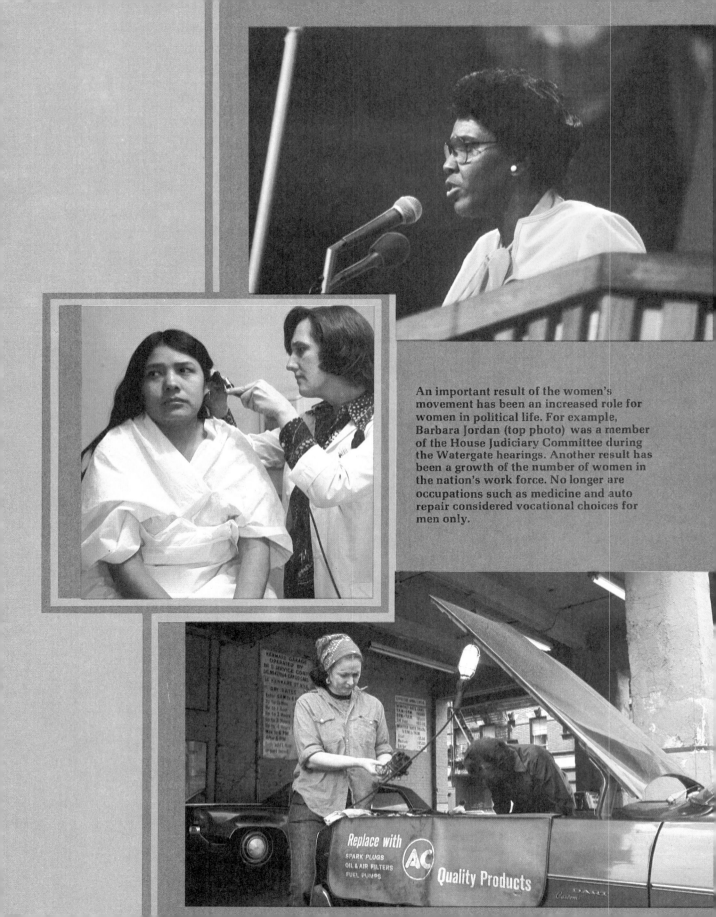

An important result of the women's movement has been an increased role for women in political life. For example, Barbara Jordan (top photo) was a member of the House Judiciary Committee during the Watergate hearings. Another result has been a growth of the number of women in the nation's work force. No longer are occupations such as medicine and auto repair considered vocational choices for men only.

★ Why Not a Woman?

The subject was not exciting in itself, but it set an important precedent for women's rights. It concerned an *estate*—the property and possessions left by someone who dies. Idaho had a law establishing a preference for men over women as administrators of estates. If, after someone died, a man and a woman were equally qualified to handle the estate, the man was automatically appointed.

Sally and Cecil Reed were the parents of Richard Reed. When he died in childhood, both parents—then legally separated—asked to be administrators of his estate. The right was given to Cecil Reed. Sally Reed challenged the automatic preference on the grounds that it violated the equal protection clause of the Fourteenth Amendment. Eventually the case reached the Idaho Superior Court, which denied Sally Reed's petition. Mrs. Reed then appealed to the United States Supreme Court. In 1971 the Court ruled unanimously that Idaho's law favoring men over women was unconstitutional. The Court returned the case to the Idaho Superior Court for a new decision. That court then made Sally Reed co-executor of the estate, with Cecil Reed.

Chief Justice Warren Burger wrote the opinion of the Court:

"The arbitrary preference established in favor of males by the Idaho code cannot stand on the basis of the Fourteenth Amendment's command that no states deny the equal protection of the law to any person within its jurisdiction."

Justice Burger made the following distinction: It is true that most laws discriminate. They apply to some groups of people and not to others. For example, if the state gives medical benefits to persons over 65, it discriminates, or makes a distinction, between persons over 65 and younger people. If the state gives social security payments only to people who have worked, it discriminates between those who have held paying jobs and those who have not.

Laws of this sort automatically discriminate between groups. But the real test is whether it is reasonable for the state to provide medical benefits for older people, or social security for workers. When such discrimination is arbitrary and serves no legitimate purpose, it is illegal.

This is what the decision meant in the case of *Reed* v. *Reed.* The Reeds were both competent adults living in similar circumstances. The only reason for discriminating against Sally Reed was her sex, which was irrelevant in this particular situation. Idaho's law was unconstitutional—and so were other laws that discriminated arbitrarily on the basis of sex alone.

1. On what grounds did Sally Reed take her case to court?
2. What was the conflict in this case?
3. In *Reed* v. *Reed,* how did the Supreme Court create change in the American political system?

The Struggle for Black Equality

While women from the beginning of American history were second-class citizens, they were at least citizens. Most black people were not. No single group in the United States has suffered so much from oppression and arbitrary discrimination. The continuing struggle for black equality has been a long and difficult one.

CHANGES over TIME   Black people first came to this country from Africa as either indentured servants or as slaves. *Indentured servants* were bound to work for their masters for a certain length of time. After the time of service was completed, they were given their freedom. In addition, many thousands of black Africans were captured and brought to this country to work as slaves.

The Constitution provides clear evidence of the legal status accorded to blacks. Article I, Section 3, established that every slave was to be counted as 3/5 of a free person for purposes of determining the number of representatives each state was to have in the House of Representatives.

The Abolitionist Movement. Beginning in the early 1800s, the movement to abolish slavery took hold. It gained supporters particularly in the North, although abolitionist societies did exist in the South. In a sense, early abolitionists can be thought of as among the first civil rights organizers in this country.

Through the mid-1800s, almost all blacks in the United States were slaves. Though not uniformly ill-treated, they were allowed no civil rights. It was even illegal in some states to teach slaves how to read and write. The few free blacks faced many barriers: job and housing discrimination and, in many states, denial of the right to vote.

As time went on, slavery became the most divisive issue in American life. It culminated in the Civil War (though the aim of many northerners, at least in the beginning, was not to free the slaves, but to restore the Union). When President Lincoln signed the Emancipation Proclamation in 1863, few slaves actually won their freedom. This did not happen until 1865, when the war ended and the Thirteenth Amendment was ratified.

At first, black Americans seemed to be making progress. They were granted citizenship by the Fourteenth Amendment, and the vote by the Fifteenth Amendment. In the South (where most blacks lived), many voted and took part in politics. Schools set up by the Freedmen's Bureau taught basic skills.

Jim Crow. A reaction to black participation soon set in. White southerners, at first kept out of government by the Reconstruction policies of the North, gradually won complete control of their states. They began a systematic program to assure white supremacy. "Jim Crow" laws (so-called after a minstrel-show song) aimed for total segregation—in schools, churches, libraries, and all other public accommodations. There were even separate Bibles for blacks to swear on in court. Black people were given low-paying jobs, and their children were denied many educational opportunities.

At the same time, most blacks were deprived of the vote through complicated literacy tests, poll taxes, and other tricks that evaded the Fifteenth Amendment. Terrorism by organizations such as the Ku Klux Klan created fear among blacks. The Supreme Court's *Plessy* v. *Ferguson* decision in 1896 further supported the separation of races.

Black Americans did not accept their second-class status passively. Educators like Booker T. Washington stressed job training and skills to raise the Negro from poverty. W. E. B. Du Bois and other black leaders believed in more direct political action. In the early 1900s they launched the Niagara Movement, aimed at ending Jim Crow discrimination in all its forms. In 1909, when some members of this group met in a large conference with other sympathizers (among them many whites), a new organization emerged, the National Association for the Advancement of Colored People (NAACP). In its early years the NAACP worked to prevent violence against blacks, to guard against unjust legal punishments for black people, and to eliminate job discrimination. The Urban League, founded in 1910, concentrated on improving social and economic conditions for black people.

Progress was slow. There was some economic improvement as blacks began to move north in large numbers during and after World War I. Supreme Court rulings in the 1930s and 1940s broadened educational opportunities for a few blacks. One ruling held, for example, that a state could not deny a black applicant admission to law school. World War II, with its high employment, benefited black workers.

Integration. A landmark in the struggle for black equality was the Supreme Court's 1954 decision in the case of *Brown v. Board of Education of Topeka.* Its ruling opposing school segregation spelled the beginning of the end for official segregation in many other aspects of American life. A new generation of black leaders arose. The best known was the Reverend Martin Luther King, Jr., who first came to prominence in the Montgomery bus boycott of 1956.

King advocated *civil disobedience*— peaceful protests against official policies believed to be unjust. This approach was followed by such newly formed organizations as the Southern Christian Leadership Conference (SCLC) and the Student Nonviolent Coordinating Committee (SNCC). The strong civil rights movement of the 1960s featured *sit-ins* (at lunch counters and similar places that would not serve blacks), *freedom rides* (on interstate transport that segregated blacks), and other demonstrations in favor of broadening black rights. The huge "March on Washington" in August 1963 brought thousands of Americans together to dramatize the cause. King's "I have a dream" speech symbolized the hopes of all those who participated.

President Johnson took the lead in the mid-1960s by exerting strong pressure on Congress to pass two legislative breakthroughs: the Civil Rights Act of 1964 and the Voting Rights Act of 1965. The former prohibited racial discrimination in public accommodations and labor unions. The latter suspended literacy tests and empowered federal examiners to investigate areas where blacks were virtually excluded from voting. The result was greatly increased black voter registration in many states and the election of a number of blacks to public office.

Economic and Social Issues. In the late 1960s, the black civil rights movement underwent a dramatic change. Early in the decade, civil rights leaders had stressed integration and achievement of political rights through legal and nonviolent actions. In the second half of the decade, attention focused on economic and social issues. Splinter groups such as the Black Panthers and the Black Muslims advocated an ideology based on black power and community control of educational and economic programs. The expression "black is beautiful" was heard often, and ethnic pride itself became an issue.

The shift in emphasis in the civil rights movement was caused by several factors.

During the 1960s, protests against Jim Crow laws and other forms of discrimination helped black Americans make gains in their struggle for civil rights.

Although many gains had been achieved in terms of legislation, these laws did not automatically change the status of blacks in America. The levels of income and employment among blacks were still far below those of whites. Moreover, during the 50s and 60s, an increasing number of blacks had become concentrated in urban ghettos. As a result, by the late 60s, the inner cities were centers of black poverty and unrest.

Because of poor social and economic conditions, some black groups no longer upheld the idea of nonviolent protest. The Black Panthers, for example, advocated militancy and an end to what they considered a subservient image of black Americans. During these years riots broke out in several western and northern cities, including Los Angeles, Detroit, Newark, and Washington. Unrest was agitated even more by the assassination of several important black leaders—Black Muslim leader Malcolm X, NAACP leader Medgar Evers, and Martin Luther King, Jr.

As a result of the violence, the President's Advisory Commission on Civil Disorders was established. Based on its investigations of urban riots, the Commission concluded that unless something was done in the next two decades, it would be impossible to unite black and white Americans.

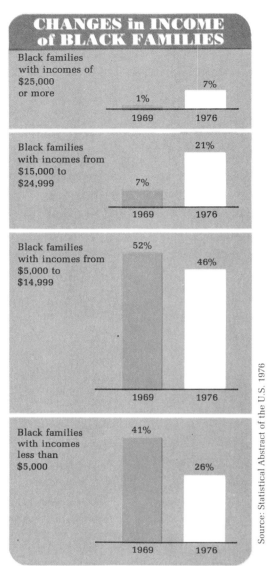

Figure 15-4 Figures are rounded percentage of total number of black families in the United States.

Figure 15-3

BLACK ELECTED OFFICIALS, 1969 to 1978	
Year	Total
1970	1,472
1971	1,860
1972	2,264
1973	2,621
1974	2,991
1975	3,503
1976	3,979
1977	4,311
1978	4,503

Source: Statistical Abstract of the U.S. 1978

Acting on the Commission's findings, the government began to set up programs to improve the economic and social conditions of black Americans. In this way, the laws of the 60s could be more fully realized.

During the 1970s, blacks continued to improve their situation, but at a slower rate than during the 60s. The average income of black families almost doubled. More blacks were in college than ever before. And the number of elected black officials greatly increased—from 103 in 1964 to 4,503 in 1978. However, problems still persisted. Some people resisted strongly the idea of busing to

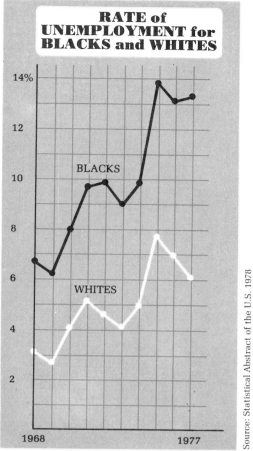

RATE of UNEMPLOYMENT for BLACKS and WHITES

BLACKS

WHITES

14%

12

10

8

6

4

2

1968   1977

Source: Statistical Abstract of the U.S. 1978

Figure 15-5

achieve racial integration in schools. Still others objected to filling employment and educational openings by the quota system. Even though black income increased, the gap widened between the average salary of whites and the average salary of blacks. Moreover, the jobless rate among blacks almost doubled during the 70s. Therefore, although the civil rights movement had achieved many of its goals, serious problems have persisted and may remain as issues during the 1980s.

1. What measures were taken to keep black Americans in a subordinate position after the Civil War?

2. What progress was made for black Americans in the early 1900s?

3. What actions were taken on behalf of black civil rights in the 1960s and 1970s? What gains were made? What problems remain?

FOCUS for ACTION In the 1960s and 1970s the areas of voting rights and busing have been the focus of important legal action and human struggle.

Voting Rights. In the mid-1960s, there were some areas in southern states where only a tiny fraction of the total black population was allowed to vote. One of these was Selma, Alabama. According to the 1960 census, there were 14,400 whites and 15,115 blacks living in the town. Of the 9,877 registered voters, 9,542 were white and 335 were black. In other words, 66 percent of the white residents, but only 2 percent of the black residents, were registered. Between May 1962 and August 1964, only 93 of the 795 blacks who tried to register were accepted as voters, compared to 945 of the 1,232 whites who applied.

The situation was summed up by President Johnson:

"Every device of which human ingenuity is capable has been used to deny voting rights. The Negro citizen may go to register, only to be told that the day is wrong, or the hour is late, or the official in charge is absent. And if he persists, and if he manages to present himself to the registrar, he may be disqualified because he did not spell out his middle name, or he abbreviated a word on the application. And if he manages to fill out the application, he is given a test. The registrar is the sole judge of whether he passes this test. He may be asked to recite the entire Constitution, or to explain the most complex provisions of statutory law. And even a college degree cannot be used to prove that he can read and write."

President Johnson put his feelings into action by asking Congress to pass a voting rights act which would prevent such discrimination. As you read the following case, think about the legal process used to promote civil rights.

★ The Voting Rights Act of 1965

In 1965, Martin Luther King and members of the SCLC and SNCC selected Selma as a target city in their efforts to win increased voting rights for black Americans. They began protest marches in January 1965 and continued them for several weeks. There was fierce opposition, as the county sheriff's police used tear gas, whips, and clubs against the demonstrators. A black civil rights worker was killed, and so was a white minister. Finally, Governor George Wallace ordered troops in to stop the marchers.

The President was angry. Clearly, events were reaching a dangerous stage. The turning point came in March, when people assembled in Selma from all over the country. With King in the lead, more than 30,000 people marched the 54 miles to Montgomery, the state capital. It took them five days. Along the way more than 80 people were injured by sheriffs' posses. Johnson ordered in 3,000 federal troops to protect the marchers.

At this critical time a voting rights bill was introduced in Congress. Its major provisions suspended literacy tests in many areas, called on the federal attorney general to appoint federal examiners where there were voting violations, and set criminal penalties for interference in the voting process. The bill passed the House with a margin of 170 to 28 votes, and the Senate by 79 to 18. It was signed into law on August 6, 1965, and became known as the Voting Rights Act of 1965.

President Johnson spoke for many Americans when he praised the black people of the United States:

> "The real hero of this struggle is the American Negro. His actions and protests, his courage to risk safety, and even to risk his life, have awakened the conscience of this nation. His demonstrations have been designed to call attention to injustice, designed to provoke change, designed to stir reform.
>
> He has called upon us to make good the promise of America. And who among us can say that we would have made the same progress were it not for his persistent bravery and his faith in American democracy?"

School Desegregation and Busing. The *Brown* decision outlawed "separate but equal" facilities for black and white students in schools across the nation. But problems still remained. How were localities to achieve desegregated schools when neighborhoods continued to be either mainly

The march of thousands of people from Selma to Montgomery, Alabama, in 1965 was an important development in gaining passage of the Voting Rights Act.

The success of the civil rights movement of the 1960s prompted other groups in American society to demand their full civil rights. Among them are Native Americans (top photo), Hispanic Americans (center photo), and Asian Americans (bottom photo).

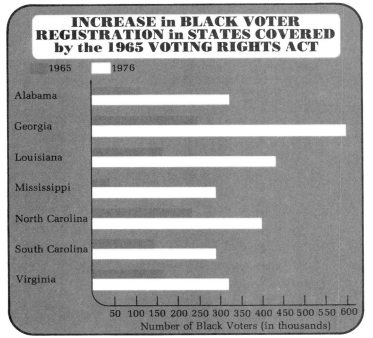

INCREASE in BLACK VOTER REGISTRATION in STATES COVERED by the 1965 VOTING RIGHTS ACT

1965 ☐ 1976

Alabama
Georgia
Louisiana
Mississippi
North Carolina
South Carolina
Virginia

50 100 150 200 250 300 350 400 450 500 550 600
Number of Black Voters (in thousands)

Figure 15-6

Source: Voter Education Project, Inc. Atlanta, Georgia.

Charlotte schools, was among those who argued that the formula was unconstitutional. Swann and others took their complaints to the federal district court. When the district court ruled against the plaintiffs, they appealed to the Supreme Court.

In 1971 the Supreme Court, in *Swann* v. *Charlotte-Mecklenburg County Board of Education,* unanimously upheld the earlier decision. The justices said that school systems could use racial quotas in unifying their school districts. They could use other formulas as well, even redrawing district boundaries in order to make schools more fully integrated. The Court, in approving the Charlotte guidelines, did not want to require any particular racial mix or formula for achieving unified schools.

The importance of the *Swann* decision was the Supreme Court's establishment of the constitutionality of busing students to accomplish a racial balance. In essence, the decision dealt a blow to the opponents of "forced busing." In a characteristic way, the Court had reaffirmed its strong civil rights stand. Legislatures and executives might quarrel and take issue with various school desegregation formulas, but the Court's position was clear. Now Americans had a further guideline for implementing the *Brown* decision.

black or mainly white, and when most students attended neighborhood schools? Was it necessary to bus students out of their neighborhoods in order to achieve racial balance? Was it legal to do so? This solution had worked in many areas. But there was also strong, sometimes bitter, opposition to "forced busing."

In the following case, a Supreme Court decision on busing is described. On what basis do you think the justices made their decision?

★ **A Decision on Busing**

The Charlotte-Mecklenburg school system in North Carolina had worked out a formula for achieving integrated schools. It had set up a ratio of 71 percent white to 29 percent black students in its schools. And it planned to institute busing in order to arrive at this particular racial balance. Mr. James E. Swann, a parent whose children attended

1. How did the Voting Rights Act result from efforts by involved citizens? the President? Congress?

2. In what way did the *Swann* decision clarify *Brown* v. *Board of Education of Topeka*?

3. How did conflict promote change in each of these cases?

4. Which of these two actions do you think was more important in changing the political system? Why?

5. According to Figure 15-6, how did the Voting Rights Act influence black voter registration?

6. Using Figures 15-3, 15-4, and 15-5 as evidence, state an hypothesis on how the status of black Americans is changing.

466

Civil Rights: Hispanic Americans

Spanish-speaking, or Hispanic, Americans make up the fastest growing ethnic minority in the United States in the 1970s. The black population is the only larger group. Census figures from March 1977 show a total of more than 11 million Hispanic Americans. This figure includes the following groups: 6,545,000 Mexican Americans; 1,742,000 Puerto Ricans; 681,000 Cubans; 872,000 Central and South Americans; and 1,428,000 "other Spanish." According to census estimates, Hispanic Americans will be the nation's largest minority group by 1990.

The various groups of Hispanic Americans share a common language and in many cases a similar cultural heritage. They also differ in significant ways such as where they live in the United States and why they have come here. Most Cubans, for example, live in the Miami, Florida, area. They have come to the United States as political refugees from the Castro regime. A majority of Puerto Ricans, on the other hand, live in the metropolitan area of New York. As American citizens they have come to the United States mainly for economic opportunity, and many return to Puerto Rico to live.

The largest number of Spanish-speaking people in the United States are Mexican Americans. The second largest ethnic minority group in the nation, they live mainly in the southwestern United States. Some Mexican Americans are the descendants of families that settled in the Southwest hundreds of years ago. Others—or their parents or grandparents—came to the United States in the first half of this century, escaping revolution and poverty in Mexico. The more recent immigrants have come mainly in search of jobs.

In the past, language acted as a strong barrier for Mexican Americans, often leading to the denial of civil rights. Mexican American citizens could not vote because of English literacy requirements. Children were unable to succeed in schools because English was the sole language of instruction. Due process was often frustrated by lack of understanding of legal proceedings conducted in English. Economic and social discrimination were added to these problems.

After World War II conditions improved for some Mexican Americans. But it was the black civil rights movement of the 1960s that gave the strongest impetus and inspiration to Mexican Americans. A new ethnic pride grew and Mexican Americans began to join together to fight for equal rights and greater power. The name "Chicano," which had been used as a slang term, was given positive meaning. It was equated with cultural and political awareness. The Chicano movement asked that Mexican Americans be recognized as bilingual and that educational, voting, and judicial laws reflect the rights of Spanish-speaking Americans.

In the 1970s important gains were achieved through legislation and court action. The 1970 Bilingual Education Act was the result of a Supreme Court case declaring that all children in the United States must be guaranteed the right to education in their native language while they are learning to speak English. Another Supreme Court case held that all grand juries must reflect a cross-section of the communities they serve. The 1975 Voting Rights Act mandated bilingual election materials and ballots. An increase in Mexican American elected officials reflects these gains.

In the past, differences kept the various groups of Hispanic Americans from uniting to fight discrimination and improve conditions. In recent years, however, this is changing. Many experts predict that a Latino movement of all Spanish-speaking people in the United States will be the strongest civil rights force in the near future.

Civil Rights: Asian Americans

In the past most Asian Americans were of Chinese or Japanese descent. Recently, however, new groups of Asians have come to the United States—primarily from the Philippines, Korea, Vietnam, Cambodia, and other countries in Southeast Asia. According to the last national census report there were 591,290 people of Japanese descent living the United States, 435,062 people of Chinese descent, and 343,060 of Philippine descent. According to later statistics, 144,758 refugees from South Vietnam, Laos, and Cambodia were admitted to the United States between April 1975 and March 1977.

Most of the first Chinese immigrants to the United States were men who came after the discovery of gold in California in 1848. Others came to build the Western railroads in the 1860s. They were well received at first, but they met hostility when they moved into cities. Because of discrimination they were forced to live together in certain sections of a city, which became know as "Chinatown."

The United States and China signed a treaty in 1868 which protected the immigration of Chinese workers to the United States. However, many American laborers resented the Chinese laborers. In the 1870s resentment increased to the point where there were riots, demonstrations, and even murders in several western states. In response to this hostility Congress passed a series of Oriental Exclusion Acts in 1882, 1888, and 1892. These laws prevented Chinese from entering the United States to live or work.

The early period of Japanese immigration was in the 1880s and 1890s. Many Japanese immigrants settled on the West Coast and became farmers, often underselling white farmers. In response, a movement was begun to drive the Japanese from farming in California. In a step similar to that taken against the Chinese, the United States and Japan arrived at a "gentlemen's agreement" in 1907. This restricted Japanese immigration to this country. The Immigration Act of 1924 went even further, and officially prohibited the entry of all Asian laborers.

During World War II Congress repealed restrictions against the Chinese. However, since the United States was at war with Japan, restrictions against the Japanese were increased. More than 100,000 Japanese citizens and American citizens of Japanese descent were held in detention camps because the government deemed them a threat to the internal security of the nation. This was a time of great sorrow for the Japanese American citizens in the United States, who suffered loss of property, humiliation, and the suspension of many of their rights as citizens.

By 1965 all discriminatory laws restricting Oriental immigration and citizenship had been repealed. In many ways Asian Americans have benefited from civil rights struggles such as the black civil rights movement. Voting rights acts and laws requiring bilingual education have helped Asian Americans exercise their civil rights. Higher job status and an increase in Asian American elected officials are gains that have far reaching effects.

Although Asian Americans today technically have all the civil rights due any American citizen, many still suffer from discrimination and ethnic isolation. However, many young Asian Americans have become more militant than their elders and have actively fought the acceptance of stereotyped roles.

Civil Rights: Native Americans

According to census reports which are admittedly an undercount, about 793,000 people consider themselves to be Native Americans. They represent about 400 recognized and unrecognized tribal groups that exist in the United States today. Of the total Native American population, about half live in or near one of the hundreds of state or federal reservations.

In the past, Native Americans have been denied many of the rights guaranteed to other Americans. Legislation, wars, and treaties forced them to give up their lands and relocate on federally controlled reservations. As reservation residents, most Native Americans were considered "wards of the government." All decisions about reservation life were made by departments of the federal government. Denied the right to vote, and with numbers too small to make a difference, Native Americans could do little to change this situation.

During the 1920s and 1930s, the federal government took the first steps toward increasing the rights of Native Americans. The 1924 Indian

Citizenship Act extended citizenship and voting rights to all Native Americans. In 1934, Native Americans were given a limited opportunity for self-rule, and sale of reservation lands by the federal Bureau of Indian Affairs was slowed down. In the same year, other legislation opened the way for federal funding of educational, agricultural, and welfare projects on reservations.

Although these acts were important precedents, they did not ensure equal rights for Native Americans. It was difficult to enforce federal laws on the local level. Many officials considered reservations to be separate governments outside of constitutional protection. As a result, it became apparent to some tribal leaders that civil rights could be achieved only through organization of Native Americans. Attempting to achieve this goal, leaders from over 50 tribes met in 1944 to form the National Congress of American Indians. Through this organization, Native Americans began to lobby for needed legislation and programs.

To accomplish their goals, some groups began to urge tribes to be more forceful. Demonstrations and protests were organized to publicize demands. In 1964, the Puyllup River "fish-in" dramatized claims to natural resources guaranteed by treaty. In 1968, two young Native Americans, Dennis Banks and Clyde Bellecourt, formed the activist American Indian Movement (AIM) for the purpose of promoting "Indian Power." In the same year, the occupation of Alcatraz prison highlighted the demand for the return of lands guaranteed to Native Americans by government treaties. In 1973, the 71-day seige of Wounded Knee and the ensuing battles between the Oglala Sioux, federal troops, and the FBI focused national attention on the Native American civil rights movement.

As a result of protests, court cases, and lobbying efforts, Native Americans have preserved some of their rights. In an effort to define the rights of Native Americans on reservations, Congress passed the 1968 Indian Bill of Rights. With the 1975 Indian Self-Determination and Educational Assistance Act, Congress recognized the right of tribal councils to supervise most businesses, schools, police forces, and public building projects on reservations. Recent court decisions have allowed some tribes to regain control over valuable natural resources on their lands.

Despite these victories, most experts agree that there are still many problems confronting the native peoples of America. Forty percent of Native Americans are unemployed. Most of those working hold low-paying jobs with an average yearly per capita income of $1,600. The education, medical care, and housing available to many reservation residents are substandard. Moreover, as Native Americans seek to regain control of treaty lands, resistance among some non-Indian groups is growing. Ultimately, the future of Native Americans will be influenced by the willingness of the federal government to commit funds to reservation projects and by battles in the courts over land titles and enforcement of existing civil rights legislation.

Changes in Basic Liberties

In dealing with the history of women and blacks in the United States, this discussion has emphasized the government as a *protector* of civil rights. In particular, the government has acted to protect the right to vote and the right to equal opportunity.

Another area of concern is that of First Amendment freedoms and other constitutional guarantees for all citizens. If you look at the Bill of Rights, you will see that these freedoms are often worded in the form of a prohibition—"Congress shall make no law . . . abridging the freedom of speech," for example. In such instances government power is viewed as a possible danger that must be *restrained*. The rights thus protected against government interference—freedom of expression and worship, the rights of the accused, and so on—are often known as civil liberties.

CHANGES over TIME In a few instances, usually in wartime, the national government has taken steps to limit individual freedom. This happened in 1798, when Federalists in Congress passed the four Alien and Sedition Acts, restricting freedom of expression. These laws were aimed at silencing Republican opponents. (The Federalists felt that the Republicans were friendly to France, at that time engaged in a sort of undeclared war against the United States.) Republican leaders Thomas Jefferson and James Madison drafted the Virginia and Kentucky Resolutions, attacking the laws as violations of free speech. At this time the Supreme Court had not handed down its historic decision (*Marbury* v. *Madison*) that first declared an act of Congress unconstitutional. As it turned out, three of the Alien and Sedition Acts lapsed, and the fourth was soon repealed.

During the Civil War, President Lincoln suspended the writ of habeas corpus.

(*Habeas corpus* is a written court order requiring legal officials who are holding a person in custody to bring the prisoner to court and to cite reasons for the prisoner's detention. Habeas corpus prevents people from being imprisoned unnecessarily for extended periods of time.) Because of President Lincoln's action, many civilian offenders were tried in military courts. This denial of a fair trial was declared unconstitutional in 1866.

After the United States entered World War I in 1917, Congress passed the Espionage Act, aimed at punishing Americans who hindered the war effort. This law resulted in the case of *Schenck* v. *United States* (1919), in which Justice Oliver Wendell Holmes held that Schenck's actions had created a "clear and present danger" to the nation. (Schenck, who was secretary of the Communist party in the United States, had mailed out thousands of flyers to American men being called into military service during World War I, urging them to resist.)

As far as the average citizen's civil liberties were concerned, however, the national government did not play an active role in the 1800s. It was widely believed that protecting these freedoms was up to the individual states. In 1833 the Supreme Court ruled specifically on this issue. In a case involving a state's violation of the Fifth Amendment (*Barron* v. *Baltimore*), the Court held that the Bill of Rights applied only to the national government.

This view did not change until the twentieth century. Then, in *Gitlow* v. *New York* (1925), the Supreme Court for the first time held that First Amendment freedoms are guaranteed to all citizens by the Fourteenth Amendment. In other words, a state that abridges a citizen's freedom of speech, for example, is depriving that individual of "due process of law." A number of decisions extended this protection to most First Amendment guarantees.

The Court was slower to apply the Fourteenth Amendment in cases having to do with the rights of accused persons, because it did not want to interfere with state judicial procedures. Beginning in the late 1940s, however, a series of decisions held that the states had to guarantee accused persons the same rights that the national government did.

During the 1950s and 1960s the Warren Court made a number of significant decisions involving civil liberties—especially those concerning the rights of the accused—such as the *Miranda* case. The chart of landmark cases on pages 434–435 outlines some of those decisions.

1. Describe three instances in which the national government restricted civil liberties. Why do you think it did so?
2. How did Supreme Court rulings in the 1900s change the application of the Bill of Rights?

MAJOR COURT DECISIONS

The cases that follow involve major court decisions in the field of civil liberties. As you read them, think about how the rights of citizens were affected.

★ What Limits to Free Speech?

In 1940, after World War II had broken out in Europe, Congress passed the Smith Act. Aimed at prohibiting subversive activities, the law made it illegal to advocate overthrowing the United States government or to organize any group that encouraged such action.

There were few prosecutions under the Smith Act until after World War II was over. Then, with the Soviet Union overrunning much of Eastern Europe, Communism seemed a dangerous threat. (One Communist teaching is that the working class should bring about revolution by force.) In 1948 Eugene Dennis, secretary general of the Communist Party of the United States, and 10 other members of the party were convicted by a New York District Court for violating the Smith Act.

What Dennis had done was to serve as a principal officer of the American Communist party. Under his direction, groups had met to talk about Communist doctrine and to consider ways in which they might strengthen the party in the United States. For holding these types of meetings, the New York court found Dennis guilty of threatening a "clear and present danger" to the American government. The decision of this court was upheld by a Circuit Court of Appeals, where Judge Learned Hand argued that the conspiracy formed by the Communist party could lead the United States into another war.

At this point the case went on to the Supreme Court on the grounds that the Smith Act was an unconstitutional limit on free speech. In 1951, in *Dennis v. United States*, the earlier rulings were upheld by a 6 to 2 decision. Chief Justice Fred Vinson wrote the majority opinion:

"The defendants have been convicted of conspiring to organize a party of persons who advocate the overthrow of the government by force and violence. The jury has found that the object of the conspiracy is advocacy as a rule or principle of action by language reasonably and ordinarily calculated to incite persons to such action, and with the intent to cause the overthrow 'as speedily as circumstances would permit.' On any scale of values which we have hitherto recognized, speech of this sort ranks low."

Chief Justice Vinson clearly felt that the mere organization of a group for the purposes of discussing adverse values constituted a danger. Justice Hugo Black disagreed in a fiery dissent:

"At the outset, I want to emphasize what the crime involved in this case is and what it is not. These petitioners were not charged with an attempt to overthrow the government. They were not charged with overt acts of any kind designed to overthrow the government. They were not even charged with saying anything or writing anything designed to overthrow the government. The charge was that they agreed to assemble and to talk and publish certain ideas at a later [time] . . . . No matter how it is worded, this is a virulent form of prior censorship of speech and press, which I believe the First Amendment forbids."

The second dissenter, Justice William O. Douglas, made a similar point: "We deal here with speech alone, not with speech *plus* acts of sabotage or unlawful conduct. Not a single seditious act is charged in the indictment."

★ Obscenity Yes, Due Process No

Late one night in May 1957, Cleveland, Ohio, police officers heard that a bombing case suspect and betting equipment might be found in the home of a woman named Dollree Mapp. The police forced their way into Ms. Mapp's home under protest. When she tried to stop them from searching her house, they handcuffed her and continued.

The officers, who had no search warrant, did not find what they were looking for. But finally, in a basement trunk, they did find books and pictures described as "lewd and lascivious." Possession of such property violated an Ohio law, and Mapp was found guilty in a Cleveland court. Her case was then appealed to the state supreme court, which upheld the earlier decision. The Ohio Supreme Court ruled that state law did not require law officers to exclude evidence that they had obtained illegally. And it was the state that had jurisdiction over this case.

Mapp v. *Ohio* then went to the Supreme Court. In 1961, by a 5 to 4 majority, it overturned the earlier decision. Forcibly obtaining evidence without a search warrant, ruled the Court, was illegal. Mapp had been unfairly tried and denied due process under the Fourteenth Amendment.

In delivering the majority opinion, Justice Tom Clark wrote, "We have no hesitation in saying that were a state affirmatively to sanction such police incursion into privacy, it would run counter to the guarantee of the Fourteenth Amendment." He made this basic point:

"Having once recognized that the right . . . to be secure against rude invasions of privacy by state officers is constitutional in origin, we can no longer permit that right to remain an empty promise. . . . Our decision, founded on reason and truth, gives to the individual no more than that which the Constitution guarantees him."

There were several important dissents in the *Mapp* case. One, by Justice John Harlan, stated:

"The ultimate result is compelled uniformity, which is inconsistent with the purpose of our federal system and which is achieved either by encroachment on the states' sovereign powers or by dilution in federal law enforcement of specific protections found in the Bill of Rights. . . . If the power of the states to deal with local crimes is unduly restricted, the likely consequence is a shift of responsibility in this area to the federal government with its vastly greater resources. Such a shift will tend to weaken the very liberties which the Fourteenth Amendment safeguards by bringing us closer to the monolithic society which our federalism rejects."

1. In *Dennis* v. *United States,* what was the reasoning behind the Supreme Court's decision? On what grounds did Justices Black and Douglas dissent?

2. What provision of the Bill of Rights was involved in the *Mapp* case? What were the main arguments of Justices Clark and Harlan, as presented in this discussion of the case?

3. What conflicts were involved in these cases?

4. What change resulted from the *Mapp* v. *Ohio* decision? What far-reaching effects could be expected from this decision?

★ **Gideon's Right to Counsel**

The case of *Gideon* v. *Wainwright* (1963) is another major civil rights case. It involved a man who was charged with breaking into and entering a poolroom with intent to commit a misdemeanor.

The following is from the Supreme Court decision, written by Justice Black.

"[Mr. Gideon] was charged in a Florida state court with having broken into and entered a poolroom with attempt to commit a misdemeanor. This offense is a felony under Florida law. Appearing in court without funds and without a lawyer, petitioner asked the court to appoint counsel for him. Whereupon the following colloquy took place:

The Court: Mr. Gideon, I'm sorry but I cannot appoint Counsel to represent you in this case. Under the laws of the State of Florida, the only time the Court can appoint Counsel to represent a Defendant is when that person is charged with a capital offense [where the defendant could be sentenced to death if found guilty]. I am sorry, but I will have to deny your request to appoint Counsel to defend you in this case.

The Defendant: The United States Supreme Court says I am entitled to be represented by Counsel."

In a trial before a jury, Gideon conducted his own defense, without legal counsel. He made an opening statement to the jury, cross-examined the state's witnesses, and presented witnesses in his own defense. He made a brief summation emphasizing that he was innocent of the charges brought against him. A prosecutor representing the state of Florida presented evidence to prove Gideon's guilt. After weighing all the evidence, the jury returned a verdict of guilty, and Gideon was sentenced to serve five years in the state prison.

Gideon filed a petition in the Florida Supreme Court attacking his conviction. He claimed that the trial court's refusal to appoint counsel for him denied him rights guaranteed by the Constitution and the Bill of Rights.

In 1963 the Supreme Court ruled in Gideon's favor. They said that in any criminal prosecution a defendant has the right to the assistance of legal counsel. Furthermore, the state must provide free legal counsel to any person accused of a felony who cannot afford a lawyer.

Justice Black wrote the Supreme Court opinion in this case. The following is from his opinion.

"The right of one charged with crime to counsel may not be deemed fundamental and essential to fair trials in some countries, but it is in ours. From the very beginning, our state and national constitutions and laws have laid great emphasis on procedural and substantive safeguards designed to assure fair trials before impartial tribunals in which every defendant stands equal before the law. This noble ideal cannot be realized if the poor man charged with crime has to face his accusers without a lawyer to assist him."

The Supreme Court *remanded,* or sent back, to the Florida Supreme Court the Gideon case. Gideon was given a new trial in Florida with a court-appointed counsel; he was acquitted and set free.

During the 1960s, many Americans used their Constitutional right to freedom of speech and assembly to protest United States involvement in the Vietnam War.

★ **Mary Beth Tinker Goes to Court**

In 1965, President Lyndon Johnson ordered American ground troops to Southeast Asia to help the government of South Vietnam in a war with Communist forces. Many citizens backed the President, but many others criticized our part in the Vietnam War.

In December 1965, sharp differences of opinion about the Vietnam War surfaced in Des Moines, Iowa. A group of high school students presented a statement criticizing American involvement in Vietnam to the editors of the Roosevelt High School newspaper. They asked the editors to print their message, which gave their reasons for opposing the presence of American troops in Vietnam. The statement also called for students who had antiwar opinions to wear black arm-bands to school as a sign of protest. The school's journalism teacher told the editor not to print the statement.

The next day, school officials in Des Moines met to discuss student protest against the war. They decided that students could not wear arm-bands to school. They said the schools were no place for political demonstration. Rather, free discussion of issues should take place in classes. They announced that any students protesting the Vietnam War by wearing arm-bands in school would be punished.

The following day, Mary Beth Tinker, an eighth-grader at Harding Junior High in Des Moines, wore a black arm-band to school. As punishment she was suspended. Three other students, including Mary Beth's 17-year-old brother, John, wore black arm-bands to school. They, too, were suspended.

School board members discussed the arm-band conflict in their next two regular meetings. Two members supported the student protesters. They said that students have the same right as other citizens, to criticize government leaders publicly. Others argued against the arm-band wearers. They said that this type of demonstration could disrupt peace and order in schools. The school principals were concerned that the arm-band wearers might incite other students to lash out at them. Thus, they advocated a ban on arm-bands in order to preserve law and order in schools.

The arm-band conflict became the talk of the town. Heated arguments broke out on street corners, at work places, and in homes over the right to wear arm-bands in school. It seemed that the majority of adults in the community as well as most students were against the protesters. One student who favored the protesters was punched in the face at a restaurant near Roosevelt High.

After hearing different points of view, the school board decided by a 5 to 2 vote to continue the ban on arm-bands. However, the students who had been suspended were allowed to return to school.

On March 15, 1966, the conflict went to the United States District Court in Des Moines. The Iowa Civil Liberties Union, an interest group which works to protect citizen rights, had offered to assume the cost of using the courts to overturn the school board's decision.

The District Court was asked to issue an injunction to stop the school officials from preventing the wearing of arm-bands. The court denied this request. The presiding judge agreed with the school board. He said that the wearing of arm-bands would create a disturbance and was a threat to discipline and security in the schools.

The Tinkers appealed their case to the 8th U.S. Circuit Court of Appeals. This higher court dismissed the case, upholding the constitutionality of the school authorities' action.

With backing from the Civil Liberties Union, the Tinker family appealed to the United States Supreme Court which heard their case on February 24, 1969, three years after the conflict began. The nine Supreme Court justices heard arguments for and against the students' right to wear arm-bands in school as a sign of protest. They then voted 7 to 2 in favor of the student protesters.

Justice Abraham Fortas wrote the majority opinion of the Court. In the case of *Tinker* v. *Des Moines School District,* Fortas stated:

"Any word spoken in class, in the lunchroom, or on the campus that deviates from the views of another person may start an argument or cause a disturbance. But our Constitution says we must take the risk. . . .

"School officials do not possess absolute authority over their students. Students in school as well as out of school are 'persons' under our Con-stitution. . . . The Constitution says that Congress (and the states) may not abridge the right to free speech. This provision means what it says.

"[The student] caused discussion outside of the classroom, but no interference with work and no disorder. In the circumstances, our Constitution does not permit officials of the state to deny their form of expression. . . . "

In a sharp dissent from the majority opinion, Justice Hugo Black argued that:

". . . after the Court's holding today, some students in the Iowa schools and indeed in all schools will be ready, able and willing to defy their teachers on practically all orders. . . . This case . . . subjects all the public schools in the country to the whims and caprices of their loudest mouths, but maybe not their brightest students."

In conclusion, Black declared that students "will soon believe it is their right to control the schools. . . . I dissent."

The Supreme Court's majority opinion as prepared by Justice Fortas represented the decision in the Tinker case. As a result of this decision, the right of students peacefully to express protest opinions in school was upheld as a constitutional right.

1. Which constitutional amendment was involved in the *Gideon* case?
2. Why did the Florida Supreme Court rule as it did in *Gideon* v. *Wainwright*? What was the reasoning behind the United States Supreme Court decision?
3. What constitutional principle was involved in the *Tinker* case?
4. How did the Tinker family and the Iowa Civil Liberties Union advocate their position on this issue?
5. What conflicts were present in the *Gideon* and *Tinker* cases? How did conflict affect change?

Civil Rights: Physically Handicapped Americans

Within the United States, approximately 35 million people suffer from some kind of handicap. Included in this number are those physically handicapped individuals who are hard of hearing, deaf, speech impaired, visually handicapped, mobility disabled, paralyzed, or suffering from other health impairments such as severe diabetes or hemophilia.

Prior to the 1960s little attention was given to the special needs of the handicapped. Lack of special transportation facilities prevented many from holding jobs, voting, serving on juries, attending public schools, or going to cultural events. The presence of a handicap often was used as a basis for denying jobs, promotions, driver's licenses, medical or health insurance, and admission to some educational programs. As a result, qualified people were denied the right to be self-supporting.

During the 1960s a movement began to end discriminatory practices against the handicapped. During this period an important issue was accessibility to the community. Without the ability to move freely, other rights would be useless. In reaction to this the federal government passed the Architectural Barriers Act of 1968. This legislation ordered designers and developers to create public facilities—particularly those owned and operated by the federal government—without the barriers that had traditionally prevented use by the handicapped. Access to these buildings must be provided, for example, by using elevators and ramps instead of stairs. Facilities such as water fountains also had to be made accessible.

Later legislation covered transportation systems in cities receiving federal funds for transportation. Cities were ordered to provide special transportation facilities such as ramps and bus lifts so that the handicapped could go to work, school, or other everyday activities.

Another important concern of the handicapped was discrimination in employment and education. One of the most important laws to address this issue was the Rehabilitation Act of 1973. This banned discrimination against the handicapped in employment by the federal government, by holders of federal contracts, and by any recipients of federal financial assistance, such as public schools, colleges, and projects that receive federal grants. The act stressed affirmative action, that is, a special effort to correct past deficiencies. In addition, in 1977 the Tax Reduction and Simplification Act offered tax credits to nongovernment businesses hiring the handicapped.

The most important development in education for the handicapped was the 1975 Education for All Handicapped Children Act. This law requires all public schools to provide appropriate free education for the handicapped. It also provides for federal funding to help meet the cost of this action. The penalty for noncompliance is the loss of federal aid. An important consequence of this act is federal approval of "mainstreaming." In other words, the handicapped are no longer to be separated from the rest of the community. They are to be integrated as much as possible with the nonhandicapped.

In 1977 physically handicapped individuals met in Washington, DC, for the White House Conference on the Handicapped. The conference gained national attention, pointing out the obstacles handicapped people still face in exercising their civil rights. Expensive changes ordered by the federal government often have not been implemented at the state and local levels. Therefore, despite gains in the 1970s, delegates to the conference expressed the need to continue working for the rights of the handicapped.

Civil Rights: Mentally Handicapped Americans

The name "mentally handicapped" is applied to people with many disabilities, such as mental illness and mental retardation, in addition to certain severe learning disabilities. Some of these handicaps, such as mental illness, are like sicknesses which can be treated and often cured. People mentally handicapped in other ways, such as mental retardation, can be helped effectively but retardation itself can never be cured.

More than 20 percent of all Americans may at some time be hospitalized for mental illness. Another 2 to 3 percent are classified as mentally retarded. Of these, a small percentage are confined to institutions.

Traditionally, those viewed by society as mentally handicapped have suffered both neglect and discrimination. They have been denied the most fundamental rights guaranteed to other citizens. If confined to institutions, mentally handicapped persons are deprived not only of their liberty but also of such basic rights as due process, privacy, and freedom to decide on their own care and treatment. Those living in the community often cannot vote, marry, or secure suitable housing or employment. In court proceedings the mentally handicapped frequently are at a disadvantage because of their inability to understand legal procedures. In addition, they have great difficulty in finding lawyers who understand their special needs well enough to represent them effectively.

Today's movement to uphold the rights of the handicapped began in the 1960s. It was initiated by organizations made up of friends or relatives acting on the behalf of the mentally disabled. Through their efforts, the federal government began to enact legislation to improve the services available to the handicapped. In the 1970s the movement grew and changed focus. Drawing on precedents from the consumer rights and civil rights movements, advocacy groups began to use the courts to fight for the legal rights of mentally handicapped persons and thereby to gain needed services.

The most important early victories were in the areas of education and institutional abuse. In the early 1970s two important cases were won in federal courts, requiring the provision of public education for mentally disabled persons. By 1975 Congress passed the Education for All Handicapped Children Act, requiring all states to educate handicapped children or lose federal funding for education.

Other court cases established the rights of individuals committed to state institutions. In 1975 the Supreme Court ruled that a state could not confine a nondangerous person against his or her will. Also in 1975 the New York State Association for Retarded Children settled a case against the state charging that the right of retarded persons to protection from harm had been violated at Willowbrook, a state institution. The federal court approved an agreement ordering improvements at Willowbrook as well as creation of alternative, community-based living arrangements for nearly all of the residents of Willowbrook. In other cases, state courts upheld retarded persons' voting rights, stating that those rights could not be denied on the basis of residence in a state institution.

In addition to court orders establishing the rights of institutionalized people, other gains were made during the 1970s. In 1973, Section 504 of the federal Rehabilitation Act prohibited discrimination on the basis of mental or physical handicaps (see page 477), although federal regulations to enforce this prohibition were not issued until 1977. Groups acting at the local level of government challenged zoning ordinances that prohibited group homes for the mentally handicapped. Organizations have also established sheltered workshops for retarded adults, ensuring their right to earn a living.

As evidenced by the victories of the 1960s and 1970s, mentally handicapped persons have gained important recognition of their civil rights. However, much remains to be done to enforce broad federal and state laws on the local level.

Civil Rights: Older Americans

Since 1900, the number of people in the United States who are over 65 has increased from 3 million to 23 million. By the year 2000, approximately 13 percent of the total population will be over 65.

The aged are a minority group to which all sexes, races, and economic groups belong; consequently, its members have a variety of concerns. Issues range from the poverty of aged women to the forced retirement of executives with yearly pensions of over $27,000. Despite this wide range of issues, the group as a whole does have some shared concerns.

The one fundamental issue common to almost all elderly Americans is the question of age equality. This means that the aged want to be regarded as individuals with the same rights and potential as younger citizens. They do not want to be denied credit, housing, or employment on the basis of age. And, as a minority group, they want state and federal groups to recognize their special needs, such as the difficulty of living on a fixed retirement income in inflationary times.

To secure these rights, older Americans are organizing on an unprecedented scale. The largest advocacy group for the aged is the American Association of Retired Persons (AARP), with a membership of over 11 million people and an annual budget of $30 million. Also active are groups like the National Council of Senior Citizens (NCSC) and the Gray Panthers. The efforts of these and other groups are devoted to making the public and the federal government aware of the special needs and rights of the aged.

As a result of increased citizen participation, the 1960s and the 1970s saw the first important legislation concerning the aged since the passage of Social Security in 1935. The enactment of Medicare and Medicaid in 1965 was designed to provide health care and medical insurance for the elderly who live on a fixed income. Discrimination in hiring, firing, and promotion of people between the ages of 40 and 65 was prohibited by the Age Discrimination in Employment Act of 1967. In addition, legislation has been passed to protect the interests of persons under private pension plans and to provide equal opportunity for loans, mortgages, and credit.

In 1965, the Administration on Aging was established within the Department of Health, Education, and Welfare. Congressional committees on the aged were set up in both houses of Congress.

The principle of forced retirement has not been overturned by courts or legislation. However, an amendment to the 1967 Age Discrimination in Employment Act would raise the upper retirement age to 70, with a few exceptions.

Perhaps the biggest problem facing the aged in the future is the fate of the total federal Social Security program. With a declining birth rate in the United States, there will be fewer people to support the elderly. Organizations such as the AARP have pointed out that giving people the right to work as long as they are willing and able may be a solution to relieve a problem that will affect the entire population in the future.

Growth of a Movement: The Montgomery Bus Boycott

You have seen that civil rights is an important area in which conflict has produced change in the United States political system. Both interest groups and individual citizens have aided in promoting civil rights change. One major example of the civil rights struggle was the 1955 bus boycott in Montgomery, Alabama.

As you read the following in-depth study of the boycott, think about what you have learned about working in groups, making decisions, bargaining, and the various roles that citizens can play. Apply your knowledge to the history of the boycott. Also analyze the political resources that citizens used to achieve their goals.

HOW IT STARTED In 1955, Montgomery, Alabama, boasted a number of distinctions. It was not only the capital of the state but, during the Civil War, it had also served as the first capital of the Confederacy. Here Jefferson Davis had been inaugurated. (Here, too, a songwriter named Daniel Emmett had performed his "Dixie" for the first time.) The city was the birthplace of people as different as Nat King Cole and Zelda Sayre, who met and married F. Scott Fitzgerald in her home town.

In many ways, though, Montgomery in 1955 was like many other southern cities. Black people—roughly 45 percent of a population of about 140,000—worked mostly at menial jobs. The median yearly income for a black family in Montgomery was $970; for a white family, $1,730. Housing, public facilities, and transportation were rigidly segregated. Nothing had been done to integrate the school system since the *Brown* decision of the previous year. Few blacks were registered to vote. And, as in many other southern communities, there was a widespread feeling that racial segregation was a way of life so ingrained that it could not be changed.

Black people supported a number of self-help organizations. These included a local branch of the NAACP, the Citizens Committee, the Women's Political Council, and a group called the Progressive Democrats. But partly because there were so many organizations, and so many different leaders, energies were not focused. As for black ministers, most wanted to avoid social problems and instead concentrate on religious matters. At least one observer felt that the black community at this time was politically apathetic.

On Thursday, December 1, 1955, just after 5:00 P.M., a seamstress named Rosa Parks walked wearily into Court Square looking for a bus that would take her home. She was tired from her day-long job in a downtown department store. She was looking not only for a bus, but a bus in which she could sit down.

That was the complicated part. For in Montgomery, as in most southern cities, strict rules governed seating on buses. A city ordinance decreed that the first four seats were to be reserved exclusively for whites. Behind them was a "no-man's-land" of two or three seats that blacks could use if there were no white demand. The back of the bus was reserved for blacks. According to another rule, blacks got on in front, paid their fare, then climbed out and boarded again in back. It was not unusual for a bus to pull away in the midst of this insane procedure, leaving blacks a dime poorer, and with no ride.

When Parks got on her bus, both the white and black sections were filled, so she sat in the first row of "no-man's-land," along with three other blacks. Then a white man got on, and the bus driver ordered the black riders in the fifth row to get up. Three of them did, but Rosa Parks refused. When the driver threatened to call the police, she replied, "Go ahead and call them." Two policemen soon arrived on the scene. One officer asked her, "Why didn't you get up?" Always dignified, Parks answered simply, "I didn't think I should have to." And then, quietly, she added a question to which the policeman had no ready answer: "Why do you push us around?"

At the police station Parks was booked, fingerprinted, and allowed one phone call. She telephoned E. D. Nixon, a black leader (president of the Progressive Democrats) with whom she had worked in the NAACP. Nixon came down with a white friend who was a lawyer and together they bailed out Rosa Parks, who by this time was very tired indeed.

At this point an idea came to Nixon and other black leaders, including Ralph Abernathy of Montgomery's First Baptist Church. Why not organize a test case to dramatize the black cause in Montgomery? Would Parks consent? After discussing the matter with her husband and her mother, she agreed. Parks commented a few months later: "It was not at all prearranged. It just happened that the driver made a demand and I just didn't feel like obeying his demand."

Sometime early Friday morning the notion of a boycott came into being. Later that day a planning committee composed mainly of clergymen met at the Dexter Avenue Baptist Church, whose new pastor was a young man named Martin Luther King, Jr. King had recently completed the course work for his Ph.D. and had moved back south from Boston. (He had grown up in Atlanta.)

The group agreed on a boycott and made the following plans: (1) A leaflet would be duplicated and distributed, urging blacks not to ride the buses on Monday. (2) Ministers would make the same announcement to their congregations on Sunday. (3) Black taxicab companies would be organized by phone to supply emergency transportation. (4) A mass meeting would be held Monday night. (Montgomery had no black-owned radio station or widely read black newspaper.)

While these plans were being carried out, the movement benefited from a stroke of luck. A black maid who could not read asked her employer for help in reading the leaflet. The outraged employer notified the local newspaper, which printed the announcement on its front page. The paper's action, motivated by a desire to expose the black "plot," carried the protesters' message to many blacks who might otherwise have missed it.

Mrs. Rosa Parks was fingerprinted by a deputy sheriff in Montgomery, Alabama, after she refused to give up her seat for a white passenger and move to the rear of the bus. This action led to a bus boycott, organized by Martin Luther King, Jr.

Black people walked, took taxi cabs, and made car pool arrangements during the 1955-56 bus boycott. They were willing to put up with inconveniences because of their goal to end discrimination against blacks on public transportation.

1. What inequalities motivated the boycott?
2. What are the advantages of a spontaneous event in triggering a mass movement of this sort? The disadvantages?
3. What political resources did the Montgomery black community have at the beginning of the boycott? What did it lack?
4. Why was speedy communication necessary for this type of protest?

ORGANIZING the MOVEMENT Martin Luther King and his wife Coretta were up early on Monday, December 5. The young minister hoped that the boycott might be 60 percent successful, and he wanted to see the first buses on the line that went past his house.

"I was in the kitchen drinking my coffee when I heard Coretta cry, 'Martin, Martin, come quickly.' I put down my cup and ran toward the living room. As I approached the front window Coretta pointed joyfully to a slowly moving bus: 'Darling, it's empty!' I could hardly believe what I saw. . . . This first bus was usually filled with domestic workers going to their jobs. Would all the other buses follow the pattern that had been set by the first? Eagerly we waited for the next bus. In fifteen minutes it rolled down the street, and, like the first, it was empty. A third bus appeared, and it too was empty of all but two white passengers.

I jumped in my car and for almost an hour I cruised down every major street and examined every passing bus. During this hour, at the peak of the morning traffic, I saw no more than eight Negro passengers riding the buses. By this time I was jubilant. Instead of the 60 percent cooperation we had hoped for, it was becoming apparent that we had reached almost 100 percent. A miracle had taken place. The once dormant and quiescent Negro community was now fully awake."

Later on Monday Rosa Parks appeared in court. To no one's surprise, she was found guilty and fined. Her lawyer appealed the case. Leaving the courtroom, Nixon and Abernathy talked about the need for an *ad hoc* organization—that is, one called into being to handle a specific situation. When they met that afternoon with other black leaders, including King, they elected King president. (Though Nixon might have seemed the natural choice, he felt that his job as a Pullman car porter would take him away from Montgomery too often.) The organization next chose a name—the Montgomery Improvement Association (MIA).

483

The group next debated a basic question: Should the boycott continue? Some argued that a one-day "miracle" was all that could be expected; better to call it off now than to have people start riding again and, little by little, erode the impression of a united community. Finally the MIA agreed to abide by the decision at the mass meeting.

An overflow crowd jammed the Holt Street Baptist Church on Monday evening. After "Onward Christian Soldiers" and a prayer, the audience leapt to its feet in tribute when Rosa Parks was introduced. Abernathy then called for a continuation of the boycott until the following three conditions were met: (1) Bus operators guaranteed courteous treatment of black passengers. (2) Passengers were to be seated on a first-come, first-served basis, blacks filling the bus from the rear and whites from the front. (3) Black drivers were to be employed on routes that were mainly black. Again the audience rose in thunderous approval. King then spoke, urging nonviolence..

Now it was time for long-term organization. The MIA set up separate committees to handle transportation and finances. On the all-important strategy committee, along with King, were Nixon, several ministers, a businessman, and two faculty members from a local Negro college. A close associate of the group was a white minister, Robert Graetz.

Improved transportation was a must. More than 17,000 black people rode the buses every day. Taxis couldn't be used for long, because a law set a minimum fare for them that was higher than what the boycotters could afford on a regular basis. Car pools were formed, and eventually 15 new station wagons were bought, each registered as the property of a different church.

Where did the money come from? At the beginning, local contributions were enough. But soon, with expenses running $5,000 a month, more help was needed. MIA leaders spoke at fund-raising meetings all over the country. Churches, especially Negro churches, sent many contributions.

Funds were also supplied by the NAACP, which in addition provided invaluable legal assistance.

As the weeks went by, MIA volunteers found it increasingly difficult to run the complex operation. So help was hired, and an office was rented. Regular mass meetings were held at least once a week, moving from church to church and denomination to denomination. Speakers kept enthusiasm high, always stressing King's nonviolent approach.

1. What is the purpose of forming an ad hoc organization to carry out a protest? What weaknesses might such a group have?
2. What advantages did King have when he was chosen as president of the Montgomery Improvement Association?
3. What initial problems did the MIA face? How did it solve them?

MOVES and COUNTER-MOVES

One white woman complained to her black maid and said to her, "Isn't this bus boycott terrible?" "Yes, ma'am, it sure is," her wise servant replied. "And I just told all my [children] that this kind of thing is white folks' business and we just stay off the buses till they get the whole thing settled."

A few "white folks" supported the boycotters. Many more were opposed to this threat to the status quo (in other words, the existing situation). Members of a group of white businessmen, the Men of Montgomery, made efforts to meet with MIA leaders. But they could get nowhere in view of the city commissioners' position on the conflict. All three city commissioners belonged to the White Citizens Council, a group dedicated to preserving Jim Crow in all its forms.

In response to the three-point resolution of the black community, the bus company took the position that courtesy on buses could be guaranteed but that the company had no intention of hiring black drivers. Seating arrangements could not be changed, since doing so would violate the law. To which King's reply was, "We will not obey unjust laws or submit to unjust practices."

When it became clear that the boycott was serious and that the protesters were well organized (even the White Citizens Council remarked on their "military precision"), some white opponents resorted to more radical methods. City policemen tailed car pool vehicles, arresting drivers for minor or imaginary violations. (King himself was arrested for allegedly speeding.) Hate mail poured in. One letter ended, "We need and will have a Hitler to get our country straightened out." Threatening phone calls deluged MIA leaders and their families. "For the first time," King admitted later on, "I realized that something could happen to me."

It almost did. On January 30 his house was bombed. Luckily he was away, and his wife and child were unhurt. Two nights later dynamite was thrown on Nixon's lawn, but he too escaped injury.

In February the authorities tried a legal measure. They arrested a number of blacks, King among them, charging them with violating a state law. This law made it illegal for two or more persons to enter into a conspiracy to prevent the operation of a lawful business without just cause—in this case, of course, the bus company. "Would this be the end of our movement?" King wondered to himself.

Far from it. The mass arrests seemed to make the black community feel more inspired than ever. "Those who had previously trembled before the law were now proud to be arrested for the cause of freedom," wrote King. At the trial, which took place in March, King was found guilty and fined $500. Charges against the 89 other defendants were suspended while King's case was appealed.

All these moves convinced the MIA that a settlement based on the original three-point resolution would be impossible to reach. Therefore in May it filed a suit of its own, charging in Federal District Court that bus segregation violated the Fourteenth Amendment. NAACP attorneys used the recent *Brown* decision as a precedent. On June 4, the three-judge panel ruled 2 to 1 that Alabama's city bus segregation laws were unconstitutional. Montgomery appealed to the Supreme Court.

Leaders of the bus boycott are shown during a planning session. Martin Luther King is facing the audience, center seat. King emerged as an important civil rights leader at this time.

The black people of Montgomery gave strong support to the bus boycott. In what way was their support a crucial resource in the boycott's success?

Through the long summer days, the black people of Montgomery walked and rode the car pools. Then a new problem arose. Insurance companies refused to insure the station wagons. Lloyds of London then took on the job. Next the city went to court again, contending that the car pools formed a private business competing in the marketplace without a franchise. But in the very midst of the hearing on this petition—December 20, 1956—word came that the Supreme Court had upheld the decision of the District Court. The MIA had won its case. "God Almighty has spoken from Washington, D.C." one bystander remarked.

In another burst of extremist resistance, the Ku Klux Klan rode that night. Carloads of robed and hooded men drove through the streets of Negro areas. But instead of retreating in fear, the blacks of Montgomery went about their business as usual. Some even sat on their porches and waved as the cars rolled by. Unable to intimidate, the Klan cut short its motorcade and rode home.

1. How did the bus company respond to the boycotters' resolution?
2. What were the political resources of the white community of Montgomery?
3. What kinds of legal action did the Montgomery authorities take? How did the protesters react?

The END of an ERA

Some weeks were to pass before the official order for desegregation reached Montgomery. In the meantime the black community prepared for integration. At mass meetings role-playing situations were set up, with rows of chairs representing a bus and men and women acting as passengers and drivers, both black and white. As earlier, leaders continually stressed nonviolence. The MIA also distributed a list of "Integrated Bus Suggestions" to help black riders make the transition. No similar steps were taken by the white community. In fact, the city commissioners issued a statement vowing not to "yield one inch" but to do everything in their power "to oppose the integration of the Negro race with the white race."

Finally, on December 20, the court order arrived. That night King addressed a joyful mass meeting, ending with these words:

"As we go back to the buses let us be loving enough to turn an enemy into a friend. We must now move from protest to reconciliation. It is my firm conviction that God is working in Montgomery. Let all men of goodwill, both Negro and white, continue to work with Him. With this dedication we will be able to emerge from the bleak and desolate midnight of man's inhumanity to man to the bright and glittering daybreak of freedom and justice."

On December 21, after 380 days of protest, makeshift arrangements, and just plain weariness, the boycott came to an end. King and other MIA leaders rode one of the first buses. For a few days there was a deceptive calm. Then, late in December, a rash of incidents disturbed the peace. A black girl was beaten by whites as she got off a bus. Other buses were fired on. The Klan rode again, although with no more effect than before. Abernathy's house and church were bombed. So were Graetz's home and three other Baptist churches. Bus schedules were curtailed. It looked as if all that had been won would soon vanish as Montgomery slipped deeper into violence.

The city cracked down. Late in January 1957, seven white men were arrested for the bombings. The first two were acquitted, in spite of confessions, and the cases against the others were dropped (along with those still pending against the black protesters). Even so, the reign of terror was over. Montgomery returned to normal, but with one big change. Rosa Parks and her family and friends and neighbors—and thousands of people who never met her—could sit wherever they pleased on the public vehicles of their communities.

1. What preparations did the black community make for integration?
2. Why do you think black leaders took such care at this time?

EPILOGUE Once during the boycott a car-pool driver stopped and asked an elderly black woman, trudging along the street, whether she wouldn't prefer to ride. She answered that she'd rather walk, and added, "I'm not walking for myself. I'm walking for my children and my grandchildren." Indeed, what happened in Montgomery, Alabama, did affect the future of black people, just about everywhere in the United States.

The boycott made Martin Luther King, Jr. famous. In January 1957, he was elected president of the newly formed Southern Christian Leadership Conference. This organization was one of the prime movers behind the civil rights protests of the late 1950s and early 1960s. King's strong and able leadership won him the Nobel Peace Prize in 1964, and death at an assassin's hands four years later.

The boycott was one factor behind congressional passage of the Civil Rights Act of 1957, which removed some of the obstacles to registration and voting by blacks. This act was strengthened by the more far reaching laws of 1964 and 1965.

The boycott made it clear that, while the *Brown* decision had spelled the beginning of the end for segregation, Jim Crow would be slow to die. In 1961 Montgomery was the scene of a riot, when a local mob attacked a group of freedom riders traveling through the town by bus. Because city police were slow to respond vigorously, the attorney general sent in several hundred federal officers to restore order. As you have read, federal troops also had to be called in at the time of the Selma-to-Montgomery voting rights march in 1965.

By the mid-1970s, Montgomery—again, like many a southern city—had changed to an extent almost undreamed of 20 years earlier. All public facilities had been desegregated. There were black bus drivers, black policemen, and even black mannequins in the store windows. Perhaps most important, four of the nine members of the city council were black. Because of increased black voter registration and participation, the political system could now serve as the chief means of bringing about changes for black people.

GENERALIZING At the heart of the
VALUES Montgomery bus
boycott were sev-
eral important
value issues. Equal opportunity in using
public transportation was the specific right
that the boycotters were fighting for; equality was a fundamental value held by participants in the boycott.

The valuing lesson in Chapter 10 (page
306) discussed the importance of evaluating
alternative positions and the consequences
of those positions when deciding a position
on a value issue. In the Montgomery bus
boycott, there were a number of alternatives
which could have been chosen. The black
community could have chosen to do nothing, to boycott, to talk with officials, or to
work through political parties. It chose
to boycott, and the boycott had consequences—both positive and negative. The
black community won its case, but there
was considerable violence and mass arrests
as a result.

Another skill in taking positions is
being able to generalize a value position to
other situations. It is an important skill, because it enables people to apply their values
consistently and in a fair way to many situations. Being able to generalize values helps
people to clearly understand the problems
and possible alternatives of new value issues when they arise. It also helps them to
decide their own position on new issues.

Many who believe in and have fought
for equality for black people have essentially generalized their value position by extending it beyond bus transportation and
into areas of housing, education, and jobs.
They have generalized their belief in equality in another way by applying it to other
minority groups in addition to blacks.

It is important to be aware that because
of circumstances, the positions you take or
decisions you make may not always be in
harmony with your basic values. For example, a person who believes that war is
wrong would probably disapprove of
United States involvement in war. However,

if the United States were attacked by another country, it would be forced to declare
war to protect itself. In this situation, many
would decide to support their country, even
though war was against their beliefs.

Read the following two case examples.
Describe the basic value issue which under-
lies each example.

1. Your school is thinking about starting a
school lunch program. The program will
be subsidized by the school and the federal government. It will give needy students in your school the opportunity to
eat nutritious food that they otherwise
could not afford. It will, however, slightly
increase the price of other food served in
the school and decrease the offerings on
the menu. Some students feel that the
lunch program is a good idea. Others
want to organize a protest because of the
changes the program will bring.

2. Your city council is debating whether or
not to build welfare housing in the downtown district. An area has been chosen in
which many poorer residents live. These
people are in need of improved housing
conditions. Some members of the city
council are against the plan. They say
that people who are not eligible for welfare have already made their way onto
the welfare housing lists. They fear that
those who need the new housing will be
shoved aside; they therefore question the
wisdom of the plan. Other members of
the city council say that the facility is absolutely necessary. They maintain that
eligibility controls can be applied.

1. What are the alternative courses of action
in examples 1 and 2? What are the consequences of these alternatives? What
course of action would you choose in
each case? Given examples 1 and 2, in
what ways can you generalize your value
position on equality?

2. Choose a civil rights issue and identify
your value position. In what other situations would that position apply?

Participation Project: Civil Rights

In this chapter you have seen that there have been conflicts over civil rights throughout United States history. Now you can construct your own study involving a civil rights issue. The steps involved in preparing your study are the same as those used in previous participation projects.

Choosing a Topic. Choose a civil rights issue that is important to you. Think about the issue in terms of how you can sample opinion on the issue in your school or community. Some broad topics for you to choose from are voting rights, discrimination, due process of the law, freedom of speech, and freedom of assembly.

Choosing a Group. This study can be done by you working alone or with other people in a group. If your teacher decides on group work, he or she will be in charge of breaking the class into groups.

Stating Objectives. You need to carefully formulate objectives for your case study. You should focus your study in one of the three following ways: Examine how the civil rights in the topic you've chosen has been either upheld or violated. Or, investigate how conflict created changes in the issue you are studying. Or, study the role of specific individuals and groups in the issue you've chosen.

Choosing Sources. Try to select a wide variety of sources in preparing your study. As suggested earlier in this book, newspaper materials, magazines, photographs, and speeches are some examples of sources to investigate. Another source could be a survey of people's attitudes on your topic.

Gathering Information. If you are working with others, divide your study into tasks. Each person should be responsible for completing a part of the assignment.

Choosing a Method of Presentation. In sharing your study with the class, decide on the best way to present your material. You may, for instance, want to combine visual materials with an oral report.

Presenting the Study. When you present your study, the following questions should be discussed.

1. Which civil right is involved in this case? Which constitutional amendment is involved?
2. How has the civil right been upheld (or violated)?
3. What is the conflict? What changes have resulted from the conflict?
4. What people and groups were studied in relation to this issue? What actions did they take?
5. If you conducted a survey, what are your findings? If you practiced observation, what are your findings?
6. What is your opinion of this issue? How did you reach that opinion? Can you generalize your opinion to any other issue?

Chapter Review

1. Define civil rights. What are some of the most important civil rights that you possess?

2. How is the Constitution an important safeguard of basic civil rights?

3. In what ways do the Supreme Court, Congress, and the president protect and extend civil rights? Give specific examples.

4. Why do citizens have a responsibility to exercise civil rights?

5. Summarize the major changes that have taken place in the rights of women since the founding of America. How does the role of contemporary women differ from that of women prior to the 1900s?

6. What forces prevented blacks from exercising rights gained by the Civil War? What tactics have black leaders used to change this?

7. Define civil liberties. What are some important civil liberties that you possess? Explain how each protects individual freedom.

8. Discuss some of the past instances when civil rights were restricted. In your opinion, are such restrictions ever justified? Explain.

9. Outline the major events in the Montgomery bus boycott.

10. What resources did Martin Luther King, Jr. use to make the bus boycott a success? What civil rights were gained as a result?

Chapter Vocabulary

Define the following terms.

civil rights	sexism	civil liberties
suffragists	Jim Crow laws	discrimination
feminism	civil disobedience	habeas corpus

Chapter Analysis

1. Of all the constitutional amendments, which two do you think are most critical in determining individual rights and liberties? Explain.

2. The right to remain silent, the right to equal educational opportunity, and the right to counsel are not explicitly stated in the Constitution; however, they are a part of constitutional law. Explain how the courts have brought this about. Do you think that they have been correct in defining these as constitutional rights? Explain.

3. How does a study of civil rights prove that the American political system is dynamic? In your opinion, does this strengthen or weaken American government? Explain.

4. Compare and contrast the women's movement and the black civil rights movement. For example, what were the goals of each? What tactics and resources did each use to bring about change? How have their gains affected American politics?

5. Describe the role of the following in the Montgomery bus boycott: local executive; local courts; federal courts; church groups; citizen organizations.

1. Make a list of civil rights that you believe should regulate school policy. Then, using constitutional amendments as a model, compose a student bill of rights.

2. Many men and women have sought to protect and extend civil rights, even though it meant unpopularity and possible personal danger. Choose one such individual and write a report profiling his or her actions. Some possible choices are Martin Luther King, Jr., Mary Beth Tinker, Daniel Ellsberg, Alice Paul, Oliver Brown, or Dorothea Dix.

3. "Legally, blacks and women have made many gains in the past century. However, in reality, true equality still does not exist." Research the current status of blacks and women in the United States. Based on your findings, comment on the above statement.

4. The American Civil Liberties Union (ACLU) has been very active in defending the rights and liberties of many people. Sometimes its actions have been very controversial. Select one such case and present it to the class. Be prepared to discuss your reactions with other class members.

Civil Rights: A Current Guide to People, Organizations, and Events, A. John Adams and Joan Martin Burke (R.R. Bowker Company: New York, NY), 1974.

An alphabetical guide to individuals and organizations active in the area of civil rights.

The Souls of Black Folk, W.E.B. Dubois (Fawcett Publications, Inc.: Greenwich, CT), 1976.

Originally published in 1903, contains essays which provide a background for viewing the civil rights struggle of black Americans.

Civil Rights: 1960–66, (Facts on File, Inc.: New York, NY), 1967.

An informative work that is a useful chronological description of key events in the civil rights movement between 1960 and 1966.

Getting Justice: The Rights of People, Stephen Gillers (New American Library: New York, NY), 1973.

Focuses on the citizens rights within our system of criminal justice. Topics include arrest, search, seizure, wire tapping, and the right to a lawyer.

" . . . To Form a More Perfect Union . . . " Justice for American Women (Report of the National Commission on the Observance of International Women's Year, Washington, DC), 1976.

An examination of the current role of women in such areas as mass media, the ERA, work, parenting, and the law. Each short section is very readable and contains quotes and illustrations.

Stride Toward Freedom: The Montgomery Story, Martin Luther King, Jr. (Harper & Row: New York, NY), 1958.

A personal account of the Montgomery bus boycott by the famous civil rights leader. This is the first of several books written by King.

unit 4

Global Political Systems

Chapter Objectives

★ To identify major global actors and issues
★ To understand the term "global political system"
★ To identify the factors behind change in the global political system
★ To understand the concept of interdependence

chapter 16

ONE SYSTEM or MANY?

Chapter 16 introduces you to the study of politics on another, wider level—global politics. The chapter opens with a discussion of major political actors on the global scene. Global political actors include nations, international organizations and businesses, and voluntary associations. Since individual citizens can have an important impact on world affairs, they too can be viewed as global political actors. As you read, you will see that the interactions among these groups form systems, in the same way that schools, communities, and national governments also form their own systems.

A major concept in the study of international politics is interdependence. When people, groups, or nations are interdependent, they rely upon one another for different needs, and they are affected by one another's actions. Because of growing interdependence in today's world, global political actors are relying more and more on one another to solve problems. Global interactions are increasing.

As you study global politics, you will see that our lives are affected in many important ways by what goes on in other countries. Not only are we citizens of our own country, but in many important respects we are also citizens of the world.

495

Global Actors and Issues

Often when people think about the world, they first consider its geography. If asked to describe Africa, some may speak of a continent made up of rivers, forests, and deserts. Perhaps they will name a few of the many nations on the African continent.

Also, many people think of the world in terms of national leaders. Most Americans can identify the leaders of our neighboring countries and those of our allies in Western Europe. Because the Soviet Union and the People's Republic of China are large, have many resources, and can threaten the security of the United States, many Americans can identify Soviet and Chinese leaders.

People often think of the world in terms of international organizations. (An *international organization* is one in which at least two nations are members.) Probably more Americans know about the United Nations than about any other international organization.

Some people think that events that happen many thousands of miles away do not affect their lives. In recent times, however, many people have begun to change the ways they think about the world. Americans have come to realize that the United States is not independent of the rest of the world. If the Soviet Union increases its production of weapons, many Americans are concerned. If one nation provides nuclear knowledge to a nonnuclear nation, many Americans fear the possibility of nuclear war.

As more and more Americans realize their involvement with the rest of the world, they view the globe in terms of international issues. People are concerned with how these issues will influence their own lives. American farmers worry about how foreign wheat deals will affect the price of wheat in the United States. American steel workers fear that increased imports of foreign steel could eliminate their jobs. All Americans are concerned with United States dependency on foreign oil supplies.

Most Americans now understand that decisions and actions in other countries can have a direct effect on their lives. As a result, people are beginning to think of the world more in political terms than in geographical terms.

This chapter will demonstrate how decisions and actions taken in one part of the world can directly affect people in your community. It will also show that decisions and actions taken in the United States and sometimes in your own community may affect people in other lands.

GLOBAL ACTORS As you have learned in previous chapters, the United States government makes many decisions that affect the lives of American citizens. Does the United States also make decisions that affect the people of other nations? If the United States decides to send technical advisers to India, does this influence the Indian government and the Indian people? The answer, of course, is yes.

Do decisions made by other governments affect American citizens? Think about what happens when the government of China decides to conduct a test explosion of a nuclear weapon. As a result, fallout from this explosion reaches the United States. Does this decision of the Chinese government affect the United States? The answer, again, is yes.

There are more than 160 nations in the world today. (A map of the world appears on pages 498–499.) When a nation takes action that affects another nation, it can be considered a *global actor*. When the United States requests an international nuclear arms agreement with the Soviet Union, it operates as a global actor. If the United States refuses to sell grain to the Soviet Union, it also operates as a global actor.

496

International organizations such as the United Nations also can take actions that affect the lives of the people in many nations. After the Middle East War of 1973, the United Nations sent peace-keeping forces to separate the armies of Israel and Egypt and of Israel and Syria. By doing so, the United Nations was operating as a global actor.

Corporations such as Volkswagen, General Motors, and U.S. Steel are also global actors. They have both manufacturing and distribution plants in several nations. They employ workers from many countries. They have a direct impact on the economic development of communities and states across the globe.

Individuals can be considered global actors when their actions affect other nations. For example, the president of an American company may decide to move one or several factories to another nation. This will have an impact on the lives of the people in that country. New jobs will be created, and new goods will be marketed.

Have you ever thought of yourself as a global actor? If you buy a Japanese television or use Brazilian coffee, you are functioning as a global actor. Your decision to buy or not to buy these products affects the economics of Japan and Brazil.

To sum up, a *global actor* is an individual, group, or nation that uses resources and takes actions that affect other nations of the world.

1. If your family spends a vacation in another country, is your family a global actor? In what ways can your actions affect the lives of the people of the nation you are visiting?

2. If the United States and the Soviet Union sign a nuclear arms agreement to limit the production of certain weapons, can other nations be affected? In what ways?

3. Suppose there is a factory in your town that makes jeans. The factory sells jeans to a number of foreign countries. Is it a global actor? In what ways can the lives of people who live in these countries be affected?

ISSUES in GLOBAL POLITICS

Global issues are problems and situations that affect the people of many different countries. The solutions to these issues often require cooperation among nations.

Today, many issues confront the nations of the world. Pollution of the oceans is a global problem, as is the danger of nuclear war. Another global problem is scarce resources. Some people estimate that many of the world's resources, especially oil, will run out in the next 100 years. This certainly affects the entire global community.

Sometimes global problems are linked to one another. For example, many people worry about the world's population growth. One estimate is that in the latter half of this century, the world's population will double every 30 years. If this prediction comes true, there might not be enough food and natural resources to meet the needs of a growing population. Therefore, the problems of increasing the world's food supply and conserving natural resources are linked to the problem of overpopulation.

Many nations, organizations, and individuals are involved in global issues today. The following cases describe a variety of issues which have existed on the global scene in recent years. As you read, identify the global actors involved. Also, summarize for yourself the issues around which they interact.

★ United Nations Membership for the People's Republic of China

On October 25, 1971, the United Nations General Assembly voted to admit the People's Republic of China as a member of the United Nations. At the same time, the General Assembly voted to expel the Chinese Nationalist government of Taiwan. The seat in the General Assembly and the Security Council that had once belonged to the

Figure 16-1

Nationalist government now belonged to the government that ruled from the city of Peking. (All nations which are members of the United Nations belong to the General Assembly, which serves as an open forum for discussion. The Security Council is another body of the United Nations to which only 15 members belong. The Security Council makes important recommendations regarding the role the United Nations should take in peace-keeping activities.)

What were some of the factors that led to this decision? How did there come to be "two Chinas"?

First, it is important to know that when the United Nations was founded in 1945 there was only one China. At that time China was considered one of the five major powers in the world. Along with the four other big powers (the United States, Great Britain, the Soviet Union, and France), China was given a permanent seat in the Security Council of the United Nations.

In 1946, a revolution began in China that lasted for three years. Communists, led by Mao Tse-tung, fought the Nationalist government which then ruled China. The leader of the Nationalist government was Chiang Kai-shek.

In 1949, the Communist army defeated the Nationalist troops. On October 1, 1949, the People's Republic of China was offi-

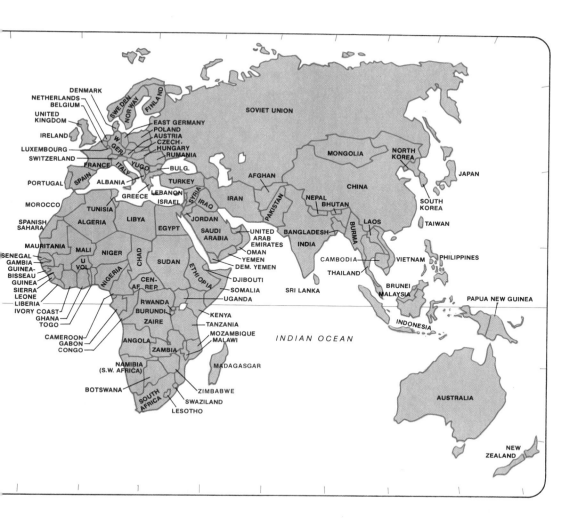

The map shows countries of Europe, Asia, Africa, and Oceania, including labels such as DENMARK, NETHERLANDS, BELGIUM, UNITED KINGDOM, IRELAND, LUXEMBOURG, SWITZERLAND, SWEDEN, NORWAY, FINLAND, EAST GERMANY, POLAND, AUSTRIA, CZECH., HUNGARY, RUMANIA, FRANCE, ITALY, YUGO., BULG., PORTUGAL, SPAIN, ALBANIA, TURKEY, GREECE, LEBANON, ISRAEL, SYRIA, IRAQ, IRAN, MOROCCO, TUNISIA, LIBYA, EGYPT, JORDAN, SAUDI ARABIA, SOVIET UNION, MONGOLIA, NORTH KOREA, JAPAN, CHINA, NEPAL, BHUTAN, SOUTH KOREA, TAIWAN, AFGHAN, PAKISTAN, UNITED ARAB EMIRATES, OMAN, YEMEN, DEM. YEMEN, BANGLADESH, INDIA, BURMA, LAOS, THAILAND, CAMBODIA, VIETNAM, PHILIPPINES, SRI LANKA, BRUNEI, MALAYSIA, PAPUA NEW GUINEA, INDONESIA, SPANISH SAHARA, MAURITANIA, MALI, NIGER, CHAD, SUDAN, ETHIOPIA, DJIBOUTI, SOMALIA, SENEGAL, GAMBIA, GUINEA-BISSAU, GUINEA, SIERRA LEONE, LIBERIA, IVORY COAST, GHANA, TOGO, U. VOL., NIGERIA, CEN. AF. REP., CAMEROON, GABON, CONGO, UGANDA, RWANDA, BURUNDI, ZAIRE, KENYA, TANZANIA, ANGOLA, ZAMBIA, MOZAMBIQUE, MALAWI, NAMIBIA (S.W. AFRICA), BOTSWANA, ZIMBABWE, SOUTH AFRICA, SWAZILAND, LESOTHO, MADAGASGAR, INDIAN OCEAN, AUSTRALIA, NEW ZEALAND.

cially formed. The defeated Nationalist army left the Chinese mainland. Under the leadership of Chiang Kai-shek, the refugees formed the Republic of China on the island of Taiwan. Figure 16-2, on the next page, is a map of mainland China and Taiwan.

The United States, along with other nations, did not recognize the People's Republic. Instead, close ties were maintained with the government on Taiwan. The Chinese government on Taiwan continued to represent China in the United Nations. In this way, there came to be two Chinas.

The People's Republic is the third largest country in the world in physical area. Moreover, it has the world's largest popu-

lation—an estimated 900 million people by the year 1982. In contrast, the island of Taiwan is small in area. It is projected that in 1982 it will have a population of about 18 million people. Because of its large size and population, many nations believed the People's Republic should have the seat at the United Nations instead of the Taiwan government. For many years, the United States opposed this action and supported the right of its ally to the seat at the United Nations.

From 1949 to 1971 the membership of the United Nations increased greatly. Most of the new member countries were friendly with the People's Republic. These nations

499

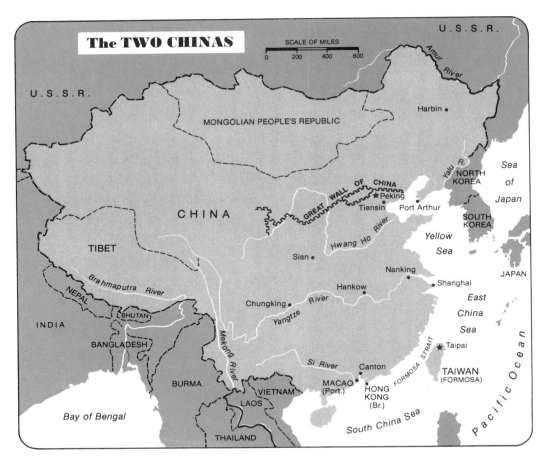

The TWO CHINAS

SCALE OF MILES
0   200   400   600

Figure 16-2

urged that the mainland government represent China at the United Nations.

In October 1971, Albania and 20 other nations proposed a resolution to give Taiwan's seat at the United Nations to the People's Republic of China. The resolution was passed by a 76 to 35 majority. Seventeen nations did not vote. Some nations, including the United States, believed both Chinas should have seats at the United Nations, but this idea was not supported by the majority.

Although the United States government opposed the action to replace one China with the other, it accepted the final decision. President Nixon said in an address, "We believe that a mistake of major proportions has been made in expelling the Taiwan government from the United Nations, but the United States recognizes that the will of the majority has been expressed. We, of course, accept that decision."

★ **Solzhenitsyn and Human Rights**

On February 13, 1974, the Soviet Union deported Alexander Solzhenitsyn. (*Deport* means to force a person to leave the nation in which he or she is living.) At the same time, the government took away his Soviet citizenship.

According to the Soviet press, Solzhenitsyn was deported for "systematically performing actions that are incompatible with being a citizen." Many people in the United States and other nations believed that Solzhenitsyn was deported because of a book he wrote—*Gulag Archipelago, 1918–1956*. In this book, Solzhenitsyn wrote about murders and prison camp deaths that occurred in the Soviet Union during those years.

This was not the first time that Solzhenitsyn had written a book in which he criticized the Soviet Union. Because of earlier critical writings, Solzhenitsyn had been put in prison for 11 years.

On June 30, 1975, Solzhenitsyn came to a dinner in Washington at the invitation of AFL-CIO leader George Meany. At the dinner, Solzhenitsyn attacked President Ford's policy of detente. (*Detente* is a policy to relax tensions between nations so that problems can be negotiated.) Solzhenitsyn said the United States should not seek peaceful relations with the Soviet Union as long as the Eastern European nations remained under Soviet control.

Because of Solzhenitsyn's view of detente, President Ford at first refused to meet with him. The President claimed that Solzhenitsyn was too strong in his criticisms of detente.

Many Americans who did not support the policy of detente said that the President was wrong not to meet with Solzhenitsyn. Even some Americans who supported the policy to improve relations with the Soviet Union criticized this action. As a result of the controversy, President Ford did offer an open invitation to the Soviet writer to come to the White House. Solzhenitsyn refused, saying he would accept only a formal invitation. During Ford's presidency, the two never met.

★ **The Civil War in Lebanon and the Role of the Red Cross**

In 1918, at the end of World War I, Great Britain was given administrative control over certain Middle Eastern areas, including Palestine. Palestine was populated primarily by Arabs—both Moslems and Christians. There was a small Jewish population as well.

The Jews living in Palestine had emigrated there, mainly from Eastern Europe, since the late 1800s. In the period between the end of World War I and the end of World War II the Jewish immigration into Palestine increased, as Jews sought a homeland. After the devastating events of World War II, in which 6 million Jews died in concentration camps in Europe, many more Jews came to Israel. They sought to establish a Jewish state there.

On November 29, 1947, the United Nations voted to end the British control of

Alexander Solzhenitsyn is shown giving the 1975 speech in which he criticized American policies toward the Soviet Union. Solzhenitsyn now lives in this country.

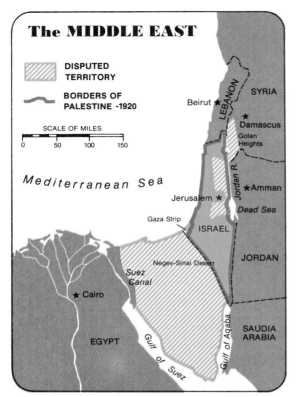

The MIDDLE EAST

DISPUTED TERRITORY

BORDERS OF PALESTINE -1920

SCALE OF MILES

0   50   100   150

SYRIA

Beirut

LEBANON

Damascus

Golan Heights

Mediterranean Sea

Jordan R.

Jerusalem

Amman

Dead Sea

Gaza Strip

ISRAEL

JORDAN

Negev-Sinai Desert

Suez Canal

Cairo

Gulf of Aqaba

Gulf of Suez

EGYPT

SAUDIA ARABIA

Figure 16-3

Palestine, calling for a division of the land into an Arab and a Jewish section. Although Great Britain and the Jewish population of Palestine agreed to this division, Palestinian Arabs did not. In their eyes, their land was being taken away.

Under the plan agreed to by Britain, British control ended and the Jewish state of Israel came into being on May 14, 1948. The next day it was attacked by troops from Egypt, Iraq, Lebanon, Syria, and Jordan. The fighting lasted for nine months and ended in a truce. However, Israel was able to remain as an independent state. (Figure 16–3 is a map of the Middle East, showing Israel and its Arab neighbors.)

After this war, many Moslem and Christian Palestinians were displaced from their homes in Israel. A large number of these Palestinians sought refuge in neighboring Lebanon. Temporary camps were set up outside of major cities such as Beirut, Lebanon. Few permanent homes were established, because many Palestinians hoped

and expected to regain their homelands in Israel.

Although Lebanon is in the Arab world, it frequently does not agree with other Arab nations because of its religious makeup. There are two major religious groups in Lebanon—Moslems and Christians. Conflict between the two groups has built up over a long period of time. In the 1970s, the presence of many Palestinian refugees in Lebanon—many of whom were armed—triggered open hostilities. Lebanese Moslems and Christians did not agree on the question of the Palestinian efforts to regain their land. In general, Lebanese Moslems supported the Palestinian efforts while most Lebanese Christians did not. In 1976, fighting broke out between these two factions. A majority of Lebanese Christians fought against a combined force of many Lebanese Moslems and the Palestinian refugees.

As a result of the fighting, many people were wounded. A number of the injured were in the Palestinian refugee camps around Beirut. To help the injured, the International Committee of the Red Cross stepped in. The Red Cross, founded in the last century, has worked to help many victims of war. It is a nongovernmental organization; in other words, it is not attached to any government. Its sole objective is to help victims of conflicts, regardless of their side in the battle.

In times of war, the parties involved may be resistant to having other governments enter the conflict area. They may fear that this will be of help to the other side. Because the Red Cross is *neutral*—it does not take sides—it sometimes can help victims of conflict when outside governments cannot.

In the Lebanese civil war, the Red Cross tried a number of times to arrange a cease-fire. (A *cease-fire* is a temporary agreement to stop fighting.) Both sides had to agree to a cease-fire, or the Red Cross would not allow its workers to enter the area.

A cease-fire agreement was reached in August 1976. At this time the Red Cross was able to evacuate 334 people from the fighting area.

Even though both sides to the fighting had agreed to the cease-fire, there still was some shooting during the evacuation. Some Red Cross vehicles were hit by bullets, but no Red Cross workers were injured. Because of the danger to its volunteers, the Red Cross had to stop the operation. Six hundred wounded people were left behind. Without a cease-fire, the Red Cross would not operate in Beirut.

An end to the fighting was later achieved, though the situation is still dangerous. The seeds of conflict remain.

★ Foreign Cars in the United States

On almost every American street, it is possible to see a foreign car. For many years, the best-selling foreign cars in the United States were manufactured by Volkswagen, a large West German corporation. In 1970, Volkswagen sold 569,695 cars in the United States.

How have sales of Volkswagens and other foreign cars in the United States affected American automakers? In 1974, the American auto industry was in a deep sales slump. Unemployment in the auto industry was very high. The United Autoworkers Union complained that many American jobs were being lost because of unfair competition from foreign cars. To investigate these charges, the United States Treasury Department began a study of 28 foreign firms that sold automobiles in the United States.

The study found that many of these foreign automakers were "dumping" their cars in the United States. (*Dumping* means that a product is sold more cheaply in a foreign market than in the country where it is made.) According to the Treasury Department, dumping was the reason why foreign cars were selling so well in the United States. A person living in Illinois could buy a Volkswagen car for less than someone living in West Germany.

The Treasury Department agreed to drop its investigation if the car makers involved promised to raise prices of their cars in the United States. The Treasury Department dropped its investigation for several other reasons as well. Foreign car sales had fallen in the United States because more small inexpensive cars were being made in the United States. In addition, if the Treasury Department had gone through with the investigation and imposed fines, foreign car companies would have had to pay large sums of money. This action might well have complicated relations between foreign governments and the United States.

★ The TAN-ZAM Railroad

Zambia is a nation located in the southern part of Africa. Because Zambia is a landlocked country, it must ship its goods to the rest of the world across other African nations. For many years, Zambia used trade routes running through Rhodesia and South Africa. Because the Zambian government came to disagree with many of the policies of these two nations, it sought new trade routes.

In 1970, President Kenneth Kaunda announced that Zambia had signed an agreement with the People's Republic of China and Tanzania. The agreement called for mutual cooperation in building a 1,163-mile railroad link to the sea. The Chinese government was to supply a $400 million loan, advisers, and workers. Tanzania was to allow the railroad to pass through its territory, to the seaport at Dar es Salaam.

On October 23, 1975, the TAN-ZAM railroad was officially opened. Today, more than 50 percent of the country's exports are sent to other countries via TAN-ZAM, including a major portion of Zambia's copper exports. Figure 16-4, on the following page, shows the railroad's route.

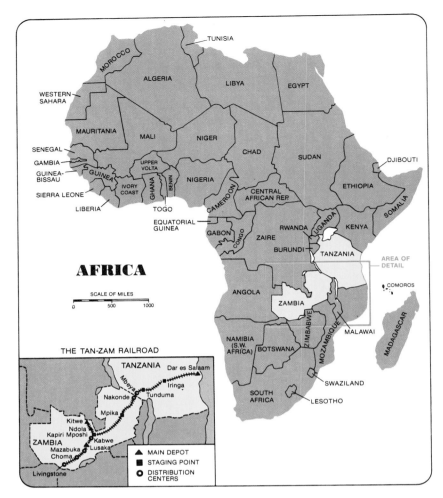

Figure 16-4

1. List the global actors in the cases you just read. Identify each actor as either a nation, international organization, corporation, or individual.

2. Identify the global issues in the preceding cases. Place each issue in one of the following categories: war and peace, international economics, human rights. There may be more than one issue in each case.

3. Describe how each of the issues you've identified can affect you.

4. Which of the following could be considered a global issue? In what ways?

   a. An oil spill in the middle of the Atlantic Ocean

   b. An insect that destroys crops

   c. Air pollution from factories

   d. The space race among nations

5. Explain why the word *complexity* is an appropriate word to explain global politics today.

Global Political Systems

Nations interact with one another over peace treaties, trade agreements, cultural exchanges, and scientific cooperation. Leaders of nations meet at special conferences, and heads of large corporations have business meetings in large cities around the world. Citizens around the world travel abroad for pleasure, business, or study.

Global political activity is based on interactions such as these. Because of the growth of such interactions in today's world, it is possible to view the world as one political system. Of course, no single official government operates for the globe. The control of global political activity depends on the voluntary agreement of individuals, groups, nations, and international organizations. Yet the growth of such agreements does signal increased joint activity and resource exchange among global actors.

ONE GLOBAL SYSTEM In what sense is the globe a political system? Remember that a system is made up of interrelated parts. Nations, international organizations and businesses, heads of state, and even individual citizens can be thought of as important parts of the global political system. A system is further defined by certain patterns of activity. Decision-making, leadership, communication, and participation take place on an international scale. Because many nations are involved in such activities, these form the backbone of global politics.

Think of major issues that concern the world today—the depletion of natural resources, the threat of nuclear war, demands on the world food supply, and the protection of human rights. These are concerns which affect the people of all countries. The interaction which occurs over these concerns creates patterns of activity that are characteristic of one global political system.

The Issue of Food Production. Let's examine food production as an issue of major global concern. Many nations have interacted to seek solutions to this problem. Here are several examples of interaction that has occurred over this issue in recent years:

1. In November 1974, the United Nations sponsored a world food conference in Rome. Representatives from many nations attended. One major purpose of the conference was to discuss ways to in-crease food production to feed a growing world population.

2. For more than 20 years, the United States has been sending technical advisers to countries in Asia and Africa. These advisers have demonstrated modern farming methods in an effort to improve agricultural yields.

3. Grain sales by grain-producing nations such as the United States and Canada to countries in need of grain are an effort to equalize food distribution in the world.

4. Nations are cooperating in investigating the potential of ocean plant life as a future source of food.

5. In times of severe crisis, individual nations, the United Nations, and private agencies send assistance to countries in need. For example, in 1973 and 1974, there was a terrible drought in the Sahel region of Africa (below the Sahara Desert). Many thousands of people died from starvation and malnutrition. Many nations sent food to this region as relief for the stricken people. The United Nations and private agencies were active in similar efforts.

Interactions such as these involve a great deal of political activity among world leaders, scientists, and technicians. Leadership is exercised, important decisions are made, communication is carefully handled, and participation is opened to many nations. Individuals such as farmers and businessmen are also involved in these political activities; they too participate in the global political system. As a result of these activities, resources are distributed to people across the globe.

The Issue of Boundaries. The Helsinki agreements of 1975 represent another example of global politics. In July 1973, the United States, Canada, the Soviet Union, and 32 nations of Western and Eastern Europe met in Helsinki, Finland. The meeting, initiated by Moscow, was known as the

Conference on Security and Cooperation in Europe. The main purpose of this meeting was to accept on an official basis the boundaries of post–World War II Europe. In addition, the Western nations wanted to discuss concrete ways to improve relations among the peoples of Europe.

A series of agreements were signed on August 1, 1975. One section, known informally as Basket 3, called for the freer movement of people, ideas, and information between East and West. This section is not a treaty or legally binding agreement, but a single statement of intent. The discussions and negotiations which helped produce the Helsinki agreements are an example of the global system at work.

Other Issues. As another example of global politics, consider the case of the TAN-ZAM railroad. As you know, the nations of Zambia, Tanzania, and China cooperated to build a railroad that would export Zambian goods, most importantly copper. Because copper is used by many industrial nations, its distribution has a direct effect on the economy of other nations.

In the same way, we can think of the Red Cross as being part of a global political system. The Red Cross distributes resources such as medical supplies and medical knowledge to crisis areas around the world. The Red Cross makes decisions on how and where its resources are to be sent. These decisions can save lives and help people across the world.

Some global concerns have less worldwide impact than others. For example, if the people of a nation do not produce or consume large quantities of coffee, the nation will probably be less concerned about the price of coffee than a country in which a lot of coffee is exported and/or consumed. However, the issues of food production and relations among nations previously discussed are examples of issues that are of significant global concern.

In summary, because of the growing amount and kinds of interactions among global political actors, we can, in one sense, view the world as a single political system. In other words, many global actors are interacting with one another in political activity—using political resources and affecting the distribution of resources throughout the world as well. As nations and people interact to find solutions to global problems, they are participating in the politics of a global political system.

1. Explain how the need to increase world food production involves a nation in a global political system.
2. Explain how large corporations can be involved in the global political system.
3. What other issues can you name that involve many global actors? Explain.

ONE SYSTEM MADE UP of OTHERS Are all patterns of activity between global actors part of the global political system? Suppose the Mexican and American governments decide to increase the number of police patrolling their common border. Does this activity affect the global system? The answer is no. In this instance, it makes sense to think in terms of the United States–Mexican subsystem of the global system.

Suppose that France and Switzerland decide to increase the number of telephone lines that connect the two nations. This activity does not affect the global system either. Again, it makes more sense to think in terms of a France-Switzerland political subsystem.

These examples illustrate that global politics can also be viewed in terms of independent political systems, or subsystems. In other words, there are some issues that concern two or perhaps several nations but that do not affect the global system.

United States negotiations with the Soviet Union, Saudi Arabian investments in Great Britain, discussions of fishing rights between Iceland and Great Britain—each of these is an example of a single political subsystem operating within the global system. Of course, if any one of these situations should eventually involve other nations, the global political system would come into play.

1. Compare the United States–Mexican political system with the global political system. In which system do you think there is more activity? Why?
2. Name at least two other political subsystems involving two nations. The newspaper and news reports on radio or television can be helpful sources of information.

GROWING COMPLEXITY

In the past 20 years, the global political system and its subsystems have expanded. In other words, there are more participants in the global community. In 1945, there were about 40 nations in the world. By the late 1970s, there were 162. The number of international organizations and businesses has grown as well.

Unfortunately, the number of problems confronting the global community has also increased. World War II introduced the threat of nuclear war, a type of warfare with obvious global implications. Pollution, maintaining a balance in world trade, overpopulation, and the distribution of scarce natural resources are also problems that require global cooperation.

The idea of one global community has been advanced further by innovations in transportation and technology. Today it is possible to cross the Atlantic Ocean in three hours on the supersonic airplane, the Concorde. Because of satellite broadcasts, it is possible to watch programs and major news items as they are televised in other countries.

As a result of all these developments, global interactions are much more common. Many of these interactions are also more complex because of the number of global is-

sues and actors. Basically every nation interacts with other nations in the world on a daily basis. Few nations can remain isolated today.

1. Highlight three ways in which the increasing oneness of the global political system can have an impact on your life.
2. In what ways do you think the world is smaller today than it was in 1945?

CHANGE in the GLOBAL SYSTEM

No political system is static. Change occurs on a regular basis. New officials are elected; new laws are enacted; court decisions establish new precedents. In other words, change is a continual process.

In Unit 3 you studied some examples of change in the American political system. You saw how the civil rights movement extended the rights of black Americans. Through new voting legislation in the nineteenth and twentieth centuries, black Americans have been guaranteed the opportunity to take full part in this country's political process. As they entered politics, changes occurred. Elected officials began to address the needs of black voters. And black people gained election in increasing numbers to local, state, and national offices.

Global political systems also change over time. The problems resulting from limited natural resources have been one source of change in global politics. The 1973 oil crisis, for example, made many people realize that nations are increasingly dependent upon one another. It became apparent that the decisions of oil-producing nations can affect many other countries. As a result, new relationships have been established in the global community. Countries controlling limited natural resources have been recognized as important global actors.

Change in a political system is often the result of many factors. Three forces that usually produce change are conflict, cooperation, and development.

Conflict. Disagreements between nations or groups can result in conflict. When conflict takes the form of war, the entire global political system may be changed. World War II certainly brought about major changes in global politics. The United States and the Soviet Union emerged as world powers. Germany was divided into two nations, and parts of Eastern Europe fell under communist control.

Conflict does not have to be violent, however. Two nations can experience conflict over trade regulations, for example, but they will not necessarily go to war against one another. Instead, the conflict may take the form of angry verbal exchanges or new trade restrictions.

Another type of action which nations in conflict may follow is breaking diplomatic ties with one another. For example, the United States broke diplomatic relations with Cuba in the late 1950s when Fidel Castro came to power. Many African nations have broken diplomatic ties with Israel.

The result of conflict on the global level is often new relationships of friendship or hostility among nations. These relationships have further impact on the internal politics and economies of individual nations. In any case, when one part of the global system is affected by conflict, the system as a whole may also be affected.

Cooperation. Another force of change is cooperation. Trade agreements and military alliances require cooperation, as do scientific and cultural exchanges. There are many examples of cooperation between two nations in today's world. The United States and Canada, for example, cooperate in maintaining a border free from armed control. The United States and Great Britain cooperate by not requiring their citizens to have visas (official authorization) when traveling between one country and another.

There are also instances of cooperation among several nations acting as a group.

The European Common Market, an economic and trade association, is an example of such cooperation. Members of the European Common Market are Belgium, France, Italy, Luxembourg, the Netherlands, West Germany, Denmark, Ireland, and Great Britain.

Cooperation can be a positive force behind global change. It can lead to improved economies, scientific advancement, and increased military security for those who cooperate with one another.

Development. A third factor that has created global change is economic and political development. As nations develop their natural resources and industrialize, they become more powerful on the global scene. Their ability to control the distribution of resources in the world brings about further changes in international politics.

The new nations of Africa are a prime example of how the growth and development of nations can affect the global scene. As voting members of the United Nations General Assembly, they can form a strong voice in passing certain resolutions. United as a group and with the backing of other countries, they can succeed in accomplishing their goals. Such was the case when the People's Republic of China was admitted to the United Nations.

The following case study illustrates how the processes of conflict, cooperation, and development produced changes in the relationships among five nations in Central America. As you read, try to identify the changes that occurred in the Central American political system. Determine whether each change was the result of conflict, cooperation, or development.

★ The Formation of the Central American Common Market

The people of Central America have close ethnic and social ties. The entire region (with the exception of British Honduras, or

Figure 16-5

Belize) was a Spanish colony from 1525 to 1821. As a result, most people share a blend of Spanish and Indian ancestries. Spanish is the official language, and many Central American customs and institutions are of Spanish origin.

In 1821, Central American nationalists united to resist Spanish rule. Independence was declared, and five nations were formed—Costa Rica, El Salvador, Honduras, Guatemala, and Nicaragua. (Belize remained a British colony until recently. Panama was part of the South American nation of Colombia until it became an independent state in 1903.) Figure 16–5 shows Central America as it is today.

Despite the common histories of the five nations, rivalries over trade and territory soon developed. Many attempts were made to resolve these disputes. However, until the 1940s most of these efforts were unsuccessful. Most leaders were dictators who were unwilling to give up complete jurisdiction over their nations.

In 1945, when the dictators of Guatemala and El Salvador lost power, the new heads of state met to work out a plan for economic cooperation. They tried to remove trade barriers and immigration restrictions between the two countries. Although the union later was dissolved, it was an important step toward economic cooperation in Central America.

In 1951, another attempt was made to establish unity. The heads of all five nations met in San Salvador, the capital of El Salvador, to discuss common problems and the need for closer ties. The charter signed at this conference was a formal basis for stronger relationships between Central American nations.

The United Nations reinforced this move toward Central American unity. Studies by the United Nations' Economic Committee for Latin America demonstrated the advantages of cooperation. This group worked out measures for easier exchange of money among the five nations. Also, the

Committee established guidelines so that the nations could exchange goods.

On the basis of the San Salvador conference and United Nations suggestions, El Salvador and Nicaragua agreed to cooperate. In 1951, a free trade treaty was signed between the two nations. In 1953, another bilateral treaty was signed by El Salvador and Costa Rica. (A *bilateral treaty* is an agreement between two nations.) During 1955 and 1956, Guatemala and Honduras signed two treaties, and in 1957, El Salvador and Honduras signed a trade agreement. These treaties formed the basis for working out political and economic problems among the Central American nations.

In 1958, two multilateral treaties were ratified by the legislatures of participating nations. (A *multilateral treaty* is an agreement among three or more nations.) These treaties established free trade for ten years. They also set up the Central American Trade Commission. This Commission sought to abolish all customs duties among Central American countries, equalize tariffs for outside trade, and create better transportation throughout Central America.

These multilateral agreements were the first of their kind in Central America. Within three years after the treaties were signed, trade had tripled among Central American countries. The advantages of multilateral cooperation were clear.

In 1960, another meeting was called. There had not been equal economic development in all Central American nations. The General Treaty of Central American

Economic Integration, proposed to make rules for all trade, was signed by Guatemala, El Salvador, Nicaragua, and Honduras in 1961. Costa Rica signed the treaty in 1963. (Panama elected to stay out of the agreement until it had completed negotiations with the United States on the status of the Panama Canal. Belize, with its continued ties to Great Britain and the Commonwealth also did not join.)

The treaty set up trade guidelines for a period of 20 years. It also established the Central American Common Market. The purpose of this organization was to work on free trade, provide equal tax incentives for industrial development, and centralize banks so money could flow more freely.

The creation of the Central American Common Market was the result of decades of work by diplomats and economists. Since the development of this organization, trade in Central America has increased, and the economic picture in this region has improved.

1. What events in the Central American case study show that political systems can change over time?
2. How did conflict first produce change in Central American politics?
3. In what ways has cooperation helped the development of Central American nations?
4. What new political relations developed as a result of the formation of the Central American Common Market? How do these differ from former political relationships?

Global Interdependence

You have seen how Central American nations cooperated to solve common economic and political problems. This cooperation reduced tensions. As a result, new relationships were established among participants in the Central American political system.

This kind of cooperation also occurs on a global scale. In recent years, global issues have required the cooperation of many global actors. Issues such as nuclear war, pollution, and scarce natural resources cannot be solved by one nation acting alone. Many

The international exchange of products, knowledge, and natural resources is a key part of today's global interdependence. These German cars, imported into Brazil, are among the thousands of products traded around the world (top photo). The United Nations sends technical advisors to many countries. This agricultural specialist is advising Indonesian farmers on rice-growing techniques (center photo). The need of nations for natural resources like oil has had a powerful effect on the global political system (bottom photo).

groups must cooperate. As a result, the global political system has become more interdependent. Interdependence on the global level means that global actors rely upon one another and are affected by one another. They must work together to solve common problems.

ANALYZING INTER-DEPENDENCE

A number of criteria can be used to determine whether a political system is interdependent. For example, in an interdependent system, the same issue affects many groups. Because of this, one group's decision affects the other groups. Many links between groups also signify interdependence. This means that within the system there are many ways to communicate and to exchange resources. Also, in an interdependent system, no one political actor can control the other groups. Political participants in an interdependent system must consider others' actions and reactions.

Using these criteria, we can establish the role of the United States in the global political system. First, is the United States affected by issues that concern other nations? The answer is yes. Global issues such as pollution, trade, and war involve many nations, including the United States. Because of this, the United States government makes some decisions only after it has conferred with other governments. For example, before extending fishing rights in the ocean, the American government made sure other nations would respect the United States decision.

Are there important links that tie the United States to the rest of the world? Again, the answer is yes. There are American ambassadors in almost every nation. Each year many thousands of American citizens travel to other countries. American goods are sold throughout the world. Therefore, the United States has many ways to communicate and to exchange resources with the rest of the world.

Finally, even though the United States is a rich and powerful nation, can it control other nations? The answer to this question is no. The United States cannot tell the Soviet Union to stop producing weapons. If a particular resource is running out, the United States cannot make other nations adhere to conservation rules. Because the United States does not control other countries, it must rely on cooperation among the participants in the global system.

Despite its interdependence, the United States still can act independently and make some decisions that affect only one or two nations. For example, the United States can impose pollution controls on American industries without consulting other governments. Grain can be sold to the Soviet Union without affecting the entire global system. But an increasing number of global problems require the cooperation of many nations. This need for cooperation is producing a much more interdependent world in which the United States participates.

The following case study shows that even 1/50th of the United States has important links to the rest of the world. The case illustrates the many contacts and interactions that the state of Indiana has with other nations. A similar case could be written about each of the other states in our country and their relationship to global affairs. As you read, think about the ways in which the state of Indiana is part of an interdependent global system. Think about how interdependence affects you in your state and community.

★ Indiana in an Interdependent World

Indiana, located in the midwestern part of the United States, is the 11th largest state in population size. Like other midwestern states, Indiana is a leading producer of agricultural goods. Indiana's wheat, flour, and soybeans are exported to many nations, including Japan, India, South Korea, Iran, Mexico, Brazil, Algeria, and the Soviet Union. If Indiana's farmers decide to raise the price of farm products, other nations will be affected. If a nation buys less grain from the United States, Indiana's farmers are concerned. In this sense, farmers in Indiana are linked to the rest of the world.

Agricultural products are not Indiana's only export. Indiana also sells many manufactured goods to other areas of the world. If the president of an Indiana corporation decides to sell a new product to another country, the lives of people in that nation may be affected. If another country produces the same products more cheaply than those made in Indiana, the state's business may be affected. Thus, the business community is interdependent with other nations.

Within Indiana's business community, many companies are owned by foreign firms. For example, both the Libby Company in Kokomo and the Alcan Aluminum Corporation in Indianapolis are owned by Canadians. Japanese, Belgian, Italian, West German, and English companies own other industries in Indiana.

The lives of Indiana's citizens are linked to other parts of the world in another way. Besides the economic links, there are educational links with the rest of the world. High school students in Indiana go abroad to study, while their counterparts from other nations are in Indiana high schools.

Students in Indiana colleges and universities may spend a semester or a school year at foreign universities. While in another country, students meet the people of other nations, share ideas, and explain what life is like in the United States.

Foreign students also study at Indiana's colleges and universities. At Indiana University in Bloomington, there are students from almost every nation of the world.

It is apparent that Indiana has many links to the world. It is an international actor, as Indiana citizens, corporations, and farmers interact with other nations.

Sometimes the interdependence benefits Indiana. Ties between the economies of many nations may mean new customers for products made or grown in Indiana. The attendance of foreign students at Indiana University means an increase in students who support the university. Moreover, the students from the United States may benefit from the opportunity to share ideas and to learn about life in other nations.

On the other hand, interdependence can have certain negative effects. If an Indiana company is owned by a foreign firm, some of the profits will be spent in other nations. If the people in Indiana can buy foreign products for less money, they may buy less from Indiana companies. Moreover, Indiana's businessmen may have little control over the economic decisions made in other countries.

Therefore, Indiana's interdependence has many positive and many negative effects. Future interactions will tell how these effects balance out. Cooperation among global actors will be needed to solve any future international problems faced by the state of Indiana.

1. Who are the major global actors in the Indiana case? What are some of the major issues over which they interact?

2. The Indiana case is an example of interdependence in the global political system. What are some positive and negative effects of such interdependence?

3. Consider the students, teachers, and administrators to be the three main political groups in your school. Decide whether this is an interdependent system by answering the following questions.

   a. Are there issues that affect all three groups? If so, name two of these.

   b. Are there important links of communication that tie these groups?

   c. Can one group make decisions for all the others concerning mutual problems? Explain why or why not.

   d. Can one group control all the others? In other words, can one group avoid being influenced by the other groups?

Students, teachers, schools, and families in 60 countries take part in the exchange programs sponsored by the American Field Service. In the photos on this page American students are welcomed in their host countries. Learning a new language and new customs are important parts of the AFS experience (page 515, top). Since 1947 more than 53,000 young people have been AFS exchange students to the United States. They have attended American high schools and lived with American families (page 515, center and bottom).

515

Chapter Review

1. What are some of the ways in which people think about the world? How do these ideas compare and/or contrast with your perceptions?
2. Review the meaning of a global actor, and list several ways in which you can be a global actor.
3. Describe several situations or problems that are examples of global issues.
4. In what ways is the world one global political system?
5. Review the case studies in Chapter 16. Then, in chart form, identify examples of leadership, communication, participation, and decision-making.
6. Summarize the ways in which the world has become more complex during the past 20 years. How have these factors promoted the idea of one global community?
7. Review the forces that usually produce change in a political system. In your opinion, which of these bring about the most constructive changes? Explain.
8. What criteria determine whether or not a system is interdependent?
9. "The United States is a global superpower; however, it is not free to set global policy." Explain the meaning of this statement.
10. In your opinion, what are the positive and negative effects of living in an interdependent political system?

Chapter Vocabulary

Define the following terms.

interdependence	global issue	bilateral treaty
international organization	detente	multilateral treaty
global actor	cease-fire	

Chapter Analysis

1. Select a global issue that you consider to be very important to the future of the global community. Then, in essay form, suggest ways in which nations might interact to resolve this issue. If possible, note the role that you can play.
2. Explain what is meant by the term *political system*. Then analyze the ways in which all the nations of the world form a global political system.
3. Discuss the positive and negative effects of change on the global system. Give examples to support your analysis.

1. Keep a notebook in which you record information that shows how you are affected by other nations. Consider the foreign products that you use, foreign policy decisions that influence your life, events in other countries that could have an impact on you and your community, etc.

2. Political cartoons express a viewpoint in a visual manner. Examine several such cartoons on the editorial page of your local paper. Then prepare your own political cartoon expressing your views on America's role in an interdependent system.

3. Investigate the number of countries that possess the technology to build nuclear weapons and/or reactors. Then in a class discussion, suggest policies that you think the global community should adopt to regulate this knowledge.

Chapter Bibliography

Columbus in the World: The World in Columbus, Chadwick F. Alger (Transnational Intellectual Cooperation Program, Columbus, OH).
> Materials that demonstrate the connections which one American city, Columbus, Ohio, has to many nations throughout the world.

The Dilemma Facing Humanity, International Symposium I (Battelle Memorial Institute, Columbus, OH), 1974.
> Contains statements of various national leaders from around the world, each considering growing interdependence from a different point of view.

Mankind at the Turning Point, Mihajlo Mesarovic and Eduard Pestel (Hutchinson: London, England), 1975.
> Describes the current problems in global politics and poses alternatives for future problem-solving, arguing for the cooperation of national and international organizations.

Toward the 21st Century: Education for a Changing World, Edwin O. Reischauer (Alfred A. Knopf: New York, NY), 1973.
> A straightforward book that presents problems inherent in an increasingly interdependent world and ends with a discussion of world citizenship.

Toward a Politics of the Planet Earth, Harold and Margaret Sprout (Van Nostrand Reinhold: New York, NY), 1971.
> Cites increasing interdependence and the resulting need for international cooperation.

Spaceship Earth, Barbara Ward (Columbia University Press: New York), 1966.
> Presents a good background to a consideration of the global political system. It details how the world has become increasingly interdependent and considers the implications for the distribution of wealth and power in the global political system.

Chapter Objectives

★ To identify reasons for peace and war in global politics

★ To analyze the work of the United Nations, regional alliances, and nations in keeping the peace

★ To develop skill in hypothesizing

★ To develop skill in settling group differences

chapter 17

The POLITICS of PEACE

Although war has been a recurring event throughout recorded history, nuclear weapons have given war a global dimension. If a nuclear war were to occur, nations could be totally devastated. Directly or indirectly, every nation would be affected. Because of this, the entire global community has a vital interest in maintaining world peace.

After World War II, the United Nations was created in an attempt to prevent future global wars. However, because the United Nations was not given the power to enforce its decisions, nations still remain the central political actors in issues of war and peace.

Chapter 16 discussed the growing interdependence among the nations of the world. Sometimes nations cooperate to solve common problems; however, at other times they have conflicting interests. In an interdependent world in which the danger of nuclear war exists, it is crucial that differences be settled peacefully.

In this chapter, you will study some of the causes for war and the ways in which global political actors have sought to prevent war. You will also learn how diplomacy and negotiation play important roles in maintaining peace in an interdependent world. Through the use of these skills, all participants in the global system, including individual citizens, can contribute to worldwide cooperation and peace.

Peace and War in Global Politics

There have been few periods since 1850 in which there has not been a major war somewhere in the world. The same has been true all through history. If you marked on a map all the countries ever affected by war, virtually every country would be included.

These facts raise a major question: Why do wars occur? People have thought about this for centuries, and it remains an important question in international politics today. Political scientists and historians have developed different theories about the causes of war. Some of the most accepted of these theories are presented here.

The ROOTS of WAR

Keep in mind that no one factor causes war. Usually there are many reasons behind the start of a war. Some of the causes of a particular war may have deep historical roots. Others are those events that immediately bring about the conflict. Therefore, the analysis of war is a complicated question. Solutions vary with the situation and the nations involved.

Human Nature. There are those who believe that people are basically aggressive. In other words, they believe it is more natural for people to fight about differences than to try to settle them peacefully. This theory is supported by the fact that foreign policies today are likely to be aimed at competition rather than at cooperation, and war is often chosen as a solution to a dispute.

National Goals. Some theorists believe that wars are brought about because of national goals. A nation may, for example, develop a policy that is best achieved by war. Suppose a nation wants more territory or more trade. War may be the best means for advancing this goal. Viewed in this manner, the decision to go to war is not made for reasons of national security; it is made because war accomplishes a goal. Moreover, when citizens of a country have a strong sense of *nationalism,* or feeling of loyalty toward their country, many may be willing to support a war effort. People who see national goals as a cause of war believe that as long as nations exist, the chances of war will be great.

Arms Race. This theory has gained increasing acceptance since World War II and the development of nuclear warfare. Advocates of this point of view assert that if a nation believes itself to be threatened, it will build up its supply of weapons. Other nations see this and they in turn feel threatened. As a result, they increase the size of their armed forces. The race goes back and forth, and each side grows more fearful of an attack. One side may become so certain that an attack is coming that it will strike first in what it considers to be self-defense. In a sense, the preparation for war produces a threat, which then causes the war itself.

Some people apply this theory to nuclear build-ups in the United States and in the Soviet Union. They argue that unless the arms race is slowed, nuclear war will result.

Economic Gains. Another prominent theory on the cause of war is that wars are fought to protect economic interests. Within a nation many people may have military careers or work in industries that provide weapons, services, or supplies to the armed forces. As a result, war or military preparedness creates jobs and a demand for certain domestic products. This helps to support the national economy.

A nation might also go to war to protect its foreign economic interests. For example, if one country tries to take control of all foreign industries within its borders, another nation might declare war to protect its investments in that country. Or, if one nation seeks to control trade with a bloc of countries, another nation might be willing to declare war to protect its trading rights.

Growing Interdependence. Some theorists believe that interdependence is a cause of war. They argue that as nations know more about each other, enter into common activities, and depend upon each other for protection and resources, they are bound to have conflicts which would not occur if nations were independent of one another. Moves toward energy independence in the United States in the 1970s have been motivated by concerns about economics and also by a fear of war over scarce resources.

Multiple Causes of War. It is important to remember that a number of reasons influence a government's decision to go to war. Therefore, when people analyze the causes of a particular war, all possible factors must be considered.

The 1973 war in the Middle East illustrates the complexity of war. No one cause led to the war. Hostility between Arabs and Israelis had existed for 25 years over claims to the area known as Palestine, now part of Israel. During the 1967 war between Israel and the Arab states, Israel had captured territory belonging to both Syria and Egypt. As of 1973, Israel still held this land, and Syria and Egypt wanted to reclaim it. There had been significant arms build-ups in all three countries, and each government was supported by a loyal and nationalistic citizenry. Together, these factors helped initiate open warfare. Any peace solution had to take into account all these forces.

1. Explain the theories of war presented in this section.
2. Think of a decision recently made by your family. What factors influenced this decision? Why should you examine all the forces that play a role in any decision?

The Skill of Hypothesizing

You have read several theories that offer answers to the question "Why do wars occur?" These theories are based on evidence that people have gathered by studying past wars. In other words, if someone notices that nationalism has been an important factor in many wars, that person may reasonably conclude that nationalism is a cause of war.

A theory that is based on evidence and that tentatively answers a question is called a *hypothesis*. A hypothesis is a statement that explains why something happens, on the basis of knowledge about similar events.

ceded rain. Because of this knowledge, whenever you see a lot of dark clouds, you say that it is going to rain whether you are in Chicago, Peoria, Denver, or Richmond.

The general form of a hypothesis is: If X, then Y. In other words, if there are dark clouds (X), then it will rain (Y). This statement not only expresses a relationship between two things, it also can be applied to all cases in which certain weather conditions exist. This is the format for a good hypothesis. It expresses some kind of relationship, and this relationship can be expected to occur in all similar situations.

FORMING HYPOTHESES You form hypotheses all the time. For example, if the sky is filled with dark clouds, you might predict that it will rain. Your hypothesis is based on your past experience in which dark clouds preceded

HYPOTHESIZING about WAR and PEACE When people talk about global war and peace, they also form hypotheses on the basis of their experiences. Through your study of some causes of past

521

wars, you could form your own hypotheses about what might cause future warfare. For example, you might say "If nationalism does not decline in Middle Eastern nations, then future wars may occur." Or, "If nations continue to pursue their individual national goals, then global conflict probably will continue." Still another hypothesis could be, "If nations feel threatened by one another, then the possibility of war is high."

Such hypotheses can be useful in working to prevent future wars and to promote peace in the world. In other words, if certain conditions have produced war in the past, people can try to keep these situations from recurring. For example, an arms build-up was one factor in the outbreak of World War I. Therefore, based on this past experience, an attempt might be made to get nations to agree to limit current arms productions.

Just as certain hypotheses can be formed about the probable causes of war, similar hypotheses can be made about the reasons for peace. This means that on the basis of past experience, tentative answers can be offered to the question "What conditions will promote world peace?" For example, recall how cooperation among Central American nations led to the formation of the Central American Common Market. This paved the way for reduced conflicts among the five member nations. Based on this case study, you might hypothesize that if nations cooperate more, the chances for another global war are reduced.

1. If nations have been able to settle differences peacefully, would you hypothesize that it will be easier to settle the next difference peacefully? Explain.
2. Review the six theories on the causes of war. Put each of these into the hypothesis form of "if X, then Y."
3. Formulate your own hypotheses about the reasons nations go to war. Next, formulate hypotheses about the conditions that might promote global peace. You will test these hypotheses throughout this unit.

Nations and Foreign Policy

Today's global political system bears little resemblance to the one that existed 30 years ago. To begin with, the number of global political actors has greatly increased. Since 1945, the global community has grown from 40 to more than 160 nations. Moreover, these nations are no longer the only force in global politics. In recent years, large business corporations, international organizations, and citizen groups have become influential participants in world affairs. Although new types of global political actors have begun to influence international politics, the nations of the world still remain the most important global actors today.

In today's world, interactions among nations are varied and also frequent. This situation has brought about a critical problem: How should the relations between nations be managed to avoid conflict?

MAKERS of FOREIGN POLICY The way in which a nation manages its relations with other nations is called its *foreign policy*. Through its foreign policy, each nation pursues its own interests while trying to influence the policies of other nations to its advantage.

A nation's foreign policy is not static. It changes over time. For example, new leaders may come into office and decide to change a particular policy. Or, new global events may make a government reexamine its relations with other nations.

In the foreign policy process, decisions are made continually. These decisions involve choosing the best alternatives and then understanding the consequences of each decision. In an interdependent system, the long-range effects of every foreign policy decision need to be assessed carefully.

Because a nation's foreign policy can affect the people of many nations, it is important to know who makes these decisions. Bearing in mind the differences in the forms of national governments, at least five types of actors are involved in making a nation's foreign policy: heads of state, foreign ministers, ambassadors, citizens, and the news media.

Heads of State. Countries have different titles for their heads of state, depending on their form of government. Some countries have a president, some have a prime minister, others have a king and/or queen, and still others may be ruled by a military leader.

In many nations, the head of state plays an active role in the foreign policy process and in conducting a nation's relations with other countries. This is only one of the many duties of a head of state. (Remember, as you read in Chapter 13, that acting as head of state is one of the six main roles of a president of the United States.)

Foreign Ministers. A head of state cannot possibly attend to all the details of making and conducting foreign policy. There are too many demands on his or her time. The responsibility for foreign policy therefore falls to the foreign minister. The foreign minister is responsible for monitoring crisis situations around the world and for implementing the nation's foreign policy.

In the United States, the foreign minister is called the secretary of state. During the Nixon and Ford administrations, Secretary of State Henry Kissinger played an important role in world affairs. He was very active in trying to work out peace solutions to crises in the Middle East, Africa, Vietnam, and Latin America. Secretary Kissinger traveled a great deal between Israel, Egypt, Jordan, and other Middle East countries in what is sometimes called "shuttle diplomacy." In effect, he shuttled from one country to another, talking to leaders individually and trying to put together compromise solutions.

Not all secretaries of state have been as influential as Kissinger. In some cases, presidents have not worked closely with their secretaries of state and have not sought their views in the decision-making process.

Ambassadors. Ambassadors represent their nation in other countries. They act as

Working aboard his plane, Secretary of State Henry Kissinger often shuttled between Egypt and Israel.

channels of communication to relay messages between national governments. If necessary, ambassadors also assist citizens of their nation who are either visitors or residents in foreign countries. The United States has ambassadors in almost all nations of the world.

Citizens. In some nations, individual citizens play an important role in making foreign policy. They can do this in several ways. In nations where there are free elections, citizens may elect leaders who support a particular foreign policy. During the Vietnam War, American foreign policy was a major campaign issue. People often decided which candidate to vote for based on that person's position on the Vietnam War.

Individual citizens can communicate their views on foreign policy in other ways as well. For example, if a person does not approve a decision to build more defensive aircraft, he or she can express that view by sending letters to government leaders, or organizing citizens to sign petitions.

Sometimes citizens as members of groups have special interests that they want the government to pursue in its relations with other nations. These groups may lobby, talk to national leaders, and try to influence foreign policy decisions. For example, labor unions may want the government to limit the amount of foreign goods that come into the country.

News Media. In some nations, the news media may affect foreign policy decisions. Editorials which evaluate foreign policy moves are read by a wide audience. Television broadcasts make viewers aware of events abroad. The positions of leaders on foreign policy issues are regularly reported. As a result, citizens and government leaders may be influenced by media reports.

Many observers believe that the news media were responsible for the change in United States foreign policy in Vietnam. For the first time in history, actual war scenes were broadcast on television. Regular reports on American wins and losses made citizens aware that victory was not going to be easy.

1. Describe the different types of people involved in making a nation's foreign policy. What function does each have?
2. What are three reasons that explain why a nation might change some foreign policy decision?
3. The head of a labor union writes a critical letter to the secretary of state. A private citizen does the same. Which letter is likely to receive more attention? Why?

FOCUS on POLITICAL CRISIS The following case study about a political crisis illustrates the efforts of different people and groups to keep peace. As you read, identify the types of people who were involved in peace negotiations. Also, determine the factors that led to war and to the cease-fire.

★ Crisis in Cyprus

Cyprus is a small island in the Mediterranean Sea, located about 40 miles south of Turkey. (See Figure 17–1 on page 526.) Ever since its independence in 1960, there have been disputes between the island's two main ethnic groups—Greek Cypriots and Turkish Cypriots. Most of these disputes have centered around the question "How should Cyprus be ruled?" Most Greek Cypriots favor a union with Greece; most Turkish Cypriots do not.

Fighting between these two groups first broke out in 1964. Although peace was reestablished, relations remained tense. Archbishop Makarios, the Greek Cypriot leader who was then ruler of Cyprus, tried to ease hostilities. However, because he opposed the union of Cyprus and Greece, Makarios angered many Greek Cypriots.

On July 15, 1974, Makarios was forced out of office. The operation was carried out by Greek Cypriots, but it was directed by the Greek government. As a result, Turkey

Greek and Turkish Cypriot villagers discuss a local dispute. Yet even a meeting like this was attended by military representatives from Great Britain, Greece, and Turkey.

intervened to protect Turkish Cypriots and to prevent the union of Greece and Cyprus.

Turkish forces invaded Cyprus by air and by sea. Troops spread out throughout the island and eventually took more than 40 percent of the island's territory. About 200,000 Greek Cypriots were forced to become refugees. Greece stepped up its protection of Greek Cypriots, and it seemed that Greece and Turkey might declare war on each other.

With the intervention of Greece and Turkey, the Cyprus controversy became an international issue. Both nations were members of the NATO alliance. A war between these two member nations could destroy the southern defense of the alliance, and the security of Europe might be threatened. Moreover, both Greece and Turkey had central geographic locations in the Mediterranean. Turkey's common border with the Soviet Union offered a unique opportunity for Western allies to observe activities within that nation. Greece provided a strategic location of Western naval and military bases.

Because of these factors, many nations were concerned about the conflict on Cyprus. The three nations most active in peace efforts were Great Britain, France, and the United States. In seeking to promote peace, these nations had to be careful not to offend the foreign policies of either Greece or Turkey. To antagonize either country

could have meant the possible weakening of Western influence in the Mediterranean.

In the days following the ouster of Makarios, American, British, French, Greek, and Turkish leaders tried to settle the Cyprus issue and avoid war between Greece and Turkey.

Turkey's head of state, Bulent Ecevit, flew to London to consult with the British, who, along with Greece and Turkey, had guaranteed the independence of Cyprus in 1960. He spoke with British Foreign Secretary James Callaghan and wanted Callaghan to intervene in the situation. Ecevit's goals were to remove the new head of Cyprus, to remove from Cyprus the Greek soldiers who had ousted Makarios, and to be certain that Cyprus would be governed by a system which would respect Turkish Cypriot rights.

Joseph Sisco, Undersecretary of State for the United States, was sent to help calm the crisis. Sisco listened to Ecevit's proposals in London. He then promised to take the proposals to the Greek government in Athens. Sisco spent considerable time shuttling between Athens and Ankara, the capital of Turkey, trying to work out a settlement for the crisis.

On July 20, 1974, a cease-fire between Greece and Turkey was arranged. Joseph Sisco, having negotiated with the Prime Minister of Turkey, the Greek Prime Minister, the Foreign Minister of the United

525

Kingdom, and the French Foreign Minister, had been active in helping to reach a settlement.

In a news conference on that day, United States Secretary of State Henry Kissinger described the negotiating activities which led to the cease-fire as follows:

"The United States concentrated on getting a cease-fire. The United Kingdom will concentrate on getting the negotiating process started after the cease-fire. . . .

"The difficulties during the day arose because, as always, in the cease-fire negotiations, there were infinite technical disputes—for example, at one point the Turks thought that a Greek fleet was approaching Cyprus and were reluctant to make a cease-fire while the Greek fleet was approaching Cyprus. . . .

"And so about six o'clock yesterday afternoon, we thought it might be time to come up with an American proposal; and therefore at the consultation with Foreign Minister Callaghan and the French Foreign Minister, we proposed to the Turkish Foreign Minister that a cease-fire go into effect.

"We gave the time at 14:00 today Greenwich Mean Time, and that this should be followed almost immediately by negotiations between Greece and Turkey under United Kingdom auspices. This was supported by the United Kingdom and by France. Turkey accepted this around nine o'clock last night ... and then we had to get Greek acceptance.

". . . the problem was to find the means between two parties that have no great confidence in each other to achieve a simultaneous announcement. . . . And this led to the solution that we

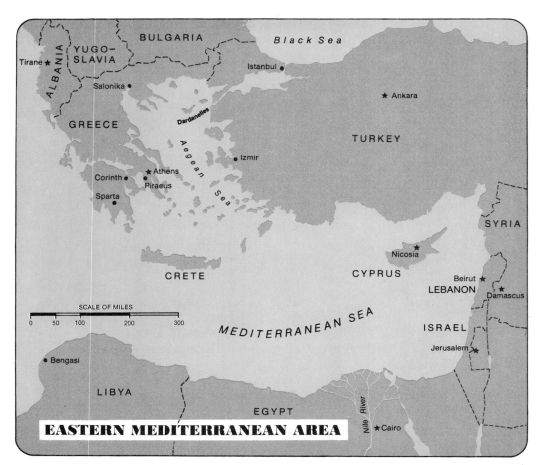

EASTERN MEDITERRANEAN AREA

Figure 17-

would make the announcement here, and after that each party would confirm our announcement."

As Kissinger's comments show, the cease-fire was the result of efforts by several nations. The United States, Great Britain, and France actively pursued a policy to prevent a further build-up of fighting on Cyprus. This was not easy. Although an end to fighting was achieved, a negotiated settlement was not agreed upon. Throughout 1974–1977, a resolution to the Cyprus issue was still being sought.

1. Who were the major actors in the Cyprus case? What actions did they take to establish a cease-fire?
2. State two hypotheses about war and two hypotheses about peace that would help explain the Cyprus situation.
3. What evidence in the Cyprus case proves that the world is becoming more interdependent?

Alliances and Collective Security

Sometimes several nations share a common interest or problem; they may see that it is in their interests to unite and set joint foreign policies. Through cooperation they can coordinate their efforts and reduce the chances of conflict. Such an organization of nations toward a common purpose is called an *alliance*.

Alliances usually have a formal structure and rules for decision-making. Representatives from each member nation meet at a central headquarters and determine alliance policies. Once resolutions are agreed upon, member nations act as a bloc.

Although nations ally for many reasons, the most common reason is for *collective security*. This means that a group of nations pool their military resources to provide a line of defense against a common enemy. In this type of arrangement, if one nation is attacked, the rest of the allied countries will come to its defense.

Some people assert that collective security is an important principle in maintaining world peace. Through alliances, nations cooperate with each other and, as a result, relations are improved. If conflict does occur, the alliance organization affords a means for nations within the alliance to settle their disputes peacefully. In the Cyprus case, members of the NATO alliance intervened to prevent a war between Turkey and Greece. In this case, the alliance played an important peace-keeping role.

Other people believe that alliances promote global peace because they establish a balance of power in the international political system. Since no nation can predict the outcome of a war between two powerful alliances, aggression is deterred.

Despite the role that alliances can play in maintaining world peace, some people still think that alliances increase the probability of war. In other words, being prepared for war makes it easier to go to war. Furthermore, once two nations from different alliances declare war on each other, there is a chance that the conflict will escalate into a world war. People who agree with this theory think that war can be prevented only by cooperation among alliances.

FIVE ALLIANCES On the following pages, you will study five different alliances. As you read, try to determine the goals of each alliance. Consider how decisions are made in each alliance, and identify each alliance as an elite, a bureaucratic, a participant, or a coalitional system.

North Atlantic Treaty Organization (NATO). After World War II, the Soviet

Union took control of the governments in Eastern European countries. The United States and the nations of Western Europe feared that the Soviet Union might try to extend its domination to Western Europe as well. To prevent this, in 1949 the United States and 11 Western European nations met to form the North Atlantic Treaty Organization (NATO). Members of NATO pledged to support the principle of collective security. Article V of the treaty details the obligations in such an arrangement:

> "The Parties agree that an armed attack against one or more of them in Europe shall be considered an attack against them all and consequently they agree that, if such an armed attack occurs, each of them . . . will assist the Party or Parties so attacked."

As Article V states, each member of the alliance has agreed to support each other in time of attack. So that they are prepared, NATO nations have built up military forces which stand in reserve all through Europe. Much of the equipment and troops have been supplied or paid for by the United States. This does not, however, entitle the United States to more power in the NATO decision-making process. Each country has one vote, and all decisions must be unanimous. If any nation vetoes a plan, it is not carried out.

The major goal of the United States as a member of NATO is to ensure against further Soviet takeover in Europe. European member nations share this goal. They have sought to keep ties with the United States for their protection, and also to receive assistance from the United States in the form of economic aid and military equipment.

NATO is seen as a necessary military bond between the United States and Western Europe. Many believe that NATO has helped deter aggression on the part of the Soviet Union.

The Warsaw Treaty Organization (WTO). The Warsaw Treaty Organization was created in 1955 by the Soviet Union. It is a mutual defense organization made up of the Soviet Union and its satellite states in Eastern Europe. (*Satellite nations* are economically or politically dependent on a larger, more powerful nation.)

The WTO was created for the specific purpose of deterring aggression against the Soviet Union. As protection, the Soviet government stationed troops along border areas throughout Eastern Europe. Because of this, the Soviet government not only has a line of defense, it also has a means of retaining control over the satellite nations.

Most WTO decisions are made by the Soviet Union. Unlike NATO, members of WTO do not have equal voting and veto rights. The satellite states are dominated by the Soviet Union, and they have only limited freedom to pursue their own foreign policies.

The Organization of American States (OAS). The Organization of American States (OAS) was created in 1948 by the Act of Bogota. Its membership includes 25 nations in North and South America. Initially, the United States played a dominant role in this alliance; however, in recent years this has changed.

Decisions on all important issues must be passed by a two-thirds majority vote. Therefore, the OAS can act over the objections of a few members, including the United States.

The OAS was started for a number of reasons, one of which was to strengthen the security of the Western Hemisphere. In 1962, when President John F. Kennedy demanded that Soviet missile sites be removed from Cuba, OAS members pledged to take the necessary measures to prevent the spread of communism in the West.

A second goal of the alliance is to ensure that member nations resolve their differences peacefully. In recent years, the OAS has been successful at this task. There have been complaints on 18 different occasions, and in no instance has prolonged conflict broken out.

The OAS also promotes economic, cultural, and social cooperation among nations. In 1961, OAS nations met in Uruguay to write a charter for an Alliance for Progress. Objectives in the charter included improving the literacy rate among Latin American citizens, encouraging agricultural reforms, and curbing inflation. All these items indicate that the OAS is more than just a military alliance.

Although the OAS has achieved certain of its goals, political stability within Latin America is still elusive. Since 1962, several democratic governments have been replaced by military rulers. To date, none of these new governments has withdrawn from the OAS, nor does it seem likely that they will do so in the future. However, the membership of these new governments may have an effect on the OAS since their goals may differ from those of previous governments.

The Arab League. In October 1944, seven Arab nations met to discuss the possibility of forming an alliance among the Arab states. The outcome of the meeting was the Protocol of Alexandria, in which participating nations agreed to form an Arab League. The final pact establishing the alliance was signed on March 22, 1945, in Cairo, Egypt.

The original purpose of the League was to promote Arab unity. Membership in the League was restricted to independent Arab states, and any decisions reached by these nations had to be unanimous. Unlike other alliances, the Protocol of Alexandria did not even mention defense against external attack. A mutual defense agreement was not signed until 1950. Instead, the Protocol called for "strengthening the relations among member nations and coordinating their policies to further cooperation."

Decisions made by the League are not binding upon member states; therefore, the League has been handicapped by differences in thinking among Arab countries. For example, there has been continual competition over which nation should play a leadership role in the League. Moreover, Arab nations pursue their individual foreign policies, and sometimes these conflict, especially on issues such as relations with Israel, the United States, or the Soviet Union. Therefore, although the League has been successful in promoting economic unity, it has not been as successful in achieving political unity.

The Organization of African Unity (OAU). In May 1963, 34 African nations met at Addis Ababa in Ethiopia to form the Organization of African Unity. One of the factors that prompted these nations to meet was their common opposition to white minority rule in Rhodesia, the Republic of South Africa, and in the remaining colonial territories. Because all of the member nations, except Ethiopia and Liberia, had at one time or another been under colonial rule, a central goal of the OAU was to erase any remaining colonial influence in Africa. Then, through cooperation, the OAU members hoped to promote the growth and independence of all African states.

The charter adopted by the OAU nations reflected their shared concerns. To maintain the rights of each member state, the OAU charter gave each nation equal decision-making power. Moreover, members agreed that the OAU would not interfere in the internal affairs of any OAU country. Instead, it would confine itself to improving the relations among African nations. To further this goal, a key task of the OAU was to resolve peacefully all disputes among member states. To ensure the independent development of Africa, the charter also pledged that the OAU would not align itself with either the Western or the Communist blocs of power. Instead of concerning itself with global affairs, the OAU would direct its efforts toward solving African social, economic, educational, and health problems.

To date, the OAU has successfully achieved some of its goals. On several issues at the United Nations, the OAU has coordinated its members to speak with one voice, especially on resolutions dealing with white

Representatives from Nigeria attend a 1977 meeting of the Organization of African Unity in Libreville, Gabon.

minority rule. The OAU also has settled several disputes among its members. For example, in 1964, the OAU played an important role in the peaceful settlement of a conflict between Morocco and Algeria. Other accomplishments include mutual agreements on trade and river navigation.

These successes have not solved all problems, however. For example, all member nations do not agree on how colonial influence in Africa should be ended. Also, many new nation-states are unwilling to surrender any of their new power to a central alliance. In spite of these difficulties, the OAU is making strides toward improving relations among African nations, and it remains a symbol of African unity.

The success of alliances in keeping world peace is a much debated issue. For example, many people argue that alliances are centered toward keeping the peace in a region rather than across the globe. Others maintain that such alliances are a cause of war. They say that when nations pool their resources in preparation for war, the chances for war are increased. Finally, there are those who believe that alliances promote global peace because they provide the means for cooperation and the peaceful resolution of conflict.

1. What type of political system does each alliance represent? What are the major goals of each?
2. If relations improve between the Soviet Union and the United States, is it likely that the United States will want to expand NATO forces? Explain.
3. In what ways do the goals of the alliances described in this section differ from one another? How are they similar?
4. State several hypotheses about how alliances might contribute to peace or war. How do these hypotheses relate to others you have made about peace and war?

The United Nations and Voluntary Cooperation

Through alliances, conflict among member nations may be reduced, thus promoting world peace. However, alliances can be powerless in the face of conflict among members of that alliance. And, it still is possible for conflict to occur between members of different alliances or between an alliance and a major world power such as the United States or the Soviet Union. Thus, there is a need for some type of peacekeeping organization to mediate disputes on a global scale—a forum in which all nations can participate. To date, the only organization that operates in this capacity is the United Nations (UN).

The United Nations was founded after the end of World War II. At the conclusion of this war, many nations were eager to ensure that such a major world war would never again occur. The allies who had won the war—the United States, the Soviet Union, Great Britain, France, and China—made an agreement to establish an international organization that would secure peace. In April 1945, representatives from these five nations met in San Francisco to work out a plan for a new world organization dedicated to preventing future global wars. In October 1945, the United Nations was officially established. Its headquarters were set up in New York City.

Fifty-one nations joined the United Nations as charter members. Today, the membership has grown to include 149 members. On page 533 there is a list of the United Nations members and the years in which they joined the organization.

The United Nations is dedicated to two major goals: peace and human dignity. In seeking peace, the United Nations may try to stop war if it breaks out between nations. It may also send in peace-keeping troops after the fighting stops to prevent a fresh outbreak of conflict. Most important, the United Nations tries to deal with problems and disputes before they escalate into war.

STRUCTURE of the UN

As outlined in the United Nations Charter, there are six major bodies through which the United Nations operates. They are the General Assembly, the Security Council, the Secretariat, the Economic and Social Council, the International Court of Justice, and the Trusteeship Council.

The General Assembly. Every member of the United Nations is automatically a member of the General Assembly. The Assembly may discuss any question of importance to the United Nations. It may also recommend action to be taken by United Nations members or by other United Nations organs, including the Security Council. In addition, the General Assembly has control over the United Nations budget.

The recommendations of the General Assembly to the member nations are not binding or enforceable. They do, however, carry considerable moral force. The weight of world opinion can be strong enough so that nations will act in accordance with United Nations resolutions.

The General Assembly meets in regular session once each year, usually beginning in September and lasting for about three months. Voting in the Assembly is based on a one-nation, one-vote rule. All nations large and small are each entitled to one vote. No nation has veto privileges. Most decisions in the General Assembly are made by majority rule. Those involving questions of finance or elections, however, require a two-thirds vote.

The Security Council. The Security Council is a 15-member council composed of major and minor powers in the United Nations. The job of the Security Council is to investigate any dispute or situation which might endanger international peace and security. It is the role of the Security Council to develop policies and recommend actions which the United Nations will carry out.

Five members of the Security Council are permanent members. The other ten are selected by the General Assembly for two-year terms each. Five are selected each year. The five permanant members are the United States, the Soviet Union, France, Great Britain, and China. These nations were the allied victors after World War II. Because of their position in the world after World War II and their role in establishing the United Nations, they hold permanent seats on the Security Council. (You will recall from the case study in Chapter 16 that the Nationalist Chinese held the Security Council seat until they were replaced in the UN by the People's Republic of China.)

The primary responsibility of the Security Council is to maintain world peace. The Security Council can act to reduce tensions or halt aggressions in instances where conflict exists.

Voting procedures in the Security Council are crucial to that body's ability to act. Each of the permanent members on the Security Council has the power to veto any decision of the Council. The other 10 members can vote, but they do not have veto power. On important matters, 9 of the 15 Security Council members must agree, including all 5 permanent members. Therefore, decision-making in the Security Council is controlled by the 5 permanent members; the use of the veto can prevent the Security Council from taking action.

The Security Council may investigate a conflict and suggest ways to settle it. It may also ask members to supply troops. However, the Council has no power to make member nations abide by its decisions.

Figure 17-2

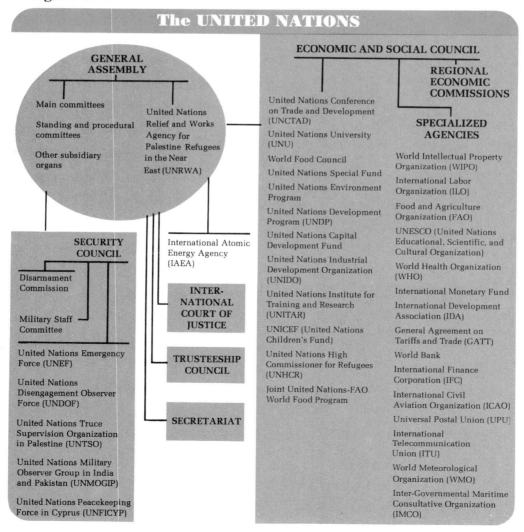

The UNITED NATIONS

GENERAL ASSEMBLY
- Main committees
- Standing and procedural committees
- Other subsidiary organs
- United Nations Relief and Works Agency for Palestine Refugees in the Near East (UNRWA)

SECURITY COUNCIL
- Disarmament Commission
- Military Staff Committee
- United Nations Emergency Force (UNEF)
- United Nations Disengagement Observer Force (UNDOF)
- United Nations Truce Supervision Organization in Palestine (UNTSO)
- United Nations Military Observer Group in India and Pakistan (UNMOGIP)
- United Nations Peacekeeping Force in Cyprus (UNFICYP)

International Atomic Energy Agency (IAEA)

INTERNATIONAL COURT OF JUSTICE

TRUSTEESHIP COUNCIL

SECRETARIAT

ECONOMIC AND SOCIAL COUNCIL
- United Nations Conference on Trade and Development (UNCTAD)
- United Nations University (UNU)
- World Food Council
- United Nations Special Fund
- United Nations Environment Program
- United Nations Development Program (UNDP)
- United Nations Capital Development Fund
- United Nations Industrial Development Organization (UNIDO)
- United Nations Institute for Training and Research (UNITAR)
- UNICEF (United Nations Children's Fund)
- United Nations High Commissioner for Refugees (UNHCR)
- Joint United Nations-FAO World Food Program

REGIONAL ECONOMIC COMMISSIONS

SPECIALIZED AGENCIES
- World Intellectual Property Organization (WIPO)
- International Labor Organization (ILO)
- Food and Agriculture Organization (FAO)
- UNESCO (United Nations Educational, Scientific, and Cultural Organization)
- World Health Organization (WHO)
- International Monetary Fund
- International Development Association (IDA)
- General Agreement on Tariffs and Trade (GATT)
- World Bank
- International Finance Corporation (IFC)
- International Civil Aviation Organization (ICAO)
- Universal Postal Union (UPU)
- International Telecommunication Union (ITU)
- World Meteorological Organization (WMO)
- Inter-Governmental Maritime Consultative Organization (IMCO)

MEMBERS of the UNITED NATIONS

MEMBER NATION*	DATE OF ADMISSION	MEMBER NATION*	DATE OF ADMISSION	MEMBER NATION*	DATE OF ADMISSION
Afghanistan	1946	Ghana	1957	Oman	1971
Albania	1955	Greece	1945	Pakistan	1947
Algeria	1962	Grenada	1974	Panama	1945
Angola	1976	Guatemala	1945	Paraguay	1945
Argentina	1945	Guinea	1958	Papua New Guinea	1975
Australia	1945	Guinea-Bissau	1974	Peru	1945
Austria	1955	Guyana	1966	Philippines	1945
Bahamas	1973	Haiti	1945	Poland	1945
Bahrain	1971	Honduras	1945	Portugal	1955
Bangladesh	1974	Hungary	1955	Qatar	1971
Barbados	1966	Iceland	1946	Romania	1955
Belgium	1945	India	1945	Rwanda	1962
Bhutan	1971	Indonesia	1950	São Tome and Príncipe	1975
Bolivia	1945	Iran	1945	Saudi Arabia	1945
Botswana	1966	Iraq	1945	Senegal	1960
Brazil	1945	Ireland	1955	Seychelles	1976
Bulgaria	1955	Israel	1949	Sierra Leone	1961
Burma	1948	Italy	1955	Singapore	1965
Burundi	1962	Ivory Coast	1960	Somalia	1960
Byelorussian SSR	1945	Jamaica	1962	South Africa	1945
Cameroon	1960	Japan	1956	Spain	1955
Canada	1945	Jordan	1955	Sri Lanka	1955
Cape Verde	1975	Kenya	1963	Sudan	1956
Central African Republic	1960	Khmer Republic	1955	Surinam	1975
Chad	1960	Kuwait	1963	Swaziland	1968
Chile	1945	Laos	1955	Sweden	1946
China	1945	Lebanon	1945	Syria	1945
Colombia	1945	Lesotho	1966	Tanzania	1961
Comoro Islands	1975	Liberia	1945	Thailand	1946
Congo	1960	Libya	1955	Togo	1960
Costa Rica	1945	Luxembourg	1945	Trinidad and Tobago	1962
Cuba	1945	Malagasy Republic	1960	Tunisia	1956
Cyprus	1960	Malawi	1964	Turkey	1945
Czechoslovakia	1945	Malaysia	1957	Uganda	1962
Dahomey	1960	Maldive Islands	1965	Ukranian SSR	1945
Denmark	1945	Mali	1960	USSR	1945
Djibouti	1977	Malta	1964	United Arab Emirates	1971
Dominican Republic	1945	Mauritania	1961	United Kingdom	1945
Ecuador	1945	Mauritius	1968	United States	1945
Egypt	1945	Mexico	1945	Upper Volta	1960
El Salvador	1945	Mongolia	1961	Uruguay	1945
Equatorial Guinea	1968	Morocco	1956	Venezuela	1945
Ethiopia	1945	Mozambique	1975	Vietnam	1977
Fiji	1970	Nepal	1955	Western Samoa	1976
Finland	1955	Netherlands	1945	Yemen	1947
France	1945	New Zealand	1945	Yemen (Democratic)	1967
Gabon	1960	Nicaragua	1945	Yugoslavia	1945
Gambia	1965	Niger	1960	Zaire	1960
Germany (Fed. Rep.)	1973	Nigeria	1960	Zambia	1964
Germany (Dem. Rep.)	1973	Norway	1945		

*Roster as of October 1977.

Figure 17-3

The Secretariat. The Secretariat is the organ that manages the administrative work of the United Nations. The Secretariat is headed by a secretary-general, who is therefore the chief United Nations administrative officer. Approximately 9,000 people are employed by the Secretariat, and about half of them work at UN headquarters in New York City. (A majority of the Secretariat employees not in New York work at UN offices in Geneva, Switzerland. In addition there are Secretariat employees at UN information centers throughout the world.)

The secretary-general is in charge of managing the day-to-day business of the UN. In addition, the secretary-general is responsible for taking on special assignments, giving advice to governments, and helping to solve international problems. The secretary-general also has the power to bring to the attention of the Security Council any situation which might threaten world peace.

The secretary-general is nominated by the Security Council and appointed by the General Assembly. Approval by the Assembly requires a majority vote. The Assembly determines the length of term at the time of selection. In 1977 Kurt Waldheim of Austria was reelected to a second five-year term as secretary-general.

The Other UN Organs. As mentioned earlier, the other three organs of the United Nations are the Economic and Social Council (ECOSOC), the International Court of Justice, and the Trusteeship Council. Briefly stated, the functions of these bodies are as follows. The Economic and Social Council works for improvement of living standards and health, educational, and social conditions in general around the world. The International Court of Justice deals with international legal disputes. And the Trusteeship Council was established to administer territories that were not self-governing when the United Nations was created.

Commissions and Agencies. As you can see in Figure 17-2 on page 532, the United Nations also includes many commissions and specialized agencies. These are independent bodies, each with its own membership and its own budget. Among the specialized agencies are the World Health Organization, the Food and Agriculture Commission, and UNICEF. These groups are concerned with problems such as disease control, family planning, food production, and finding ways to combat droughts and famines.

1. Describe the major objectives of the United Nations.
2. Compare the structure and function of the General Assembly and the Security Council.
3. What is the Secretariat? The Economic and Social Council? The International Court of Justice?

The UN as a POLITICAL SYSTEM

A great deal of interaction occurs among member nations of the United Nations. Groups with mutual interests meet on a regular basis to plan a common policy on issues before the General Assembly.

In order to ensure a majority on any issue, various groups interact to form a coalition large enough to pass or defeat a resolution. Therefore, policy-making is often the result of which nations are able to assemble the largest coalition. United Nations General Assembly activities can therefore be described as operating under a coalitional system.

Different blocs, or groups, of nations operate within the United Nations. For example, some groups are formed around regional alliances. NATO nations sometimes form one bloc at the United Nations, and Eastern European Communist countries usually form another. There are also important groupings of Asian, African, Arab, and Latin American countries.

There are also other groups based on common interests. For example, members of the Islamic group meet on a regular basis, as do members of the Nordic group of nations. So do the nine Western European members who share common economic and political concerns.

On many issues the non-aligned group of nations who belong neither to the Western or Eastern bloc vote together. Today this group forms a majority of the General Assembly membership. This situation increases their power in the United Nations.

1. Explain why the United Nations General Assembly can be described as a coalitional system.
2. What part do alliances play in United Nations activities?
3. What advantages might the non-aligned nations have in General Assembly decision-making?

KEEPING PEACE It is important to understand that the United Nations is based on the principle of voluntary cooperation of its members. Unlike the decisions of the United States government, which all citizens must obey, the decisions of the United Nations are not binding on member nations. It is up to each member of the United Nations to decide whether or not to carry out the decisions of the United Nations.

Although there is no legal authority that forces nations to comply with the decisions of the United Nations, there is pressure from the community of nations to carry out the will of the majority. Few nations like to stand alone in opposing the will of the majority. As a result, member states do go along with most decisions. However, on issues of great importance to a nation, particularly if that nation believes a decision will threaten its security, nations may refuse to carry out the will of the majority.

It was hoped by the founders of the United Nations that nations would voluntarily give up some of their authority to the United Nations as the years went on. It was believed that nations would see it in their interests to do so. However, in the years since the United Nations was established, nations have not shown any willingness to turn over decision-making authority to the United Nations.

Because the United Nations has certain restrictions on its peace-keeping efforts, it has met with only partial success. It has been able to keep some disputes from escalating into major wars. And it has improved the quality of life for many people around the world. However, the continued power of individual nations has prevented the organization from doing a thorough job of maintaining world peace. To date, United Nations forces have been used only in certain limited situations. Nevertheless, the United Nations still plays an important peace-keeping role in that it provides a place where nations can meet and settle differences before they result in war. Many people think that this ongoing discussion of global issues is the major function of the United Nations.

Following are three case studies describing incidents in which the United Nations intervened to end or to avoid a crisis situation. As you read these cases, think about the ways in which the United Nations tried to keep the peace. Determine whether its efforts were successful or unsuccessful. Based on the evidence presented in these cases, begin to form hypotheses about ways the United Nations might be more successful in its efforts as an international peace-keeping agency.

★ **The Korean War**

During World War II, as part of the Allied effort to defeat Japan, both the United States and the Soviet Union fought on the Asian continent. They worked to defeat the Japanese in the Asian countries that they had

Figure 17-4

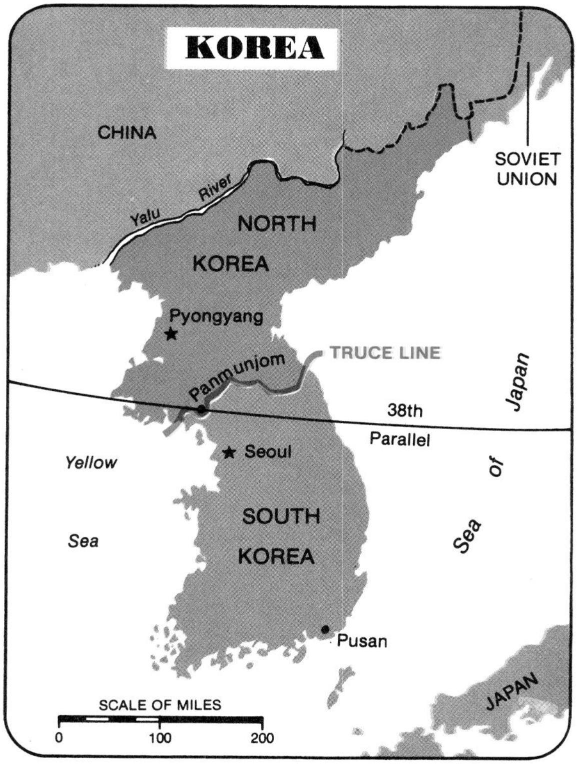

conquered. By the end of the war, they had freed Korea from Japanese control. The United States and the Soviet Union arbitrarily divided the country at the 38th parallel, with Soviet troops occupying the part of Korea north of the parallel. American troops were stationed in the southern part of the country. (Figure 17–4, on page 535, is a map of Korea.)

In 1947, the United Nations appointed a commission to investigate ways in which the country could be reunited. The northern part of Korea refused to participate in these efforts. With Soviet support, a separate government and military force were set up in North Korea. In the south, elections were held under United Nations supervision, and the Republic of Korea was established. In 1948, the UN General Assembly voted to recognize the southern government as the only legitimate Korean government. By 1949, Soviet and American troops had left their respective zones, but tensions remained between the two Korean governments.

In June 1950, the Communist-sponsored regime in North Korea crossed the 38th parallel to attack South Korea. Many people asserted that the action was prompted by the Soviet Union and the People's Republic of China, although the two governments denied any involvement.

At the onset of fighting, the United States prevailed upon the Security Council to take immediate military action to protect South Korea. The Soviet Union could not veto this proposal because it had recalled its delegate in protest of the United Nations refusal to admit the People's Republic of China. A United Nations agency certified the facts of aggression and asked North Korea to withdraw its troops. It refused, and, with the Soviet delegate absent, the Security Council voted to send forces to South Korea.

On July 7, 1950, a United Nations force was formed. Although 16 nations sent troops and 41 sent supplies, the major part of the war effort was supported by the United

General Douglas MacArthur, shown here talking with U.S. marines, was Commander of the United Nations forces in Korea.

States. An American commander, General Douglas MacArthur, was appointed to head the joint United Nations force.

In October 1950, Communist Chinese troops entered the conflict in support of North Korea. The Security Council again met, but this time the Soviet delegate was present. He vetoed any further United Nations attempts to intervene in the Korean controversy. With the Security Council blocked, the General Assembly demanded that the Chinese withdraw their forces from Korea, but the Peking government refused.

The war became a major issue in the 1952 presidential election in the United States, with General Eisenhower promising to go to Korea if elected. As president he did visit the area and convinced South Korea to supply more troops. Eisenhower withdrew the U.S. 7th fleet, sent more jet planes to the Far East, and placed atomic weapons in strategic areas in the Pacific. While these changes occurred, Josef Stalin, head of the Soviet Union, died, and a more flexible leader came into power. Many feel that all of these factors helped renew the peace talks.

On June 26, 1953, an armistice was signed creating a 4-kilometer demilitarized zone along the 38th parallel. A force of UN and Communist troops were placed in charge of the zone. Talks were held in late 1953 to discuss the reunification of Korea, but they quickly broke down. Today, North Korea and South Korea remain divided; each is a separate nation.

This was the only conflict in which a joint military action was undertaken by United Nations members to stop an aggressor. Since the Korean War, vetoes by Security Council members have hindered United Nations intervention. As a result, the General Assembly has assumed a greater responsibility in crisis situations.

★ **The Suez Crisis**

Stretching about 100 miles in Egypt to connect the Mediterranean and the Red Seas,

the Suez Canal was opened in 1869. The waterway was built and operated by the private Suez Canal Company. From 1875 the principal stockholders in the company were British and French.

Both Great Britain and France depended on the canal for shipping goods and oil from the Middle East, vital to both nations. Because of the canal's strategic importance, an international agreement was signed in 1888 stating that the canal should be open to all nations in peace and war.

In July 1956, Great Britain and the United States claimed that Egypt was following a pro-Soviet foreign policy, and they withdrew their offers to help Egypt construct the Aswan High Dam, a project important to Egypt's president at that time, Gamal Abdel Nasser. In reaction, Nasser quickly took control of the Suez Canal Company, announcing that he would use canal tolls to build the dam.

Great Britain and France tried unsuccessfully to reach an agreement with Egypt. They then asked the UN Security Council to intervene. However, before the Council could reach a decision, war broke out between Israel and Egypt.

Israel took this action because it feared a strong Egypt. Since the establishment of the Israeli state in 1948, relations between Israel and Egypt had been tense. As a result, Israel believed that Egyptian control of the canal could weaken its position in the Middle East. Because the French and British governments also had important interests in the canal, they attacked Egypt by air and then sent troops to join the Israelis.

The Security Council met to consider the conflict. Great Britain and France vetoed the resolution for a cease-fire. A majority of the Council members then voted to convene a special session of the General Assembly. When the General Assembly met, it called upon Israel, France, and Great Britain to withdraw their forces from Egypt. Both the Soviet Union and the United States gave strong support to this decision. The Assembly then agreed that United Nations troops should be stationed along the border of Israel and Egypt to prevent future attacks and to protect Israeli canal rights. By 1957, the attacking nations had left Egypt. Although Israel did not permit UN troops in its territory, Nasser gave his permission for the United Nations to station troops in Egypt.

The United Nations Emergency Force (UNEF) was made up of 6,500 officers and troops representing eight nations. This was the first instance of what came to be known as "consensual peace-keeping." In other words, parties on both sides agreed to the presence of peace-keeping forces. This differed from the collective military action in Korea, in which no such consent was required.

For 11 years, UNEF helped to keep peace between Egypt and Israel. In 1967, Egypt requested its withdrawal. Because the forces could remain only with the consent of parties, they were recalled. Unfortunately, the area did not remain peaceful after the UNEF troops left. War broke out in June 1967 and again in October 1973 between Israel and the Arab nations.

★ The Congo Emergency

In June 1960, the Republic of Congo—now called Zaire—became independent after 55 years of Belgian rule. Unlike many colonial powers, Belgium had given the Congolese little preparation for independence. Although some of the new Congolese leaders had local administrative experience, few, if any, had governing experience on the national level. Also, the people were unprepared for national unity. Their first loyalty was still to tribe and locality. Moreover, there were no national political parties to help transfer allegiances to a new national government.

As the Belgian forces withdrew, riots broke out between conflicting factions in the Congo. A complete breakdown of government threatened the new nation, and Belgian troops returned to restore order. Shortly thereafter, the rich province of Katanga seceded, or withdrew, from the Congo. The Congolese government was forced to call upon the United Nations for military assistance.

After much debate, the Security Council asked Belgium to withdraw its troops from the Congo. In their place, the Council proposed an international force made up of troops from Ghana, Ethiopia, Morocco, and Tunisia. Following this decision, Soviet vetoes blocked further actions by the Security Council, and the General Assembly assumed responsibility for the Congo peace-keeping operation.

For the next four years, 20,000 United Nations troops attempted to unite the country under a national parliamentary government. During this period Katanga seceded on several occasions, and major African leaders were assassinated. Independent foreign intervention by nations such as the Soviet Union made the situation even more complicated. As a result, the United Nations was unable to withdraw its forces until 1964.

Although the United Nations restored some degree of stability to the Congo, factional conflicts and rebellions continued. It was not until 1969 that some evidence of a stable government appeared, and the Congo began to recover from years of civil war, foreign intervention, and economic distress.

Clearly the United Nations has used many different methods to resolve global crises. However, many of these activities are different from those originally anticipated by the writers of the United Nations Charter. For example, nations have not given the United Nations a large standing military force to preserve world peace. But considering the continued power of nations, the United Nations has been able to adapt to the wishes of member states. And, although it has not stopped global wars, the United Nations has intervened successfully in several major conflicts that might not otherwise have been resolved.

1. What was the United Nations' peace-keeping role in each of these three cases?

2. In your opinion, what are some of the major strengths and weaknesses of the United Nations as a global peace-keeping agency?

3. Based on your study of past global conflicts, form two hypotheses about how the United Nations might be more effective in its peace-keeping efforts.

The Skill of Settling Group Differences

Throughout history, groups of people have been unable to settle their differences peacefully, and they have gone to war. In this chapter you have read about some of the conditions that observers believe lead to war, and you have studied some examples of recent wars such as the Cyprus and Korean incidents. You also have learned how nations, alliances, and international organizations try to prevent war through peace-keeping efforts such as collective security.

Settling group differences is a skill, a series of techniques that can be applied to conflicts among and within many different kinds of groups. The basic principles of settling group differences apply to conflict between nations as well as to conflict between members of a club or other group.

WHY NEGOTIATE? As you have seen, any peaceful settlement of a conflict depends upon the willingness of nations to cooperate and to compromise. Central to this is the process of *negotiation*. It is a skill that all global actors must have if nations are to come to terms on an issue. It also is a process that characterizes the successful interactions among all people involved in any group relationship.

In any large group, such as a school, community, or corporation, there are usually differences of opinion. Even within a family, there are disagreements. If someone has the authority to make decisions that everyone must follow, these disputes are quickly resolved. However, in the absence of such a person, people must come to some kind of agreement among themselves. Through discussion, bargaining, and compromise they finally reach a solution. This is the process of negotiation.

In the global political system today there is no central authority regulating the relations among nations. Therefore, the negotiation process is very important in promoting world peace. When differences occur among global actors who agree to discuss rather than to fight about them, the parties enter into the negotiation process. As a result, in proposing any solution to global conflict, it is essential to understand how negotiations are successfully conducted.

Negotiations can be easy if one nation wants something that the other party does not care about. But if this is not the case, it may be much harder to come to some kind of peaceful agreement. If neither side will change its position, then an issue becomes nonnegotiable. This means that compromise between the nations is impossible.

On nonnegotiable issues, a mediator can be helpful as a neutral third party in suggesting ways to settle a difference. Because they do not have their own interests at stake, mediators may be able to see problems more clearly. Quite often this is the role played by the United Nations.

1. Why is the negotiation process important in promoting world peace?
2. What role does a mediator play in settling disputes?
3. Do you think negotiations are more difficult among many nations than between two? Explain.

STEPS in NEGOTIATION Many methods are used in negotiation. However, the following principles can be used by negotiators in almost all situations, from international diplomacy to the conflicts in a small school group. These basic principles are

1. Think about the interests of each side.

2. Offer a "yesable" proposition.

3. Do more than make threats.

4. Ask for a different decision.

5. Make the outcomes desirable and just.

Think about the Interests of Each Side. You have learned that in the bargaining process you must think about the other person's point of view. In the same way, a negotiator must determine the primary interests of each party. Then it may be possible to find some way to work out a compromise. In other words, the negotiators can predict the issues on which the parties are most likely to concede, and some progress can be made. Once tensions are reduced, parties may be more willing to cooperate on more important issues.

Quite often failure in negotiation occurs because of poor communications. Therefore, it is necessary that negotiators not only understand the interests of all parties, but also that they express these. Then the issues can be discussed and realistic compromises suggested. People are more ready to accept peace proposals if they feel that their most important interests are not jeopardized by settlement. In the same way, if you are negotiating a settlement of differences in a group in your school or community, it is important to understand the positions of all parties involved. Suppose, for example, you were trying to settle a difference between two groups in your neighborhood association. One faction wants to use all group resources to plant trees along neighborhood streets. The other group wants to concentrate all resources on improving city garbage collection in the neighborhood. There may be a common interest—neighborhood attractiveness—shared by the two groups. But until that shared interest is understood, the two groups will work at cross purposes.

Offer a "Yesable" Proposition. Once you have acknowledged the positions of opposing parties in a negotiation, you need to offer a proposition or solution to which it is possible and likely for the parties to answer "yes." If you present a vague idea for discussion, or an impossible proposal, your negotiations will not go very far.

In the Cyprus situation, for example, Henry Kissinger called for a cease-fire. This was a suggestion to which parties could say "yes." However, had Kissinger suggested a discussion of a total peace settlement or division of territory, the two sides would undoubtedly have become involved in complex discussions in which they could not have found a common ground for agreement. By offering a "first step" on which both parties could agree, Kissinger ensured the progress of negotiations.

In the same way, a negotiator trying to settle differences between the two groups in the hypothetical neighborhood association described earlier might suggest that the disagreeing parties work together on a study of all the ways to improve the neighborhood's appearance. Both groups could accept this proposal without having to give up their positions. And, in working together, the two groups might find common interests.

Do More than Make Threats. People often want to make threats in situations in which they themselves feel threatened. However, threats may backfire. They often are not effective in either changing people's behavior or encouraging them to compromise.

A more effective negotiating technique is to demonstrate how the parties will benefit from a course of action which will peacefully settle their differences. Sometimes a promise of a reward or assistance also may make people more willing to compromise.

"... HOWEVER, IT'S EXTREMELY IMPORTANT THAT WE KEEP TALKING!"

How does this cartoon illustrate the importance of negotiation for world peace?

If you were negotiating a settlement between the groups in the hypothetical neighborhood association, how would you handle threats? What benefits could you point out as a result of peaceful settlement?

Ask for a Different Decision. Sometimes a negotiator may ask one party to agree to something that it already has said it would not do. For instance, if a government has publicly taken a stand on an issue, changing this position may force it to "lose face." In cases like these, it is often best to ask the party to make a somewhat different decision. This may make it easier to reach an agreement.

Some techniques for leading people to make a different decision are to ask them to do the following:

1. Make us an offer.

2. Respond to our offer.

3. Explain your position.

4. Do something else.

Make the Outcomes Desirable and Just. Often, we do not make the payoffs high enough when we negotiate. In order to settle differences, both sides must see sufficient advantages in the solutions. They must see that those solutions are more desirable than the existing conflict. Both groups in the neighborhood association must see that a cleanup campaign is preferable to doing nothing. Or, in the Cyprus conflict, the division of rule between the Greeks and the Turks could be seen by both sides as preferable to continued war. Since neither side was able to overpower the other, divided rule was a preferable solution for both than total rule by one party.

Equally important is the need for outcomes to be seen as just. If either party considers a settlement grossly unfair, it may, as a result, have great difficulty abiding by that settlement.

1. What does each of the five principles of negotiation offer to the negotiation process?

2. Suppose negotiation breaks down because one party to a conflict threatens the other. What action would you recommend be taken so that negotiation can begin again?

Headquarters of the United Nations is in New York City (top photos). Working at the UN is one way people take part in the global political system. Monica Ladd (center left) is an economic officer at the United States Mission to the UN. She works with a commission on multinational corporations and discusses economic issues with delegates from other nations.

Valerie Jo Bradley is the Deputy Counselor for Public Affairs at the United States Mission to the UN. She is responsible for providing the press with information about United States positions on UN issues. To do this she writes press releases, holds frequent briefings, and gives speeches.

Chapter Review

1. In analyzing the causes of a particular war, why is it necessary to consider all possible causes?

2. Make a list of the major causes of war. Then select one of these and offer proposals on how you would attempt to prevent this from being a cause of future wars.

3. Why is the skill of hypothesizing important in maintaining peace?

4. Summarize the activities of government leaders who determine and conduct a nation's foreign policy. How can citizens influence the decisions of these individuals?

5. List some of the positive and negative effects of alliances upon the peace-keeping process. In your opinion, do alliances increase or decrease the possibilities of a global war? Explain.

6. Identify the two major goals of the United Nations. Then summarize the ways in which the UN tries to achieve these goals.

7. Compare and/or contrast decision-making in the Security Council and the General Assembly.

8. Explain how the continued power of individual nations has limited the ability of the UN to act effectively as an international peace-keeping agency.

9. Summarize the basic principles of negotiation.

10. Identify the principles that played important roles in the Cyprus talks.

Chapter Vocabulary

Define the following terms.

nationalism	ambassador	collective security
hypothesis	secretary of state	shuttle diplomacy
foreign policy	alliance	negotiation
foreign minister		

Chapter Analysis

1. For centuries, people have been analyzing the causes of war; however, wars continue to occur. In your opinion, why has the prevention of war been so difficult?

2. "As long as there are nations, war—rather than peace—will typify international politics." In essay form, attack or defend this statement.

3. Based on your understanding of the causes of war and peace, form hypotheses about what the following global actors can do to promote peace: nations, alliances, international organizations, individual citizens. In paragraph form, defend each of your theories.

4. Using specific examples from the textbook, evaluate the success of the United Nations in promoting global peace. In your opinion, how might the United Nations be more effective?

5. Both the United States and the Soviet Union are actively involved in exploring outer space. As a negotiator for the United States, how would you secure an agreement to ban the use of space for military purposes?

Chapter Activities

1. With a group of students, make a list of foreign policy objectives that you think the United States should fulfill in the next 20 years.

2. The Central Intelligence Agency (CIA) is an arm of the National Security Council. Its main function is to collect information on foreign affairs for the executive branch of the federal government. Research the duties and responsibilities of the CIA.

3. Interview some people who were in or affected by World War I, World War II, the Korean War, or the Vietnam War. Design questions to determine how the respondents viewed American involvement in the war. Present your findings to the class, comparing and/or contrasting your report with those of other students. Then analyze the reports, considering questions such as how the American attitude toward war has changed over time.

4. Practice the skill of settling group differences in a group to which you belong.

Chapter Bibliography

Basic Documents in United States Foreign Policy, Thomas P. Brockway (Van Nostrand Reinhold: New York, NY), rev. ed., 1968.
>   Contains important documents of United States foreign policy from the Declaration of Independence to 1968.

United Nations Journal: A Delegate's Odyssey, William F. Buckley, Jr. (G.P. Putnams Sons: New York, NY), 1974.
>   A chronicle, of the author's work as a member of the United States delegation to the United Nations General Assembly. It is both readable and informative, providing a unique view of international diplomacy.

The United Nations: Sacred Drama, Conor Cruise O'Brien and Feliks Topolski (Simon and Schuster: New York, NY), 1968.
>   Excellent descriptive information about the actions taken by the UN. It also chronicles the UN in session and highlights the account through many drawings and paintings.

Chapter Objectives

★ To identify economic systems and important economic blocs
★ To analyze how interdependence is changing the global economy
★ To identify major economic processes and actors
★ To analyze the roles citizens can take in the global economy
★ To develop skills in participating as an organizer

chapter 18

The POLITICS of SCARCITY

As you have learned in previous chapters, resources are scarce. This is true on both the local and national levels in the United States. It is also true of the world at large. There are shortages of food, raw materials, money, energy, skills, and information. Not only that, but these resources are distributed unequally among the nations of the world.

In this chapter, you will learn about the two chief ways in which nations allocate their resources. You will learn too about the impact of growing interdependence on the global economy. As you will see, economic interdependence has led to cooperation among some nations and conflict among others.

This chapter also deals with some of the major groups that participate in the global economy. These include international organizations where nations work together and huge corporations with operations in many foreign countries. Citizens, too, can have an impact on the global economy. You will see how citizens played influential roles during a coffee boycott. And finally, you will have an opportunity to study the organizer role.

The Global Economy

Economics is the study of how goods and services are produced and distributed. Economic decisions are those decisions that people make about how to use their limited resources in the production and distribution of goods and services. As you have learned, political decisions also involve the allocation of scarce resources; therefore you can see that economic decision-making can be considered political. In fact, in many people's minds, the two processes of decision-making are identical.

This was not always the case. At one time, people drew sharp distinctions between political and economic issues and rated economic issues as secondary. They thought, for instance, that nations would go to war over disputed territory, but not over disputed trade. We now know how important economic issues are to a nation's security, to its ability to protect its people from outside attack. They are so important that nations are prepared to fight over them.

TWO WAYS of ALLOCATING RESOURCES It is important to remember that all nations are not at the same stage of economic development. Nor do they all have the same economic system.

An economic system, like a political system, is based on resources and activities. Resources include human resources, natural resources, and capital. Human resources, or labor, consist of men and women as workers. Natural resources are the sources of wealth provided by nature—land, water, minerals, and so on. Capital is not only money but also such means of production as factories and farms. Political activities are used to distribute these resources within the economic system.

There are two main types of economic systems. One is a *command economy*. In this system a few strong political leaders make most basic decisions about what will be produced, the cost of goods and services, and how things will be distributed. (You can see why this system is sometimes called a *planned economy*.) The Soviet Union has a command economy, with government leaders making most important decisions.

The other main type of economic system is a *market economy*. In such a system, decisions about production and allocation of resources are the result of competition in a free market. This system is also called the "free enterprise" system. Producers and consumers interact to "decide" what gets produced—how, for whom, and in what amounts. For example, if the price of pocket calculators is high, more firms may decide to manufacture them. Production is expanded, competition increases, prices fall, and more people can buy calculators.

Command economies are most common under *socialism*. Under this form of government, it is the government that owns and controls the means of production and sets prices for goods and services. If government control of the economy is combined with democratic political institutions, the system is called *democratic socialism*. Scandinavian countries such as Sweden have democratic socialism. The Swedish people have a choice among leaders, whom they elect to make important decisions, including those about their economy.

Socialism as an economic system also operates under *communism*. Theoretically, communism is a classless society in which all property and means of production are owned by everyone. In practice today, however, nations with communist governments have been dictatorships in which all economic decisions are made by a small group of government leaders.

Market economies are usually associated with *capitalism*. Under capitalism the means of production are owned by private individuals, who also interact to determine prices. In a system of pure capitalism there would be no government controls at all. However, no country has ever had a purely capitalistic, purely free enterprise system. Every government has exercised some control. These economies—mixtures of free enterprise and government control—are often called *mixed economies*.

1. Describe the two major types of economic systems.
2. What are the differences between them?

GROWING INTER-DEPENDENCE

As you read in Chapter 16, global interdependence is increasing in the political arena. As the case study about Indiana showed, economic interdependence is also on the rise. In earlier times, the countries of the world were relatively self-sufficient. The people of each nation grew and made most of what they needed. But the global economy is now more integrated. There are at least three reasons for this trend.

One important factor is trade. During the 1960s, for example, international trade increased 8 percent annually, doubling in nine years. Also on the increase is the amount of each nation's gross national product that is traded. (*Gross national product*—GNP—is the value of all the goods and services produced by a nation in a given year.) Money crosses borders, so to speak, when it is used to buy goods. It also does so when people invest in other countries by buying shares in industries.

A second factor contributing to economic interdependence is the fact that raw materials are unevenly distributed throughout the world. Oil is one such resource. It is in great demand but produced by only a few nations. Some countries, like Japan, are very poor in natural resources and could hardly survive without imports. Even nations rich in natural resources are not self-sufficient. For instance, in 1970 the United States had to import more than half its supplies of six vital natural resources: bauxite, manganese, nickel, tin, zinc, and chrome.

A third factor that has increased interdependence is the hope for economic progress. Money and resources have always been distributed unequally. But no longer are poor nations willing to accept poverty as inevitable. They want to live better than they do. This increased desire for economic betterment is often called the *revolution of rising expectations*.

What evidence does this photograph provide to support the theory of growing interdependence among nations?

Increased economic interdependence has produced both benefits and burdens. It has brought prosperity to many nations. But it also transmits shocks and upsets from one country to another. For instance, the failure of a big company in the United States could spell economic disaster for a whole community in Bolivia whose economy depended on a local tin mine the company owned.

1. What three factors have increased economic interdependence?
2. In what ways is your everyday life affected by economic interdependence?

MAJOR ECONOMIC BLOCS

Each nation has its own unique blend of resources and its own variety of economic system. There are, however, groups of nations that share characteristics. In the economic sphere, we often speak of three major blocs, or subsystems of the global economic system: the Western bloc, the Eastern bloc, and the Third World.

The Western Bloc. The Western bloc consists of the United States, Canada, the countries of Western Europe, Japan, Australia, and New Zealand. (Japan, although culturally an Asian country, has many economic and political ties with the United States and Western Europe. Thus it is considered part of the Western bloc.)

The Western group is not a solid bloc, but a loose association of countries with similar economies and political values. Most of the nations have democratically elected governments. But the economic systems vary, from the capitalistic system of the United States to the planned socialistic economies of Scandinavia.

As a group, the Western nations are the world's wealthiest. They have the highest *per capita income* (income per person per year), have the most advanced technical knowledge, and are highly industrialized.

These nations produce about three-fourths of the world's total exports.

The Western nations have long dominated the world's trading and monetary system. American dominance was especially evident after World War II, when the United States poured large sums of money into the devastated economies of Western Europe and Japan as part of the Marshall Plan.

During the postwar period, the Western system was in many ways an elite one, with the United States making most basic decisions. This situation began to change in the 1970s. The Western bloc moved toward a more coalitional system, with a number of nations influencing each other in the conduct of economic policy. Western nations also worked together to coordinate their economic decisions.

Wealthy as they are, the Western nations are not without problems. After decades of rapid growth and almost continual prosperity, many were troubled by an economic slowdown in the 1970s. One problem was *inflation*—a constantly rising level of prices. In the United States, the dollar in the 1970s was worth less than half what it had been in 1940. Another problem was unemployment.

The Eastern Bloc. This group, consisting of nations in Eastern Europe, is dominated by the Soviet Union. Economies in these nations are planned and centralized. The Eastern bloc produces about 20 percent of the global world products, and is generally poorer than the Western bloc nations.

The economies of the Eastern bloc nations have problems of their own. It is very difficult to centrally coordinate a large economy in an efficient way. People are plagued by shortages, particularly of consumer goods.

For years, the Eastern bloc tried to restrict trade with the Western nations. But by the mid-1960s, it was clear that some interdependence was necessary. For one thing, the Communist nations wanted to buy

Contrasts between wealth and poverty exist around the world. In Rio de Janeiro, Brazil, expensive apartments are bordered by slums (top photo). In rural areas, both rich and poor farm the land, but under very different circumstances. Some, like the owner of a South African sugar plantation, live in elegance (center photo). Others, like these Filipinos, live in discomfort (bottom photo).

Western technology. Soviet computer technology, for example, is estimated to be about 10 years behind American knowledge. They also need Western goods. When the Soviet Union had severe grain shortages in the 1970s, the Russians bought wheat from the United States.

The Third World. The nations that are not members of the Western or Eastern blocs are known as the Third World. As a group, all these nations are less developed than either the Western or Eastern bloc. Not all of them are poor, however. In the past few years, oil-producing states such as Saudi Arabia and Kuwait have become very rich. (Differences in wealth have led some observers to speak of a Fourth World of nations—the Third World nations, without resources, that are the world's poorest and least developed.)

In spite of prosperity in some Third World nations, the bloc as a whole is poor. Per capita income in 1977 was extremely low. The 115 countries in this bloc contain two thirds of the world's population, yet they account for only 10 percent of total world production.

Unemployment is high. In some countries 25 percent of the work force is jobless. The inflation that has affected the West has also hit these nations hard. In the poorest of them, there is widespread disease, hunger, and malnutrition.

The Third World nations have a wide variety of economies. Some—such as Thailand and Morocco—have market economies like the Western nations. Others—like Cuba and Vietnam—are command economies like those of the Eastern bloc.

The overwhelming majority of Third World countries gained independence after World War II. Most of them are active participants in the global economy because they are highly dependent on foreign trade, investment, and loans. (The case study about the TAN-ZAM railroad in Chapter 16 described one example of foreign investment in the Third World.)

Third World nations have been urging adjustments in the global economy that will meet their interests. They feel that the structure and institutions of the global economy have discriminated against them. The major causes of their poverty, they say, need to be corrected through trade liberalization, monetary reform, and access to supplies. And they want special aid to help them develop their economies.

Some people believe that industrialized nations must do all they can to promote their own economic well-being. While Third World poverty is of concern to them, it is not their responsibility. According to this point of view, it is up to poor nations to work hard, without special advantages. Others disagree. They think that the Third World has legitimate grievances. The industrialized nations, they say, should engage in a cooperative effort to accommodate differences.

1. What are the three major economic blocs?
2. How do these blocs compare in size? In population? In wealth?

The PROBLEM of UNEQUAL DISTRIBUTION Probably the single most important characteristic of the global economy is the unequal distribution of resources. (Figure 18–1 provides data on world oil reserves.) World reserves of energy, food, and raw materials are not equally available to everyone. As a result, there are big gaps between the poor and rich nations of the world. Rich nations have capital to build new factories and other productive units while poor nations lack money to develop their economies.

There are dramatic extremes in wealth. Kuwait, an oil-producing nation in the Middle East, has a population of 1 million. Its per capita income is almost $12,000—the world's highest. In Mali, however, where the

CRUDE OIL: PRODUCING AREAS, RESERVES, and ANNUAL SHIPMENTS

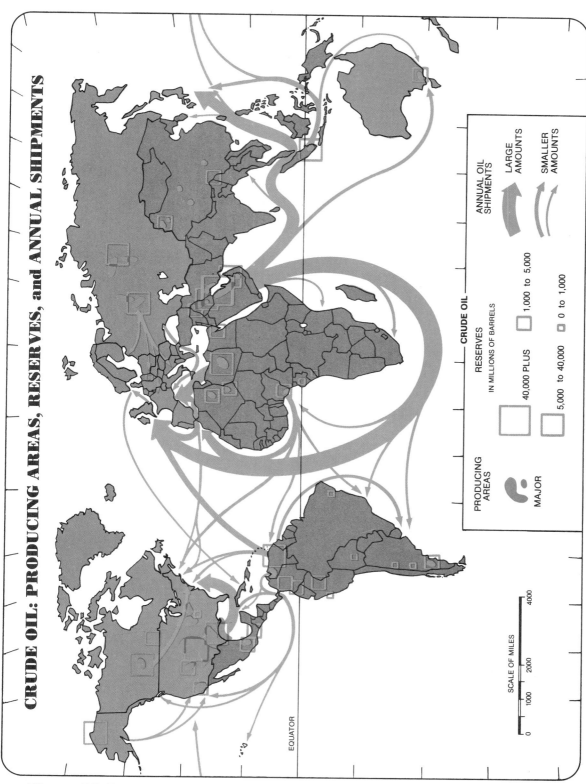

Figure 18-1

population of 6 million people suffers from drought and famine, the per capita income is about $70.

Unequal distribution is a problem within nations, too. In the United States, although there are the very rich and the very poor, most people belong to the middle class. In Ecuador, on the other hand, one fifth of the population receives 73 percent of the nation's income.

1. What are the major groups of nations that participate in the global economy?
2. What are some of the factors that have led to the increasing interdependence of the global economy?
3. Form a hypothesis about how growing interdependence will affect economic relations between nations. In other words, in your view, if there is growing interdependence, will it lead to conflict or cooperation?

Managing Global Economic Resources

A number of important processes influence the global economy. In this section you will read about three of them: money, trade, and aid. They are interrelated, and together they affect the stability of the entire world economy.

MONEY There is a lot of truth in the saying that "Money makes the world go round." Indeed, it affects every nation on earth. Two individuals may be able to barter for goods each wants, perhaps exchanging a cow for flour and salt. But if two nations want to do business, they need a reliable medium of exchange—in other words, money.

Exchange Rates. One important element in the flow of money from one country to another is the *exchange rate*. This determines what a given currency is worth in terms of another. If you were to buy a German camera directly from Germany, you would have to pay in marks, the standard monetary unit of Germany. What is a mark worth in relation to the standard American monetary unit, the dollar? On May 11, 1978, for example, the exchange rate was 2.0 marks to a dollar, so that a mark equaled 50 cents. (Though you personally may not have

to pay for foreign goods in foreign currency, the importer does.) Figure 18-2 contains statistics on the exchange rates of various currencies in early 1978.

In 1944 a group of Western nations met in Bretton Woods, New Hampshire, in an attempt to establish international monetary cooperation. At this time they agreed to set exchange rates in terms of gold and the American dollar. But this system broke down in 1971 for a number of reasons. Other nations complained that using the dollar as the standard for other currencies gave the United States too much power. At the same time, the United States felt that its independence was hampered. When other nations accumulated dollars, the American economy was affected.

Figure 18-2

VALUE of the DOLLAR	
ONE DOLLAR EQUALS	
.5	British pounds
1.9	Swiss francs
2.0	German marks
4.4	French francs
2.2	Dutch guilders
806.5	Italian lira
215.1	Japanese yen

as of May 11, 1978

IMPORTS/EXPORTS of SELECTED COUNTRIES

COUNTRY	IMPORTS (in millions of dollars)	EXPORTS	BALANCE OF TRADE
U.S.	128.872	113.323	—
Brazil	13.622	10.128	—
Canada	37.910	38.128	+
France	64.404	55.817	—
West Germany	87.782	102.032	+
India	5.515	5.424	—
Indonesia	5.673	8.547	+
Iran	12.894	23.480	+
Iraq	3.470	8.841	+
Israel	4.052	2.310	—
Ivory Coast	1.296	1.620	+
Japan	64.799	67.225	+
Kuwait	3.321	9.842	+
Liberia	399	476	+
Mexico	6.030	3.298	—
Netherlands	39.574	40.167	+
Nigeria	8.199	10.565	+
Peru	2.183	1.365	—
Poland	13.867	11.017	—
Romania	6.095	6.138	+
Saudi Arabia	11.759	38.286	+
South Africa	6.751	4.776	—
Sweden	19.334	18.440	—
USSR	38.108	37.169	—
United Kingdom	55.986	46.271	—
Venezuela	6.023	9.149	+
Zambia	780	1.046	+

(1977 figures)

Figure 18-3

Source: Statistical Abstract of the U.S. 1978

The result was that currencies were allowed to "float." Exchange rates were not fixed, but allowed to shift up and down.

The Balance of Payments. The *balance of payments* is another important aspect of the international money system. This is the difference between the total amount of money a nation pays out to other countries and what it receives back from them. When a nation buys products abroad, it spends money. When it sells goods overseas, it earns money. If a nation spends more money abroad than it earns, there is a deficit in its balance of payments. If it earns more than it spends, there is a surplus in its balance of payments. A country with a surplus in its balance of payments has good credit. In other words, it can borrow funds because lenders are fairly certain of being repaid.

Mainly because of enormous increases in the price of oil in the 1970s, many nations are now suffering from huge deficits in their balance of payments. Poorer nations with balance-of-payments deficits have trouble paying their debts. At the same time, some of the oil-producing nations have built up big surpluses in their balance of payments. Also in the 1970s the United States ran up a deficit in its balance of payments for the first time since World War II.

Many experts believe that, in order to be sound, the international monetary system needs to be managed. They say there must be a stable exchange rate and a relatively stable balance of payments. This was not the case in the 1970s. The most urgent need was for cooperation among nations to fix exchange rates and to deal with the imbalance in the international monetary system.

1. Why do some nations have a deficit in their balance of payments? Why do others have surpluses?

2. How would you use money to adjust the unequal resources among nations? How would your solution to this problem affect interdependence?

TRADE International trade involves buying and selling raw materials, goods, and services. Figure 18–3 provides data on international trade.

A nation might trade to acquire something it doesn't have. Every country in the world that wants to import cocoa has to buy it from a few countries because they are the only countries that sell it.

A nation also might trade to acquire something it has, but in insufficient quantities. For instance, Great Britain raises some livestock, but not enough to feed all its people, so it must import meat. A nation may trade to acquire goods that can be produced abroad better (as when Brazil buys American computers) or more cheaply (as when the United States buys Korean textiles).

Unequal Trade Relations. Many of the developing nations export only one commodity. This may be an agricultural crop such as sugar or coffee, or a mineral such as tin or copper. If the price of this commodity falls, the economy of the nation suffers greatly. Commodities are important to many Third World nations because they have not yet acquired the technical know-how to produce enough manufactured goods. These countries are at a disadvantage when compared with industrialized nations. They need manufactured goods more than the developed nations need their commodities.

Another factor that causes unequal trade relations is a shortage of capital. If a country's credit is poor its ability to trade is limited because it cannot borrow the money it needs to develop new markets.

Government Actions. Governments frequently intervene in international trade. Sometimes they want to promote it. At other times they want to restrain it.

A primary method of government regulation is the *tariff,* a tax on imports. High tariffs are often set on imported products in order to protect a country's own industries. For instance, if India wanted to encourage its textile companies, it might set very high tariffs on fabrics made in Korea or Japan. Few Indians could afford to buy the imports, so they would have to buy those made domestically.

A government may also set quotas on certain imports, decreeing that only a cer-

tain number may be brought in during a given year. Or it may ban imports for political reasons, as the United States does Cuban cigars, or the Soviet Union does most American periodicals.

Economists disagree about whether there should be *free trade,* with relatively limited management, or a *fully managed economy.* Free trade is the system as it exists today. Nations are free to invest, trade, and make loans more or less as they please. Those who favor free trade believe that world economic relations will balance out because of differences in supply and demand. A free-trade economy, however, does very little to correct the imbalance in natural resources, and it has not brought economic growth to less developed nations.

People who favor a fully managed economy argue that if trade could be completely regulated, money could be invested in developing countries. This approach would promote industrialization, and the world economy could be brought into better balance. Developing nations favor this kind of global economy, but they have not yet convinced the industrialized nations.

1. Why do nations trade?
2. What methods do governments use to regulate trade?
3. Do you think Third World nations should have special advantages in trading? If so, what types? If not, why not?

AID Aid is a third important process in managing international economic relations. It may take several different forms. Money may be given for relief, as in grants to American allies after World War II. It may be lent at low interest rates to build up industry. Aid may also be in the form of technical assistance, with experts teaching their skills to others.

The motives for aid are varied. One developed out of the politics of the Cold War.

Western countries wanted developing nations to align themselves on the side of democracy. The Soviet Union's activities in developing areas stimulated competition. Western aid increased in order to keep the balance between Communist and non-Communist countries in the Third World at least even.

Another motive was a desire for increased trade to provide markets for the developed nations. The United States, for example, established the Development Loan Fund to aid Latin America. In 1958, it lent Latin American nations $300 million. By 1961, the sum had doubled. In 1961 the Agency for International Development (AID) took over the Development Loan Fund's functions. In 1976 AID gave Latin American nations $307.7 million.

In the late 1960s and early 1970s, the United States and European nations cut back dramatically on foreign aid. It seemed to have little economic impact. Because of population increases, the economic level of most developing nations did not rise. In fact, the gap between rich and poor widened. Massive unemployment continued. And many nations became even more dependent on the developed countries.

Aid did not seem to work from a political point of view either. Nations that received aid either continued as dictatorships or even joined the Communist camp.

Forms of aid may be increasing as the desire for new markets grows. However, the impact of aid formulas has yet to be tested. New ideas and strategies will be needed before massive aid is used again as an economic and control device for developing nations.

1. Describe three forms of foreign aid.
2. Why have developed nations given foreign aid? Why did they cut back beginning in the late 1960s?

Global Economic Actors

In Chapter 17 you read about the importance of the more than 160 sovereign nations in making decisions affecting the global system. The major global decisions are made by these sovereign states, each pursuing its own national interest.

Other actors also play an important role in the global economy, however. Among them are several institutions that make rules for international economic activities and a group of large corporations with a worldwide scope. You will read about both of these in the following sections.

INTERNATIONAL ECONOMIC ORGANIZATIONS As you read about these global economic actors, think about how they contribute to conflict, cooperation, and development in the global economy. Think too about how they stimulate and respond to increasing interdependence.

The International Monetary Fund. At the 1944 conference at Bretton Woods, Western nations set up the International Monetary Fund (IMF). Its main purpose was to manage the international money system by keeping exchange rates relatively stable. The IMF has also extended credit to nations.

As you have read, the exchange rates set at Bretton Woods broke down in 1971. Since then, a major concern of the IMF has been to reform the international money system. Its aim is to devise a stable exchange rate to replace the system of floating currencies that now exists. Figure 18–4 provides information on fluctuations in currency value.

Today 25 industrialized nations and nearly 100 developing nations participate in the IMF. The fund is run by an executive

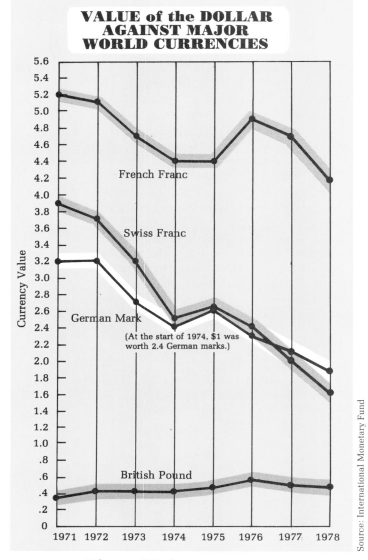

VALUE of the DOLLAR AGAINST MAJOR WORLD CURRENCIES

French Franc

Swiss Franc

German Mark

(At the start of 1974, $1 was worth 2.4 German marks.)

British Pound

Currency Value

5.6 5.4 5.2 5.0 4.8 4.6 4.4 4.2 4.0 3.8 3.6 3.4 3.2 3.0 2.8 2.6 2.4 2.2 2.0 1.8 1.6 1.4 1.2 1.0 .8 .6 .4 .2 0

1971 1972 1973 1974 1975 1976 1977 1978

Source: International Monetary Fund

Figure 18-4

board and a board of governors. Votes in the fund are weighted by member contributions to the fund. Therefore, the 25 leading industrialized nations have controlled three quarters of the vote. Because of this imbalance, Third World members have argued that the fund has not been responsive to their needs.

In 1976, in response to a suggestion by the United States, the IMF set up a trust fund of $2 billion to aid the poorest nations burdened with increasing debts. In 1977, the IMF announced the creation of an additional $10 billion fund to lend money to the poorest nations. Nearly half of the money is to come from the group of oil-producing nations known as OPEC. (See pages 559–560.)

The IMF also took steps to increase the voting shares of OPEC members. This action could reduce the influence of Western nations and affect future decisions of the fund.

The World Bank. The meeting at Bretton Woods also resulted in the creation of the International Bank for Reconstruction and Development (IBRD), or World Bank. Like any bank, it makes loans—in this case loans to nations unable to finance developments through private sources. The World Bank loans have been used to build roads, medical clinics, and seaports, among other projects. In 1960, the World Bank established the International Development Agency (IDA) which makes loans to poorer nations on special terms that make repayment easy. Since its establishment IDA has made loans totaling more than $11 billion.

In the period since World War II, the World Bank has been the chief source of official development aid. Like its sister institution, the IMF, the bank has made changes in its structure that will give a greater voice in decision-making to nations of the Third World.

Trade Agreements. In 1947, twenty-three countries met at Geneva to form the General Agreement on Tariffs and Trade (GATT). GATT drew up a code of fair trading practices. It is also the institution through which member nations negotiate to reduce tariffs and other barriers to trade. Negotiations by GATT have resulted in the lowering of tariffs.

Nearly 100 nations participate in GATT. The group is governed informally by a council of representatives. A secretary carries out most executive functions. GATT has been controlled by countries in the Western bloc. The most prominent are the so-called Group of Ten: Belgium, France, Germany, Italy, the Netherlands, Sweden, Canada, Japan, Britain, and the United States.

The Common Market. In 1957, six nations met at Rome to form the European

Economic Community (EEC), or Common Market. The original members were Belgium, the Netherlands, Luxembourg, West Germany, France, and Italy. In later years they were joined by Denmark, Ireland, and Great Britain. The group is thus sometimes called The Nine.

The purpose of the EEC was to remove trade barriers among member nations and to establish a single commercial policy toward nonmembers. The first reduction in tariffs among members occurred in 1959. By 1968, all internal tariffs had been removed. At the same time, a common tariff for nonmember countries was put in operation.

The EEC has developed a common agricultural policy to block imports from coming into the community. Agreements make it cheaper for France, for instance, to buy butter from Denmark than from Norway. The EEC has also encouraged trade agreements that allow members to export commodities at favorable rates. The Common Market's policy aims toward creating the most favorable balance of trade for its members. This policy has created difficulties in trading relations with the United States, which has complained about unfair barriers against American exports and investments.

In the United Nations and other international institutions, The Nine try to formulate common policy on economic and some political concerns. However, they do not agree on all economic decisions. For instance, Denmark usually supports Third World economic demands, while Germany often opposes them.

The OECD. The Organization for Economic Cooperation and Development (OECD) was founded in 1961. This organization of 24 Western nations, including Canada and the United States, was set up to ensure continued economic growth among members. Such growth, it was believed, would contribute to the development of the world economy. It was to be fostered in part by liberalizing trade among members. Another goal was to coordinate aid to devel-

OPEC RESERVES and CAPACITY

COUNTRY	RESERVES[1] (billions of barrels)	PRODUCTION CAPACITY (millions of barrels a day)
Saudi Arabia	170	11.5
Kuwait	70	3.5
Iran	63	6.7
Iraq	35	3.0
United Arab Emirates	31	2.4
Libya	26	2.5
Nigeria	20	2.3
Venezuela	14	2.6
Indonesia	14	1.7
Algeria	7	1.0
Qatar	6	0.7
Gabon	2	0.3
Ecuador	2	0.2

Figure 18-5

[1]Estimated proved and probable reserves as of April 1977. Source: Central Intelligence Agency

oping nations. The OECD is a consultative body, and its decisions are not binding.

Members of the OECD, led by the United States, have tried to coordinate economic policies, particularly those concerned with energy and foreign aid. In 1973 the International Energy Agency (IEA), a 19-nation group with the OECD, was set up to integrate members' energy policies.

OPEC. In 1960, five oil-producing nations founded the Organization of Petroleum Exporting Countries (OPEC). They were distressed because oil-refining companies had just lowered the price they were paying for crude oil. Although each nation could do little on its own, OPEC hoped that group action could influence the oil companies. Therefore they organized to set a common price for oil. The five founding nations—Saudi Arabia, Venezuela, Iran, Iraq, and Kuwait—were later joined by eight other oil-producing nations. These were Algeria, United Arab Emirates, Libya, Indonesia, Nigeria, Ecuador, Qator, and Gabon. (See Figure 18-5 for statistics on OPEC oil reserves.)

At first, OPEC had very little influence. Initial attempts to coordinate policies failed, and members watched the price for other commodities soar. Then in one electrifying action, OPEC nations changed the entire international scene. Their action—the embargo of 1973—dramatically demonstrated that the West no longer held all the economic cards. A case study on the embargo appears on pages 561–562.

OPEC is run on a majority rule. A majority must agree in order to arrive at decisions, such as those to raise prices. When majority agreement cannot be reached, prices remain frozen.

There are policy differences within OPEC. Some members want to hold prices down, fearing that increases will weaken Western economies. Those who have heavy investments in the West and want Western manufactured goods and technology feel it is in their own best interests to keep prices frozen. Other OPEC members want to get as much money as they can while supplies last.

UNCTAD. Third World nations for some time felt that the world's economic relationships were dominated by GATT. The trade rules it established, they believed, did not work to their benefit. So in 1964 a group of them met at Geneva to take part in a United Nations Conference on Trade and Development (UNCTAD). After this conference, UNCTAD became a permanent United Nations institution.

In the early 1960s, 77 developing nations belonged to UNCTAD. Members are still called the Group of 77, although the nations in the group number well over 100.

The UNCTAD Secretariat is part of the United Nations Secretariat. Basically, the organization has served as a pressure group for developing nations that want reforms in trade policy which will benefit them.

1. Name five major international economic organizations and describe their goals.
2. What political systems operate in each of the organizations?
3. What policy matters divide the members of the EEC? Of OPEC?

MULTI-NATIONAL CORPORATIONS

Multinational corporations, another major international actor, are large companies with operations in more than one country. This definition contains an important element. Not only does a company trade abroad, it must also have production facilities in at least one other nation.

There are several reasons why corporations choose to be multinational. One is profits. Using labor and manufacturing facilities in other nations can lower production costs substantially. For example, an American company can pay Mexican workers lower wages than those earned by Americans.

A second reason is tariffs. A British multinational corporation can manufacture products in a country from which it normally buys the raw materials needed. In this way importing is avoided—and tariffs as well.

A third benefit is lower taxes. An underdeveloped nation may offer tax breaks to a corporation so that it will set up a factory there. For instance, a multinational corporation may not have to pay any taxes on its profits for a number of years.

A fourth benefit for the multinational corporation is freedom from regulation. Because these firms operate in more than one nation, it is difficult for any one nation to control them. A multinational corporation can simply move its operations out of a nation if the climate for business there is not right.

People disagree about the impact of multinational corporations on the global economy. Their supporters say that they bring technology and technical know-how to developing nations. This transfer contributes to the equalizing of resources among rich and poor nations. Multinational corporations, say supporters, have made major investments in developing nations, and have created thousands of new jobs. All these activities increase economic development.

Critics of multinational corporations argue that they create unemployment. They say that a company that sets up operations where labor is cheap is shortchanging its own people. American labor leaders have criticized corporations for moving their factories to Taiwan, where wages are low. Another criticism of multinational corporations is that they allow foreign business executives too much control over the economies of developing nations.

1. What is a multinational corporation?
2. What are the arguments in favor of multinational corporations? Against?

A GLOBAL CRISIS

You have seen how various actors operate in the international economy. Sometimes these actors are in conflict; at other times they cooperate. As you read the following case about the oil crisis of 1973, identify the major actors. Think about how their varying interests led to cooperation and conflict and how these processes created changes in the global economy.

★ The Crisis of 1973

During the summer of 1973 tensions between the state of Israel and its Arab neighbors were high. On October 6, Egypt and Syria launched a simultaneous attack on two fronts. After heavy initial losses, Israel pushed back the invaders. It was during this conflict that the Arab members of OPEC decided to use their oil resources as a political and economic weapon.

On October 17, 1973, representatives of 11 members of OPEC assembled in the small Persian Gulf country of Kuwait. They decreed a 5 percent cutback in oil production each month. A few days later they announced an *embargo* (a total trade prohibition) on oil sold directly or indirectly to nations friendly to Israel. Initially this included the United States and the Netherlands; later Portugal, Rhodesia, and South Africa were cut off as well. (Figure 18–5 on page 559 presents statistics on OPEC oil reserves and production capacity.)

The resulting crisis was immediate and severe. Japan, dependent on the Mideast for more than 80 percent of its oil, was hurt badly by the decision. The European nations were also hard hit. Oil companies found themselves with decreasing energy reserves. The price of oil skyrocketed, up some 400 percent from its price at the beginning of 1973. Many countries were forced to curtail energy use. Competition for oil supplies from other areas was keen.

The oil embargo led to a scramble for energy supplies. The Western nations were unable to coordinate their policies. Nor could the EEC work out a concerted response to the price increases. Cooperation was hampered by individual nations who focused on their own problems rather than seeking a joint solution. The OECD was not much better off. Its machinery was weak, and there had been little planning for an energy crisis.

As early as Christmas 1973, Arab OPEC members were easing their embargo, which lasted only a few months altogether. But prices continued to rise. In January 1978 the price for a barrel of crude oil stood at $12.70.

It seemed clear to the Western nations that they had to take steps to deal with their energy weaknesses. One result was the formation of the International Economic Agency. As you read earlier, IEA, an agency within the OECD, sought to make Western nations less dependent on OPEC oil. With this goal in mind, it developed a comprehensive plan for dealing with the oil crisis. IEA's first recommendation was that each nation should become more self-sufficient by increasing its production and through strict conservation measures. The

In the oil-dependent nations of North America and Western Europe, the 1973 oil embargo created severe inconveniences. Limited supplies of gasoline often forced gas stations to close.

second recommendation was to share burdens equally, with participating nations helping each other.

The full consequences of the oil crisis are probably still to be felt. Many regard it as the prime cause of the worldwide recession that began in 1974. Developing nations have run up a $170 billion deficit in paying for oil. The United States, in the three-year period between 1973 and 1976, paid an additional $225 billion for crude oil. It lost over $60 billion in GNP and over 2 million jobs.

When is the oil situation likely to improve? Not very soon, according to a 1977 OECD report. Unless production and conservation are dramatically increased, the report warns, members of OECD will have to import 35 million barrels a day from OPEC in 1985. This would be a big increase over the 23 million barrels imported in 1975.

One fact is certain: the actions of OPEC in 1973 dramatically changed the global economy. The wealth of OPEC nations increased greatly. At the same time, oil-buying countries found themselves with huge deficits due mainly to soaring oil bills. A small group of nations controlling a vital resource showed in an unforgettable way the power they could wield on an international scale.

1. Who were the major international actors in this crisis? What roles did they play?
2. What interests of the OPEC nations affected their decisions in 1973? What interests of Western nations were in conflict with OPEC?
3. How did Western nations cooperate during the oil crisis? What conflicts were there among them?

"There's only one answer to the dwindling supply of oil, gentlemen . . . smaller barrels!"

GRIN AND BEAR IT by Lichty and Wagner. © Field Enterprises, Inc., 1977. Courtesy of Field Newspaper Syndicate.

CITIZEN ACTORS: the COFFEE BOYCOTT

You have seen that many different kinds of actors are important in the politics of the global economy. Citizen actors can also be important.

Roles that citizens take on the international level are similar to those they take on the local or national level. Many citizens are observers. They read newspapers and magazines and watch television and determine their positions on such economic issues as energy or industrial growth. They may express their opinions informally or formally.

People take supporter roles as consumers. For example, a family may decide not to buy a foreign car in order to help the American economy. A group of students may form a car pool to conserve gasoline.

Advocates on the international economic level have been active in voicing their concerns over American economic decisions in the United Nations. Citizens also try to influence congressional decisions about foreign aid and trade.

Organizers on the international scene may be business executives who influence the global economy by organizing corporations. Or they may be people who organize citizens in order to affect the decisions of government.

In the two cases that follow, you will see individual actors participating in international economics. The first case illustrates American reaction to high coffee prices after the 1975 freeze in Brazil. The second case concerns a businessman who built a flourishing coffee firm. As you read the cases, think about how the actors have an impact on the global economy.

★ A Citizen Protest

In July 1975, one of the worst freezes in the history of Brazil devastated the nation's coffee crop. (This was winter in the Southern hemisphere, as the seasons there are reversed from what they are in the Northern hemisphere.)

At the same time, a war in Angola halted the harvest of that country's coffee crop. Droughts and floods in Colombia damaged much of its coffee, and an earthquake in Guatemala interfered with its coffee shipments out of the country.

As a result of all these conditions, the price of coffee rose dramatically. Brazil produces a third of the world's coffee, and a fifth of what Americans consume. Because the Brazilian coffee prices rose in the United States, people had to pay three to four times more for a pound of coffee than they had paid before.

Was the steep increase justified? Whenever there is a big demand for a product in short supply, prices do go up. But it was common knowledge that the Brazilian government had tripled its export price of coffee. Because they were in a "seller's market," the Brazilian growers had raised their prices. They defended their action, saying that Brazilians were paying more for the coffee they bought too.

Many Americans, angry about the steep rise, decided to take action. One of them was New York City's Commissioner of Consumer Affairs, Elinor Guggenheimer. In January 1976, she urged American consumers to boycott coffee. By January 11 organized consumer groups across the nation joined in and urged the American people to cut their use of coffee 25 percent. Protesters argued that if United States consumption was reduced by one quarter, thus cutting the demand, coffee prices would go down.

Restaurants across the United States offered free tea to customers instead of coffee. Supermarkets advertised tea and set special prices for tea and cocoa. They also posted signs urging consumers not to buy coffee because of the high price.

Whether because of high prices or the boycott, coffee consumption did drop 15 percent by 1977. And the lessened demand did have an impact. Although the price of coffee did not go down to pre-1975 levels, it did not hit predicted highs either.

1. What roles did citizens play in the coffee boycott?
2. How would you have acted if you had been part of the coffee-drinking population in January 1977?

★ A Businessman's Story

The family of Jorge Wolney Atalla moved from Lebanon to Brazil in 1898. Atalla's grandfather worked as a longshoreman and peddler before buying a farm. Though he lost his business with the worldwide depression of the 1930s, he held on to the farm. After the grandfather's death, Atalla's father went to medical school while his mother tended the farm. Atalla himself studied petroleum engineering in the United States before returning to Brazil to help his mother run the farm. There, he increased its size by buying land at low prices.

Atalla was joined in business by his three brothers. Beginning in the 1950s, they built a major firm that has had a large impact on Brazil and on the international economy.

The Atalla brothers started by producing sugar. Then they bought Hills Brothers, a major processor of coffee in the United States. The Atalla brothers now owned a multinational corporation, and by 1975 their firm was the largest coffee grower in Brazil and in the world.

On an evening in July 1975, Atalla was warned by the weather station of a possible freeze that could endanger his 8½ million coffee trees. It happened as predicted, and there was nothing Atalla could do. By the next morning more than 6½ million trees—some 75 percent of his total crop—had died. Each of them was worth more than $10.

Since then, the Atallas have been replacing the coffee trees. In the meantime they have relied on sugar and other industries they own to support their activities.

According to Atalla, the huge increase in the price of Brazilian coffee was justified by the frost. Costs went up simply because coffee was in short supply. To prove his point, Atalla even sponsored a tour of Brazil for American consumer advocates to show them the extent of the destruction and convince them that no coffee was being kept off the market to force prices up.

Atalla, an influential businessman, says that his chief purpose is

". . . to build things up for the country, to help the country grow, to help our economy, to see if one day Brazil can be among the greatest countries in the world. We have a very good chance, but we have to work more and we have to work harder."

1. What citizen role did Attala play in the coffee boycott?
2. How did Attala have an impact on the global economy?

CITIZENS as ORGANIZERS In the global economy, citizen actors can play important roles as organizers. For example, people who arranged for a coffee boycott acted as organizers. Jorge Wolney Atalla also acted as an organizer by building a small farm into a huge, billion-dollar industry with multinational connections.

As you read in Chapter 1, organizers plan activities and work with others in carrying them out. To participate effectively as an organizer, follow these guidelines. A successful organizer:

1. Plans group activities.
2. Helps set group goals.
3. Influences people to work together in reaching their goals.
4. Makes sure that decisions are carried out.

The exercise on the following two pages will help you develop skills in acting as an organizer. The situation involves coffee prices in one community. Read the description carefully. Be prepared to place yourself in an organizer role in the situation described.

In group activity, a successful organizer structures the effective use of group resources. An organizer must be able to communicate well with group members and must be a respected member of the group.

★ *The Organizer Role*

High Coffee Prices

Mayberry High School is located in a residential district of a suburban town. Nearby are three restaurants where students often meet after school. They may eat lunch there, too, if they decide not to eat in the school cafeteria.

Over a period of a few weeks during the fall semester, coffee prices have risen from 15¢ to 50¢ a cup. In answer to complaints, the restaurant managers claim that they have to raise prices because their own costs for coffee have gone up.

The local newspaper has carried stories about a freeze destroying much of the coffee crop in Brazil, and about troubles in other coffee-growing countries. Apparently, there is not enough coffee to meet the de-

mand, and prices will keep going up until more coffee is produced.

But there is another factor. According to some accounts, the government of Brazil has raised the price of raw coffee beans to an artificially high level, knowing that people will pay it because there is such a big demand. It may be that the Brazilian government is taking advantage of the situation in order to rake in extra profits.

One citizen, in a letter to the local newspaper, said he thought the only way to stop soaring coffee prices was to convince people to drink less coffee. If the demand fell off, coffee growers could not charge such high prices. Maybe, he wrote, someone in the community should organize a boycott.

Profile: Paul / Paula Tinello

You are a junior at Mayberry High. An honor student, you're shy and hard-working. You think most meetings are a waste of time. But you are very good at organizing your thoughts and presenting them clearly.

You're a confirmed coffee drinker and think that prices are way out of line. You favor the idea of a boycott, and have collected news items about citizen-sponsored protests in other communities.

Profile: Debbie / Don Brucker

A sophomore at Mayberry, you are the head of the school's pep club. You are enthusiastic and well-liked, and have gotten bigger turnouts at pep rallies and other school events than any pep club leader in recent memory.

You don't like coffee, but you've heard your parents complain about high prices. You think a boycott is a good idea. Besides, you'd like to run for student body president next year, and working on a boycott campaign would make you even better known.

Profile: Chuck / Sharon Sullivan

As a Mayberry senior, you have an easy course load this year, and are enjoying your leisure. Last summer you worked part-time in the city manager's office and got to know quite a few important people around town.

After college, you might want to enter politics. For now you'd rather not get involved. You don't drink coffee, but you realize that a boycott might help to bring prices down.

Profile: the Organizer

A junior at Mayberry High School, you want to organize a coffee boycott. You don't believe that the Brazilian government is trying to force prices up, but you do think that if demand goes down, prices will too.

Assignment 1

a. Write a letter to the local newspaper, thanking the other letter writer for his suggestion that someone organize a boycott. Summarize why you agree with him.

Assignment 2

a. With three of your classmates, form a group of four to organize a coffee boycott. One person should play the role of Paul/Paula Tinello, one of Debbie/Don Brucker, a third that of Chuck/Sharon Sullivan. The fourth person should play the organizer.

Reread the characteristics of a good organizer on page 565. Then review the material you have just read and complete one of the following assignments. Your teacher will tell you which one to follow.

b. Outline the steps you would take in organizing a local coffee boycott. Include ideas that would appeal to citizens as observers, supporters, and advocates.

b. The organizer should articulate the goals of the boycott. Then he or she should divide up the main tasks among the members of the group. Discuss details that will be part of carrying out the tasks.

c. At the end of the discussion, each person should answer these questions:

1. What are the major parts of the boycott plan? Is the plan a feasible one?
2. How did the organizer handle his/her role?
3. What suggestions do you have for improving the plan?

Chapter Review

1. How are major economic decisions made in a command economy? In a market economy? In a mixed economy?
2. Why is economic interdependence greater now than it used to be?
3. How do the Western bloc and Eastern bloc differ?
4. What is the Third World of nations? The Fourth World?
5. When was the dollar established as the standard medium of exchange? When was it abandoned? Why?
6. What factors cause unequal trade relations in the global economy?
7. What are the major international economic organizations and what is the purpose of each?
8. What are the main advantages a multinational corporation has in doing business?
9. Summarize the main events of the 1973 oil crisis.
10. What are the important characteristics of the organizer role?

Chapter Vocabulary

Define these terms.

economic system   capitalism   exchange rate
command economy   mixed economy   balance of payments
market economy   gross national product   credit
socialism   embargo   tariff
democratic socialism   per capita income   multinational corporation
communism   inflation   revolution of rising
    expectations

Chapter Analysis

1. Which system do you think would be best for a Third World nation—a command economy or a market economy? Give reasons for your answer.
2. How has interdependence made the Eastern bloc less isolated from the rest of the world economically? Do you think such economic interdependence can ease political tensions? Why or why not?
3. Which of the international economic organizations discussed in this chapter do you think has done most to promote international cooperation? Why?
4. If you were a Third World leader, would you want multinational corporations to set up operations in your country? Why or why not?

1. Collect tables and charts showing the unequal distribution of the world's resources. Study one major economic actor and how it affects this inequality. Report to the class on your findings.

2. Create a currency for your class. Design a game, using this currency, that your class can play for a short period each day. Its purpose should be to simulate global economic processes.

3. Make a list of ways in which the energy shortage has affected you. Beside each item, jot down whether you think the change is for better or worse.

4. Develop a plan for a way in which you could act in the organizer role. Discuss with your teacher the possibility of putting your plan into action.

Chapter Activities

The Limits to Growth, Donella H. Meadows, Dennis L. Meadows, Jørgen Randers, William W. Behrens III (New American Library: New York, NY), 1972.

Discusses the global effects of rapid and continued technological growth. Based upon careful predictions, this book outlines the potential catastrophy of continued uncontrolled growth.

Small Is Beautiful: Economics as if People Mattered, E.F. Schumacher (Harper & Row, Inc: New York, NY), 1973.

A comprehensive economic analysis of the global political system focusing, in part, on the uses of resources such as education, land, and nuclear energy.

Bread for the World, Arthur Simon (Paulist Press: New York, NY), 1975.

Focuses on the general problem of world hunger, discussing issues including food production, population, and the use of natural resources. It devotes a large section to the role of the United States and concludes with a section on what citizens can do about the hunger problem.

Chapter Bibliography

Chapter Objectives

★ **To analyze the role of justice in global political systems**

★ **To identify some of the global actors involved in the search for justice**

★ **To understand the process of seeking international justice**

★ **To develop skills in forecasting alternative futures**

chapter 19

The POLITICS of JUSTICE

When we think of global politics, we tend to concentrate on political or economic situations. We talk about war, or about oil. It is less common to talk about the role of justice in global political systems.

But a concern for justice is a vital part of the American political heritage, whether in our school, our community, our nation, or in the global system. Americans are concerned about discrimination and equal opportunity for everyone. So are the citizens of other nations. But all the world's people do not share a common idea of justice.

One problem in reaching a global definition of justice is that there are very few formal rules. How can we formulate principles of justice that will apply to people from different cultures, of different religions, and with different political and economic goals?

A number of official global actors are involved in the process of seeking justice. Ordinary citizens like you can also make known their views on justice and can influence changes in the global political system. You will see how the process of bringing about such change actually works.

Finally, this chapter will give you a chance to use what you have learned about global politics, economics, and justice to examine possible future alternatives for global political systems.

What Is Justice?

Justice may be defined as a fair standard that is applicable to everyone within a group. A group can be a family, a school, a nation, or the international community. More simply put, justice is equivalent to fairness.

When we speak of justice we are usually concerned with a conflict of interests. More than one person or group is making a claim on a limited resource. Justice is the standard we use in trying to settle claims and counterclaims. The law aims to ensure justice. But not all laws are just. Today in the United States, for instance, most people believe that laws enforcing racial segregation are unjust. This was not always the case.

To most of us, justice is closely involved with the idea of equality—that all people should be treated the same. Think about being accepted as a student in a medical school or law school. Competition is keen for openings. If a woman were admitted because she was a niece of the admissions director, we would regard this as unequal treatment. It is unjust (though it might not be illegal).

Take the case of an election in your state. One party bribes the election commis-sioners to falsify the returns. If a man won election this way, we would regard this as unequal treatment. It is unjust (and illegal as well).

CONFLICTING IDEAS Deciding what is just in a given situation is a complicated process. What seems just to one person may seem highly unfair to another. Suppose you believe in equality. This is a good idea and a common principle for American justice. Suppose you believe, too, that people can pursue their own interests as long as they don't hurt anyone else. These two principles can conflict under certain circumstances.

We may think of equality as meaning that everyone has relatively equal income, status, and ability in society. Yet when people pursue their interests independently of other people, they may gain an advantage in wealth, status, or skills. Therefore, they will enjoy more of society's benefits. Inequality is the result.

The situation is more complex when we think about group justice, or *social justice*. When we use this term, we mean that

A student judicial council is responsible for dealing with the question of justice. Here, council members hear the case of a student accused of breaking a major school rule.

The issue of capital punishment produces great conflict. Supporters claim that the death penalty helps prevent crime. Opponents view it as inhumane. Here California college students show their protest.

society makes decisions about what is fair. Many people have to agree. What makes this complicated is that people have to decide first how they will decide what is the best rule. Does the majority rule? Do the best educated decide? Or must the decision be unanimous?

The American people have had to cope with many decisions involving social justice. The income tax is one. The nation made a decision (which required a constitutional amendment) that everyone should pay income tax. But how much should people pay? According to what standard? The answer was a *graduated income tax*—one in which payments are calculated according to a scale (graduated). Theoretically, at least, people pay more income tax the wealthier they are. But not everyone agrees that this is the best system. Some people believe that everyone should pay the same amount of income tax. Others think that the rich should pay more than they pay now. Because of deductions and various special provisions, some millionaires pay very little income tax. What is socially just in this case?

Another example involving social justice is the death penalty. Some people believe that capital punishment is fair in the case of a person convicted of murder—taking the life of another. Other people believe that the death penalty is not fair under any circumstances because it is absolutely

wrong to take a human life. What is socially just in this case?

The political nature of justice can most clearly be seen in human rights cases. Political prisoners are in jail because they hold political beliefs that are different from those of people in power and are threatening to them. Some people believe that jailing those with widely deviant political opinions is just because they are a threat to society. Others feel that all people have the right to think and speak as they please, regardless of how disagreeable their ideas are to others.

The rights of women may also be viewed as human rights, though they are less obviously political. Women have traditionally been discriminated against just because they are women. Some people feel that certain types of discrimination—for instance, limiting the kinds of jobs women can hold—are necessary in order to preserve the family. Others believe that sex discrimination is wrong, even if family life does undergo change.

We have talked about individual justice and social justice. Let us now think about the problem in international terms. Views on justice vary widely around the globe. There are many reasons for this, but we will concentrate on three main reasons: culture, religion, and ideology.

Culture is the shared ideas and ways of acting of a group of people. People with the same cultural heritage share common customs and values. They share many common beliefs about what is just. Among most Americans, for example, it is accepted that when someone accuses another person of serious wrongdoing, the matter will be taken to court. In the Eskimo culture, on the other hand, it is common for accusations to be made before a group of villagers. The conflict is resolved by a contest in which the two parties hurl insults at each other.

Religious teachings also affect standards of justice. Among Muslims it is legal for a man to have as many as four wives (although few men do). Most Christian countries, however, have laws prohibiting a man or woman from being married to more than one person at a time.

Our *ideologies*—the doctrines that underlie our political and economic systems—also affect our ideas of justice. For example, Western nations place a high value on individual political and civil rights. Individual freedoms are guaranteed by such documents as the Bill of Rights of the American Constitution.

In the governments of the Communist bloc, however, the state is regarded as more important than the individual. Citizens have little protection against the vast power of the government—as you saw in the case of Alexander Solzhenitsyn.

Many of the countries of the Third World regard political rights as less important than economic rights. What use, they ask, is freedom of speech to a starving person? A Jamaican woman active in the feminist cause says, "Equal pay for equal work is a fine concept, but the main priority for Jamaica's women is first getting work for *any* kind of pay."

1. Why is it difficult to achieve social justice?
2. How do ideologies affect our ideas of what is fair?
3. Which do you think is more important, political or economic justice? Why?

INTER-NATIONAL AGREEMENT

In the past, nations have sometimes agreed to common standards of justice on a voluntary basis. In the 1860s a group of countries met in Geneva to agree on the care and treatment of wounded during wartime. Out of this meeting grew the International Red Cross. At subsequent conferences several agreements were signed providing for wartime protection of civilians and prisoners of war.

Before World War II, however, the protection of citizens within a nation was considered to be the concern only of the nation itself. Although one country might have criticized another's treatment of its citizens, no international action was taken. But some of the events of the war—such as the violations of human rights committed by Adolf Hitler—were too appalling to be disregarded by other nations.

The Need for Standards. Determining justice in the global system is much more complicated than it is within one nation, where it is complex enough. There are more than 160 nations in the global system, each with its own system of laws. And, as you have read, ideas of justice can also be affected by factors such as culture, religion, and ideology.

Sometimes nations may be able to settle their differences without too much trouble. However, sometimes differences are not easy to resolve. The Middle East, for example, has been torn by warfare since the state of Israel was created.

The United Nations was formed with the hope of preventing further bloodshed between nations. An earlier organization—the League of Nations, established after World War I—had failed, in part because the United States had never joined. Now, with a broader membership, it seemed realistic to hope for greater cooperation. There was also a hope that nations would agree on a standard of justice, embodied in rules and regulations drawn up by the UN.

As you have read in earlier chapters, hopes for the United Nations as a great peace-keeper have not been fulfilled. There are still many disputes, some of which lead to war. Nor do all nations share common standards of what is just and fair.

Why is it important to decide what is fair in the global political system? It seems to be an impossible task. It is a very important one, however, for at least three reasons.

First of all, the peoples of the globe are becoming more interdependent economically. They are increasingly linked to each other for their very survival. Resources are scarce in the global economy. In the past they were very often distributed simply on the basis of power. The strongest contender got the land, or the coal, or the rubber. But global problems cannot be solved this way any longer. The danger of war, especially nuclear war, is too great.

A second reason for agreeing on international standards of justice concerns technology. Technological changes, such as advances in transportation and communication, have international effects. In 1978, for example, a radioactive Russian satellite fell into Canadian territory. How can such accidents be prevented in the future—justly? Standards of justice must be clear in order to control technological advances for peaceful and humanitarian means.

A third reason for the importance of developing global standards of justice is the effect of global politics on every person on earth. Just as you are affected by standards of fairness in your family, school, or community, so you are also affected by standards of justice in the international community. Humanity itself is diminished when people anywhere are denied the opportunity to live secure and useful lives.

The following case illustrates some of the problems in international justice that are a result of global interdependence. As you read the case, think about the economic, technological, and humanitarian factors involved in skyjacking.

★ Policing the Sky

Like many other phenomena of the twentieth century, it seemed to require a new word—skyjacking. The practice of commandeering a plane in mid-flight was, obviously, a side effect of the air age. It was also closely tied in with the instant mass communications of the time, for skyjackers wanted their demands known quickly by as many people as possible. The other necessary component, the threat of harm to hostages, was as old as warfare, and as unjust to the innocent as it had always been.

Apparently the first skyjacking occurred in Peru in 1931, when forces opposed to the regime in power seized a plane in midair. (Their coup succeeded.) The practice did not pose much of a danger for several years. Then, after World War II, it became a favorite tool of terrorists, especially radical nationalists wishing to draw attention to their cause. For example, Palestinians who wanted a state of their own used skyjacking against Israel. They and others also used it as a way of obtaining ransom money and the release of prisoners.

When a skyjacking does occur, most experts feel it is best not to give in to skyjackers' demands. Successful blackmail breeds more blackmail. Two especially daring commando rescues in the 1970s seemed to prove that skyjackers could be resisted.

Clearly, it is far preferable to prevent skyjacking in the first place. One method is to screen passengers before boarding to make sure they are not carrying concealed weapons. Metal detection systems have been quite successful when used consistently. In the United States, skyjackings dropped from a record high of 40 in 1969 to 5 (all unsuccessful) in 1975. But many countries are unable or unwilling to expend the time and money needed for this procedure. In 1977 there were 30 skyjackings in the world.

A second approach is to encourage international agreements which would deny

HIJACKERS HOLD JET WITH 256

Newspaper headlines like this one have become less frequent as more countries have taken precautions against skyjacking.

skyjackers "havens." Many planes hijacked in the United States were landed in Cuba. This practice all but ceased after 1973, when the two nations signed a treaty guaranteeing to prosecute skyjackers. Unfortunately, several countries, far from condemning skyjacking, condone and even applaud it.

Since 1963, there have been six major international conventions dealing with skyjacking and other aspects of terrorism. None has provided for punishment. In November 1977, the UN General Assembly passed a resolution condemning skyjacking. However, there was little optimism that it would lead to any drastic change in the situation.

1. How is skyjacking related to modern technology? What human rights are involved?
2. What are the two main methods of preventing skyjacking? Why have they not been more successful?
3. Which of the international actors mentioned in this case do you think could best provide a just solution to skyjacking?

Three Approaches. If we agree that it is useful to have international standards of justice, how do we arrive at them? There are three main approaches: the utilitarian, the elite, and the egalitarian.

Utilitarian theory is built on the basic goal of seeking the greatest good for the greatest number. In practice, this often means that decisions are made by majority rule. The result can be to discount the poor in a mainly rich society, or Catholics in a mainly Protestant society.

The word "utilitarian" means "useful." This theory is concerned with practical needs, not long-term solutions. If it is thought that a lumber mill will benefit a community, it is built, regardless of future depletion of forests. Utilitarianism provides the means for making decisions about specific situations rather than the principles behind them. Thus this theory can be accommodated to almost any ideology.

Elite theory is very different. It is based on the idea that society should be in the hands of a few outstanding people, whether the wisest, the richest, or the best educated. Because of their special qualities, they can carry out goals more easily. Thus they have the right to make decisions for everyone.

Obviously elitism leads to inequality. Privileged groups are favored over the masses of people. The huge gap between rich and poor in many countries today is built upon elitism, though the theory may not be the stated goal of the nation.

Egalitarian theory is based on the idea that everyone is equal. (*Egal* means "equal" in French.) This theory leads to consensus rule. Either everyone has a veto over what can be done, or everyone must be satisfied before an action can be carried out.

Society as a whole is the focus of egalitarianism. Every single participant makes a difference. Egalitarian theory is concerned with the most good for *society*. Goods and services should be distributed not to benefit the majority, or the privileged few, but everyone in the community. No nation today operates under an egalitarian system of justice, although many aspire to it.

1. Why should we try to reach international agreement on standards of justice?
2. Summarize the three major theories regarding the nature of justice in society.

WHO SEEKS JUSTICE?

Many actors are involved in the search for international justice. Some are formal, official organizations. Others are private, unofficial groups seeking justice for members of the global community.

Over the years, a body of international law has grown up to govern the conduct of nations toward each other. Some of it is in the form of treaties, such as the 1963 agreement reached by Britain, the United States, and the Soviet Union to ban nuclear tests in the atmosphere, under water, and in space.

International law may also take the form of *conventions* or *covenants*. These are pledges nations make to each other, usually involving a rather specific issue, such as copyright. The series of agreements regarding wartime treatment of the wounded, prisoners, and noncombatants are usually known as the Geneva Conventions.

If any of these agreements are to last, the signing parties must believe that they are just. Rules on nations are binding only insofar as nations allow them to be.

As in other arenas of international politics, there is no single international judicial system. There is, rather, a series of coalitions that interact from time to time. A group of nations may agree during a crisis, such as the allies during World War I or II. When the crisis is over, they tend to go their separate ways.

The International Court of Justice. One of the first attempts to set up an international court was the Permanent Court of Arbitration, established in 1899 by The Hague Peace Conference. (*Arbitration* is a method of settling disputes by having a third party, such as a court or a neutral nation, make a decision.) After World War I, the League of Nations went a step further with the Permanent Court of International Justice, or World Court. It could hand down judicial decisions as well as arbitrate. In 1945 the World Court became the International Court of Justice, the principal judicial organ of the United Nations. The court sits today, as then, at The Hague, in The Netherlands.

The Palace of Peace, home of the ICJ, was built in the 1920s as a symbol of international peace. American industrialist and philanthropist Andrew Carnegie gave the money to build it.

The International Court has 15 regular justices. It can also seat additional temporary judges when it is hearing cases. The justices of the court come from many nations and are distinguished members of the legal profession.

All signers of the United Nations Charter are under the jurisdiction of the court. But there are limitations on what the court can do. No member nation can be forced to bring a dispute to the International Court. And even when the court rules on disputes, its decisions are not mandatory; a nation cannot be forced to comply. However, 44 nations have voluntarily signed a declaration to submit to mandatory jurisdiction.

The International Court has ruled on questions of treaties, such as the relationship between the Organization of African Unity and the UN. It has also judged technical cooperation between Israel and Turkey.

The court has ruled on conventions, such as those on human rights and on social and economic equality made by the United Nations. In addition it has ruled on recommendations made by the United Nations regarding higher standards of living, as well as on economic, social, health, and related problems in respect for human rights.

1. What is the International Court of Justice?
2. In what ways are the powers of the International Court limited?

Other Groups. There are many other official groups concerned with questions of justice. Most deal specifically with human rights. The United Nations itself has always been deeply involved with the question of human rights. The UN Charter mentions human rights in the preamble and in six different articles. The Universal Declaration of Human Rights, adopted in 1948 by the General Assembly, defined and elaborated on these provisions. It affirms the inherent dignity and equal rights of human beings as a foundation for freedom, justice, and peace. It defends the right to life, human dignity, and self-determination. The Declaration has become a standard of reference, and many new governments have included parts of it in their constitutions.

The 1966 United Nations Covenant on Economic, Social, and Cultural Rights and the International Covenant on Civil and Political Rights were the first international bill of human rights. Signers agreed to be legally bound by their provisions.

Although the United Nations has taken a strong stand in support of human rights, the actual record of member states is far from UN ideals. Few nations can measure up to the standards set by the Universal Declaration. Many nations do not protect their citizens from government oppression. In others, protection is officially guaranteed but means little in practice.

Several regional organizations have tried to encourage justice on an international scale. The Council of Europe, composed of 19 European nations, was founded in 1949 to deal with questions of war and peace. It has taken a strong stand on human rights, and was the first group to set up a judicial body to investigate violations of human rights on a regional level. This judicial body, the European Convention for the Protection of Human Rights and Fundamental Freedoms, was joined by all of the member states of the Council of Europe.

In the western hemisphere the major regional grouping is the Organization of American States (OAS), formed in 1948. Though designed mainly to provide security for the American continents, this group too formed a special humanitarian organization, the Inter-American Commission on Human Rights. The OAS adopted the American Convention on Human Rights in 1969. Figure 19–1 itemizes the points of the agreement. Other regional organizations, such as the League of Arab States and the Organization of African Unity, also support human rights provisions.

AMERICAN CONVENTION on HUMAN RIGHTS

1. The right to life.
2. Freedom from torture and inhuman treatment.
3. Freedom from slavery and servitude.
4. The right to liberty and security.
5. The right to a fair trial.
6. Freedom from the retroactivity of criminal law.
7. The right to respect private and family life.
8. Freedom of conscience and religion.
9. Freedom of thought and expression.
10. Freedom of assembly and association.
11. Freedom to marry and form a family.
12. The right of property.
13. Freedom of movement.
14. Freedom from exile.
15. Prohibition of collective expulsion of aliens.
16. The right to free elections.
17. The right to an effective remedy when one's rights are violated.
18. The right to recognition as a person before the law.
19. The right to compensation for miscarriage of justice.
20. The right of reply.
21. The right to a name.
22. The right of a child.
23. The right to a nationality.
24. The right to equality before the law.
25. The right of asylum.

Figure 19-1

---

1. What UN actions have been especially concerned with human rights?
2. What other official organizations have taken a stand on human rights? How?

Justice is promoted and supported by many nongovernmental groups, such as the International Committee of the Red Cross and the World Council of Churches. Amnesty International, another such group, reports on human rights violations around the world. In 1977 Amnesty International was awarded the Nobel Peace Prize for its work.

Citizens try to achieve justice by speaking out against wrongs and by joining together for collective action. For example, people around the world, both independently and as members of groups, have condemned South Africa for its policies of racial discrimination.

Many citizens are also concerned about human rights for women. The UN Charter is committed to the goal of equal rights, and so is the Universal Declaration of Human Rights. But millions of women today have these rights in name only.

As you read the case that follows, think about the main international actors involved in the case, the processes they use, and the consequences of their actions.

★ "I Belong to No-Man's Land"

In most nations of the world, women do not enjoy the same advantages and rights that men do. From the moment a girl is born, custom and tradition usually limit her educational opportunities and other rights.

Statistics indicate the discrimination many women have suffered. In some nations 80 to 85 percent of the people who cannot read are women. Because they cannot read, women are locked into the lowest positions—if they are even allowed to work outside the home. With few skills, they get low pay. Even in developed nations like the United States, women's wages are only 50 to 80 percent of what men get for the same work.

In many nations, sex discrimination is embedded in the culture, and has been for countless generations. Changing people's attitudes is a very slow process. Princess Ashraf of Iran put it this way:

"Since the beginning of this century when women started fighting to raise their status in society, we have seen remarkable changes in the lawbooks of many nations. However, changing a written law is one thing; changing deep-seated attitudes is another. New feelings and attitudes cannot be legislated, and merely changing a law will not change people's mental outlooks."

An organized international movement to improve the status of women began after World War II. The United Nations was the first international organization to mention the rights of men *and women* in its charter. The preamble asks member countries to reaffirm their faith in "fundamental rights and the dignity and worth of the human person, and the equal rights of men and women and of nations, large and small." In 1946 the United Nations established the Commission on the Status of Women as part of its Economic and Social Council. The commission makes recommendations to the Economic and Social Council, which in turn brings resolutions before the General Assembly.

The United Nations has taken five major steps to break down barriers and promote women's rights. First, it has tried to establish standards of justice for women. Second, it has prepared studies on the position of women across the world. Third, it has worked to include women in the work force in developing nations. Fourth, it has attempted to develop training programs for women. Finally, it has worked to gather information on women's rights.

The United Nations has adopted a number of resolutions designed to strengthen women's rights. In a 1954 resolution, it supported women's right to vote and to hold public office. The Convention of Consent to Marriage, adopted in 1964, prohibited child marriage under 15 years of age, and set up rules against forced marriages. The Declaration of Discrimination Against Women, unanimously adopted by the General Assembly in 1967, extended all political, social, and economic rights to women.

Of special importance was the Teheran Conference on Human Rights, held in 1968. It passed a unanimous resolution that gave priority to problems of educating women in developing societies. It called for more education to enable women to join the work force and thus make real contributions to the development process. In 1974 training programs were established to teach women to work in domestic agriculture, in paying jobs, and in income-producing sectors of the economy. They also trained women in community development programs so that they could train others.

The General Assembly also set up an International Women's Year Conference, which was held in Mexico in 1975 to examine how effective the UN had been in carry-

More than 1,000 official delegates and 6,000 unofficial delegates attended the two-week International Women's Year Conference in 1975. The opening ceremonies were held in a large Mexico City gymnasium.

RESOLUTIONS of INTERNATIONAL WOMEN'S YEAR CONFERENCE

1. Marked increased in literacy and civic education of women, especially in rural areas.

2. The extension of coeducational technical and vocational training giving basic skills to women and men in industrial and agricultural centers.

3. Equal access at every level of education, compulsory primary school education and measures necessary to prevent school dropouts.

4. Increased employment opportunities for women, reduction of unemployment, and increased efforts to eliminate discrimination in terms of conditions of employment.

5. The establishment and increase of services in both urban and rural areas.

6. The enactment of legislation on voting and eligibility for elections on terms equal with men.

7. Encouragement of greater participation of women in policy-making positions at local, national and international levels.

8. Increased provisions for comprehensive measures for health education services, sanitation, nutrition and family education.

9. Provisions for parity in the exercise of civil, social, and political activities, such as those pertaining to marriage, citizenship, and commerce.

10. A recognition of the economic value of women's work in the home, in food production, in marketing and voluntary activities.

11. The direction of formal, non-formal and life-long education for the reevaluation of men and women in order to insure their full realization as an individual in the family and in society.

12. The development of modern rural technology, cottage industry, pre-school day centers, time- and energy-saving devices so as to help reduce the heavy workload of women, particularly those living in rural sections and for the urban poor and thus facilitate the full participation of women in community, national, and international affairs.

13. The establishment of an interdisciplinary and multi-sectural machinery within the government for accelerating the achievement of equal opportunities for women and their full integration into national life.

Figure 19-2

ing out the recommendations of the Commission on the Status of Women. A total of 133 nations sent representatives. Figure 19-2 lists the resolutions of the International Women's Year Conference.

The conference, and events throughout International Women's Year, stressed advancement toward three goals—equality, development, and peace. Lack of equality for women, it was held, affects both the individual and the nation. It has had an especially negative impact on the development process. If large numbers of women cannot read, and are not allowed to learn, the process of improving the society is made more difficult.

Members of the United Nations were encouraged to adopt national measures to improve the position of women. In the United States, President Ford appointed a special commission, noting that "opening up new doors to approximately half the world's population is vital to solving many of our international problems."

The long-run impact of UN activities is hard to determine. Even where laws have been passed, changes in attitudes lag behind. Until they come, women may well echo the sentiments of one delegate in stating her citizenship at a conference: "I belong to no-man's land."

1. Who are the actors involved in this case?
2. What steps have been taken by the United Nations in order to advance women's rights?
3. What are some of the possible consequences of the actions to improve women's rights?
4. What effect do you think increasing interdependence has had on the women's movement?

How Is Justice Pursued?

How do individuals and nations seek justice? We shall examine a series of steps in the process in an effort to see how major international actors try to change unjust situations. This process will then be related to your own problem-solving on an everyday basis as a citizen of the international community.

MAIN STEPS in the PROCESS The first step is for a violation to occur, or at least for a situation to be seen as a violation. People may feel discriminated against because of their religion, as in Northern Ireland. Or citizens may want to leave a country but be prohibited from doing so, as in the Soviet Union. Or political prisoners may be held in jail without trial, as in Brazil. Whatever the situation, it raises a value issue. And it usually embodies a conflict of interest, since both sides believe their actions to be just.

The alleged violation is publicized. Generally this happens first in the nation where it is occurring. Then the situation comes to the attention of the international community through the mass media. In fact, it is largely because of technological advances in communication that value questions are more widely known now than they were in the past.

The publicized situation causes a reaction among people in other nations. This reaction is an important component of the process of seeking justice. Remember that there is no official institution for seeking justice. Therefore, unless there is some type of reaction to a violation it may be disregarded.

The reaction to a publicized violation usually spurs people to seek organized help. They may turn to an existing organization, like the United Nations. Or they may form an ad hoc organization, such as those created when Greece was ruled by a military junta from 1967 to 1973.

The organization must determine its goals and how to implement them. It may try to bring about change through the pressure of public opinion. This can be mobilized by increased media publicity, demonstrations, and letter-writing campaigns. Organized opposition may also take the form of boycotts or trade embargoes. It is important to remember again that actions will have a consequence only if the nation in question is influenced. There is no formal standard that can force an offending nation to change its policies.

Action taken by an organization may lead to a rule or principle—a standard of behavior for members of the international community. The principle may state, for instance, that all people have a right to self-determination. The offending nation may agree to carry out the standard because of world pressure. The rule or principle then may lead to a new situation, especially if the nation that had begun the chain reaction again reacts to the actions of the other nations.

1. What are the main steps in seeking to correct an unjust international situation?

2. Why are modern communications techniques important in the politics of justice?

HOW YOU FIT IN This process of seeking justice can apply to international organizations and to nations. It can also apply to individual citizen actors like yourself. You can have an impact in two chief ways.

First, your decision on value issues furnishes a model of behavior for others. If you are uninterested and apathetic, you implicitly set a model for apathy about questions of justice in the international community. If you are interested and have clear values, you set a model of concern for others. This is especially true, of course, if you take some action, either individually or collectively.

Second, as a citizen of the global community, you can fulfill an organizer role. You can put together people and groups who are concerned about a particular issue of international justice. You have considered ways in which you might act as an organizer in a coffee boycott. You can play the same kind of role in a situation involving what you see as injustice.

Applying Valuing Skills. How do you apply valuing skills in cases involving the global politics of justice? Here it is helpful to review what you already know.

In previous units you learned how to recognize a value issue. The value issues in this chapter involve justice, especially human rights. As you have read, a question of justice is usually one of equality.

You have also learned to place value issues in a social context. In this case, the social context for justice is the global political system. We are concerned with the economic, political, and social rights of peoples in a variety of settings. It is important in considering a global value issue to consider both local cultural values and the more generalized global values common to humankind.

You have also learned about alternative consequences of actions that you might take in reference to a value position. In a variety of situations throughout the course, you have learned about ways in which you can generate alternatives and evaluate the pros and cons of taking actions. The sections of this unit on the organizer role have shown you how taking such a role requires taking actions based on your value position.

You have also learned to consider the consequences of actions you might take. Considering the consequences of making a value decision is one of the most important parts of the process.

And you have also been concerned about how you might generalize your values. You want to be sure that your actions in a variety of situations are consistent. If you believe in equality as a general principle, then you should hold to it in specific instances, whether they concern race, or religion, or sex.

The case study that follows focuses on racial discrimination in South Africa. As you read it, think about how the process of seeking justice is operating here. Think too about your own value position on the question of apartheid. Also keep in mind how difficult it is to implement a standard of justice if a nation doesn't want to comply.

★ Apartheid in South Africa

The Republic of South Africa is a large nation rich in resources. Its population of more than 26 million people consists of almost 19 million blacks, about 4.5 million whites, 2.4 million "coloreds" (people of mixed racial parentage), and about 800,000 Asians. The whites can be divided into two groups. About two fifths are of British descent. The others, of Dutch, German, and French descent, are known as Afrikaners and speak a form of Dutch called Afrikaans.

The first white settlers came to Capetown, at the tip of the African continent, in 1652. (See Figure 19-3 on the following page.) This settlement was established by the Dutch East India Company to protect Dutch trade to Asia. In 1806 the British seized Capetown from the Dutch to protect their own trade route to India, and in 1814 the British gained official ownership of the territory. By 1910 the Union of South Africa was formed as a self-governing part of the British Empire. In 1931 Great Britain gave South Africa independence as a member of the British Commonwealth. In 1961, as a result of Commonwealth criticism of South African racial policies, South Africa left the Commonwealth and became the Republic of South Africa.

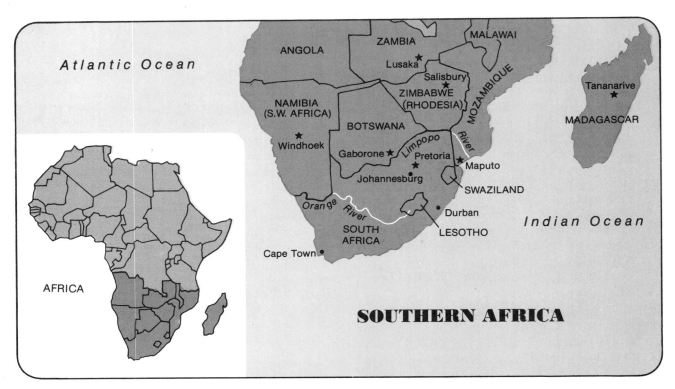

Figure 19-3

Discrimination against blacks had existed for hundreds of years. They received lower wages for the same work and were excluded from trade unions, for example. But an official government policy of racial discrimination did not become law until the Nationalist party, the party of the Afrikaners, rose to power in 1948. Since that time the South African government, under the Nationalist party, has carried out a policy of apartheid (pronounced *ah PART* hite)—an Afrikaans word meaning "apartness."

Apartheid is designed to (1) ensure white supremacy and (2) separate the races. This means that nonwhites are denied certain rights and privileges. Strict segregation separates the races on trains and buses, on the job, and in schools, hospitals, residential areas, and recreational facilities. Apartheid is a system of legal discrimination embodied in law and custom.

From a bare majority of the national parliament in 1948, the Afrikaners have grown in power. In 1976 they held 123 seats in a house of 171. They have strictly enforced apartheid.

The South African policy of racial discrimination has drawn worldwide attention. In the 1940s the Nationalist party attempted to limit the voting rights of Indians, to establish separate Indian residential areas, and to reduce the number of Indian traders in non-Indian areas. Because of these injustices toward Indians, India brought a complaint before the United Nations in 1952. Later the Indian question was included in the larger issue: how South Africa's racial policy violates the human rights of all nonwhite citizens.

Every year since 1946, the United Nations has taken action of one sort or another against South Africa's policy of racial discrimination. In 1950 the General Assembly adopted a resolution equating the apartheid policy with racial discrimination, which is against the principles of the UN Charter.

In 1960 the policy of apartheid came before the Security Council at the request of 29 member states. The council passed a resolution stating that the apartheid situation led to international friction, and, if continued, might endanger peace and security.

AFRICAN BATHING BEACH

The rules of apartheid affect all aspects of life in South Africa. Public facilities are strictly segregated (top photo). Nonwhites are allowed to live only in certain areas, where housing is often substandard (center photo). Black workers (bottom photo) have limited job choices. They have long been discriminated against in many ways.

In 1962 the General Assembly requested that UN members break off diplomatic relations with South Africa, close their ports to South African vessels, prohibit their ships from entering South African ports, boycott South African trade, and refuse landing rights to South African aircraft. Although most members did not comply with these requests, this was the strongest statement yet made on apartheid.

In 1962 the General Assembly established a Special Committee on the Policies of Apartheid in South Africa to keep these policies under review when the General Assembly was not in session. This committee became a moving force for action against apartheid. Unlike other human rights questions at the United Nations, apartheid was actively opposed by many member states.

In 1963 the Security Council ruled again that apartheid was a basic threat to international peace and security, and called on UN members to stop selling military equipment to South Africa. All members did not comply. The Security Council also asked South Africa to release all its political prisoners.

South Africa has consistently refused to comply with UN resolutions urging an end to apartheid, insisting that they are a direct interference in its domestic affairs. The UN Charter prohibits such interferences, yet it also establishes certain fundamental human rights and calls on members to support them. In 1971 the International Court of Justice ruled in an advisory opinion that human rights provisions are binding on member states.

In South Africa itself, protestors have staged many demonstrations against the government's apartheid policy, sometimes with small but positive results. In June 1976, for example, blacks violently protested a government rule requiring students to study their subjects in Afrikaans. As a result the government eventually revoked this law. In 1978 they even agreed to provide black students between the ages of 10 and 17 with free textbooks. But the basic policy of apartheid did not change.

South Africa stands alone in the world community because of its apartheid policy. Other southern African nations that were once ruled by white minorities have become independent, with the black majorities assuming power. In the late 1970s, South Africa's neighbor Rhodesia—the only other African nation controlled by a white minority—began a process of transferring political power to the black majority.

In 1977 the United Nations Security Council, acting with the General Assembly, censured South Africa. This was the first time in United Nations history that the assembly actually censured a member. The ruling called for UN member nations to stop supplying any form of arms to South Africa. The impact of the embargo was uncertain because South Africa was making many of its own arms.

What are the policy alternatives available to the United States in this controversy? It could continue voicing opposition to the policy of apartheid in principle, and putting quiet pressure on South Africa to change. Other possible actions include an economic boycott of South Africa or the use of military force. Neither seems feasible.

Economic withdrawal on the part of the United States might well disrupt the South African economy. This would harm the nonwhite population, the very people for whom such a step would be taken. In addition, the United States financial involvement in South Africa is great. American firms carry on a great deal of trade there, both exporting raw materials and manufacturing goods sold in South Africa.

If the United States used military force against South Africa it would definitely be in a position of interfering in another nation's internal affairs. This policy of interference, which was so widely criticized by the world community in the case of Vietnam, would certainly be challenged in the case of South Africa.

The moral position of the United States is clear. No American official has approved of apartheid since its beginning in 1948. The world community joins in the moral condemnation of South Africa. The question of what else can be done remains.

Certain nations and organizations have taken a variety of actions. Venezuela, for example, broke all ties with South Africa in 1976. The World Council of Churches sold all of its stock in any companies doing business with South Africa. Amnesty International has made public charges and publicized torture of political prisoners in South Africa.

A majority of the white population of South Africa resists any change in the situation of nonwhites. South African law supports them. Since the country has ample resources, it can resist economic pressure.

Not all South Africans support their government's policies, however. Some, unable to change established law, have left the country rather than live under apartheid. Others, like Donald Woods, have been in a position to make their protest public. Woods, a white South African, was the influential editor of the East London Daily Dispatch and vocal critic of apartheid. In October 1977 he was officially banned, which meant that he was unable to publish his views, in addition to other strict restrictions on his private life. On December 30, 1977, Woods escaped to nearby Lesotho and then to Great Britain.

In the late 1970s it seemed to many observers that the only way change could occur in South Africa was through the efforts of its own black majority. In the meantime apartheid continues. Clearly, there is no easy solution to the problem.

1. What process and what principles of justice are involved in the apartheid issue?
2. What do you think the United States should do in this situation?
3. What actions would you take in this case? How might your value position on apartheid be generalized to other cases in which you are involved every day?

The Future of Global Political Systems

You have seen how politics, economics, and the search for justice are all woven together in the fabric of global political systems. Of the many actors in the global system, nations are still the most important. But some observers believe that others will grow in importance. Because of increased interdependence, some people predict one increasingly integrated system for global politics.

What would this system be like? Numerous theories have been proposed. We will outline briefly four possible models: elite, bureaucratic, coalitional, and participant. (Review the discussion of these systems on pages 332–341.)

The elite model is based on a single organization that would provide a structure for the entire international system. In order for this system to exist, nations would have to give up much of their sovereignty to a higher body. One person or governing body would have the authority to make decisions on all questions that were regarded as international in scope.

The bureaucratic model of a global political system would feature a chain of command. A central body would coordinate separate international organizations supervising different functions. One group, like the International Monetary Fund, might be in charge of economic matters. Another, such as the International Court of Justice, might handle judicial matters. At the base of the hierarchy would be the individual nation-states and their own economic, political, and judicial institutions.

A coalitional system would be similar in many ways to the global political system that operates today. Depending upon the issue, coalitions would form, break apart, and form again. There would be no central organization.

When writers talk about "one world," they are usually thinking of a participant system. In this system, every nation or group would participate and there would be a unanimous rule. Everyone would have to agree before a decision could be made. An elected general assembly, with a unanimous rule, would probably govern this system.

> 1. How might resources and activities be divided in each of the four models?
> 2. What might the advantages and disadvantages of each system be?

The Skill of Forecasting

How can we choose among these four alternative models of possible futures for the global political system? What is possible and what is preferred? These are very different questions. Finding the answers involves a skill called forecasting.

Forecasting, or suggesting alternative futures, is extremely important. It can influence our positions on issues. If we could determine what the future of the globe was going to be in terms of energy supplies, for example, we could make intelligent decisions in terms of the next hundred or even the next thousand years. Instead we live with risk, uncertainty, and the possibility of natural disasters.

Forecasting can also influence the actions we take. If we have an image of the future—or what we would like the future to be—we naturally have a much better idea of the correct steps to take in getting there.

There are four basic steps involved in suggesting alternative futures. The first is identifying a trend in the political experiences of one or more political systems. The second is projecting alternative future events in that political system or systems. The third is determining the likelihood of the alternative futures. A fourth consideration is that of preferred alternatives.

IDENTIFYING a TREND Identifying a trend in the political experience of global political systems involves tracing history in terms of a set of concepts. For example, in our desire

Population growth is a trend which has a powerful effect on the future of global political systems.

to decide which of the four models the global political system might adopt, we need to look at the history of the world. It has evolved from a very disparate system, with increasing interdependence, into a relatively coalitional system. What made it evolve the way it is? We can use our concepts of interdependence, conflict, cooperation, and development in order to trace these trends.

1. Identify three trends in the global political system today. For example, you might say that there has been a trend toward increasing interdependence. If this is a trend, then it will be the basis for your prediction about the future of the globe.
2. What concepts—such as conflict—help describe each trend?

PROJECTING FUTURE EVENTS The second step in suggesting alternative futures is to project alternative future occurrences in the political experiences of global political systems. To do this, you need to think about your trend and ask yourself questions about whether or how it will continue. Basically, there are three different types of alternative futures.

First, a trend can continue. In the case of interdependence, it can continue to increase. You then say that there will be more multinational and transnational activity and less national activity. This will influence your projection about the global political system. On this basis, you might say that it would become increasingly coalitional and perhaps even participant.

As a second alternative you might predict that a future event would change the trend you have identified. Within the global system, a new trend would develop—for example, a trend toward less interdependence.

A third alternative future would occur if the global political system moved in some entirely new direction, in other words if the entire global system changed. What if national and multinational corporations faded out of existence, to be replaced by one single international conglomerate? In this case, the global system might become an entirely corporate-directed system. This would affect economic development in one way and political development quite differently.

1. Project a series of alternative future events and match them with the trends you have identified in the global political system. List at least three future events
2. In what direction would each event move the global political system?

DETERMINING LIKELIHOOD The final step in projecting alternative futures is to determine the likelihood of alternative futures in one or more political systems. Probabilities can be assigned to the alternatives so that you can judge what is most likely to occur. You might determine, for example, that there is a 10 percent chance two nations will sign a treaty and a 60 percent chance of increasing interdependence. This would influence your predictions about the future of the global political system. These probabilities are not written in stone. They are based on as much evidence as you can gather about the global political system.

1. What evidence would you need to gather or generate in order to determine the likelihood of each of the alternative futures you have described?
2. If you had the resources of a presidential advisor, how would you go about determining the likelihood of the alternative futures you have described?

DECIDING on a PREFERENCE There is another step that is not part of the scientific procedure of forecasting, but is very important for citizens in the international community. This is considering which alternatives you value or prefer. In this case you do not choose the alternative future that seems to be most probable, but the one you feel is most fair according to a system of human values. You may need to compare the most likely future with the one you most prefer. You might, for example, think it highly unlikely that the future you prefer will come about. At the same time you may find that your least preferred alternative is also highly unlikely. Therefore you will decide to work for a middle ground.

Take each of the three steps in the procedure for forecasting and apply it to the current global political system. Decide which type of system (or which new type of system not described here) you think is the most likely and most preferable future for the global political system. Then answer the following questions.

1. Which type of organization do you think is the most possible in the future of the global political system?
2. Which type of system do you think is the most preferable future?
3. How could citizens participate in the global community in your model?
4. How might you work toward this model as a citizen of the international community in your own everyday life?

Chapter Review

1. What is justice? How is it related to law?
2. How did World War II affect concerns about global justice?
3. How is the search for international justice affected by scarce resources? by advances in technology? by interdependence?
4. What is the position of the individual in utilitarian, elite, and egalitarian theories?
5. Give two examples of international law.
6. Summarize three decisions handed down by the International Court of Justice.
7. What are the major steps in seeking justice in the case of a human rights violation?
8. Why has the United States not taken a leadership role in the apartheid controversy?
9. Summarize what you think might be the major advantages and disadvantages of the elite, bureaucratic, coalitional, and participant models of a global political system?
10. What are the steps in the skill of forecasting?

Chapter Vocabulary

Define these terms.

social justice	utilitarian theory	conventions
culture	elite theory	covenants
ideologies	egalitarian theory	arbitration

1. What are the major consequences that action in regard to human rights questions would have for the global political system?

2. Can universal value principles be generalized across many cases in different parts of the world? Why or why not?

3. Do issues in the areas of the politics of peace, scarcity, and justice require different forms of political organization or can they be integrated together into one global political system?

4. How does increasing interdependence affect the possibilities for the future political organization of the international system?

5. What are alternative roles you could take in the future of the international system?

1. Research a human rights case currently in the news. Show how various actors are responding to the case. Show how the global judicial system you have designed might apply. Point out similarities and differences between what is actually happening and what could happen in this system.

2. Keep a diary of your own actions during a week. See how they fit the value principles you have formulated in this unit. Discuss various alternative actions you might have taken that would violate or better uphold your principles.

International Human Rights and International Education, Thomas Buergenthal and Judith V. Torney (U.S. National Commission for UNESCO: Washington, DC), 1976.

> Focuses on education for "international understanding"; reviews international education from a historical perspective; discusses the role of the global systems, regional systems, and the United States in the protection of human rights. The book contains a large and very useful annotated selection of student materials.

The Pattern of Human Concerns, Hadley Cantril (Rutgers University Press: New Brunswick, NJ), 1965.

> Uses a psychological approach to determine the major concerns of people living in various parts of the world.

Documents of Fundamental Human Rights, Zechariah Chafee, Jr. (Atheneum: New York, NY), 1963.

> Provides in two volumes a historical background of human rights conflicts. The volumes are composed entirely of documents.

Footsteps Into the Future, Rajni Kothari (The Free Press: New York, NY), 1974.

> Presents an excellent analysis of the problems of regional organization and justice.

Chapter Objectives

★ To understand how multinational corporations are organized and how they operate
★ To apply the concept of interdependence
★ To describe global corporations in the global political system
★ To identify how global corporations can affect the lives of citizens
★ To develop and apply skills in valuing

chapter 20

CITIZEN PARTICIPATION in the GLOBAL ECONOMY

Chapter 18 introduced you to the topic of the multinational, or global, corporation. This chapter examines multinational corporations in more detail, analyzing them as political systems and describing their role in the global arena. Global corporations are powerful business giants today. They use people, money, and technology from around the world. These firms are not confined by national boundaries, but rather view the entire world as their marketplace.

Think about your own community for a moment. Do you see any evidence there of global corporations? Your town may have a factory connected with a multinational corporation. If not, you undoubtedly use products that are made by multinational businesses.

As you read this chapter, think about giant corporations as political systems. You will see a number of ways in which they can affect the lives of citizens everywhere, including your own.

An Overview of Multinational Corporations

"In the process of developing a new world, the managers of firms like GM, IBM, Pepsico, GE, Pfizer, Shell, Volkswagen, Exxon, and a few hundred others are making daily business decisions which have more impact than those of most sovereign governments on where people live; what work, if any, they will do; what they will eat, drink, and wear; what sorts of knowledge schools and universities will encourage; and what kind of society their children will inherit."

From *Global Reach,* © 1974 by Richard L. Barnet and Ronald E. Huller. Reprinted by permission of Simon & Schuster.

Businesses have carried on overseas trade for centuries. Some companies have had production facilities abroad for many years. Ford and the Singer Sewing Machine Company are just two of many firms that have done so throughout this century. Since World War II, however, the scope of multinational corporations—businesses with significant operations in more than one country—has expanded enormously. Many more companies are engaging in multinational op-

erations. And much more money is involved. In 1950 the value of American multinational foreign investments was $11.8 billion. By the mid-1970s it was more than $100 billion.

An example will indicate the extent of global corporate activities. Massey-Ferguson, a Canadian-based corporation, has a plant in Detroit. There it assembles transmissions made in France, axles made in Mexico, and engines made in Britain to turn out tractors for sale in Canada. In this example, Canada is the *parent country.* The nations where its foreign operations are located—that is, the *host countries*—are the United States, France, Mexico, and Britain.

The key to understanding multinational corporations is realizing that they are not restricted by national boundaries. They make use of people, money, and technology wherever they exist to produce goods and provide services for markets wherever they exist. Multinational corporations are systems that extend throughout the world.

Today many global corporations have become bigger than entire nations in terms of wealth. Figure 20–1 lists the 100 largest

One impact of the growth of multinational corporations is the spread of modern technology into all parts of the world.

100 LARGEST ECONOMIC ENTITIES

	(In billions of dollars)		(In billions of dollars)		(In billions of dollars)
1. United States	1,779.3	39. Nigeria	25.0	70. *Cie Française des Pétroles (France)	9.1
2. U.S.S.R.	865.0	40. *Texaco	24.5	71. Algeria	9.2
3. Japan	614.3	41. *Ford Motor	24.0	72. *Nippon Steel (Japan)	8.7
4. West Germany	504.5	42. Greece	23.4	73. *August Thyssen-Hütte (Germany)	8.7
5. France	346.0	43. Bulgaria	23.1	74. Bangladesh	8.7
6. China	223.0	44. *Mobil Oil	20.6	75. Malaysia	8.6
7. United Kingdom	216.6	45. *National Iranian Oil (Iran)	18.8	76. *Hoechst (Germany)	8.4
8. Canada	184.5	46. Indonesia	18.7	77. *ENI (Italy)	8.3
9. Italy	169.0	47. South Korea	18.7	78. *Daimler-Benz (Germany)	8.1
10. Spain	102.8	48. *British Petroleum (Britain)	17.2	79. *U.S. Steel	8.1
11. Brazil	93.8	49. Nationalist China	17.1	80. *BASF (Germany)	8.1
12. Australia	92.2	50. *Standard Oil of California	16.8	81. *Shell Oil	8.1
13. Poland	89.9	51. Portugal	15.8	82. Chile	7.9
14. Netherlands	87.2	52. Philippines	15.4	83. *Renault (France)	7.8
15. India	80.2	53. *Unilever	15.0	84. *Siemens (Germany)	7.7
16. Mexico	78.8	54. *International Business Machines (IBM)	14.4	85. *Volkswagenwork (Germany)	7.6
17. Sweden	74.2	55. *Gulf Oil	14.2	86. *Atlantic Richfield	7.3
18. East Germany	70.2	56. *General Electric	13.3	87. *Continental Oil	7.2
19. Belgium	68.1	57. Thailand	12.2	88. *Bayer	7.2
20. Iran	67.4	58. Pakistan	12.2	89. *E.I. DuPont de Nemours	7.2
21. Switzerland	59.5	59. Columbia	12.1	90. *Toyota (Japan)	7.1
22. Romania	51.4	60. Israel	12.0	91. *ELF/Aquitane (Paris)	7.1
23. Czechoslovakia	56.6	61. Libya	11.9	92. *Nestlé (Switzerland)	7.0
24. *Exxon	44.8	62. *Chrysler	11.6	93. *Imperial Chemical Industries (London)	6.8
25. Turkey	41.2	63. *International Telephone and Telegraph (ITT)	11.3	94. *Petrobrás (Venezuela)	6.6
26. Saudi Arabia	41.0	64. New Zealand	11.2	95. *Western Electric	6.5
27. Austria	40.4	65. Iraq	11.0	96. Vietnam	6.5
28. Argentina	36.7	66. Kuwait	11.0	97. Ireland	6.2
29. Denmark	37.8	67. *Philips' Gloeilampenfabrieken (Netherlands)	10.7	98. *British American Tobacco (London)	6.1
30. *General Motors	35.7	68. Peru	10.6	99. Cuba	6.1
31. South Africa	35.3	69. *Standard Oil of Indiana	9.9	100. North Korea	6.1
32. Yugoslavia	35.0				
33. *Royal Dutch/Shell Group (Netherlands/Britain)	32.1				
34. Norway	30.2				
35. Sri Lanka	29.8				
36. Finland	28.5				
37. Hungary	27.8				
38. Venezuela	27.6				

Source: Fortune

Figure 20-1

*Multinational corporations
Unless otherwise noted corporations have headquarters in the United States.
The figures for nations represent Gross National Product in 1975. The figures for corporations represent 1975 sales.

economic entities in the world in 1975, with the annual sales of each corporation and the gross national product of each nation.

1. Based on Figure 20–1, what was the largest multinational corporation in the world in 1975? How much money did this corporation make in annual sales?
2. How much influence do you think global corporations have on the global political system? Give several reasons for your response.
3. Describe the resources that you think a company would need in order to operate as a global corporation.

GROWTH of MULTI-NATIONALS

Multinational corporations are not new. Large corporations, especially those with headquarters in the United States, have worked for years with foreign firms. Some of these were *affiliates*—independent companies associated with the large corporation. Others, called *subsidiaries,* were owned outright by the corporation.

In the 1930s the United Fruit Company, distributor of Chiquita Bananas among other products, was active on four continents: North and South America, Europe, and Africa. At the same time, the International Telephone and Telegraph Corporation (ITT) also was investing heavily in foreign utilities and manufacturing firms.

Mining companies have had global interests throughout the twentieth century. In 1916 the Anaconda Copper Company, fearful that mineral resources in the United States were dwindling, began mining operations in Chile. The company then expanded into Europe as well. By 1970 Anaconda had sales offices in England, Germany, Italy, France, Brazil, Japan, and India.

It was mining in Chile, Mexico, Canada, Jamaica, and Australia; refining in Chile and Mexico; and manufacturing in Canada, Mexico, and Brazil.

The most dramatic growth of global corporations occurred after World War II. Between 1950 and 1966, the number of affiliates of American-based corporations rose from around 7,000 to more than 23,000. American investment throughout the world tripled. In Europe it increased more than 10 times.

1. Give some examples of multinational activity before World War II.
2. How has multinational business activity grown since World War II?

ORGANIZA-TION and MANAGEMENT

Though the hundreds of multinational corporations in the world vary in size and engage in many different businesses, they have several characteristics in common. Many of these have to do with organization and management.

Integration. Most global corporations have a high degree of *integration*. This means that the firm itself controls the production and assembly of its final products, rather than relying on other independent companies for parts or assembly.

A company that produces television sets might make transistors in Hong Kong, picture tubes in Taiwan, channel selectors in Mexico, and the remainder of the needed parts in the United States. The parent company arranges for the parts produced in each country to be transported to one main location for final assembly. Thus the parent company *integrates production* by organizing work done throughout the system. (See Figure 20-2.)

Centralized Decision-Making. Because production occurs in so many places, decision-making has become an especially difficult problem for multinational corporations. Global activities must be carefully coordinated. In the case of the television sets, once the parent company decides how many sets to manufacture in one year, each overseas plant must make the proper number of parts. All of them must then be shipped on schedule to be assembled.

As corporations have expanded their activities throughout the world, decision-making has become centralized. Most important policy decisions are made by the parent company. They are then implemented by plants in host countries. Many important choices, however, are made by foreign offices. Activity is often assigned on the basis of a person's position in a company. Many corporations thus operate as bureaucratic systems.

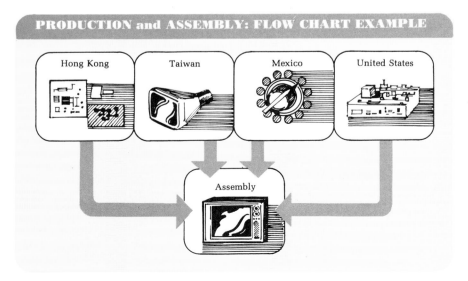

PRODUCTION and ASSEMBLY: FLOW CHART EXAMPLE

Hong Kong | Taiwan | Mexico | United States

Assembly

Figure 20-2

Ranan R. Lurie/King Features Syndicate.

Interdependence. Another similarity of global corporations is their interdependence, both among themselves and in relation to nations. For example, the Ford Motor Company must cooperate with companies in Mexico in order to get the parts it needs to assemble automobiles. At the same time, some people in Mexico depend upon Ford to provide them with jobs and certain kinds of technical assistance.

Ford must also cooperate with the government of Mexico itself. The trend is for host countries to place an increasing number of restrictions on activities of foreign companies. The countries of Latin America have become particularly strict in this regard.

1. Describe the three characteristics that most multinational corporations share.
2. What kind of political system do many multinational corporations have?

CITIZENS and the LABOR MARKET What do foreign operations mean in terms of ordinary citizens and their jobs? By regarding the whole world as a marketplace, global corporations draw on resources both inside and outside the United States. A common move, as you have read, is to locate production facilities on foreign soil.

Labor leaders in the United States claim that practices like this simply export jobs that Americans might have. But the managers of multinational corporations argue that these actions often lead to more jobs for Americans than would otherwise exist.

Suppose, they say, that a company makes automobiles. According to company executives, the engine is the most expensive part of the automobile to produce. The company discovers that engines can be produced more cheaply in Iceland, and moves its engine production facilities there. Finished engines are shipped to the United States for installation in automobiles. This practice results in job losses for Americans who made engines in the United States. But, because engines can be produced so cheaply in Iceland, the company can afford to buy more of them, to produce more automobiles, and thus to employ more Americans overall in the production process.

1. Why do American firms locate production facilities in other countries?
2. How, according to multinational managers, does foreign production lead to more jobs for Americans? Do you find this argument convincing? Explain.

The Cummins Engine Company

Automotive companies are among the largest multinational corporations because of the increasing demand for automobiles and trucks, especially since World War II. These corporations depend on a variety of other companies to supply them with the parts they need—air conditioners, radios, and even entire engines. One supplier is the Cummins Engine Company, which makes diesel engines for trucks.

A small group of inventive men in Columbus, Indiana, founded the Cummins Engine Company on February 3, 1919. Clessie Cummins, one of the men, wanted to build diesel engines, invented 30 years earlier in Europe. Neither Cummins nor W. G. Irwin, the man who put up the money to start the business, could predict the future of the company. When it began, it employed fewer than 40 people and made engines that few Americans considered useful.

Between 1920 and 1936, Cummins did not make a penny of profit. It kept going largely because of funds supplied by the Irwin family. But diesel engines proved especially useful in heavy-duty trucks (those weighing over 26,000 pounds), and demand for them began to increase. As a result, Cummins grew rapidly in size and strength. By the early 1970s, the firm employed 9,000 people in the Columbus, Indiana, area. Today, Cummins engines power more heavy-duty trucks than those of any other engine manufacturer in the United States. Every American maker of trucks, including Ford, General Motors, White, Mack, and International Harvester, buys engines from Cummins.

Through its engine business and related interests, Cummins employs about 20,000 people throughout the world. In 1974, company sales totaled $83,977,000. Three years later its annual sales surpassed $1 billion.

1. Shown here in 1931 is almost the entire manufacturing staff of Cummins Engine Company.
2. Heavy duty trucks, like these, use diesel engines.
3. The growth of Cummins Engine was directed from Columbus, Indiana.
4. This woman is one of 20,000 Cummins employees today.

While Cummins has its headquarters and several main plants in the United States, its activities are worldwide in scope.

Until the 1950s Cummins Engine Company built all its engines in the United States. Then it began to manufacture them in plants elsewhere. In 1957 Cummins made an agreement with the Chrysler Corporation, which owned a plant in Darlington, England, to produce engines for Britain and continental Europe. Cummins in Columbus sent engine designs, engine parts, and investment money to the plant in Darlington. In return, Darlington sent some of its profits as well as certain engine parts to Cummins in Columbus. Darlington also produced completed Cummins engines for the British and European markets.

The Darlington venture led to other international activities on the part of Cummins. In 1962 the firm entered into a partnership with an Indian company called Kirloskar. It is located in Poona, a large city in western India. In 1963 Cummins signed an agreement with a Mexican company called Diesel Nacional (DINA). The company, owned by the Mexican government, produces trucks, buses, and other kinds of vehicles.

In each of these two situations, Cummins worked out arrangements similar to the one it had in England. It supplied designs, investment, and some parts. In return it received certain parts and a share of the profits. Each company also shipped out its own exports. In addition, the three foreign affiliates had arrangements with each other, as you can see by the diagram in Figure 20–3.

1. What resources did Cummins Engine Company rely on most heavily when it began? How did its resources change over the years?
2. Describe the international operations of Cummins Engine.
3. How do these operations illustrate interdependence?

5. Darlington, England, was one of the first locations of Cummins overseas.
6. This man works for Cummins in Poona, India.
7. The DINA plant in Mexico is part of Cummins worldwide operations.
8. Cummins has also expanded into São Paulo, Brazil.

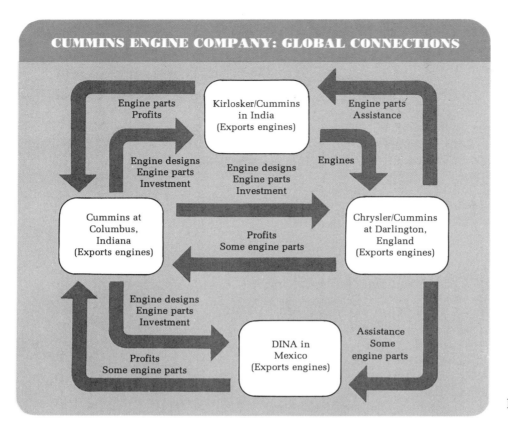

CUMMINS ENGINE COMPANY: GLOBAL CONNECTIONS

Engine parts
Profits

Kirlosker/Cummins
in India
(Exports engines)

Engine parts
Assistance

Engine designs
Engine parts
Investment

Engine designs
Engine parts
Investment

Engines

Cummins at
Columbus,
Indiana
(Exports engines)

Profits
Some engine parts

Chrysler/Cummins
at Darlington,
England
(Exports engines)

Engine designs
Engine parts
Investment

Profits
Some engine parts

DINA in
Mexico
(Exports engines)

Assistance
Some
engine parts

Figure 20-3

WORKING at a MULTINATIONAL CORPORATION

When a business, like Cummins Engine Company, develops into a large multi-national corporation, many things are affected. The very organization of the company changes in order to meet new demands. Employees also notice a change even if they never leave Columbus, Indiana. An individual worker is no longer isolated, he or she is tied to developments in India, England, or Mexico.

CHANGES in In the early years
ORGANIZATION at Cummins, all
major decisions
were made by
three men—Clessie Cummins; H. L. Knudsen, the chief engineer; and W. G. Irwin, the man who supplied the money. The decisions of these three men went directly to the plant

superintendent and were passed on by him to the foremen and the production workers. Cummins, Knudsen, and Irwin controlled all the political activities and resources of the company. Thus, Cummins was an elite political system.

In 1919 Clessie Cummins probably knew everything that happened in the engine plant. Only the plant superintendent and the foremen worked more closely with the production crew. The company produced only one size engine, and the same men worked on it from beginning to end.

Cummins grew, beginning in the late 1920s, when it started to produce several different engines. It then became necessary to have separate production lines, one for each type of engine.

Because each line made a different engine, it was necessary to add new manage-

600

ment positions to the Cummins system: line foremen. Each line foreman reported to a general foreman. As the number of lines increased, so did the number of line foremen and general foremen. The gap between Clessie Cummins and the production workers grew larger and larger.

As additional engine plants were opened in Columbus and elsewhere in the United States, a new position, plant manager, was created. Plant managers are responsible for the activities of all the employees in their plants, including foremen and production workers.

More positions were added when Cummins began to expand overseas. Various managers today have responsibility for Cummins' activities abroad. For instance, one man oversees the operation of the four Cummins plants in the United Kingdom. He and other similar managers are responsible to executives in charge of the company's international activities.

The employees at Cummins Engine Company are divided into levels. At the first level are the production workers who assemble the engines. Approximately 5,000 production people work in the Columbus area. All of them belong to the Diesel Worker's Union (DWU), which was established in 1937. The DWU seeks higher wages, better working conditions, and benefits such as health insurance.

Foremen form the next highest level of employees at Cummins. They do not belong to the DWU. Because production workers report to them, foremen generally have more status than DWU members. They make more money, too. At the next level are superintendents, who receive higher salaries and have more influence than foremen. (As you move up the pyramid chart, you will find that in general, personnel at each higher level have more resources than personnel who occupy a lower level.)

Today Cummins is no longer an elite system. It has become instead a bureaucratic system.

> 1. How were political resources and activities distributed in the Cummins system in 1919?
> 2. How are they distributed today?

SOME CUMMINS EMPLOYEES SPEAK

The history of the Cummins Engine Company is the story not just of engines and divisions, but also of people. The two case studies that follow consist of interviews with Cummins employees. In the first one, a man named Ben talks about the early years at Cummins when it was a struggling young firm.

★ The Early Years

In 1928 there were around 60 people employed here. Then, in the depression years of the early thirties, we had a layoff and the work force went down to about 45.

When I began working, my starting salary was 25¢ an hour. I was fortunate to get that much. At that time people were working on farms for $1 a day. The first year I worked at Cummins I received three 2½¢ raises. Back in those days, to get a raise you had to stop the superintendent and ask for one. That's the only way we got raises then. If he said "no" that was it.

We had very little machinery—a milling machine, external grinder, radial drills, lathes—but nothing like today's modern equipment. In those days, we had to fit everything by hand. Sometimes, to make things fit right we had to grind pieces, and we did quite a bit of filing and reaming; very much done by hand. Back in the old days we didn't know what an automatic machine was. Everything was manually operated.

Now back in those days we didn't have a research department. We did all our experimental work in the factory. Mr. Cummins was the most important man at the company. He had us build engines, put them

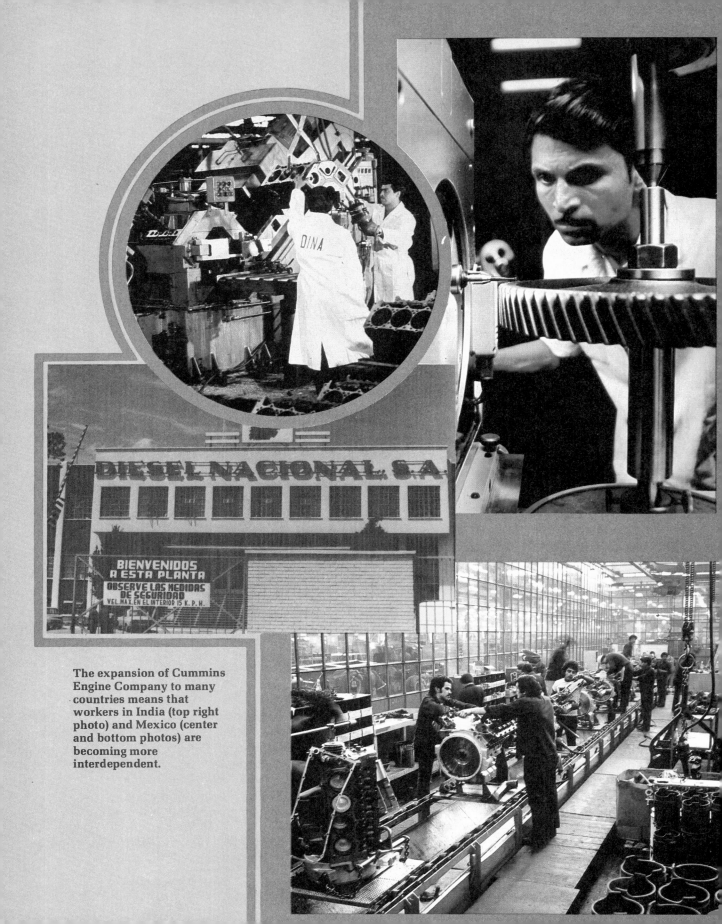

The expansion of Cummins Engine Company to many countries means that workers in India (top right photo) and Mexico (center and bottom photos) are becoming more interdependent.

on tests, and run them until they quit. Then we tore them down to find out what failed and repaired them. They figured that by using that method, when business looked up again, we would have good engines to go on the market. It worked and it allowed most of us to keep our jobs.

The last time that I could say that I knew everyone at Cummins was around 1945.

---

1. What did Ben like about his first years at Cummins?
2. What were the disadvantages of working at Cummins in the early period?

In the following case study, four actual Cummins employees discuss their feelings about the expansion of the company.

★ Expansion at Cummins

Ray: The company should be giving some more to their people here before expanding like they have been expanding. You know, I'd like for them to expand and get big, but still they gotta take care of how they're gettin' there.

Mark: I think that when they branch out into other plants—other countries—somebody's got to pay for it. They should think about the employees back here. They kind of let their people down for as big as they got and for expanding as much as they have.

Steve: Well, I think most of outside or overseas business to me is just more business. In Mexico, for example, our main operation has created a lot of work for us because we furnish a lot of parts to build those engines. Some of the parts they make, some of them we make. To me, that's more job security. If you only sell engines within the United States, you don't have the volume and you're entirely dependent on the U.S.

John: Ah, expanding into foreign countries doesn't affect my job to any extent—we make a lot of parts—ship a lot of parts. Normally [at our company] down there in Mexico, they build and assemble. They're an assembly plant virtually. They don't do a whole lot of machining. We do most of the machining. They're trying to get their capabilities up where they can machine there but that's just business. I mean that doesn't affect me, but I like to see everything kept in the United States. I'm the type of guy who hates to buy anything made overseas. I guess we have to have foreign trade to a certain extent to make the world go round so that's just part of life.

---

1. How does each of these four men feel about Cummins' expansion?
2. What major differences exist between Cummins before 1940 and Cummins today?
3. How has expansion into foreign countries affected the job security of workers at Cummins?

SPECIAL PROBLEMS Because Cummins is a multinational corporation, it has some special problems that arise from its overseas expansion. One of them has to do with jobs.

Jobs. DINA in Mexico needs many engine parts from Cummins in Columbus and Darlington. Even if business were bad in the United States or England, workers there might be kept busy making parts for Mexico. Suppose, however, that there is a strike at the DINA plant that shuts it down for weeks. Or suppose that, because of poor planning, DINA produces too many buses and trucks and has to cut production until it sells its surplus. In either case, DINA would not need new parts from Cummins plants elsewhere. Some American or English workers might well be laid off.

Consider the situation from the viewpoint of an English worker at Darlington.

Many Darlington employees make engine parts for DINA. Without DINA, they might not have jobs at all. But if the situation in Mexico forces DINA to reduce production, workers in England could be directly affected.

Consider the situation from a DINA worker's position. In the case of one type of engine, the Mexican company assembles it entirely out of parts sent from Columbus. What if Cummins makes a design error at Columbus and has to stop making these parts until the error is fixed? Many Mexican workers might lose their jobs, at least temporarily.

DINA could also be in trouble if there were a strike at Darlington, a strike in Columbus, or even a strike of workers in England. DINA has virtually no control over such situations, which could affect many Mexican workers.

Government Relations. Another special problem arising out of multinational operations involves foreign governments. A company doing business abroad must be sure to abide by the regulations it imposes.

Take the case of Kirloskar-Cummins, in India. Unlike DINA, the firm is not owned by the national government. But it must obey Indian government regulations. And so must Cummins. It must know about government regulations and be careful to obey them. Otherwise, its agreement with Kirloskar could be canceled.

Cummins must also demonstrate a willingness to work with Indians. Its people need to learn new languages, respect customs different from their own, and cooperate with foreign managers. Kirloskar-Cummins has no Americans on its staff. All of its management is Indian.

1. What are some of the problems resulting from interdependence at Cummins?
2. Do you think that the benefits of such interdependence outweigh the disadvantages? Give reasons for your answer.

The Future of Multinational Corporations

Global interdependence has many benefits. It calls for increased communication among various actors in the global political system. It requires decision-making that takes into account the views of people throughout the world. It leads to increased political participation by more than just a handful of countries and individuals. As long as multinational corporations can make this kind of participation constructive, they contribute to the well-being of citizens of all nations.

GOVERNMENT SUPPORT and REGULATION Multinational corporations can do a great many things that benefit the global political system. They can quickly distribute needed resources throughout the world. They can provide developing countries with industries. They can bring the countries of the world closer together through their modern systems of communication. They can help to simplify decision-making in the global political system through the increased coordination of governments and corporations. They can provide needed leadership on the world scene.

But multinational corporations also cause concern. As they become more and more powerful, they can become involved in the internal politics of foreign countries.

Official United States policy has been to foster the overseas investment of American corporations. The government helps such firms through the Overseas Private Investment Corporation (OPIC). It offers "risk insurance" to cushion companies against ex-

propriation—takeover of a foreign operation by the host country. This insurance guarantees that if an overseas facility is taken over by a host country, the government will pay the multinational corporation for its losses.

Many Americans, both in and out of government, are worried about potential dangers posed by multinational corporations. For several years a Senate subcommittee has been investigating them for evidence of corrupt practices. Its most noted probe was its 1973 investigation into the activities of ITT in Chile. In 1974 the committee began a careful investigation of the large oil companies and their relationship with governments in the Middle East. It followed this investigation by looking into the sale of weapons to nations in the Persian Gulf area.

International organizations have also begun to study the activities of multinational corporations. The United Nations established a Commission on Multinational Corporations that would investigate the activities of these companies and control them when necessary. In 1976 the commission established a working group of five to draft an agreement aimed at controlling possible corrupt practices. Later in 1976, the UN General Assembly adopted Resolution 3514, which condemned the practice of any illegal activities by global corporations.

Will the managers of multinational corporations respond more to the rulings of international political bodies, or to their own personal values? Many people say that citizens cannot depend only upon national and international bodies to regulate the activities of multinational corporations. They feel citizens should exert their own influence over activities of these giant businesses.

1. How has the United States government aided the growth of multinational corporations?
2. What are the potential benefits of multinational corporations? What are the potential dangers to citizens?

SUMMARY of VALUING SKILLS

The growth of multinational corporations is a very important issue. It will probably affect your life more and more over the next several decades. Important ethical issues will be raised as companies become involved with governments throughout the world.

Based on what you've read about the Cummins Engine Company, think about some of the value issues that result from the growth of such a corporation. On a separate sheet of paper, identify several of these. Remember that such issues should be based upon either your preferences or your feelings about what is right and wrong.

After you have made a list of several value issues, outline the fundamental values that underlie each one. Next, you will want to identify alternative ways of dealing with each issue and describe the possible consequences of each alternative.

So far you should have a list of issues, a list of fundamental values for each issue, a set of alternatives for dealing with each issue, and a set of consequences for each alternative.

Now go on to select one alternative for each value issue you've identified. Pick the one that is most acceptable to you after you have weighed the consequences of each alternative.

After you have identified your preferred alternative for each issue, think about how you can generalize your position. To what other situations can your value position be applied? As you work through each of the value issues you identified, be sure to list other situations to which your value position might be applicable.

Next suggest several ways in which you might take responsibility for implementing each alternative you chose. Taking responsibility for a value involves suggesting several activities that might implement it.

It is important in doing this exercise to recognize and apply all the important steps in considering a value question. Before going on to the final section of this chapter, make sure you know them by reviewing the list below.

1. Identify a value issue.
2. Identify fundamental values underlying it.
3. Speculate on alternatives to the issue.
4. Identify the consequences of each alternative.
5. Choose the desired alternative.
6. Generalize your value position.
7. Take responsibility for your choice.

Participation Project: The Impact of Multinational Corporations

This chapter has provided you with information about the size and scope of multinational corporations. You have learned about the ways in which they can affect the daily lives of citizens. Increasingly, these large companies have an effect on the international political system, the national political system, and the local political system.

The purpose of the project described below is for you to do a study of a global corporation that has an impact on your community. You will be applying the knowledge and skills you have learned in this unit. For example, the skills associated with managing group differences will help you in seeing how various groups within corporations interact. These skills will also help you to understand how multinational corporations can come into conflict with national governments and international political bodies.

Forecasting skills will be useful, too. You will want to speculate about the future of the multinational corporation you are studying. Will it expand? If so, how? Or might it lose its importance? Why?

There are seven basic steps involved in preparing your own case study.

Choosing a Topic. The first step is to choose a topic. You will want to focus on the activities of a global corporation that has an impact on your community.

Choosing a Method of Working. You may decide that you can work best by yourself. However, it may be more valuable to work with several other people who are interested in the same topic.

Stating Objectives. What are the purposes of your case study? Of course, you will be studying the activities of a multinational corporation. You will want to see how it controls political resources and engages in political activities. You should observe how the corporation manages conflicts in groups with which it has contact. (For example, has it ever had any difficulty in cooperating with a specific country? If so, be sure to determine how the conflict was managed.)

Formulate the objectives of your study carefully. You might want to explore an issue that relates to how a corporation deals with the United

States government, or how it distributes its products. Whatever objectives you choose, be certain to state them clearly.

Choosing Sources. Make use of as wide a variety of sources as you can in preparing your study. These can include newspaper articles, magazines, and books from the library. Helpful information can usually be obtained by writing directly to the headquarters of the corporation.

Skills used in other parts of this book should be useful to you in creating your case study. For example, you may want to interview people who work for the corporation. Or you may want to analyze the way in which personnel and corporations make decisions.

One part of your study should be a forecast of the future of the corporation you are studying. To do this, you will need to gather information about the history of the corporation as well as its present activities. Using this information, combined with the steps involved in forecasting alternative futures, you should determine the likeliest future of the corporation. This statement should appear at the end of the study.

Gathering Information. If you are working with others, divide the project into tasks. Each person should be responsible for completing a part of the assignment. It might be best to divide the work among the group members according to objectives (third step above).

Choosing a Method of Presentation. In sharing your study with the class, you may choose to make a short oral report or a written report. You may want to make an entirely visual presentation. What do you think is the best way to present your case study? Discuss your ideas with your teacher before you make your presentation.

Presenting Your Findings. When you present your findings, have the class answer the following questions:

1. What issue or issues does this project focus on?
2. Who are the major groups involved in the project?
3. What resources does the corporation have and how does it use them?
4. What activities does the corporation carry out?
5. What resources are redistributed as a result of the firm's activities?
6. How does the corporation affect the international political system?
7. How does the corporation affect this community?

1. What are some key factors in understanding multinational corporations?

2. What similarities in organization and management characterize multinational corporations?

3. How do multinational corporations affect the U.S. labor market?

Chapter Review

4. Summarize the early history of the Cummins Engine Company.

5. When did Cummins begin to expand overseas? Why?

6. Why and how did Cummins change from an elite to a bureaucratic system?

7. What effect did Cummins' expansion have on workers' feelings about their jobs at the company?

8. How does OPIC help multinational corporations based in the United States?

9. Name three multinational activities that the Senate investigated in the 1970s.

10. What action has the United Nations taken to control multinational corporations?

Chapter Vocabulary

Define the following terms.

parent country   affiliates   integration

host countries   subsidiaries   expropriation

Chapter Analysis

1. Describe several political activities engaged in by most global corporations.

2. Looking back at Chapter 18, review the benefits a corporation receives by doing business overseas. How would you add to this list?

3. Describe how global corporations can affect the distribution of resources in the global political system.

4. Summarize the advantages and the disadvantages the Cummins Engine Company would offer you as (a) an American employee in Columbus, Indiana; (b) an English employee in Darlington; (c) the owner of a French trucking firm in need of engines; (d) a German manufacturer of diesel engines.

5. If you were president in a Third World country where Cummins wanted to set up an operation, what rules would you establish to regulate it?

6. Describe how global corporations have led to a more interdependent world.

7. Throughout this book, you have studied how citizens can influence the activities of political actors. Describe how you might try to affect the actions of multinational corporations.

1. Bring to class at least three pieces of evidence showing the influence of multinational corporations on your community. Give an oral report stating whether or not this influence is likely to continue.

2. Work carefully with a partner to draft a letter to the Senate Subcommittee on Multinational Corporations. Ask for additional information about the activities of this committee so that you will know more about the position of the United States government with respect to global corporations. Send your letter to the Subcommittee at the Senate Office Building, Washington, DC.

3. Draft a similar letter to the chairman of the United Nations Commission on Multinational Corporations (at the United Nations in New York). Try to get recent information about what the United Nations has been doing in regard to multinational corporations.

What's Good for GM . . . , Edward Ayres (Aurora Publishers, Inc.: Nashville, TN), 1970.
> Describes the growth and present role of General Motors in American society and the global political system. Also discusses the impact of the automobile industry on all levels of government.

Global Reach: The Power of the Multinational Corporations, Richard J. Barnet and Ronald E. Muller (Simon and Schuster: New York, NY), 1974.
> Presents one of the best available overviews of global corporations. It is very readable and covers many aspects of this important topic.

Guide to Corporations: A Social Perspective, Council on Economic Priorities (The Swallow Press: Chicago, IL), 1974.
> In large part an indexed guide to profiles of some of the world's largest global corporations.

The Corporation in American Politics, Edwin M. Epstein (Prentice-Hall, Inc.: Englewood Cliffs, NJ), 1969.
> Offers a historical overview of the involvement of corporations in American politics, then focuses on the period after World War II. Highlights how corporations are active in elections and other aspects of government and politics.

An American Company: The Tragedy of United Fruit, Thomas P. McCann (Brown Publishers, Inc.: New York, NY), 1976.
> A description of the growth of this global corporation by a former executive of United Fruit Company. Provides an insider's view of a global corporation.

glossary

The page number following each definition refers to the page on which the word or term is first discussed.

advocacy group a group which supports a particular issue or program (p. 296)

alien a foreign-born person who is not yet a citizen of the country in which he or she resides (p. 33)

alliance an agreement made among people or groups to further their common interests (p. 222)

ambassador a nation's official representative in another country (p. 523)

amendment a change or addition to an original document (p. 34)

appellate jurisdiction the authority to review the decisions of a lower court (p. 422)

apportion to distribute in shares according to a plan; for example, to distribute seats in legislature in a proportionate manner (p. 288)

arbitration a method of settling disputes by having a third party, such as a court or a neutral nation, make a decision (p. 577)

article one part or division of a document (p. 176)

balance of payments the difference between the total amount of money a nation pays to other countries and what it receives back from them (p. 555)

bargaining a political activity in which two or more individuals attempt to influence each other to support different alternatives (p. 372)

bias slant; a prejudice sometimes based on the selective use of evidence (p. 236)

bicameral a two-chamber legislature (p. 228)

bilateral treaty an agreement between two nations (p. 510)

bill a draft of a law presented to a legislature for enactment (p. 230)

bureaucratic political system a political system with many different levels of authority in which persons at higher levels have more power than those at lower levels (p. 334)

canvass to contact citizens to ask them their party and candidate preferences (p. 97)

capitalism an economic system in which all or most of the means of production and distribution are privately owned and operated for profit (p. 24)

charter the official plan of government for a municipality (p. 263)

checks and balances a system by which each branch of government can check or stop the actions of the other branches (p. 319)

citizenship the duties, rights, and privileges of being a citizen (p. 32)

city council an elected legislature in a municipal government (p. 260)

civil disobedience peaceful protests against official policies believed to be unjust (p. 461)

civil rights rights and freedoms guaranteed to citizens (p. 452)

civil service any government service in which a job is obtained through competitive public examination (p. 239)

civil suit a dispute between individuals or groups concerning their respective rights (p. 244)

closed primary a primary election in which only voters who have identified themselves as party members can take part (p. 82)

coalition a group of people with similar interests or goals (p. 89)

coalitional political system a political system in which the majority usually rules, with each person or group having an equal vote (p. 337)

collective security a pooling of military resources by a group of nations to provide a line of defense against a common enemy (p. 527)

command economy an economic system in which a few leaders make most basic decisions about what will be produced, the cost of goods and services, and how things will be distributed; also called a planned economy (p. 548)

communism in theory, an economic system in which all property and means of production are owned by society as a whole; in practice today, a form of government in which economic decisions are made by a small group of government leaders (p. 548)

concurrent powers powers shared by the national and state governments (p. 194)

confederation a union of groups; an alliance (p. 23)

conference committee a committee of members from both houses of a legislature which tries to resolve differences in the house and senate versions of a bill (p. 231)

constituent a person who chooses another as his or her representative (p. 228)

constitution a set of basic rules and principles for a government (p. 26)

decision-making an activity through which choices are made from two or more alternatives (p. 204)

defendant a person who has been accused or sued (p. 245)

delegated powers powers specifically assigned to the national government in the United States Constitution (p. 194)

democratic socialism a form of socialism where government control of the economy is combined with democratic political institutions (p. 548)

denied powers powers specifically forbidden to national or state governments in the United States Constitution (p. 194)

detente a policy to relax tensions between nations so that problems can be negotiated (p. 501)

elastic clause a clause in the Constitution that allows Congress to make all laws necessary for the functioning of government (p. 194)

electoral college a body of people chosen to elect the president and vice-president of the United States (p. 102)

elite political system a political system in which one person or small group controls the system and makes all important decisions (p. 332)

executive agreement a treaty made by the president that does not require Senate approval (p. 385)

federalism the division of power between a central government and a number of regional governments (p. 194)

felony a major crime such as murder, burglary, or arson (p. 244)

feminism the movement to gain equal rights for women (p. 455)

foreign policy the way in which a nation manages its relations with other nations (p. 522)

general election an election in which voters make their final choices in the selection of government officials (p. 83)

global actor an individual, group, or nation that uses resources and takes actions that affect other nations (p. 496)

global issue a problem or situation that affects the people of many countries (p. 497)

government an organization that makes and enforces rules to guide a group of people (p. 20)

gross national product (GNP) the value of all the goods and services produced by a nation in a given year (p. 549)

gubernatorial of or relating to a governor (p. 89)

habeas corpus a written court order requiring legal officials who are holding a person in custody to bring the prisoner to court and to cite reasons for the prisoner's detention (p. 471)

hypothesis a theory that is based on evidence and that tentatively answers a question (p. 521)

ideologies the doctrines that underlie political and economic systems (p. 574)

impeach to accuse an official of wrong conduct in doing his or her job (p. 321)

incumbent a person currently holding an office (p. 53)

inflation a constantly rising level of prices (p. 550)

initiative a process that permits citizens to propose laws to their state or local governments (p. 84)

interdependence a condition in which people, groups, or nations rely on one another for different needs and are affected by one another's actions (p. 495)

interest group a group that acts in order to influence the distribution of resources in favor of its members (p. 118)

interim committee committees that meet between legislative sessions (p. 230)

item veto the rejection of specific items in a bill (p. 240)

---

joint committee a committee with members from both houses of a legislature (p. 230)

judicial review the process by which federal courts can declare laws or actions of the legislative and executive branches unconstitutional (p. 418)

jurisdiction the authority to interpret and apply the law (p. 418)

---

lobby a group that promotes its own interests by trying to influence public government (p. 118)

---

majority decision-making a decision-making process by which more than half the people in a group must agree on a decision for it to become the decision of the whole group (p. 356)

majority party the party with more than half the members in a legislative body (p. 360)

market economy an economic system where decisions about production and allocation of resources are the result of competition in a free market (p. 548)

megalopolis a heavily populated region, including several cities and their surrounding suburbs (p. 276)

metropolitan area a central city and its surrounding suburbs (p. 276)

minority party the party with fewer than half the members in a legislative body (p. 360)

misdemeanor a crime less serious than a felony; for example, shoplifting or trespassing (p. 244)

mixed economy an economic system that combines free enterprise with government control (p. 549)

multilateral treaty an agreement among three or more nations (p. 510)

multinational corporation a large company with operations in more than one country (p. 560)

multiparty system a system in which a number of political parties compete through elections for control of a government (p. 87)

---

nationalism a feeling of loyalty citizens have toward their country (p. 520)

naturalization the legal process by which a person changes citizenship from one country to another (p. 33)

negotiation the process of reaching a solution through discussion, bargaining, and compromise (p. 539)

nominate to select or to put forward (p. 82)

nominating convention a meeting of delegates who represent other party members and who decide which candidates the party will support for various offices (p. 95)

nonpartisan election an election in which candidates who run for office do not run on party tickets (p. 52)

---

one-party system a system in which there is only one legal political party (p. 87)

open primary a primary election in which voters do not have to declare their party preference in order to vote (p. 82)

ordinance a law (p. 301)

original jurisdiction the authority to hear or try a case for the first time (p. 420)

---

participant political system a political system in which each member has equal power and decisions must be unanimous (p. 338)

partisan election an election in which candidates run for office on the basis of political party identification and support (p. 82)

party platform a statement of beliefs for which a party's candidates stand during an election campaign (p. 94)

petition a formal, written request (p. 206)

plaintiff a person who brings a suit into a court of law; complainant (p. 421)

pocket veto the process by which a governor or president rejects a bill by not signing it before the end of a legislative session (p. 240)

political party an organization whose main purpose is to win elections for the candidates it sponsors (p. 82)

politics activity in which resources are used and distributed in a group (p. 50)

presidential succession the order in which the office of president is filled if a president dies, resigns, or is removed from office (p. 389)

primary election an election in which voters nominate candidates for office (p. 82)

ratification formal approval (p. 187)

recall election a process by which citizens may remove government officials from office before their terms are finished (p. 83)

referendum a process by which citizens may vote on laws that have been passed by a legislative body (p. 83)

republic the form of government in which citizens elect representatives to manage the government (p. 22)

reserved powers powers reserved to state governments according to Amendment 10 of the United States Constitution (p. 194)

resources something that is used to satisfy needs or accomplish goals (p. 50)

roll call vote a method of voting in a legislature in which members record their vote as their names are read (p. 231)

satellite nations nations that are economically or politically dependent on a larger, more powerful nation (p. 528)

select committee a committee that examines matters that do not fall within the exact area of any standing committee (p. 362)

separation of powers the division of power among different branches of a government (p. 314)

socialism an economic system in which the government owns and controls the means of production (p. 24)

sovereignty supreme and independent political authority (p. 178)

special district a unit of local government that is formed for a specific need such as education (p. 267)

special election an election held to fill an office that is vacated before a regularly scheduled election (p. 83)

special session a special meeting of a legislature called by a governor or a president (p. 229)

split ticket the situation of voting for candidates of one party for some offices and candidates of other parties for other offices (p. 86)

standing committee a permanent legislative committee that specializes in different types of legislation (p. 230)

state the power or authority represented by a group of people living in a defined geographical area and organized under one government (p. 24)

straight ticket the situation of voting only for the candidates of one party (p. 86)

suffragists advocates of the right to vote for women (p. 454)

two-party system a system in which there are two major political parties (p. 87)

unicameral a one-chamber legislature (p. 228)

urban related to, or part of, a city (p. 260)

veto to reject (p. 231)

voice vote a method of voting in a legislature in which the volume of responses for or against an issue determines the outcome (p. 231)

ward an administrative area of a city, made up of several precincts (p. 89)

writ a written, legal order (p. 419)

write-in vote a vote for a person whose name is not on the ballot cast by writing his or her name on the ballot (p. 86)

The Declaration of Independence

When in the course of human events it becomes necessary for one people to dissolve the political bands which have connected them with another and to assume, among the powers of the earth, the separate and equal station to which the laws of nature and of nature's God entitle them, a decent respect to the opinions of mankind requires that they should declare the causes which impel them to the separation.

We hold these truths to be self-evident, that all men are created equal; that they are endowed by their Creator with certain unalienable rights; that among these are life, liberty, and the pursuit of happiness. That, to secure these rights, governments are instituted among men, deriving their just powers from the consent of the governed; that, whenever any form of government becomes destructive of these ends, it is the right of the people to alter or to abolish it, and to institute a new government, laying its foundation on such principles, and organizing its powers in such form, as to them shall seem most likely to effect their safety and happiness. Prudence, indeed, will dictate that governments long established should not be changed for light and transient causes; and, accordingly, all experience hath shown that mankind are more disposed to suffer, while evils are sufferable, than to right themselves by abolishing the forms to which they are accustomed. But when a long train of abuses and usurpations, pursuing invariably the same object, evinces a design to reduce them under absolute despotism, it is their right, it is their duty, to throw off such government and to provide new guards for their future security. Such has been the patient sufferance of these colonies, and such is now the necessity which constrains them to alter their former systems of government. The history of the present King of Great Britain is a history of repeated injuries and usurpations, all having, in direct object, the establishment of an absolute tyranny over these States. To prove this, let facts be submitted to a candid world:

He has refused his assent to laws the most wholesome and necessary for the public good.

He has forbidden his governors to pass laws of immediate and pressing importance, unless suspended in their operation till his assent should be obtained; and, when so suspended, he has utterly neglected to attend to them.

He has refused to pass other laws for the accommodation of the large districts of people, unless those people would relinquish the right of representation in the legislature; a right inestimable to them and formidable to tyrants only.

He has called together legislative bodies at places unusual, uncomfortable, and distant from the depository of their public records, for the sole purpose of fatiguing them into compliance with his measures.

He has dissolved representative houses, repeatedly for opposing, with manly firmness, his invasions on the rights of the people.

He has refused, for a long time after such dissolutions, to cause others to be elected; whereby the legislative powers, incapable of annihilation, have returned to the people at large for their exercise; the state remaining, in the meantime, exposed to all the danger of invasion from without and convulsions within.

He has endeavored to prevent the population of these States; for that purpose, obstructing the laws for naturalization of foreigners, refusing to pass others to encourage their migration hither, and raising the conditions of new appropriations of lands.

He has obstructed the administration of justice by refusing his assent to laws for establishing judiciary powers.

He has made judges dependent on his will alone for the tenure of their offices and the amount and payment of their salaries.

He has erected a multitude of new offices and sent hither swarms of officers to harass our people and eat out their substance.

614

He has kept among us, in time of peace, standing armies, without the consent of our legislatures.

He has affected to render the military independent of, and superior to, the civil power.

He has combined with others to subject us to a jurisdiction foreign to our Constitution and unacknowledged by our laws, giving his assent to their acts of pretended legislation—

For quartering large bodies of armed troops among us;

For protecting them by a mock trial from punishment for any murders which they should commit on the inhabitants of these States;

For cutting off our trade with all parts of the world;

For imposing taxes on us without our consent;

For depriving us, in many cases, of the benefit of trial by jury;

For transporting us beyond seas to be tried for pretended offences;

For abolishing the free system of English laws in a neighboring province, establishing therein an arbitrary government, and enlarging its boundaries, so as to render it at once an example and fit instrument for introducing the same absolute rule into these colonies;

For taking away our charters, abolishing our most valuable laws, and altering, fundamentally, the powers of our governments;

For suspending our own legislatures and declaring themselves invested with power to legislate for us in all cases whatsoever.

He has abdicated government here by declaring us out of his protection and waging war against us.

He has plundered our seas, ravaged our coasts, burnt our towns, and destroyed the lives of our people.

He is, at this time, transporting large armies of foreign mercenaries to complete the works of death, desolation, and tyranny already begun with circumstances of cruelty and perfidy scarcely paralleled in the most barbarous ages, and totally unworthy the head of a civilized nation.

He has constrained our fellow citizens, taken captive on the high seas, to bear arms against their country, to become the executioners of their friends and brethren, or to fall themselves by their hands.

He has excited domestic insurrections amongst us and has endeavored to bring on the inhabitants of our frontiers, the merciless Indian savages, whose known rule of warfare is an undistinguished destruction of all ages, sexes, and conditions.

In every stage of these oppressions, we have petitioned for redress in the most humble terms; our repeated petitions have been answered only by repeated injury. A prince whose character is thus marked by every act which may define a tyrant is unfit to be the ruler of a free people.

Nor have we been wanting in attention to our British brethren. We have warned them, from time to time, of attempts made by their legislature to extend an unwarrantable jurisdiction over us. We have reminded them of the circumstances of our emigration and settlement here. We have appealed to their native justice and magnanimity, and we have conjured them, by the ties of our common kindred, to disavow these usurpations, which would inevitably interrupt our connections and correspondence. They, too, have been deaf to the voice of justice and consanguinity. We must, therefore, acquiesce in the necessity which denounces our separation, and hold them, as we hold the rest of mankind, enemies in war, in peace, friends.

We, therefore, the representatives of the United States of America, in general Congress assembled, appealing to the Supreme Judge of the world for the rectitude of our intentions, do, in the name and by the authority of the good people of these colonies, solemnly publish and declare, that these united colonies are, and of right ought to be, free and independent states: that they are absolved from all allegiance to the British Crown, and that all political connection between them and the state of Great Britain is, and ought to be, totally dissolved; and that, as free and independent states, they have full power to levy war, conclude peace, contract alliances, establish commerce, and to do all other acts and things which independent states may of right do. And, for the support of this declaration, with a firm reliance on the protection of Divine Providence, we mutually pledge to each other our lives, our fortunes, and our sacred honor.

The Constitution of the United States

We the people of the United States, in order to form a more perfect union, establish justice, insure domestic tranquility, provide for the common defense, promote the general welfare, and secure the blessings of liberty to ourselves and our posterity, do ordain and establish this Constitution for the United States of America.

Article I

SECTION 1. All legislative powers herein granted shall be vested in a Congress of the United States, which shall consist of a Senate and House of Representatives.

SECTION 2. 1. The House of Representatives shall be composed of members chosen every second year by the people of the several States, and the electors in each State shall have the qualifications requisite for electors of the most numerous branch of the State legislature.

2. No person shall be a representative who shall not have attained to the age of twenty-five years, and been seven years a citizen of the United States, and who shall not, when elected, be an inhabitant of that State in which he shall be chosen.

3. Representatives and direct taxes[1] shall be apportioned among the several States which may be included within this Union, according to their respective numbers, which shall be determined by adding to the whole number of free persons, including those bound to service for a term of years, and excluding Indians not taxed, three fifths of all other persons.[2] The actual enumeration shall be made within three years after the first meeting of the Congress of the United States, and within every subsequent term of ten years, in such manner as they shall by law direct. The number of representatives shall not exceed one for every thirty thousand, but each State shall have at least one representative; and until such enumeration shall be made, the State of New Hampshire shall be entitled to choose three, Massachusetts eight, Rhode Island and Providence Plantations one, Connecticut five, New York six, New Jersey four, Pennsylvania eight, Delaware one, Maryland six, Virginia ten, North Carolina five, South Carolina five, and Georgia three.

4. When vacancies happen in the representation from any State, the executive authority thereof shall issue writs of election to fill such vacancies.

5. The House of Representatives shall choose their speaker and other officers; and shall have the sole power of impeachment.

SECTION 3. 1. The Senate of the United States shall be composed of two senators from each State, chosen by the legislature thereof,[3] for six years; and each senator shall have one vote.

2. Immediately after they shall be assembled in consequence of the first election, they shall be divided as equally as may be into three classes. The seats of the senators of the first class shall be vacated at the expiration of the second year, of the second class at the expiration of the fourth year, and of the third class at the expiration of the sixth year, so that one third may be chosen every second year; and if vacancies happen by resignation, or otherwise, during the recess of the legislature of any State, the executive thereof may make temporary appointments until the next meeting of the legislature, which shall then fill such vacancies.[4]

3. No person shall be a senator who shall not have attained to the age of thirty years, and been nine years a citizen of the United States, and who shall not, when elected, be an inhabitant of that State for which he shall be chosen.

4. The Vice President of the United States shall be President of the Senate, but shall have no vote, unless they be equally divided.

[1]See the Sixteenth Amendment.
[2]See the Fourteenth Amendment.
[3]See the Seventeenth Amendment.
[4]See the Seventeenth Amendment.

5. The Senate shall choose their other officers, and also a president pro tempore, in the absence of the Vice President, or when he shall exercise the office of the President of the United States.

6. The Senate shall have the sole power to try all impeachments. When sitting for that purpose, they shall be on oath or affirmation. When the President of the United States is tried, the chief justice shall preside: and no person shall be convicted without the concurrence of two thirds of the members present.

7. Judgment in cases of impeachment shall not extend further than to removal from office, and disqualifications to hold and enjoy any office of honor, trust or profit under the United States: but the party convicted shall nevertheless be liable and subject to indictment, trial, judgment and punishment, according to law.

SECTION 4. 1. The times, places, and manner of holding elections for senators and representatives, shall be prescribed in each State by the legislature thereof; but the Congress may at any time by law make or alter such regulations, except as to the places of choosing senators.

2. The Congress shall assemble at least once in every year, and such meeting shall be on the first Monday in December, unless they shall by law appoint a different day.

SECTION 5. 1. Each House shall be the judge of the elections, returns and qualifications of its own members, and a majority of each shall constitute a quorum to do business; but a smaller number may adjourn from day to day, and may be authorized to compel the attendance of absent members, in such manner, and under such penalties as each House may provide.

2. Each House may determine the rules of its proceedings, punish its members for disorderly behavior, and, with the concurrence of two thirds, expel a member.

3. Each House shall keep a journal of its proceedings, and from time to time publish the same, excepting such parts as may in their judgment require secrecy; and the yeas and nays of the members of either House on any question shall, at the desire of one fifth of those present, be entered on the journal.

4. Neither House, during the session of Congress, shall, without the consent of the other, adjourn for more than three days, nor to any other place than that in which the two Houses shall be sitting.

SECTION 6. 1. The senators and representatives shall receive a compensation for their services, to be ascertained by law, and paid out of the Treasury of the United States. They shall in all cases, except treason, felony, and breach of the peace, be privileged from arrest during their attendance at the session of their respective Houses, and in going to and returning from the same; and for any speech or debate in either House, they shall not be questioned in any other place.

2. No senator or representative shall, during the time for which he was elected, be appointed to any civil office under the authority of the United States, which shall have been created, or the emoluments whereof shall have been increased, during such time; and no person holding any office under the United States shall be a member of either House during his continuance in office.

SECTION 7. 1. All bills for raising revenue shall originate in the House of Representatives; but the Senate may propose or concur with amendments as on other bills.

2. Every bill which shall have passed the House of Representatives and the Senate, shall, before it becomes a law, be presented to the President of the United States; If he approves he shall sign it, but if not he shall return it, with his objections, to that House in which it shall have originated, who shall enter the objections at large on their journal, and proceed to reconsider it. If after such reconsideration two thirds of that House shall agree to pass the bill, it shall be sent, together with the objections, to the other House, by which it shall likewise be reconsidered, and if approved by two thirds of that House, it shall become a law. But in all such cases the votes of both Houses shall be determined by yeas and nays, and the names of the persons voting for and against the bill shall be entered on the journal of each House respectively. If any bill shall not be returned by the President within ten days (Sundays excepted) after it shall have been presented to him, the same shall be a law, in like manner as if he had signed it, unless the Congress by their adjournment prevent its return, in which case it shall not be a law.

3. Every order, resolution, or vote to which the concurrence of the Senate and the House of Representatives may be necessary (except on a question of adjournment) shall be presented to the President of the United States; and before the same shall take effect, shall be approved by him, or

being disapproved by him, shall be repassed by two thirds of the Senate and House of Representatives, according to the rules and limitations prescribed in the case of a bill.

SECTION 8.   The Congress shall have the power

1. To lay and collect taxes, duties, imposts, and excises, to pay the debts and provide for the common defense and general welfare of the United States; but all duties, imposts, and excises shall be uniform throughout the United States;

2. To borrow money on the credit of the United States;

3. To regulate commerce with foreign nations, and among the several States, and with the Indian tribes;

4. To establish an uniform rule of naturalization, and uniform laws on the subject of bankruptcies throughout the United States;

5. To coin money, regulate the value thereof, and of foreign coin, and fix the standard of weights and measures;

6. To provide for the punishment of counterfeiting the securities and current coin of the United States;

7. To establish post offices and post roads;

8. To promote the progress of science and useful arts, by securing for limited times to authors and inventors the exclusive right to their respective writings and discoveries;

9. To constitute tribunals inferior to the Supreme Court;

10. To define and punish piracies and felonies committed on the high seas, and offenses against the law of nations;

11. To declare war, grant letters of marque and reprisal, and make rules concerning captures on land and water;

12. To raise and support armies, but no appropriation of money to that use shall be for a longer term than two years;

13. To provide and maintain a navy;

14. To make rules for the government and regulation of the land and naval forces;

15. To provide for calling forth the militia to execute the laws of the Union, suppress insurrections and repel invasions;

16. To provide for organizing, arming, and disciplining the militia, and for governing such part of them as may be employed in the service of the United States, reserving to the States respectively, the appointment of the officers, and the authority of training the militia according to the discipline prescribed by Congress;

17. To exercise exclusive legislation in all cases whatsoever, over such district (not exceeding ten miles square) as may, by cession of particular States, and the acceptance of Congress, become the seat of the government of the United States, and to exercise like authority over all places purchased by the consent of the legislature of the State in which the same shall be, for the erection of forts, magazines, arsenals, dockyards, and other needful buildings; and

18. To make all laws which shall be necessary and proper for carrying into execution the foregoing powers, and all other powers vested by this Constitution in the government of the United States, or any department or officer thereof.

SECTION 9.   1. The migration or importation of such persons as any of the States now existing shall think proper to admit, shall not be prohibited by the Congress prior to the year one thousand eight hundred and eight, but a tax or duty may be imposed on such importation, not exceeding ten dollars for each person.

2. The privilege of the writ of habeas corpus shall not be suspended, unless when in cases of rebellion or invasion the public safety may require it.

3. No bill of attainder or ex post facto law shall be passed.

4. No capitation, or other direct, tax shall be laid, unless in proportion to the census or enumeration hereinbefore directed to be taken.[5]

5. No tax or duty shall be laid on articles exported from any State.

6. No preference shall be given by any regulation of commerce or revenue to the ports of one State over those of another; nor shall vessels bound to, or from, one State be obliged to enter, clear, or pay duties in another.

7. No money shall be drawn from the treasury, but in consequence of appropriations made by law; and a regular statement and account of the receipts and expenditures of all public money shall be published from time to time.

8. No title of nobility shall be granted by the United States: and no person holding any

[5]*See the Sixteenth Amendment.*

office of profit or trust under them, shall, without the consent of the Congress, accept of any present, emolument, office, or title, of any kind whatever, from any king, prince, or foreign State.

SECTION 10. 1. No State shall enter into any treaty, alliance, or confederation; grant letters of marque and reprisal; coin money; emit bills of credit; make any thing but gold and silver coin a tender in payment of debts; pass any bill of attainder, ex post facto law, or law impairing the obligation of contracts, or grant any title of nobility.

2. No State shall, without the consent of the Congress, lay any imposts or duties on imports or exports, except what may be absolutely necessary for executing its inspection laws: and the net produce of all duties and imposts laid by any State on imports or exports, shall be for the use of the treasury of the United States; and all such laws shall be subject to the revision and control of the Congress.

3. No State shall, without the consent of the Congress, lay any duty of tonnage, keep troops, or ships of war in time of peace, enter into any agreement or compact with another State, or with a foreign power, or engage in war, unless actually invaded, or in such imminent danger as will not admit of delay.

Article II

SECTION 1. 1. The executive power shall be vested in a President of the United States of America. He shall hold his office during the term of four years, and, together with the Vice President, chosen for the same term, be elected, as follows:

2. Each State shall appoint, in such manner as the legislature thereof may direct, a number of electors, equal to the whole number of senators and representatives to which the State may be entitled in the Congress: but no senator or representative, or person holding an office of trust or profit under the United States, shall be appointed an elector.

The electors shall meet in their respective States, and vote by ballot for two persons, of whom one at least shall not be an inhabitant of the same State with themselves. And they shall make a list of all the persons voted for, and of the number of votes for each; which list they shall sign and certify, and transmit sealed to the seat of the government of the United States, directed to the president of the Senate. The president of the Senate shall, in the presence of the Senate

and House of Representatives, open all the certificates, and the votes shall then be counted. The person having the greatest number of votes shall be the President, if such number be a majority of the whole number of electors appointed; and if there be more than one who have such majority, and have an equal number of votes, then the House of representatives shall immediately choose by ballot one of them for President; and if no person have a majority, then from the five highest on the list the said House shall in like manner choose the President. But in choosing the President, the votes shall be taken by States, the representation from each State having one vote; a quorum for this purpose shall consist of a member or members from two thirds of the States, and a majority of all the States shall be necessary to a choice. In every case, after the choice of the President, the person having the greatest number of votes of the electors shall be the Vice President. But if there should remain two or more who have equal votes, the Senate shall choose from them by ballot the Vice President.[6]

3. The Congress may determine the time of choosing the electors, and the day on which they shall give their votes; which day shall be the same throughout the United States.

4. No person except a natural born citizen, or a citizen of the United States, at the time of the adoption of this Constitution, shall be eligible to the office of President, neither shall any person be eligible to that office who shall not have attained to the age of thirty-five years, and been fourteen years a resident within the United States.

5. In case of the removal of the President from office, or of his death, resignation, or inability to discharge the powers and duties of the said office, the same shall devolve on the Vice President, and the Congress may by law provide for the case of removal, death, resignation or inability, both of the President and Vice President, declaring what officer shall then act as President, and such officer shall act accordingly, until the disability be removed, or a President shall be elected.

6. The President shall, at stated times, receive for his services a compensation, which shall neither be increased nor diminished during the period for which he shall have been elected, and he shall not receive within that period any other emolument from the United States, or any of them.

[6]*Superseded by the Twelfth Amendment.*

7. Before he enter on the execution of his office, he shall take the following oath or affirmation:—"I do solemnly swear (or affirm) that I will faithfully execute the office of President of the United States, and will to the best of my ability, preserve, protect and defend the Constitution of the United States."

SECTION 2.   1. The President shall be commander in chief of the army and navy of the United States, and of the militia of the several States, when called into the actual service of the United States; he may require the opinion, in writing, of the principal officer in each of the executive departments, upon any subject relating to the duties of their respective offices, and he shall have power to grant reprieves and pardons for offenses against the United States, except in cases of impeachment.

2. He shall have power, by and with the advice and consent of the Senate, to make treaties, provided two thirds of the senators present concur; and he shall nominate, and by and with the advice and consent of the Senate, shall appoint ambassadors, other public ministers and consuls, judges of the Supreme Court, and all other officers of the United States, whose appointments are not herein otherwise provided for, and which shall be established by law: but the Congress may by law vest the appointment of such inferior officers, as they think proper, in the President alone, in the courts of law, or in the heads of departments.

3. The President shall have power to fill up all vacancies that may happen during the recess of the Senate, by granting commissions which shall expire at the end of their next session.

SECTION 3. He shall from time to time give to the Congress information of the state of the Union, and recommend to their consideration such measures as he shall judge necessary and expedient; he may, on extraordinary occasions, convene both Houses, or either of them, and in case of disagreement between them with respect to the time of adjournment, he may adjourn them to such time as he shall think proper; he shall receive ambassadors and other public ministers; he shall take care that the laws be faithfully executed, and shall commission all the officers of the United States.

SECTION 4.   The President, Vice President, and all civil officers of the United States, shall be removed from office on impeachment for, and conviction of, treason, bribery, or other high crimes and misdemeanors.

Article III

SECTION 1.   The judicial power of the United States shall be vested in one Supreme Court, and in such inferior courts as the Congress may from time to time ordain and establish. The judges, both of the Supreme and inferior courts, shall hold their offices during good behavior, and shall, at stated times, receive for their services, a compensation, which shall not be diminished during their continuance in office.

SECTION 2.   1. The judicial power shall extend to all cases, in law and equity, arising under this Constitution, the laws of the United States, and treaties made, or which shall be made, under their authority;—to all cases affecting ambassadors, other public ministers and consuls;—to all cases of admiralty and maritime jurisdiction;—to controversies to which the United States shall be a party;[7]—to controversies between two or more States;—between a State and citizens of another State;—between citizens of different states;—between citizens of the same State claiming lands under grants of different States, and between a State, or the citizens thereof, and foreign States, citizens or subjects.

2. In all cases affecting ambassadors, other public ministers and consuls, and those in which a State shall be party, the Supreme Court shall have original jurisdiction. In all the other cases before mentioned, the Supreme Court shall have appellate jurisdiction, both as to law and fact, with such exceptions, and under such regulations as the Congress shall make.

3. The trial of all crimes, except in cases of impeachment, shall be by jury; and such trial shall be held in the State where the said crimes shall have been committed; but when not committed within any State, the trial shall be at such place or places as the Congress may by law have directed.

SECTION 3.   1. Treason against the United States shall consist only in levying war against them, or in adhering to their enemies, giving them aid and comfort. No person shall be convicted of treason unless on the testimony of two witnesses to the same overt act, or on confession in open court.

[7]See the Eleventh Amendment.

2. The Congress shall have power to declare the punishment of treason, but no attainder of treason shall work corruption of blood, or forfeiture except during the life of the person attainted.

Article IV

SECTION 1. Full faith and credit shall be given in each State to the public acts, records, and judicial proceedings of every other State. And the Congress may by general laws prescribe the manner in which such acts, records and proceedings shall be proved, and the effect thereof.

SECTION 2. 1. The citizens of each State shall be entitled to all privileges and immunities of citizens in the several States.[8]

2. A person charged in any State with treason, felony, or other crime, who shall flee from justice, and be found in another State, shall on demand of the executive authority of the State from which he fled, be delivered up to be removed to the State having jurisdiction of the crime.

3. No person held to service or labor in one State under the laws thereof, escaping into another, shall, in consequence of any law or regulation therein, be discharged from such service or labor, but shall be delivered up on claim of the party to whom such serfice or labor may be due.[9]

SECTION 3. 1. New States may be admitted by the Congress into this Union; but no new State shall be formed or erected within the jurisdiction of any other State; nor any State be formed by the junction of two or more States, or parts of States, without the consent of the legislatures of the States concerned as well as of the Congress.

2. The Congress shall have power to dispose of and make all needful rules and regulations respecting the territory or other property belonging to the United States; and nothing in the Constitution shall be so construed as to prejudice any claims of the United States, or of any particular State.

SECTION 4. The United States shall guarantee to every State in this Union a republican form of government, and shall protect each of them against invasion; and on application of the legislature, or of the executive (when the legislature cannot be convened) against domestic violence.

Article V

The Congress, whenever two thirds of both Houses shall deem it necessary, shall propose amendments to this Constitution, or, on the application of the legislatures of two thirds of the several States, shall call a convention for proposing amendments, which in either case, shall be valid to all intents and purposes, as part of this Constitution, when ratified by the legislatures of three fourths of the several States, or by conventions in three fourths thereof, as the one or the other mode of ratification may be proposed by the Congress; Provided that no amendment which may be made prior to the year one thousand eight hundred and eight shall in any manner affect the first and fourth clauses in the ninth section of the first article; and that no State, without its consent, shall be deprived of its equal suffrage in the Senate.

Article VI

1. All debts contracted and engagements entered into, before the adoption of this Constitution, shall be as valid against the United States under this Constitution, as under the Confederation.[10]

2. This Constitution, and the laws of the United States which shall be made in pursuance thereof; and all treaties made, or which shall be made, under the authority of the United States, shall be the supreme law of the land; and the judges in every State shall be bound thereby, any thing in the Constitution or laws of any State to the contrary notwithstanding.

3. The senators and representatives before mentioned, and the members of the several State legislatures, and all executive and judicial officers, both of the United States and of the several States, shall be bound by oath or affirmation to support this Constitution; but no religious test shall ever be required as a qualification to any office or public trust under the United States.

Article VII

The ratification of the conventions of nine States shall be sufficient for the establishment of this Constitution between the States so ratifying the same.

[8]*See the Fourteenth Amendment. Sec. 1.*
[9]*See the Thirteenth Amendment.*

[10]*See the Fourteenth Amendment. Sec. 4.*

Done in Convention by the unanimous consent of the States present the seventeenth day of September in the year of our Lord one thousand seven hundred and eighty-seven, and of the independence of the United States of America the twelfth. In witness whereof we have hereunto subscribed our names.

[Names omitted]

* * * * *

Articles in addition to, and amendment of, the Constitution of the United States of America, proposed by Congress, and ratified by the legislatures of the several States, pursuant to the fifth article of the original Constitution.

FIRST AMENDMENT [*First ten amendments ratified December 15, 1791*]

Congress shall make no law respecting an establishment of religion, or prohibiting the free exercise thereof; or abridging the freedom of speech, or of the press; or the right of the people peaceably to assemble, and to petition the government for a redress of grievances.

SECOND AMENDMENT

A well regulated militia, being necessary to the security of a free State, the right of the people to keep and bear arms, shall not be infringed.

THIRD AMENDMENT

No soldier shall, in time of peace be quartered in any house, without the consent of the owner, nor in time of war, but in a manner to be prescribed by law.

FOURTH AMENDMENT

The right of the people to secure in their persons, houses, papers, and effects, against unreasonable searches and seizures, shall not be violated, and no warrants shall issue, but upon probable cause, supported by oath or affirmation, and particularly describing the place to be searched, and the persons or things to be seized.

FIFTH AMENDMENT

No person shall be held to answer for a capital, or otherwise infamous crime, unless on a presentment or indictment of a grand jury, except in cases arising in the land or naval forces, or in the militia, when in actual service in time of war or public danger; nor shall any person be subject for the same offense to be twice put in jeopardy of life or limb; nor shall be compelled in any criminal case to be a witness against himself, nor be deprived of life, liberty, or property, without due process of law; nor shall private property be taken for public use, without just compensation.

SIXTH AMENDMENT

In all criminal prosecutions, the accused shall enjoy the right to a speedy and public trial, by an impartial jury of the State and district wherein the crime shall have been committed, which district shall have been previously ascertained by law, and to be informed of the nature and cause of the accusation; to be confronted with the witnesses against him; to have compulsory process for obtaining witnesses in his favor, and to have the assistance of counsel for his defense.

SEVENTH AMENDMENT

In suits at common law, where the value in controversy shall exceed twenty dollars, the right of trial by jury shall be preserved, and no fact tried by a jury shall be otherwise reexamined in any court of the United States, than according to the rules of the common law.

EIGHTH AMENDMENT

Excessive bail shall not be required, nor excessive fines imposed, nor cruel and unusual punishments inflicted.

NINTH AMENDMENT

The enumeration in the Constitution of certain rights shall not be construed to deny or disparage others retained by the people.

TENTH AMENDMENT

The powers not delegated to the United States by the Constitution, nor prohibited by it to the States, are reserved to the States respectively, or to the people.

ELEVENTH AMENDMENT [January 8, 1798]

The judicial power of the United States shall not be construed to extend to any suit in law or equity, commenced or prosecuted against one of the United States by citizens of another State, or by citizens or subjects of any foreign State.

TWELFTH AMENDMENT
[September 25, 1804]

The electors shall meet in their respective States, and vote by ballot for President and Vice President, one of whom, at least, shall not be an inhabitant of the same State with themselves; they shall name in their ballots the person voted for as President, and in distinct ballots, the person voted for as Vice President, and they shall make distinct lists of all persons voted for as President and of all persons voted for as Vice President, and of the number of votes for each, which lists they shall sign and certify, and transmit sealed to the seat of the government of the United States, directed to the President of the Senate;—The President of the Senate shall, in the presence of the Senate and House of Representatives, open all the certificates and the votes shall then be counted; —The person having the greatest number of votes for President, shall be the President, if such number be a majority of the whole number of electors appointed; and if no person have such majority, then from the persons having the highest numbers not exceeding three on the list of those voted for as President, the House of Representatives shall choose immediately, by ballot, the President. But in choosing the President, the votes shall be taken by States, the representation from each State having one vote; a quorum for this purpose shall consist of the member or members from two thirds of the States, and a majority of all the States shall be necessary to a choice. And if the House of Representatives shall not choose a President whenever the right of choice shall devolve upon them, before the fourth day of March next following, then the Vice President shall act as President, as in the case of the death or other constitutional disability of the President. The person having the greatest number of votes as Vice President shall be the Vice President, if such number be a majority of the whole number of electors appointed, and if no person have a majority, then from the two highest numbers on the list, the Senate shall choose the Vice President; a quorum for the purpose shall consist of two thirds of the whole number of Senators, and a majority of the whole number shall be necessary to a choice. But no person constitutionally ineligible to the office of President shall be eligible to that of Vice President of the United States.

THIRTEENTH AMENDMENT
[December 18, 1865]

SECTION 1.   Neither slavery nor involuntary servitude, except as a punishment for crime whereof the party shall have been duly convicted, shall exist within the United States, or any place subject to their jurisdiction.

SECTION 2.   Congress shall have power to enforce this article by appropriate legislation.

FOURTEENTH AMENDMENT
[July 28, 1868]

SECTION 1.   All persons born or naturalized in the United States, and subject to the jurisdiction thereof, are citizens of the United States and of the State wherein they reside. No State shall make or enforce any law which shall abridge the privileges or immunities of citizens of the United States; nor shall any State deprive any person of life, liberty, or property, without due process of law; nor deny to any person within its jurisdiction the equal protection of the laws.

SECTION 2.   Representatives shall be apportioned among the several States according to their respective numbers, counting the whole number of persons in each State, excluding Indians not taxed. But when the right to vote at any election for the choice of electors for President and Vice President of the United States, representatives in Congress, the executive and judicial officers of a State, or the members of the legislature thereof, is denied to any of the male inhabitants of such State, being twenty-one years of age, and citizens of the United States, or in any way abridged, except for participating in rebellion, or other crime, the basis of representation therein shall be reduced in the proportion which the number of such male citizens shall bear to the whole number of male citizens twenty-one years of age in such State.

SECTION 3. No person shall be a senator or representative in Congress, or elector of President and Vice President, or hold any office, civil or military, under the United States, or under any State, who having previously taken an oath, as a member of Congress, or as an officer of the United States, or as a member of any State legislature, or as an executive or judicial officer of any State, to support the Constitution of the United States, shall have engaged in insurrection or rebellion against the same, or given aid or comfort to the enemies thereof. But Congress may by a vote of two thirds of each House, remove such disability.

SECTION 4. The validity of the public debt of the United States, authorized by law, including debts incurred for payment of pensions and bounties for services in suppressing insurrection or rebellion, shall not be questioned. But neither the United States nor any State shall assume or pay any debt or obligation incurred in aid of insurrection or rebellion against the United States, or any claim for the loss or emancipation of any slave; but all such debts, obligations, and claims shall be held illegal and void.

SECTION 5. The Congress shall have power to enforce, by appropriate legislation, the provisions of this article.

FIFTEENTH AMENDMENT
[March 30, 1870]

SECTION 1. The right of citizens of the United States to vote shall not be denied or abridged by the United States or by any State on account of race, color, or previous condition of servitude.

SECTION 2. The Congress shall have power to enforce this article by appropriate legislation.

SIXTEENTH AMENDMENT
[February 25, 1913]

The Congress shall have the power to lay and collect taxes on incomes, from whatever source derived, without apportionment among the several States, and without regard to any census or enumeration.

SEVENTEENTH AMENDMENT
[May 31, 1913]

The Senate of the United States shall be composed of two senators from each State,

elected by the people thereof, for six years; and each senator shall have one vote. The electors in each State shall have the qualifications requisite for electors of the most numerous branch of the State legislature.

When vacancies happen in the representation of any State in the Senate, the executive authority of such State shall issue writs of election to fill such vacancies: Provided, That the legislature of any State may empower the executive thereof to make temporary appointments until the people fill the vacancies by election as the legislature may direct.

This amendment shall not be so construed as to affect the election or term of any senator chosen before it becomes valid as part of the Constitution.

EIGHTEENTH AMENDMENT[11]
[January 29, 1919]

After one year from the ratification of this article, the manufacture, sale, or transportation of intoxicating liquors within, the importation thereof into, or the exportation thereof from the United States and all territory subject to the jurisdiction thereof for beverage purposes is thereby prohibited.

The Congress and the several States shall have concurrent power to enforce this article by appropriate legislation.

This article shall be inoperative unless it shall have been ratified as an amendment to the Constitution by the legislatures of the several States, as provided in the Constitution, within seven years from the date of the submission hereof to the States by Congress.

NINETEENTH AMENDMENT
[August 26, 1920]

The right of citizens of the United States to vote shall not be denied or abridged by the United States or by any State on account of sex.

Congress shall have the power to enforce this article by appropriate legislation.

TWENTIETH AMENDMENT
[January 23, 1933]

SECTION 1. The terms of the President and Vice President shall end at noon on the 20th day of January, and the terms of Senators and Representatives at noon on the 3rd day of January, of the years in which such

[11]Repealed by the Twenty-first Amendment.

terms would have ended if this article had not been ratified; and the terms of their successors shall then begin.

SECTION 2. The Congress shall assemble at least once in every year, and such meeting shall begin at noon on the 3rd day of January, unless they shall by law appoint a different day.

SECTION 3. If, at the time fixed for the beginning of the term of President, the President-elect shall have died, the Vice President-elect shall become President. If a President shall not have been chosen before the time fixed for the beginning of his term, or if the President-elect shall have failed to qualify, then the Vice President-elect shall act as President until a President shall have qualified; and the Congress may by law provide for the case wherein neither a President-elect nor a Vice President-elect shall have qualified, declaring who shall then act as President, or the manner in which one who is to act shall be selected, and such person shall act accordingly until a President or Vice President shall have qualified.

SECTION 4. The Congress may by law provide for the case of the death of any of the persons from whom the House of Representatives may choose a President whenever the right of choice shall have devolved upon them, and for the case of the death of any of the persons from whom the Senate may choose a Vice President whenever the right of choice shall have devolved upon them.

SECTION 5. Sections 1 and 2 shall take effect on the 15th day of October following the ratification of this article.

SECTION 6. This article shall be inoperative unless it shall have been ratified as an amendment to the Constitution by the legislatures of three-fourths of the several States within seven years from the date of its submission.

TWENTY-FIRST AMENDMENT
[December 5, 1933]

SECTION 1. The Eighteenth Article of amendment to the Constitution of the United States is hereby repealed.

SECTION 2. The transportation or importation into any State, Territory, or possession of the United States for delivery or use therein of intoxicating liquors in violation of the laws thereof, is hereby prohibited.

SECTION 3. This article shall be inoperative unless it shall have been ratified as an amendment to the Constitution by conventions in the several States, as provided in the Constitution, within seven years from the date of the submission thereof to the States by the Congress.

TWENTY-SECOND AMENDMENT
[March 1, 1951]

No person shall be elected to the office of the President more than twice, and no person who has held the office of President, or acted as President, for more than two years of a term to which some other person was elected President shall be elected to the office of the President more than once.

But this article shall not apply to any person holding the office of President when this article was proposed by the Congress, and shall not prevent any person who may be holding the office of President, or acting as President, during the term within which this article becomes operative from holding the office of President or acting as President during the remainder of such term.

This article shall be inoperative unless it shall have been ratified as an amendment to the Constitution by the legislatures of three-fourths of the several States within seven years from the date of its submission to the States by the Congress.

TWENTY-THIRD AMENDMENT
[March 29, 1961]

SECTION 1. The District constituting the seat of Government of the United States shall appoint in such manner as the Congress may direct:

A number of electors of President and Vice President equal to the whole number of Senators and Representatives in Congress to which the District would be entitled if it were a State, but in no event more than the least populous State; they shall be in addition to those appointed by the States, but they shall be considered, for the purposes of the election of President and Vice President, to be electors appointed by a State; and they shall meet in the District and perform such duties as provided by the twelfth article of amendment.

SECTION 2. The Congress shall have power to enforce this article by appropriate legislation.

TWENTY-FOURTH AMENDMENT
[January 23, 1964]

SECTION 1.   The right of citizens of the United States to vote in any primary or other election for President or Vice President, for electors for President or Vice President, or for Senator or Representative in Congress, shall not be denied or abridged by the United States or any State by reason of failure to pay any poll tax or other tax.

SECTION 2.   The Congress shall have power to enforce this article by appropriate legislation.

TWENTY-FIFTH AMENDMENT
[February 10, 1967]

SECTION 1.   In case of the removal of the President from office or of his death or resignation, the Vice President shall become President.

SECTION 2.   Whenever there is a vacancy in the office of the Vice President, the President shall nominate a Vice President who shall take office upon confirmation by a majority vote of both Houses of Congress.

SECTION 3.   Whenever the President transmits to the President pro tempore of the Senate and the Speaker of the House of Representatives his written declaration that he is unable to discharge the powers and duties of his office, and until he transmits to them a written declaration to the contrary, such powers and duties shall be discharged by the Vice President as Acting President.

SECTION 4.   Whenever the Vice President and a majority of either the principal officers of the executive departments or of such other body as Congress may by law provide, transmit to the President pro tempore of the Senate and the Speaker of the House of Representatives their written declaration that the President is unable to dis-charge the powers and duties of his office, the Vice President shall immediately assume the powers and duties of the office as Acting President.

Thereafter, when the President transmits to the President pro tempore of the Senate and the Speaker of the House of Representatives his written declaration that no inability exists, he shall resume the powers and duties of his office unless the Vice President and a majority of either the principal officers of the executive departments or of such other body as Congress may by law provide, transmit within four days to the President pro tempore of the Senate and the Speaker of the House of Representatives their written declaration that the President is unable to discharge the powers and duties of his office. Thereupon Congress shall decide the issue, assembling within forty-eight hours for that purpose if not in session. If the Congress, within twenty-one days after receipt of the latter written declaration, or, if Congress is not in session, within twenty-one days after Congress is required to assemble, determines by two-thirds vote of both houses that the President is unable to discharge the powers and duties of his office, the Vice President shall continue to discharge the same as Acting President; otherwise, the President shall resume the powers and duties of his office.

TWENTY-SIXTH AMENDMENT
[June 30, 1971]

SECTION 1.   The right of citizens of the United States who are eighteen years of age or older to vote shall not be denied or abridged by the United States or by any State on account of age.

SECTION 2.   The Congress shall have power to enforce this article by appropriate legislation.

acknowledgments/sources

Continued from copyright page.

UNIT THREE Page 340: Judy Stevens, (ed.), *Ward Assembly Manual* (Chicago: 44th Ward Service Office, 1976). **351t:** Reprinted from 'U.S. News & World Report.' Copyright 1977 U.S. News & World Report, Inc. **379:** From *Guide to Congress* (Washington, D.C.: Congressional Quarterly, Inc.), 1976, p. 590. **408-409:** Courtesy of H & R Block, Inc. and the Roper Organization, Inc. **466t:** With permission of Voter Education Project, Inc., Atlanta, Georgia. **483b:** From *Stride Toward Freedom* by Martin Luther King, Jr. Copyright © 1958 by Martin Luther King, Jr. Reprinted by permission of Harper & Row, Publishers, Inc.

UNIT FOUR Page 553: Adapted from *The Oxford Economic Atlas*, 4th edition, © 1972, p. 35. **594:** From Richard L. Barnet and Ronald E. Muller, *Global Reach*. Copyright © 1974 by Richard L. Barnet and Ronald E. Muller. Reprinted by permission of Simon & Schuster, A Division of Gulf & Western Corporation. **601, 603:** Adapted from the May, 1973, *Power Team*, employee magazine of Cummins Engine Company, Inc., Columbus, Indiana.

photo identifications

Key to position of photographs: t-top, b-bottom, c-center, l-left, r-right, tl-top left, tr-top right, bl-bottom left, br-bottom right.

TITLE PAGES Page 1: *t* United States Congress; *bl* Mount Rushmore National Memorial near Rapid City, South Dakota; *br* Supreme Court Justice John P. Stevens (left) in conference. **Page 2:** *l* Rally in Central Park, New York City; *tr* Austin, Texas; *br* Deborah Stabenow (left), Ingham County Board of Commissioners in Michigan.

UNIT 1, pp. 16-17: 1976 Republican National Covention.

Chapter 1, p. 18: *l* American flag; *r* Taking an oath of naturalization.

Chapter 2, p. 48: *t* Distributing campaign literature; *b* The County Election, painting by George Caleb Bingham.

Chapter 3, p. 80: *l* Mayoral election headquarters in Miami, Florida; *r* Connecticut campaign rally.

Chapter 4, p. 116: *l* Cesar Chavez at a farm workers' meeting; *r* NEA button.

Chapter 5, p. 140: *t* UMWA bumper sticker; *b* Coal miners about to enter a mine.

UNIT 2, pp. 172-173: Municipal Building in Corpus Christi, Texas.

Chapter 6, p. 174: *l* Portrait of James Madison; *r* Detail from painting of the Constitutional Convention.

Chapter 7, p. 202: *l* Civil rights rally; *r* Distributing Literature.

Chapter 8, p. 220: *l* Dome of the State Capitol in Austin, Texas; *r* From the State Assembly in Albany, New York.

Chapter 9, p. 258: *t* Detail of community map; *b* Election poster.

Chapter 10, p. 288: *both* Views of Santa Barbara.

UNIT 3, pp. 310-311: United States Congress.

Chapter 11, p. 312: *l* Detail from the United States Constitution; *r* Inaugural celebration at the United States Capitol, 1976.

Chapter 12, p. 346: *l* Congressman Peter Rodino (right) confers during presidential impeachment hearings in the House of Representatives, 1974; *r* United States Congress.

Chapter 13, p. 382: *l* White House; *r* Mount Rushmore, South Dakota.

Chapter 14, p. 416: *l* Supreme Court building; *r* Supreme Court Justice William H. Rehnquist at work.

Chapter 15, p. 450: *l* American flag; *r* Civil rights rally in Washington, D.C.

UNIT 4, pp. 492-493: Display of flags at Rockefeller Center, New York City.

Chapter 16, p. 494: *l* General Assembly meeting of United Nations delegates; *r* View of Earth.

Chapter 17, p. 518: *t* United Nations peacekeeping troops in the Sinai Desert; *b* President Ford and Soviet leader Leonid I. Brezhnev sign an agreement.

Chapter 18, p. 546: *l* Oil derricks; *r* Rice farming in Japan.

Chapter 19, p. 570: *both* Internationl Court of Justice at The Hague, The Netherlands.

Chapter 20, p. 592: *l* Port of San Francisco; *r* Factory workers at the Cummins Engine Company in Poona, India.

Index